ORAL AND POSTER PRESENTATIONS

Chairpersons: Lis Alban, Alex Cook

ORAL PRESENTATIONS

7th

INTERNATIONAL SYMPOSIUM

on the epidemiology & control of foodborne pathogens in pork

MAY 9-11, 2007
VERONA (Italy)
Palazzo della Gran Guardia

Proceedings

Grafica: KROMATOS - Padova

Stampa: CLEUP Cooperativa Libraria Editrice Università di Padova
           Via Belzoni, 118/3 - Padova

ISBN 978-88-6129-083-9

Chairpersons: Rob Davies, Thomas Blaha

ORAL PRESENTATIONS

POSTERS

Chairpersons: Franco Ruggeri, Edoardo Pozio

ORAL PRESENTATIONS

POSTERS

Control strategies

Chairpersons: Peter van der Wolf, James McKean

ORAL PRESENTATIONS

Chairpersons: Philippe Fravalo, Antonia Ricci

ORAL PRESENTATIONS

SIXTH SESSION

Antimicrobial resistance

Chairpersons: Peter Davies, Antonio Battisti

PRESENTATIONS

ORAL & POSTER

FIRST SESSION

Risk assessment and Public Health

Understanding on-farm prevalence and risk factor knowledge base for *Salmonella* in swine: a systematic review-meta-analysis approach

Sanchez, J., [1,2]* Dohoo, I., [1] Christensen, J. [3] and Rajić, A[2,4]

[1]Population Health Research Group, Atlantic Veterinary College, 550 University Avenue, Charlottetown, PE, Canada, C1A 4P3.
[2]Laboratory for Foodborne Zoonoses, Public Health Agency of Canada, Guelph, Ontario N1G 3W4
[3]Canadian Food Inspection Agency, Charlottetown, PE, Canada Canadian Food Inspection Agency,
[4]Department of Population Medicine, University of Guelph, Ontario N1G 2W1

Methods of research synthesis – the process of bringing together the results of individual research to better map the knowledge base – have developed over the last couple of decades. Systematic review-meta-analysis (SR-MA) has been used in agri-food public health to a limited extent. The main purpose of this study was to evaluate the suitability of SR-MA in this area using *Salmonella* issue in pigs. Three areas were identified as potentially suitable for MA, prevalence, diagnostic test performance, and risk factor data.

Prevalence MA. A comprehensive literature search (Jan. 1990 and March 2005) was conducted using the principles of SR methodology. Among 216 articles that met the inclusion criteria, 104 articles did not contain data suitable for a quantitative MA. A logit transformation was used to normalize the prevalence estimates (outcome variable). The effects of different factors on estimates of the prevalence were investigated. The MA was stratified according to the sampling unit (eg. herd, pen and animal). Each of the predictors was evaluated unconditionally; all significant predictors ($P > 0.15$) were presented to a multi-variable model. Random effects meta-regression models were fit to investigate the association between a set of predictors related to study design quality and to study design characteristics. Results from models for herd and animal-level prevalence will be presented and discussed.

Feed MA. Three specific feed-related factors were investigated: meal vs. pelleted, dry vs. wet, and coarse vs. fine. Out of a total of 70 articles suitable for MA, only 26 contained enough information for computing both the Odds Ratio (OR) and the precision of the OR. MA was performed at the herd, pen and animal levels. Results from these analyses will be presented and discussed. The needs, gaps and opportunities for utilizing this method in agri-food public health will be highlighted and discussed.

*Population Health Research Group
Atlantic Veterinary College
50 University Avenue, Charlottetown
PEI, Canada, C1A 4P3.
Tel: +1 902.566.0803
Fax : +1 902.566.0823
e-mail: jsanchez@upei.ca

An evidence based ranking system for multiple studies designs for informing public policy. An example using interventions associated with Salmonella in swine.

O'Connor, A.M. *[1], Denagamage, T., [1] Sargeant, J., [2] McKean,. J.,[1]

[1]Department of Veterinary Diagnostic and Production Animal Medicine, College of Veterinary Medicine, Iowa State University, Ames, 50011, IA, USA.
[2]Department of Clinical Epidemiology and Biostatistics, McMaster University, 1200 Main St. W., Hamilton, L8N 3Z5, ON, Canada.
*corresponding author: oconnor@iastate.edu

Abstract

Using the association between feed characteristics and Salmonella prevalence we will present an approach to combining data with multiple outcomes from multiple studies designs. The approach may be a method of informing policy makers in the area of food safety when a large amount of heterogeneous literature is available about a topic. The procedure for a systematic review of the literature was followed until the synthesis component. However, to combine the evidence we modified of the FDA Interim Evidence Ranking System for Scientific Information. Each study was characterized as one of 5 study design types based on evidentiary value. After classification by evidentiary value, the studies were considered collectively to rate the strength of the body of evidence based on quantity and consistency. The quantity ranking considered the number of studies, the number of individuals studied and generalizability to the target population. The consistency ranking considered whether studies with different designs reported similar findings. After ranking the body of evidence, an overall ranking was assigned for the strength of the evidence. The final ranking system had four levels. For example, the highest rank of scientific evidence, reflects a high level of comfort among qualified scientists that the association/relationship is scientifically valid. This level ranked relationship would be considered to have a very low probability of significant new data overturning the conclusion that the relationship is valid or significantly changing the nature of the relationship.

Quantitative risk assessment of human salmonellosis through consumption of pork in Belgium: a modular risk model

Grijspeerdt, K.[1], Messens, W.[1], Bollaerts, K.[2], Van Dessel, P.[3], Delhalle, L.[4], Maes, D.[5], Boone, I.[6], Mintiens, K.[6]

[1]Institute for Agricultural and Fisheries Research (ILVO), Technology and Food Unit, Brusselsesteenweg 370, 9090 Melle, Belgium
[2]University Hasselt, Center for Statistics (CENSTAT), Agoralaan 1 Gebouw D, 3590 Diepenbeek, Belgium
[3]Scientific Institute of Public Health (IPH), Epidemiology Unit, J. Wytsmanstraat 14, 1050 Brussels, Belgium
[4]University of Liege, Faculty of Veterinary Medicine, Food Science Department, Food Microbiology, Sart-Tilman, Bât B43bis, 4000 Liege, Belgium
[5]Faculty of Veterinary Medicine, Ghent University, Salisburylaan 133 9820 Merelbeke, Belgium
[6]Veterinary and Agrochemical Research Centre (VAR), Coordination Centre for Veterinary Diagnostics, Groeselenberg 99, 1180 Brussels, Belgium
*corresponding author: Koen.Grijspeerdt@ilvo.vlaanderen.be

Abstract

As *Salmonella* Typhimurium (STM) is the major source of human salmonellosis in Belgium, a quantitative microbial risk assessment (QMRA) to evaluate the health risks associated with the consumption of minced pork meat contaminated with STM in Belgium was initiated. The QMRA model describes the chain from farm-to-fork, dividing the exposure pathway into several modules (1) primary production, (2) transport & holding, (3) slaughter & processing, (4) distribution & storage and (5) consumer. Both fresh and frozen minced meat products prepared at home are considered and human illness is estimated for both inadequately cooking and cross-contamination during preparation. Data relevant to the Belgian situation was incorporated into the model where available, international and literature data was used otherwise. First baseline results of the model are presented and the impact of some scenarios was investigated. These first results show that there seems to be more potential in reducing the STM load on the carcasses, rather then reducing the prevalence.

Introduction

In 2006, *Salmonella* was the second most common cause of gastrointestinal disease in Belgium and was isolated from 3670 human cases of gastroenteritis. *Salmonella* Typhimurium (STM) contributed to 49.4% of these human cases (personal communication with Nadine Botteldoorn). As STM is the most common serovar isolated from pigs (Botteldoorn et al., 2003), it is clear that the consumption of pig meat is an important risk factor. Therefore, a quantitative microbial risk assessment (QMRA) was developed to evaluate the health risks associated with the consumption of minced pork meat contaminated with STM in Belgium. The main objectives of this QMRA are threefold: (1) the development of a modular risk model, (2) the investigation of the quality of information and assumptions of the risk model and (3) the optimization of the risk model and the implementation of mathematical and statistical refinements. There are several QMRA's estimating the risk to human health from STM originating from pigs meat (Hill et al., 2003; Ranta et al., 2004; van der Gaag, 2004; Alban & Stärk, 2005) using different approaches.

The approach followed in this project is based on the Hill-model. Data relevant to the Belgian situation was incorporated into the model where available, international and literature data was used otherwise. Some adaptations to the model were made in among others the partitioning, cross-contamination and dose response models. To take the imperfect nature of the available data as much as possible into account, a methodology for assessing the quality of data and information sources (based on a multi criterion pedigree matrix) was developed in parallel.

The model

The model is based on the model of Hill (2003) (Figure 1). The current model is only applicable to minced pig meat.

Several adaptation were made to the original model. Some are highlighted in this paper. (1) Primary production. The mechanistic farm model in the original model was replaced by a seroprevalence estimation based on data from the national *Salmonella* surveillance program. This estimation was done by using generalised estimating equations, taking into account the sensitivity and specificity of the test used. The data differentiates between the weight category of the pigs and the time of sampling. The farm model is used to calculate the ratio between infected and carrier animals.
(2) Module transport. During the transport & holding phase there is a possible state transition of animals. Since the average time in this module is very similar to the current practice in the UK, the original model seems to be applicable for Belgium.
(3) Slaughter & processing. The slaughter process has not been modified, apart from the carcass weight which has significantly increased in recent years.

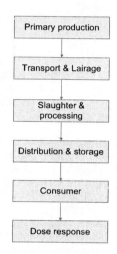

Figure 1: Schematic overview of the modular QRMA

Data obtained by a survey of 11 Belgian pig meat processors has been incorporated in the processing model. The partitioning of the meat mix is completely redone according to the concept introduced by Nauta *et al.* (2001): BetaBin(N_{mix},b,$b(n$-1)) with N_{mix} the number of *Salmonella* in the meat mix, b a cluster parameter (b=0.22 (Nauta *et al.*, 2001)) and n the number of units.
(4) Distribution & storage. For this module, data obtained by surveys among four Belgian retailers (comprising > 50% of the market) and 3000 consumers (Devriese *et al.*, 2006) concerning the time/temperature of storage were used.
(5) Preparation & consumption. Consumer data was used to make the model applicable for the Belgian condition. Cross contamination in the kitchen was modeled analogously to the WHO model of *Salmonella* Enteritidis in eggs (World Health Organization, 2003), adapted with the concepts described by Nauta *et al.* (2005) in their risk assessment of *Campylobacter* in broilers (CARMA).
(6) Dose-response. Based on the *Salmonella* outbreak data described in World Health Organization (2003), a novel dose response model was developed based on fractional

polynomials. This model differentiates between a normal and a sensitive population, and between the different *Salmonella* serovars.

(7) Data. The quality of data to be used in a QMRA is very diverse, but has a large impact on model results. One of the goals of the project was to develop a methodology to allow for an as objective as possible quantification of data quality. This methodolgy is based on pedigree scoring (Boone *et al.*, 2007) and was applied to identify these data sources that are most likely to yield the most reliable and useful data.

Results

Preliminary results of the risk model are summarized in Table 1, where the risk of salmonellosis per serving of minced pork meat is shown. This risk is in general so small that a large number of iterations is needed to obtain a reasonably reliable estimation of the output distribution. The numbers presented here are the result of one million iterations. The average value of the risk was calculated as $2.08×10^{-4}$ (sd. $6.16×10^{-3}$) and the corresponding number of yearly cases, based on the estimated number of servings, is then 67076 (sd. 17123). The reported number of cases due to STM is 1813 in 2006. Taking into account that there is an estimated underreporting of about 90%, the model output is in fact quite realistic. The risk is mainly determined by cross contamination $2.06×10^{-4}$ (sd. $6.15×10^{-3}$) and only to a small extent to undercooking $2.83×10^{-6}$ (sd. $5.85×10^{-4}$).

Table 1: The effect of mitigation strategies on the risk of illness from minced pork meat

	Scenario	Mean	Standard deviation
Baseline*		$2.02×10^{-4}$	$5.74×10^{-3}$
Seroprevalence at the farm	20% reduction	$1.69×10^{-4}$	$5.01×10^{-3}$
	40% reduction	$1.60×10^{-4}$	$5.04×10^{-3}$
	60% reduction	$1.59×10^{-4}$	$5.25×10^{-3}$
	80% reduction	$5.68×10^{-5}$	$2.68×10^{-3}$
Salmonella load on carcass after stunning and killing	1 log reduction	$1.52×10^{-5}$	$1.79×10^{-3}$
	2 log reduction	$3.29×10^{-7}$	$1.04×10^{-4}$
	3 log reduction	0	0
Salmonella load on carcass after meat inspection	0.5 log reduction	$6.36×10^{-5}$	$2.80×10^{-3}$
	1 log reduction	$2.1×10^{-5}$	$1.79×10^{-3}$
	2 log reduction	$1.69×10^{-7}$	$4.41×10^{-5}$
Prevalence of *Salmonella* carcass contamination after meat inspection	10% reduction	$2.02×10^{-4}$	$5.80×10^{-3}$
	20% reduction	$2.08×10^{-4}$	$5.85×10^{-3}$
	30% reduction	$2.13×10^{-4}$	$5.97×10^{-3}$
Probability of ineffective cleaning during jointing (30% baseline)	20%	$1.74×10^{-4}$	$5.35×10^{-3}$
	10%	$2.19×10^{-4}$	$6.36×10^{-3}$
	0%	$1.89×10^{-4}$	$5.69×10^{-3}$

Percentage of minced meat destined for the frozen market (26% baseline)	100%	0	0
	75%	6.96×10^{-5}	3.51×10^{-3}
	50%	1.66×10^{-4}	5.19×10^{-3}
	0%	2.74×10^{-4}	6.78×10^{-3}
Storage temperature of fresh minced meat at home	-1°C reduction	1.57×10^{-4}	5.57×10^{-3}
	-2°C reduction	1.02×10^{-4}	4.27×10^{-3}
	-3°C reduction	8.58×10^{-5}	4.15×10^{-3}
	-4°C reduction	5.90×10^{-5}	3.24×10^{-3}
	-5°C reduction	4.69×10^{-5}	3.23×10^{-3}
	-6°C reduction	4.82×10^{-5}	2.83×10^{-3}
Percentage who defrost minced meat product at room temperature (48.8% baseline)	40%	2.22×10^{-4}	5.89×10^{-3}
	30%	2.09×10^{-4}	6.05×10^{-3}
	20%	1.91×10^{-4}	5.81×10^{-3}
Percentage of change in behaviour during food preparation (cross contamination)	3% reduction	1.96×10^{-4}	3.55×10^{-3}
	7% reduction	2.05×10^{-4}	5.81×10^{-3}
	25% reduction	1.94×10^{-4}	5.58×10^{-3}
	50% reduction	1.90×10^{-4}	5.54×10^{-3}

Discussion

The model in its current state produces already realistic results and allows testing mitigation strategies. The results of these indicate that there are certain strategies that are possibly more worthwhile to pursue than others. Reducing the STM-load seems to be much more efficient than trying to reduce the overall prevalence. This raises the question whether the monitoring program in place today, based solely on *Salmonella* seroprevalence of pigs and *Salmonella* prevalence of pig carcasses, pork meat and minced pork meat, is the most effective way of following up the problem. In this context, it has to be remarked here that the modeling of the slaughter process appears to be one of the weakest links of the model: it is based on only two data sources (Berends *et al.*, 1998; Davies *et al.*, 1999). Since the STM concentration has such a large impact there is a definite need to collect more quantitative data in the slaughtering plants.

Another important factor is the percentage of minced meat destined for the frozen market. Freezing has a profound positive impact on the risk and could thus be considered as a valid mitigation strategy. However, there are economic and consumer consequences to be considered as well, which falls outside the scope of this paper.

Storage conditions (time and temperature) in retail and especially households prove to be important factors, and could be improved by stringent controls and conscience raising campaigns. There seems to be less to gain by trying to improve food handling in the kitchen. The cost to reach consumers is large whilst only a small fraction (0-7%) of the consumers is willing to change their behaviour. Moreover the risk is not reduced significantly.

Conclusion

The current QMRA model for STM in pigs is already usable and allows assessing the most efficient intervention strategies. There is still room for improvement though, and especially the description of the slaughtering process requires more data.

Acknowledgements

This study has been carried out with the financial support of the Belgian Federal Public Service of Health, Food Chain Safety, and Environment research programme (R-04/003-Metzoon) 'Development of a methodology for quantitative assessment of zoonotic risks in Belgium applied to the 'Salmonella in pork' model'.

References

ALBAN, L. and STÄRK, K. D., 2005, Where should the effort be put to reduce the Salmonella prevalence in the slaughtered swine carcass effectively? Preventative Veterinary Medicine, 68 (1), 63-79.

BERENDS, B. R., VAN KNAPEN, F., MOSSEL, D. A., BURT, S. A. and SNIJDERS, J. M., 1998, Impact on human health of Salmonella spp. on pork in The Netherlands and the anticipated effects of some currently proposed control strategies. International Journal of Food Microbiology, 44 (3), 219-229.

BOONE, I., VAN DER STEDE, Y., BOLLAERTS, K., VOSE, D., DAUBE, G., AERTS, M. and MINTIENS, K., 2007, Belgian 'farm-to-consumption' risk assessment-model for Salmonella in pigs: methodology for assessing the quality of data and information sourcesquality of data and information sources. In: Proceedings Safepork. Verona, Italy. 9-11 May.

BOTTELDOORN, N., HEYNDRICKX, M., RIJPENS, N., GRIJSPEERDT, K. and HERMAN, L., 2003, Salmonella on pig carcasses: positive pigs and cross contamination in the slaughterhouse. Journal of Appied. Microbiology, 95, 891-903.

DAVIES, R. H., MCLAREN, I. M. and BEDFORD, S., 1999, Distribution of Salmonella contamination in two pig abattoirs. In: Proceedings 3rd International Symposium on the Epidemiology and Control of Salmonella in pork. Washington, D.C. August 5-7. ISECP. 267-272.

DEVRIESE, S., HUYBRECHTS, I., MOREAU, M. and VAN OYEN, H., 2006, De Belgische Voedselconsumptiepeiling 1 - 2004, Afdeling Epidemiologie, Wetenschappelijk Instituut Volksgezondheid Report.

HILL, A. A., ENGLAND, T. J., SNARY, E. L., KELLY, L. A., COOK, A. J. C. and WOOLDRIDGE, M., 2003, A 'farm-to-consumption' risk assessment for the adverse effects to human health of Salmonella Typhimurium in pigs, Centre for Epidemiology and Risk Analysis, Veterinary Laboratories Agency Report. Pages 102.

NAUTA, M. J., EVERS, E. G., TAKUMI, K. and HAVELAAR, A., 2001, Risk assessment of Shiga-toxin producing Escherichia coli O157 in steak tartare in the Netherlands, RIVM Report. Pages 169.

NAUTA, M. J., JACOBS-REITSMA, W. F., EVERS, E. G., VAN PELT, W. and HAVELAAR, A., 2005, Risk assessment of Campylobacter in the Netherlands via broiler meat and other routes, Report. Pages 128.

RANTA, J., TUOMINEN, P., RAUTIAINEN, E. and MAIJALA, R., 2004, Salmonella in pork production in Finland - A quantitative risk assessment, National Veterinary and Food Research Institute, EELA, Finland Report. Pages 104.

VAN DER GAAG, M. A., 2004, Epidemiological and economic simulation of Salmonella control in the pork supply chain, PhD Thesis. Wageningen, The Netherlands. Pages 174.

WORLD HEALTH ORGANIZATION, 2003, Risk assessments of Salmonella in eggs and broiler chickens. Microbiological risk assessment series; no. 2. World Health Organization. Pages 303.

An updated transmission model for *Salmonella* in grower-finisher pigs

Hill, A.A.[1]*, Snary, E.L.[1], Alban, L.[2], Cook, A.J.C.[1]

[1]Centre for Epidemiology and Risk Analysis, Veterinary Laboratories Agency, Woodham Lane, KT15 3NB, New Haw, Surrey, United Kingdom
[2]Danish Bacon & Meat Council, Vinkelvej 11, DK8620 Kjellerup, Denmark
*Corresponding Author: a.hill@vla.defra.gsi.gov.uk

Abstract

A model describing the transmission of *Salmonella* between pigs on a British continuous-production grower-finisher pig farm has previously been developed (Hill et al, 2005). We will describe improvements to the model and updates to the parameter estimation. In addition, the model has been expanded to include all-in-all-out production, a much more detailed model of serological response, and all *Salmonella spp.* rather than just *Salmonella* Typhimurium. The model now also differentiates between farms with slatted and solid flooring.

The average prevalence of infection in slaughter-age pigs (13-15%) did not change significantly given the model updates. A key feature of this model is that, almost independently of peak infection levels, equilibrium in the prevalence of infection is generally reached around the same level (~15%) and time. Therefore, while meat-juice ELISA (MJE) prevalence estimates for slatted and solid flooring show a significant difference, the model results for the prevalence of true infection at slaughter shows little difference between the flooring types.

Introduction

The UK Food Standards Agency have set a target of achieving a 50% reduction in the incidence of *Salmonella* infection in slaughter-age pigs by 2010. In order to meet this target for *Salmonella*, the British Pig Executive, BPEx, in association with Defra and the Food Standards Agency, has introduced a Zoonoses Action Plan (ZAP) programme (British Pig Executive 2003). This nationwide surveillance scheme is used to monitor all pig farms sending pigs to assured slaughterhouses and uses a meat-juice ELISA (MJE) test. Farms are categorised into 3 groups based on the level of MJE-positive pigs at slaughter. By targeting the worst-offending farms (i.e. those farms within ZAP 2 and 3 categories) with financial penalties and control programmes, the ZAP programme ultimately aims to reduce the prevalence of *Salmonella* in pigs at slaughter; in turn a reduction in the burden of human salmonellosis should be observed.

In support of this effort to reduce the incidence of *Salmonella* infection in pigs of slaughter-age, a farm-to-consumption risk assessment was developed (Hill et al, 2003). The aim of this risk assessment was to estimate the risk of *Salmonella* Typhimurium infection from the consumption of three types of pig-meat products; pork, bacon and mixed meat products. As part of this risk assessment a farm transmission model for *Salmonella* in grower-finisher pigs was developed, with the aim of estimating the prevalence of infected pigs at the age of slaughter. This farm transmission model has been further developed since the original risk assessment was finished, primarily by using meat-juice ELISA (MJE) data that has become available from the ZAP monitoring programme to improve parameter estimation (Hill et al, 2005). In this paper we report on a further update to the farm transmission model, using data from a Danish longitudinal study to improve a number of critical parameters within the model, such as the finisher pig's individual time to a detectable serological response after initial infection with *Salmonella*.

Material and methods

A fuller description of the modeling methods used can be found in Hill et al (2005), and a full paper has been submitted for external peer-review (Hill et al, submitted). In brief, the farm transmission model is a modified Reed-Frost SI (Susceptible-Infected) model, which includes pen-to-pen transmission of *Salmonella* (assumed to be either by the faecal-oral or airborne routes). The model output is the prevalence of infection in slaughter-age pigs, which is broken down further into the prevalence of pigs actively excreting the organism in their faeces, and the prevalence of carrier pigs. The model output also includes an estimate of the prevalence of MJE-positive slaughter-age pigs.

The model requires estimation of parameters that were/are weakly supported by data (primarily due to the size of the field studies that would be required to fill these data gaps). Examples of parameters where data are lacking include: the probabilities of an "effective" contact from one pig to another (i.e. one which results in the successful transmission of infection from one infected pig to a susceptible pig) within and between pens, denoted p_w and p_b respectively; and the variation in the duration of infection and the duration of time any serological response is detectable by the MJE test.

As described previously (Hill et al, 2005) data from the British ZAP monitoring programme were used to estimate the transmission parameters p_w and p_b by using maximum-likelihood methods (essentially the values of p_w and p_b were varied over a number of model simulations until the resulting distribution of MJE-positive pigs produced from the simulation model was as close as possible to the actual distribution of MJE-positive pigs recorded by the ZAP monitoring programme). However, a number of unsatisfactory assumptions were used to estimate these parameters due to a lack of knowledge about the development of the serological response in pigs; namely that once infected pigs would immediately develop a serological response detectable by the British MJE test, and that this serological response would continue to be detectable until the infected pig was slaughtered.

The two assumptions about a pig's serological response were able to be removed from the model when the raw data from a Danish longitudinal study (Kranker et al, 2003) became available. Briefly, the authors of this study took monthly faecal and blood samples from three herds, for a total of 180 finisher pigs over the course of their rearing to slaughter weight. Using standard survival analysis methods, this dataset enabled us to generate "survival curves" for the duration of *Salmonella* excretion, the time to a detectable serological response and the duration of this detectable serological response. The parameter estimation of the transmission parameters was then redone using the updated model and the same maximum-likelihood methods as before.

The model was also modified to simulate all-in-all-out (AIAO) production: briefly, the modifications taken were to populate the grower-finisher farm with weaners all of the same age at $t = 0$, remove the continuous repopulation of pens over time, and remove all pigs from the farm at slaughterage. In addition, the ZAP programme dataset was split by farms that used solid and slatted flooring: we were therefore able to estimate transmission parameters for both types of farm.

Results

Epidemic curves for continuous and all-in-all-out production
The average epidemic curves for continuous and AIAO production are presented in Figures 1a and 1b. The average prevalence of MJE-positive pigs on AIAO farms is reduced by approximately 5% compared to continuous production over the range of t (the time pigs will be taken to slaughter). There are marked changes in the average prevalence of excretion and carriage for AIAO farms at slaughter age: the average prevalence of excretion within the range of slaughter age is approximately 1%, which is 2-4% lower than for continuous production, and the prevalence of carriage is reduced by around 5-6%. However, it must be noted the variation between individual farms' epidemic curves is much greater than the difference between the average epidemic curves for continuous and AIAO production.

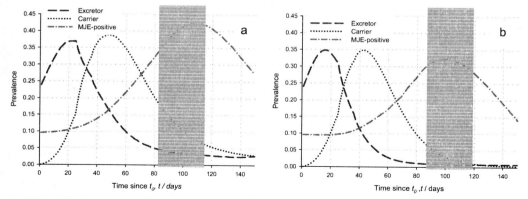

Figure 1: Average prevalence of excretion, carriage and MJE-positive pigs for a) continuous production farms and b) all-in-all-out production farms, for 150 days post arrival (slaughter age between 84-116 days after the time of introduction to the grower-finisher farm, t_0, denoted by red shading).

Epidemic curves for slatted- and solid-floored farms.

The average epidemic curves for solid-floored and slatted-floored farms are illustrated in Figures 2a and 2b respectively (the solid-floored farm curve is very similar to the epidemic curve for all flooring-type farms). Again, as above, there is significant variation between farms, such that the prevalence of infection at slaughter age may typically vary between 0 and 30-40%. Slatted-floored farms tend to have less MJE-positive pigs sent to slaughter, which translates into lower transmission parameters for this type of farm compared to solid-floored farms. These lower transmission parameters result in less pigs become infected during the course of the growing/finishing period. However, there is no significant decrease in the prevalence of infected pigs being sent to slaughter from slatted-floored farms compared to solid-floored farms.

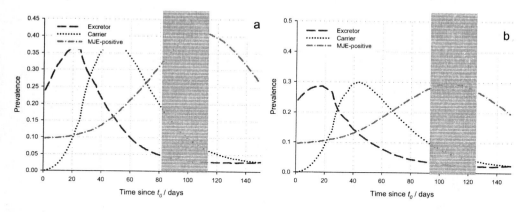

Figure 2: Average prevalence of excretion, carriage and MJE-positive pigs for a) solid-floored farms and b) slatted-floored farms, for 150 days post arrival (slaughter age between 84-116 days after the time of introduction to the grower-finisher farm, t_0, denoted by red shading).

Discussion

We have updated the previous farm transmission model (Hill et al, 2005) to remove key assumptions from our parameter estimation. This has increased our confidence in the results of the model, and allowed us to include a model describing the serological response within pigs and the related MJE test within the farm transmission model. In addition, we have investigated different types of grower-finisher farms, such as those with AIAO production, and compared those farms with solid and slatted flooring.

An interesting result of the model is that while solid-floored farms have, on average, a higher peak prevalence of infection, the average prevalence of infection at slaughter is very similar to that of slatted-floored farms, even though overall less pigs are infected on slatted-floored farms. This is because the main phase of the epidemic lasts the same time in both farm types (as duration of infection is independent of how many pigs are infected), leaving a residual infection period afterwards which is driven by a much smaller population of excreting and susceptible pigs than in the main epidemic period. AIAO production follows the same trends as continuous production, but has a lower "equilibrium" prevalence of infection at the end of the finishing period, presumably due to the proportionally lower number of excreting pigs on the farm at this time compared to continuous farms.

The European Commission is expected to require that all Member States introduce National Salmonella Control programmes for pigs, in order to achieve a prescribed reduction in prevalence. Our model can be adapted to compare the predicted response to different interventions by assuming how these might impact on key parameters, such as contact rate. In addition, our model allows a comparison of MJE results with prevalence of infection at slaughter, which could enable a national control programme to consider the use of MJE tests to monitor response of the national herd to a control programme where the definitive criterion was to achieve a targeted reduction in the prevalence of infection at slaughter.

An important point to note is that the farm transmission model still contains assumptions (an important one being the initial conditions of the model) and further research is required to confirm the results of this model, and apply the results to the risk assessment model as a whole. Improvements to the risk assessment and the farm transmission model are currently underway, and the knowledge these models provide on the dynamics of *Salmonella* infection in pigs and its relation to human risk can only be of added value to the current monitoring programme.

Conclusions

To our knowledge we have modeled the epidemic curve of *Salmonella* infection in grower-finisher pigs as comprehensively as has yet been done. The main result of this updated model, that the dynamics of infection appear to reach an equilibrium towards the point where pigs reach slaughter age, has potential implications for any monitoring programme. This result therefore requires further research, which is currently underway.

References

BRITISH PIG EXECUTIVE, 2003. ZAP *SALMONELLA*: an update: A zoonoses action plan for the British pig industry. Available at: http://www.bpex.org/technical/zap/zapupdate.pdf. Last accessed: 18th May 2005.
HILL, A.A., ENGLAND, T.E., SNARY, E.L., COOK, A.J.C., 2003. A Farm-to-Consumption Risk Assessment for *Salmonella* Typhimurium in pigs. Report to the Department of Environment, Food and Rural Affairs (available on request from authors).
HILL, A.A., SNARY, E.L., ARNOLD, M.A., COOK, A.J.C., 2005. A transmission model for *Salmonella* in grower-finisher pigs. *Proceedings of Safepork 2005*.

HILL, A.A., SNARY, E.L., ARNOLD, M.A., ALBAN, L., COOK, A.J.C., submitted. Dynamics of *Salmonella* transmission on a British pig grower-finisher farm: a stochastic model. *Epidemiology and Infection*.
KRANKER, S., ALBAN, L., BOES, J. AND DAHL, J., 2003. Longitudinal study of *Salmonella enterica* subtype Typhimurium infection in three Danish farrow-to-finish swine herds. *Journal of Clinical Microbiology*, 41, 2282-2288.

A Quantitative Risk Assessment of the Human Health Impacts Due to Macrolide Use in Swine

Hurd HS*, Malladi S

Food Risk Modeling and Policy Lab, College of Veterinary Medicine, Iowa State University, Ames, Iowa, USA
*Corresponding author: shurd@iastate.edu

Abstract

We used a retrospective modeling approach instead of the traditional farm to fork model; back calculating (C_m), the number of human macrolide resistant C. coli infections caused by eating contaminated pork, due to specific macrolide use in swine. We used the estimated number of culture confirmed human infections (C_t). As a measure of human health risk, we then calculated the expected number among the (C_m) cases that experience an adverse treatment outcome (prolonged illness) due to macrolide resistance, using estimates for fluoroquinolone. We divided the model into Release, Exposure and Consequence assessment sections according to FDA guidance 152 and utilized @Risk software with 20,000 iterations for simulation. The results show the human health risks are negligible. For example, the predicted annual risk, for prevention and growth promotion uses is only 1 in 92 million per U.S. resident, with a 5% chance it could be as high as 1 in 52 million. Our model focuses on the impact of resistance on human treatment. It assumes that macrolide resistance C. coli infection reduces treatment efficacy. However, it is possible that risks less than our estimates.

Introduction

Campylobacter is considered an important food-borne pathogen. Erythromycin, a macrolide antibiotic, is recommended for the treatment and control of severe culture confirmed campylobacteriosis. Recent studies have reported higher frequencies of resistant Campylobacter in conventional swine farms compared to antibiotic free farms. There are concerns that macrolide antibiotic use on swine farms may increase human health risk. Our objective was to conduct a stochastic quantitative risk assessment of potential adverse health outcomes due to macrolide resistant C. coli infection originating from macrolide use on the swine farm.

Materials and Methods

We chose a retrospective modeling approach instead of the traditional farm to fork model which is significantly more data intensive. Hence, we back calculated (C_m), the number of human macrolide resistant C. coli infections caused by eating contaminated pork, due to a specific type of macrolide use in swine. We started with estimated number of total culture confirmed human infections (C_t). As a measure of human health risk, we then calculated the expected number among the C_m cases that might experience an adverse treatment outcome due to macrolide resistance. An adverse treatment outcome refers to ineffective treatment resulting in prolonged illness such as extra days of diarrhea or fever. We divided our model into Release, Exposure and Consequence assessment sections according to FDA guidance 152 (www.fda.gov/cvm/guidance/fguide152.DOC). We utilized a variety of uncertainty distributions for the parameters and simulated with @Risk software (20,000 iterations).

Release Assessment: In this section, we calculated the fraction of C. coli population in swine that is macrolide resistant due to different types of macrolide (r_m). Following we describe the estimation of r_m for prevention and growth promotion uses (Tylan Premix® and Tylan Sulfa-G ®) followed by the estimation for treatment and control uses (Tylan Injection®, Tylan Soluble® and Pulmotil Premix®)

Let r_b be the background resistant fraction that exists without exposure to macrolide, and r_t be the steady state resistant fraction in a conventional farm in which a fraction (α) of the swine have been exposed to a specific macrolide. The total resistant fraction (r_t) is linearly related to the fraction exposed (α) as a first order approximation shown in Equation 1.

$$r_t = r_b + \alpha(1 - r_b)p \tag{1}$$

Where, the constant (p) corresponds to the probability that a bacterium among the fraction $\alpha(1\text{-}r_b)$ of the C. coli population that is susceptible, acquires resistance or is replaced by a resistant bacterium. The term $\alpha(1\text{-}r_b)p$ is equal to (r_m), the fraction resistant due to macrolide use.

To estimate p, we used the difference in the resistant fractions between antibiotic free (ABF) farms and conventional farms (using macrolide). Two studies reported 38% of 745 C. coli isolates from ABF farms and 77% of 347 C. coli isolates from conventional farms (r_t) were resistant (Gebreyes et al., 2005 and Thakur and Gebreyes 2005). Hence, we estimated r_b = 38% and r_t = 77% (Mean of the Beta distributions in Table 2). We assumed that all the animals in the conventional farms were exposed to macrolide i.e. α =1. By solving Equation 1, we calculated p = 62% for prevention and growth promotion uses. From industrial usage data, the overall national fraction of swine exposed for prevention and growth promotion uses was 58% (Doane, 2005). Finally, we computed, r_m =21% (resistance in C. coli in swine that is due to macrolide use).

For estimation of p due to treatment uses, we had to use data on Enterococci spp. Jackson et al., 2004 found that the resistant fraction in Enterococci spp. from farms that used macrolide for prevention alone was twice of that in farms with treatment uses. Therefore, we assumed (p) for treatment uses is 31% or half of the (p) for prevention or growth promotion uses.

Exposure assessment: For the Exposure assessment, we estimated the number of culture-confirmed human C. coli infections that are resistant due to macrolide use in swine (C_m) utilizing Equation 2.

$$C_m = C_t \eta \, r_m \tag{2}$$

Where, the population etiologic fraction (η) is defined as the fraction of human infections caused by C. coli from swine. Total number of culture confirmed human C. coli infections per year is C_t.

To calculate the etiologic fraction (η) for swine, we conservatively (Risk increasing) assumed that all the C. coli infections (C_t) are caused by eating only chicken or pork, then distributed the cases according to relative carcass contamination rates. Table 1 provides the data sources, and the estimated values of the parameters utilized in calculating η. To estimate the kilograms of contaminated pork, we assumed that all ground pork from a contaminated swine carcass is contaminated, while the non ground pork is not. For kilograms of contaminated chicken we assumed all servings from a contaminated carcass were contaminated. As a result, we calculated that 12.4% of the human C. coli infections are caused from swine.

Table 1 Estimation of etiologic fraction for C. coli for swine and chicken

Parameter Details	Chicken	Swine
Carcass contamination rate of Campylobacter spp (Food safety and Inspection service 1994)	88% Beta(1149, 190)	32% Beta(666,1448)
Fraction of C.coli among Campylobacter spp isolates (NARMS: National Antimicrobial Resistance Monitoring System retail 2002-2003)	30% Beta(231,527)	1 (assumption)
Fraction of carcasses contaminated with C.coli	27%	32%
Expected Fraction of swine carcass processed into ground meat (Hurd et al., 2004)	100%	21%
Overall fraction C.coli contaminated meat servings after slaughter	27%	6.72%
Annual kilograms of meat produced (National Agricultural Statistics Service, 2006)	16 billion	9.3 billion
Annual kilograms of C. coli contaminated servings	4.4 billion	0.620 Billion
Etiologic fractions for C. coli from chicken and swine	87.6%(86-89)%	12.4(11 -14)%

Consequence assessment: We calculated the annual number of adverse outcomes due to macrolide use (C_{ao}) according to Equation 3. Where τ is the joint probability that a culture confirmed infection is treated with an antibiotic and the prescribed antibiotic is macrolide. The parameter, ρ, is the probability that adverse outcome occurs due to macrolide resistance.

$$C_{ao} = C_m \rho \tau \tag{3}$$

We are unaware of any evidence that macrolide resistant *Campylobacter* causes any more illness days than susceptible or that erythromycin treatment has any clinical benefit, i.e. ρ is likely zero. However, to be conservative, we utilized fluoroquinolone data to estimate ρ; erroneously assuming that macrolide and fluoroquinolone resistant infections have identical clinical consequences.

Table 2 Parameter estimates and risk assessment of adverse treatment outcomes to *C.coli* infections that are resistant due to macrolide use in swine

Parameter	Prevention and Growth promotion	Treatment	All uses	Data sources
Release Assessment				
α, Fraction of animals exposed to macrolide	58%	17.3%		Doane marketing survey (2005)
r_b, Background resistance	38% Beta(229,518)*	--		Gebreyes et al., (2005);Thakur and Gebreyes (2005)
r_t, Resistant fraction in farms utilizing macrolide	r_t=77% Beta(12,823)*	--		
P, Probability of resistance development	62%	31.2%		
r_m, Fraction resistant due to macrolide use	21%	3.3%		
Exposure Assessment				
Annual number of *Campylobacter spp* cases (culture-confirmed)	38,315 Gamma(5665,1)6.76*			Foodnet 2004
Fraction of human *Campylobacter* cases caused by C. *coli*	4.3% Beta (64,1409)*			Gupta et al., 2004
C_t, Annual number of C. *coli* cases	1647			
η, Etiologic fraction	12.40%			
C_m, number of cases resistant due to macrolide use/year	46	7	53.0	
Consequence Assessment				
τ Probability that a culture confirmed case is treated with a macrolide	32% Beta(320,501)Beta(938,193)*			Nelson et al., 2004
ρ Probability of an adverse outcome given macrolide resistance	22% Beta(7,24)*			Kushner et al., 1995; Sanders et al., 2002
C_{ao} Annual number of adverse outcomes (median)	3.23 (1.61-5.65)	0.5(0.23-0.84)	3.7 (1.8-6.4)	
Annual risk of an adverse outcome for a person in the US (median)	1 in 92 (52-184) million	1 in 620(354-1250) million	1 in 80 (45-162) million	

Confidence intervals provided are two sided at 90% confidence. The human health consequences are given as medians. Annual risk was calculated as the ratio of the US population of 298 million/C_{ao}. * These are uncertainty distributions for the parameter estimates which were simulated using @Risk® software.

Results

The parameter estimates, their distributions, data sources, the results for the risk assessment are summarized in Table 2. The median risk of an adverse treatment outcome due to macrolide use induced resistance in C. *coli* from swine is less than 1 in 80 million. The risk is less than 1 in 45 million with 95%. The risk due to treatment uses is negligible and is less than 1 in 354 million with 95% confidence.

Discussion

Our results show that at worst, the human health risk due to macrolide induced resistance in C. *coli* from swine is very low even with the conservative assumptions we made. Reasons for the low risk include the low fraction of human infections caused by C. *coli* and the relatively higher C. *coli* contamination rate of chicken carcass. Furthermore, the risk due to treatment uses is negligible as only a very small fraction of swine is exposed to it. We had to make very conservative assumptions such as that all the C. *coli* infections are caused from chicken or swine due to the lack of data on the etiologic fraction. More data on the etiologic fraction and the clinical consequences of erythromycin resistance is required. In addition, Sensitivity analysis showed that the fraction of human infections caused by C. *coli* and macrolide resistant fractions in conventional and ABF farms are other parameters leading to a significant uncertainty in the resulting risk estimates, demonstrating the need for further research in this area.

References

DOANE MARKETING RESEARCH (2005). "Doane Marketing Research Animal Health Market Study (2003-2005)".

GEBREYES, W., A., et al., 2005. Campylobacter coli: prevalence and antimicrobial resistance in antimicrobial-free (ABF) swine production systems. *Journal of Antimicrobial Chemotherapy,* 56(4), 765-768.

GUPTA, A., et al., 2004. Antimicrobial resistance among Campylobacter strains, United States, 1997-2001. *Emerging Infectious Diseases,* 10(6), 1102-1109.

HURD, H. S., et al., 2004. Public health consequences of macrolide use in food animals: a deterministic risk assessment. *Journal of food Protection,* 67(5), 980-992.

JACKSON C.R, et al., 2004. Effects of Tylosin use on erythromycin resistance in enterococci isolated from swine. *Applied Environmental Microbiology,* 70:4205-10.

KUSCHNER, R. A., et al., 1995. Use of azithromycin for the treatment of Campylobacter enteritis in travelers to Thailand, an area where ciprofloxacin resistance is prevalent. *Clinical Infectious Diseases,* 21(3), 536-541.

NELSON, J. M., et al., 2004. Prolonged diarrhea due to ciprofloxacin-resistant campylobacter infection. *Journal of Infectious Diseases* 190(6), 1150-1157.

THAKUR, S. AND GEBREYES, W. A. (2005). Prevalence and antimicrobial resistance of Campylobacter in antimicrobial-free and conventional pig production systems. *Journal of Food Protection,* 68(11), 2402-2410.

SANDERS, J. W., et al., 2002. An observational clinic-based study of diarrheal illness in deployed United States military personnel in Thailand: presentation and outcome of Campylobacter infection. *American Journal Tropical Medicine and Hygiene,* 67(5), 533-538.

Risk assessment for antibiotic resistance: use of macrolides in Danish pig production

Alban, L.*[1], Nielsen, E.O. [1], Dahl, J.[1]

[1]: Danish Meat Association, Vinkelvej 11. DK-8620 Kjellerup, Denmark
* Lis Alban: lia@danishmeat.dk

Abstract

What is the risk that use of antibiotics in farm animals will result in treatment failure in humans? Different approaches can address this. One approach is to make a risk profile and another to conduct a risk assessment. Use of macrolides in Danish pigs will be used as an example that demonstrates how the conclusion depends on the approach. A risk profile includes a description of the hazard and a qualitative assessment of the risk, similar to hazard identification. Accordingly, macrolide-resistant *Campylobacter* might develop as a result of usage of macrolides in pig production. This is of concern for human health, because it might reduce the effect of erythromycin, a macrolide used in children for treatment of *Campylobacter* infections. A full risk assessment contains an assessment of release, exposure, and consequences related to the unwanted outcome. Release deals with the probability that *Campylobacter* will be present in the gut, and how often the isolates found are resistant to macrolides. Exposure relates to the probability of a person being exposed to macrolide-resistant *Campylobacter*, and here the prevalence in pork - and not live pigs - is of interest. The consequences deal with the outcome of exposure: likelihood of disease/adverse effects. *Campylobacter* is commonly occurring in the pig gut, and so is macrolide-resistance in *Campylobacter* in pigs. However, the prevalence of *Campylobacter* in Danish pork at retail is negligible because of use of blast-chilling after slaughter. Human campylobacteriosis is usually self-limiting. One study describes adverse effects related to infection with macrolide-resistant *Campylobacter* – but the effect was severely confounded with age and co-morbidity, and no children got adversely affected. So according to the risk assessment, the risk associated with veterinary use of macrolides in Danish pigs for the health of humans seemed low. This is contrary to the result obtained by the risk profile.

Introduction

Veterinary usage of antibiotics might result in development of resistance among zoonotic bacteria or non-pathogenic microorganisms. The fear is that treatment failure of humans will occur as a result of infection with zoonotic bacteria originating from e.g. pigs or poultry treated with antibiotics. Moreover, transfer of resistance from non-pathogenic microorganisms to human pathogens might occur, and examples of this have been observed. The World Health Organization (WHO) has re-servations about veterinary use of macrolides, because of the risk of development of macrolide-resistant *Campylobacter*. In particular, children are of concern, because macrolides are the drug of choice for treatment of intestinal disorders in children (WHO, 2005). In line, The US Federal Drug Agency (FDA) considers veterinary usage of macrolides as a risk for human health (FDA, 2003). To mitigate this risk, usage of antibiotics as growth promoters has gradually been banned within the European Union (EU) (Anon., 1998; Anon., 2003). In July 1999, the EU suspended four antimicrobial growth promoters: bacitracin, virginiamycin, spiramycin and tylosin (Anon., 1998).

In 2006, the Danish Veterinary & Food Administration decided to redraw macrolides from the list of drugs recommended for treatment of diarrhea in pigs. The decision was driven by a political interest in reducing the antibiotic consumption *per se* as well as evidence pointing at a specific risk related to macrolides. The decision to leave out macrolides was taken based on a risk profile, in line with the precautionary principle, which can be used to take preliminary decisions.

A full risk assessment is then a natural step – to study whether in fact the decision taken is justified or not. Therefore, a risk assessment following international guidelines was conducted by the Danish Meat Association aiming at assessing the risk for human health associated with usage of macrolides in Danish pigs. In the following it will be demonstrated how the estimated risk depends on the approach taken: risk profile or quantitative risk assessment.

Materials and Methods

Initially, we identified macrolide–resistant *Campylobacter* as the agent of interest based on two criteria: 1) it should be a zoonotic bacterium that causes disease in humans and 2) macrolides should be the drug of choice for treatment of disease. Data on prevalence of *Campylobacter* in beef, pork, poultry meat and humans as well as on macrolide-resistant *Campylobacter* were obtained from national and international surveys primarily from 2004. In particular, data from EU surveillance were obtained from the EFSA report (EFSA, 2005). Moreover, information on antibiotic consumption, meat import statistics and consumptions patterns were obtained. Information from published papers on the consequences related to human infection with *Campylobacter* was also incorporated.

We decided to include pork and poultry in the analysis, whereas we interpreted pets as carriers of *Campylobacter* from pork and poultry, because pets often share food with their owners. Beef was ruled out because it was an insignificant source of macrolide-resistant *Campylobacter*.

A risk profile includes a description of the hazard and a qualitative assessment of the risk, similar to hazard identification. A risk assessment is an extension because is implies an evaluation of each of the following steps:

1. Hazard identification
2. Release assessment
3. Exposure assessment
4. Consequence assessment
5. Risk estimation

A quantitative model was constructed in the software programme @Risk

Results

Risk profile
According to the risk profile, macrolide-resistant *Campylobacter* might develop as a result of usage of macrolides in animal production. This is of concern for human health, because it might reduce the effect of erythromycin, a macrolide used in children for treatment of *Campylobacter* infections. In 2004, approximately 13t of macrolides were used for therapeutic treatment in Denmark (DANMAP, 2004). Around 92% of this was used for a production of 23m finishers as well as an export of 2m piglets (DANMAP, 2004; Anon., 2005b). This corresponds to around 0.5g macrolides per produced pig (13t x 0.92 /25m pigs = 0.48g macrolides / pig). The main part (87%) of the consumption in pigs was used for weaners and finishers. Only around 50kg of macrolides were used in cattle, and here, half of it was used in adult cattle and half in calves <12months of age. In poultry, around 15kg were used (DANMAP, 2004). This common use selects for development of macrolide-resistance in *Campylobacter* (Frimodt-Møller and Hammerum, 2004). Secondly, a Danish study, recently published, demonstrated an excess risk of invasiveness or dying among patients infected with macrolide-resistant *Campylobacter* (Helms et al., 2005). Based on this information it was judged that use of macrolides for treatment of pigs might lead to development of macrolide-resistant *Campylobacter* which again constitutes an increased risk for humans.

Risk assessment
The release assessment showed that thermophilic *Campylobacter* spp. are widespread in nature and the principle reservoirs are the alimentary tract of wild and domestic birds and mammals. In poultry and cattle, *C. jejuni* is the most commonly found species, whereas *C. coli* is most common in pigs (Stern & Line, 2000). There is a moderate to high prevalence of macrolide-resistant *Campylobacter* in live pigs, including Danish pigs, presumably as a result of usage of macrolides in pig production. In poultry, the macrolide-resistance in *Campylobacter* is less common and probably

a result of the use of antimicrobial growth promoters (virginiamycin and spiramycin) in broilers in EU before year 2000.

The exposure assessment showed that the prevalence of *Campylobacter* in pork is low, and especially low in Danish pork due to blast chilling. In poultry, the proportion of *Campylobacter* isolates that are macrolide-resistant is much lower than in pork however; this is counteracted by the high prevalence of *Campylobacter* found in poultry in general. The exposure model for 2004 data showed that the usage of macrolides in Danish pig production was associated with seven human cases only. The main part of the cases was related to imported meat; pork (83 cases) or poultry meat (74 cases).

Table 1
Description of input parameters used in a model describing the source of exposure of Danes to macrolide-resistant *Campylobacter* due to consumption of pork or poultry meat, 2004

Variable	Parameter estimate	Derived distribution	Source
Relative consumption of pork compared to poultry	1.4 times more pork is consumed than poultry in Denmark on average	a	GfK Consumer Scan, GfK Denmark
Distribution of origin of pork	Domestic: 75% Imported: 25%	a	Statistics from Danish Meat Association, 2006
Distribution of origin of poultry	Nationally: 65% Imported: 35%	a	Statistics from Danish Meat Association, 2006
Prevalence of *Campylobacter* in pork	Domestic: 0.2% Imported: in general 5% or lower, however higher prevalences also observed	Beta(s=5, n=2,413) Pert (0%; 5%; 20%)	EFSA, 2005
Proportion that is macrolide-resistant	Domestic: 23% Imported: varying greatly	Beta(s=23,n=100) Pert(16%;24%;78%)	DANMAP, 2004 EFSA, 2005 Authors' best guess
Prevalence of *Campylobacter* in poultry	Domestic: 23.5% Imported: varies greatly	Beta(s=137, n=584) Pert(2%; 30%, 89%)	DANMAP, 2004 EFSA, 2005
Proportion[b] that is macrolide-resistant	Domestic: *C. jejuni*: 0.5% *C. coli*: 3% Imported: *C. jejuni*: 3% *C. coli*: 12%	1.0%[ab] 4.8%[ab]	DANMAP, 2004
Human cases due to macrolide-resistant (Mres) campylobacteriosis	3,724 human *Campylobacter* cases in 2004 1997-2000: 5.9% Mres C. 1997-2004: 0-5% Mres C.	5% ≈ 186 cases[a]	Anon., 2005a; Helms et al., 2005

a: No attempt was made to model the variability associated with these parameters.
b: The distribution between *C. jejuni* and *C. coli* in poultry meat was assumed to be 80:20 in line with Nielsen et al. (2005), hence in domestic produced poultry the proportion of *Campylobacter* isolates that is macrolide-resistant is 0.8 x 0.5% + 0.2 x 3.0% = 1%. Similarly, for imported poultry: 0.8 x 3% + 0.2 x 12% = 4.8%. In pork, all isolates were assumed to be *C. coli*.

The consequences assessment showed that in 2004 an incidence of human campylobacteriosis of 68.8 cases per 100,000 inhabitants in Denmark corresponding to 3,724 cases (Anon., 2005a). The disease is usually self-limiting with symptoms lasting less than seven days. Apparently, an excess risk of invasiveness and death among patients infected with *Campylobacter* has been observed by Helms et al. (2005). However, the effect of macrolide-resistance found in that study was confounded by age (only old people at risk) and co-morbidity, and non-significant when evaluated for 0 to 30 days of infection (Helms et al., 2005). In addition, in the study by Helms et al. (2005) no children infected with macrolide-resistant *Campylobacter* had invasive infection or died, and these were the ones that WHO were concerned with. Overall speaking, the consequences seemed to be negligible for children and adults, and low for old people. The crude data showed that patients infected with macrolide-resistant *Campylobacter* had a probability of 3.4% of experiencing invasive infection or death (Helms et al., 2005). This implies that for the year 2004, 7 cases x 0.034 = 0.2

human cases with adverse effect due to Danish pork could have been expected – when disregarding the confounding effect of age and co-morbidity, and the baseline risk associated with *Campylobacter*.

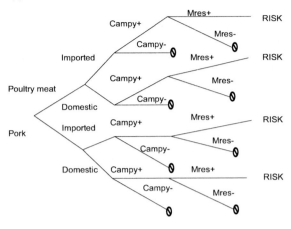

● : No risk

Figure 1
Graphical description of model used to assess the distribution of exposure of humans in Denmark to macrolide-resistant *Campylobacter* in pork or poultry meat of domestic or imported origin based on data from 2004

Discussion

The present study demonstrates that the use of the pre-cautionary principle is a preliminary activity that should be utilized when there is concern about a given activity/hazard. However, a full risk assessment is also required because it might yield a different conclusion about the concerned risk than when only undertaking a risk-profile. When performing risk assessments, international guidelines should be followed. Ideally, the assessment should be subjected to peer-review and an open debate should be held among stakeholders to ensure quality, validity and common understanding of the risk assessment. The results of such a risk assessment constitute the optimal scientific basis of management decisions (Vose et al., 2001).

Conclusions

The risk associated with veterinary use of macrolides in Danish pigs for human health because of macrolide-resistant *Campylobacter* seems to be negligible to low. A further reduction in the usage of macrolides in Danish pig production will therefore have limited effect on the number of human cases with adverse effects due to exposure of Danes to macrolide-resistant *Campylobacter*.

References

EFSA, 2005. http://www.efsa.eu.int/science/monitoring_zoonoses/reports/1277_en.html.
WHO, 2005.
http://www.who.int/foodborne_disease/resistance/amr_feb2005.pdf accessed January 2007
HELMS ET AL., 2005. Adverse Health Events Associated with Antimicrobial Drug Resistance in *Campylobacter* Species: A Registry-based Cohort Study. *J. Inf. Diseases.* 191, 1050-1055.

Please, contact the presenting author for a reference list for the remaining references.

Quantification of the informative value of meat inspection to detect biological hazards for pork consumers in Europe

Fosse, J. *[1, 2], Seegers, H.[2], Magras, C.[1]

[1] National Veterinary School, National Institute of Agronomic Research (INRA), Unit of Food Safety, Route de Gachet, BP 40706, 44307 Nantes cedex 3, France
[2] National Veterinary School, National Institute of Agronomic Research (INRA), Unit of Animal Health Management, Route de Gachet, BP 40706, 44307 Nantes cedex 3, France
* corresponding author: j.fosse@vet-nantes.fr

Abstract

Meat inspection at slaughterhouse was the main mean of control used historically to protect consumers from biological hazards transmitted by the consumption of pork. The epidemiological evolution of biological hazards led the European Union to promulgate new food safety legislation in the form of the Hygiene Package, based on a risk analysis approach. This package authorizes Member States to develop new meat inspection methods in order to accentuate consumer health protection. However, the levels of detection of biological hazards during traditional meat inspection have not been established, particularly in quantitative terms. Such an assessment is needed to define risk-based meat inspection schemes. The aim of this study was to provide elements to quantify the lack of detection of biological hazards by current meat inspection methods. A literature review of 440 references was undertaken to summarise information on the incidence of foodborne zoonoses and the prevalence of biological hazards on/in pork carcasses. Then for each hazard, the incidence rate of zoonosis induced by pork consumption (I_{pork}) and the ratio of non-control of hazard at and after meat inspection (NC) were calculated. The comparison between incidence rates and non-control scores shew that the three most frequent hazards Salmonella enterica, Campylobacter spp., Yersinia enterocolitica (I_{pork} = 3.374; 2.170 and 2.826 cases per 100,000 inhabitants per annum, respectively) cannot be detected by macroscopic examination of carcasses (NC = 1.19223; 0.27756; 0.08341, respectively). Consequently, new means of hazards control are needed to complete the classical macroscopic examination.

Introduction

Pork is the most consumed meat in the European Union (DEVINE, 2003). Management of hazards transmitted to humans by consumption of pork is therefore of major health significance. Meat inspection is the oldest means used at slaughterhouse to protect the consumer health. It is based on an *ante mortem* clinical examination and a macroscopic *post mortem* examination of the carcass, including incision or palpation of lymph nodes and organs to detect clinical signs or macroscopic lesions potentially correlated with the presence of hazards (THORNTON, 1957). Additional bacteriological or chemical analyses can also be performed if relevant to assess the safety of carcasses. In 2002 the European Commission promulgated the Food Law (regulation (EC) 178/2002) whose main objective is to apply risk analysis to food safety legislation, with risk assessment - a "*scientifically based process consisting of four steps: hazard identification, hazard characterisation, exposure assessment and risk characterisation*" - as primary step. A preliminary study concerning hazard identification has shown that 35 biological hazards may be transmitted to humans by the consumption of pork: 12 are parasitic, 14 bacterial and 9 viral (FOSSE *et al.*, 2005). Of these, 12 were defined as current established European hazards, *i.e.*

hazards whose presence on pork and whose transmission to humans by food consumption is established today in the countries of the European Union. Three were parasitic (*Sarcocystis suihominis, Toxoplasma gondii* and *Trichinella spiralis*) and nine were bacterial (thermophilic campylobacters, *Clostridium botulinum, Clostridium perfringens, Listeria monocytogenes, Mycobacterium* spp., *Salmonella enterica, Staphylococcus aureus,* shiga-toxin producing *Escherichia coli* or STEC, *Yersinia enterocolitica*). The impact on human health of biological hazards transmitted by the consumption of contaminated pork, which may be assessed by the consecutive incidence of clinical cases in humans, is closely linked with their occurrence on pork carcasses, and also their detectability during meat inspection. However, levels of contamination of carcasses are often not fully known, whereas risk analysis has to include such information, especially to estimate the detectability of biological hazards at meat inspection. Moreover, few studies have included data from all the countries of the European Union to assess the mean impact of biological hazards transmitted by pork on human health. The purpose of this article was to explore the informative value of the epidemiological indicators available in European countries in order to apply risk assessment to pork meat inspection. Assessment of the mean occurrence of hazards transmitted to humans by the consumption of pork in Europe was therefore first implemented. Mean levels of prevalence of biological hazards on pork carcasses was also estimated. A ratio for non-control (NC) of risks for consumers after meat inspection was calculated.

Material and methods

A review of four hundred and forty-nine papers was carried out to collect information regarding the prevalence of biological hazards potentially transmitted to humans by the consumption of pork on carcasses and the exposure of humans to these hazards due to the consumption of pork. These articles were searched on CAB and Medline databases. This study only addresses the main category of pig produced in Europe, *i.e.* indoor reared and finished pig. To assess the occurrence of clinical cases in humans induced by biological hazards, only information concerning western European countries (former EU-15) population was studied.

For each current established European hazard: *i)* from 3 to 43 values of rates of prevalence on pork carcasses were compiled and from this information, a mean rate of prevalence on pork carcasses (P_{car}) was calculated for each hazard; *ii)* from 1 to 58 data regarding the incidence of the foodborne disease in humans induced by biological hazards in western European countries were collected. A mean incidence rate (I) was calculated for each hazard. The pork attributable proportion (PAP), *i.e.* for each current established European biological hazard responsible for foodborne disease in humans, the proportion of clinical cases induced by the consumption of contaminated pork, was calculated from: *i)* data concerning the number of clinical cases of foodborne disease according to the food vehicle of transmission (OLSEN *et al.*, 2000; DANSK ZOONOSECENTER, 2001): $PAP = n_{pork} / n_{total}$ with n_{pork} and n_{total}, for one given hazard, the number of human cases due to pork consumption and the total number of human cases due to food consumption, respectively; *ii)* or, when exhaustive data was lacking, from data concerning the proportion of outbreaks induced by pork according to the mean number of clinical cases per outbreak (SOCKETT *et al.*, 1993; SCHMIDT and GERVELMEYER, 2003; HAEGHEBAERT *et al.*, 2002; HAEGHEBAERT *et al.*, 2003): $PAP = (o_{pork} / o_{total}) \times N$ with o_{pork} and o_{total}, for one given hazard, the number of outbreaks due to pork consumption and the total number of outbreaks due to food consumption, respectively; *N*: the mean number of human cases per outbreak; *iii)* or, when those information was lacking, PAP was the estimate given by an expert panel in a study performed in the United States in 2006 (HOFFMANN *et al.*,

2006). The incidence rate of clinical cases in humans induced by the consumption of pork (I_{pork}) may be considered in relation to the mean incidence rate (I) and the estimate of the pork attributable proportion (PAP):

$$I_{pork} = I \times PAP$$

Moreover, I_{pork} may also be considered as a function of the level of consumption of pork ($Cons_{pork}$), the mean prevalence of the biological hazard in pork carcasses (P_{car}), the score of non-detection of hazards at meat inspection (ND), the potential secondary contamination of meat from inspection step to consumption step (SC) and the susceptibility of consumers to the hazard (Su):

$$I_{pork} = f\ (Cons_{pork},\ P_{car},\ ND,\ SC,\ Su)$$

Variations in levels of consumption of pork between European countries are small (DEVINE, 2003). So we considered $Cons_{pork}$ as a constant. Sensitive subpopulations are usually described: Young children, Olderly, Pregnant and neonates, and Immunocompromised (YOPI) (GERBA et al., 1996). But today quantitative information about the mean susceptibility of a whole population to a specific biological hazard is often lacking. So we considered here the value of Su for the whole population as a constant for each hazard in each European country. Consequently, a score of non-detection of hazards at meat inspection (ND) and a ratio of non-control of hazards (NC) at and after meat inspection were calculated by the following equations:

$$ND\ =\ \int\left(\frac{I_{pork}}{P_{car} \times SC}\right) = \int\left(\frac{I \times PAP}{P_{car} \times SC}\right)\ \text{and then: } NC\ =\ \int(ND \times SC)\ =\ \frac{I_{pork}}{P_{car}}$$

Results

Yersinia enterocolitica and *Clostridium perfringens* are the two main hazards identified on pork carcasses, with mean rates of prevalence higher than 30%. *Listeria monocytogenes* (P_{car} = 25.8%) and *Staphylococcus aureus* (23.8%) have the next highest prevalence rates, before *Sarcocystis suihominis* (15.7%) and *Toxoplasma gondii* (12.5%), whereas the mean prevalence rates of other hazards are lower than 10% (Table 1).
Salmonella enterica, *Yersinia enterocolitica* and *Campylobacter* spp. are the three most frequent hazards reported in human clinical cases which may be related to the consumption of pork, with I_{pork} of 3.374, 2.826 and 2.170 cases per 100,000 inhabitants per annum, respectively. The other hazards have I_{pork} lower than 1 case per 100,000 inhabitants per annum (Table 1).

Table 1. *Mean rate of incidence of human clinical cases (I), mean Pork Attributable Proportion (PAP), mean rate of incidence of human cases due to the consumption of pork (I_{pork}), mean rate of prevalence of biological hazards on pork carcasses (P_{car}) and ratios of non control (NC) after meat inspection according to biological current established European hazards.*

Hazard	I	(n)	PAP	I_{pork}	P_{car}	(n)	$minP_{car}$	$maxP_{car}$	NC
Parasitic hazard									
Sarcocystis suihominis	0.0025	(1)	10.0	0.00025	15.7	(7)	0.8	32.0	0.000016
Toxoplasma gondii	4.250	(2)	10.0	0.425	12.5	(8)	0.9	33.0	0.03395
Trichinella spiralis	0.025	(29)	55.9	0.014	0.4	(9)	$3x10^{-6}$	1.2	0.03911
Bacterial hazard									
Campylobacter spp.	62.980	(35)	3.6	2.170	7.8	(12)	0	31.5	0.27756
Clostridium botulinum	0.117	(35)	23.8	0.028	32.6*	-	-	-	0.00086
Clostridium perfringens	0.730	(21)	20.3	0.148	32.6	(3)	10.4	66.0	0.00454
Listeria monocytogenes	0.305	(34)	13.8	0.042	25.8	(6)	10.7	48.0	0.00163
Mycobacterium spp.	0.003	(2)	33.3	0.001	5.8	(2)	0.7	10.9	0.00017
Salmonella enterica	51.537	(58)	6.6	3.374	2.8	(43)	0	45.6	1.19223
Staphylococcus aureus	0.547	(29)	12.2	0.067	23.8	(5)	10.3	57.7	0.00282
STEC	1.292	(33)	2.2	0.029	7.2	(9)	0	50.0	0.00402
Yersinia enterocolitica	3.654	(15)	77.3	2.826	33.9	(5)	0	80.0	0.08341

*(n): number of data used to calculate the mean value; $_{min}$: minimal value; $_{max}$: maximal value; *: estimated value, considering that C. botulinum and C. perfringens have the same biological characteristics, notably in their digestive origin. Thus, the prevalence of C. botulinum may be considered similar to the prevalence of C. perfringens.*

Salmonella enterica is characterized by the highest non-control ratio (1.19223), before *Campylobacter* spp. (0.27756) and *Yersinia enterocolitica* (0.08341).

Discussion

Information regarding the prevalence rates for hazards on pork carcasses and the occurrence of the clinical disease they induce in humans is needed to assess risks due to pork consumption. However, although many hazards have a huge impact on public health, such information is not yet available, mainly because of the cost and difficulties of detection of these hazards in food. Moreover, even when enough information is available to calculate mean rates of prevalence or incidence, and when it is obtained with sensitive and efficient methods, the range of available values is often huge. This variation may be due to differences in: *i)* sensitivity of analytical methods, *ii)* recording of clinical cases, or also *iii)* actual incidence of clinical cases in humans in the area or country. Consequently, the incidence of some hazards may be underestimated, particularly when the hazard mainly result in isolated cases.

Evaluation of the non-control of hazards at and after meat inspection was considered both according to the presence of the hazard on pig carcasses, and to the incidence of clinical cases induced by pork consumption. This evaluation overlooks the effects of pork processing and such an approach may therefore be considered as a first step in evaluation. The secondary contamination of pork after meat inspection and before consumption is indeed not quantitatively assessable.

Conclusion

This study demonstrated that hazards with high rates of incidence due to pork consumption (I_{pork}) are those which have the highest non-control ratios. Such a result should lead to changes in meat inspection methods to take account of hazards which cannot be detected by macroscopic examination of carcasses. Consequently, to reduce the human exposure to these hazards, either a reduction of their prevalence in pigs entering the slaughterhouse or a carcass sampling design to identify their presence by analytical tools are needed. However, given that systematic sampling to look for all main hazards is not reasonably feasible, the assessment of on-farm existing pre-harvesting information and / or a dedicated on-farm pre-harvesting sampling protocol for laboratory analyses seem to be useful.

Acknowledgements

The authors thank the Directorate of Food Safety (DGAI) of the French Ministry of Agriculture.

References

DANSK ZOONOSECENTER, 2001. Annual Report on Zoonoses in Denmark 2000. Available online at: http://zoonyt.dzc.dk/annualreport2000/index.html.
DEVINE, R., 2003. Meat consumption trends in the world and the European Union. *INRA Productions Animales*, 16, 325-327.
FOSSE, J., MAGRAS, C., SEEGERS, H., 2005. Identification of biological hazards transmitted to humans by pork consumption: the first step of a risk analysis approach in european slaughterhouses. In : *5th Congress of the ECVPH*, Glasgow, 10-13. Available online at: http://www.sapuvetnet.org/Pdf%20Files/Proc-abstrCONF2005.pdf
FOSSE, J., MAGRAS, C., SEEGERS, H., 2007. Evaluation quantitative des risques biologiques pour le consommateur de viande de porc. *39èmes Journées de la Recherche Porcine* (on press).
GERBA, C., ROSE, J.B., HAAS, C.N., 1996. Sensitive populations: who is at the greatest risk? *Int. J. Food Microbiol.*, 30,113-123.
HAEGHEBAERT, S., et al., 2002. Les toxi-infections alimentaires collectives en France en 2001. *Bull. Epidemiol. Hebd.*, 50:249-53.
HAEGHEBAERT, S., CARLIER, J-P., POPOFF, M., 2003. Caractéristiques épidémiologiques du botulisme humain en France, en 2001 et 2002. *Bull. Epidemiol. Hebd.*, 29:129-130.
HOFFMANN, S., et al., 2006. *Eliciting information of uncertainty from heterogenous expert panels. Attributing U.S. foodborne pathogen illness to food consumption.* Washington: Ressources For the Future. Available online at: www.rff.org/rff/Documents/RFF-DP-06-17-REV.pdf.
OLSEN, S.J., et al., 2000. Surveillance for foodborne diseases outbreaks - United States, 1993-1997. *MMWR Surv. Sum.*, 49:1-64.
SCHMIDT, K., GERVELMEYER, A., 2003. *WHO surveillance programme for control of foodborne infections and intoxications in Europe. 8th report 1999-2000.* Geneva: World Health Organization. Available online at: http://www.bfr.bund.de/internet/8threport/8threp_fr.htm.
SOCKETT, P.N., et al., 1993. Foodborne disease surveillance in England and Wales: 1989-1991. *Commun. Dis. Rep. CDR Rev.*, 3:R159-174.
THORNTON, H., 1957. *Textbook of meat inspection.* London: Baillere, Tindall and Cox, 47-64.

Microbiological criteria – Danish experience with use of the food safety criteria on minced meat and meat preparations

Olsen, A-M.*[1], Sørensen, L.L.[1], Alban, L[2]

[1]: Danish Meat Association, Axeltorv 3, 1609 Copenhagen, Denmark.
[2]: Danish Meat Association, Vinkelvej 11, 8620 Kjellerup, Denmark
*Anne-Mette Olsen: mol@danishmeat.dk,

Abstract

The recently introduced EU Commission regulation 2073/2005 on microbiological criteria for foodstuffs sets food safety criteria on Salmonella in minced meat and meat preparations. Products intended to be eaten cooked are to be sampled weekly by five samples of 10g each. If Salmonella is found and the product is on the market, a recall will take place.

Data from several EU countries in 2005 show a Salmonella prevalence varying from 0-8% in minced pork and 0-4% in minced beef. In Denmark, a total of 32 recalls were performed in 2006. This is costly, and it is questionably whether it has any impact on food safety, since the meat is supposed to be heat-treated prior to consumption

If surveillance for Salmonella is conducted it is usually at slaughterhouse or herd level. This makes it impossible to source all raw materiel from Salmonella-free animals. Even if Salmonella is not found in samples from live animals, there is no guarantee that Salmonella might not be present in the meat from the same animal, because e.g. cross-contamination might have taken place at the abattoir.

Following a request from the UK, the Commission has agreed to ask EFSA for a quantitative risk assessment by December 2008 to possibly review the microbiological criteria in meat, based on data provided by the Member States. In line, the Danish Meat Association has decided to initiate a project on collection of semi-quantitative Salmonella data in minced pork and beef and meat preparations. There is a need for other Member States to provide equal information to ensure that representative data will be available for EFSA.

Introduction

The Commission Regulation No 2073/2005 (Commission, 2005) has been in force since January 1, 2006, and according to this regulation minced meat and meat preparations intended to be eaten cooked must fulfil the food safety criteria on absence of Salmonella in five samples of each 10g.

According to Article 8 of the regulation, Member States are granted a possible transitional derogation related to the food safety criteria for Salmonella, allowing, until 31/12 2009, one of the five samples to be positive for products placed on the national market. This opportunity is used in some Member States, not in others and at present discussed in some. Denmark does not make use of the derogation.

The preamble (9) to the EU regulation 2073/2005 highlights the relevance of basing microbiological criteria on formal risk assessment and internationally approved principles. However, it is questionable whether this has taken place for the microbiological criteria, e.g. it is unknown what the effect of the criteria is on the number of human cases of salmonellosis – and other more cost-effective means have not been evaluated.

This paper describes the Danish experience on dealing with the microbiological food safety criterion on minced pork and beef and meat preparations (pork and beef) intended to be eaten cooked. A food safety criterion applies for products on the market, meaning that the focus is on the consumer. Sampling is done at least weekly (5 x 10g samples). The demand is absence of Salmonella in the five samples, and if Salmonella is found the sampled batch must be withdrawn or recalled. A withdrawal means that the compagny shall withdraw the food in question from the market where the food has left the immediate control of that initial food business operator and inform the competent authorities. A recall means that consumers are also informed in order to recall from them products already supplied to them. In Denmark only recalls are performed.

Following a request by the UK, the Commission has agreed to ask EFSA for a quantitative risk assessment by December 2008 to possibly review the microbiological criteria in meat, based on data provided by the Member States.

UECBV, avec and CLITRAVI, the main meat industry federations working with this dossier in EU, support this possibility for the requirements to be reconsidered in the light of a quantitative risk assessment.

The Danish Meat Association has decided to initiate a project including performing of semi-quantitative analyses when finding Salmonella in minced pork and beef and in meat preparations in the surveillance programme described in Regulation No 2073/2005. These data will subsequently be made available for EFSA. With other words: we are interested in knowing how contaminated a positive sample is; are we talking about few bacteria or high loads?

The aim of the project is to:
1. Provide semi-quantitative data for a risk assessment
2. Based on semi-quantitative data to support introduction of risk-based regulation if possible, because this will have a larger impact on food safety in a more cost-effective manner.

Materials and Methods

The samples included in this study consist of the samples taken routinely according to Regulation No 2073/2005. The ratios of the different kinds of products are not laid down from the start, as the production is dependent on orders. An estimate is that 40% of the samples will consist of minced pork, 40% of minced beef and 20 % of meat preparations. The Danish study will include a minimum of 500 samples, and hopefully up to 1000 samples.

The industry finances the extra costs for analysis of the dilution line. If the plan described above does not supply a sufficient number of positive samples, an additional study may be initiated at the Danish Meat Research Institute.

The five samples that are collected weekly from one batch according to 2073/2005 are kept cooled during transport to the laboratory. Because Denmark does not make use of the derogation the five samples are pooled to one sample adding to a total of 50 grams at the laboratory. Next, 450 ml buffered peptone water is added to the pooled sample. This is the original sample, the 0-dilution. From this sample a dilution line is made. The dilution line is kept at chilling temperature (0-5 °C), until the result of the original sample is available. If the original sample is positive for Salmonella the dilution line is taken into analysis.

For analysing the original sample the laboratory uses their own routine method(s). In Denmark these are the PCR method BAX, the immunoassay system Vidas, or the NMKL no 71, 5th Edition, 1999. For verification of Salmonella-suspect samples the laboratories use NMKL no 71.

Results

Table 1
Variation in prevalence of Salmonella in different EU member states, (EFSA, 2005)

	Carcasses (swabs)	Cuts of meat	Minced meat (10-25g) non RTE*	RTE*
Pork	0-9%	0-18%	0-8%	0-3%
Beef	0-0.6%	0-8%	0-2%	0-4%

*: RTE= Ready to eat

According to Table 1 it can be seen that Salmonella is present in carcasses (pig and beef). Also Salmonella can be found in cuts of meat and in minced meat.

In Denmark, Salmonella is found in app. 1 % of the carcass swabs (Annual report 2005). An earlier Danish study showed that the number of Salmonella bacteria on positive Salmonella carcasses generally is low (Olsen and others). The prevalence in the minced meat is presumably lower due to grinding and mixing. Nevertheless Salmonella will be found from time to time due to the sporadic occurrence.

According to 2073/2005 a batch means a group or set of identifiable products obtained from a given process under practically identical circumstances and produced in a given place within one defined production period. It is important for the producers to well-define a batch in order to identify products that must wait for results and/or eventual recall or withdrawal. If possible, testing of batch is done prior to shipping. This is possible for products with a shelf-life of e.g. 7-8 days or frozen products and when using rapid testing methods. However, this is a problem for retailers, where products have a 24 hour shelf-life.

In Denmark, we have had 32 recalls of batches of minced meat in 2006 due to finding of Salmonella in minced meat, see Table 2. A total of 19 batches derived from wholesale production and 13 batches derived from retail production.

Table 2
Recalls conducted according to Regulation 2073/2005 in different types of meat, Denmark, 2006

	Minced pork	Minced beef	Mixed pork and beef
Number of batches	13	17	2

Discussion

Salmonella may be present in an animal in a herd delivering animals for slaughter. Usually, there are no clinical symptoms of infection, because infection is subclinical.

The Danish surveillance-and-control program for Salmonella for pigs is based on seroligcal testing of pigs at slaughter. Thereafter, the herd is allocated to one out of three herd levels (Alban et al., 2002). This implies that the exact Salmonella-status of each single animal is not known at the time of slaughter. Hence, it is impossible to source all raw material from Salmonella free animals, Even if Salmonella is not found in samples from live animals, it is no guarantee that Salmonella might not be present. Cross-contamination at the abattoir might e.g. occur.

Salmonella action plans in other EU countries also operate on herd level, meaning that the Salmonella status is known on herd level and not on animal level. Even animals from e.g. seronegative herds can be positive for Salmonella (Alban et al., 2002). This can e.g. be a result of recent infection, where antibodies have not yet been developed.

Our experience is that the food safety criteria on Salmonella do not improve food safety, since withdrawal or recalls of batches, where Salmonella is found do not influence the prevalence. Often Salmonella is found by chance and it is not an indicator that this batch is unsafe compared to the batch right beside it.

Focus should rather be on the intended use e.g. ready-to-eat products or not. Moreover, focus should be on ways of controlling the process and minimizing contamination with Salmonella or other enteric pathogens.

Recent contacts with meat producers in EU have shown that there is a great need to revise the current microbiological criteria. However, EFSA will need comparative data to perform a quantitative risk assessment. Therefore it is important for industry and member states to provide semi-quantitative data.

The challenge is to develop a regulation that will ensure food safety in a cost-effective manner for the sake of both consumers and industry.

References

Alban, L., Stege, H., Dahl, J., 2002. The new classification system for slaughter-pig herds in the Danish Salmonella surveillance-and-control program. Prev. Vet. Med., 53:133-146.

Annual report 2005: Annual report on Zoonoses in Denmark 2005: http://www.dfvf.dk/Default.aspx?ID=9606

Commission, 2005: EU Regulation 2073/2005 of 15 November 2005 on microbiological criteria for foodstuffs.

EFSA, 2005: EFSA's Second Community Summary Report on Trends and Sources of Zoonoses, Zoonotic Agents, Antimicrobial resistance and Foodborne outbreaks in the European Union in 2005:
http://www.efsa.europa.eu/en/science/monitoring_zoonoses/reports/zoonoses_report_2005.html

Olsen, A-M., Jensen, T., Dahl, J., Christensen, H. 2001. Level of Salmonella on swine carcasses after slaughter dressing with and without splitting of the head. Proceeding, Salinpork 2001, Leipzig

Identification of *Salmonella* high risk pig farms in Belgium using semi-parametric quantile regression

Bollaerts, K.*[1], Aerts, M.[1], Ribbens, S.[2], Van der Stede Y.[3], Boone, I.[3] & Mintiens, K.[3]

[1]Center for Statistics, Hasselt University, Diepenbeek, Belgium
[2]Ghent University, Faculty of Veterinary Medicine, Merelbeke, Belgium
[3]Veterinary and Agrochemical Research Centre, Brussels, Belgium
*corresponding author: kaatje.bollaerts@uhasselt.be

Abstract

Since consumption of pork contaminated with *Salmonella* is an important source of human Salmonellosis in Belgium, policy makers implement the identification of the 10%
most *Salmonella* problematic pig herds. These herds are then encouraged to take control measures to reduce the *Salmonella* infection burden. To identify high risk herds, serological data were collected, reported as Sample to Positive ratios (SP-ratios).
Objectives of the current study are to identify the 10% highest risk herds and to investigate risk factors associated with high *Salmonella* prevalence. We propose to identify risk herds using semi-parametric quantile regression. The risk factor analysis is conducted using Generalized Linear Mixed Models. Finally, practical rules to identify risk farms are deduced.

Introduction

Salmonellosis is a disease affecting most livestock production worldwide. Nowadays national *Salmonella* surveillance programmes are implemented and encouraged within the European Union. The Belgian Federal Agency for the Safety of Food Chain (FASFC) started with a national *Salmonella* surveillance programme in pig herds. The surveillance programme started in January 2005 and consists of the collection of serological data to classify pig herds in *Salmonella* high risk herds. Then, these high risk herds are encouraged to take part in the surveillance programme. In this programme, high risk herds are (financially) supported to implement control measures. Because of financial and practical constraints, the Belgian government decided that only 10% of the Belgian pig herds can participate in the surveillance programme. The identification of the 10% high risk herds is currently based on a mean SP-ratio which is calculated for each herd during consecutive sampling rounds. However, SP-ratios are heavily (positively) skewed. Therefore, least squares based measures and methods are not appropriate and the sample mean does not provide a good summary of the data.

As an alternative, we propose to select the 10% high risk farms based on the number of animals in that herd for which very high SP-ratios are observed. Very high SP-ratios are then defined as SP-ratios above a specific upper quantile. An additional complication is the presence of confounding factors such as seasonal effects with higher expected SP-ratios throughout the summer months and animal age with the older the animal, the higher the expected SP-ratio. To deal with all these issues, conditional quantile curves of animal SP-ratios are estimated while accounting for confounding seasonal and animal age effects. However, it is not easy to model seasonal effects and most parametric models do not provide a good fit. Therefore seasonal effects are modelled in a flexible way using P-splines (Eilers & Marx, 1996). P-splines belong to the family of non-parametric models that provide a data driven and smooth fit to the data.

Finally, since high risk farms are encouraged to implement control measures, a *Salmonella* risk factor analysis is conducted. To this end, the serological data are linked with data from a survey on biosecurity in Belgian pig herds conducted in 2005 (Ribbens et al, 2006). The risk factor analysis is conducted using Generalized Linear Mixed Models (Molenberghs & Verbeke, 2005). The use of mixed models is motivated by the presence of clustering in the data due to the sub-sampling of animals within herds.

Material and methods

Serological data from the *Salmonella* surveillance programme (FASFC) are used. Within this programme, blood samples are taken and analysed using an indirect ELISA. The results are reported as SP-ratios. Every herd is monitored 3 to 4 times a year. Each time, 10 or 12 samples from pigs of different weight categories are collected (within the frame of the eradication programme of Aujeszky disease). For every blood sample taken, the herd identification number, animal estimated weight (<40kg, 40-59kg, 60-80kg and >80kg) and sampling time are recorded. The serological data are linked to data from a survey on biosecurity (Ribbens et al, 2005) by herd identification number (Sanitel). The objective of the survey was to describe the degree of measures taken in Belgian pig herds to minimize the risk of introducing infectious agents into herds (external biosecurity measures) and of spreading an infectious agent within herds once it has been introduced (internal biosecurity measures). The combined dataset contains data on 314 pig herds. In total, 13649 serological observations sampled from January 2005 to July 2006 are retained for analysis.

The 10% high risk farms are identified based on the number of animals in that herd for which very high SP-ratios are observed (also called risk animals). It is natural to define very high SP-ratios by means of quantiles. To account for confounding seasonal and animal age effects, quantile curves of animal SP-ratios are estimated as a function of time and animal weight (proxy for animal age). In particular, the following semi-parametric model is used to estimate the θ x 100% quantile of animal SP-ratio for animal 'i' in function of sampling time and animal weight

$$\hat{S}_{\theta,i} = h(time)_i + I(weight)_i$$

with h being a smooth P-splines function and I an indicator matrix. As such, seasonal effects are modelled in a very flexible way whereas the effect of age is assumed to be additive. Risk animals are defined as animals for which the observed SP-ratio is higher than the corresponding θ x 100% quantile or

$$R_{\theta,i} = \begin{cases} 1 & if \ S_{\theta,i} > \hat{S}_{\theta,i} \\ 0 & otherwise. \end{cases}$$

Then, high risk herds are defined as herds 'k' having a large proportion of risk animals or

$$P_{\theta,k} = \frac{1}{n_k} \sum_{i=1}^{n_k} R_{\theta,i}$$

However, proportions do not take the total number of observations n_k into account nor the correlated nature of the data due to the subsampling of animals within herds. As an alternative, beta-binomial p-values can be calculated. Under the null hypothesis that high levels of SP-ratios are equally likely in all herds, the number of risk animals $Y_{\theta,k}$ is beta-binomially distributed and the p-value corresponding to the alternative hypothesis that high levels of SP-ratios are more likely in herd 'k' compared to the other herds equals

$$p_{\theta,k} = P\{Y_{\theta,k} \geq y_{\theta,k} | Y_{\theta,k} \sim BB(n_k, 1 - \theta, \rho)\}$$

with ρ being the intra-herd correlation coefficient under the null hypothesis.

A risk factor analysis using Generalized Linear Mixed Models is conducted with the number of risk animals in the herd being the response variable of interest. Random intercepts are included in the model to account for clustering due to subsampling of animals within herds. In total, 20 potential risk factors coming from a study on biosecurity (Ribbens et al, 2006) are investigated using forward selection.

Results

A conservative choice is made to define risk animals by choosing $\theta = 0.90$. These 90% quantile curves of animal SP-ratios in function of sampling time and animal weight are graphically represented in Figure 1. By means of comparison, the conditional median functions are given as well. Clearly, strong seasonal effects are observed with higher expected values of SP-ratios during the summer months. Furthermore, weight (age) effects are observed as well. Except for the weight categories 40-59kg and 60-79kg, for which the 90 % quantile curves are identical, higher SP-ratios are observed for higher weight categories. The proportion risk animals as well as the corresponding beta-binomial p-values are displayed in Figure 2. In this figure, herds are ordered following increasing proportion of risk animals. Clearly, large differences in proportion risk animals between herds exist with a large number of herds having a proportion of zero whereas for one herd the proportion equals one. Similarly, large differences between herds can be observed when looking at the beta-binomial p-values. Selection of exactly 10% most problematic pig herds corresponds to selecting herds with a proportion risk animals > 0.30 or with beta-binomial p-values < 0.0005.

Based on the estimated quantile curves, practical identification rules can be deduced. For each month by weight category, the average estimated quantile SP-ratios are calculated. By means of example, the average SP-ratios for the months January and February are displayed in Table 1. This can be used to identify risk animals. Then, high risk herds are defined as herds having a proportion risk animals > 0.30.

Finally, from the risk factor analysis it can be concluded that the number of risk animals increases with farm size (OR 95%CI [1:1.004]). Furthermore, nose contact between pigs from different pens (OR 95%CI [1.14:3.45]) is an important risk factor whereas systematic insect control (OR 95%CI [0.28:0.0.74]) and regularly cleaning the stables (OR 95%CI [0.13:0.0.89]) are found to be remedial measures.

Tab 1. Average estimated quantile SP-ratios ($\theta = 0.90$) by month and weight category.

	< 40kg	40-79kg	>80kg
January	0.97	1.19	1.49
February	1.01	1.23	1.52
...			

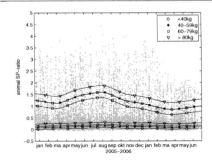

Fig 1. Estimated quantile curves 0.90 and 0.50.

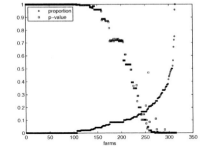

Fig 2. Proportion risk animals and beta-binomial p-values per herd.

Discussion and Conclusion

Currently, the identification of the 10% high risk herds as recommended by the Belgian government is based on a mean SP-ratio. However, SP-ratios are extremely skew implying that the mean does not provide a good summary of the data. Furthermore, the current approach does not account for confounding seasonal and animal age effects. Therefore, we propose to identify high risk herds using estimated quantile curves of SP-ratios conditional on sampling time and animal age. This method does not suffer from the afore mentioned shortcomings. However, the choice of upper quantiles θ is to a certain extent arbitrary. Therefore, a sensitivity analysis is conducted (results not shown here), from which it can be concluded that θ = 0.80, θ = 0.90 and θ = 0.95 yield similar results. From the risk factor analysis, it is concluded that nose contact is an important risk factor and regularly cleaning and insect control are remedial measures. Finally, in the current study, the longitudinal aspect of the data has not been investigated as such. This way, increasing or decreasing trends of SP-ratios could be investigated. However, analyzing longitudinal data poses important new challenges for quantile regression.

References

Bollaerts, K., Eilers, P. & Aerts, M. (2006). Quantile regression with monotonicity constraints using P-splines and the L1-norm. *Statistical Modelling, 6, 189-207.*
Eilers, P. and Marx, B. (1996). Flexible smoothing using B-splines and penalized likelihood (with comments and rejoinder). *Statistical Science, 11(2), 89-121.*
Molenberghs, G. & Verbeke, G. (2005). *Models for Discrete Longitudinal Data.* New York, Springer.
Ribbens, S. et al (2006). A survey on biosecurity in Belgian pig herds. *Preventive Veterinary Medicine,* submitted.

Acknowledgement

This study has been carried out with the financial support of the Belgian Federal Public Service of Health, Food Chain Safety, and environment research programme (R-04:003-Metzoon) ' Development of a methodology for quantitative assessment of zoonotic risks in Belgium applied to '*Salmonella* in pork' model'.

Belgian 'farm-to-consumption' risk assessment-model for *Salmonella* in pigs: methodology for assessing the quality of data and information sources

Boone, I.*[1,4], Van der Stede, Y.[1], Bollaerts, K.[2], Vose, D.[3], Daube, G.[4], Aerts, M.[2], Mintiens, K.[1]

[1] Veterinary and Agrochemical Research Centre (VAR), Coordination Centre for Veterinary Diagnostics, Groeselenberg 99, 1180 Brussels, Belgium
[2] Hasselt University, Center for Statistics, Universitaire Campus, 3590 Diepenbeek, Belgium
[3] Vose Consulting, Iepenstraat 98, 9000 Gent, Belgium
[4] University of Liege, Faculty of Veterinary Medicine, Food Science Department – Microbiology Section, Sart-Tilman, Bât B43, 4000 Liege, Belgium
*corresponding author: ides.boone@var.fgov.be

Abstract

Quantitative Microbiological Risk Assessment (QMRA) is a scientific tool that can be used to evaluate the level of exposure and subsequently the risk to human health. However, using this technique one should be aware of the limits of the QMRA model due to data quality, limited amount of time, model uncertainty and quality of assumptions. In addition, each information source may have different study designs, sampling methods, diagnostic tools, etc. Within the Belgian *Salmonella* QMRA-model in pigs, following exposure pathways were identified: primary production, transport, slaughterhouse & post processing, distribution & storage, consumer, dose response. From more than 60 available data sources, information was available for up to 101 potential input parameters, which were essential for building up the model-framework. For each parameter different specifications were summarised. In order to evaluate the quality of these input parameters and to measure their importance and possible impact on the outcome of the risk assessment model, a NUSAP/Pedigree methodology was chosen. Four different criteria used in the matrix include: proxy representation, empirical basis, methodology and validation. Every input parameter was scored by a panel of experts using these pedigree criteria. The overall scores or strength (aggregate of the 4 criteria) for each parameter was obtained by using appropriate weighted methods. The obtained strengths for each parameter should be taken into account when building the QRMA model. This scoring exercise showed for the first time the use of the NUSAP/Pedigree method as an essential tool in QRMA. It showed to be enhancing the credibility of the model in its communication towards decision makers.

Introduction

Quantitative microbial risk assessment (QMRA) is a scientifically based process used to evaluate quantitatively the exposure and adverse effects of microorganisms to human health. Often QMRAs rely on poor data with gaps and deficiencies (Gardner, 2004). This article aims to provide a novel approach in assessing the quality of data involved in QMRA. Quality of data is defined here as a measure of the fitness for the purpose for which the data will be used (Southgate, 2002). Gardner (2004) indicates that in microbial risk assessment, quality of data is related to the amount, the completeness, validity, relevance, comparability and timeliness of data, as well as to sampling methods and the use of (imperfect) diagnostic tests. We used a Pedigree assessment to address this problem. It emerged in the context of the Numeral Unit Spread Assessment Pedigree (NUSAP) notational system which aims to provide a better management and communication of uncertainty in science for policy (Funtowicz and Ravetz, 1990). The Pedigree evaluates the scientific underpinning of numbers used in a risk assessment. It is expressed by a set of pedigree criteria in a pedigree matrix. The pedigree matrix is used to code each criterion on a discrete numeral scale from 0 (weak) to 4 (strong). Assessment of pedigree involves qualitative expert judgment (van der Sluijs et al., 2005a).

The Pedigree method was applied to a Belgian farm-to-fork model aiming to assess the risk of *Salmonella* due the consumption of pig meat (Metzoon project). Scoring the parameters with this method intended a clear documentation and a structured selection of input parameters used for this model.

Material and methods

Stakeholders of the Metzoon project described following model pathways: primary production, transport slaughterhouse & post processing, distribution & storage, consumer. These pathways form the backbone of the QMRA model, and have to be supplied with available input parameters originating from various sources of information such as epidemiological, observational studies, surveys, (un)published literature and expert opinion. The potential model parameters were specified in an Access database as an ID-card by means of their reference, the used sampling frame (study population, sample size, non-response, diagnostic test,..), information for central tendency, range, and distribution. The pedigree matrix was adapted from van der Sluijs (2005b) and the criteria used to evaluate the parameter strength are summarised in Table1.

Table 1: Parameter matrix for parameter strength

Score	Proxy	Empirical	Method	Validation
4	Exact measure of the desired quantity (e.g. geographically representative)	Large sample direct measurements, recent data, controlled experiments	Best available practice in well-established discipline (accredited method for sampling / diagnostic test)	Compared with independent measurements of the same variable over long domain, rigorous correction of errors
3	Good fit or measure (measurements used from another geographical area but representative)	Historical/field data, small sample, direct measurements, less recent data, uncontrolled experiments, low non-response rate	Reliable method common within established discipline, best available practice in immature discipline (sampling / diagnostic test)	Compared with independent measurements of closely related variable over shorter period
2	Well correlated but not measuring the same thing (large geographical differences)	Very small sample, historical data, Modelled/derived data / indirect measurements, organised expert elicitation	Acceptable method but limited consensus on reliability of sampling & diagnostic test	Compared with measurements not independent, proxy variable, limited domain
1	Weak correlation (very large geographical differences)	1 Expert opinion, rule of thumb estimate	Preliminary methods with unknown reliability	Weak very indirect validation
0	Not clearly correlated	Crude speculation	No discernible rigour	No validation

The 101 parameters were scored using the information from the parameter ID-cards by 10 Metzoon experts. The strength of each parameter is calculated taken into account: (a) the expertise of the experts, (b) the consistency in rating between experts and (c) the number of experts actually rating the characteristic. In particular, the strength of a parameter is defined as the mean of the strengths of its pedigree criteria. The latter are calculated as $S_i = \frac{1}{4} R_i C_i \overline{X}_{weight,i}$ (with $i = 1, \ldots, 4$) where (a) $\overline{X}_{weight,i}$ is a weighted mean of the ratings with the weights reflecting the expertise of the experts, where (b) $C_i = 1 - s_i/E_i$ with s_i being the observed standard deviation of the ratings and E_i is the entropy or the maximal standard deviation possible and where (c) $R_i = N_i/N$ with N_i being the number of experts actually rating criterion i and N is the number of experts involved in the study ($N = 10$). Finally, note that an alternative (often used) way to account for raters consistency is dividing the mean by its standard deviation. However, when all raters agree, the standard deviation is zero and division by zero leads to undefined results. This problem is avoided when using formula (b).

Results

The resulting strength of the 101 parameters scored by 10 experts is graphically represented for the different modules in figure 1. The majority of the experts attributed low scores for the validation-criterion, partly because no validation was performed and partly because they were not sure if there had been a validation of the parameters. We will overview most important examples of parameter strengths.

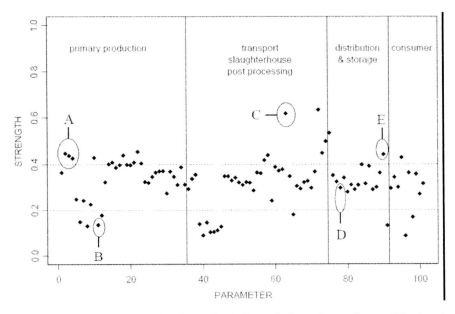

Figure 1: Overall parameter strength distributed according to the production pathways. Scores <0.2 = low strength, between 0.2 and 0.4 = moderate/high strengths, >0.4 = very high strength. A complete legend with definitions of the represented parameter numbers (1-101) can be obtained from the first author.

High parameter strengths were attributed to parameters representing the prevalence of *Salmonella* spp. in pig feed (figure 1, A). The data used to estimate these parameters were provided by an association of feed producers and by the Belgian Federal Agency for the Safety of the Food Chain (FASFC). These parameters obtained very high scores for the proxy criterion, and moderate to high scores for the criteria empirical rigour and methodology. This is due to the fact that the values are considered representative for the Belgian situation, sufficiently recent, obtained by a large sample size and that a coherent sampling methodology as well as a good diagnostic test procedure was used throughout to obtain the data. The parameter B in figure 1 represents the duration of shedding of *Salmonella* Typhimurium & Choleraesuis in pig. The low strength of this parameter can be explained by a low score for the proxy criterion, because the duration of shedding was estimated from population of pigs in the USA, using the Choleraesuis serotype which is not common in the Belgian pig population. Low empirical scores resulted from the use of indirect aggregated measurements from different studies. In addition, low scores were given for the methodological rigour and scores for validation. Within the slaughterhouse & post processing module (figure 1, C), the parameter estimating the prevalence of *Salmonella* spp. at the end of the slaughter line (provided by the FASFC) was attributed a high parameter strength. Next to very high scores for proxy, empirical basis, methodological rigour, the parameter was also considered as sufficiently validated. The data could be validated with *Salmonella* prevalence data originating from private companies. Concerning the distribution & storage module, a number of parameters were obtained through questionnaires (figure 1, D). The parameter "duration of pig carcass storage in the storage room" (D, figure 1) obtained a moderate strength. Hereby, the empirical basis did not reach very high scores, due to the fact that values were obtained indirectly by means of an oral interview with the quality managers from the cutting plant visited instead of measurement by the interviewers themselves. The experts gave high scores to the parameter estimating the temperature of pig meat in the fridge (E, figure 1). This parameter was obtained through a national Belgian Food Consumption Survey among 3001 households. Although the temperature was not measured in the pork meat itself, but in the lowest drawer of the fridge, it still yielded a high proxy score. Likewise, the empirical basis (due large sample size and direct measurements), and the methodological rigour received very high scores.

Discussion and conclusions

The proposed Pedigree methodology for assessing quality of data permits a structured reflection on the quality of data used for a QMRA. When several options are available for a same parameter, originating from different information sources, the pedigree process can help in choosing the parameters with highest strength to be included in the QMRA model. The real impact of the quality of input parameter can only be assessed after the parameters themselves are actually filled in into the model. Hereby, it might be decided to leave out high quality parameters if they don't fit into the model. To evaluate the impact of the strength of the parameters used in the model, the strengths will be combined with the results of a sensitivity analysis to produce a "Diagnostic Diagram" (van der Sluijs et al., 2005a). Plotting both the sensitivity and the strength of the parameters on this type of diagram will allow identification of the weak parameters in the model, i.e. those parameters with a low strength and having a high contribution to the sensitivity of the output. Describing and critically evaluate the quality of data used in a QMRA is essential step to allow an effective peer-review process. The use of the NUSAP/Pedigree will absolutely improve the decision-makers' awareness of and the confidence in their conclusions from QMRA. The above described process is recommended by the authors and it is advised to implement generally in risk assessment. The process should be regarded as an essential step for quality assurance in (QM)RA.

Acknowledgements

This study has been carried out with the financial support of the Belgian Federal Public Service of Health, Food Chain Safety, and Environment research programme (R-04/003-Metzoon) 'Development of a methodology for quantitative assessment of zoonotic risks in Belgium applied to the 'Salmonella in pork' model'. We wish to thank Dr. Jeroen van der Sluijs (Copernicus Institute, Utrecht University, The Netherlands) and Mr Matthieu Craye (KAM, JRC, Ispra, Italy) for their contribution.

References

FUNTOWICZ, S.O., RAVETZ, J.R., 1990. Uncertainty and Quality in Science for Policy. Kluwer, Dordrecht, 229 p.
GARDNER, I.A., 2004. An epidemiologic critique of current microbial risk assessment practices: the importance of prevalence and test accuracy data. Journal of Food Protection 67, 2000-2007.
SOUTHGATE, D.A.T., 2002. Data Quality in Sampling, Analysis, and Compilation, Journal of Food Composition and Analysis (15), 507-513.
VAN DER SLUIJS, J.P., et al., 2005a. Combining Quantitative and Qualitative Measures of Uncertainty in Model-Based Environmental Assessment: The NUSAP System, Risk Analysis (25), 481-492.
VAN DER SLUIJS J.P., RISBEY, J.S., RAVETZ, J., 2005b. Uncertainty Assessment of VOC Emissions from Paint in the Netherlands Using the Nusap System, Environmental Monitoring and Assessment (105), 229-259.

Exploring the risk factors for *Salmonella* in the ten biggest Belgian pig slaughterhouses

Delhalle L. [(1)]*, De Sadeleer L. [(2)], Farnir F. [(3)], De Zutter L. [(2)], Daube G. [(1)]

[(1)] University of Liege - Faculty of Veterinary Medicine - Food Science Department – Food Microbiology - Sart-Tilman, Bât B43bis, 4000 Liege, Belgium
[(2)] Ghent University - Faculty of Veterinary Medicine - Department of Veterinary Public Health and Foodsafety - Salisburylaan 133, 9820 Merelbeke, Belgium
[(3)] University of Liege - Faculty of Veterinary Medicine - Animal Production Department – Biostatistic, Economy and Animal Selection - Sart-Tilman, Bât B43bis, 4000 Liege, Belgium

*Corresponding author : l.delhalle@ulg.ac.be

Abstract

The goal of this work is to identify the risk factors related to *Salmonella* in the porcine die at the stage of the slaughterhouse. Thanks to investigations carried out into the ten biggest Belgian slaughterhouses, data concerning the manufacturing process and the working methods were gathered. Moreover, an access to the microbiological results carried out on these companies within the framework of the official plans of monitoring was asked to the Belgian Food Agency. A data base allowing to test the influence of risk factors on the presence of *Salmonella* was established. To quantify a relation between a risk factor and the presence of *Salmonella*, statistical methods such as the logistic regressions were used.

Introduction

In Belgium, the monitoring of *Salmonella* by the Federal Food Agency at the level of the slaughterhouses found a prevalence in 2005 of 9.3% (Korsak et al., 2006). Prevalence from 0,8% to 17,5% on the pig carcasses was brought back in Europe and in the world (Anonymous, 2003). Other studies undertaken in Belgium slaughterhouses presented different percentages: two independent studies (Botteldoorn et al., 2003; Korsak et al., 2003) found respectively 37% and 27% of contaminated carcasses. However, since 2000, a reduction in the prevalence at all the stages of the die is to be noted (Ghafir et al., 2005).
Many authors consider that the most important stage for the contamination of the pig meat is the slaughterhouse. Many sources of contamination were brought back with the installations and the method of work (Bolton et al., 2003; Korsak et al., 2003; Pearce et al., 2004; Swanenburg et al., 2001).

Material and methods

The ten biggest Belgian slaughterhouses were visited for the study. These slaughterhouses represent 60 % of the total volume of pig meat production in Belgian (Source: National Instute of Statistics in Belgium). A detailed questionnaire was created based on the Hazard Analysis Critical Control Point (HACCP) with headings relating to the manufacturing methods, the technical description of the installations, the traceability of the carcasses and the methods of cleaning and disinfection.
An access to the microbiological results concerning the monitoring of the zoonotic agents of the ten biggest slaughterhouses was requested from the Federal Food Agency in Belgium. Carcass swabbing areas were based on those described by Korsak et al. (1998). For one carcass, the area swabbed, including four different zones for a total area of 600 cm². The official method SP-VGM002 from the Ministry of Public Health (based on semi-solid enrichment) was used for the detection of *Salmonella*. The detection of *Salmonella* was registered as absence or presence.
The data base was created by gathering the microbiological results of the Federal Food Agency and the results of our investigations into the slaughterhouses. It was structured and organized in order to facilitate the exploitation. Technical description and descriptive statistics on *Salmonella*

were carried out for each slaughterhouse. Then logistic regressions were calculated with different variables in order to try to explain the presence of *Salmonella*.

Results and Discussion

The microbiological results of the ten biggest slaughterhouses in Belgium are presented for *Salmonella* in table 1. A great variability exists between the slaughterhouses with prevalence coming from 2.63% for the best slaughterhouse and with 34.33% for the worst.

Table 1: Prevalence of *Salmonella* in the selected slaughterhouses with data from the Federal Food Agency from 2000 to 2004

		Salmonella		
	n	Prevalence (%)	Low CI	High CI
1	76	2,63	0,32	9,18
2	46	4,35	0,53	14,84
3	39	5,13	0,63	17,32
4	47	6,38	1,34	17,54
5	54	11,11	4,19	22,63
6	66	21,21	12,11	33,02
7	55	21,82	11,81	35,01
8	60	26,67	16,07	39,66
9	74	27,03	17,35	38,61
10	67	34,33	23,15	46,94
All the ten abattoirs	**584**	**16,07**	**8,75**	**27,49**

The results of prevalence from 2000 to 2004 are observed for each slaughterhouse. The companies with high levels of prevalence remain high along the years and inversely for the companies with weak prevalence.

There is also a great variability with the working methods between the slaughterhouses (see table 2). These methods can protect against *Salmonella* or can be a risk factor.

For example, in the best case, the slaughterhouse with the lowest prevalence for Salmonella use a double flaming, steam for the scalding, removing the head before the splitting of the carcass, etc. In the worst case, the slaughterhouse with a high prevalence have a temperature of disinfection of the knives not hot enough, wash the carcase if there is a problem of contamination, etc.

Table 2: Technical data sheet of the slaughterhouses

Steps	Abattoirs	1	2	3	4	5	6	7	8	9	10
Lairage											
	Spraying	x		x	x	x	x	x	x	x	x
Stunning											
	Electric	x			x	x		x	x		
	Carbonic gas		x	x			x			x	x
Sticking											
	Temperature of disinfection for the knives	87,0	65,8	80,0	73,5	n.m.	n.m.	79,8	n.m.	52,0	76,0
	Trocard			x			x			x	
	Channel used for collecting blood	x	x		x	x		x	x		x
	Lay down	x			x	x		x	x		
Scalding											
	Basin		x	x		x	x	x	x	x	x
	Steam	x			x						
	Temperature (°C)	62	61	64	59	61	60	60	61	59	60
	Time (seconds)	556	435	n.m.	360	345	470	325	480	405	360
	hood	x					x		x		
Dehairing											
	Temperature (°C)	38	13	40	40	48	13	52	13	13	30
Singeing											
	Time (seconds)	7	12	14	6	12	8	5	n.m.	15	16
	Second flaming (after polishing)	x									
Polishing											
	Time (seconds)	90	35	n.m.	45	60	35	97	n.m.	55	75
	Temperature (°C)	17	13	30	13	13	13	13	13	13	13
Evisceration											
	Boring machine	x	x		x	x	x	x	x		x
	Another line system if there is a problem	x	x	x			x	x		x	
	Washing the contaminated meat		x	x		x	x		n.m.	x	x
	Temperature of disinfection for the knives	n.m.	70	81,5	77	66	n.m.	78	n.m.	47	76,8
Splitting											
	Splitting without the head	x									
	Cleaning between two carcases	x	x			x	x	x	x		x
	Disinfection between two carcases	x				x	x				
	Cleaning/Disinfection three times per day	x									
Chilling											
	Automatic	x	x	x	x	x	x	x	x		x
	Time to reach 7°C (hours)	19	n.m.	n.m.	16,5	15	15	n.m.	24	n.m.	n.m.
New hooks		x	x	x	x			x		x	x

n.m. = not measured

The first logistic regressions show that several variables seem significant for risk factors or for protection. But in spite of the great number of microbiological results, they were not enough to explain many variables. These tests must be still validated and moreover, the methods of regressions logistic must be adapted by using mixed logistic regressions.

Conclusions

The originality of this work is to combine in a single data base, not only the microbiological results obtained by the public authorities from 2000 to 2004, but also to the data of investigations in the slaughterhouses. A high number of results of microbiological analyses has been collected for *Salmonella* for the different slaughterhouses visited (n=584).

We have observed differences for the working methods between the slaughterhouses and they can explain the differences of prevalence.

In this study, we will use an analysis by multivariate logistic regression on several variables observed in order to establish a relation between the absence and the presence of *Salmonella*. In the state of the researches, the multivariate logistic regressions must be still validated.

Acknowledgments

We thank the Federal Food Agency of Belgium for their help and their advices. This study has been carried out with the financial support of the Belgian Federal Public Service of Health, Food Chain Safety, and Environment research programme (R-04/003-Metzoon) 'Development of a methodology for quantitative assessment of zoonotic risks in Belgium applied to the '*Salmonella* in pork' model'.

References

ANONYMOUS. 2003. Opinion of the scientific committee on veterinary measures relating to public health on *Salmonellae* in foodstuffs. European commission health consumer and protection directorate. Bruxelles

BOLTON, D. J., R. PEARCE, J. J. SHERIDAN, D. A. MCDOWELL, and I. S. BLAIR. 2003. Decontamination of pork carcasses during scalding and the prevention of *Salmonella* cross-contamination. *Journal of Applied Microbiology,* 94, 1036-1042.

BOTTELDOORN, N., M. HEYNDRICKX, N. RIJPENS, K. GRIJSPEERDT, and L. HERMAN. 2003. *Salmonella* on pig carcasses: Positive pigs and cross contamination in the slaughterhouse. *Journal of Applied Microbiology,* 95, 891-903.

GHAFIR, Y., B. CHINA, N. KORSAK, K. DIERICK, J. M. COLLARD, C. GODARD, L. D. ZUTTER, and G. DAUBE. 2005. Belgian surveillance plans to assess changes in *Salmonella* prevalence in meat at different production stages. *Journal of Food Protection,* 68, 2269-2277.

KORSAK, N., G. DAUBE, Y. GHAFIR, A. CHAHED, S. JOLLY, and H. VINDEVOGEL. 1998. An efficient sampling technique used to detect four foodborne pathogens on pork and beef carcasses in nine Belgian abattoirs. *Journal of Food Protection,* 61, 535-541.

KORSAK, N., J. N. DEGEYE, G. ETIENNE, J. M. BEDUIN, B. CHINA, Y. GHAFIR, and G. DAUBE. 2006. Use of a serological approach for prediction of *Salmonella* status in an integrated pig production system. *Int. Journal Food Microbiology,* 108, 246-254.

KORSAK, N., B. JACOB, B. GROVEN, G. ETIENNE, B. CHINA, Y. GHAFIR, and G. DAUBE. 2003. *Salmonella* contamination of pigs and pork in an integrated pig production system. *Journal of Food Protection,* 66, 1126-1133.

PEARCE, R. A., D. J. BOLTON, J. J. SHERIDAN, D. A. MCDOWELL, I. S. BLAIR, and D. HARRINGTON. 2004. Studies to determine the critical control points in pork slaughter hazard analysis and critical control point systems. *International Journal of Food Microbiology,* 90, 331-339.

SWANENBURG, M., B. R. BERENDS, H. A. P. URLINGS, J. M. A. SNIJDERS, and F. V. KNAPEN. 2001. Epidemiological investigations into the sources of *Salmonella* contamination of pork. *Berliner und Munchener Tierarztliche Wochenschrift,* 114, 356-359.

Quantitative Microbiological Risk Assessment of *Salmonella* in pigs: an EFSA initiative towards constructing a European QMRA approach.

Robinson, T.P., Hugas, M.

Biological Hazards Unit, European Food Safety Authority, Largo N. Palli 5/A, I-43100 Parma, Italy.
corresponding author : tobin.robinson@efsa.europa.eu

Summary
To date, the scientific opinions of EFSA's Scientific Panel on Biological Hazards (with the exception of those on BSE/TSE) are mainly based on qualitative and in some cases semi-quantitative risk assessment. As a first step towards developing a European approach on Quantitative Microbiological Risk Assessment (QMRA), EFSA is now preparing to carry out a QMRA on *Salmonella* in pigs, at a European level, via a consortium of European institutes funded through a grant.

What is EFSA ?
EFSA was established by the European Parliament in 2002 following a series of food scares in the 1990s (BSE, dioxins....) which undermined consumer confidence in the safety of the food chain. EFSA's two main areas of work are: Risk Assessment and Risk Communication. Risk management measures and the operation of food control systems are not within EFSA's remit and remain the responsibility of the European Commission and Member States.
EFSA's Scientific Committee, its Scientific Expert Panels and other expert groups provide risk assessments on all matters linked to food and feed safety, including animal health and welfare and plant protection. EFSA's Scientific Expert Panels provide the European Commission, the European Parliament and Member States with a sound scientific basis on which to base legislation and policies related to food and feed safety. The Authority is also consulted on nutritional issues in relation to Community legislation.
EFSA is committed to ensuring that all interested parties and the public at large receive timely, reliable, objective and meaningful information based on the risk assessments and scientific expertise of its Scientific Committee and Expert Panels. Communicating its own initiatives and ensuring collaboration and coherence across the Member States are crucial to maintaining consumer confidence in the risk assessment process.

Elaborating a strategy on QMRA at the European level
To date, the scientific opinions of EFSA's Scientific Panel on Biological Hazards (with the exception of those on BSE/TSE) are mainly based on qualitative and in some cases semi-quantitative risk assessment. However, in September 2004, EFSA launched a project tender to formulate a strategy for QMRA at the European level taking into account: i) the expectations from interested parties, ii) the advantages and disadvantages of the application of QMRA at European level, iii) the available resources at European level and iv) existing international experience. The conclusions from this project were:
- There is broad support in the European Commission, among Member States and scientists for development of QMRA at the European level. EFSA is considered to be the appropriate organisation to organise the process on a European scale.
- QMRA is expected to promote structured, evidence-based decision making in food safety and to improve the transparency of the process. This will result in better risk communication and help to build trust among stakeholders. Careful consideration of regional differences is a prerequisite for QMRA studies at the European level.
- Three important tasks were identified for EFSA:
  o creating a network of European institutes for QMRA
  o harmonisation of QMRA
  o developing and maintaining databases to support QMRA
- EFSA can build its QMRA activities on completed and on-going work in Member States and may aim to organize the process on a European scale, while keeping a community perspective and

taking into account the needs of Member States. It needs to be aware of the diversity in Europe, both with respect to technical development as well as to cultural and consumption habits.
- It is expected that there will be a limited number of questions that require full farm-to-fork risk assessments. More questions requiring quantitative assessment of specific stages in the food chain are anticipated.
- A structured, interactive process is necessary to assure a purpose-oriented QMRA process and to prevent wasting of scarce resources.

A variety of applications of QMRA will be required, such as in helping risk managers to set priorities for control at different stages of production, to establish control measures and to defend them in an international context and towards stakeholders.

The development of a strategy for conducting QMRA at European level is a challenge and will require taking into account the limited resources available, time constraints, the risk of duplication of existing or ongoing national QMRA studies, the needs of the individual Member States and regional variations (e.g. nutritional habits, local products, and prevalence variability). The effective interaction between risk assessors and risk managers is also an essential factor.

As a first step, and taking into account the conclusions from the project formulating a strategy for QMRA, and in response to a demand from the Commission, EFSA is proposing to fund a collaborative project to carry out a QMRA on *Salmonella* in pigs, from the farm to the table, involving a consortium of European institutes. This will be carried out through Article 36 of EFSA's founding regulation, that provides for networking with organizations operating in the field of EFSA's mission. Funding for the consortium will be in the form of a grant, details of which can be found on the EFSA website (http://www.efsa.europa.eu/en/about_efsa/cooperation.html). The list of competent organisations with which EFSA may collaborate with through this type of funding have also been published on the EFSA website (http://www.efsa.europa.eu/etc/medialib/efsa/about_efsa/cooperation/art_36_cooperation/1065.Par .0005.File.dat/Art36_list.pdf).

QMRA *Salmonella* in slaughter and breeder pigs

A total of 192 703 human cases of salmonellosis were reported in the EU in 2004, food being the main source of infection. It is estimated that several thousand people die each year in the EU due to salmonellosis. Eggs and egg products, poultry meat and pig meat are the main source of outbreaks in humans from products of animal origin.

Commission Regulation (EC) No 2160/2003[1] lays down provisions for the control of *Salmonella* and other specified food-borne agents. The scope of the Regulation is limited to agents which pose a public health concern. The Regulation required that the Commission targets for the reduction of the prevalence of Zoonoses and zoonotic agents at the level of primary production and where appropriate, at other stages of the food chain. Target setting in poultry populations (breeding hens, laying hens, broilers and turkeys) is ongoing. However, the current provisions also require the setting of targets for *Salmonella* in live pigs within a fixed time schedule.

In view of this future cost/benefit analysis, it seems appropriate to carry out quantitative risk assessments on *Salmonella* in slaughter and breeder pigs. In accordance with Article 15 of Commission Regulation (EC) No 2160/2003, EFSA shall be consulted before a target for reduction is set. Therefore EFSA, in particular its Panel on Biological Hazards, is requested to carry out this quantitative microbiological risk assessment. The cost/benefit analysis itself is not part of this mandate.

---

[1] OJ L 325, 12.12.2003, p. 1. Regulation as amended by Commission Regulation (EC) No 1003/2005 (OJ L 170, 1.7.2005, p. 12)

Background of the call for proposals

EFSA is seeking proposals from the competent bodies identified in the approved list of competent organizations approved by the Management Board on the 20th December 2006 to carry out a quantitative microbiological risk assessment (QMRA) on *Salmonella* in slaughter (fattening) and breeder pigs.

EFSA's Scientific Panel on Biological Hazards adopted in March 2006 a Scientific Opinion on "Risk Assessment and mitigation options of *Salmonella* in pig production", which can be found on the following webpage:http://www.efsa.europa.eu/en/science/biohaz/biohaz_opinions/1430.html.

The objectives of this Call for proposals are as follows:
A QMRA model that covers the whole food chain is required, beginning with a baseline model for the farm-to-fork-chain, including risk characterisation. While slaughter (fattening) pigs are the main object of this risk assessment, the role of piglets as a source of *Salmonella* also needs to be considered. During transport and lairage, cross-contamination might occur, both between-animal and between-batches (i.e. between-herds) due to carry-over of *Salmonella* on surfaces from one day to the next. The model will concentrate on primary production through to raw pig meat and raw pig meat products arriving in the kitchen. The model will also include (a) module(s) accounting for preparation and consumption of raw pig meat and raw pig meat products, and a dose response model, thus allowing numbers of human cases to be assessed.

Variability at all stages of the farm to fork chain, in and between Member states is a major consideration and needs to be explored. The end point of the QMRA will be, where possible, human cases of salmonellosis, which will, where possible, be compared with human incidence data. In addition, intermediate outputs such as prevalence/numbers on pork meat and antibody detection in meat juice should also be included and compared with surveillance data from both animals and meat. All assumptions on which the assessment is based and the uncertainties will be clearly identified, as will data gaps, with a view towards improving surveillance.

Terms of reference

The QMRA will address the terms of reference given by the European Commission, described below:

- *The expected reduction of Salmonella cases in humans (or pig meat at retail) by a reduction (e.g. 5- or 10-fold) of Salmonella prevalence in slaughter pigs (based on bacteriology in lymph nodes or serology at slaughter).*
- *The sources of infection for fattening pigs at farm level.*
- *The reduction of the prevalence in slaughter pigs by the most important potential treatments or control measures at farm level.*
- *The impact of transport, lairage and slaughter processes on contamination of carcasses.*
- *The expected reduction of Salmonella cases in humans (or pig meat) by the most important control measures during transport, at lairage or during the slaughter process.*

If quantitative data are not available and if such data can be generated with the limited resources and in the limited time of this project, then such data generation may also be included in the proposal.

EFSA also intends that the QMRA should build on existing models as much as possible and take into account;

- The variation in primary production within the EC, including factors such as herd size, access to the external environment, etc. Likewise, variations in slaughter practices and related primary production types should be characterised.
- Different behaviour between different serotypes of *Salmonella enterica*, if known should be taken into account.

- Differences in preparation and consumption_within the EU, in the amount of pork and pork products consumed, and also in the major types of products consumed should be considered. Whereas most pork is eaten cooked, some traditional pork and pork products are consumed raw. Poor hygiene and differences in handling raw pork in the kitchen may lead to different probabilities of cross-contamination and undercooking and should also be considered.

For further details of this and future collaborations funded by EFSA through Article 36 grants, the corresponding page on EFSA's website should be consulted (http://www.efsa.europa.eu/en/about_efsa/cooperation.html).

Acknowledgements
The authors gratefully acknowledge the extensive contributions of the members of EFSA's Scientific Panel on Biological Hazards to the development of this project.

Potential Human Health Implications of Swine Health

Hurd, HS.*[1], Brudvig, J.[1], Dickson, J.[2], Patton, B[2], Mirceta, J[3], Polovinski, M[3], Matthews, J[4], Griffith, R[5].

[1]Food Risk Modeling and Policy Lab, Iowa State University, College of Veterinary Medicine, Ames (IA), USA
[2]Iowa State University, College of Agriculture, Ames (IA), USA
[3]University of Novi Sad, Novi Sad, Serbia Montenegro
[4]Premium Standard Farms, Milan (MO), USA
[5]Iowa State University, College of Veterinary Medicine, Ames (IA), USA
*corresponding author: shurd@iastate.edu

Abstract

This study measured the relationship between subclinical pig health at slaughter and carcass contamination. 280 randomly selected carcasses were swabbed at three points during slaughter: skin pre-scald; pelvic cavity following removal of the distal colon and rectum; and pleural cavity, immediately before the final carcass rinse. Swabs were cultured quantitatively for *Campylobacter* spp. and *Enterococcus* spp. *Campylobacter* spp. were recovered from the pleural cavity in 58.9% (33/56) and 44.6% (25/56) of pools from the bung cavity. *Enterococcus* spp. were recovered from 66.1% (37/56) and 38.7% (22/56) of pleural and bung samples, respectively. The most common lesion identified was pleuritis/adhesions, with a total of 7.1% (186/2,625 total head). Linear regression showed that for every percentage point increase in lesions, there was a significant 4.4% increase in *Enterococcus* spp. and 5.1% increase in *Campylobacter* spp. contamination. Additionally, significant relationships were identified between pleuritis and the quantity (log CFU) of *Enterococcus* spp. present in the bung cavity or *Campylobacter* spp. in the pleural cavity.

This study shows a connection between animal health and human health risk, as measured by bacterial contamination on the carcass. If disease is not outwardly evident during processing, subclinically ill animals may go undetected until slaughter, and lesions may interfere with processing. If swine carcass contamination is indeed a reasonable proxy for human health risk of bacterial foodborne illness, and the findings from this study can be supported by further research, then management decisions on-farm, such as antibiotic use, housing, and veterinary care directly impact public health.

Survival of Campylobacter spp. on inoculated pork skin or meat.

Laroche, M., Kaiser, J, Magras, C.

National Veterinary School, National Institute of Agronomic Research (INRA), Unit of Food Safety, Route de Gachet, BP 40706, 44307 Nantes cedex 3, France
* corresponding author: laroche@vet-nantes.fr

Abstract

Campylobacter is one of the main causes of human foodborne bacterial zoonoses due to food consumption in developed countries. Nine to 32% of pig carcasses are contaminated by *Campylobacter.* The purpose of the study was to improve our knowledge of the survival of implanted campylobacters from the two kinds of pork matrix meat (skin, muscle) during meat cold domestic storage. One hundred and twenty pork skin and 120 skinless chine samples (25 cm^2/sample) were inoculated with two *C. jejuni* and four *C. coli* strains and stored in closed box at 4 °C for 1, 4, 8, 15 and 22 days. *Campylobacter* were isolated from sample suspensions after mechanical pummeling and numbered by direct plating. We calculated the shoulder time (ST), the D value (the time for one log decrease) and the R_1 value (the time to reach 10% of the initial population R_1 = ST + D). We compared them in a stratified approach according to pork matrix and strain. According to matrixes, mean D, TS and R_1 value varied significantly between pork skin (4.3 days, 1.3 days, 5.6 days, respectively) and spare rib (7.2 days, 3.5 days, 10.8 days, respectively). On spare rib, R_1 was higher (16 days) with one *C. coli* strain (CCV55). Statistical effects between TS and R_1 value on spare rib and strain were noticed. This study shows that the survival of campylobacters on pork meat is similar to the survival of *Campylobacter* on poultry meat. Consequently, good hygiene practices are needed to manage the risk of pork *Campylobacter* contamination and further studies focusing on survival factors may complete this risk analysis on the pork food chain.

Introduction

Campylobacter jejuni and *C. coli* are responsible for the main foodborne bacterial zoonoses in developed countries (OMS 2000). Only around one hundred bacteria are needed to induce abdominal pain or gastro-enteritis and even Guillain – Barré (ROBINSON et al. 1979, BLACK et al. 1988). The prevalence of meat contamination by thermophilic *Campylobacter* has been reported to reach 90% for poultry meat and 60% for red meat (pork, bovin). Pork is the most consumed meat in the European Union (DEVINE, 2003). In pork primary production, *Campylobacter coli* carriage is high (PAYOT et al. 2004, PEARCE et al. 2003, HARVEY et al. 1999, WIETJENS et al. 1999) and many studies have reported that from 9 to 32% of pig carcasses are contaminated. Even if slaughterhouse hygiene is a determining factor for managing pig carcass contamination (MAGRAS et al. 2006), little information is available about the survival of *Campylobacter* on pork during meat cold domestic storage.

Previous studies performed on chicken (LEE et al. 1998, SOLOW et al. 2003, YOON et al. 2004) and pork (SOLOW et al. 2003, FOSSE et al. 2006) have shown a protective effect of the matrix (skin versus muscle). But among all the factors affecting campylobacters survival, two other factors can be quoted: i) endogen flora level which can compete with campylobacters, ii) a meat matrix / *Campylobacter* spp. strain competition. Furthermore excepted Yoon et al. (2004), studies on survival of *Campylobacter* described only the survivor curve without fitting the data to a linear model. To our knowledge, such a definition of *Campylobacter* survival on the two kinds of pork matrix (skin and meat) has not been carried out to date. This kind of data must be taken into account to apply risk analysis for food safety.

The purpose of the study was to improve our knowledge of the survival of different implanted *Campylobacter* strains on retailed pork skin and meat during the meat cold domestic storage.

Material and methods

Campylobacter strains. Six strains of *Campylobacter* were studied: *C. jejuni* NCTC 11168, a sequenced human feces strain (28); wild *C. jejuni* isolated in human campylobacteriosis (CjBOF); *C. coli* CIP 70.81, a pig feces strain; three *C. coli* wild strains (CcV055, CcV639 et CcV782) isolated from pig carcasses in a slaughterhouse (Magras et al. 2006).

Pork meat samples. Two meat matrices were tested: skinless chine (*trapezius* muscle, *serratus ventralis cervicis* muscle, and *semispinalis capitis* muscle) and pork skin. The cooled retail meats were purchased from a local butcher, and 5- by 5-cm pieces were excised as samples. Samples of both pork skin (120 samples) and chine (120 samples) were the same thickness, i.e., 0.5 cm. The homogeneity of the thickness of samples was controlled randomly.

Experimental inoculation of meat samples. A calibrated quantity of *Campylobacter* colonies from a 48-h culture on Karmali plates (AES Laboratoires, Combourg, France) was inoculated into 20 mL of BHI broth (Oxoid, Dardilly, France). After 24 h of incubation under microaerophilic conditions, 1 mL of this liquid culture was inoculated into 100 mL of BHI and incubated for 48h under microaerophilic conditions to obtain the parent culture. To assess the absence of bacterial contamination of parent cultures, 0.1 mL of the culture was streaked onto Karmali and PCA plates and then cultured. The surfaces of the meat samples (5- by 5-cm piece of chine or pork skin) were inoculated with 0.1 mL of parent culture. After inoculation, samples were stored for 1, 4, 8, 15 and 22 days in hermetically sealed boxes at 4°C. In each series of four analyses, the sample clusters contained inoculated samples and noninoculated samples.

Bacterial analysis. Recovery method for separating *Campylobacter* from meat samples and obtaining a bacterial suspension was mechanical homogenization (pummeling with 10 mL of sterile peptone water for 60 seconds in a stomacher bag with a filter). A 0.1 mL volume of two dilutions of bacterial suspensions obtained was streaked on two Karmali with a spiral plater (Eddyjet, IUL SA, Barcelona, Spain) and incubated under microaerophilic conditions at 42°C. After 72 h of incubation, colonies on plates were enumerated.

Survivor curves and parameters calculation: Each survivor curve was generated by fitting the data (5 samples/curve, 1 sample/time) to the linear model developed by Buchanan et al. (1993) (figure 1).

$$Y = Y_0 + s(t - ST)$$

Y = log count of bacteria at time t (log (CFU/sample)); Y_0 = log count of bacteria at time t = 0 represents the number of Campylobacter inoculated on the sample (log (CFU/sample); s = slope of the survivor curve (log (CFU/sample)/day); t = time (days); ST = duration of lag period prior to initiation of inactivation or the shoulder time (days).

The D values were then calculated by taking the negative reciprocal of s. The time (days) to a 1-D (the time for one log decrease) inactivation (R_1) was calculated using the equation:

$$R_1 = ST + D$$

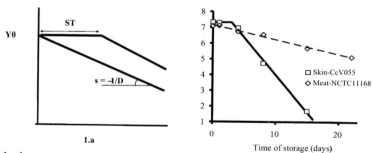

Figure 1: 1.a The linear model of survivor curve of Buchanan et al. (1993) used to calculate the 3 parameters (ST, D, R_1); **1-b** example of one of the 24 survivor curves of *Campylobacter sp.* on pork meat and of the 24 survivor curves on pork skin generated.

Statistical analysis. Data were analyzed with SAS software (SAS Institute, Cary, North Carolina) using a general linear model (PROC GLM) which is a sum of squares difference analysis of variance. We compared them in a stratified approach according to pork matrix and strain.

Results

Twenty four survivor curves of *Campylobacter* on skinless chine (meat) and 24 survivor curves of *Campylobacter* on pork skin were generated. According to matrices, mean D, TS and R_1 value varied significantly (table 1) between pork skin: 4.3 days, 1.3 days, 5.6 days, respectively and pork meat: 7.2 days, 3.5 days, 10.8 days, respectively.

Table 1: Mean values of *Campylobacter* survivor parameters (D, ST, R_1) according to pork matrices.

		D (days)	ST (days)	R_1 (days)
Pork skin	n	24	24	24
	mean value	4.3	1.3	5.6
	σ	2.0	2.2	2.9
	Minimal value	2.1	0	2.3
	Maximal value	10.5	7.5	11.8
Pork meat (skinless chine)	n	24	24	24
	mean value	7.2	3.5	10.8
	σ	3.4	4.6	4.4
	Minimal value	2.6	0	3.7
	Maximal value	16.4	15.1	18.6
p value of matrix effect Pr > F		0.001	0.04	<.0001

n: number of survivor curves generated; D: negative reciprocal of slope of the survivor curve; ST: duration of lag period prior to initiation of inactivation or the shoulder time; R_1 the time for one log decrease = ST + D

On pork meat, R_1 varied from 8.0 to 16.1 days for the different strains. On pork skin, R_1 for the different *Campylobacter* strains are not statistically different (table 2).

Table 2: Comparisons of adjusted mean R_1 obtained on pork skin and pork meat for the different *Campylobacter* strains.

Strain		Pork skin			Pork meat		
	n	R_1	Pr>F	n	R_1		Pr>F
CCV055	4	7.6	NS	4	16.1	a	0.013
CCV639	4	5.5	NS	4	8.6	b	0.18
CCV782	4	4.7	NS	4	11.3	ab	0.07
CIP7081	4	4.2	NS	4	8.7	b	0.38
CJBOF	4	6.7	NS	4	8.0	b	0.62
NCTC11168	4	4.2	NS	4	10.3	b	0.007

a, b : statistical difference with α = 5%, NS: no statistical difference with α = 5%.

Discussion

We confirm the high survivability of *Campylobacter* on pork meat during cold domestic storage conditions (SOLOW et al. 2003). Furthemore this survivability of *Campylobacter* on pork meat appears similar to the survivability of *Campylobacter jejuni* on poultry meat (with mean ST 7 days, D 4 to 5 days, YOON et al. 2006). However our study shew variations of the three survivor parameters (D, ST, R_1) in function of pork matrix, since parameters obtained from pork meat were significantly higher than parameters obtained from pork skin. The less survivability of *Campylobacter* on pork skin could be explained by skin nature (malpighian epithelium). This tissue has less directly available nutriments, which can stress trophical competition. Mean mesophile flora contamination levels were not different on pork skin and pork meat (results not shown). Endogenous flora can not explain differences between those two kinds of pork matrix.

Conclusion

Data of the present study confirm that the survivability of *Campylobacter sp.* on pork matrix (skin and meat) in cold domestic storage conditions is similar to the survivability of *Campylobacter jejuni* on poultry meat. Consequently, good hygiene practices are needed to manage the risk of pork contamination by *Campylobacter* and further studies focusing on survival factors may complete this risk analysis on the pork food chain.

Acknowledgements

The authors thank A. Rossero, F. Jugiau and F. Rama for their technical assistance.

References

- BLACK, R. E., M. M. LEVINE, M. L. CLEMENTS, T. P. HUGHES, AND M. J. BLASER., 1988. Experimental *Campylobacter jejuni* infections in humans. *J. Infect. Dis.*, 157: 472-479.
- BUCHANAN R.L., GOLDEN M.H., WHITING R.C., 1993. Differentiation of the Effects of pH and Lactic or Acetic Acid Concentration on the Kinetics of Listeria monocytogenes Inactivation. *Journal of Food Protection* 56(6): 474-478,484.
- DEVINE, R., 2003. Meat consumption trends in the world and the European Union. *INRA Productions Animales*, 16, 325-327.
- FOSSE J., LAROCHE M., ROSSERO A., FEDERIGHI M., SEEGERS H., MAGRAS C., 2006. Recovery methods for detection and quantification of Campylobacter depend on meat matrices and bacteriological or PCR tools. *Journal of Food Protection* 69(9): 2100-2106.
- HARVEY R.B., ANDERSON R.C., 1999. Prevalence of Campylobacter, Salmonella, and Arcobacter species at slaughter in market age pigs. *Adv. exp. med. biol.* 473 : 237-239
- MAGRAS C., LAROCHE M., MIRCOVICH C., FOSSE J., DESMONTS M.H., FEDERIGHI M., 2006. Quantitative analysis of *Campylobacter* hazard in the pork food chain. CAMPYCHECK, European Commission Research Project, 8th February, Dublin, UK.
- PAYOT S., DRIDI S., LAROCHE M., FEDERIGHI M., MAGRAS C., 2004. Prevalence and antimicrobial resistance of *Campylobacter coli* isolated from fattening pigs in France. *Veterinary Microbiology.* 101 : 91-99
- PEARCE R.A., WALLACE F.M., CALL J.E., DUDLEY R.L., OSER A., YODER L., SHERIDAN J.J., LUCHANSKY J.B. 2003. Prevalence of *Campylobacter* within a swine slaughter and processing facility. *Journal of Food Protection.* 66 (9) : 1550-1556
- ROBINSON, D. A., W. J. EDGAR, G. L. GIBSON, A. A. MATCHETT, AND L. ROBERTSON. 1979. Campylobacter enteritis associated with consumption of unpasteurised milk. *Br. Med. J.*, 1: 1171-1173.
- SOLOW B.T., CLOAK O.M., FRATAMICO P.M., 2003. Effect of temperature on viability of Campylobacter jejuni and Campylobacter coli on raw chicken or pork skin. *Journal of Food Protection* 66(11): 2023-2031.
- WEIJTENS M.J.B.M., REINDERS R.D., URLINGS H.A.P., VAN DER PLAS J. 1999. *Campylobacter* infections in fattening pigs ; excretion pattern and genetic diversity. *Journal of Applied Microbiology.* 86 : 63-70
- YOON K.S., BURNETTE C.N., OSCAR T.P., 2004 Development of predictive models for the survival of *Campylobacter jejuni* (ATCC 43051) on cooked chicken breast patties and in broth as a function of temperature. *Journal of Food Protection* 67(1): 64-70.

Quantification of Salmonella and Yersinia on pork carcasses by simulation modelling

Lo Fo Wong, D.M.A.*, Emborg, H.D., Sørensen, A.H., Sørensen, G., Aabo, S.

National Food Institute, Mørkhøj Bygade 19, DK-2860, Søborg, Denmark
*corresponding author: dwo@food.dtu.dk

Abstract

Stagnation in the success of control programmes in pig production in Denmark has led to an increased interest in the development of alternative control strategies such as decontamination of carcasses to further decrease the attribution of pork meat to human foodborne illness. This project sets out to develop a model for quantitative estimation of slaughterhouse output of *Salmonella* and *Yersinia*. Distributions of the occurrence of *Salmonella*, *Yersinia* and *E. coli* on pork carcasses are based on the analysis of paired faecal samples and carcass swabs from 2880 animals originating from four abattoirs. By combining the estimated quantity of faecal contamination of carcasses with a semi-quantitative distribution of the number of *Salmonella* or *Yersinia* per gram faeces, an output distribution describing the number of *Salmonella* or *Yersinia* bacteria per carcass can be established. In order to validate the model, carcass swabs, analysed for *Salmonella* and *Yersinia* serve as control. After the model has been validated, the effect of various decontamination methods on human exposure to foodborne pathogens in pork will be evaluated in both economic terms as well as with regard to public health impact.

Introduction

During the last decade, control programmes in pig production have contributed considerably to improving food safety in Denmark. However, stagnation is currently observed in the *Salmonella* control programme which has led to an increased interest in the development of alternative control strategies from both the industry and the authorities to further decrease the attribution of pork meat on human foodborne illness.

Faecal contamination of carcasses during the slaughter process is unavoidable and the degree of contamination depends on the applied slaughter techniques and manual handling of the carcasses. Faecal material on the carcass surface can contain pathogens that, if not removed during further processing, pose a threat to food safety at the point of consumption. Surface decontamination of carcasses can lead to a significant reduction of pathogens on carcasses. Our believe in the potential benefit of decontamination of fresh meat at the harvest level of pig production on food safety forms the basis of our control efforts at this stage of pig production.

A prerequisite for a general acceptance of the implementation of general endpoint decontamination processes at the slaughter line is that there is firm scientific evidence available on the consequences of these procedures on food quality and safety, as well as risk perception of consumers, for the decision-making process for the industry and the authorities. In order to provide science-based decision support, a project was initiated to evaluate the ability of several carcass decontamination methods in eliminating pathogens on the surface as well as in deep-skin structures on the carcass. As part of this project, we are developing a simulation model to produce quantitative estimates of *Salmonella* and *Yersinia* contamination of pig carcasses by linking quantitative measurements of these pathogens in faeces to faecal *E. coli* contamination of carcass surfaces. Though *Salmonella*, *Yersinia* and *E. coli* are used as model organisms, our findings regarding pathogen reduction and decontamination are expected to be applicable more broadly.

Materials and Methods

Data
Four abattoirs were selected to participate in this study, two with a level of contamination above average and two with a lower level as determined by routine hygiene control procedures. For a period of 18 months, each abattoir is sampled six times. At each sampling, 120 animals are selected randomly. This will give a total of 2880 animals sampled, 720 for each abattoir.

From each selected animal a faecal sample is collected from the rectum or colon after evisceration and marked for identification later at the slaughter line. Further down the slaughter line, the same carcass is sampled by the swabbing of both half carcasses (ca. 2800 cm2) prior to any surface cleaning procedures. Samples are analysed quantitatively for *E. coli*, and semi-quantitatively for *Yersinia* and *Salmonella*. The results of faecal and swab samples are paired for each animal. The objective of the sampling is to determine the distribution of faecal contamination on carcasses and the distribution of pathogens and indicator organisms in faeces.

The models
For the development of the simulation models, Microsoft Excel (Microsoft Corp., USA) and @RISK software (@RISK 4.5, Palisade Corp., USA) were utilised. The principle of the models is to draw random paired results of the concentration of *E. coli* in faeces and in carcass swab samples to estimate the faecal contamination of the carcass in two steps.

1. The total number of cfu on the carcass is estimated from the swab sample concentration as follows:
   cfu/ml in swab $\Rightarrow$ *cfu on 2800 cm^2 swabbed surface* $\Rightarrow$ *cfu on total carcass surface*

2. The total number of cfu on the carcass is linked to the concentration of *E. coli* found in faeces of the same animal:
   total cfu / (cfu/gram faeces) = gram faeces

Finally, the estimated carcass faecal contamination is combined with the concentration of *Salmonella* or *Yersinia* that the animal harboured in its faeces to give an estimated number of pathogens per carcass, e.g.:
   gram faeces x (cfu Salmonella/gram faeces) = total cfu Salmonella

Since *Salmonella* and *Yersinia* concentrations are analysed semi-quantitatively (i.e. given in intervals), a random concentration is selected within the observed concentration interval where all values have an equal probability of being selected (i.e. a uniform distribution).

To explore any association between concentrations of *E. coli*, *Salmonella* and *Yersinia*, regression models were built to provide estimates that can be used to link the various distributions in the model. The simulation results will be validated through carcass measurements of *Salmonella* contamination.

Statistical analysis
Data were clustered in space (i.e. slaughterhouse) and time (i.e. sampling round) as paired faecal and swab samples from pigs. Regression analyses were performed to determine associations between the occurrences of different bacterial species in the paired samples. The type of regression analysis was determined by the nature of data. The statistical package SAS was used for the analysis.

E. coli *in swab and faecal samples*

A mixed model was used to analyses the association between the dependent variable *E. coli* in swab samples and the explanatory variable *E. coli* in faecal samples. Abattoir and sampling date within abattoir were included as random effects.

Salmonella *in faeces and* E. coli *in faeces*

An ordinal multinomial model was used to analyse the association between the semi-quantitative measures of *Salmonella* in faeces (dependent variable) and the explanatory variables *E. coli* in faecal samples and abattoir

Salmonella *in swab samples and in faecal samples*

The occurrence of *Salmonella* in swab and faecal samples was coded Yes/No and a binomial model was used to analyse the association between *Salmonella* in swab samples (dependent variable) and the explanatory variable *Salmonella* in faecal samples.

Results

At this time, results from 2520 animals (i.e. from 21 sampling days) are available for fitting preliminary distributions of *E. coli* and pathogen populations in faeces and on contaminated carcasses. As not all samples are analysed for all pathogens, 1008 paired samples are available for modelling *Salmonella*, and 600 paired samples for *Yersinia*. Two models have been developed so far.

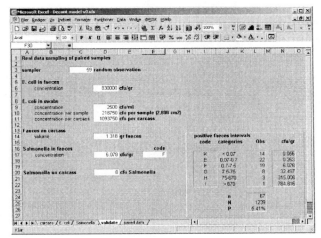

Model I draws random observations from the collected data, estimates carcass contamination as described above and picks a random pathogen concentration within the observed interval. Carcass contamination and pathogen concentration are linked as described above to give an estimate of the number of pathogens on the carcass (Fig. 1).

Since the observed data are used directly in Model I, any underlying dependencies that may exist between the various parameters in the model are assumed to be accounted for.

Figure 1. Model I - quantification of *Salmonella* on a pork carcass based on observed paired samples of *E. coli* in faeces and swabs and a random *Salmonella* concentration within the observed semi-quantitative concentration interval.

Model II draws random values from log-transformed distributions for *E. coli* concentrations in faeces (RiskNormal(5.73, 0.95)) and in swab samples (RiskNormal(2.38, 1.10)) that were defined based on the properties of the raw data.

The estimated carcass faecal contamination is derived from the *E. coli* concentration in faeces and the total number of cfu estimated from swab samples as described above (Fig. 2).

Figure 2. Model II - quantification of the volume of faeces on a pork carcass based on simulated paired samples of *E. coli* in faeces and swabs.

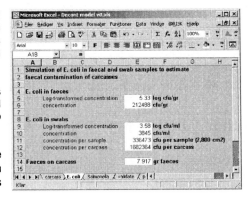

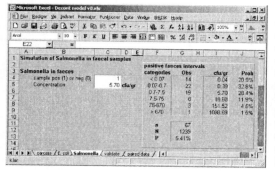

For *Salmonella* and *Yersinia*, each iteration during simulation of the model has a probability of returning a positive sample equal to the prevalence of positive carcasses found in this study (RiskBinomial(1,0.0541)). For each positive sample, a semi-quantitative concentration interval is selected (column F, Fig. 3) with a probability equal to the distribution of positive faeces intervals observed in this study (column J, Fig. 3). Then, a random concentration is selected within the selected interval as described above.

Figure 3. Model II – Simulation of the concentration of *Salmonella* in faeces of a single animal, taking the prevalence of positive samples and the distribution of semi-quantitative concentrations observed in this study into account.

Currently in Model II, the various distributions from which values are drawn are not linked to each other. Preliminary results from the regression analyses suggest that some of the distributions can be modelled independent from each other, whereas others need to be linked to produce realistic results.

We found a positive and significant association (P<0.0001) between the number of *E. coli* in faeces and the number of *E. coli* in the paired swab sample. The covariance parameter estimate for sampling date within abattoir (0.6065) was almost twice as large as the covariance parameter estimate for abattoir (0.3646) indicating that day-to-day variation within the slaughterhouse contributes to the observed variation.

There was an indication of a positive association between the number of *E. coli* and *Salmonella* bacteria found in faeces, however this association was not significant. In this analysis abattoir was significant (P<0.0001) which means that the number of *Salmonella* bacteria the pigs are shedding varies between slaughterhouses.

The final analysis also indicated a positive, but non-significant association between the number of *Salmonella* bacteria found in swab samples and in faecal samples.

Discussion

From 2001, the estimation of human exposure to *Salmonella* from contaminated pig carcasses in Denmark has been based on qualitative and/or quantitative results of carcass swabs. However, the sensitivity of swab sampling is generally considered lower than that of faecal sampling. The perspective of the model under development, where the pathogen analysis is restricted to faecal samples, is that faecal sampling is simple, several pathogens can be monitored simultaneously from a single sample, and the results from faecal samples also provide information on the distribution of the pathogen at farm level. This makes faecal sampling an attractive monitoring method, especially for low-level pathogen contamination.

When the models are finalised, results from Model II will be compared to results from Model I, as well as to the *Salmonella* and *Yersinia* distributions obtained through swab sampling of carcasses. However, the obtained swab sample distributions will also need to be adjusted for non-perfect sensitivity of the diagnostic methods used. Given the importance of day-to-day variation and between-abattoir variation, these factors will be incorporated into Model II. Furthermore, we may want to allow for cross-contamination in Model II. After Model II has been validated, the effect of various decontamination methods can be simulated and their relative decrease in human exposure to foodborne pathogens in pork will be evaluated in both economic terms as well as with regard to public health impact.

The knowledge of zoonotic diseases in swine producers, veterinarians and swine industry allied personnel in Ontario, Canada

Marvin, D.,[1] Dewey, C.,[1*] Rajić, A.,[1,2] Deckert, A.,[1,2] Poljak, Z.,[1] and Richardson, K.[1]

[1]Department of Population Medicine, University of Guelph, Guelph, Ontario, Canada
[2]Laboratory for Foodborne Zoonoses, Public Health Agency of Canada, Guelph, Ontario, Canada

More than 70% of swine marketed in Canada come from the Canadian Quality Assurance (CQA®) program, established in 1998 with the main purpose of demonstrating the implementation of on-farm good production practices (GPP). To employ effective farm-level control measures that prevent and control the transmission of pig/pork related zoonotic diseases it is important that producers, veterinarians and swine allied personnel are knowledgeable about these diseases. A mail questionnaire was distributed to selection of 409 individuals representing this target group, with the main purpose to determine the knowledge level in the Ontario swine industry about zoonotic diseases, and the self-reported prevalence of on-farm GPP. A response rate of 53% was observed (range 38-74%). Veterinarians and allied industry personnel appeared to be more familiar with Campylobacter *spp.*, *S. suis*, *T. gondii*, Swine influenza virus(SIV), *Trichinella*, and *Y. enterocolitica* than producers. A higher proportion of respondents within the all groups believed that *Campylobacter, Strep. Suis, T. gondii*, Erysipelas, SIV, *Salmonella, Trichinella*, and *Y. enterocolitica* can spread between pork and people. On average, within all four groups of respondents *Salmonella* (71%) was the disease agent they were the most concerned regarding spread from pigs/through pork to humans. Most of the respondents believed that the government should pay for testing pigs/pork for *Salmonella*. More Ontario swine veterinarians and allied personnel believed that antibiotic resistance is a problem compared to producers. On average, random producers, sentinel producers, industry professionals and veterinarians preferred to receive information on new diseases, control measures for diseases and/or results of research projects via a producer magazine. Our preliminary findings indicate that producers, allied professional and veterinarians are not sufficiently aware of all zoonotic diseases. An effective implementation of OFFS programs might require the development of effective education and communication strategies dealing with the risks associated with zoonotic diseases.

*Department of Population Medicine
Ontario Veterinary College, University of Guelph
Guelph, ON, N1G 2W1, Canada
Tel.1-519-824-4120 ext.4070, e-mail: cdewey@uoguelph.ca

Quantitative risk assessment of human salmonellosis from the consumption of typical pork products in the Veneto Region of Italy

Barrucci, F.*, Cibin, V., Busani, L., Ricci, A.

National Reference Laboratory for Salmonella, Istituto Zooprofilattico Sperimentale delle Venezie, Italy
*corresponding author: fbarrucci@izsvenezie.it

Abstract

ARSIS is a pilot scheme commissioned by the Veneto Region aimed at evaluating the risk of salmonellosis for Veneto region inhabitants due to the consumption of 'insaccati', typical pork sausages. The quantitative risk assessment (QRA) approach was used to assess the risk of human salmonellosis and to estimate the number of cases in a year among Veneto inhabitants, divided into sex and age classes.

Introduction

Salmonellosis is one of the most common foodborne infections worldwide, and particularly Salmonella Typhimurium and Enteritidis are the serotypes more frequently isolated from humans (Herikstad H. *et al.*, 2002).

It is estimated that in 2004 S. Enteritidis caused 76% and S. Typhimurium caused 14% of human salmonellosis in the EU. It is generally accepted that infection caused by S. Enteritidis are related to poultry products and specially tables eggs. Important sources of S. Typhimurium infections are broiler meat, pig meat and cattle. Results from Denmark and The Netherlands indicate that the greater part of the human S. Typhimurium infections are attributable to pig meat (EFSA, 2006).

In the Veneto Region the situation in 2001 was different and opposite: 19% of the isolated strains were typed as S. Enteritidis while 41% were typed as S. Typhimurium (Enter-net Italy, http://www.simi.iss.it/Enternet/index.asp).

Data from Enter-net Italy demonstrate that during the years 2000-2002 pig meat and pork products accounted for 6,6 to 12,3% of human reported and investigated cases of salmonellosis in Italy (Busani L., personal communication).

In Italy pork production is extremely varied and products are consumed both raw (ripened sausages) and cooked (raw sausages and cuts of meat), in particular in the Veneto region the production as well as the consumption of both raw and ripened sausages is relevant.

Therefore in 2002 Regione Veneto, as the institution in charge of safeguarding public health, commissioned a pilot scheme (denominated ARSIS) aimed at evaluating the risk of salmonellosis for Veneto region inhabitants due to the consumption pork sausages.

A risk model, based on a *farm-to-fork* approach, was developed to estimate the exposure to *Salmonella* from pork sausages and the number of human cases associated with this exposure.

Material and methods

Information and data for the development of the risk model were appropriately collected with a sampling scheme. The sampling was conducted at retails to estimate prevalence and concentration of Salmonella in both raw wand ripened sausages.

To determine the sample size necessary to estimate the frequency of contaminated sausages, we supposed an expected prevalence of 30% for raw sausages and 20% for ripened sausages. Sample sizes equal to 325 and 250 respectively were fixed to catch the expected frequencies with 95% confidence and 5% accuracy.

Moreover we supposed that the number of meat retailers and the amount of sold meat were proportional to the population living in a particular district, therefore the total number of samples was divided proportionally to the number of district residents.

When information was not available, published data were used to establish input settings for the model.

Whenever possible, the data were represented by probabilistic distributions rather than single point estimates, as they were to be integrated in a probabilistic estimation of the risk using Monte Carlo simulation. The software R and @Risk have been used to estimate parameters and run simulations.

Exposure assessment

A mathematical models was developed to estimate the likelihood and magnitude of exposure to Salmonella due to the consumption of sausages. The framework of the model is described in figure 3.

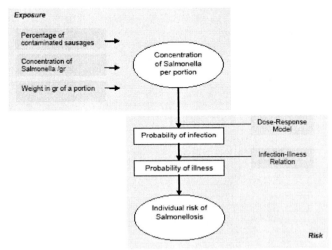

Fig. 3: Framework of the model for the exposure assessment and for the risk characterization

Using the collected data, the percentage of contaminated sausages at retails was modelled as a Beta distribution with parameters $\alpha=s+1$ and $\beta=N-s+1$, where N is the total number of sausages and s the number of contaminated sausages. The most appropriate distribution to describe concentration data was the Poisson distribution with estimated parameter $\lambda=0.161$ and $\lambda=0.085$ for raw and ripened sausages. To estimate the number of microorganisms to which consumers were exposed, we supposed that the weight of a portion is 50gr for raw sausages and 20gr for ripened sausages.

For each iteration the exact number of organisms ingested (n) was estimated and the probability that at least one of the n organisms would infect the host could be determined as $P_{inf}=1-(1-p)^{n}$. We assumed that p follows a Beta(α,β) distribution, taking into account variability between individual humans, that is we assumed that the dose-response relationship could be described by the Beta-Poisson model. For the Beta parameters we used the estimates proposed by Rose and Gerba (1991), $\alpha_{,}=0.33$ and $\beta=139.9$.

From the feeding trial data presented by McCullough and Eisele in 1957, the probability of infection followed by illness is between 0 and 75%. Because of the high doses administered in this study, in the present dose-response model it was assumed that independently of the dose ingested, if a person becomes infected, there is a reduced 10% probability that the person will become ill. The uncertainty on the probability of illness was described by a Beta distribution.

Risk characterization

The risk of salmonellosis from the consumption of a single portion of both raw and ripened sausages was estimated using the results of the previous steps.

The probability of exposure to Salmonella is obtained as one minus the probability of not being exposed to any Salmonella cells in a serving multiplied with the fraction of positive sausages. Given exposure, and the number of Salmonella cells, the probability of infection for each individual person from a serving is calculated. The probability of illness was calculated by multiplying the probability of infection with the probability of illness given the person has been infected.

In the present work we have not included the variability in the probability of getting illness from each individual serving containing Salmonella. Instead the average probability of getting illness was determined.

Finally, the frequency of consuming data were linked to census data (Table 1) to obtain the estimates of the number of human cases of salmonellosis associated with the consumption of sausages.

AGE	MALE	FEMALE	%MALE	%FEMALE
3-5	64998	62046	53,1	50,3
6-14	189134	178372	74,4	72,2
15-24	227577	216971	80,3	67,1
25-44	759341	720325	72,1	61,5
45-65	587805	594328	66,3	56,3
>65	337782	509223	51,8	41,9
Tot	2166637	2281265	68	57,3

Table 1: People living in Veneto on 1st of January 2003 divided in age and sex groups (data obtained from ISTAT, Census 2001 updated to 2003). Fraction of people who eats salami at least once a week divided in age and sex groups (data based on "Aspetti della vita quotidiana" survey on family from ISTAT, 2003)

Results

563 samples were collected at retails (315 raw sausage samples and 248 ripened sausage samples) and 53 were found positive to Salmonella, with a frequency of 11.4% (CI [8.85;14.77]) for raw sausages and 6.8% (CI [4.72;10.07]) for ripened sausages. Results of the enumeration using most probable number (MPN) method are shown in Figure 2.

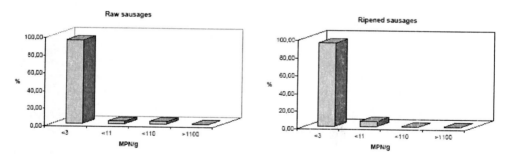

Fig. 2: Quantitative detection of Salmonella in raw and ripened sausages sampled at retail.

Using the previous results as input for the model, the risk of salmonellosis from the consumption of a single portion of sausages was estimated to vary from 0 to 8.24×10^{-3} with a mean of 1.79×10^{-4} for raw sausages and from 0 to 1.79×10^{-3} with a mean of 2.59×10^{-5} for ripened sausages.

The number of human cases of salmonellosis associated with the consumption of both raw and ripened sausages was estimated to be approximately 18 case out of 100.000 servings.

The expected number of cases associated with the consumption of Salmonella contaminated sausages was estimated to be approximately 229 per year (95% confidence interval: from 176 to 282 cases).

The simulation also showed that especially 25-44 aged men and 25-44 aged women were at higher risk than other groups (Fig. 4).

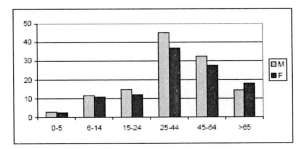

Fig. 4: Age distribution of estimated human cases of salmonellosis associated with the consumption of sausages divided in sex groups in Veneto.

Discussion and conclusions

The presented model provides us with some good indications of how relevant is the consumption of pork sausages in relation to the risk of salmonellosis.
However it should be kept in mind that the model needs to be further developed by taking into account the exclusion of several steps of the "farm-to-fork" approach as well as the uncertainty about some of the parameters.
Furthermore, some of the assumptions made in the development of the model need to be discussed.
In particular, due to the lack of data on infective dose of Salmonella, we chose to use the BetaPoisson model proposed by Rose and Gerba (1991). The probability of illness was assumed by reducing the report attack rate in feeding studies on human volunteers (McCullough and Eisele, 1957).
In the presented model, collected data as well as published data were used to establish input settings.
Concerning the consumption data, we referred to ISTAT survey on family in which the frequencies of generic salami consumption are registered.

References

EFSA – European Food Safety Authority, 2006. Trends and sources of zoonoses, zoonotic agents and antimicrobial resistance in the European Union in 2004. *The EFSA Journal*, 310,23-95.
N.B.McCullough, C.W.Eisele, 1951. Experimental human salmonellosis: III. Pathogenicity of strains of Salmonella newport, Salmonella derby and Salmonella bareilly obtained from spraydried whole egg. *Journal of Infectious Diseases*, 89 (3), 209–213.
J.B.Rose, C.P.Gerba, 1991. Use of risk assessment for development of microbial standards. *Water Science and Technology*, 24, 29– 34.

Ante mortem comparative evaluation of different ELISA systems for diagnosis of porcine *Salmonella* Infantis infection.

Roesler, U.*, Matthies, C., and Truyen, U.

Institute of Animal Hygiene and Veterinary Public Health, An den Tierkliniken 1, 04103 Leipzig, Germany
*corresponding author: roesler@vetmed.uni-leipzig.de

Introduction

Salmonellosis is one of the most important enteric infections in man and in livestock. Various serotypes of *Salmonella enterica* can cause a variety of clinical and subclinical infections, which are mainly self-limiting gastroenteritis or systemic diseases. Beside *Salmonella* (*S.*) Typhimurium, *S.* Derby and *S.* Infantis are the most important cause of porcine *Salmonella* infections. Although pigs usually do not develop clinical salmonellosis, they become carriers and shedders resulting in a substantial disease-causing potential for humans via meat and faeces.

Salmonella infections can be directly diagnosed in the piggery or at the slaughterhouse by isolating salmonellae with various established cultural methods or by serodiagnosis using lipopolysaccharide (LPS)-based ELISA-systems or a whole-cell-lysate based standard ELISA test. These serological results are used to classify pig herds in one of three categories. Category 3 has the highest prevalence of *Salmonella* infection, defined as at least 40 percent of the pigs examined being seropositive. Cateory 2 herds have a moderate number of antibody-positive pigs, whereas, herds of category 1 have no or only a low prevalence of antibody-positive pigs.

Material and Methods

The object of this study was the comparative evaluation of four indirect *Salmonella* ELISA tests approved in Germany to detect *Salmonella* Infantis infection of pig. Three tests are based on a LPS-antigen mix and directed against specific IgG antibodies. The fourth test is based on a purified *S.* Typhimurium whole-cell-lysate antigen and discriminates between *Salmonella* specific IgM-, IgA-, and IgG- antibodies. In a longitudinal study sixteen 6 weeks old hybrid piglets were orally infected with *Salmonella* Infantis. During an observation period of 120d clinical and bacteriological parameters were weekly monitored and serum samples were in parallel investigated by the respective ELISAs.

Results and discussion

During the comparing evaluation (sensitivities) of the four ELISA tests it became obvious that the tested LPS-based ELISA systems failed to detect *S.* Infantis infected pigs (which shed the pathogen in high amounts throughout the study) until day 80 after infection. The isotype specific *Salmonella* whole-cell-lysate based ELISA showed the best results in detection of *S.* Infantis infected pigs. Furthermore, it became obviously that the often used cutoff value of 40 OD% is not suitable for *intra vitam* detection of *S.* Infantis infected pigs. In contrast, the cutoff values given by the suppliers of the ELISAs would result in a eminent higher detection rate.

Our findings indicate that the most of the currently used ELISA systems have diagnostic uncertainties in detection of porcine *S.* Infantis infection when combined with the cutoff of 40 OD%. Therefore, future *intra vitam Salmonella* control measures should use the cutoff of 20 OD% or alternatively use a protein based ELISA system like the isotype specific *Salmonella* whole-cell-lysate based ELISA used in this study.

Presence of *Salmonella* spp. in retail pork in Northern Ireland

Spence*[1], S., Naughton, P.J.[3,4], Egan, D.[3] and Madden, R.H.[1,2]

[1]Food Science Department, Queen's University of Belfast, Belfast, Northern Ireland.
[2]Food Microbiology Branch, AFBI, Belfast, Northern Ireland.
[3]Northern Ireland Centre for Food and Health, University of Ulster, Coleraine, Northern Ireland.
[4]Microbial Biotechnology Group, University of Ulster, Coleraine, Northern Ireland.
*Corresponding author: sspence04@qub.ac.uk

Abstract

As part of an investigation into the potential hazard presented to the population of Northern Ireland by *Salmonella* spp. in raw pork products a survey was designed and conducted. Two geographical locations were chosen for the purchase of samples; Belfast and Coleraine. At both locations on each sampling day ten sample consisting of retail packs of fresh, chilled pork products were purchased. At both sites three supermarkets were sampled plus two butchers shops. Two different products were purchased at each premises. Where possible one sample of organically produced meat was obtained. Samples were taken immediately to the laboratory and analyses commenced within two hours of purchasing the samples. Analysis was according to ISO 6579:2002: Microbiology of food and animal feeding stuffs-Horizontal method for the detection of *Salmonella* spp.. Following enrichment samples were plated onto brilliant green agar and xylose lysine desoxycholate agar. Isolated salmonellas were serotyped by the UKAS accredited *Salmonella* reference laboratory, AFBI, Belfast. Overall two hundred samples were analyzed with 5.5% of samples being positive, indicating a relatively low prevalence of this pathogen. Since there is a UK-wide scheme aimed at reducing the incidence of salmonellas in pigs i.e. the Zoonoses Action Plan or ZAP scheme, the results imply that such measures are having a beneficial effect. Working in conjunction with abattoir HACCP schemes such measures appear to significantly reduce potential for the transfer of salmonellas from pigs to retail pork.

Introduction

Salmonellosis in the human population of Northern Ireland (NI) reached peak numbers in 1999) but has since fallen with the figure for 2005 being 26% that of the 199 peak (Anon. 2006a. This is largely due to the control measures on poultry reducing the incidence of *Salmonella* Enteritidis. However, studies on pigs at slaughter in Great Britain (Davies et al. 2004) found that 23% of animals (n=2509) carried *Salmonella* spp. hence raw pork could be contaminated with these pathogens. Giovannaci et al. (2001) noted that pork slaughter and cutting plants could give rise to cross-contamination of meat with salmonellas and found that the French abattoirs they studies were receiving pigs, 65% of which (n=89) carried salmonellas. Further, they noted that 32% of cutting room samples carried salmonellas (n=32%). Thus a significant proportion of the meat leaving the plants would carry salmonellas. Previous salmonellosis outbreaks due to contaminated pork have been reported (Maguire et al.1993, Smerdon et al. 2001).

In order to determine the potential threat presented to the human population of NI by raw pork carrying *Salmonella* spp. a survey of retail pork was conducted. The survey was based on sampling based at two population centres, the city of Belfast and the town of Coleraine. Sampling took place at supermarkets and butchers shops.

Materials and methods

Retail pork meat samples (200) were purchased over a 3 month period to establish the prevalence of *Salmonella* positive packs in Northern Ireland. Half of the samples were obtained in the vicinity of the city of Belfast and half in the vicinity of the town of Coleraine. The sampling locations were approximately 90km apart. Raw pork was purchased prepacked in supermarkets and from open trays in butchers shops. To ensure as wide a range of meat sources as possible samples were purchased with different 'use by' dates and comprised a variety meat cuts. Testing of the samples commenced less than 2 hours after leaving the retailer.

All media were obtained from Oxoid (Basingstoke, UK).

The presence and confirmation of salmonellas was determined using ISO method (ISO 6579:2002) with *S.* Nottingham NCTC 7832 and *Yersinia enterocolitica* NCTC 10460 being used as positive and negative controls, respectively.

Pre-enrichment. A 25 ±0.5g sample of pork was excised and carved into pieces aseptically using sterile disposable forceps and sterile, disposable scalpels (Swann-Morton, Sheffield, UK). The excised region was weighed, transferred into a sterile stomacher bag (Seward, Worthing, UK) and blended (Seward 400) for 30s with 225 ml of buffered peptone water (BPW, ISO: Oxoid, CM 1049). The contents of the stomacher bag were transferred to a 300ml sterile plastic jar, and incubated at 37± 1°C for 18 ± 2 h.

Following incubation, BPW (0.1 ml) was transferred to 10ml Rappaport Vassiliadis soya broth (RVS: Oxoid, CM 0866) and incubated at 42±1°C for 24±3 h and 1ml of BPW transferred to10ml Muller-Kaufmann tetrathionate/novobiocin broth (MKTTn broth, ISO: Oxoid CM 1048). The enriched samples were streaked onto brilliant green agar (BGA: Oxoid CM 0329) and xylose lysine desoxycholate agar (XLD, ISO: Oxoid CM0469), which were incubated for 24±3 hrs at 37°C. A minimum of 3 presumptive *Salmonella* colonies per plate were selected and streaked to purity on nutrient agar, for subsequent confirmatory tests.

Biochemical confirmatory tests included growth on MacConkey broth, triple sugar iron and SLUMS (sucrose, lactose, urea, mannitol and salicin) media. Colonies were streaked onto nutrient and MacConkey agar to confirm purity, and incubated at 37°C for 20-24hrs. In addition API 20E strips (Biomerieux, UK) were inoculated to ensure an accurate identification.

Poly O and Poly H antisera (Pro lab, Neston, South Wirral, UK) were used to confirm isolates as *Salmonella* spp, before full serological testing was carried out to determine the *Salmonella* serovar. All confirmed *Salmonella* spp. were serotyped by The Northern Ireland Reference Laboratory for *Salmonella* in Belfast, United Kingdom Accreditation Service (UKAS) accredited.

Results

A total of 200 retail pork products were examined for the presence of *Salmonella*; 120 prepacked supermarket retail samples and 80 butcher samples. The range of pork products investigated included mince, loin, chop, escalope, medallion, diced, and fillet depending on what was available on the day of sampling at the particular retailer.

Overall the prevalence of *Salmonella* spp in retail pork was found to be 5.5% i.e. eleven samples were positive. Six packs contained *Salmonella* Kentucky and five contained *Salmonella* Typhimurium. Of the 11 positive samples, three were obtained from butchers shops and eight were prepacked supermarket products.

Discussion

A major survey of the level of *Salmonella* contamination in retail pork obtained across the U.S. showed that 9.6% of samples were positive (n=384) (Duffy et al. 2001) whilst a survey limited to the Greater Washington D.C. Area found only 3% of samples (n=209) positive (Zhao et al. 2001). In Edmonton, Canada Bohaychuk et al. (2006) examined 100 samples of retail raw pork and found that none contained salmonellas. Thus a considerable variation was seen in the U.S. with prevalences varying from almost double the rate found in NI to almost half whilst Canadian samples appeared to be *Salmonella*-free. A small survey conducted in Ireland (Duffy et al. 1999) found 10% of 22 samples to be positive whilst studies in Italy (Busani et al.) noted that 4.9% of 3182 samples were positive, similar to the incidence found in this study. Thus it appears that raw pork on retail sale is not commonly contaminated with salmonellas, and the level found in NI is unexceptional.

Considering the serovars found in NI, *S.* Typhimurium is frequently associated with pigs and pork (Botteldoorn et al. 2003, Davies et al. 2004, Giovannacci et al. 2001) and also human illness (Anon. 2006b). It is regarded as a virulent zoonotic organism (Davies et al. 2004) hence should be absent from foodstuffs. *S.* Kentucky can also cause human illness although it is rarely isolated from patients in Northern Ireland (Anon. 2004). Thus both serovars found in retail pork in NI capable of infecting man. Further study will be required to asses the hazard presented to consumers by raw pork products since in NI they now have higher frequency of salmonella contamination than that of 1.5% found in raw poultry (Soultos et al. 2003).

Conclusions

The prevalence of *Salmonella* spp. in retail packs of raw pork in Northern Ireland was found to be similar to that noted in Italy. Only two serovars were isolated from the samples but both *Salmonella* Kentucky and *Salmonella* Typhimurium are zoonotic pathogens

References

Anonymous. 2004. Communicable Diseases, Provisional Summary 2003. Available at: http://www.cdscni.org.uk/publications/MonthlyReports/Volume_12_2003/Prov%20Summary%2020 03.pdf

Anonymous. 2006a. Laboratory reports of *Salmonella* sp (all specimen types). Available at: http://www.cdscni.org.uk/surveillance/Gastro/Salmonella_sp.htm

Anonymous. 2006b. Salmonella in humans (excluding *S.* Typhi & *S.* Paratyphi). Available at: http://www.hpa.org.uk/infections/topics_az/salmonella/data_human.htm

Berends, B.R., Van Knappen, F., Mossel, D.A.A., Burt, S.A. and Snijders, J.M.A., 1998. Impact on human health of *Salmonella* spp.on pork in The Netherlands and the anticipated effects of some currently proposed control strategies. *International Journal of Food Microbiology,* 44 (3), 219-229.

Bohaychuk, V.M., Gensler, G.E., King, R.K., Manninen, K.I., Sorensen, O., Wu, J.T., Stiles, M.E., McMullen and L.M. 2006. Occurance of pathogens in raw and ready -to -eat meat and poultry products collected from the retail market place in Edmonton, Alberta, Canada. *Journal of Food Protection,* 69(9), 2176-2182.

Botteldoorn, N., Heyndrickx, M., Rijpens, N., Grijspeerdt, K. and Herman, L. 2003. *Salmonella* on pig carcasses:positive pigs and cross contamination in the slaughterhouse. *Journal of Applied Microbiology,* 95, 891-903.

Busani, L., Cigliano, A., Taloli, E,. Caligiuri, V., Chiavacci, L., Di Bella, C., Battisti, A., Duranti, A., Gianfranceschi, M., Nardella, M.C., Ricci, A., Rolesu, S., Tamba, M. and Marabelli, R. 2005. Prevalence of *Salmonella enterica* and *Listeria monocytogenes* contamination in foods of animal origin in Italy. *Journal of Food Protection,* 68 (8), 1729-1733.

Davies, R.H., Dalziel, R., Gibbens, J.C., Wilesmith. J.W., Ryan, J.M.B., Evans, S.J., Byrne, C., Paiba, G.A., Pascoe, S.J.S., Teale and C.J. 2004. National survey for *Salmonella* in pigs, cattle and sheep at slaughter in Great Britain(1999-2000). *Journal of Applied Microbiology* , 96, 750-760.

Duffy, E.A., Belk, K.E., Sofos, J.N., Bellinger, G.A., Pape, A. and Smith, G.C. 2001. Extent of microbial contamination in United States pork retail products. *Journal of Food Protection,* 64(2), 172-178.
Duffy, E.A., Cloak, O.M., O'Sullivan, M.G., Guillet, A., Sheridan, J.J., Blair, I.S.and McDowell, D.A. 1999. The incidence and antibiotic resistance profiles of *Salmonella* spp on Irish retail meat products. *Food Microbiology,* 16, 623-631.

Giovannacci, I., Queguiner, S., Ragimbeau, C., Salvat, G., Vendeuvre, J.L., Carlier, V. and Ermel, G. 2001. Tracing of *Salmonella* spp. in two pork slaughter and cutting plants using serotyping and macrorestriction genotyping. *Journal of Applied Microbiology,* 90, 131-147.

Jorden, E., Egan, J., Dullea, C., Ward, J., McGillicuddy, K., Murray, G., Murphy, A., Bradshaw, B., Leonard, N., Rafter, P. and McDowell, S. 2006. *Salmonella* surveillance in raw and cooked meat and meat products in the Republic of Ireland from 2002 to 2004. *International Journal of Food Microbiology,* 112, 66-70.

Maguire, H. C., Codd, A. A., Mackay, V. E., Rowe, B. and Mitchell, E. 1993. A large outbreak of human salmonellosis traced to a local pig farm. *Epidemiology and Infection* 110, 239-246.

Smerdon, W.J., Adak, G.K., O'Brien, S.J., Gillespie, I.A. and Reacher, M. 2001. General outbreaks of infectious intestinal disease linked with red meat, England and Wales, 1992-1999. Communicable *Disease and Public Health.* 4, 259-67.

Sorensen, L.L., Wachmann, H. and Alban, L. 2007. Estimation of *Salmonella* prevalence on individual-level based upon pooled swab samples from swine carcasses. *Veterinary Microbiology,* 119, 231-220.

Soultos,N., Koidis, P., Madden, R.H. 2003. Presence of *Listeria* and *Salmonella* spp. in retail chicken in Northern Ireland. *Letters in Applied Microbiology* 37, 421–423.

Maguire, H.C.F., Codd, A.A., Mackay, V.E., Rowe, B. and Mitchell,E. 1993. A large outbreak of human salmonellosis traced to a local pig farm. *Epidemiology and Infection,* 110, 239-246.

ORAL & POSTER

SECOND SESSION

Epidemiology

ZAP: The role of routine surveillance data in understanding the geography and timing of *Salmonella* on UK pig farms.

Clough, Helen*[(1)], Sanderson, Jean[(2)], Brown, Patrick[(3)], Miller, Alexander[(4)] and Cook, Alasdair[(4)]

[(1)]National Centre for Zoonosis Research, University of Liverpool, Liverpool, UK
[(2)]Department of Mathematics, University of Bristol, Bristol, UK
[(3)]Department of Public Health Sciences, University of Toronto and Cancer Care Ontario, Toronto, Canada
[(4)]Centre for Epidemiology and Risk Analysis, Veterinary Laboratories Agency, Weybridge, UK

*corresponding author: h.e.clough@liv.ac.uk

Abstract

The Zoonoses Action Plan (ZAP), at its inception in 2002, sought to reduce prevalence of *Salmonella* infection in quality assured pigs at slaughter by 25% within three years. *Salmonella* levels are monitored by Meat Juice ELISA tests on samples from individual pigs and aggregated to indicate farm-level *Salmonella* status. By combining the ZAP scheme and quality assurance scheme datasets we generated a large geographically referenced data set which allows us to investigate aspects of the spatial and temporal epidemiology of *Salmonella* on GB pig farms. We seek in this study to address two questions. First, is there evidence that *Salmonella* in GB pigs varies seasonally? Secondly, do close farms tend to have similar levels of *Salmonella*? We suggest explanations for spatial and temporal effects where evidenced. Knowledge of seasons or GB regions which have atypically high *Salmonella* risk informs the design of control strategies.

Geostatistical and statistical modelling techniques provide evidence that (i) farm *Salmonella* status varies by season, with a peak in Autumn and early Spring and (ii) farm *Salmonella* burden is spatially structured, having allowed for seasonality and all currently available explanatory variables. This latter may indicate a true spatial effect, or may reflect as yet unmeasured explanatory variables. These latter are currently being collected.

Introduction

The Zoonoses Action Plan (ZAP) *Salmonella* monitoring scheme was introduced by the British Pig Executive in 2002. It sought to reduce prevalence of *Salmonella* infection in pigs slaughtered at British Quality Assured Pork (BQAP) abattoirs by 25% within three years. Farms which wish to sell their meat through BQAP abattoirs must participate in ZAP. This initiative supports a target set by the UK Food Standards Agency to reduce human food-borne infectious intestinal disease by 20% by 2006 and to reduce *Salmonella* infection in pigs by 50% by 2010.

Previous epidemiological studies have identified factors associated with increased levels of *Salmonella* on-farm, for example herd size (Mousing et al, 1997). We hypothesise *a priori* other risk factors for elevated *Salmonella* levels; amongst these is herd type (breeder/finisher or specialist finisher), and interest concerns whether finisher herds, experiencing a greater level of movement of pigs on- farm, might show higher *Salmonella* levels. Of further interest is whether, having taken account of explanatory variables, there remains any evidence of spatial (or temporal) structure – so that farms which are close together geographically (or measurements close in time) have inherently more similar *Salmonella* levels than those further apart. Evidence of this nature is valuable for designing control strategies which are efficiently targeted; an awareness of high-risk times of year, for example, is valuable for determining when resources should be targeted, and an enhanced knowledge of intrinsically high-risk regions is similarly informative. An understanding of spatial or temporal trends may also contribute to our general epidemiological understanding of this infection – clustering may indicate a common exposure, spread between neighbouring units, an effect of climate, or shared management practices.

Material and methods

The data consist of longitudinal records from two Government Office Regions; East of England, (Cambridgeshire, Norfolk, Suffolk, Essex, Hertfordshire and Bedfordshire) and Yorkshire and the Humber (North, South, East and West Yorkshire). These represent the two highest density pig farming regions in the UK and we are interested in any similarities (and discrepancies) between them. ZAP scores are assigned on the basis of number of samples positive according to a mix-ELISA which detects antibodies against Group B and C1 *Salmonella* in meat juice samples collected from every batch of pigs slaughtered in BQAP abattoirs. The MJ ELISA results are indicative of levels of circulating antibodies, not of infection and thus, peak exposure to Salmonella infection on farm will have preceded the peak ELISA result noted in the abattoir. Antibody levels are not well correlated with shedding so the peak risk of Salmonella shedding from pigs at the abattoir may precede or co-incide with the peak of antibody positives. However, knowledge of both associations between ELISA levels and risk factors and an understanding of inherent spatial and temporal variation is useful for interpreting this surveillance data and informing a targeted approach to monitoring and control in the future.

Previous studies of these data (Clough *et al.*, submitted) aggregated the data by year,fitted a common mean prevalence of MJ-ELISA positive pigs to all farms in a given year in a given region using a generalized linear model; constructed residuals (observation minus fitted mean) quantifying how different each farm was from the common average; farm-level residuals were then investigated using the variogram (Cressie, 1993) for any evidence of spatial structure, so that farms which are close together have more similar residuals (unexplained variation) than those far apart. Spatial structure is common in such applications and may indicate shared risk factors, either spatially (e.g. weather, topography) or non-spatially structured (farms in the same region may be of similar types (for example, all outdoor herds) or may share common management practices), or of transmission. Some evidence of spatial structure in the residuals from farms in the East of England was discovered, warranting the development of a model-based approach (described fully in Sanderson (2005) and being prepared for publication).

For each sample, several variables (MJ-ELISA concentration, date of sample, holding number, holding location, breeder/finisher status of holding) are recorded. The outcome is MJ-ELISA concentration; predictors are seasonal effects (modelled using smooth terms representing 12-month and 6-month cycles) and finisher status. We take a three-tiered approach.

• First, we fit a linear regression model (model 1) to the MJ-ELISA test result data to search for preliminary evidence of either seasonality or an association with breeder/finisher status. The MJ-ELISA data were logged to assist in analysis. This simple approach ignores both the geographical element and the fact that there are repeated measurements at each holding.

• Secondly, we extend the first approach to reflect the fact that multiple observations from the same premises are present and hence that our observed sample results may not be independent. We achieve this by incorporating a holding-level random effect, which is a standard statistical approach for any kind of clustering (model 2).

• Thirdly, we extend model 2 to include a spatial component (model 3). Our approach had to take into account three aspects of our data: time, location and multiple observations at each location. We had to consider time and location together and we had to consider that farms close together might still be more similar than expected by chance. These added complexities preclude the use of many published spatial statistics approaches. Consequently, we designed a method which included a spatially-varying random effect term at the same time as the farm-level random effect. We do not describe the spatial methodology in detail; description of the statistical approaches is in preparation for publication in a statistical journal.

• In summary, our novel approach to the data allowed us to analyse spatial, temporal and farm-level effects whilst taking account of clustering and repeated measures.

All analyses are implemented in the statistical package R (http://www.r-project.org) and using the libraries geoR (Ribeiro and Diggle, 2001) and lme4 (Bates and Sarkar, 2007).

Results

There was evidence of a seasonal component to *Salmonella* levels from all three modelling approaches, in both the East of England and Yorkshire and Humber regions. In most models, a primary peak in September with a secondary peak in February were evidenced in the East of England, with similar peaks occurring marginally later (October and March) in Yorkshire and Humber (Fig. 1 shows seasonal components from model 2).

Figure 1: Seasonal components of models for *Salmonella* levels in East of England and Yorkshire and Humber

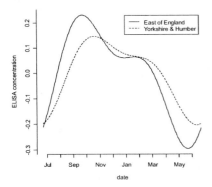

There was a suggestion of an effect of being a breeder farm by comparison with finishers; breeders have lower infection levels (from model 2, in East of England $\hat{\beta}_{breeder}$ = -0.2389 (SE = 0.0830); in Yorkshire and Humber $\hat{\beta}_{breeder}$ = -0.2716 (SE = 0.0710)). Note that the analysis at this stage does not consider confounders; we discuss their possible effects below.

Having taken account of seasonality and breeder/finisher effect, there was some preliminary evidence of a differential spatial component to the distribution of *Salmonella* levels; in the East of England, for a given separation, farms were likely to have more similar intrinsic *Salmonella* levels than farms in Yorkshire and Humber separated by the same distance.

Having identified a component of spatial variation, we assess relatively the amount of unexplained between-farm variation which can be explained by spatial structure, by comparing the variance of spatial and non-spatial farm-level random effect terms. Spatial variation was small by comparison with farm-level non-spatial variation, indicating that unexplained spatial variation, though present, has a limited role to play in explaining total variability by comparison with other sources. The largest source of variation is between samples over time.

Table 1: Contributions to variance in *Salmonella* levels in the two regions, having controlled for seasonality and farm type. $\square^2$ = between-animal within-farm (non-spatial); $\square^2$ = between-farm (non-spatial); $\square^2$ = between-farm (spatial).

Region	$\square^2$	$\square^2$	$\square^2$	Ratio $\left(\dfrac{\alpha^2}{\sigma^2}\right)$
East of England	1.3567^2	0.6370^2	0.4084^2	2.4343
Yorkshire & Humber	1.3884^2	0.5984^2	0.3504^2	2.9161

Discussion

Our analysis has provided a suggestion of a seasonal component to the behaviour of *Salmonella* levels on UK pig farms, with the most pronounced peak in Autumn and a secondary peak in late Winter/early Spring. This finding of a double peak is in support of previous findings of Hald and Anderson (2001) in Denmark, but only the Autumn peak is consistent across studies. Note that this work has been conducted with only two years' data so that conclusions regarding seasonality, and the secondary peak in particular, are tentative. Studies are ongoing which use a longer data series; these will clarify the seasonal profile.

It is interesting that farms which had atypically high intrinsic *Salmonella* levels (quantified as random effect values) were the same farms which had atypically high maximum-over-time-period ZAP scores via the ZAP categorisation scheme. Small discrepancies occurred in that two farms which were never awarded ZAP 3 scores achieved high random effects; these were farms from which small numbers of samples were taken and this disagreement therefore makes sense because a minimum number of sample requirement (15 samples in a given quarter) must be fulfilled before a ZAP score of 2 or 3 can be awarded. This demonstrates that our novel approach is useful for quantifying risk in the same broad terms as the ZAP scoring, but has the added advantage that it is taking into account factors such as seasonality, covariate effects and spatially varying factors before classifying farms as high risk.

There is evidence in both regions that breeder-finisher herds experience lower *Salmonella* levels than specialist finishing herds, which purchase weaners from one or more breeding unit. One explanation is that breeding herds see less animal movement; since a major route of *Salmonella* introduction is through intake of sub-clinically infected animals (Cook, 2004), the probability of introducing infection into a previously uninfected herd will increase with the number of animals introduced. For breeding herds, the population is more self-contained and so a lower risk of infection might be expected. Further studies explicitly examining pig movement could strengthen this hypothesis. The matter is complicated further by possible confounding via associations between herd health (including PMWS), finisher status, herd size and whether any part of the production cycle was maintained outdoors. There is a theoretical (though as yet unreported) possibility that this effect is further confounded with herd size. For example, if finisher herds were larger, more samples would be taken from these herds which would hence have a greater probability of testing positive when prevalence is non-zero. These problems can be alleviated by incorporation of relevant covariates.

An important finding is that the variation between animals within farms over time contributed to the greatest extent to the farm level non-spatial variation; batches of pigs from the same farm at different times may have a different prevalence of MJ ELISA positive pigs, indicating that sampling multiple animals per batch is warranted.

Collection of more information about confounders and explanatory variables is ongoing, and these will be incorporated into the models, enhancing understanding further. Outputs will feed into risk assessment models; insight provided by our novel approaches represents an important step toward a fully integrated risk-based approach to the control of *Salmonella* on UK pig farms.

References

BATES, D. AND SARKAR, D., 2007. lme4: Linear mixed-effects models using S4 classes.

CLOUGH, H. E., FENTON, S. E., FRENCH, N. P., MILLER, A. AND COOK, A. J. C.. Evidence from the UK Zoonoses Action Plan in favour of localised anomalies of Salmonella infection on UK pig farms. Submitted.

COOK, A. J. C., 2004. Measuring the impact of *Salmonella* control in finishing pigs – lessons from a pilot study. Pig Journal 53 157-163

CRESSIE, N.A.C., 1993. Statistics for Spatial Data, revised Edition, Wiley Series in Probability and Mathematical Statistics, Wiley, New York.

HALD, T. AND J. STRODL ANDERSEN, 2001. Trends and seasonal variations in the occurrence of Salmonella in pigs, pork and humans in Denmark, 1995- 2000. Berl. Münch. Tierärztl. Wschr. 114, 1–5.

MOUSING, J., THODE JENSON, P., HALGAARD, C., BAGER, F., FELD, N., NEILSEN, B.,NIELSEN, J.P. AND BECH-NEILSEN, S., 1997. Nation-wide *Salmonella* enterica surveillance and control in Danish slaughter swine herds. Preventive Veterinary Medicine 29 pp. 247-261.

RIBEIRO JR., P.J. AND DIGGLE, P.J., 2001. geoR: a package for geostatistical analysis. R-News Vol. 1 (2) pp. 15-18.,

SANDERSON , J., 2005. Spatial and temporal modelling of Salmonella surveillance data from UK pig farms. Unpublished MSc. thesis.

Risk factors for the detection of *Salmonella* in ileocolic lymph nodes in US slaughtered pigs.

Bahnson, P. B., [1]* Troutt, H. F. [2], Weigel, R. M. [2], Miller G. Y. [2] and Isaacson, R. E. [3]

[1] School of Veterinary Medicine, University of Wisconsin-Madison, Madison, Wisconsin, U.S.A.
[2] College of Veterinary Medicine, University of Illinois at Urbana-Champaign, Urbana, Illinois, U.S.A.
[2] College of Veterinary Medicine, University of Minnesota, St. Paul, Minnesota, U.S.A.
*corresponding author: pbbahnson@wisc.edu

Abstract

Salmonella harborage at slaughter can be viewed as a risk for human health through contamination of the pork food chain. Better understanding of herd level factors associated with this harborage would be useful to prioritize further study of epidemiology and control of *Salmonella* in pork production. Ileocolic lymph node samples collected at slaughter from 115 Midwest US swine herds were assayed for *Salmonella enterica*. A subset of these herds was collected sequentially one or two additional times. Herd characteristics and management factors were assessed by a written survey. Risk factors were screened at the univariate level (p < 0.3), then offered for inclusion by stepwise analysis including herd / sample as a random statistical effect. Pigs at increased risk of *Salmonella* harborage at slaughter included those placed in finisher barns at heaver weights (OR 1.2 per 10 kg increased weight), those from larger herds (OR 2.0 comparing upper quintile to lower quintile of herd size), those from herds that allowed visitors with recent (<8 h) contact with other herds (OR 2.2), or those fed pelleted feeds (OR 2.1). Further investigation of these risk factors and potential biological mechanisms will require further study.

Introduction

Salmonella enterica has been commonly identified on U.S. pig farms, with 38.2% of farms testing positive in a 1995 survey of the major swine producing states in the U.S. (Anon., 1997). Risk factors for *Salmonella* shedding have been identified in different countries and production systems. Risk factors identified in studies reviewed by Funk and Gebreyes included not using automated liquid feeding of by-products, not having membership of an Integrated Quality Control production group, trough feeding, high proportion of solid flooring surfaces, concurrent Lawsonia or Porcine Reproductive and Respiratory Syndrome virus infection, and infrequent removal of sow dung failure to empty manure pits. More recently *Salmonella* shedding or harborage in tissues at or near the time of slaughter slaughtered was associated with provision of dry-only diets or use of bowl rather than nipple drinkers.

The following study was designed to assess for a broad range of potential risk factors for *Salmonella enterica* harborage in the ileocolic lymph nodes of slaughtered pigs from Midwest US swine herds. Ileocecal lymph nodes were chosen for microbial *Salmonella* culture since they drain an area of the GI tract often colonized by *Salmonella*, were conveniently and economically collected at slaughter, and because harborage in these nodes has been associated with increased shedding on farm and in fecal samples collected at slaughter (Bahnson et al., 2005, Bahnson et al., 2006).

Material and Methods

Samples were collected from pigs at two US slaughter plants. Thirty pigs were sampled from each herd studied; only herds supplying ≥ 30 pigs on a given day were enrolled. Herds were identified prior to sampling from a pre-existing slaughter plant herd supplier list, a U.S. state pork-producer association, coordinated marketing groups, and swine-dedicated veterinary practices. Pigs were sampled on the basis of availability of technical personnel at the time of delivery to the slaughter plant. The target was to sample up to 150 herds for the first sample collection period. At 3-9 month intervals these same herds were sampled up to two additional times as they marketed additional pigs to the same slaughter plants. The slaughter plant deliveries were a part of normal marketing practices of the herds.

After humane slaughter and evisceration, GI tracts were moved to a separate area. A minimum of 10 g from the ileocolic lymph node chain was aseptically collected. After the overlying mesentery was removed the lymph node tissue was extracted using sterile gauze. For the first two sample collections each lymph node was split, with ≥5 g frozen at -70°C. Samples (~1 g) from each of five pigs were pooled in plastic bags, smashed by a mallet, then blended with tetrathionate broth using a paddle blender. For the third sample collected, 2 g of lymph node tissue was cultured from each pig individually within 24 h of collection.

After completing pooled sample cultures, a subset of frozen paired to samples contributing to culture positive pools were identified. These were thawed overnight at 2°C, then individually cultured using the laboratory process described for fresh samples, except that 2 g lymph node from each individual was blended with 20 mL tetrathionate broth.

A survey, mailed to herd managers the day after collection of samples, included questions on facilities, husbandry, management, and slaughter-transport practices. Non-respondents were sent a reminder card, a second copy of the survey, and were contacted by telephone.

For samplings for which culture results were at the individual-pig level, *Salmonella* prevalence was defined as the number of culture positives / number sampled. Where only pooled sample were tested, prevalence was estimated from a formula derived by regression analysis. (Bahnson et al., 2006). Statistical models were developed using SAS PROC GLIMMIX, including herd of origin as a random effect to adjust for expected clustering of results within herd. Putative risk factors were screened for univariate association; those with $p < 0.3$ were considered for a multivariate model using forward stepwise approach, with $p < 0.05$ to enter the model, and $p > 0.10$ to leave.

Results

Valid survey responses and microbiologic data were available for 115 herds for sample 1, 77 herds for sample 2, and 19 herds for sample 3. Salmonellae were detected in 73% of sample sets. Mean *Salmonella* prevalence across herds and samples was 8.4%; the unweighted mean prevalence by sample number was as follows: Sample 1, 6.4%, sample 2, 9.0%, and sample 3, 18.3%. The mean herd size, reported as the number of slaughter weight pigs sold in the prior 12 months was 9,275. The mean weight at slaughter and at entry to the barn from which pigs were sold to slaughter (finisher) was 112.2 and 33.9 kg, respectively. Strict batch pig flow was reported by 42% and 16% of respondents by barn and by herd site, respectively. Dry feed was provided in 62% of finisher groups, while 15% reported pelleted feeds. Birds, mice and rats were reported in 39%, 47% and 97% of finishing facilities, respectively. *Salmonella* vaccine was administered to pigs post-weaning in 6% of samples. Thirty variables passed the screening criteria to be considered in multivariate statistical models.

The final model described increased risk of harborage associated with pelleted finishing feeds (OR = 2.1, 95% CI 1.06-4.2), allowing visitors with same day contact to other herds (OR 2.2, 95% CI 1.15-4.3), increasing weight of pigs entering the finishing phase and increasing herd size. Finisher entry weight was associated with odds ratio of 1.2 (95% CI 1.01-1.58) per 10 kg increased weight. The upper and lower quintiles of herd size were 11,755 and 1,800 slaughter weight pigs sold per year, and was associated with a 2.0 (95% CI 1.3 – 3.2) when comparing the larger to the smaller herds.

Discussion

The prevalence of *Salmonella* (8.4%) is comparable to that of three other reports on intestinal lymph node tissues collected at slaughter from pigs of Midwest US herds. One study of 73

Midwest US herds estimated 14.5% prevalence (Bahnson et al., 2006a) and a second study of 25 herds which 3.4% prevalence (Carlson and Blaha).

Pelleting of feed can increase feed to gain efficiency. However, feed form has been linked to changes in *Salmonella* carriage in observational and experimental settings. Pelleted feed has been associated with higher *Salmonella* seroprevalence in commercially produced pigs (Leontides et al., Wong et al.) and increased bacterial culture prevalence in an experiment (Mikkelsen et al.). Although feed pelleting has been shown to effect adherence of S. Typhimurium on the intestinal epithelium (Hedemann et al.), a more complete understanding of the underlying mechanisms have not been adequately explained.

Herds that allow visitors with recent with other herds increase the chance of spreading infectious agents such as *Salmonella*. In addition to the potential for people clothing and transporation vehicles to act as fomites, other biosecurity precautions or lack there of may be associated. Taking the precaution of prohibiting visitors with recent contact to other herds is seems logically associated with awareness of the importance of other biosecurity practices. Consequently, the variable may also be a proxy for other correlated biosecurity practices, which in turn may contribute to lowered *Salmonella* harborage.

Increased weight of pigs placed in the finisher barns was associated with increased prevalence at slaughter. Increased weight would logically be associated with older pigs, more rapid growth in a prior stage, or with systems that break growth into more stages, such as nursery and growers at locations separated from the finisher barn. It should be noted that weight of pigs at slaughter was included as a potential risk factor, was not associated with harborage when considered at the univariate level ($p > 0.3$).

Herd marketing larger numbers of pigs of pigs per year tended to have higher *Salmonella* prevalence. Etiologic or explanatory biological mechanisms by which herd size is associated go beyond the findings of the current report; however, further investigation seems warranted, especially given the increasing market share of larger herds in US pork production.

Conclusions

Salmonella shedding in ileocecal lymph nodes in slaughtered pigs was associated with provision of pelleted feed, allowing entry of visitors with recent (<8 h) contact with other herds, increasing weight of pigs when entering the last (finisher) pre-slaughter growth phase, and increasing herd size. These findings suggest the need for further study of these factors and potential underlying mechanisms of effect.

References

Anon., 1997. Shedding of *Salmonella* by finisher hogs in the USA. Info Sheet #N223.197, eterinary Services, United States Department of Agriculture, Animal Health and Plant Inspection Service. Accessed September 26, 2005:
http://www.aphis.usda.gov/vs/ceah/ncahs/nahms/swine/swine95/sw95salm.pdf.

Bahnson P.B., Damman D.J., Isaacson R.E., Miller G.Y, Weigel, R.M., Troutt H.F. 2006a. Prevalence and serovars of *Salmonella enterica* isolated from ileocecal lymph nodes of market pigs reared in selected Midwest US swine herds. J. Swine Health and Production, 14:182-188.

Bahnson, P.B., Fedorka-Cray, P.J., Ladely, S.R., Mateus-Pinilla, N.E. 2006b. Herd-level risk factors for *Salmonella enterica* subsp. *enterica* culture prevalence in U.S. market pigs. Prev. Vet. Med. 76:249–262.

Bahnson P.B., Kim J.Y., Weigel R.M., Miller G.Y., Troutt H.F. 2005. Associations between on-farm and slaughter plant detection of *Salmonella* in market-weight pigs. J. Food Protect. 68:246-251.

Carlson, AR, Blaha T. 2001. In-herd prevalence of *Salmonella* in 25 selected Minnesota swine farms. J Swine Health Prod. 9:7-10.

Fedorka-Cray PJ, Dargatz DA, Thomas LA, Gray JT. Survey of *Salmonella* serotypes in feedlot cattle. *J Food Prot.* 1998;62:525–530.

Funk, J., Gebreyes, W.A., 2004. Risk factors associated with *Salmonella* prevalence on swine farms. J. Swine Health Prod. 12, 246–251.

Hedemann, M.S., Mikkelsen, L.L., Naughton, P.J., Jensen, B.B. 2005. Effect of feed particle size and feed processing on morphological characteristics in the small and large intestine of pigs and on adhesion of *Salmonella enterica* serovar Typhimurium DT12 in the ileum in vitro. J. Anim. Sci. 83:1554-1562.

Leontides, L.S., Grafanakis, E., Genigeorgis, C. 2003. Factors associated with the serological prevalence of *Salmonella enterica* in Greek finishing swineherds. Epidemiology and Infection. 131:599-606.

Mikkelsen, L.L., Naughton, P.J., Hedemann, M.S., Jensen, B.B.2004. Effects of physical properties of feed on microbial ecology and survival of *Salmonella enterica* serovar Typhimurium in the pig gastrointestinal tract. Applied & Environmental Microbiology. 70:3485-3492.

Wong, D.M.A.L.F., Dahl, J., Stege, H., van der Wolf, P.J., Leontides, L., von Altrock, A., Thorberg, B.M. Herd-level risk factors for subclinical *Salmonella* infection in European finishing-pig herds. Prev. Vet. Med. 62:253-266.

In-depth investigations into Salmonella infection sources, reservoirs, and intervention measures in herds with a high hygiene level

Bode, K.[*][(1)], Baier, S.[(2)], Blaha, T.[(1)]

[(1)]Field Station for Epidemiology, University of Veterinary Medicine Hannover, Buescheler Str. 9, 49456 Bakum, Germany.
[(2)]Animal Health Service, Chamber of Agriculture for Lower Saxony, Sedanstr. 4, 26121 Oldenburg, Germany.
*corresponding author: kerstin.bode@tiho-hannover.de

Abstract

The paper describes the in-depth analysis of the reasons for an extreme high Salmonella load of a high-health and well-managed pork production system and the measures that were taken to reduce the prevalence of Salmonella antibody positive finisher pigs produced by the system. The results and experiences gained during the study are discussed.

Introduction

In September 2002, the first German nation-wide quality management and assurance system for food production was launched. This QS-System ("QS" stands for "Quality and Safety") started with the pork production chain in response to a series of scandals and a growing distrust of the consumers in meat, especially in pork. QS is a non-governmental voluntary quality management system developed and established solely by the following five sectors of the food production chain: the feed industry, farming, the slaughter industry, the meat processing industry and retail.

One of the major modules of the QS-System is a Salmonella monitoring programme. Due to the fact that slaughter plants and meat processors have already good hygiene procedures (GHP) and good manufacturing procedures (GMP) which include activities targeted at Salmonella reduction, the Salmonella monitoring within the QS-System focuses on the primary production, i.e. mainly on the finishing phase of the pig production. The QS Salmonella monitoring programme aims at categorising the participating herds according to the risk of introducing Salmonella into the pork chain via infected slaughter pigs. The following three categories are differentiated: Cat. I = low risk, Cat. II = medium risk, and Cat. III = high risk. The classification into the categories is calculated quarterly based on the percentage of salmonella antibody positive meat juice samples during the last 12 months for each farm (ANONYMOUS, 2007a).

The presented study is a contribution to a better understanding of Salmonella infection sources and reservoirs in pig production systems, especially in those with remarkably high hygiene levels, where producers and their farm veterinarians are often at a loss convinced of the idea that nothing can be improved. The objective of this study was to detect "hidden" Salmonella infection sources and reservoirs in a well-managed group of pig herds with a hygiene level far above average.

Material and methods

Three very cooperative owners of well-managed herds with a high hygiene level, but continuously categorised into Cat. III, were chosen for this study. All of them did not see any of the traditionally accepted risk factors (e.g. frequent diarrhoea, rodent infestation, hygiene deficiencies, pets in the barn etc.) on their farms. Furthermore, they themselves and their veterinarians did not know where to start with intervention measures.

The study herds are:
-   a breeding herd with 680 sows with an extremely well-run biosecurity system (only shower-in access to the barn, separate isolation barn for gilts, ectoparasite-free status),
-   a well-managed, visually always clean separate nursery (1000 piglets with 6 to 18 kg on flat decks, 1000 grow-finishers with 18 to 30-40 kg on slatted floors), and

- three finisher herds that receive exclusively weaner pigs from this breeding herd through the described nursery.

In the first phase of the study, selected and earmarked sows, piglets, weaners and finishers were repeatedly tested serologically (SALMOTYPE® Pig Screen ELISA, Labor Diagnostik Leipzig, Leipzig) and bacteriologically (DIN ISO 6579) for identifying the time and location of the infection. 42 sows were included into the study representing animals of different litter numbers ranging from sows with one litter to sows with 12 litters. All 42 sows farrowed within three weeks. Per sow three piglets were chosen, earmarked with individual numbers and blood was drawn from each of these sentinel animals at various points in time until slaughter. All together, 694 blood samples, 41 colostrum samples and 66 meat juice samples were investigated.

Simultaneously, along the first phase of the study, diverse faeces samples, environmental samples (floors, walls, fans, troughs, drinkers, transport vehicles and cleaning tools) and slaughter samples (tonsils, Lnn. mandibulares and Lnn. iliaci) were cultivated for Salmonella, all together 538 samples.

In the second phase, targeted intervention measures were implemented according to the findings of phase 1. The major measures are:

Cleaning and disinfection (ANONYMOUS, 2007a)
- intensifying cleaning and disinfection of floors, walls, troughs, drinkers etc. and other pig contact areas in the pens
- adding disinfection to already existing cleaning of floors and walls of areas with no or rare pig contact (ante-rooms for changing clothes and boots, alleys for pig movements, tools for cleaning and devices for moving pigs, transport vehicles)
- cleaning and disinfection of areas that are not regularly included in cleaning and disinfection (fans and air ducts, upper parts of walls and ceilings, scales, loading and unloading ramps)

Implementing "black and white" principles (ANONYMOUS, 2007a)
- optimising animal and people movement targeting for salmonella transmission
- ante-rooms with a strict and obvious separation between normal and farm clothes and boots (e.g. installing solid separation between "black" and "white")
- installing boots use in only one building
- increasing awareness of crossing walkways between stables and farmyard

Watering system
- chlorination of the drinking water, if taken from a well (ANONYMOUS, 2007b)
- switch to municipal water supply instead of well

Changing feed structure, composition, and feed acidification (VISSCHER, 2006)
- rough grinding of grain components (largest possible particle size)
- increase of barley in the ration (about 35%)
- adding of 0.6 to 1.2% K-diformate (Formi®)

Optimising rodent control (ANONYMOUS, 2007a)
- Improving cleanliness outside barns
- Engaging a professional pest control company

For controlling the efficacy of these measures, 360 serological samples (300 blood samples and 60 meat juice samples) were taken during phase 2. Twenty weaning pigs per finishing herd (n = 60) were randomly selected and earmarked as sentinel animals and five times serologically investigated.

Simultaneously, along the second phase of the study, diverse faeces samples, environmental samples and slaughter samples (similar as described for phase 1) were cultivated for Salmonella, all together 549 samples.

Results

Bacteriology:
1. The isolated Salmonella strains in all herds and all age groups belonged to the serovar Salmonella Typhimurium [4, (5), 12 : i : 1, 2] and the same phage type.

2. All gilts were Salmonella negative, 8.3% of the pooled faeces samples taken from the productive sows were Salmonella positive.
3. None of the faeces samples taken from the weaned piglets in the flat deck were Salmonella positive (see Figure 1).
4. Whereas 4.5% of the grow-finisher samples in phase 1 were Salmonella positive, none of these faeces samples were Salmonella positive in phase 2 (see Figure 1).
5. The drastic increase of Salmonella positive faeces samples from grow-finishers to the finishers in phase 1 from 4.5% to 27.8% was remarkably reduced in phase 2 to 10.2% in the finishers (see Figure 1).
6. The bacteriological results of samples (faeces and environmental) taken from the finisher herds 1, 2 and 3 show only in herds 1 and 2 significant reductions between phase 1 and phase 2, whereas in herd 3 an increase occurred (see Figure 2):
-   herd 1, phase 1: faeces 56.3%, environmental 31.1%
-   herd 1, phase 2: faeces 6.3%, environmental 10.0%
-   herd 2, phase 1: faeces 25.0%, environmental 7.5%
-   herd 2, phase 2: faeces 6.3%, environmental 0%
-   herd 3, phase 1: faeces 15.6%, environmental 5.0%
-   herd 3, phase 2: faeces 21.9%, environmental 26.1%

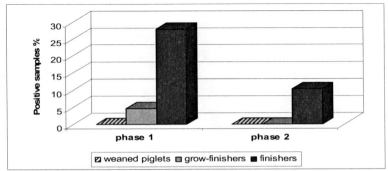

Figure 2. Bacteriological results of faeces samples of all three finisher herds in phase 1 and 2

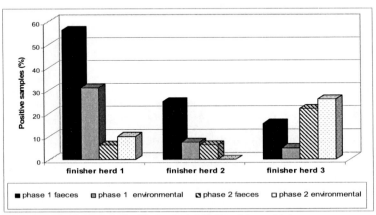

Figure 2. Bacteriological results of faeces and environmental samples in finisher herds 1, 2 and 3 in phase 1 and 2

Serology:
1. The serological results of the blood samples of the sows, of their colostrum, and the blood samples of the corresponding 7-day piglets correlated highly significantly.

2. The colostral antibodies in piglets decreased drastically during the suckling period; even piglets with the highest antibody level were negative at weaning.

3. The percentage of Salmonella antibody positive samples of all three herds in phase 1 increased over time and exceeded the 40%-threshold (category III) in the end of the finishing period, whereas the overall percentage of the positive samples in the end of the finishing period of phase 2 remained below 40% (see Figure 3).

4. The reduction of the overall percentage of the Salmonella antibody positive samples in phase 2 is exclusively due to the remarkable decrease of positive samples in herd 1 and 2 (see Figure 4).

5. The reduction (herds 1 and 2) and non-reduction (herd 3) of the serological results correlated strongly with the reduction (herds 1 and 2) and non-reduction (herd 3) of the bacteriological results in faeces samples (see Figure 2 and 4).

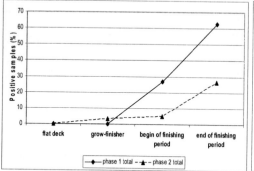

Figure 3. Serological results of blood samples of all three herds in phase 1 and 2

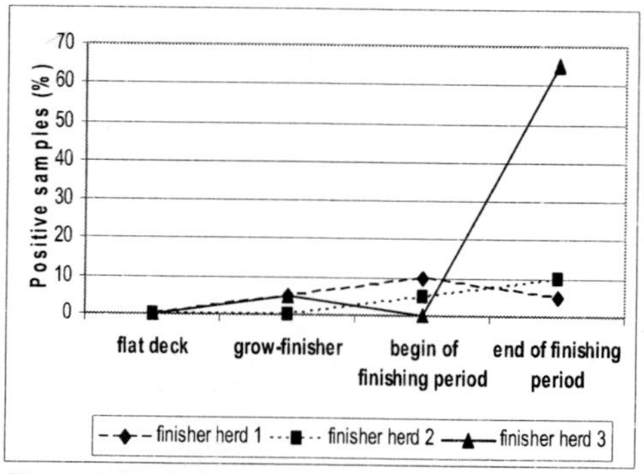

Figure 4. Serological results of blood samples of herd 1, 2 and 3 in phase 2

Discussion and conclusions

As for its Salmonella infection pattern before any intervention measures, the investigated three-site pork production system (one sow herd, one flat deck with grow-finishers, and three finisher herds) can be characterised as follows:

- The "Salmonella problem" of the production system is obviously not a constant introduction of Salmonella into the system at various points of entry, but rather the circulation of one "quasi" hospitalised Salmonella serovar.
- This serovar is already found in the sow herd, but the Salmonella prevalence of the weaned piglets in the flat deck and in grow-finishers on the same site as the flat deck is relatively low.
- This low prevalence in the flat deck and grow-finisher period, however, leads to a varying increase of the Salmonella infection rate in the three finisher herds, with remarkable differences in the resulting prevalence in the end of the finishing period.

The intervention measures taken on flat deck and grow-finisher site as well as in the three finisher herds (specific measures on each site according to the results of the in-depth analysis of phase 1 as described in material and methods) are capable of drastically reducing the infection pressure and environmental contamination in Salmonella infected pork production systems (herds 1 and 2). However, it is unrealistic to expect a complete "sanitation" during one production cycle – only the stringent repetition of the specific measures necessary to be defined for every herd can lead to a sustainable success. Any failure in reducing the Salmonella load (as in finisher herd 3) must result in another in-depth analysis of the hygiene, biosecurity and the daily working procedures on the farm in question. Such analysis will identify the reasons for the failure, if "everything that happens" on the farm is taken into consideration; in case of herd 3 a non-planned construction in the barn without biosecurity measures, and a liquid manure transfer from a cattle shed to the deep pit of the pig barn led to severe hygiene and biosecurity break-downs.

References

ANONYMOUS, 2007a. QS-Guidelines on "Monitoring and Reduction of Zoonotic Pathogen – Salmonella Monitoring". *www.q-s.info*

ANONYMOUS, 2007b. Easy Des Chlordioxid. *www.hdd-technik.de*

VISSCHER, C., P. WINTER, J. VERSPOHL, J. STRATMANN, T.V. MÜFFLING u. J. KAMPHUES, 2006. Field study on effects on coarsely ground diets and/or organic acids as feed additives on *Salmonella* prevalence in fattening pigs before and at slaughtering. *Proc. 19th IPVS Congress, Copenhagen, Denmark*, <u>1</u>, 127

Longitudinal study of Salmonella infection in four Italian farrow-to finish swine herds

Merialdi G.[1], Tittarelli C.[1], Bonilauri P.[1], Bonci M.[1], Barbieri G.[2], Casali M.[2], Franchi L.[2], Granito G.[3], Guerzoni S.[3], Dottori M.[1]

[1]Istituto Zooprofilattico Sperimentale della Lombardia e dell'Emilia Romagna, Sezione Diagnostica di Reggio Emilia, 42100, Reggio Emilia, Italy
[2]Progeo scrl, Reggio Emilia, 42100 Reggio Emilia, Italy
[3]Veterinario Aziendale, 41100 Modena, Italy

Corrisponding Author: Giuseppe Merialdi, Via Pitagora 2, 4200 Reggio Emilia, Italy, e-mail: giuseppe.merialdi@bs.izs.it

Abstract

A longitudinal study of Salmonella enterica infection was carried out in 4 Italian farrow-to-finish swine herds. In each herd 5 litters were randomly selected and in each litter 6 piglets ear tagged. Thus, on each farm 30 pigs were included in the study. Individual blood samples were collected for serologic examination at weaning from all piglets and in the same day from all sows in the farrowing unit. Piglets were bled again at approximately 60, 90, 150, 210 and 270 days of life with the last blood sample collected at slaughtering. In one herd, in which the duration of productive cycle was about 12 months, the last blood samples was collected at 350 days of life. 5 pen pooled faecal samples were collected from each herd for bacteriological examination with the same time schedule of blood samples. At slaughtering mesenteric lymph nodes were collected from each ear tagged pig. Sero-prevalence (cutoff S/P ratio 0,25) in sows varied from 93,8% to 100%. In all herds sero-prevalence in piglets showed a similar profile with complete decline of maternal antibodies at day 60 and clear sero-conversion between day 90 and day 150. The peak of sero-prevalence was observed between day 210 and day 270. Sero-prevalence at slaughtering varied from 66% to 100%. Salmonella was isolated from faecal samples in 3 out of 4 herds. No Salmonella was isolated from mesenteric lymph nodes at slaughter in 2 herds. Culture prevalence from mesenteric lymph nodes in the other herds was respectively 3,3% and 30%. This longitudinal study provides original information about epidemiological dynamics of Salmonella enterica infection in Italian swine herds in consideration of the typical longer fattening cycles.

Introduction

Salmonella enterica infection is a potential cause of disease in pig, but in most cases it is subclinical. The possibility that asymptomatic carrier pigs reach the slaughterhouse contaminating the food chain is a matter of concern for Pubblic Health. Regulation (EC) No 2160/2003 requires Member States to establish national control programs in order to achieve community targets in the reduction of zoonotic agents in animals, including Salmonella enterica in swine. Some Member States as Denmark, Great Britain, Germany and Netherland (Anonimous, 2006), have established Salmonella control programs in pigs. Others countries, including Italy, have been acquiring information about the epidemiology of the infection for the implementation of the national programs. Further need of investigation also derives from the peculiar Italian production system, characterized by a slaughter live weight of 160-180 kg that means 3-4 additional months in the duration of the production cycle. This make observations about herd epidemiology recorded in other countries not fully complying to the Italian situation. This kind of information will also be necessary in order to establish control measures at farm level in those herds that will need to reduce the infective pressure in the future in consideration of the application of a National program. The principal aim of this study was to investigate the dynamics of Salmonella infection in Italian farms with different characteristics in herd dimension and organization. The Authors wanted as well to evaluate the efficacy and feasibility of different diagnostic approaches in the Italian situation.

Material and methods

Four Italian farrow-to-finish herds were selected for the study. The herds were known to be infected by *Salmonella* from previous bacteriological findings. The farms had the following characteristics: farm 1) 100 sows, single site operation, farm 2) 550 sows, single site operation, farm 3) 1100 sows, two sites operation, farm 4) 1500 sows, three sites operation. In each herd 6 litters were randomly selected, and in each litter, the ears of five piglets were tagged. Thus, a total of 120 piglets were involved at the beginning of the study. All ear-tagged pigs were supposed to be raised together for the entire observation period. The day before weaning individual blood and faecal samples were collected from all sows in the farrowing unit, including the mothers of tagged piglets. In herds 1,2,3 and 4, 9,9, 17 and 20 sows were respectively submitted to blood and faecal sample collection. The same day in each herd a pool of faeces from the five boxes with tagged piglets was collected and tagged piglets were bled. In addition, tagged piglets were bled at day 60, 90, 150, 210. In herd 4 in which pigs are raised until the age of 350-360 days, a supplementary blood sample was collected at day 270. The same days of blood sampling, five faecal pools were collected in each herd from the floor of boxes in which the identified pigs were housed. Each faecal pool was composed of five faecal drops collected from the box floor. The maximum variation in effective sampling from schedule was 7 days. At slaughter, individual blood samples from tagged pigs were collected at bleeding (day 270 for herd 1,2,3 and 350 for herd 4) and ileocecal lymph nodes from corresponding carcasses were collected. Tagged pigs that died during the study period were replaced by other pigs of the same age and reared in the same conditions. Blood samples were analyzed by using a commercial ELISA test (Swine Salmonella Antibody Test, IDEXX) with a cutoff fixed at S/P ratio ≥ 0,25 (OD% =10). Faecal pools (25 g, except samples at day 30 that reached 5-10 g) were cultured as recommended by Lo Fo Wong and Hald , 2000. Ileocecal lymph nodes were submitted to bacteriological examination following superficial decontamination with ethanol (Anonimo, 2006). Differences in S/P ratio values and in sero-prevalence were compared by using respectively ANOVA and Fisher's Chi^2.

Results

In table 1 serologic results are reported as single herd and as aggregated average data of all herds. The serologic aggregated average data of all herds are reported graphically in figure 1

Table 1. Serologic results expressed as % of sero-positives and mean S/P ratio value.

herd	sows	day 30	day 60	day 90	day 150	day 210	day 270	day 350
	% (S/P)	% (S/P)	% (S/P)	% (S/P)	% (S/P)	% (S/P)	% (S/P)	% (S/P)
1	100 (0,66)	20 (0,12)	0 (0,02)	3 (0,06)	82,7 (0,61)	75,9 (0,45)	96,7 (0,56)	nd (nd)
2	100 (0,92)	26 (0,15)	0 (0,01)	0 (0,03)	51,7 (0,25)	52,6 (0,29)	93,3 (0,42)	nd (nd)
3	93,8 (0,52)	20 (0,09)	0 (0,01)	3 (0,04)	35,7 (0,29)	59,3 (0,32)	65,8 (0,58)	nd (nd)
4	95 (0,70)	19 (0,12)	0 (0,03)	4 (0,04)	55,2 (0,49)	100 (1.06)	100 (0,93)	100 (0,81)
1+2+3+4	96,2 (0,67)	21,4 (0,12)	0 (0,01)	2,7 (0,04)	56,5 (0,47)	74,3 (0,56)	87,2 (0,62)	nd (nd)

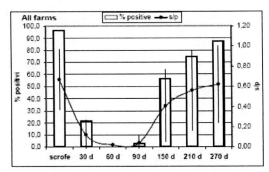

Fig. 1 Aggregated average serologic results (herds 1,2,3,4)

Sows sero-prevalence varied from 100% to 93,8%. Percentage of sero-positive piglets at day 30 of life was in average 21,4% (19%-26%). No significant differences were observed between herds. At day 60 of life all pigs in all herds were sero-negative and at day 90 only 2,7% (0-4%) showed S/P ratio values higher than the cutoff. Between day 90 and day 150 a high number of sero-conversions was observed. At day 150 the average sero-prevalence reached 56,5% (35,7-82,7%) with an average S/P ratio value 0,4 (0,25 – 0,61). The differences in terms of sero-positive pigs and S/P ratio value at day 90 and 150 were significant. ($Chi^2_{(1)}$Fisher's exact p< 0.01; $F_{1,1954}$= 129,65 p<0.01). From day 150 and 270 a further increase in sero-prevalence was recorded in all herds. Average differences in terms of sero-positive pigs and S/P ratio value were significant ($Chi^2_{(1)}$Fisher's exact p<0.05; $F_{1,211}$= 8.16 p<0.01). Bacteriological results obtained from faecal samples an ileocecal lymph nodes are reported in table 2.

Table 2. Results of bacteriological examination of faecal samples and ileocecal lymph nodes (ND= not determined).

	Herd 1 (ratio of positive samples)	Herd 2 (ratio of positive samples)	Herd 3 (ratio of positive samples)	Herd 4 (ratio of positive samples)
Sows	1/5 (S. Llandoff)	0/5	0/5	1/5 (S. 1,4,5,12:i:-)
day 30	0/5	0/5	0/5	0/5
day 60	0/5	0/5	0/5	0/5
day 90	0/5	0/5	0/5	0/5
day 150	1/5 (S. Derby)	0/5	2/5 (S. 1,4,5,12:i:-)	0/5
day 210	0/5	0/5	0/5	0/5
day 270	ND	ND	ND	1/5 (S. Bredeney)
Lymph nodes at slaughter	9/30 (S.Thompson, S. Umbilo, S. Typhimurium, S. Derby)	0/30	1/30 (S. Choleraesuis)	0/30

Discussion

The results of serology provide new information about epidemiology of *Salmonella* infection in Italian herds with different characteristics of organization. In all herds sero-prevalence in sows was high. The role of breeding animals in the epidemiology of the infection has been investigated in several studies and results are not always concordant (Dahl et al., 1997; Fedorka-Cray et al., 1997, Funk et al., 2001). In our study faecal samples collected from piglets at day 30 of life were all negative irrespective of *Salmonella* excretion by sows at the same day. S/P ratio value and sero-prevalence at day 30 was not influenced by evidence of faecal excretion in sows in the same herd. Serologic profile from day 30 to day 90 was similar in the four herds. Sero-prevalnce in piglets at weaning ranged from 19% to 26% (average S/P ratio value 0,12) in spite of the high rate of sero-positive sows (93,8-100%, average S/P ratio value 0,67). These results could be explained by low transfer of detectable antibodies with colostrum or by their rapid decline. In all herds the minimum number of sero-positive pigs was recorded between day 60 and 90 of life. As previously described by others Authors (Beloeil et al., 2003; Kranker et al., 2003), a clear increase in sero-prevalence was observed from day 90 to day 150. Assuming approximately an interval of 30 days from the peak of faecal excretion and maximal incidence of seroconversion (Kranker et al., 2003), it can be suggested that the highest number of infections took place in all herds approximately between day 60 and 90 of life. This hypothesis is supported by other studies (Funk et al., 2001; Beloeil et al., 2003; Kranker et al., 2003). Furthermore in that period usually animals are mixed and hygienic and environmental conditions worsen in coincidence with the transfer from weaning to early fattening units. Surprisingly, and in contrast with serologic results and with the previously mentioned reports, all faecal pools collected in that period (60-90 days of life) were negative at bacteriological examination. In feed medication was almost continuous in these groups at that age and antibiotic intake might have lowered the sensibility of the test without preventing spreading of the infection. In contrast with the observations of Kranker et al. (2003), who reported a decrease of sero-prevalence in 5 of 6 cohorts from 3 Danish herds in proximity of slaughter after a peak in the early fattening period, in this study the sero-prevalence increased until slaughter. The serologic results together with the detection of *Salmonella* in faeces at 150-270 days in three herds suggest that the spread of infection was not confined in the early finishing period. In consideration of this evidence the longer fattening period typical of the Italian swine production system could be an additional point of concern for the control of infection at herd level. The results of bacteriological investigation of ileocecal lymph nodes confirm what previously described by various Authors (Berends et al.,1996; Davies et al., 2000; Hurd et al., 2001; Gebreyes et al., 2004) about the contrasting results in terms of serotypes detected from samples collected at farm and at the slaughterhouse.

Conclusions

This study provides three major considerations about *Salmonella* infection in Italian herds: 1) the infection is highly diffused in breeding animals of commercial farms irrespective of number of sows and operating sites, 2) the early fattening period is, as expected, the moment of massive spread of the infection, 3) the long fattening period of Italian herds could make even more difficult the implementation of control strategies at herd level when farms will be called to reduce prevalence. The sampling protocol for blood samples was practicable and the serologic test results provided useful information about infection dynamics in herds. The protocol used for faecal samples collection was probably inadequate for the same purpose and the sensitivity of the test might have been influenced by in feed medication.

Acknowledgements

This study was founded by Italian Health Ministry within the research project IZSLE 05-04 RC.

References

Anonimous, 2006. *Risk Assessment and mitigation options of Salmonella in pig production.* The EFSA Journal, 341, 1-131.

Beloeil P.A., et al., 2003. *Longitudinal serologic responses to Salmonella enterica of growing pigs in a subclinically infected herd.* Preventive Veterinary Medicine, 60, 207-226.

Berends B.R., et al., 1996. *Identification of risk factors in animal management and transport regarding Salmonella in pigs.* International Journal of Food Microbiology, 30, 37-53.

Dahl J., et al., 1997. *Elimination of Salmonella Typhimurium infection by strategic movement of pigs.* The Veterinary Record, 140, 679-681.

Davies P.R., et al., 2000. *Comparison of methods for isolating Salmonella from faeces of naturally infected pigs.* Journal of Applied Microbiology, 89, 169-177.

Fedorka-Cray P. J., et al., 1997. *Using isolated weaning to raise Salmonella free swine.* Veterinary Medicine, 92, 375-382.

Funk J.A., et al., 2001. *Longitudinal study of Salmonella enterica in growing pigs rared in multiple-site swine production systems.* Veterinary Microbiology, 83, 45-60.

Gebreyes W.A., et al., 2004. *Salmonella enterica serovars from pigs on Farms and after slaughter and validity of using bacteriological data to define herd Salmonella status.* Journal of Food Protection, 67, (4), 691-679.

Hurd H.S., et al., 2001. *The effect of lairage on Salmonella isolation.* Journal of Food Protection, 64, 939-944.

Kranker S., et al., 2003. *Longitudinal study of Salmonella enterica Serotype Typhimurium in three Danish farrow-to-finish Swine Herds.* Journal of Clininical Microbiology, 41, (6), 2282-2288.

Lo Fo Wong D.M.A. and Hald T. (2000). *Salmonella in Pork (SALINPORK): pre-harvest and harvest control options based on epidemiologic, diagnostic and economic research.* Final Report to European Commission of project FAIR1 CT95-0400, Appendix II.1, Microbiological Standard Operating Procedures, 194-207.

Modelling the prevalence of *Salmonella* carrier pigs at slaughtering age: influence of management systems and of the *Salmonella* status of replacement gilts

A. Lurette[(1)*], **C. Belloc**[(1)], **S. Touzeau**[(2)], **T. Hoch**[(1)], **H. Seegers**[(1)] and **C. Fourichon**[(1)]

[(1)] *UMR708 Unit of Animal Health Management, Veterinary School, INRA, F-44000, ENVN, Nantes, France*
[(2)] *UR341 Unit of Applied Mathematics and Computer Science, INRA, F-78350, Jouy-en-Josas, France*
corresponding author: lurette@vet-nantes.fr

Abstract

To reduce *Salmonella* contamination of pork food chain at the farm level, control actions can aim at preventing the introduction of the bacteria into herds or/and at preventing the in-herd transmission. Our aim is to estimate the influence of (i) the decontamination efficiency and (ii) the *Salmonella* status of replacement gilts on the prevalence of carrier pigs at slaughtering age. We developed a stochastic mathematical model to simulate the pig population dynamics and the *Salmonella* transmission within a farrow-to-finish herd. Results show a different prevalence of carriage in groups of delivered pigs according to the scenarios tested. The prevalence of carriage in the groups of replacement gilts had more impact on the increase of the prevalence of carrier finishers than the decontamination process. Given the expected objectives of control programs, these results emphasized the need for producers to implement a high level of room floor decontamination between consecutive batches and to avoid introduction by carrier replacement gilts in *Salmonella*-free herds.

Introduction

The *Salmonella* contamination of the pork food chain is initiated by the presence of carrier pigs at slaughtering age. To reduce *Salmonella* prevalence in pigs, control actions can aim at preventing the introduction of the bacteria into herds or/and at preventing the in-herd transmission. Carrier and shedder gilts are considered as the main risk factor for introduction of *Salmonella* into herds (Berends *et al.*, 1996, EFSA, 2006). Several authors have shown in risk factors studies the influence of herd management systems on *Salmonella* prevalence in commercial herds (Dahl *et al.*, 1997, Lo Fo Wong *et al.*, 2004). A modelling approach allows to represent both management system, sow replacement and *Salmonella* transmission. In prospect of implementation of *Salmonella* control programs, this approach enables to identify the key processes to reduce *Salmonella* prevalence in pig herds. However, previously published models describing *Salmonella* transmission considered only the growing and the finishing periods without representing the all-in/all-out housing system in use with the batch management and the sows and their replacement (Ivanek *et al.*, 2004; van der Gaag *et al.*, 2004). Our aim is to simulate and to estimate the influence of (i) the decontamination efficiency of

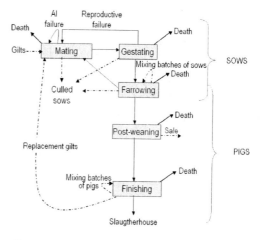

Figure 1. Simplified flow diagram of the farrow-to-finish herd production system.

→ flows linked to demographic process
--·-·→ flows controlled by producer.

the room floor and (ii) the *Salmonella* status of replacement gilts on the prevalence of carrier pigs at slaughtering age.

Material and methods
We developed a stochastic mathematical model to simulate the pig population dynamics (Fig.1) and the *Salmonella* transmission within a farrow-to-finish herd. In this herd, the farrowing batch system was used. We considered both the reproduction cycle of sows and the growth of pigs from birth to slaughterhouse delivery. The sow herd was divided into groups called batches. The reproduction cycle of sows was represented by the occupation of three successive rooms: the mating room (4 weeks), the gestating room (12 weeks) and the farrowing room (5 weeks). The duration in each room and the transfer between rooms were governed by the animals' physiological stage. The cycle ended in the farrowing room at the weaning of piglets. The growth of pigs corresponded to the occupation of three successive rooms: the farrowing room (4 weeks), the post-weaning room (8 weeks) and the finishing room (between 12 and 16 weeks). In farrowing, post-weaning and finishing rooms, pigs of a batch, which had the same age, entered and left the room at once. This all-in/all-out housing system allowed a cleaning-disinfecting process and a rest of one week between two batches defined as the decontamination process.

The making up of groups of delivered finisher pigs and kinetic of slaughterhouse deliveries were considered. Given that producers had to deliver finisher pigs with a homogeneous weight and knowing the variability in pig growth, the groups of delivered pigs consisted in pigs coming from several batches.

To model the infection of *Salmonella* in sows and pigs, three states were distinguished: (i) the susceptible state (*Salmonella*-free pigs); (ii) the shedder carrier state (infected pigs shedding *Salmonella* in the environment) and (ii) the non shedder carrier state (infected pigs not shedding). We considered an indirect transmission of *Salmonella* by the environment. The bacteria originated from shedder pigs in the batch or from other batches having previously contaminated the room floor. Input parameter values for *Salmonella* transmission were estimations from literature (Beloeil *et al.*, 2003; Fravalo *et al.*, 2003; Kranker *et al.*, 2003; Nielsen *et al.*, 1995) and from expert opinions.

For an effective control of *Salmonella* transmission within a farrow-to-finish herd, biosecurity interventions simulated here were prevention of batch mixing while raising pigs and implementation of decontamination process between two consecutive batches. We tested the strict all-in/all-out housing system with four different decontamination efficiencies (0.8, 0.9, 0.99 and 0.999 which corresponded to the proportion of bacteria eliminated by the decontamination process in a room).

For each scenario, results were obtained from 100 runs over 400 weeks. We considered the prevalence of carriers in groups of delivered pigs, *i.e.* the sum of shedder and non shedder carrier pigs. On the one hand, we tested the influence of the decontamination process efficiency on two outputs: (i) the prevalence of carrier finisher pigs over time and the mean of this prevalence for the six last months of the simulation (weeks 376 to 400), and (ii) the frequency of groups of delivered pigs with a prevalence higher than 0.40 during the whole simulation. In the Danish *Salmonella* plan, this prevalence value corresponds to the threshold for the

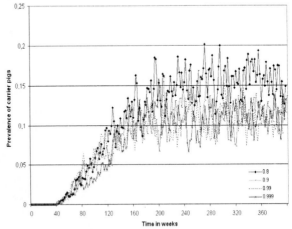

Figure 2. *Prevalence of carriage in groups of delivered pigs according to the cleaning-disinfecting process efficiency under the all-in/all-out housing system.*

herd contamination level at which producers have to implement control actions and have financial penalties. Simulations were run from a herd initially *Salmonella*-free with only one introduction of *Salmonella* in the mating room at the initial time.

On the second hand, we assessed the influence of the prevalence of carrier replacement gilts on the prevalence of carrier finishers in groups of delivered pigs in a herd *Salmonella*-free. Simulations were run with the introduction of carrier gilts at three fixed prevalence levels (0.05, 0.15 and 0.5) at each time of replacement for the all-in/all-out housing system.

Results

Prevalence of carriage in groups of delivered pigs differed according to the efficiency of the decontamination process (fig. 2). The mean 6-month prevalence was significantly higher ($p<0.001$) for the decontamination efficiency equal to 0.8 than for all the others decontamination efficiencies (fig. 2).

The frequency of groups of delivered pigs with a prevalence higher than 0.4 was more than twice higher for a cleaning-disinfecting efficiency of 0.8 than for one of 0.999 (tab. 1).

Table 1. Frequency of groups of delivered pigs with a prevalence higher than 0.4 according to the decontamination efficiency and the level of prevalence of carriage in groups of replacement gilts.

Values of parameters	Decontamination efficiency (proportion of bacteria removed by the process)				Prevalence of carriage in groups of replacement gilts		
	0.8	0.9	0.99	0.999	0.05	0.15	0.5
Frequency in % of groups of delivered pigs with a prevalence higher than 0.4	6.3 [b] (3.8)	3.3 [ab] (2.8)	2.8 [a] (1.8)	2.3 [a] (1.8)	1.8 [a] (1.7)	2.6 [a] (1.7)	11.0 [b] (3.3)

Mean (SD), data of one result with a common superscript within a line were not significantly different (p<0.001).

A higher prevalence of carriage in groups of replacement gilts increased significantly the prevalence of carrier delivered pigs (fig. 3). The mean 6-month prevalence of carrier pigs differed significantly when prevalence of carriage in groups of replacement gilts was equal to 0.05 and 0.5.

The frequency of groups of delivered pigs with a prevalence of carriers higher than 0.4 was significantly higher ($p<0.01$) when the prevalence of carriage in groups of replacement gilts was 0.5 than for a prevalence of 0.05 and 0.15 (tab. 1).

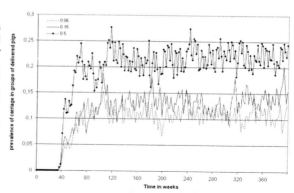

Figure 3. Prevalence of carriage pig in groups of delivered pigs according to the prevalence of carrier replacement gilts.

Discussion

The decontamination process influences the prevalence of *Salmonella* carriage in groups of delivered pigs. A good implementation of this process allowed to maintain a low *Salmonella* prevalence in the herd. Decontamination experiments in field conditions can result in removing more than 99% of bacteria (Morgan-Jones, 1987). However, this decontamination efficiency is not always reached in commercial pig herds where conditions of cleaning and disinfectant actions are not always optimal. Whatever the decontamination process efficiency tested, an only one introduction of *Salmonella* was sufficient to induce the set up of this bacteria in the herd. This was related to the persistence of *Salmonella* in the environment and to the continuous transmission by the room floor for sows in the mating room.

High prevalence of carriage in groups of replacement gilts induced an increased prevalence of carrier finisher pigs. Given that the repeated introduction of carrier gilts at each replacement time did not induce an increased prevalence of carrier delivered pigs which tended to an equilibrium, efforts should be put on avoiding the first introduction of carrier animals in *Salmonella*-free herds. This introduction was especially important as once the bacteria were set up in the herd, it is difficult to eradicate *Salmonella* even if decontamination level is well implemented.

Conclusion

These results showed the influence of the decontamination process and the prevalence of carrier gilts on the prevalence of carriage in groups of delivered pigs. Given the expected objectives of control programs, these results emphasized that control actions have to combine the efficiency of the decontamination of the room floor and the possibility for producers to know the *Salmonella* prevalence of their suppliers to avoid the introduction of replacement gilts with a high *Salmonella* prevalence.

References

BELOEIL, P.A., CHAUVIN, C., PROUX, K., ROSE, N., QUEGUINER, S., EVENO, E., HOUDAYER, C., ROSE V., FRAVALO P., MADEC F. (2003). Longitudinal serological responses to *Salmonella enterica* of growing pigs in subclinically infected herd. *Preventive Veterinary Medicine*, 60, 207-226.

BERENDS, B.R., URLINGS, H.A.P., SNIJDERS, J.M.A., VAN KNAPEN, F., 1996. Identification and quantification of risk factors in animal management and transport regarding Salmonella spp. in pigs. International Journal of Food Microbiology, 30, 37-53.

DAHL, J., WINGSTRAND, A., NIELSEN, B., BAGGESEN, D.L., 1997. Elimination of *Salmonella* typhimurium infection by the strategic movement of pigs. *The Veterinary Record*, 140, 679-681.

EFSA, 2006. Opinion of the scientific panel on biological hazards on "Risk assessment and mitigation options of Salmonella in pig production". *The EFSA journal*, 341, 1-131.

FRAVALO P., CARIOLET R., PROUX K., SALVAT G. (2003). Le portage asymptomatique de *Salmonella* enterica par les porcs : résultats issus de la constitution d'un modèle en conditions expérimentales. Journées de la recherche porcine, 35, 393-400.

IVANEK, R., SNARY, E.L., COOK, A.J., GROHN, Y.T. (2004). A mathematical model for the transmission of *Salmonella* Typhimurium within a grower-finisher herd in Great Britain. *Journal of Food Protection*, 11, 2403-2409.

KRANKER S., ALBAN L., BOES J., DAHL J. (2003). Longitudinal study of *Salmonella enterica* serotype Typhimurium infection in three Danish farrow-to-finish swine herds. *Journal of Clinical Microbiology*, 41, 2282-2288.

LO FO WONG, D.M.A., DAHL, J., STEGE, H., VAN DER WOLF, P.J., LEONTIDES, L., VON ALTROCK, A., THORBERG, B.M., 2004. Herd-level risk factors for subclinical Salmonella infection in European finishing-pig herd. Preventive Veterinary Medicine, 62, 253-266.

MORGAN-JONES, S., 1987. Practical aspects of disinfection and infection control. In: Linton A.H. et al., eds. Disinfection in Veterinary and Farm Animal Practice. Oxford: Blackwell Scientific Publications, 144.

NIELSEN B., BAGGESEN D., BAGER F., HAUGEGAARD J., LIND P. (1995). The serological response to *Salmonella* serovars Typhimurium and Infantis in experimentally infected pigs. The

Session 2

time course followed with an indirect anti-LPS ELISA and bacteriological examinations. *Veterinary Microbiology*, 47, 205-218.

VAN DER GAAG , M.A., VOS, F., SAATKAMP, H.W., VAN BOVEN, M., VAN BEEK, P. and HUIRNE, R.B.M., 2004. A sate-transition simulation model for the spread of *Salmonella* in the pork supply chain. European Journal of Operational Research, 3, 782-798.

Tracking of *Salmonella* Positive Pigs from Farm to Fork in the Republic of Ireland

Duggan, S.J.*[1], Prendergast, D.M.[1], Leonard, N.[2], Mannion, C.[2], Butler, F.[3], Fanning, S.[2] and Duffy, G.[1]

[1]Food Safety Department, Ashtown Food Research Centre, Teagasc, Ashtown, Dublin 15, Ireland.
[2]School of Agriculture, Food Safety and Veterinary Medicine, University College Dublin, Belfield, Dublin 2, Ireland.
[3]Department of Biosystems Engineering, University College Dublin, Belfield, Dublin 2, Ireland.

*Corresponding author: Sharon.duggan@teagasc.ie

Abstract

In this study, individual pigs from selected herds of known *Salmonella* serological status were tracked through the slaughter and dressing process. From all tracked animals, caecal contents, rectal faeces, carcasses (before washing and chilling and after chilling) and pork primal cuts were examined for the presence of *Salmonella*. All samples were screened for *Salmonella* using real time PCR and all suspect positive samples were confirmed using the ISO 6579 method for *Salmonella*. To determine the relationship between *Salmonella* isolates from different parts of the chain, all isolates are being characterised by Pulse Field Gel Electrophoresis (PFGE). The results suggest that the slaughter and dressing operations have a significant effect on the incidence of *Salmonella* and that even if pigs are presented for slaughter with caecal or rectal carriage of *Salmonella* then good slaughter practices can prevent carcass contamination. All data generated in the study is being fed into a quantitative risk assessment model for *Salmonella* in pork.

Introduction

In Ireland, salmonellosis is one of the most common zoonotic diseases in humans and the two predominant serovars associated with human illness are *S.* Enteriditis and *S.* Typhimurium (Health Protection Surveillance Centre). Recent surveillance data indicates that *S.* Enterica was identified in 3 and 2% of raw pork respectively in 2002 and 2003 (FSAI, 2005) and in 2.3% of raw pork in 2004 (FSAI, 2006). In keeping with this trend, at retail level, *S.* Enterica was identified in 3 and 0% of raw pork respectively in 2002 and 2003 (FSAI, 2005) and 0.2% of raw pork in 2004 (FSAI, 2006).

In the Republic of Ireland there is an ongoing *Salmonella* pig herd monitoring programme which is operated by the Department of Agriculture and Food (DAF). The meat juice from twenty four pigs in each herd are tested serologically three times a year at slaughter plants and herds are assigned a category (1-3) based on a calculated weighted average of the three most recent tests. A certificate is issued grading the herd as Category 1 (< 10% of herd serologically positive for *Salmonella*), Category 2 (≥ 10%, ≤ 50% positive) or Category 3 (> 50% positive). Category 3 herds are slaughtered separately from other pigs to minimise the risk of cross contamination. The head meat and offals of category 3 pigs may not be sold in the raw state and must be heat treated in an approved manner before being passed fit for human consumption or else it must be destroyed. Pigs with no valid certificate are treated as category 3 pigs at slaughter.

The aim of this study was to determine the correlation between the *Salmonella* status of the pigs presented for slaughter and the *Salmonella* status of the pork following slaughter and dressing operations.

Materials and Methods

Pigs from nine different herds were tracked through three commercial pork abattoirs. Each pig to be tracked was slap marked for identification purposes. The serological status of each herd presented for slaughter was a historical value based on the rolling average of the three most recent serological tests. Each marked pig was examined for the presence of *Salmonella* at key stages during slaughter and dressing, namely, caecal contents, rectal faeces, carcasses (left side before washing and chilling and right side after overnight chilling) and pork primal cuts.

All samples were screened for *Salmonella* using real time PCR based on the method developed by Catarame *et al.*, 2005, for the detection of the 16S rRNA gene (Trkov and Avgustin, 2003). Suspect positive samples were plated from the enrichment broth (Rappaport Vassiliadis Soya broth) onto brilliant green agar and xylose lysine desoxycholate (BGA and XLD; Merck, Germany) and incubated for 24 h at 37°C. Suspect positives were confirmed using the ISO 6579 method for the detection of *Salmonella*. Figure 1 below outlines the method employed in this study.

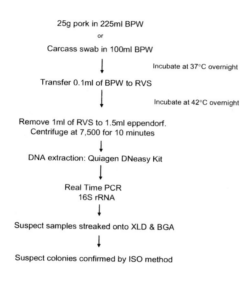

Figure 1: *Salmonella* detection method

Results

The summarised results are shown below in Table 1. The historical serological *Salmonella* status of the nine herds tracked in this study ranged from 0% to 95%. The number of pigs tracked from each herd ranged between thirteen and twenty one animals.

Of the 147 pigs tracked only 69 (46.9%) had *Salmonella* in their caecal contents and 50 (34.0%) had *Salmonella* in their rectal faeces. In general, if a pig showed rectal carriage of *Salmonella* then it was also present in the caecal contents, the exception being the pigs tracked from herd six, from which three pigs tested positive for *Salmonella* in rectal faeces but all their caecal contents tested negative.

As the pigs progressed through the slaughter and dressing procedures there was a marked decrease in the incidence of *Salmonella*. Only sixteen pork carcasses examined after evisceration and before chilling and washing tested positive for *Salmonella* and this decreased to only four

Salmonella positive carcasses after chilling. Only two pork primal cuts were positive for *Salmonella*. This suggests that the slaughter and dressing operations significantly reduce the incidence of *Salmonella*.

Table 1: Number of *Salmonella* positive animals as they were tracked from individual pig herds through the slaughter process at different plants.

Abattoir	A	A	A	B	C	C	A	B	B	Total no. sampled	Total no. positive (%)
Stage	Herd 1	Herd 2	Herd 3	Herd 4	Herd 5	Herd 6	Herd 7	Herd 8	Herd 9		
Category (rolling average of herd)	2 (49%)	2 (21%)	2 (44%)	3 (62%)	3 (95%)	1 (6.7%)	1 (7.3%)	1 (0%)	3 (60%)		
No. animals sampled	16	21	13	19	16	14	16	16	16	147	
No. positive rectal samples	10	11	1	5	2	3	2	0	16	147	50 (34.0)
No. positive caecal samples	16	17	4	6	7	0	2	1	16	147	69 (46.9)
No. positive carcasses (pre-chill)	0	0	0	7	2	1	1	0	5	145	16 (11.0)
No. positive carcasses (post-chill)	1	0	0	0	1	0	0	0	2	131	4 (3.05)
No. positive pork primal cuts	0	0	0	0	2	0	0	0	0	135	2 (1.48)

Discussion

Overall, 46.9% of the caecal samples tested positive for *Salmonella* in relation to 11.0 and 3.05% of carcasses before washing and chilling, and after chilling respectively. These results are in agreement with other workers who found a poor correlation between caecal carriage and carcass contamination (Davies *et al.*, 2004; Vieira-Pinto *et al.*, 2005). A larger study carried out in the UK (Davies *et al.*, 2004), reported a carriage of *Salmonella* in 23% of caecal contents but on only 5.3% of carcasses.

In the present study, all pigs tracked from herds 1 (n=16) and 9 (n=16) had *Salmonella* in their caecal contents. Of the corresponding carcasses none of the pigs from herd 1 had a positive carcass pre washing and chilling and only one carcass was positive post chilling while from herd 9, five of the pre washing and chilling carcasses and two of the post chill carcasses tested positive for *Salmonella*. Of these, only one animal was positive for *Salmonella* at both stages of carcass sampling. It should be noted that herds 1 and 9 were slaughtered at different pork plants with differences in abattoir practices and production days.

The tracking study on pigs from herd 5 (n=16) showed *Salmonella* was present on the pork primal cuts with two of the sixteen animals testing positive. One of these contaminated pork primal cuts was also positive at the pre chill carcass stage, however the second positive pork cut was not positive at the pre or post chill carcass stage. This would indicate that cross contamination may have occurred. When complete, molecular characterisation will inform us if the *Salmonella* strains carried by the pigs are the same *Salmonella* strains recovered from the carcass or if contamination is as a result of cross contamination within the pork slaughter process.

Other workers concluded that cross contamination accounted for 29% of the entire carcass contamination and that improvements in slaughter house hygiene as well as measures to decrease the *Salmonella* contamination both in the slaughterhouse and at pig level was needed (Botteldoorn *et al.*, 2003).

According to Giovannacci *et al.*, 2001, *Salmonella* transmission to carcasses occurs by pig to pig contact and exposure to the contaminated physical environment and as long as contaminated carcasses are being processed, about 90% of cross contamination that occurs is unavoidable.

Conclusions

The results of this present study suggest that the slaughter and dressing operations have a significant effect on the incidence of *Salmonella* and that even if pigs presented for slaughter have caecal or rectal carriage then good slaughter practices can prevent carcass contamination.

References

Botteldoorn, N., Heyndrickx, N., Rijpens, N, Grijspeerdt, K and Herman, L., 2003. *Salmonella* on pig carcasses: positive pigs and cross contamination in the slaughterhouse. Journal of Applied Microbiology, 95, 891-903.

Catarame, T.M.G., O'Hanlon, K.A., McDowell, D.A., Blair, I.S. and Duffy, G., 2006. Comparison of a real time polymerase chain reaction assay with a culture method for the detection of *Salmonella* in retail meat samples. Journal of Food Safety 26 1-15.

Davies, R.H., Dalziel, R., Gibbens, J.C., Wilesmith, J.W., Ryan, J.M.B., Evans, S.J., Byrne, C., Paiba, G.A., Pascoe, S.J.S. and Teale, C.J., 2004. National survey for *Salmonella* in pigs, cattle and sheep at slaughter in Great Britain (1999-2000). Journal of Applied Microbiology, 96, 750-760.

Food Safety Authority of Ireland, 2005. Report on zoonoses in Ireland, 2002 and 2003.

Food Safety Authority of Ireland, 2006. Report on zoonoses in Ireland, 2004.

Giovannacci, I., Queguiner, S., Ragimbeau, C., Salvat, G., Vendeuvre, J.L., Carlier, V., and Ermel, G., 2001. Tracing of *Salmonella* spp. in two pork slaughter and cutting plants using Serotyping and macrorestriction genotyping. Journal of Applied Microbiology, 90, 131-147.

Trkov, M. and Avgustin, G., 2003. An improved 16S rRNA based PCR method for the specific detection of *Salmonella* enterica. International Journal of Food Microbiology 80 (1) 67-75.

Vieira-Pinto, M., Temudo, P. And Martins, C., 2005. Occurrence of *Salmonella* in the Ileum, Ileocolic Lymph nodes, Tonsils, Mandibular Lymph nodes and Carcass of pigs slaughtered for consumption. Journal of Veterinary Medicine B 52, 476-481.

Observations on the distribution of *Salmonella* on primary pig breeding farms

Davies, R.*, McLaren, I., Wales, A., Bedford, S.

Department of Food and Environmental Safety, Veterinary Laboratories Agency - Weybridge, Surrey, KT15 3NB, UK
Corresponding author: r.h.davies@vla.defra.gsi.gov.uk

Abstract

Salmonella infection in pigs has emerged as an important potential public health issue in recent years and several countries have introduced monitoring and control programmes. However, the *Salmonella* status of most primary breeding herds remains unknown. This paper describes the results of intensive sampling carried out on four occupied primary pig breeding farms and one breeding farm which was purchased and cleaned and disinfected before being used for primary breeding. All premises were sampled intensively by taking large gauze swab samples from every pen of breeding sows, boars and rearing gilt and boar progeny. Samples of equipment and faeces plus carcases of wildlife vectors were also collected. On one farm (A) *S.* Derby, *S.* Kedougou and *S.* Newport were found in all locations whereas *S.* Typhimurium (DT104, DT20) was restricted to gilts retained for the herd and gilts and boars being reared for sale. There was considerable involvement of rodents and evidence of ineffective disinfection of farrowing crates. On a second farm (B), owned by the same company, there were similar findings, with *S.* Meleagridis also present. Improvements to rodent control but not disinfection produced no reduction in the overall prevalence of *Salmonella*. On two other farms, belonging to a separate company, *S.* Give predominated in adult breeding stock and rearing gilts and boars but some *S.* Typhimurium (DT104, DT193) was also present in the young stock on the larger unit (C). In the smaller unit (D), in which hygiene and rodent control was much better, only *S.* Give and *S.* Kedougou were found. In another farm (E) *S.* Stanley, *S.* Bredeney, *S.* Mbandaka and *S.* Typhimurium were found before total depopulation. Cleaning and disinfection was poor initially but successful after improvements, but no sampling was permitted in the new primary breeding herd by the new owners of the farm.

Introduction

Salmonella infection in pigs has emerged as an important potential public health issue and several countries have introduced monitoring and control programmes. However, there is limited data on *Salmonella* colonisation in pig herds above the commercial production tier of the breeding pyramid. The few survey reports (van der Wolf et al., 2001, Grafanakis et al., 2001, Mejia et al., 2006), suggest that the herd and individual prevalence of *Salmonella* excretion or serological response may be broadly similar between genetic and production breeding herds. Such rates are also comparable to those observed amongst young fattening stock. Data from bacteriological sampling in Denmark (Christensen et al., 2002) showed similar herd-level prevalences of *Salmonella* (around 12%) in genetic breeder herds and in finished pigs before slaughter. The present report concerns intensive sampling for *Salmonella* on five premises in England: four occupied primary pig breeding farms and one breeding farm which was purchased to be used for primary breeding.

Materials and Methods

Farms A and B were both 700-sow primary breeding units producing boars and under common ownership. Farms C and D were primary gilt-producing units of 550- and 150-sow size respectively, also under common ownership. Farm E was at the first visit a 400-sow unit producing slaughter pigs, and at the second visit a unit undergoing depopulation, cleaning and disinfection (C&D). The strategy was to sample representative groups of pigs from all age groups present, plus empty and cleaned accommodation, equipment, walls and floors in pig-handling and staff areas, and wildlife vectors, particularly rodents. Samples taken on each unit included 25 g bulked faeces from groups of pigs, surface swabs of sterile medical gauze soaked in buffered peptone water (BPW) from empty pens and cleaned surfaces (approx 0.5 m^2), plus rodent droppings and dead mice. Faeces and swabs were placed directly into 225 ml BPW. Rodent droppings (1-10 g) and the liver, intestine and spleen from aseptically dissected mouse carcases (2-3 g) were placed in an approximately tenfold volume of BPW at the processing laboratory. Samples were taken to the laboratory under ambient temperature conditions and processed on the day of collection.

Samples in BPW were pre-enriched for 24 h, inoculated onto modified semi-solid Rappaport-Vassiliadis agar with 0.01 % novobiocin (MSRV; Difco 218681) and incubated at 41.5 °C for 16 to 24 h. A 1 µl loop from the edge of any opaque growth on MSRV was inoculated onto Rambach agar (Merck 107500). Rambach and associated MSRV plates were incubated at 37 °C and 41.5 °C respectively for 24 h. Any MSRV plates on which the growth had spread widely, but which were negative for *Salmonella* on the Rambach plates, were subcultured again onto Rambach agar. Serotyping of representative *Salmonella* isolates was performed at the *Salmonella* reference laboratory at VLA – Weybridge.

Results

Farms A and B were each visited on three occasions between 1998 and 2000, Farm C on two occasions between 1999 and 2000, Farm D on one occasion in 2000 and Farm E on three occasions in 1996. Figure 1 shows the prevalences (total positive samples / total samples) for each visit, together with the *Salmonella* serotypes and *S*. Typhimurium definitive phage types isolated. Figure 2 illustrates the proportion of positive samples over all visits and the range of prevalences at each visit, broken down by the sample categories.

At **Farm A**, salmonella was isolated from all categories on all occasions. *S*. Typhimurium DT104 was initially found at high frequency among young boars and gilts, rodents, and less often among weaners. This declined over two years to zero prevalence. Serotypes Derby and Kedougou were found on all visits, whilst Newport, Senftenburg and Agona were detected at lower frequencies on single visits. Non-Typhimurium serotypes occurred at high prevalences, between 15% and 78%. Seven of 10 samples from cleaned & disinfected areas were positive, and serotypes from rodents (Derby, Kedougou and Typhimurium DT104) reflected the predominant pig serotypes.

A high prevalence of *Salmonella* was also encountered on **Farm B**, with all categories yielding positive samples on all occasions. *S*. Typhimurium DT104 was present initially among young stock only, but extended into dry sows and rodents at the final visit. Within affected categories, prevalences ranged from 4% to 30%. Serotypes Derby, Kedougou and Newport were all frequently found on multiple visits whilst Meleagridis was isolated from one group on one occasion. Non-Typhimurium serotypes were persistently highly prevalent across all categories. Improved rodent control during the study had little effect in the face of poor C&D efficacy.

From **Farm C**, *S*. Typhimurium was initially isolated amongst weaners, fatteners and associated rodents, but one year later it was detected much more widely. Within-category prevalences ranged from 10% to 50%. Phage type DT104 predominated. S. Give had a high prevalence on both visits and across all categories. Serotypes Agona, Kedougou and Rissen were occasional isolates in single areas on single visits. Rodent control was notably poor, and *Salmonella* types from rodents reflected those from pigs. **Farm D** received some stock from Farm C, and *S*. Give was again the predominant serotype although at a more moderate prevalence (14% overall) than on Farm C. *S*. Kedougou was also present. C&D appeared effective (phenolic disinfectant, none of 27 samples positive) but rodent control was inadequate in the sow yards, where the highest prevalence was found. *S*. Typhimurium was not found.

Initially, **Farm E** showed a low (4.5%) prevalence of *S*. Typhimurium (untyped) among growers, plus carriage by rodents. Eight months later, it was present at high prevalence across all categories except dry sows. There was a high prevalence of serotypes Bredeney, Mbandaka and Stanley among older stock on both visits, but of these only Stanley was found amongst weaners, finishers and rodents. Kedougou was also detected on equipment on the second visit. C&D using a peroxygen disinfectant was ineffective but repeat disinfection of the whole site using 5% formalin after total depopulation (data not shown) resulted in no isolates from 240 samples.

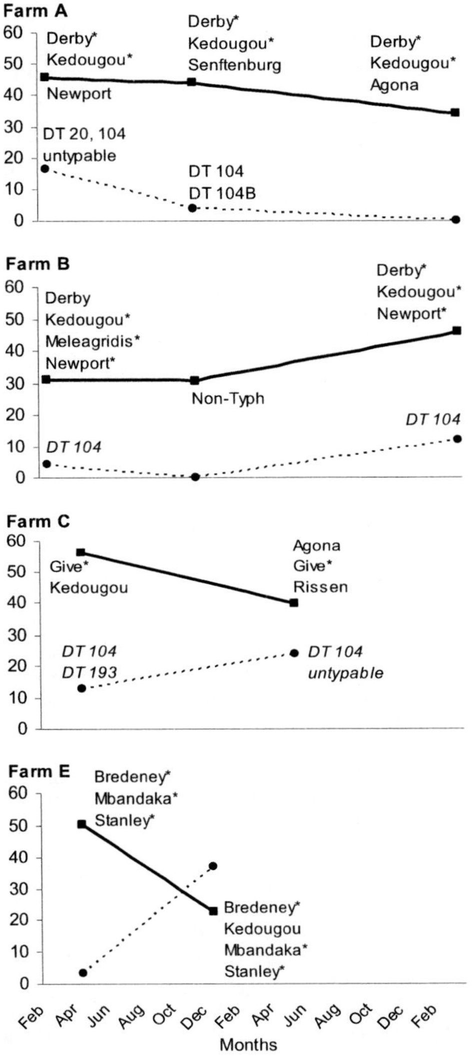

Farm A

Farm B

Farm C

Farm E

Farm A
- ◆ Non-Typhimurium overall % positive samples.
- ● Typhimurium overall % positive samples.
- | Range of prevalence (single visit) values (%).

Farm B

Farm C

Farm E

Farm D

Figure 1 (above): Overall farm-level prevalence values of *Salmonella* Typhimurium (dotted lines) and non-Typhimurium serotypes (solid lines) over time, for farms visited more than once (A, B, C, E). The time scale for all charts is on the bottom chart. * Predominant serotypes.

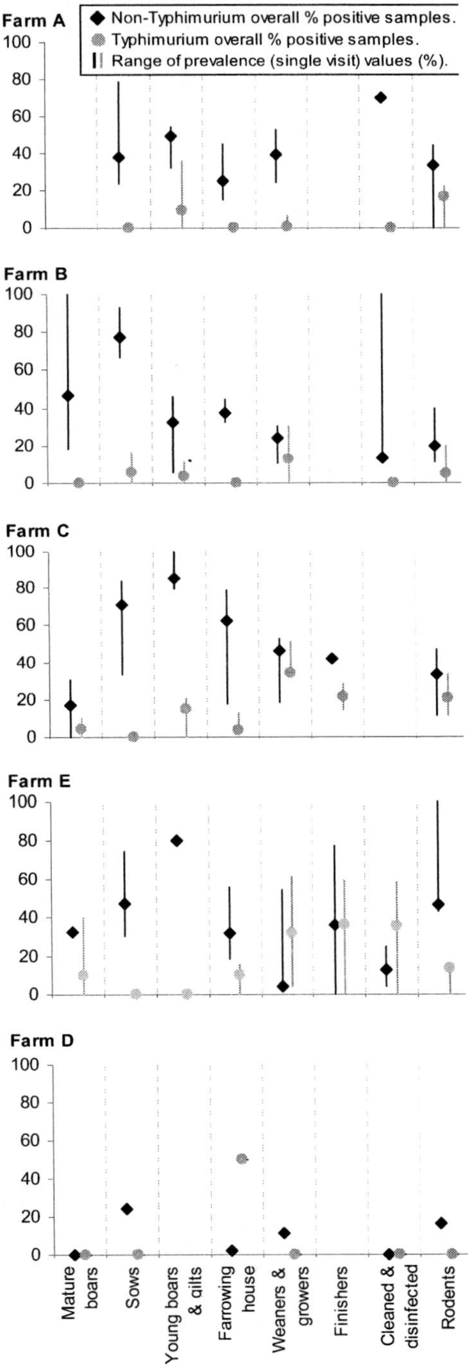

Figure 2 (above right): *Salmonella* within groups/areas on farms A to E. Point markers show the percentage of positive samples from all visits combined; lines show the range of individual visit prevalence values. Category labels are on the bottom chart.

Salmonella prevalence (%)

Discussion

The present findings show a substantial prevalence of several *Salmonella* serotypes, including Typhimurium, among four primary breeder establishments (A to D), and on another farm (E) shortly before conversion to a primary breeder. The within-herd prevalence rates are comparable to those found within production herds at slaughter in the UK (Davies et al., 2004). Certain serotypes and phage types (Derby, Stanley, Give, Bredeney, Mbandaka, Typhimurium DT104) appeared stably persistent on premises, others (Senftenburg, Agona, Rissen, Meleagridis, Typhimurium DT104B, DT20, DT193) were infrequent or transient, and some (Kedougou, Newport) appeared persistent on some premises and not on others. The smallest unit (D) had fewest concurrent serotypes present and the lowest overall prevalence of *Salmonella*, despite receiving stock from a farm (C) with a comparatively high prevalence and number of strains. Principal serotypes appeared to be shared among the farms with common ownership, i.e. A and B, C and D.

Aside from transient strains, temporal patterns of prevalence varied widely. Where *S.* Typhimurium was seen to increase over time (farms B, C and E), it apparently extended from weaners and growers, and in some cases young gilts and boars, into older groups. Where it decreased over time (Farm A), initial colonisation was restricted to these same young age groups, and spread no further.

Cleaning and disinfection of buildings, pens and equipment was generally found to be poor, except on one premises (D) where a concentrated phenolic disinfectant was used rather than the more commonly used peroxygen products, and on farm E after repeat disinfection with formalin. There was circumstantial evidence of the importance of rodent vectors, inasmuch as rodent results correlated with prevailing pig *Salmonella* types and prevalences, at both unit and group levels.

Conclusions

Breeding units potentially may act as a source of *Salmonella* contamination for units that they supply, and the primary breeding units examined appeared to be as susceptible to persistent *Salmonella* colonisation as units further down the production pyramid, especially on large farms with a high genetic turnover rate. Persistent and transient strains of *Salmonella* were observed and temporal patterns were highly variable. Juvenile growing and breeding stock appeared to be important in the epidemiology of at least one important serotype (Typhimurium). The unit with best control of *Salmonella* was small and had good separation of age groups, reasonable rodent control and practised effective C&D. Effective disinfection under farm conditions has become more difficult since the withdrawal of phenolic products.

References

CHRISTENSEN, J., BAGGESEN, D. L., NIELSEN, B. & STRYHN, H. (2002) Herd prevalence of *Salmonella* spp. in Danish pig herds after implementation of the Danish Salmonella Control Program with reference to a pre-implementation study. *Veterinary Microbiology*, 88, 175-188.

DAVIES, R. H., DALZIEL, R., GIBBENS, J. C., WILESMITH, J. W., RYAN, J. M. B., EVANS, S. J., BYRNE, C., PAIBA, G. A., PASCOE, S. J. S. & TEALE, C. J. (2004) National survey for *Salmonella* in pigs, cattle and sheep at slaughter in Great Britain (1999-2000). *Journal of Applied Microbiology*, 96, 750-760.

GRAFANAKIS, E., LEONTIDES, L. & GENIGEORGIS, C. (2001) Seroprevalence and antibiotic sensitivity of serotypes of Salmonella enterica in Greek pig herds. *Veterinary Record*, 148, 407-11.

MEJIA, W., CASAL, J., ZAPATA, D., SANCHEZ, G. J., MARTIN, M. & MATEU, E. (2006) Epidemiology of *Salmonella* infections in pig units and antimicrobial susceptibility profiles of the strains of *Salmonella* species isolated. *Vet Rec*, 159, 271-6.

VAN DER WOLF, P. J., ELBERS, A. R. W., VAN DER HEIJDEN, H. M. J. F., VAN SCHIE, F. W., HUNNEMAN, W. A. & TIELEN, M. J. M. (2001) *Salmonella* seroprevalence at the population and herd level in pigs in The Netherlands. *Veterinary Microbiology*, 80, 171-184.

Association of Pathogen Load in Pigs with Retail Pork Contamination.

Abley, M.J.[1]*, Wittum, T.E.[1], Zerby, H.N.[2], Moeller, S.J.[2], Funk, J.A.[3]

[1]Department of Veterinary Preventive Medicine, The Ohio State University, 1900 Coffey Road, 43210, Columbus, OH
[2]Department of Animal Sciences, The Ohio State University, 2029 Fyffe Road, 43210, Columbus, OH
[3]National Food Safety and Toxicology Center, Michigan State University, 165 Food Safety and Toxicology Building, 48824, East Lansing, MI

*corresponding author: abley.1@osu.edu

Abstract

Salmonella and *Campylobacter* are estimated to cause 3.9 million illnesses annually in the United States, and most of these illnesses are food-related. Pigs can be sub-clinically infected with these pathogens and fecal contamination of meat during processing is a food safety risk. Quantitative measures of foodborne safety risk are rarely reported and are a critical data gap for development of quantitative risk assessments. The goal of this study was to determine the association between the concentration of *Salmonella* and *Campylobacter* in porcine feces and hide with concentrations in meat. Samples were collected 5 times from 100 individually identified pigs during the peri-harvest period. Feces were collected on the farm and in lairage. A hide swab was collected before scalding and the entire carcass was swabbed immediately before chilling. For each individually identified carcass a meat sample was collected. *Salmonella* and *Campylobacter* were cultured and quantified at each stage using the Most Probable Number Method (MPN). At the time of submission, 20 pigs have been sampled. *Salmonella* was cultured from one farm and one lairage sample. The proportion (%) of samples that were *Campylobacter* positive was 95, 100, 100, 100, and 37 for farm, lairage, hide, carcass and rib samples respectively. The mean *Campylobacter* concentration for each sample type was: farm, 227,785 cfu/g; lairage,1,946,294cfu/g; hide, 476cfu/100cm^2; carcass, 470 cfu/half carcass; and ribs, 820cfu/lb.

Introduction

Salmonella and *Campylobacter* are estimated to cause 3.9 million illnesses annually in the United States, and most of these illnesses are food-related (Mead et. al.). Pigs can be sub-clinically infected with these pathogens and fecal contamination of meat during processing is a food safety risk. Qualitative measures of contamination have been used in the past to assess food borne safety risk, but this can be problematic because it does not consider the quantity of bacteria contaminating the product, which is important for the risk of human infection as it relates to infectious dose. Quantitative measures of contamination could be utilized to evaluate interventions and to collect data for public health risk assessments. Quantitative measures of foodborne safety risk are rarely reported in the literature, most likely as a consequence of the substantial labor and media requirements of traditional culture based methods for determining pathogen concentration. The goal of this study was to determine the association between the concentration of *Salmonella* and *Campylobacter* in porcine feces and hide with concentrations in meat.

Material and methods

Samples will be collected 5 times from 100 individually identified pigs during the peri-harvest period. Feces were collected on the farm and in lairage. A hide swab was collected before scalding and the entire carcass was swabbed immediately before chilling. For each individually identified carcass a meat sample was collected. *Salmonella* and *Campylobacter* were cultured and quantified at each stage. Samples that were cultured for *Salmonella* were placed in Tetrthionate Broth (TTB) with Iodine added only for 48h at 37C. The samples were then transferred to Rapport-

Valsides (RV) Broth and incubated at 42 C for 24h and then spread-plated onto Xylose Lactose Tergitol 4 (XLT4) plates. Plates were then read yes/no for the presence of a *Salmonella* suspect colony. Four 10-fold dilutions were made and the 3 tube MPN method was used to quantify the samples. Calculations were performed using the excel spreadsheet from the FDA's Bacteriological Analytical Manual. The farm and lairage samples were enumerated using the direct dilution method for *Campylobacter*. The fecal samples were mixed with buffered peptone water (BPW) and plated onto Campy-Cefex plates. After incubation under microaerophilic conditions at 42 C for 48h the suspect *campylobacter* colonies were counted. The hide, carcass and meat samples were incubated in Bolton Broth for 48h under microaerophilic conditions at 42 C and were then spread plated onto Campy-Cefex the plates were read and the MPN was calculated as described previously. Descriptive statistics will be performed on the results (prevalence and mean concentration). Determination of association between concentrations will be preformed using the Spearman's Rank Coefficient. The risk of a meat sample being positive will be calculated using odds ratios.

Results

At the time of submission, 20 pigs have been sampled. *Salmonella* was cultured from one farm and one lairage sample. The proportion (%) of samples that were *Campylobacter* positive was 95, 100, 100, 100, and 37 for farm, lairage, hide, carcass and rib samples respectively. The mean *Campylobacter* concentration for each sample type was: farm, 227,785 cfu/g; lairage,1,946,294cfu/g; hide, 476 cfu/100cm^2; carcass, 470 cfu/half carcass; and ribs, 820 cfu/lb. Further results will be given at presentation.

Discussion

Based on the preliminary results at every stage peri-harvest the pigs have had *Campylobacter* recovered.

Conclusions

References

Mead P. S., Slutsker L., Dietz V., McCaig L. F., Bresee J. S., Shapiro C., Griffin P. M., and Tauxe R. V. 1999. Food-Related Illness and Death in the United States. Emerging Infectious Diseases 5(5):607-625.

Prevalence of *Campylobacter* spp. and Yersinia enterocolitica in Fattening Pig Herds in Lower Saxony, Germany

Altrock, A. v.*[1], A. L. Louis[1], U. Roesler[2], T. Alter[3], M. Beyerbach[4], L. Kreienbrock[4], K.-H. Waldmann[1]

[1]Clinic for Pigs, Small Ruminants, Forensic Medicine and Ambulatory Service, University of Veterinary Medicine Hannover, Foundation, D-30173 Hannover, Germany
[2]Institute of Animal Hygiene and Veterinary Public Health, University of Leipzig, D-04103 Leipzig, Germany
[3]Institute for Food Hygiene, University of Leipzig, D-04103 Leipzig, Germany
[4]Department of Biometry, Epidemiology and Information Processing, University of Veterinary Medicine Hannover, Foundation, D-30559 Hannover

*Corresponding author: Alexandra.von.Altrock@tiho-hannover.de

Abstract

The results of a study on the occurrence of two bacteria that cause zoonoses, *Campylobacter* spp. and *Yersinia enterocolitica* were presented and the results of bacteriological and serological methods of detection were compared. The study was carried out on 30 fattening herds in Lower Saxony, Germany. Bacteriological findings of *Campylobacter* spp. in the faeces indicated that 69.7 % of the fattening pigs were positive, but 81.2 % tested positive serologically. All herds tested here were both bacteriologically and serologically positive for *Campylobacter* spp. Furthermore, only 8.4 % tested positive for *Yersinia enterocolitica* in the faecal samples, but 66.8 % of the animals were serologically positive for that bacterium. At herd level 43.3 % of the herds tested bacteriologically positive for *Yersinia enterocolitica*, whereas serological testing showed that 83.3 % of the units had one or more reacting animal.
Although both agents take the same route of infection there was no statistical correlation between bacteriological and serological findings for *Campylobacter* spp. and *Yersinia enterocolitica*.
The great difference between the results of bacteriological and serological testing, especially in the case of *Yersinia enterocolitica,* can be explained by the intermittent intestinal excretion and predominance of this bacterium in the animals' tonsils. Low faecal excretion is also the reason for the low detection rate of 3.4 % of *Yersinia enterocolitica* in the environmental samples, while that of *Campylobacter* spp. was 33.3 %. These results indicate that the environment plays only a secondary role in the distribution of *Yersinia enterocolitica* in pig herds.

Introduction:

Infections with *Campylobacter* spp. and *Yersinia enterocolitica* are the two most frequently occurring zoonoses in Europe. Both bacteria are potential pathogens and can cause acute enteritis in humans. In pigs the infection with each of these bacteria is characterised by latent, i.e. clinically unapparent herd infections that do not result in visible tissue changes. Therefore, food products from pigs represent a potential source of human infections. Pigs are an important reservoir for *Yersinia enterocolitica* as well as *Campylobacter* ssp.. Especially *Campylobacter coli* can be isolated from the intestinal tract of pigs. This agent represents the second most common cause of human campylobacteriosis (TAM et al., 2003) with part of 20 % in Germany (SCHULZE et al, 2000, GUERTLER et al., 2005a). .

In Germany, the reported prevalence of *Campylobacter* spp. in faeces of slaughter pigs is up to 96 % with *Campylobacter coli* strains as the major isolate (V. ALTROCK et al., 2004). According to studies from GUERTLER et al. (2005b), the prevalence of *Yersinia enterocolitica* ranges between 0 % and 65.4 % in fattening pig herds. The prevalence of anti-Yersinia-antibodies in Bavarian slaughter pigs was about 45 % (HENSEL et al., 2004). In German blood-donors the prevalence of *Yersinia enterocolitica* O3/O9-specific antibodies has been reported to be 33 % and 43 % by immunoassay and immunoblotting, respectively (MAEKI-IKOLA et al., 1997).

The purpose of this work was to increase the knowledge of the epidemiology of the occurrence of *Campylobacter* spp. and *Yersinia enterocolitica* in fattening herds with particular emphasis on the comparison of serological and bacteriological findings.

Material and methods
Blood and faecal samples were taken from 30 fattening herds in Lower Saxony. From each herd samples from 30 pigs, shortly before being slaughtered, were examined. In addition one swab at a time was taken from drinking and feeding troughs, from the boots of the person in charge of the pigs, and from a water tap near the entrance of the stable.

Swabs and faecal samples were investigated bacteriologically. *Campylobacter* spp. were grown in enriched Bolton bouillon, isolated on modified charcoal cefoperazone deoxycholate agar (mCCDA), and identified by PCR (VAN DOORN et al., 1998; GONZALEZ et al. 1997). *Yersinia enterocolitica* were grown in Irgasan-Ticarcillin-Potassium-Chlorate (ITC) bouillon, isolated on Cefsulodin-Irgasan-Novobiocin (CIN) agar, and identified with the API 20E system.

The serological investigation of antibodies against *Campylobacter* spp. was carried out using a method based on immunoblot analysis developed by the Institute of Animal Hygiene and Veterinary Public Health, University of Leipzig. *Yersinia enterocolitica* infections were detected serologically with an enzyme-linked immunosorbent assay (ELISA) of *Yersinia* outer proteins (YOPs) (Pigtype® YOP-Screen™).

Results

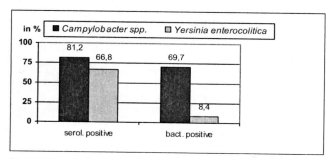

Figure 3: part of serologically and bacteriologically positive pigs

A total of 69.7 % of the investigated faecal samples and 81.2 % of the blood samples were positive for *Campylobacter* spp. (Fig. 1). In the herds, prevalence of *Campylobacter* spp. varied from 10 % to 100 %. *Yersinia enterocolitica* was found in 8.4 % of faecal samples, and antibodies against *Yersinia enterocolitica* in 66.8 % of the blood samples (Fig. 1). The results of bacteriological testing indicated prevalence of *Yersinia enterocolitica* in herds between 0 % and 53 %, and serological testing showed prevalence up to 100 %. Five herds tested bacteriologically and serologically negative for *Yersinia enterocolitica*. One herd tested bacteriologically negative, while serological testing showed a prevalence of 100 % and *Yersinia enterocolitica* was detected in one of the environment samples for this herd.

While one-third of the environment samples (N = 117) were positive for *Campylobacter* spp., with the troughs in particular showing contamination, only four environmental samples were found to contain *Yersinia enterocolitica* (Fig. 2). All *Yersinia enterocolitica* isolates belong to bioserotype 4/O : 3.

There was no statistical correlation between bacteriological and serological findings for *Campylobacter* spp. and *Yersinia enterocolitica*.

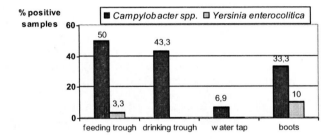

Figure 2: part of bacteriological-positive environmental samples

Discussion

The aim of the study was to compare the serological and bacteriological prevalence of *Campylobacter* spp. and *Yersinia enterocolitica* in fattening pig herds in Lower Saxony, Germany. There are strong differences between the serological and bacteriological findings especially for *Yersinia enterocolitica*. Only 8.4 % of the investigated fatteners were bacteriologically positive for *Yersinia enterocolitica*, but 66.8 % tested serologically positive. As the agent is excreted intermittently the detection of the agent is more or less by chance. In six herds *Yersinia enterocolitica* was not found in the faeces, but in one of these herds we could isolate the agent from the boots of the person in charge of the pigs. That means the bacteriological investigation of the faeces lead to a false negative result. But, although faecal shedding stopped after infection, pigs carry *Yersinia enterocolitica* in the tonsils (KAPPERUD, 1991). During slaughter the rinse water of the tonsils spreads the agent and contaminated offal (FREDRIKSSON-AHOMAA et al., 2001), whereby pork becomes the source of infection for humans. In order to discover subclinically infected pigs it can be concluded that serological testing is more precise than culture methods.

So as to investigate the prevalence of Campylobacter-antibodies, the Institute of Animal Hygiene and Veterinary Public Health, University Leipzig, developed an immunoblot method. In comparison to the cultural procedure the sensitivity was about 93 % but the specifity only about 46 %. One reason is the intermittent shedding of the agent, but also the difficulty in finding pig serum without antibodies. In this examination serum from gnotobiotic pigs was used as a negative control. In our study about 54 % of the bacteriologically negative pigs were serologically positive. At present no statement can be made either about the moment of seroconversion or the persistence of antibodies. Further investigations are mandatory.

The contaminated environment can be a source for the infection of the pigs. Therefore, in each herd samples were taken from four different locations. Altogether, *Campylobacter* spp. was found in 33.3 %, whereas *Yersinia enterocolitica* was isolated only from 3.4 % of the samples. PILON et al. (2001) reported about 0.6 % of positive environment samples. The authors concluded that the environment does not represent the main source of contamination of pigs by *Yersinia enterocolitica*, whereas WINGSTRAND and NIELSEN (1996) assumed that pigs are infected by the environment rather than by the sow. In contrast to the findings of *Yersinia enterocolitica*, *Campylobacter* ssp. was found in a third of the taken samples. The contamination of the environment with faeces seems to have the same importance for the prevalence of *Campylobacter* ssp. among the pigs as direct contact.

There was no statistical correlation between bacteriological and serological findings for *Campylobacter* spp. and *Yersinia enterocolitica*, which means that a high prevalence of one agent in a herd did not necessarily mean a high prevalence of the other occurring.

Conclusion

Although *Campylobacter* spp. and *Yersinia enterocolitica* have the same route of infection, differences were found in their distribution. Concerning the status of infection of the herd serological results seem to be more useful than bacteriological results since both agents are not excreted continuously. Nevertheless, further studies on differences and similarities of

Campylobacter spp. and *Yersinia enterocolitica* are needed in order to create a consistent surveillance programme for both zoonotic agents.

References

ALTROCK, A. V., WEBER, R. M., GLUENDER, G., WALDMANN, K.-H. (2004): Investigation into the occurrence of *Campylobacter* spp. on pig carcasses. Proceedings of the 18th Int. Pig Vet. Soc. Congress, Hamburg, Germany, 683

FREDRIKSSON-AHOMAA, M., BUCHER, M., HANK, C., STOLLE, A., KORKEALA, H. (2001): High Prevalence of *Yersinia enterocolitica* 4/O:3 on Pig Offal in Southern Germany: A Slaughtering Technique Problem. System. Appl. Microbiol. 24, 457-463.

GONZALEZ, I., GRANT, K. A., RICHARDSON, P. T., PARK, S. F., COLLINS, M. D. (1997): Specific identification of the enteropathogens *Campylobacter jejuni* and *Campylobacter coli* by using a PCR test based on the *ceuE* gene encoding a putative virulence determinant. J. Clin. Microbiol. 35, 759-763.

GUERTLER, M., ALTER, T., KASIMIR, S., FEHLHABER, K (2005a): The importance of *Campylobacter coli* in human campylobacteriosis: prevalence and genetic characterization. Epidemiol. Infect. 133, 1081-1087.

GUERTLER, M., ALTER, T., KASIMIR, S., LINNEBUR, M., FEHLHABER, K (2005b): Prevalence of Yersinia enterocolitica in fattening pigs. J. Food Prot. 68, 850-854

HENSEL, A., NIKOLAOU, K., BARTLINIG, C., PETRY, T., ROESLER, U., CZERNY, C. P., TRUYEN. U., NEUBAUER, H. (2004): Zur Prävalenz von Anti-Yerinia-Outer-Protein-Antikörpern bei Schlachtschweinen in Bayern. Berl. Muench. Tieraerztl. Wschr. 117, 30-38.

KAPPERUD, G. (1991): *Yersinia enterocolitica* in food hygiene. Int. J. Food Microbiol. 12, 53-66.

PILON, J., HIGGINS, R., QUESSY, S. (2000): Epidemiological study of *Yersinia enterocolitica* in swine herds in Québec. Can. Vet. J. 41, 383-387.

MAEKI-IKOLA, A., HEESEMANN, J., TIOVANEN, A., GRANFORS, K. (1997): High frequency of Yersinia antibodies in healthy populations in Finland and Germany. Rheumatol. 16, 227-229

SCHULZE, F., BARTELT, E., MÜLLER, W. (2000): CAMPYLOBACTER. in: Molekularbiologische Nachweismethoden ausgewählter Zoonoseerreger. Hrsg.: SACHSE, K., GALLIEN, P., BgVV-Hefte 02/2000, 13-28.

TAM, C. C., O'BRIEN, S. J., ADAK, G. K., MEAKINS, S. M., FROST, J. A. (2003): *Campylobacter coli* – an important foodborne pathogen. J. Infect. 47, 28-32

VAN DOORN, L. J.,VERSCHUUREN-VAN HAPEREN, A., VAN BELKUM, A., ENDTZ, H. P., VLIEGENHART, J. S., VANDAMME, P., QUINT, W. G. (1998): Rapid identification of diverse *Campylobacter lari* strains isolated from mussels and oysters using a reverse hybridazation line probe assay. J. Appl. Microbiol. 84, 545-50.

WINGSTRAND, A., NIELSEN, B (1996): Cross-sectional investigation of pig herds for *Yersinia enterocolitica*. 14th Int. Pig Vet. Society Congress, Bologna, 320.

Acknowledgements: The study was financially supported by the German Federal Ministry for Consumer Protection, Nutrition, and Agriculture.

Evaluation of the use of serological and bacteriological investigation for monitoring and controlling Salmonella in Italian pig herds

Lisa Barco[1*], Veronica Cibin[1], Dellamaria Debora[2], Valerio Giaccone[3], Stefano Nardelli[2], Cristina Saccardin[1], Claudio Minorello[1], Antonia Ricci[1]

[1]*National Reference Laboratory for Salmonella, [2] Virology and Serology Laboratory
Istituto Zooprofilattico Sperimentale delle Venezie, Viale dell'Università 10, 35020 Legnaro (PD), Italy, Ph:0039 049 8084283 Email:lbarco@izsvenezie.it
[3] Department of Public Health, Comparative Pathology and Veterinary Hygiene, Faculty of Veterinary Medicine, University of Padua, Italy

Abstract
At the European level the control of foodborne diseases is defined by the new zoonoses legislation (Directive 2003/99/EC and Regulation (EC) No 2160/2003), which points out the necessity to establish surveillance programmes for zoonotic agents in animal populations. Recently Commission Decision 2006/668/EC concerning a baseline study on the prevalence of Salmonella in slaughter pigs has been published.
Many different strategies have been developed and applied by EU Member States in order to implement monitoring and/or control programmes for Salmonella in pigs; these strategies are mainly based on bacteriological analysis (performed on caecal content, ileo caecal lymph nodes or carcass swabs collected at slaughterhouse) and/or on serological analysis (mainly performed on meat juice obtained from diaphragm muscle).
Very few data are published about the comparison among different strategies so that it is still difficult for a country wanting to implement a monitoring/control programme to choose the most cost-effective methodology.
The objective of the present study was to develop an effective methodology to evaluate Salmonella spp. prevalence in slaughter pigs comparing bacteriological and serological strategies with the aim of identifying the most effective methodology to apply.
To detect the presence of the infection, both bacteriological examination of faeces and ileocaecal lymph nodes and serological investigation of meat-juice and blood sera were used.
Samples of diaphragm muscle, blood, caecal content and mesenteric lymph nodes were collected from 150 pigs of 10 batches in two slaughterhouses of the Veneto Region of Italy and comparisons were made between isolation of Salmonella in faeces and lymph nodes and the capability to detect Salmonella antibodies in sera and meat juice using three different commercial ELISA kits.
In this paper the results of bacteriological and serological investigations are presented emphasising the comparison among the three different commercial ELISA kits.

Introduction
Salmonella spp. is one of the major causes of foodborne illnesses in humans. According to the Community Summary Report on Trends and Sources of Zoonoses a total of 192703 cases of human salmonellosis were reported by the 25 EU Member States in 2004. Pork, after eggs and poultry meat, is a major source of human foodborne salmonellosis in the European Union (EU) (EFSA 2005). The zoonoses legislation (Directive 2003/99/EC and Regulation EC No 2160/2003) points out the necessity to establish specific monitoring programmes at primary production for some zoonotic agents. Two very different approaches for Salmonella detection in pigs can be applied: bacteriological or serological analysis. The choice of method to use depends mainly on the epidemiological situation of the monitored population. The bacteriological method detects all the spreading serovars and allows to define the actual infection _status_ of the animal, but this analytic procedure is laborious.
The serological analysis expresses the previous exposure to the infection agent by detecting specific antibodies against Salmonella; it is cheaper and easier to perform.

Therefore the use of bacteriological investigation is a prerequisite to estimate exactly the prevalence of infection and the serovars involved in order to identify the suitable ELISA kit to employ for large scale monitoring programmes.

To date in Italy only few serological monitoring programmes have been performed in swine population (Cibin et al. 2005, Magistrali et al. 2005), so in this study we tried to compare bacteriology and serology in order to assess the possibility of serological application in future monitoring programmes.

Materials and Methods

The study was carried out in two slaugtherhouses located in the Veneto region of Italy. Samples were collected from 10 batches (15 pigs/batch). From each pig, on the slaughter line, blood samples were taken at the exsanguination, ceacal content and mesenteric lymph nodes after evisceration and cubes of approximately 3 cm of edge of diaphragmatic muscle at the post-mortem inspection.

For bacteriological examination 5 g of faeces and 5 g of lymph nodes were cultured according to the Amendment of ISO 6579:2002. Colonies with typical *Salmonella* morphology were screened biochemically and serotyped following the Kauffman-White scheme.

Serology was performed on serum and meat juice by means of three commercial indirect mix-ELISA tests (Kit 1: Salmonella Covalent Mix-ELISA-SVANOVA; Kit 2: Porcine Antibody ELISA Vestigen™ –GUILDAY-; Kit 3: HerdCheck Swine Antibody Test Kit –IDEXX) following the manufacturer's recommendations.

Meat juice for the serological analysis was obtained by freezing and thawing the diaphragmatic muscle as described by Nielsen et al. (1998).

Results

Bacteriological analysis

Considering as positive one batch in which Salmonella was detected in at least one sample of faeces or/and lymph nodes, 100% of the batches resulted positive.

The prevalence of positive cultures was higher for lymph node samples (44%; IC 35,91-52,32) than for faecal samples (20% IC 13,91 – 27,3) and this discrepancy between the bacteriological results obtained from the two matrixes (table 1) was confirmed also by the statistical analysis (k value: –0.0057). Although several serovars were identified in lymph nodes and in faeces, S. Typhimurium, S. Derby, S. Anatum and S. London represented the great majority of the strains isolated from both the matrixes.

Bacteriological analysis		LYMPH-NODES		
		pos	neg	Tot
FAECES	Pos	14	17	31
	Neg	52	67	119
	Tot	66	84	150

Table 1: Comparison between bacteriological detection of Salmonella on faeces and on lymph nodes

Comparison between serological and bacteriological tests

In order to evaluate the correlation between the bacteriological and serological analysis, the sensitivity and the specificity of the three ELISA kits on serum and meat juice were calculated considering as "gold standard" the bacteriological test performed both in faeces and in lymph nodes. Since the three ELISA kits are specific for serovars belonging to serogroups B, C1 and D1, the sensitivity of serological tests was calculated considering as positive only the samples in which strains belonging to serogroups B, C1 and D1 were isolated (from lymph nodes or faeces). The specificity was determined considering as negative the samples in which *Salmonella* was not isolated from faeces or lymph nodes and those in which *Salmonella* strains belonging to serogroups different from B, C1 and D1 were identified.

For all the three serological tests the specificity values are generally higher than the sensitivity ones. Considering the bacteriological results obtained from lymph nodes instead of the results obtained from faeces, both the sensitivity and the specificity of the serological tests (both in serum and meat juice) were generally better.

Comparison between serum and meat juice for serological tests
The three ELISA kits were performed both on serum and meat juice and the results were compared. Serological analysis on serum was considered as "gold standard" (Nielsen et al. 1998). The Cohen Kappa value obtained comparing serum and meat juice for the three ELISA kits were respectively k: 0,46 (Kit 1), k: 0,31 (Kit 2) and k: 0,28 (Kit 3).

	Ser. MJ/ Bact. F	Ser. MJ/Bact. L	Ser. S/Bact. F	Ser. MJ/Bact. L
SENSITIVITY				
Kit 1	0,09	0,41	0,65	0,79
Kit 2	0,17	0,16	0,78	0,68
Kit 3	0,09	0,20	0,57	0,88
SPECIFICITY				
Kit 1	0,65	0,79	0,69	0,71
Kit 2	0,78	0,68	0,70	0,79
Kit 3	0,57	0,88	0,83	0,59

Table 2. Values of sensitivity and specificity of the three ELISA kits on serum and meat juice determined compare serology with bacteriology
(Ser. MJ/Bact. F: serological test on meat juice compared to bacteriological test on faeces; Ser. MJ/Bact. L: serological test on meat juice compared to bacteriological test on lymph nodes; Ser. S/Bact. F: serological test on serum compared to bacteriological test on faeces; Ser. S/Bact. L: serological test on serum compared to bacteriological test on lymph nodes)

Discussion
The bacteriological results indicated that analysis of lymph nodes could be more sensitive than analysis of faeces for *Salmonella* detection, since lymph nodes represent the tissues most consistently colonised by *Salmonella* in infected animals and these organs often harbour *Salmonella* in carrier animals (Nollet et al., 2005) .
Comparing bacteriology and serology for *Salmonella* diagnosis, a weak agreement was found but the sensitivity and the specificity of serological tests (in serum and meat juice) were generally higher when the results of serology were compared with those of bacteriological analysis of lymph nodes. This data confirm what was previously observed by other authors, who demonstrated that in a herd a better estimation of the *Salmonella* prevalence can be carried out by isolation of the bacterium in the lymph nodes (Nollet et al., 2005).
Several explanations for these discrepancies can be hypothesized.
A positive serological result in a bacteriological negative animal may be due to:
- the cross reactivity between *Salmonella* and other bacteria of the *Enterobacteriaceae* family (Van Der Hejden 2001);
- the use of a too low cut off value of the serological test adopted;
- the presence in the herd of intermittent shedders that may harbour infection, produce antibodies against Salmonella without excreting the bacterium (Lo Fo Wong et al., 2003);
- the persistence of a detectable level of antibodies in pigs that may be no longer infected.
On the other side, a negative serological result in a bacteriological positive animal may be due to:
- the stage of infection: the interval between the peak of the bacteriological and serological response ranges from one to approximately two months (Kranker et al., 2003);
- the antibody clearance in infected animals;
- the presence of animals with a low serological response to *Salmonella* spp. (Lo Fo Wong et al., 2003);
- the presence of Salmonella strains that doesn't belong to the serogroups detectable by the ELISA kit used.
- the adoption of a too high cut-off value of the serological test used.

This weak agreement between the two methods demonstrates that no prediction concerning the *Salmonella* carrier *status* can be made with confidence using serological tests at the individual level.–Other previous studies agree that serology is suitable for the screening on a herd basis (Nollet et al., 2003, Lo Fo Wong et al., 2003).

The sensitivity and the specificity values obtained by the three serological tests were very different and these results confirm the great variability between the serological tests previously observed by other authors (Mejia et al. 2005).

Serological test performed on meat juice is considered an alternative to the analysis of serum to estimate the *Salmonella* prevalence and several studies have documented a clear correlation between antibody levels in serum and in meat juice (Nielsen et al., 1998). However in our study a low concordance between the serological results obtained on serum and meat juice was found. The reason for this discrepancy is not completely clear but it is possible that factors such as stress or the state of hydration of animals may influence the meat juice results (Davies et al., 2003). Another possible reason for this could be found in the quality of the meat juice samples (for instance presence of small blood clots on the meat surface, blood vessels in the meat sample) that could influence the ELISA' s results (Feld N.C. et al., 2005).

Conclusion

Based on the results obtained in our study we can conclude that:

- the analysis of lymph nodes seems to be more sensitive for the detection of *Salmonella* than the analysis of faeces;
- as expected the agreement between bacteriology and serology is low, since these two methods measure different phenomena and are suitable to be used in different situations and with different purposes;
- we found a low concordance between serological results obtained analysing serum and meat juice;
- large differences exist between the serological results obtained using the three ELISA kits.

Bibliography

- CIBIN V., TONON F., MANCIN M., BARCO L., ZAVAGNIN P., RICCI A. 2005 Uso di metodi batteriologici e serologici per stimare la prevalenza di *Salmonella* spp. nei suini - XXXI meeting annuale SIPAS, Mantova Italy pp. 197-203
- DAVIES R.H., HEATH P.J., COXON S.M., SAYERS A.R. 2003 Evaluation of the use of pooled serum, pooled muscle tissue fluid (meat juice) and pooled faeces for monitoing pig heards for Salmonella. *J. of Applied Microbiology* 95 1016-1025
- FELD N.C., EKEROTH L., MØGELMOSE V., NIELSEN B. 2005 Correlation between colour of meat juice samples and Salmonella antibody levels in the Danish Mix-ELISA In proceedings Book (243-245) of 6th International Symposium on the epidemiology and control of foodborne pathogens in pork. California 6-9 September 2005
- LO FO WONG D.M.A., DAHL J., VAN DER WOLF P.J., WINGSTRAND A., LEONTIDES L., VON ALTROCK A. 2003 Recovery of *Salmonella enterica* from seropositive finishing pig herds. *Vet. Microbiol.* 97 201-214
- MAGISTRALI C., DE CURTIS P., PANCCIÀ M., CUCCO L., PEZZOTTI G., FOGLINI A. An Epidemiological survey on the prevalence of Salmonella in swine in central Italy. In proceedings Book (243-245) of 6th International Symposium on the epidemiology and control of foodborne pathogens in pork. California 6-9 September 2005
- MEJÌA W., CASAL J., MATEU E., MARTIN M. 2005 Comparison of two commercial ELISAs for the serological diagnosis of salmonellosis in pigs. *Vet. Rec.* 157 47-48
- NIELSEN B., BAGGESEN D., BAGER F., HAUGEGAARD J., LIND P. 1995 The serological response to *Salmonella* serovars Typhimurium and Infantis in experimentally infected pigs. The time course followed with an indirect anti-LPS ELISA and bacteriological examinations. *Vet. Microbiol.* 47 205-218.

- NIELSEN B., EKEROTH L., BAGER F., LIND P. 1998. Use of muscle fluid as a source of antibodies for serologic detection of *Salmonella* infection in slaughter pig herds. *Journal of Veterinary Diagnostic Investigation* 10, 158-163

NOLLET N., MAES D., DUCHATEAU L., HAUTEKIET V., HOUF K., VAN HOOF J., DE ZUTTER L., DE KRUIF A., GEERS R. 2005. Discrepancies beween the isolation of *Salmonella* from lymph nodes and the results of serological screening in slaugther pigs. *Vet Res* 36, 545-555

VAN DER HEIJDEN H.M. 2001 First International Ring Trial of ELISAs for *Salmonella*-antibody Detection in Swine. *Berl. Munch. Tierarztl. Wochenschr.* 114 389-392

Prevalence of foodborne pathogens in rural pigs and in derived cold pork meats - preliminary report

Cereser, A.*[1], Capelli G.[1], Favretti M.[1], Marchesan, D.[2], Marchesan R.[2], Marcati, M.[1], Rossetto, K.[1], Furlan F[1].
[1]Istituto Zooprofilattico Sperimentale delle Venezie, Padova, Italy
[2]ASL 10 Veneto Orientale

*corresponding author: acereser@izsvenezie.it

Introduction

The "rural" breeding of one or two pigs and their domestic slaughtering is a significant reality in the Veneto Region, as a consequence of an ancient tradition still surviving in the countryside.

In the eastern part of the Venice Province, about 2.500 rural pigs are bred and slaughtered every year in the period between November and February.

Many data are available on industrial breeding and processing, whereas very little is known about the prevalence of foodborne pathogens both in live animals and in derived food, mainly sausages, salami and cold pork meats.

The present paper shows the preliminary results of a project during which about 400 samples are collected at different steps: faeces, muscle and lymph nodes during slaughtering, fresh sausages just after sacking and fermented salami at the end of the seasoning period.

Samples are examined for several parameters, including bacteria (*Enterobacteriaceae*, *Salmonella*, *Listeria monocytogenes*, *Campylobacter* spp., β-glucuronidase-positive *Escherichia coli*, Lactic Acid Bacteria, Coagulase-positive *Staphylococci* and Sulphite-Reducing Clostrides) and parasites (*Trichinella* spp., *Giardia duodenalis*, *Cryptosporidium* spp and others).

The aim of the research is to define: 1) the pathogens prevalence during breeding, 2) the hygienic conditions during slaughtering and processing, mainly considering pathogen carry-over effects, and 3) the microbiological profile of sausages and salami, the latter being conditioned by proper seasoning practices and environmental contamination.

The research will continue involving microbiology laboratories of the local hospitals since we would like to know if any case of illness due to foodborne pathogens was detected and recorded; moreover we will collect data about products (ingredients, salt percentage, use of preservatives...) and processing (temperature, drying conditions, seasoning conditions...) to know the relationships between these conditions and pathogen prevalence in pork products.

Material and methods

Samples are processed in San Donà di Piave and Padua Parasitology Laboratories.

Almost all deliveries are composed of the following samples: faeces and mesenteric lymph nodes taken during slaughter and a fresh sausage produced usually in the same day of slaughter; another sample of fermented salami, belonging to the same lot of the previous samples, are delivered after 60-70 days of seasoning.

In total, 70 faeces, 70 lymph nodes, 70 diaphragms, 69 fresh sausages, 12 seasoned salami samples were examined.

Salami were examined for the following parameters: *Salmonella* spp. (ISO 6579:2002/Cor 1:2004E), *Listeria monocytogenes* (ISO 11290-1:1996/Amd 1 2004), *Enterobacteriaceae* (ISO 21528-2:2004), Sulphate-Reducing *Clostridia* (ISO 7937:2004), *Campylobacter* spp. (FDA BAM), Lactic Acid Bacteria (internal method), β-glucuronidase-positive *Escherichia coli* (ISO 16649-2:2001), Coagulase-positive *Staphylococci* (ISO 6888-2:1999 Amd 1 2003), Inhibitory Substances Research (only from fresh sausage, DM 10.03.1997).

Diaphragms were examined for the detection of *Trichinella* spp. (magnetic stirrer method for pooled sample digestion, according to Regulation 2075/2005).

Lymph nodes and faeces were examined for the detection of *Salmonella* spp. (in 25 g), *Listeria monocytogenes* (in 25 g) and *Campylobacter* spp. (in 25 g).

pH was measured in all fresh sausages.
62 faecal samples were examined by flotation technique and modified Zhiel-Neelsen staining for gastrointestinal parasites, and *Cryptosporidium* oocysts. For 50 sample an Immunofluorescence (IF) kit (Merifluor, Meridian) for both *Giardia* cyst and *Cryptosporidium* oocysts was performed too.

Results

8 faeces samples (11,4 %) were positive for *Campylobacter* spp., (in 5 cases *Campylobacter coli*); 2 samples (2,8 %) were positive for *Salmonella* spp. (*Salmonella derby* and *Salmonella typhimurium*); *Listeria* spp. has never been detected.
25 faecal samples (40%) were positive for gastrointestinal parasites, in particular 15 (24.2) for coccidia, 9 (14.5%) for ascarids, 5 (8.0%) for trichurids and 4 (6.5%) for gastrointestinal strongyles. 7 animals showed mixed infection of 2 or more parasites. *Giardia* cysts were found in 5 animals (8.2%); 13 animals were found positives for *Cryptosporidium* oocysts at the stained smears, but only 8 of them (13.11%) were confirmed by IF.
5 lymph nodes samples (7,3%) were positive for *Campylobacter* spp. (1 *Campylobacter coli* and 1 *Campylobacter jejuni*). 2 samples (2,9 %) were positive for *Salmonella* spp. (1 Salmonella derby). No samples were positive for *Listeria monocytogenes*. 2 samples were not examined due to the small quantity.
All diaphragm samples were negative for *Trichinella* spp.
Fresh sausage samples (69) showed a *Enterobacteriaceae* count between 0 (7 samples) and 39.000.000 CFU/g; a Coagulase-positive *Staphylococci* count between 0 (6 samples) and 12.000 CFU/g; a β-glucuronidase-positive *Escherichia coli* between 0 (25 samples) and 910.000 CFU/g; a Sulphate-Reducing *Clostridia* count between 0 (40 samples) and 840 CFU/g. Lactic Acid Bacteria were counted between 270 and 1.300.000.000 CFU/g.
Salmonella spp. and Campylobacter spp. were not detected in any sample (in 25 g) while *Listeria monocytogenes* was detected in 1 sample (1,4%).
Inhibitory Substances have never been detected.
In all samples, pH values of fresh sausages ranged between 5.0 and 6.3.
Fermented salami samples (12) showed a *Enterobacteriaceae* count between 0 (5 samples) and 3.900 CFU/g; a Coagulase-positive *Staphylococci* count between 0 (8 samples) and 280 CFU/g; a β-glucuronidase-positive *Escherichia coli* between 0 (8 samples) and 4.000 CFU/g; a Sulphate-Reducing *Clostridia* count between 0 (9 samples) and 250 CFU/g. Lactic Acid Bacteria were counted between 67 and 500.000.000 CFU/g.
Salmonella spp. and Campylobacter spp. have not been detected (in 25 g) in any of the examined fermented salami; 2 samples (16,7%) were positive to *Listeria monocytogenes*.
In all samples, pH values of fermented salami ranged between 5.1 and 6.1.

Discussion

Even if only a few number of fermented salami has been examined (many of the others are still seasoning) preliminary results showed hygienic situation of alive rural pigs and derived meats.
Some pathogens (*Salmonella* spp., *Campylobacter* spp.) were detected in faeces and lymph nodes but not in derived products.
This is probably due to good hygienic practices during slaughtering and processing.
Enterobacteriaceae and β-glucuronidase-positive *Escherichia coli* reduction during seasoning says that this phase is, in most cases, correctly done.
In other situations this did not appear, probably as a consequence of not appropriate processing and seasoning conditions (temperature, humidity).
Listeria monocytogenes presence in fermented salami is probably linked to a high water activity value, due to a low salt content or to a short seasoning period.
It will be important, by the end of the research, to correlate the presence of *Listeria monocytogenes* to these products and process characteristics.

Conclusions

Notwithstanding the research is not concluded, pathogens presence at different stages of production outlines the importance of continuing the exam of other samples.

According to the final results, HACCP principles will be used to establish where a CCP phase can help operators to avoid the risk of *Listeria* and other pathogens in final products.

For each CCP, critical limits will be set, i.e.: salt percentage in the recipe, use of microbial starter cultures, seasoning conditions: time, temperature, humidity...

All these factors will be adequately considered since environmental conditions cannot be completely controlled since these products are usually stored in private basements and not in refrigerating rooms.

References

Commission Regulation (EC) N° 2075/2005 of 5 December 2005 laying down specific rules on official controls for *Trichinella* in meat.

Salmonella monitoring in pigs in the Veneto Region of Italy: results of three monitoring campaigns from 2002 to 2006

Veronica Cibin*, Marzia Mancin, Lisa Barco, Keti Antonello, Paola Zavagnin, Antonia Ricci

*National Reference Laboratory for Salmonella,
Istituto Zooprofilattico Sperimentale delle Venezie, Viale dell'Università 10, 35020 Legnaro (PD), Italy, Ph:0039 049 8084283 Email:vcibin@izsvenezie.it

Abstract
From 2002 to 2006 three monitoring campaigns have been performed in the Veneto Region of Italy to define the prevalence of Salmonella in pigs slaughtered in this area.

The monitoring scheme applied allowed to assess the prevalence for Salmonella, and was adjusted after each year of application in order to detect defined variations in prevalence, with a reduced number of samples.

In the first (2002-2003) monitoring campaign the sample size (384 slaughtered batches) was assessed on the basis of the following criteria: expected prevalence = 50%; accuracy = 5% and confidence interval = 95%. Samples were stratified according to the capacity of each slaughterhouse, and equally distributed in a 12 months period. One animal was sampled for each batch, collecting 25 grams of caecal content.

During the following year (2004), starting from the results of the previous campaign the sample size was reduced in order to be able to evaluate a prevalence variation of at least 12%.

In 2005 a new monitoring campaign was set up and the sample size was established on the basis of the results of the previous campaign, as previously described; this new study started in September 2005 and finished in December 2006.

In this last campaign it was decided to sample 15 animals for each slaughtered batch, when possible, in order to be able to detect at least a 20% within batch prevalence; moreover, with the aim of avoiding any risk of cross-contamination of samples during slaughtering, it was decided to collect a sample of ileocaecal lymph nodes for each selected animals. The bacteriological investigation on lymph nodes should better reflect the sanitary status of the herd of origin than the information obtained analysing the caecal content.

In this paper the results of the three monitoring campaigns in the swine populations are described and compared.

Introduction
Salmonella is one of the major causes of foodborne illnesses in humans and in 2004 nearly 200.000 human cases of salmonellosis were notified in the 25 EU Member States (EFSA 2005).

The zoonoses legislation (Directive 99/2003/EC and Regulation EC No 2160/2003) obliges all Member States to carry out monitoring programmes for zoonoses and zoonotic agents all along the food chain. Data from the surveys will be used by the Commission to set Community targets for the reduction of the prevalence of Salmonella in animal populations. For this perspective in the Veneto Region of Italy a monitoring programme, involving all the major animal species farmed in the area, has been carried out since 2002. This monitoring programme aims to establish Salmonella and Campylobacter levels across the region and the diffusion of the antimicrobial resistance in pathogen and indicator bacteria. The data collected can be used as a baseline against which future changes in prevalence at slaughter can be monitored and specific control strategies can be defined. The programme was adjusted progressively in order to define the better methodology to estimate as accurately as possible the Salmonella status of animals slaughtered in our region.

In this paper the sampling methods adopted to monitor Salmonella in swine population and the results obtained are presented.

Material and methods
Sampling scheme
A three-step monitoring programme was used to accurately estimate the prevalence of Salmonella. In the first campaign (2002-2003) the number of samples to be collected was calculated considering an expected prevalence of 50%, an accuracy of 5% and a confidence level of 95%. Since accurate information regarding the Salmonella status of swine population in our region was not available, we supposed a predicted prevalence of 50%, which is the situation with the highest variance.

In the second (2004) and third campaigns (2005-2006) it was possible to reduce the number of samples considering the prevalence obtained in the previous phases of the study. The sample sizes adopted allowed to detect either the increase or the decrease of prevalence of 12% (bilateral interval).

The criteria used for the definition of the three sampling schemes are summarized in table 1.

Sampling campaign	Prevalence	IC confidence limit	Accuracy	Difference of prevalence to be detected	Interval	Sample size (number of batches to be sampled)
2002-2003	(expected prevalence) 50%	95%	5%			384
2004	prevalence obtained in the previous campaign	95%	5%	12%	Bilateral	187
2005-2006	prevalence obtained in the previous campaign	95%	5%	12%	Bilateral	171

Table 1. Criteria adopted to define the sample size in the three campaigns of the monitoring programme

In the first and second campaigns of the monitoring programme one sample of faeces was taken from one animal per batch, while in the third phase, in order to increase the sensitivity of the sampling plan, samples of mesenteric lymph nodes were taken from 15 pigs per batch.

Laboratory methods for detection and typing of Salmonella spp.
The samples were collected in major regional pig slaughterhouses irrespective of the origin of the animals (either regional or extra-regional) and were transported to the Italian National Reference Laboratory for Salmonellosis where the samples were analysed.

For each sample (faeces or lymph-nodes) the presence of Salmonella spp. was qualitatively determined according to the Amendment of the ISO 6579:2002. In summary 5 g of sample were added to 45 ml of Buffered Peptone Water and incubated for 18 ± 2 h at 37 ± 1°C. 0,1 ml (3 drops) of pre-enriched broth-culture was inoculated on MSRV and incubated for 24/48 ± 2 h at 41,5 °C ± 1°C. Suspect white culture around the inoculation spots in MSRV were plated on XLD and BGA and after 18 ± 2 h of incubation at 37 ± 1°C colonies with morphology typical of Salmonella were screened biochemically and serotyped following the Kauffman-White scheme. Salmonella Enteritidis and Salmonella Typhimurium strains were then phagetyped following the method provided by HPA, Colindale, London.

Results

During the first campaign of the programme 208 batches were sampled and the prevalence of Salmonella resulted to be 29.33%. The most frequent serotypes were S. Typhimurium (24,21%), S. Derby (18,95%), the monophasic strain 4,5:l:- (10,53%).

In 2004, a total of 173 pig faecal samples, representing the same number of batches, were analysed for the detection of Salmonella spp., and the prevalence of the bacterium resulted to be 25.43%. The stains isolated were serotyped mainly as S. Typhimurium (22,22%), S. Anatum (20%), S. Derby (13,33).

In the last campaign of the monitoring 1557 samples of lymph nodes were collected from 107 batches. A total of 65 batches resulted to be positive for Salmonella (prevalence of 60,75%), and 442 strains of Salmonella were isolated and serotyped. The most prevalent serotypes were S. Derby (21,48%), S. Typhimurium (14,09%), S. Anatum (10,74%), S. London (6,71%), S. Rissen (5,37%). In 28 of the 65 positive batches one or more strains belonging to the same serovar were isolated, while in the other batches two or more serovars were identified. In the 9% of the positive batches 5 (2 batches), 6 (2 batches) and also 7 (2 batches) different serovars were identified.

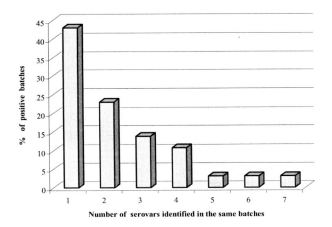

Figure 1 Number of serovars isolated in the same batch simultaneously during the third campaign of the monitoring programme

Discussion

In the last campaign of the monitoring programme a Salmonella prevalence almost three times higher than the one obtained in the previous phases (2002-2003 and 2004) was detected. The reason for this increase of prevalence is clearly due to the rise in the number of samples collected from each batch. Such increase in the number of samples per batch was decided in order to improve the sensitivity of the sampling plan, to assess the extent of the infection within the single groups and to estimate whether different serovars are spread within the single groups.

Another possible explanation for the increase in Salmonella prevalence can be found in the type of matrix investigated, since in the first two phases of the programme we analysed faecal samples while in the last campaign we collected samples of lymph nodes. Usually Salmonella infect swine herds subclinically so pigs at slaughterhouses present chronic infection characterized by a low intermittent excretion of the bacterium in faeces (EFSA 2006). Therefore, the examination of individual faecal samples from pigs has a poor sensitivity. However a better bacteriological estimation of the Salmonella status of a swine herd seems to be obtained analysing intestinal lymph nodes (Nollet et al., 2005), since these tissues reflect a localised intestinal infection, a previous exposure to Salmonella or, possibly the spread from intestinal organs as consequence of generalised infection (EFSA 2006).

Considering the most common serovars detected in the three campaigns of the programme we can note that they are the serotypes identified most frequently in pigs also in the other EU Member States (EFSA 2005).

Conclusion

Both the high prevalence of Salmonella detected in the herds sampled and the presence in several batches of different Salmonella serovars point out the need to carry out specific preventive strategies to control Salmonella in swine production. The possible control strategies, that should be focused mainly at the primary production level, may be for instance the improvement of the hygienic and management procedures in the herds, the improvement of the health status of animals, the adoption of strict biosecurity measures, the control of Salmonella contamination of feed, the use of vaccines and eventually the implementation of specific monitoring programmes to check the effectiveness of the strategies adopted.

Finally, the reduction of Salmonella-prevalence at the primary production is one of the means which can facilitate the respect of certain microbiological criteria fixed by Regulation (EC) No 2073/2005, in force in the EU since 1st January 2006. In fact, this Regulation applies a zero tolerance policy for Salmonella contamination in meat and in particular in minced meat and meat preparations. Therefore, in order to respect these criteria, the implementation of specific control measures of Salmonella reduction in the swine population farmed and slaughtered in our region seems to be definite and urgent. In addition, at the end of 2007 the European target for the reductions of Salmonella in pigs will be fixed, and then all the Member States will have to define their control programmes.

References

EFSA 2005 Community Summary Report on Trends and Sources of Zoonoses, Zoonotic Agents and Antimicrobial resistance in the European Union in 2004, The EFSA Journal - http://www.efsa.eu.int/science/monitoring_zoonoses/reports/1277_en.html

EFSA 2006 Opinion of the Scientific Panel on Biological Hazards on the request from the Commission related to "Risk assessment and mitigation options of Salmonella in pig production" The EFSA Journal

Nollet N., Maes D., Duchateau L., Hautekiet V., Houf K., Van Hoof J., De Zutter L., De Kruif A., Geers R. 2005 Discrepancies between the isolation of Salmonella from mesenteric lymph nodes and the results of serological screening in slaughter pigs. Vet. Res. 36 545-555

Popoff M.Y., Le Milor L. 1997 Antigenic formulas of the Salmonella serovars. WHO Collaborating Centre, Institut Pasteur, Paris

Observations on the distribution of *Salmonella* on pig multiplier breeding farms

Davies, R.*, McLaren, I., Wales, A., Bedford, S.

Department of Food and Environmental Safety, Veterinary Laboratories Agency - Weybridge, Surrey, KT15 3NB, UK
Corresponding author: r.h.davies@vla.defra.gsi.gov.uk

Abstract
Centralisation of the structure of pig production in the UK has resulted in the development of large integrated companies which supply finishing pigs as well as centralised services such as compound feed, transport and veterinary services to the whole company. Typically the integration will comprise an indoor multiplier farm which supplies gilts, and other boars, to a range of large outdoor commercial breeding farms. Usually artificial insemination is used on the multiplier farm rather than natural service. Each commercial breeding farm then supplies weaned pigs either to a range of nursery farms or direct to finishing farms. It is therefore possible to disseminate *Salmonella* to tens or hundreds of other farms if the multiplier herd is infected. Longitudinal studies were carried out on the multiplier farms for two large companies and a single investigative visit was made to the multiplier farm from a third company. On one of the farms (X) *Salmonella* Typhimurium and other serovars were widespread in all age groups of pigs and environmental samples. There was a sustained reduction in *S.* Typhimurium after ongoing tetracycline medication for sub-fertility was removed but the improvement for other serotypes was transient. On the second farm (Y) *S.* Typhimurium was intermittently detected, against a background of *S.* Panama. *S.*Typhimurium DT104b and *S.*Derby were found in batches of new replacement gilts, originating from a primary breeding company, which had just been delivered to this farm. On the third farm (Z) *S.* Ohio was predominant, although *S.* Derby was present in post weaning accommodation for gilts and *S.* Typhimurium was detected in several groups. It was necessary to sample individual pens to detect *S.* Typhimurium on the site because of masking by the other serovars in pooled samples. All three of the companies had a high prevalence in their commercial breeding and finishing herds of the same *Salmonella* serovars found on the respective multiplier farms.

Introduction

Despite the potential importance of multiplier herds in the maintenance and dissemination of *Salmonella* amongst production herds, there is limited data on *Salmonella* colonisation above the commercial production tier of the breeding pyramid. Serological examination of a small number of Dutch multiplier herds by ELISA (van der Wolf et al., 2001) revealed that 100% and 91% of herds were seropositive at 10% and 40% optical density (OD) cut-offs, respectively. Similar values were obtained for production breeding sows. One of four Greek multiplier herds proved seropositive with an ELISA similar to that used in Danish monitoring (Grafanakis et al., 2001). Bacteriological sampling of 10 animals per herd in Denmark (Christensen et al., 2002) showed similar herd-level prevalences of *Salmonella* in genetic breeder herds (12%) and in finished pigs before slaughter. The present report concerns intensive sampling for *Salmonella* on three multiplier herd premises in England.

Materials and Methods

Farms X, Y and Z were, respectively, 800-, 200- and 1100-sow multiplier units. All 3 farms were multiplier units for large integrated companies and supplied maiden gilts for service on commercial breeding farms throughout the organisations.

The strategy was to sample all groups of pigs from all age groups present, plus empty and cleaned accommodation, equipment, walls and floors in pig-handling and staff areas, and wildlife vectors, particularly rodents. Samples taken on each unit included 25 g bulked faeces from groups of pigs, swabs of sterile medical gauze soaked in buffered peptone water (BPW) from empty pens and surfaces (approx 0.5 m^2), plus rodent droppings and dead mice. Faeces and swabs were placed directly into 225 ml BPW. Rodent droppings (1-10 g) and the liver, intestine and spleen from aseptically dissected mouse carcases (2-3 g) were placed in an approximately tenfold volume of BPW at the processing laboratory. Samples were taken to the laboratory under ambient temperature conditions and processed on the day of collection.

Samples in BPW were pre-enriched for 24 h, inoculated onto modified semi-solid Rappaport-Vassiliadis agar with 0.01 % novobiocin (MSRV; Difco 218681) and incubated at 41.5 °C for 16 to 24 h. A 1 μl loop from the edge of any opaque growth on MSRV was inoculated onto Rambach agar (Merck 107500). Rambach and associated MSRV plates were incubated at 37 °C and 41.5 °C respectively for 24 h. Any MSRV plates on which the growth had spread widely, but which were negative for *Salmonella* on the Rambach plates, were subcultured again onto Rambach agar. Serotyping of representative *Salmonella* isolates was performed at the *Salmonella* reference laboratory at VLA – Weybridge.

Analyses included consideration of prevalence rates (number of positive samples or pools / number of same collected) within certain sample categories, i.e. boars/service areas, sows, farrowing accommodation, weaner pens/decks, grower/finisher pens, gilt pens, rodent samples, and surfaces after cleaning and disinfection (C&D). In addition, for each visit there was an overall prevalence rate that additionally included results from samples of equipment, other wildlife and the wider farm environment.

Results

Farm X was sampled on seven occasions over seven years (Figure 1), and routine tetracycline medication ceased between the first and second visits. *S.* Manhattan was stably persistent in most sample categories throughout the seven years and *S.* Derby was widespread on the first visit and the last four visits, but not detected in the intervening period. Other non-Typhimurium serotypes were detected within several categories on two consecutive visits (Bredeney, Muenchen), or in one or two categories on one visit only (Newport, Heidelberg, Montevideo). The temporal variation of non-Typhimurium *Salmonella* prevalence was marked and without regular patterns. Of the age-group categories, weaners showed oscillations between zero and 15 to 40% detected prevalence on consecutive visits, whereas other age groups were more consistently positive, at prevalences up to 90%. *S.* Typhimurium initially was prevalent and widespread, it declined after three years and in the last eighteen months of the study was found only amongst growers or finishers, at modest prevalences of up to 15%. A number of different definitive phage types and untypable strains were isolated, some concurrently (Figure 1). Hospital pens were heavily contaminated, first with *S.* Typhimurium and latterly with other serotypes. Samples following C&D yielded zero prevalence on only three of five occasions. Initially, rodent faeces were heavily contaminated with herd serotypes, but opportunities to sample declined sharply as rodent control improved.

Farm Y was visited on five occasions over three years and showed an alternating pattern of dominance by serotypes Panama and Typhimurium (Figure 1). Initially, *S.* Panama was prevalent in the farrowing accommodation (25%) and present at a lower level amongst sows, boars and weaners. On this first visit *S.* Typhimurium DT208 was found only in wild bird faeces on site, but on the second visit nine months later it was prevalent (30%) among gilts and detected also from boars, farrowing accommodation and weaners. *S.* Panama was not found on this occasion, but a year later it was heavily prevalent in all age groups plus rodents, and no Typhimurium was found. A novel serotype (Derby) was found amongst incoming and established gilts on one occasion, and on another occasion *S.*Typhimurium DT104b was found. Five months later, the overall *Salmonella* prevalence was much lower with Panama, Derby and Typhimurium DT104b being isolated at modest frequency (3-10%) from weaners, dry sows and gilts respectively. Higher levels of contamination and excretion were once again evident a year later, dominated by *S.* Typhimurium DT208, which was heavily prevalent (30-80%) amongst farrowing and young stock but present also in older animals. A low level of S. Panama was found among sows. C&D proved to be inconsistently effective, with 8 of 43 swabs taken post-C&D throughout the study yielding *Salmonella*, and cleaning equipment itself being found to be contaminated on one visit. Few rodent faeces samples were taken, but S. Panama was found in four of five samples on one occasion.

A single visit was made to **Farm Z**, where *Salmonella* was found to be widespread, with 53% prevalence overall (Figure 2). The exception was farrowing sows, yielding no positives from 151 individual faeces samples. The commonest serotype was Ohio, but Derby was found amongst weaners and associated rodents, plus in water and effluent associated with sows and the farrowing house. Ohio was very widespread, extending to staff clothing and rooms, vehicles and a public road. S. Typhimurium was also present, although sometimes difficult to detect due to masking by other serotypes. It was found amongst weaners, rodents and in service and hospital pens, but not in sow groups. Phage type U288 was predominant.

Discussion

The three multiplier herds examined showed distinctly differing patterns of *Salmonella* contamination. Farm X had multiple serotypes simultaneously present, but only three of eight (Manhattan, Derby and Typhimurium) were persistent and recurrent. The prevalences varied widely between visits, and a reduction in prevalence of *Salmonella* spp. after the withdrawal of tetracycline medication proved to be short-lived. S.Typhimurium was the only persistent serotype to show a progressive decline over time, ultimately being restricted to less than 2% prevalence among growers only. Hospital pens consistently showed heavy contamination and might prove to be a sensitive site for detection on occasions when sampling opportunities are limited.

Farm Y had a much smaller herd, with fewer serotypes present in an apparently more dynamic relationship, oscillating between periods of dominance by S. Panama and S. Typhimurium DT208. It is difficult to estimate the relative influences of pig immunological responses and bacterial ecological competition upon the patterns observed but it is likely that some strains fell below the limits of detection rather than disappeared. S. Typhimurium DT208 was initially found only in wild bird faeces, but nine months later it was the dominant strain in the herd. This is consistent with a role for wild birds as sentinel and/or reservoir species for *Salmonella* in pigs. A further factor was the introduction of S. Derby by incoming gilts, it being found subsequently in sows. S. Typhimurium DT104B was uniquely found amongst gilts and may have been another such import.

The investigation on Farm Z provided an interesting snapshot of an untypical serotype (Ohio) appearing dominant, against a background of serotypes more typically found as residents, i.e. Derby and Typhimurium. Ohio can be found as a feedstuff contaminant, which may be the route by which it attained dominance. As there was just one visit, it is unknown whether it was persistent, but it had achieved extensive spread on the farm, even into staff areas and a roadway. The absence of *Salmonella* in the farrowing accommodation was surprising, but this area was relatively isolated from effluent and faeces from elsewhere and had a good foot-dip system in place.

Conclusions

Multiplier herds are well-placed to disseminate *Salmonella* to production herds via movement of young breeding stock, and the introduction of S. Derby, and possibly S. Typhimurium DT104B, into Farm Y by gilts illustrates the point. Reductions in *Salmonella* contamination of slaughter pigs will be difficult to achieve without good controls higher up the production pyramid. The present data shows fluctuating but persistent contamination of multiplier herds by several serotypes, including Typhimurium. Prevalence rates were similar to those found amongst slaughter-age pigs in the UK (Davies et al., 2004). As in production herds, wildlife, ineffective C&D and importation of infected stock appear to be significant factors in the maintenance and re-introduction of *Salmonella* within multiplier herds.

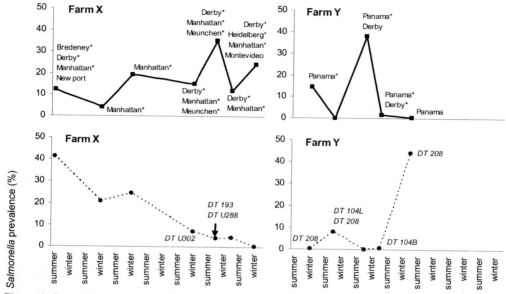

Figure 1: Overall *Salmonella* prevalence values of non-Typhimurium (solid lines) and Typhimurium (dotted lines) serotypes over time. Time scales apply to all charts. * Predominant serotypes.

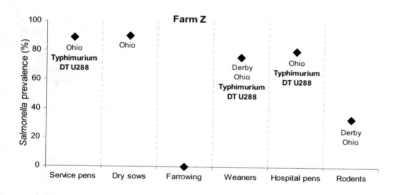

Figure 2: *Salmonella* prevalence within categories on Farm Z.

References

CHRISTENSEN, J., BAGGESEN, D. L., NIELSEN, B. & STRYHN, H. (2002) Herd prevalence of *Salmonella* spp. in Danish pig herds after implementation of the Danish Salmonella Control Program with reference to a pre-implementation study. *Veterinary Microbiology,* 88, 175-188.

DAVIES, R. H., DALZIEL, R., GIBBENS, J. C., WILESMITH, J. W., RYAN, J. M. B., EVANS, S. J., BYRNE, C., PAIBA, G. A., PASCOE, S. J. S. & TEALE, C. J. (2004) National survey for *Salmonella* in pigs, cattle and sheep at slaughter in Great Britain (1999-2000). *Journal of Applied Microbiology,* 96, 750-760.

GRAFANAKIS, E., LEONTIDES, L. & GENIGEORGIS, C. (2001) Seroprevalence and antibiotic sensitivity of serotypes of *Salmonella enterica* in Greek pig herds. *Veterinary Record,* 148, 407-11.

VAN DER WOLF, P. J., ELBERS, A. R. W., VAN DER HEIJDEN, H. M. J. F., VAN SCHIE, F. W., HUNNEMAN, W. A. & TIELEN, M. J. M. (2001) *Salmonella* seroprevalence at the population and herd level in pigs in The Netherlands. *Veterinary Microbiology,* 80, 171-184.

Estimation of the risk of Salmonella shedding by finishing pigs using a logistic model obtained from a survey

Fablet, C.[*], Robinault, C. , Jolly, J.P. , Dorenlor, V., Eono, F. , Eveno, E., Labbé, A., Bougeard, S., Fravalo, P., Madec, F.

AFSSA, French Agency for Food Safety, Zoopôle Les Croix, B.P.53, 22 440 Ploufragan, France

* corresponding author:c.fablet@ploufragan.afssa.fr

Abstract

An analytic epidemiological survey was carried out in 105 French farms to identify factors associated with Salmonella shedding by finishing pigs. This study gave out a list of 7 risk factors using a logistic model. The aim of the present survey was to validate this model on a second sample of batches of pigs in order to estimate their Salmonella status. The validation study was carried out from April 2003 to August 2005 on 64 finishing pig batches distinct from those used originally to generate the logistic model. In each farm, Salmonella shedding of a batch of pigs at the end of the finishing phase was assessed using swabs as described in the analytical study. Questionnaires were filled in with the farmer to collect data related to management routines. Blood samples from10 growing and 10 finishing pigs were taken to assess sanitary risk factors: status vs Lawsonia intracellularis and Porcine Respiratory Coronavirus. Salmonella contamination status of a finishing room before loading, a further identified risk factor, was tested by environmental swabbing procedure. The estimated risk with the standard error, of Salmonella shedding was calculated using the logistic model and compared to the bacteriological Salmonella status of each batch. Several thresholds are proposed and sensitivity, specificity, positive and negative predictive values related to each cut-off value were calculated. A cut-off value of 0.34 maximised both sensitivity (76.9%) and specificity (68.6%) of the model. Whatever the threshold, the accuracy of the Salmonella non-shedding predicted status is better than the Salmonella shedding predicted status. In a bacteriological sampling programme, this model could be a useful tool to identify batches with low risk of Salmonella shedding and to focus attention on those getting a high probability for being positive.

Introduction

Salmonella enterica is a frequent cause of bacterial food poisoning worldwide. Although outbreaks are frequently related to the consumption of contaminated eggs and egg products, contaminated pork products have been incriminated in human salmonellosis cases (Hald et al., 1999; Van Pelt et al., 2001). Contamination of pig meat is related to asymptomatic intestinal carriage of Salmonella by living pigs arriving at the slaughterhouse (Borch et al., 1996). Furthermore, the risk of Salmonella contamination of the caecal contents of pigs at the slaughter line is increased for pigs belonging to batches shedding Salmonella at the farm (Beloeil et al., 2004). Therefore, a reduction of Salmonella carriage at the farm level and/or the identification of at-risk batches delivered to the slaughterhouse with the implementation of segregated slaughtering procedures should help to decrease Salmonella contamination all along the food chain. Several epidemiological studies have been conducted to better understand circumstances associated with Salmonella contamination of finishing pig. Results of analytic surveys, with the determination of at-risk production practices, are used to identify critical points in farm management and constitute a basis for control programs. In analytical studies, logistic models are often used to identify risk factors. As far as they are sufficiently robust, these models could further be used in a predictive aim. To the best of our knowledge, no study was designed to assess the predictive value of a model dealing with the Salmonella shedding by finishing pigs. An analytic epidemiological survey was carried out in 105 French farms to identify factors associated with Salmonella shedding by finishing pigs (Fablet et al., 2003). This study gave out a list of 7 risk factors using a logistic model. The aim of the current study was to validate this model on a second sample of batches of pigs in order to estimate their Salmonella shedding status.

Material and methods

Study design

The validation study was carried out from April 2003 to August 2005 on 64 finishing pig batches distinct from those used originally to generate the logistic model. In every farm, *Salmonella* shedding of a batch of pigs at the end of the finishing phase, housed in the same room, was assessed using swabs as described in the analytical study. Briefly, overshoes, *i.e.* sterile pairs of gauze socks (Sodibox, La Forêt Fouesnant, France), were used to wipe faecal material on the slatted floor of each pen. The sampling method consisted in walking on the floor wearing the overshoes. The 7 risk factors determined in the analytic study are presented **Table 1**. They were gathered by means of questionnaires and sampling. Questionnaires were filled in with the farmer to collect data related to management routines, identified as risk factors in the first study. Blood samples from 10 growing (115 days old) and 10 finishing (batch of interest) pigs were taken to assess sanitary risk factors: infection status *vs Lawsonia intracellularis* (Knittel *et al.*,1998) and Porcine Respiratory Coronavirus. *Salmonella* contamination status of a finishing room before loading, another identified risk factor, was tested by an environmental swabbing procedure. In each pen, one sterile gauze swab (Sodibox, La Forêt Fouesnant, France) was used to wipe the bottom of the walls and the pen partitions and 1m² of the slatted floor of the pen.

Bacteriological analyses

After use, the Sodibox soiled swabs and overshoes were placed into sterile bags and brought to our laboratory on the day they were collected. The *Salmonella* detection protocol involved four steps. Environmental swabs and overshoes were incubated 20 hours at 37°C in respectively 150 mL and 300 mL of buffered peptone water (neutralised for the post cleaning and disinfection swabs) (AES Laboratoire, Combourg, France). Following the pre-enrichment step, two selective media were used: Müller-Kauffman Tetrathionate Broth (MKTB) and Modified Semi-Solid Rappaport Vassiliadis agar (MSRV), incubated respectively 24 hours at 42°C and 48 hours at 41.5°C. The migrated colonies of MSRV plates were isolated on Rambach agar plates and each MKTB on Xylose-Lysine-Tergitol4 (XLT4) agar plates. Both media were incubated 24 hours at 37°C. The presumptive colonies (at least one per selective media) were biochemically confirmed on Kligler-Hajna medium (AES Laboratoires, Combourg, France). All isolates were serotyped by agglutination following the Kauffman-White scheme using *Salmonella* polyvalent O and H antisera (Diagnostics Pasteur, Paris, France) (Popoff and Le Minor, 1992).

A batch was considered *Salmonella* shedding as soon as one of the overshoes tested positive. A room was considered *Salmonella*-residually contaminated as soon as one sample tested positive for *Salmonella*.

Statistical analyses

The logistic model built in the previous analytic study is presented next:

Logit (**SHEDDING**) = 1,3037 **FAR1** + 0,9879 **FAR2** + 1,2792 **FEED** + 1,2150 **ENVCONTAM** + 1,9392 **PRCV**+ 1,1026 **Laws** + 1,1658 **PW** - 5,5839 + residual

where **FAR1**: Frequency of sows' faeces removal in farrowing room, **FAR2**: Emptying the pit below the slatted floor between two successive batches of sows in the farrowing room, **ENVCONTAM**: *Salmonella* contamination of the finishing room prior to loading of a new batch of pigs, **PW**: Duration of the down period in the post-weaning room, **FEED**:Type of feeding during the fattening phase, **PRCV**: Infection status *vs* PRCV, **Laws:** Seroconversion against *Lawsonia intracellularis* in the second half of the fattening phase.

From this logistic model, the estimation of the probability of shedding at the end of the finishing phase was calculated according to the following formula (SAS Institute Inc., 2001):

$$p = \frac{e^{(1,X)\beta}}{1 + e^{(1,X)\beta}}$$ where (1,X) is the matrix of the variable X and β the vector of the parameters estimate of X.

The estimated risk with the standard error of *Salmonella* shedding was compared with the *Salmonella* status of each of the 64 batches under study. Several thresholds (values to classify the batches having either a "low" or a "high" risk of *Salmonella* shedding) were calculated and sensitivity, specificity, positive and negative predictive values related to each cut-off value were assessed.

Results

Among the 64 batches included in the validation survey, 12 (18.9%) tested positive for *Salmonella*. Distribution of the estimated risk for shedding and non shedding batches is presented Figure 1. Several cut-off values can be established. Figure 2 shows the evolution of sensitivity (Se) and specificity (Sp) according to the threshold retained. Overall, Sp increased when Se decreased. The best Se is obtained for low cut-off values. Sp raised with increasing cut-off values. A cut-off value of 0.34 maximised both Se (76.9%) and Sp (68.6%) of the model. The threshold maximizing Se (92.3%) is 0.12. In this case the specificity is 41.2%. Positive and Negative Predictive Values (PPV and NPV) for 3 prevalences and 6 cut off values are presented Table 1. Whatever the prevalence, PPVs are higher for threshold 0.34, 0.45, 0.40 and NPVs are higher for 0.12, 0.24, 0.34. The threshold of 0.34 is common for higher PPV and NPV, especially for prevalence around 20 and 30%.

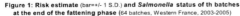

Figure 1: Risk estimate (bar=+/- 1 S.D.) and *Salmonella* status of th batches
at the end of the fattening phase (64 batches, Western France, 2003-2005)

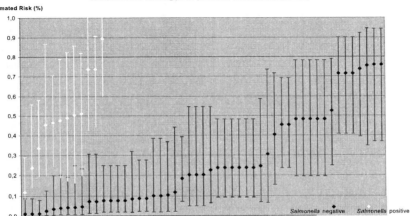

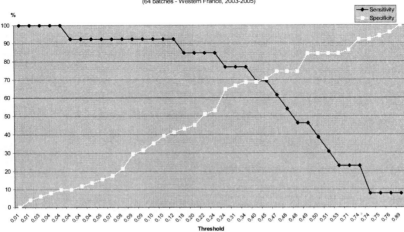

Figure 2: Sensitivity and specificity of the logistic model according to different cut-off values
(64 batches - Western France, 2003-2005)

Table 1: Positive and Negative Predictive Values (PPV, NPV) according to the prevalence and the threshold retained

Prevalence		Threshold		
		0.12	0.24	0.34
40 %	PPV	51.1	54.5	62.0
	NPV	88.9	83.8	81.7
30 %	PPV	40.2	43.5	51.2
	NPV	92.6	88.9	87.4
20 %	PPV	28.2	31	38.0
	NPV	95.5	93.2	92.2

Discussion - Conclusions

The purpose of our study was to assess the characteristics of a logistic model to predict the *Salmonella* status of batches of pigs at the end of the fattening phase. To run the mathematical model, information are needed on housing and managements practices. Blood samples and swabbing are also required. These data can be obtained before shipment to the slaughterhouse and the estimate risk of *Salmonella* shedding can be calculated. Therefore adequate slaughtering procedures might be performed for "at risk" batches. The qualification of batches having either a "low" or "high" risk depend on the cut-off value retained. Indeed, depending on the threshold chosen, a given batch may be estimated contaminated or not. The determination of the cut-off level is done according to strategic decisions: economical, technical or for food safety reasons. In a food safety assurance scheme, sensitivity of the method must be preferred to the specificity and the threshold would be low (Rumeau-Rouquette *et al.*, 1993). Therefore, a better detection of "at risk" batches is achieved. Nevertheless, the level of prevalence is not taken into account with this criteria and number of false positive and false negative evolve according to prevalence. In our study, the estimation of sensitivity was certainly complicated by the low number of negative batches in the sample. In these case, PPV and NPV are 2 other recommended criteria to define a threshold (Rumeau-Rouquette *et al.*, 1993). In the previous analytic study, *Salmonella enterica* shedding was identified in 36.2 % of the tested batches (Fablet et al., 2003). According to these data, we could speculate that the level of *Salmonella* positive batches might be around 20 to 35 %. Whatever the threshold retained in our model, the accuracy of the *Salmonella* non-shedding predicted status is better than the *Salmonella* shedding predicted status. In a bacteriological sampling programme, this model could be a useful tool to identify batches with low risk of *Salmonella* shedding and to focus attention on those getting a high probability for being positive.

Acknowledgements

We are very grateful to the farmers and the farm organisations for their cooperation in this project. The study was co-financed by the French Agency for Environmental Safety (AFSSET) and the Green Piggery (ADEME and Porcherie Verte).

References

BELOEIL, P.A. et al., 2004. Impact of the *Salmonella* status of market-age pigs and the pre-slaughter process on *Salmonella* caecal contamination at slaughter. *Vet. Res.*, 35, 513-530.

BORCH, E., et al., 1996. Hazard identification in swine slaughter with respect to foodborne bacteria. *Int. J. of Food Microbiol.* 30, 9-25.

FABLET, C., et al., 2003. Factors associated with *Salmonella enterica* shedding by finishing pigs. An epidemiological survey in French pig farms., *International Society for Animal Hygiene: XIth International Congress*, Mexico City, I, 345-350.

HALD, T., et al., 1999. Quantitative assessment of the sources of the human salmonellosis attributable to pork. *3rd International Symposium of the Epidemiology and Control of Salmonella in Pork*, Washington DC, USA. 197-199.

KNITTEL, J.P., et al., 1998. Evaluation of antemortem polymerase chain reaction and serologic methods for detection of *Lawsonia intracellularis*-exposed pigs. *Am. J. Vet. Res.* 59, 722-726.

POPOFF M. Y. and LE MINOR L., 1992. Antigenic formulas of the *Salmonella* serovars. Paris, Institut Pasteur.

RUMEAU-ROUQUETTE, C., et al., 1993. *Evaluation des méthodes de dépistage.* Médecine-Sciences: Flammarion Press.

VAN PELT, W. and VALKENBURGH, S.M. (Eds), 2001. Zoonoses and zoonotic agents in humans, food, animals and feed in the Netherlands. *Available:www.keuringsdienstvanwaren.nl.*

Study of *Salmonella* contamination of pig slurry in France

Fablet, C.[*], Robinault, C., Jolly, J.P., Dorenlor, V., Eono, F., Eveno, E., Labbé, A., Madec, F., Fravalo, P.

AFSSA, French Agency for Food Safety, Zoopôle Les Croix, B.P.53, 22 440 Ploufragan, France

* corresponding author:c.fablet@ploufragan.afssa.fr

Abstract

A study was carried out from April 2003 to August 2005 in 69 French pig farms to detect *Salmonella* contaminated pig batches and to assess the level of contamination of their slurry. In each herd, a batch of finishing pigs was included in the survey. In the selected room, *Salmonella* shedding was assessed using swabs method, pools of faecal material and 4 litres of slurry stored in the pit below the pigs. All samples were analysed for the presence of *Salmonella enterica* in a classical bacteriological four-step protocol. Quantification of *Salmonella* was performed in pools of faecal material and slurry samples according to the most probable number method. Using the swabbing procedure, 20.3% of the batches tested *Salmonella* positive at the end of the finishing phase and 11.6 % according to the pools of faeces (8/69). Quantification of *Salmonella* in faeces could be performed in 6 out of 8 positive batches with levels ranging from 2.4 to 350 *Salmonella*/gram. The slurry of 11.8% of the batches (8/68) was found to be *Salmonella* contaminated. A quantification was achieved in 3 of them. Levels of less than 110 *Salmonella*/ml were found. The study indicates that pig slurry may be contaminated by *Salmonella enterica*. However, the percentage of positive samples was rather low and *Salmonella* could only be detected in slurry stored in the pit under the slatted floor of moderately or highly shedding batches. Since storage without introduction of new fresh slurry is known to reduce *Salmonella* survival, the probability of spreading the bacteria in the environment is expected to be low as far as adequate storage conditions are applied.

Introduction

In industrialised countries, salmonellosis is one of the most important and most-frequently reported human foodborne diseases (Haeghebaert *et al.*, 2002). Salmonellosis outbreaks have been associated with the consumption of pork and pork products (Van Pelt and Valkenburgh, 2001; Hald et al., 1999). Contamination of pork products is related to asymptomatic intestinal carriage of *Salmonella* by living pigs arriving at the slaughterhouse (Borch et al., 1996). In order to reduce the occurrence of *Salmonella* in pork, a decrease of *Salmonella* carriage at the farm level is needed. On the other hand, the spread of *Salmonella* contaminated slurry on fields and crops may constitute a threat for environmental preservation. Therefore, efforts undertaken at the farm level to reduce *Salmonella* shedding contribute to increase both human food safety and environmental safety. Few data are available regarding the contamination level of finishing pigs and their slurry in France. The aim of our study was to identify *Salmonella* contaminated finishing pig batches and to assess the level of contamination of their slurry.

Material and methods

A study was carried out from April 2003 to August 2005. 69 batches of finishing pigs from farrow-to-finish French farms were involved in the survey. The farms were selected on voluntary basis. In every herd, a batch of finishing pigs was included in the survey. In the selected room, *Salmonella* shedding was assessed on the one hand with an environmental sampling procedure: sterile pairs of gauze socks (Sodibox, La Forêt Fouesnant, France) were used to wipe faecal material on the slatted floor of each pen housing the selected batch. On the other hand, in each pen a pool of faeces collected on the floor was prepared and placed into sterile bags. In addition 4 litres of slurry stored in the pit below the followed pigs were collected in sterile bottles. Environmental swabs, 25 g of the homogenized pools of faeces and 25 ml of mixed slurry were analysed for the presence of *Salmonella enterica* in a four-step protocol. Following a pre-enrichment step (20 hours at 37°C in buffered peptone water), two selective media were used: Müller-Kauffman Tetrathionate Broth (MKTB) and Modified Semi-Solid Rappaport Vassiliadis agar (MSRV), incubated respectively 24 hours at 42°C and 48 hours at 41.5°C. The migrated colonies of MSRV plates were isolated on Rambach agar plates and each MKTB on Xylose-Lysine-Tergitol4 (XLT4) agar plates. Both media were incubated 24 hours at 37°C. The presumptive colonies (one per selective media) were biochemically confirmed on Kligler-Hajna medium (AES Laboratoires, Combourg, France). All isolates were serotyped by agglutination following the Kauffman-White scheme (Popoff and Le Minor, 1992). A quantification of *Salmonella* was additionally used according to the most probable number (mpn) method to better describe positive pools of faecal material and positive samples of slurry (Fablet et *al.*, 2006).

Results

Results of positive samples are presented Table 1. At least one environmental sample tested positive in 14 out of 69 batches (20.3%). In 8/69 batches (11.6%), *Salmonella* shedding was detected in pooled faeces. *Salmonella* quantification was possible in 5 of these batches with levels ranging from 2.4 to 350 *Salmonella*/gram. *Salmonella* detection in slurry samples was attempted in 68 batches. In 8 batches (11.8%), *Salmonella* was identified in slurry samples. Quantification was achieved in 3 samples of slurry and we found 1.6, 110 and 5.8 *Salmonella*/ml. Quantification in pooled faeces or in slurry could be observed when at least 40% of environmental swabs tested *Salmonella* positive. *Salmonella* Typhimurium and *Salmonella* Derby were the most common serotypes isolated.

Table 1: Description of *Salmonella* serotypes isolated in swabs, pooled faeces and slurry samples and *Salmonella* quantification in pooled faeces and slurry (16 positive batches/69 farms, April 2003 - August 2005)

Farm	Swabs	Pooled faeces		Slurry samples	
	% Positive - *Salmonella* serotype	mpn* (S./gram and $Cl_{95\%}$)	*Salmonella* serotype	npp (S./ml and $Cl_{95\%}$)	*Salmonella* serotype
02	100 - S.T**	2,4 (0,66-8,5)	S.T	-	S.T
05	50 - S.T	350 (94-1300)	S.T	-	S.T
08	25 - S.Bredeney	-	S.Bredeney	-	-
09	41,7 - S. Derby	350 (94-1300)	S. Derby	1,6 (0,38-6,9)	S. Derby
10	16,7 - S.T	-	-	-	-
14	12,5 - S. Derby	-	-	-	-
16	8,3 - S.T	-	-	-	-
24	0	-	-	-	S. Derby
25	8,3 - S. Derby	-	-	-	-
30	37,5 - S.T	-	-	-	-
32	75 - S.T	7,6 (2,5-23)	S.T	-	S.T
45	90,9 - S. Derby	350 (94-1300)	S. Derby	110 (35-360)	S. Derby
56	0	-	S.T	-	-
58	50 - S.T	-	S.T	5,8 (1,9-19)	S.T
60	50 - S.T	-	-	-	S.T
67	16,7 - S.T	-	-	-	-

*mpn : most probable number ; ** S.T : S. Typhimurium*

Discussion - Conclusions

Our study indicates that pig slurry may be contaminated by *Salmonella enterica*. However, the percentage of positive samples and the levels of contamination were rather low. Furthermore, these results suggest that *Salmonella* could only be detected in slurry stored in the pit under the slatted floor of moderately to highly shedding batches of pigs. Since storage without introduction of new fresh slurry is known to reduce *Salmonella* survival (Guan and Holley, 2003), the probability of spreading the bacteria in the environment is expected to be low as far as adequate storage is applied.

Acknowledgements

We are very grateful to the farmers and the farm organisations for their cooperation in this project. The study was co-financed by the French Agency for Environmental Safety (AFSSET) and the Green Piggery (ADEME and Porcherie Verte).

References

HAEGHEBAERT, S., et al., 2002. Toxi-Infections Alimentaires Collectives en France en 2001. *Bulletin Epidémiologique Hebdomadaire*, 50.

BORCH, E., et al., 1996. Hazard identification in swine slaughter with respect to foodborne bacteria. *Int. J. of Food Microbiol.* 30, 9-25.

FABLET, C., et al., 2006. *Salmonella enterica* level in French pig farms effluents: experimental and field data. *Livestock Science*, 102, 216-225

GUAN, T.Y. and HOLLEY, R.A., 2003. Pathogen survival in swine manure environments and transmission of human enteric illness, a review. *J. Environ. Qual.* 32, (2), 383-92.

HALD, T., et al., 1999. Quantitative assessment of the sources of the human salmonellosis attributable to pork. *3rd International Symposium of the Epidemiology and Control of Salmonella in Pork*, Washington DC, USA. 197-199.

POPOFF M. Y. and LE MINOR L., 1992. Antigenic formulas of the *Salmonella* serovars. Paris, Institut Pasteur.

VAN PELT, W. and VALKENBURGH, S.M. (Eds), 2001. Zoonoses and zoonotic agents in humans, food, animals and feed in the Netherlands. *Available:www.keuringsdienstvanwaren.nl.*

National *Salmonella* and *E. coli* Monitoring (ESAM) data from Australian pig carcases from 2000 to 2006

Hamilton, D.R.[1]*, Smith, P.[2], Pointon, A.[1]

[1] Food Safety Research, South Australian Research and Development Institute, 33 Flemington Street, Glenside, SA 5065, Australia.
[2] Australian Quarantine & Inspection Service, GPO Box 858, Canberra, ACT 2601, Australia.
*Corresponding author: hamilton.david@saugov.sa.gov.au

Abstract

Since 1997, pig carcases produced in Australian export abattoirs have been routinely monitored for *Salmonella* spp. and *E. coli* contamination using the standard USDA method (i.e. swabbing 3x 100cm^2 areas on chilled pig carcases). The National *Salmonella* carcase prevalence and serotype isolation frequency was calculated for the years from January 2000 to September 2006. The yearly prevalence range was from 1.19% (7/586) to 2.73% (28/1025) with a 7-year average of 1.88% (132/7038). The most frequent serotypes isolated were Derby, Anatum, Havana, London, Agona and Adelaide. Overall *S*. Typhimurium was isolated in 5.3% (7/132) of the positive samples. For the same period for *E. coli* detection, overall 97.65% (21891/22417) of samples were below the Australian regulatory "m" desirable benchmark (1 cfu/cm^2), with a yearly range from 95.92% to 98.07% of samples. Overall, only 0.08% (18/22417) of samples were >"M", the upper regulatory limit (10^{2}cfu/cm^2).

Introduction

The Australian *E. coli* and *Salmonella* monitoring system (ESAM) was introduced into all Australian US listed export registered abattoirs in January 1997 in order to maintain access to the US market. In August 1997 it was extended to all Australian export registered abattoirs, which accounts for more than 80% of national slaughterings of beef, sheep and pigs. For pigs, carcases are sampled at the rate of 1 in 1000 for *E. coli* and 1 in 5000 for *Salmonella* by company QA staff, under the oversight of the on-plant officers of the Australian Quarantine & Inspection Service (AQIS). Since 1997 Total Viable Counts (TVC) have also been conducted on a voluntary basis on all *E. coli* monitoring samples (i.e. 1 in 1000 carcases). In 2005 this became mandatory for export abattoirs listed to export to the EU. Results are collated by AQIS on-plant staff and entered into a national database (Anon 2003). The purpose of this paper is to report the *E. coli* and *Salmonella* findings of this ongoing monitoring over a 7-year period.

Material and methods

The AQIS national database was examined for the years January 2000 to June 2006 to determine the *Salmonella* and *E. coli* contamination rate (Anon 2003) of pig carcases slaughtered at export establishments on a yearly basis. In 2006 only the first 9 months figures were available, but they have been included for completeness.

Results

The *Salmonella* carcase prevalence for pigs slaughtered at export abattoirs between January 2000 and September 2006 and the serovars isolated are shown in Table 1. The average carcase prevalence over the 7-year period is 1.88%. The table includes all samples, both routine ESAM monitoring and the additional "targeted" samples (i.e. the additional samples required to be taken once a positive isolation occurs) as they are not differentiated in the database. Overall *S*. Typhimurium was found in 7/132 (5.3%) of all positive isolates. Australian *Salmonella* reference laboratories do not differentiate between *S*. Typhimurium and Typhimurium var. Copenhagen.

Table 1. Australian pig carcase *Salmonella* serovar detection rates for the years 2000 to 2006 under the national ESAM sampling programme (monitoring and targeted samples)

Serovar	*Salmonella* isolates Jan 2000 -Sep 2006		# of yearly isolates						
	#	% of positives	2000	2001	2002	2003	2004	2005	2006
S. Derby	20	15.2%	2	6	5	6	1		
S. London *	14	10.6%	1	3	1	4	2	2	1
S. Anatum *	12	9.1%	1	4	1	3		1	2
S. Infantis *	7	5.3%		1		4	1	1	
S. Typhimurium	7	5.3%	1	1	1		3	1	
S. Agona *	4	3.0%		1	1	2			
S. Give *	4	3.0%		1	2	1			
S. Havana *	4	3.0%	2	1			1		
S. Ohio *	4	3.0%		1	3				
S. Muenchen	3	2.3%			1		2		
S. Bredeney *	2	1.5%	1					1	
S. Heidelberg	2	1.5%			1		1		
S. Johannesburg *	2	1.5%				1	1		
S. Livingstone	2	1.5%				1			1
S. Stanley	2	1.5%				1	1		
S. Kiambu	1	0.8%		1					
S. Kottbus	1	0.8%		1					
S. Senftenberg *	1	0.8%		1					
S. Adelaide	1	0.8%						1	
S. Alachua	1	0.8%							1
S. Bovismorbificans*	1	0.8%					1		
S. Chester	1	0.8%							1
S. Enteriditis	1	0.8%							1
S. Mbandaka *	1	0.8%							1
S. Worthington	1	0.8%						1	
untypeable	33	25.0%		5	2	8	9	6	3
Total # positives	132	100.0%	7	28	18	31	23	14	11
Total # samples	7038		586	1025	1147	1306	1278	953	743
Carcase prevalence	1.88%*		1.19%	2.73%	1.57%	2.37%	1.80%	1.47%	1.48%

* 95% Confidence Interval (1.57, 2.22)
* Relatively commonly isolated from animal feeds compared to other serovars (NEPPS 2000-2005)

The results of ESAM sampling for *E. coli* for the years 2000 to 2006 are shown in Table 2. The samples come from pigs killed at export abattoirs, which represents the majority of the approximately 5 million pigs slaughtered annually in Australia. The majority of samples in all years were below "m" (1 cfu/cm^2), the maximum desirable level of contamination. The overall prevalence of samples in this category was 97.65% (21891/22417) with a yearly range between 95.92% and 98.49%. The prevalence of samples falling in the > "M" category (10^2 cfu/cm^2-the upper regulatory limit) overall was 0.08% (18/22417) with a yearly range from 0% to 0.21%.

Table 2. Australian pig carcase *E.coli* detection rates for the years 2000 to 2006 under the national ESAM sampling programme.

Year	n	# samples < m (1 cfu/cm^2)	% < m	# samples >M (10^2 cfu/cm^2)	% > M
2000	2380	2283	95.92%	5	0.21%
2001	2768	2693	97.29%	4	0.14%
2002	3115	3052	97.98%	1	0.03%
2003	3864	3783	97.90%	3	0.08%
2004	3860	3762	97.46%	1	0.03%
2005	3575	3506	98.07%	0	0.00%
2006*	2855	2812	98.49%	4	0.14%

<m = acceptable; m≤ and ≤ M = satisfactory; >M = unacceptable
* 2006 results for 9 months to September

Discussion

Although Australia does not have a national *Salmonella* surveillance and control programme, various studies in pig herds have indicated that the infection rate of Australian pigs may be relatively low by international standards (Hamilton *et al* 2003; 2004). The 7-year average *Salmonella* carcase prevalence of 1.88% and a prevalence in 2005 and 2006 of 1.47% and 1.48% respectively, compares favourably with international findings. The US pig carcase prevalence was reported as 5.3% in 2005 (Anon 2007) and Denmark reports a carcase prevalence of 1.4% (Anon 2004).

S. Typhimurium is the most common serovar isolated in human infection in this country, as it is overseas. However, unlike Europe and the USA, recent epidemiological studies suggest it is not a common serovar in Australian pigs. This view is supported by the ESAM pig carcase *Salmonella* results, with only 5.3% of all isolates identified as Typhimurium over a 7-year period. The explanation for the differing *Salmonella* epidemiology will require further study but a number of Australian factors may have an influence, including well ventilated pens and high air quality, the non-use of slurry systems, the increasing use of deep litter housing (with a consequent increase in the consumption of bedding material - up to 10% of the diet) and climate. In addition genetics may play a part as quarantine restrictions mean the Australian pig herd has been effectively closed since the 1960's.

The national E. coli contamination rates reported here appear low (eg 98.07% <1 cfu/cm2 and 0.00% >102 cfu/cm2 in 2005) (Table 2), although data on E. coli levels from other countries are not readily available so direct comparisons are difficult. The 1997-1998 US Baseline survey found 84.1% of sponge samples had <1cfu/cm2 and 3.8% of samples had >102 cfu/cm2 (Anon 2005). The relatively low figures reported here might be due to a combination of lower chain speeds in this country and the fact that QA systems were introduced into Australian abattoirs in 1984, to be followed by HACCP a few years later.

References

ANON, 2003. Revised ESAM Program (AQIS Notice Number Meat 2003/06).

ANON, 2004. Annual report on zoonoses in Denmark 2003. Danish Zoonosis Centre, Copenhagen, Denmark pp 31.

ANON, 2007. Progress Report on Salmonella Testing of Raw Meat and Poultry Products, 1998–2005. http://www.fsis.usda.gov/science/progress_report_Salmonella_testing/index.asp.

ANON, 2005. Nationwide sponge microbiological baseline data collection program:swine. June 1997-May 1998. http://www.fsis.usda.gov/Science/Baseline_Data/index.asp.

HAMILTON, D., BOBBITT, J., LESTER, S., POINTON, A.M., 2003. Effect of pre-slaughter handling and serology on Salmonella in pigs. In: Proceedings of the 5th International Symposium on the Epidemiology and Control of Foodborne Pathogens in Pork: Crete, pp 180-183.

Session 2

HAMILTON, D.R., HOLDS, G., BOBBITT, J., KIERMEIER, A., HOLYOAKE, P., FAHY, T., DAVOS, D., HEUZENROEDER, M., LESTER, S., POINTON, A., 2004. Ecology of Salmonella Infection across Australian Pig Rearing Production Systems. APL Project No. 1836. SARDI. August 2004. NEPPS 2000-2005. National Enteric Pathogen Surveillance Scheme: Non-Human Reports.

Prevalence of *Salmonella* in minced pork meat in supermarkets and butchers' shops in Denmark and dependence on retail supply chains

Hansen, T.B.*[1], Shukri, N.M.[1], Nielsen, N.L.[1, 2], Christensen, B.B.[1], Aabo, S.[1]

[1]National Food Institute, Technical University of Denmark, Mørkhøj Bygade 19, DK-2860 Søborg, Denmark
[2]The Danish Veterinary and Food Administration, Mørkhøj Bygade 19, DK-2860 Søborg, Denmark

*corresponding author: tibha@food.dtu.dk

Abstract

In 2001/2002 a retail survey of the prevalence of *Salmonella* in minced pork, purchased in butchers' shops and supermarkets has been conducted. Also the distribution supply chain of fresh minced pork meat from slaughterhouse to retail in Denmark was mapped. Among a total of 2,172 samples, 46 (2.1%) were *Salmonella* positive. In 2,151 samples of Danish origin and in 18 samples of imported meat, 1.8% and 39% were positive for *Salmonella*, respectively. The *Salmonella* detection rates were significantly higher in minced pork packaged in atmospheric air as compared to MAP ($P = 0.014$). Samples taken from butchers' shops showed a *Salmonella* prevalence of *approx.* 3.5% compared to a prevalence of *approx.* 0.7% for samples taken from supermarkets selling pre-packed meat and *approx.* 1.6% in samples from supermarkets approved for meat processing. The distribution analysis showed that butchers' shops traded more frequently with slaughterhouses having low levels of *Salmonella* than the supermarkets. Thus, the higher *Salmonella* prevalence in butchers' shops could not be explained by their trading patterns and may, therefore, be due to poorer hygiene standard as indicated by significantly ($P = 0.004$) higher levels of faecal enterococci in the minced pork samples compared to supermarkets.

Introduction

Pork meat is a substantial source of human *Salmonella* infections in Denmark accounting for 10 to 20% of all *Salmonella* cases. An outbreak, in 1993, lead to the implementation of a *Salmonella* control program aiming at reducing the consumer risk from Danish fresh pork. The program includes serological classification of slaughter pig herds into three *Salmonella* infection levels, sanitary slaughter of pigs from herds belonging to the highest infection level, and *Salmonella* surveillance of fresh meat at the slaughterhouse. Fresh meat surveillance data from 2001/2002 showed an overall *Salmonella* prevalence of 1.7% with 1.8% positive carcasses from the large export-authorized slaughterhouses, 1.1% from medium-sized slaughterhouses and 0.6% from small slaughterhouses only approved for the domestic market. Thus, the surveillance data suggest that meat from the small slaughterhouses may be safer for the consumer compared to meat from the other two groups of slaughterhouses. The small- and medium-sized slaughterhouses are expected to provide up to 40 to 50% of the fresh pork at retail but no solid data on the distribution of pork meat to retail are available. Therefore, a survey of the prevalence of *Salmonella* in retail butchers' shops and supermarkets was initiated where also the distribution supply chain of fresh minced pork meat from slaughterhouse to retail in Denmark was established.

Materials and methods

In eleven geographic regions in Denmark, samples of at least 300 g minced pork meat were taken from butchers' shops as well as supermarkets with and without approval for meat processing. Each sample was accompanied by a questionnaire for registering of country of origin, type of retailer, type of supplier and type of packaging. For microbiological analyses, samples were transported to the Regional Food Administration Centres. Twenty-five-gram-samples where analysed for Salmonella by standard enrichment procedures. Furthermore, quantitative enumeration of faecal enterococci was performed on all samples using the method described in NMKL no. 68, second edition (1992).

Results

Salmonella prevalence. A total of 2,172 minced pork samples were collected and analysed for the presence of *Salmonella*. As shown in Table 1, 99% (2,151) of the samples were of Danish origin and 0.8% (18) originated from imported pork meat, primarily from the Netherlands (11) and Germany (5).

Table 1. Detection of *Salmonella* spp. in minced pork meat collected at retail level in Denmark in 2001 and 2002.

		Salmonella detection			
				95% confidence interval (%)	
Origin	No. of samples	No. of positives	Prevalence (%)	Lower	Upper
Danish	2,151	39	1.8	1.3	2.5
Imported	18	7	38.9	17.3	64.3
Unknown	3	0	0	0	70.8
Total	2,172	46	2.1	1.6	2.8

Among the samples of Danish origin 457 were from butchers' shops and 1,275 and 405 were from supermarkets with and without meat processing, respectively (Table 2). The prevalence of *Salmonella* was significantly (Maximum Likelihood Test, $P = 0.018$) higher in minced pork meat from butchers' shops compared to the supermarkets approved for meat processing, whereas comparison of supermarkets with and without approval for meat processing revealed no statistical difference ($P = 0.182$).

Table 2. Detection of *Salmonella* in Danish minced pork meat samples collected in butchers' shops or supermarkets in 2001 and 2002.

		Salmonella detection				
	Meat processing approval	No. of pos.	No. of neg.	Prevalence (%)	95% confidence interval (%)	
Retailer					Lower	Upper
Butchers' shops	Yes	16	441	3.5	2.01	5.62
Supermarkets	Yes	20	1255	1.6	0.98	2.45
	No	3	402	0.7	0.15	2.15
Unknown	-	0	14	-	-	-

Retail supply chain. The distribution network of fresh minced pork, from slaughter to retail, was established for the samples. Retail suppliers were divided into categories according to their authorization for slaughter and/or cutting of fresh meat as well as their organizational association (Table 3). Three main retail supply routes were identified. Six percent of pork meat was supplied directly from slaughterhouses, which were authorized only for slaughter, 36% from slaughterhouses authorized for slaughter as well as cutting and 45% were distributed from specialised cutting plants to the retailers. As seen in Table 3, each of these three routes could be divided further into three different categories, dependent on authorization and organizational association. Butcher's shops traded more frequently with suppliers approved for the domestic market (21%) compared to supermarkets (3%) in general (P < 0.001). For supermarkets, without approval for meat processing, the 92% of the samples originated from Danish Meat Association (DMA) members. In the supermarkets, approved for meat processing, this same tendency was observed with approx. 70% supplied by DMA members, whereas the major suppliers for butcher's shops were the medium-sized export approved companies outside the DMA represented by 52.5 % of the samples (Table 3).

Table 3. Distribution of the retail suppliers of fresh minced pork samples, of Danish origin, collected in butchers' shops and supermarkets in Denmark in 2001 and 2002.

	Type of retailer					
			Supermarkets			
			With meat processing		Without meat processing	
Supplier, authorization and organization	Butchers' shops					
Slaughter						
Export – members of DMA[a]	0	%	0.7	%	0	%
Export – other than DMA members[b]	9.6	%	1.3	%	0	%
Domestic[c]	7.9	%	0.9	%	1.0	%
Slaughter & cutting						
Export – members of DMA	11.4	%	26.8	%	26.9	%
Export – other than DMA members	33.3	%	4.6	%	1.0	%
Domestic	7.2	%	1.3	%	0.5	%
Cutting						
Export – members of DMA	5.7	%	42.0	%	65.4	%
Export – other than DMA members	9.6	%	3.2	%	0.7	%
Domestic	5.9	%	1.2	%	0.5	%
Other[d]	2.0	%	4.5	%	1.5	%
Unknown	7.4	%	13.5	%	2.5	%

[a] Danish Meat Association (large enterprises)
[b] Export authorized slaughterhouses outside DMA (medium sized enterprises)
[c] Slaughterhouses approved for the domestic market (small sized enterprises)
[d] This category covers samples that were delivered from other types of suppliers e.g. wholesalers

Retail hygiene level. Counts of faecal enterococci in the minced pork samples from the three different types of retailers were determined and used as an indication of faecal contamination. As shown in Table 4, faecal enterococci were detected to a significantly higher extent in meat samples from butchers' shops compared to supermarkets with (Maximum Likelihood Test, $P = 0.004$) and without meat processing ($P < 0.001$). Also the concentrations of faecal enterococci were observed to be significantly (Chi-square Test, $P = 0.008$) higher for the samples taken in butchers' shops (Table 4).

Table 4. Detection and concentration of faecal enterococci in Danish minced pork samples collected in butchers' shops and supermarkets in 2001 and 2002.

Concentration of faecal enterococci $(CFU\ g^{-1})$	Type of retailer							
			Supermarkets					
	Butchers' shops		With meat processing		Without meat processing		Total	
Not detected	266		804		294		1,364	
Detected	156		332		55		543	
<100	10.3	%	13.6	%	63.6	%	17.7	%
100 – 999	55.8	%	66.6	%	29.1	%	59.7	%
1.000 – 9.999	30.1	%	17.8	%	7.3	%	20.3	%
10.000 – 99.999	3.9	%	1.5	%	0	%	2.0	%
>100.000	0	%	0.6	%	0	%	0.4	%

Among a total of 1,919 samples, *Salmonella* was detected more frequently in those of the samples also harbouring faecal enterococci (Maximum Likelihood Test, $P < 0.001$). The prevalence of *Salmonella* was 1.1% (95% C.I.: 0.6% - 1.8%) in samples with less than 100 faecal enterococci per gram and 4.4% (95% C.I.: 2.7% - 6.8%) in samples with 100 or more faecal enterococci per gram.

Packaging. Of the collected samples of Danish origin, 20% (434) were packed in modified atmosphere (MA) and 4% (91) were L-packed, *i.e.* produced from meat with low initial microbial level, MA-packed and kept refrigerated at max. 2°C. The rest of the samples were packed in atmospheric air. A significantly higher number of the samples packed in atmospheric air were *Salmonella* positive (Fisher's exact test, *P* = 0.014). Also the occurrence of faecal enterococci was significantly higher in these samples (Chi-square Test, P < 0.001) compared to the MA-packed samples. As shown in Table 5, a significantly higher proportion of the samples, packed in atmospheric air and collected from butchers' shops, had concentrations of faecal enterococci above 1.000 CFU g^{-1} (Chi-square Test, *P* = 0.004).

Table 5. Prevalence and concentration of faecal enterococci in Danish minced pork samples, packed in atmospheric air, and collected in 2001 and 2002.

Faecal enterococci	Butchers' shops		Supermarkets with meat processing	
Prevalence (%)	37 (95% C.I.: 33 – 42)		32 (95% C.I.: 29 – 35)	
Concentraion (CFU g^{-1})				
<100	66.8	%	71.7	%
100 – 999	20.8	%	21.7	%
1.000 – 9.999	10.9	%	5.9	%
10.000 – 99.999	1.4	%	0.5	%
>100.000	0	%	0.2	%

Discussion

In the present survey, *Salmonella* was detected in 39 samples of minced pork of Danish origin corresponding to an overall prevalence of 1.8% (Table 1). Samples taken from butchers' shops accounted for 21% of all samples but 41% of the *Salmonella* positive samples, corresponding to a prevalence of 3.5% (Table 2) in meat from this type of retailer. The corresponding prevalence was 1.6% for samples taken from supermarkets approved for meat processing and 0.7% for supermarkets without this approval. From the routine surveillance of fresh pork in Denmark, it is known that the prevalence of *Salmonella* on pig carcasses was two- to three-fold higher for export-authorized slaughterhouses compared to slaughterhouses authorized for the domestic market in 2001/2002. As more than 70% of the samples, taken from supermarkets, were traced back to export-authorized companies (Table 3), it was expected to find the highest prevalence of *Salmonella* in samples from supermarkets. However, this was not the case, which could indicate a different hygienic level between butchers' shops and supermarkets, *e.g.* resulting in higher degree of cross-contamination and/or growth of *Salmonella* in butchers' shops. As it was confirmed, that *Salmonella* was found more frequently in minced pork samples also harbouring faecal enterococci, the presence of these organisms in the meat was used as a parameter for comparison of the hygiene levels between the retailers. Faecal enterococci were detected in significantly more samples as well as in higher concentrations in minced pork from butchers' shops (Table 4), indicating poorer hygiene in these shops. As the prevalence of *Salmonella* and faecal enterococci was significantly lower in MA-packaged minced pork compared to samples packaged in atmospheric air and the proportion of MA-packaged samples were higher in the case of supermarkets, this could, in part, explain the difference in *Salmonella* prevalence between butchers' shops and supermarkets. However, when comparing only the samples packaged in atmospheric air, significantly higher concentrations of faecal enterococci in samples from butchers' shops were revealed compared to those from supermarkets (Table 5).

Conclusions

Samples taken from butchers' shops in 2001/2002 accounted for 21% of all samples but 41% of *Salmonella* positive samples, resulting in a prevalence of 3.5% in minced pork from this type of retailer. The corresponding prevalence was 0.7% for samples taken from supermarkets without meat processing and 1.6% for minced pork from supermarkets approved for meat processing. This difference could not be traced back to the different supply routes observed for butchers' shops and supermarkets. Rather, the difference was a result of a poorer hygienic standard in butchers' shops as indicated by significantly higher levels of faecal enterococci in the minced pork samples.

Pork Quality Assurance Plus™ Program

Larsen S.*[1], Sundberg P.[1], Wagstrom E.[1], Niekamp S.[1], and Risa E.[1]

[1]National Pork Board, 1776 NW 114th Street, Des Moines, IA 50235, USA

*Corresponding Author: slarsen@pork.org

Abstract

Pork producers in the United States have developed a new food safety and animal care certification program that builds on the current Pork Quality Assurance (PQA®) program. Working with the pork industry's customers, pork producers have created a workable, credible and affordable solution to assure food safety and animal care and at the same time meet the needs of customers including restaurants, food retailers and, ultimately, consumers. The industry's solution is a continuous improvement system focused on producer education and premises assessment, which is called PQA Plus™.

Introduction

The PQA program was introduced in 1989 as a multi-level voluntary producer education program to increase residue avoidance awareness. Since its introduction in 1989, Pork Quality Assurance has become the pork industry's flagship educational program. The PQA Plus program provides producers with information about on-farm good production practices (GPPs) for the promotion of pork safety and pig well-being. Development of the PQA Plus program, which began in 2005, added animal well-being and site assessment components (portions of which were formerly known as the Swine Welfare Assessment Program or SWAP™) to the PQA program. The program has become a proven resource for information to improve food safety and well-being, in addition to efficiency of production and assessment of premises.

The PQA Plus Program is comprised of two main elements - food safety and animal well-being. Food safety refers to the practices that minimize physical, chemical or biological hazards. This includes the responsible use of antimicrobials to minimize the potential for the development of antimicrobial resistance. Animal well-being encompasses producer responsibilities for all aspect of animal well-being., including proper housing, management, nutrition, disease prevention and treatment, responsible care, humane handling, and when necessary, humane and timely euthanasia.

There are nine Good Production Practices (GPPs) that address food safety and/or antimicrobial resistance and one that addresses animal care. A site assessment has also been developed to assess animal care practices. While many of the GPPs were included in previous programs they were further developed through input from industry experts in food safety, production, animal welfare, and veterinary medicine. The draft GPPs, educational materials, and the assessment were then beta tested on farms of various sizes, and edits were made to address concerns identified. The program will be launched in 2007 and will have a three-year implementation period.

Discussion

The PQA Plus program comprises two main elements - food safety and animal well-being. Food safety refers to the practices that minimize physical, chemical or biological hazards that might be injurious to consumers. Animal well-being encompasses producer responsibilities for all aspects of animal well-being, including proper housing, management, nutrition, disease prevention and treatment, responsible care, humane handling and when necessary, humane and timely euthanasia. Food safety and animal well-being have become concerns for consumers, both domestic and international.

Customers are concerned about their food and how the animals are raised. The PQA Plus program sets the example for the meat commodities by showing that the U.S. pork industry is proactively addressing food safety and animal well-being issues. The participation of U.S. pork producers in PQA Plus opens markets abroad and shows to all customers that we have a commitment to a safe, wholesome food supply. The fact that numerous packers have incorporated the PQA certification into United States Department of Agriculture (USDA) approved HACCP plans shows their confidence that the PQA program will help ensure food safety.

The 10 PQA Plus GPPs are:

GPP #1 Establish and implement an efficient and effective herd health management plan.
GPP #2 Use a veterinarian/client/patient relationship (VCPR) as the basis for medication decision-making.
GPP #3 Use antibiotics responsibly.
GPP #4 Identify and track all treated animals.
GPP #5 Maintain medication and treatment records.
GPP #6 Properly store, label, and account for all drug products & medicated feeds.
GPP #7 Educate all animal caretakers on proper administration techniques, needle-use procedures, observance of withdrawal times, and methods to avoid marketing adulterated products for human food.
GPP #8 Follow appropriate on-farm feed processing and commercial feed processor procedures.
GPP #9 Develop, implement and document an animal caretaker training program.
GPP #10 Provide proper swine care to improve swine well-being.

PQA Plus Certification is certifying that the producer has completed the PQA Plus educational program with a PQA Plus Advisor. PQA Plus Certification is valid for three years from the date of issuance. To become PQA Plus Certified, an individual must attend a PQA Plus Certification training session on the 10 PQA Plus GPPs conducted by a PQA Plus Advisor. No examination is required for PQA Plus Certification but retraining is needed for recertification.

PQA Plus Site Status is a PQA Plus status assigned to a production site and stays with that site for three years from the date of the assessment. To be granted PQA Plus Site Status the production site must be identified with a premises ID. The site also must have associated with it a PQA Plus Certified individual that has a stable relationship/responsibility with the production site. Finally, the site needs to have a PQA Plus site assessment done either by a PQA Plus Advisor or an Endorsed individual. Once these criteria have been met and a PQA Plus Advisor reports the assessment data, the site will receive a PQA Plus Site Status that will be valid for three years. Reassessment is required to renew PQA Plus Site Status. The anonymous aggregate data from the PQA Plus site assessments will be used to help the Pork Checkoff direct research and educational programming.

The first step for a producer to get a PQA Plus Site Self-Assessment Endorsement is to hold a current PQA Plus Certification. A training session with a PQA Plus Advisor is the next step during which the producer will need to successfully complete and pass an examination covering PQA Plus GPP #10 and the on-farm site assessment process. The PQA Plus Site Self-Assessment Endorsement is valid for up to three years based on the date of issuance of PQA Plus Certification. Retraining and completing and passing an examination is required for re-endorsement.

Conclusion

The PQA Plus program consists of 10 GPPs to ensure that pork is free from chemical and physical hazards and that the pigs are raised in a caring manner with regard to their well-being. The 10

GPPs, when implemented, will lead to operating more efficiently and to maintaining the reputation of not only the producer, but the entire U.S. pork industry. These 10 practices are based on:

1. Hazard Analysis and Critical Control Point principles.

2. The Food and Drug Administration's Compliance Policy Guide (CPG) 7125.37 – "Proper Drug Use and Residue Avoidance by Non-veterinarians."

3. The Animal Medicinal Drug Use Clarification Act (AMDUCA) of 1994.

4. Science-based animal care and well-being guidelines.

PQA Plus is a continuous improvement system focused on producer education and premises assessment that is a workable, credible and affordable solution to assure food safety and animal care and at the same time meet the needs of customers including restaurants, food retailers and, ultimately, consumers. The program will be launched in June of 2007.

The serological Salmonella Monitoring in German pork production: the structure of the central database and preliminary results of a basic epidemiological report

Merle, R.[*][(1)], Schneider, B.[(2)], Franz, B.[(2)], Portsch, U.[(3)], May, T.[(4)], Blaha, T.[(5)], Kreienbrock, L.[(1,2)]

[(1)]WHO Collaborating Centre for Reserarch and Training in Veterinary Public Health, University of Veterinary Medicine, Buenteweg 2, 30559 Hannover, Germany
[(2)]Department of Biometry, Epidemiology and Information Processing, University of Veterinary Medicine, Buenteweg 2, 30559 Hannover, Germany
[(3)]Qualitype AG, Moritzburger Weg 67, 01109 Dresden, Germany
[(4)]QS Qualität und Sicherheit GmbH, Margaretenstr. 1, 53175 Bonn, Germany
[(5)]Field Station for Epidemiology, University of Veterinary Medicine Hannover, Büscheler Str. 9, 49456 Bakum, Germany

*corresponding author: roswitha.merle@tiho-hannover.de

Abstract

Since 2002, the Qualität und Sicherheit GmbH (QS GmbH) has carried out a serological salmonella monitoring in German finishing pig herds. This monitoring aims at reducing the risk of introducing salmonella into the meat production chain caused by infected slaughter pigs and to identify and to remove infection sources. For this purpose the farms are differentiated into three risk categories (I = low, II = middle, III = high) by their chance to introduce salmonella into the pork production chain. All data generated within the monitoring are entered into the central database Qualiproof® (Qualitype AG, Dresden).
The dataset investigated included 1 762 270 samples taken between April 1, 2003 and March 31, 2006 originating from 15 452 farms. Blood sera or meat juices are sampled at slaughterhouses following a scheme (up to 60 samples per year and farm, depending on farm size). The laboratories analyse the samples serologically using one of four ELISA-tests and report the results as OD% as well as the decision "positive"/"negative" (cut-off: 40 OD%). The categorisation is re-calculated quarterly based on the percentage of positive samples during the last 12 months for each farm. A proportion of less than 20% positive samples yields in category I, 20-40% category II, ≥40% category III.
The analysis showed that so far 12 545 farms could be categorized, and, that in quarter 1-2006, 80% of the farms were in category I, about 15% in category II, and only 5% in category III.
11.1% of all samples were serologically positive. The distributions of the OD%-values differed between the regions of Germany. The North-western parts for Germany showed higher values than other parts of Germany. Higher numbers of animals per area as well as per farm and a higher rate of participation in these intensive agricultural regions are reasons for the higher Salmonella prevalence. Apart from regions, single risk factor analyses showed an increase in prevalence by laboratory, testkit and the slaughterhouse. Due to strong interactions between these factors multivariate statistical models have to be used to describe the real influences on the OD%-values correctly.
The basic epidemiologic report can be used to optimise the salmonella monitoring by evaluating further useful information. Periodical updates of this analysis will help to control the evolution of the Salmonella prevalence in fattening pigs in Germany. Furthermore, these data can be used to define scientific hypotheses and to conduct specific studies.

Introduction

The Salmonella regulations establishment as well as the implementation of the European regulation on zoonoses requires to prepare objective and scientifically valid information about the situation of the Salmonella burden in the German pork production.

Regarding the prevalence of Salmonella in finishing pig herds, a variety of results is currently available in Germany. Some of them are presented in table 1.

Table 1:   Published data of Salmonella prevalence in Germany

Source	Samples (n)	Group	Detection	*Salmonella-Seroprevalence (%)*
Vonnahme et al. (2007)	13 511	Gilts	serological	9.9
Meyer (2004)	2 947	Fattened pigs	serological	7.3
Leyk et al. (2004)	unknown	Fattened pigs	serological	8.0
Ehlers (2003)	51 477 (1999)	Fattened pigs	serological	6.0
	68 761 (2002)	Fattened pigs	serological	11.0
	92 309 (2003)	Fattened pigs	serological	14.2
Protz et al. (1997)	11 942	Fattened pigs	serological	7.7

Since 2002, the QS Qualität und Sicherheit GmbH in Bonn/Germany (QS) has carried out a serological Salmonella monitoring in German finishing pig hers. This monitoring aims at reducing the risk of introducing Salmonella into meat production chain by infected slaughter pigs and to identify and remove infection sources.

To establish the Salmonella burden of the farms, blood serum or meat juice samples are analysed regarding the presence of antibodies against Salmonella. By this, the Salmonella burden of the farm can be estimated simply and cost-effectively. The farms are classified by their percentage of positive samples during the last year in the categories low, middle or high burdened (QS Qualität und Sicherheit GmbH 2006).

Meantime, this monitoring system is the greatest database concerning Salmonella in the German pork production. A basic epidemiological analysis has been carried out including all data from April 1, 2003 until March 31, 2006.

Material and methods

Depending on farm size, every farm has to take up to 60 blood serum or meat juice samples per year. The samples are taken on the farm by a veterinarian (blood serum samples) or at the slaughterhouse (meat juice samples) and sent to a laboratory, where they are analysed serologically. The number of samples per slaughter is given by the Qualiproof® database (Qualitype AG, Dresden/Germany) following a scheme which provides for consistent distribution over the whole year. Four ELISA-tests are registered within the Salmonella monitoring system (Enterisol, Herdcheck, Salmotpye Pigscreen, Salmotype Fleischsaft). For each sample, the laboratories report the antibody activity in OD% (optical density relative to reference) as well as the decision "positive"/"negative" (cut-off: 40 OD%) to QS.

The classification of the farms into the categories I, II, or III is made by their percentage of positive samples per year: category I, if less than 20% of the samples are positive; category II, if 20-40% of the samples are positive; and category III, if more than 40% of the samples are positive. The first classification is given after the delivery of the first 60 samples. The classification is updated quarterly basing on the data of the last 12 months.

IFor farms with few samples or if the last sampling is more than 6 months ago, the classification is not updated, but they are labelled "below quota" and "sampling gaps", respectively.

Up to March, 31, 2006, 1 762 270 valid samples from 15 452 participating farms were entered into the QS database. 203 slaughterhouses as well as 37 laboratories all over Germany were involved in the QS Salmonella monitoring.

To perform regional analyses of the data, regions within Germany were defined regarding numbers of fattening pigs and numbers of farms per area as well as farm sizes within each district. By means of their location, every farm and every sample was assigned to one of the six regions (North-west, North-east, West, South, Cloppenburg/Vechta, the Alps).

The data transmitted were analysed statistically using SAS®, version 9.1 TS level 1M3 (SAS Institute, Inc., Cary, NC, USA). Absolute and relative frequencies of farms or samples with similar attributes were determined. The results of the laboratory examinations in OD% were converted into the logarithmic scale for the statistical analyses. To display the results in tables and figures, these logarithmic values were reconverted and presented as geometric means. Several analyses of variance regarding one or more influence factors were used.

Results

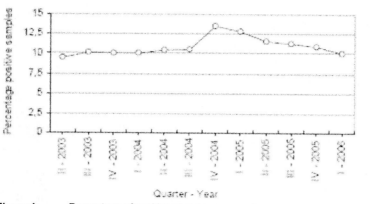

Figure 1: Percentage of positive samples per quarter

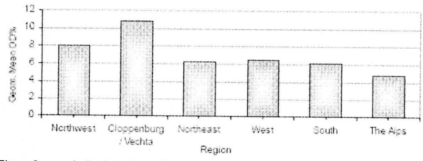

Figure 2: Antibody activity in OD% per region

Table 2: Categorisation of the farms in the quarter I/2006

	Categorisation					Overall
	I	II	III	Below quota	Gaps	
No.	5 875	1 087	407	4 458	538	12 365
%	47.5	8.7	3.2	36.0	4.3	100.0

During the first year, the number of participating farms increased strongly, and it is still increasing. The percentage of positive samples per quarter has small variation (Figure 1), but it peaked in quarter IV-2004. In quarter I-2006, the number of samples investigated was 206 327, the percentage of positive samples was 10.0%. In table 2, the categorisation of the farms in the quarter I-2006 is shown. Most of the farms were category I (47.5%), and only a small fraction (407 farms) belonged to category III. But more than 40% of the farms could not be classified because of missing samples or sampling gaps. 3 090 farms have never been classified, because they did not send the first 60 samples which are necessary for the first classification yet (e.g. participation < 12 months). The results differed between the regions, eminently the Northwest had the highest mean OD%-values of all regions (figure 2). Similar patterns of association are found due to the factors laboratory, testkit, and slaughterhouse (not presented here).

Discussion

The percentage of positive samples evaluated by the QS Salmonella monitoring was slightly higher than prevalence estimates from other studies in Germany (Pretz et al. 1997; Ehlers 1999; Leyk et al. 2004; Meyer 2004; Vonnahme et al. 2007).

The high proportion of farms with few samples reflects that the participation at this monitoring programme still is voluntarily and that participating farms are decorated with the QS certificate. To decrease this percentage of not categorised farms, control measures should be integrated into the monitoring system.

The analysis of the regions showed that mainly the North-western regions including Cloppenburg / Vechta (the districts with the highest density of animals in Germany) had the highest OD%-values as well as the highest percentage of category-III-farms in Germany. To interpret these results, it is necessary to consider that higher numbers of animals per area as well as per farm enhance the spread of pathogens within the animal population, because the transmission pathways are shorter. Furthermore, the rate of participation was higher in these regions than in the other German regions. Possibly, in the North-West of Germany, it is more necessary to participate at quality management measures to stand up to the competition. This might cause that farms participated at the QS Salmonella monitoring which participated not in the other regions.

As many laboratories analyse samples originating from only one or two regions, and as most of the laboratories use only one or two of the registered testkits, the factors testkit, laboratory, and region showed various interactions between each other. Therefore, identifying one of these factors as an initial risk factor is invalid, and additional analyses have to be performed. Specific sub-analyses are necessary to affirm the real influences of these factors on the results of the samples. Scientific studies concerning this problem are in preparation.

The epidemiological report of the QS Salmonella monitoring showed that these data are adequate to improve the quality of the German pork production. Furthermore, they fulfil the criteria of public surveillance, because changes in the Salmonella prevalence can be observed in detail basing on the continuous evaluation of data. The basic analysis of the data can be used to identify gaps of information within the database, to generate recommendations regarding the performance of the monitoring system, and to initiate scientific studies.

Session 2

References

EHLERS, J. 2003. Viel zu tun. *Landwirtschaftsblatt Weser-Ems*, 49, 27.

LEYK, W., JUNGNITZ, S., WALDMANN, K.-H., ORTMANN, R., SELBITZ, H. J., 2004. Schweinesalmonellose. *Nutztierpraxis aktuell*, 10, 20-24.

MEYER, C., 2004. *Qualitative und quantitative Risikofaktoren für die Einschleppung und Verbreitung von Salmonellen in unterschiedliche Produktionsverfahren beim Schwein.* [Thesis] Kiel, Germany: Christian-Albrechts-Universität.

PROTZ, D., STAAK, C., STEINBACH, G., KÄSBOHRER, A., HELMUTH, R., 1997. *Pilot study on the prevalence of Salmonella in slaughter pigs in Germany: IV. Field experiences using Danish serological method for detection.* Proceedings of the 2nd Int. Symp. Epidemiol. Control Salmonella Pork: Copenhagen, Denmark. 251-253.

QS QUALITÄT UND SICHERHEIT GMBH ed., 2006. *Leitfaden Salmonellenmonitoring.* Bonn, Germany: QS Qualität und Sicherheit GmbH.

SAS INSTITUE INC., 2004. *SAS OnlineDoc®*, Version 9.1.3, Cary, NC: SAS Institute Inc.

VONNAHME, J., KREIENBROCK, L., GROßE BEILAGE, E., 2007. Untersuchungen zur saisonalen Variation der *Salmonella*-Seroprävalenzen in Aufzuchtbeständen für Jungsauen. *Berl. Münch. Tierärztl. Wschr.*, 120, 61-66.

Campylobacter in the Pork Food Chain : a quantitative hazard analysis

Minvielle, B. *[1], Magras, C. [2], Laroche, M. [2], Desmonts, M.H. [3], Mircovich C. [1]

[1]Meat Quality and Safety Department, IFIP – French Institute For Pig and Pork Industry, La Motte au Vicomte, BP 35104, 35651 Le Rheu Cedex, France;
[2]Unit of Food Safety, Veterinary School-INRA,Nantes Cedex 3, France ; [3]Aérial, Rue Laurent Fries, BP 40443, 67412 Illkirch, France

*corresponding author: brice.minvielle@ifip.asso.fr ; fax: +33(0)2 99 60 93 55

Abstract

Campylobacter are one of the most frequent causes of bacterial enteritis in industrialized countries and are widespread in food animals. Pigs are known to be largely contaminated in farms, but few data exist about the status of the pork food chain.

The purpose of this study was to quantify the *Campylobacter* contamination of the French pork food chain : prevalence, contamination level, bacterial species in primary production (piglets and fattening pigs when slaughtered), and in first and second transformation process (from carcasses before chilling to deboned meat cuts).

A total of 1286 rectal samples (from 1036 piglets 25 days old, and from 250 fattening pigs) and 3500 meat samples (from 550 carcasses and 300 meat cuts, 2 or 8 samples/carcass and 2 samples/cut, 25 cm^2/sample) were collected from 9 pigs from confined farrow-to-finish farms (3 batches per farm were tested over a year), randomly selected, and five slaughterhouses and six cutting plants.

Bacteriological results showed that 77% of the piglets and 100 % of the fattening pigs were infected with high levels of contamination: 40 000 cfu/g of faeces (50 to 5 10^6 cfu/g). Before chilling, 23% of the carcasses (2 sites) were contaminated with low levels (2.3 cfu/cm^2 as a mean value) with high variations between samples (0.4 to 330 cfu/cm^2), and 9,7% of the carcasses (8 sites) after chilling were contaminated. Primal cuts contamination was lower than 1%, and no *Campylobacter* detected after deboning.

On the basis of multiplex-PCR identification, 0 isolates were identified as *C. jejuni*, 91% (1028/1128) as *C. coli* and 9% (100/1128) campylobacter-like.

From these data we concluded that *Campylobacter coli* carriage is high in pork primary production, but hygiene procedures (GHP, HACCP...) are essential to maintain the low contamination of carcasses and meat cuts.

The link between *Campylobacter* porcine and human strains remains to be established, and their virulence for humans studied.

Introduction

Campylobacter are one of the most frequent causes of bacterial enteritis in industrialized countries (OMS, 2005) and are widespread in food animals. Pigs are known to be largely contaminated in farms (Weijtens, et al., 1997 ; Magras et al., 2004 ; Payot et al., 2004) and *Campylobacter* colonization seems to occur at an early age (Weijtens, et al., 1997 ; Weijtens et al., 1999 ; Magras et al., 2004). Nevertheless, few data exist on the status of the pork food chain and particularly on the contamination level of primary products (animals) and meat (Pearce et al., 2003). The purpose of this study was to quantify the *Campylobacter* contamination of the French pork food chain: prevalence, contamination level, bacterial species in primary production (piglets and fattening pigs when slaughtered), first transformation (carcasses before and after chilling) and second transformation process (deboned meat cuts).

Material and methods

In 9 confined farrow-to-finish farms situated in the western part of France, 1036 rectal samples (5g/sample) from 25 days old piglets were collected. In each farm, 3 batches were tested over a year, and within a batch 10 nursing dams and 4 piglets by litter were randomly selected.

In 5 slaughterhouses, 250 rectal samples (5g/sample) and 500 meat surface samples from corresponding carcass (25 cm^2/sample, two samples/carcass) were collected from 10 visits during 4 months.

In 6 cutting plants, 300 randomly selected refrigerated carcasses were sampled on 8 sites (25 cm^2/site) over a 2 years period. On 75 of these carcasses, 4 primal cuts were sampled before and after deboning.

Preston broth (10 ml) was added to rectal and meat samples for selective enrichment before inoculation on Karmali and Butzler media. Plates were incubated at 42°C in microaerophilic conditions (5% O_2, 10% CO_2, 85% N_2). After 5 days, suspected colonies were confirmed by typical morphology, darting motility and Gram staining tests. Species identification of isolates was conducted by PCR-Multiplex (Van de Giessen et al. 1998).

Results and discussion

On all the 9 farms, pigs were heavily contaminated by *Campylobacter*. *Campylobacter* was recovered from 77 % (95% CI :74-79) of the faecal samples collected from the 1036 piglets. Nevertheless some differences between the 9 farms in the number of pigs tested positive for *Campylobacter* were statistically significant (p < 0.005 SNK test). On the basis of identification with multiplex-PCR, *C.coli* was the only species recovered from the faecal samples.

The high prevalence rates reported in this study agree with other results indicating prevalence of *Campylobacter* of 85 % amongst piglets (Weijtens, et al., 1997 ; Young et al., 2000). This study confirms that piglets are already intestinal carriers of *C. coli* at the age of 25 days on the piggeries. Young et al. (2000) have described a predominant infection of pigs by *C.jejuni* in the USA. In our study and in agreement with Nesbakken et al. (2003), *C.jejuni* had never been isolated from the faecal samples. These findings suggest that the prevalence of the respective species might differ considerably between countries. An other explanation may be the use of different identification procedures.

At slaughter, bacteriological results showed that 100 % of the pigs were infected with high levels of contamination : 40 000 cfu/g of faeces on average (50 to 5 10^6 cfu/g). Before chilling, 23% (95% CI : 18-29) of the carcasses (2 sites) were contaminated with low levels (2.3 cfu/cm^2 as a mean value) with high variations between samples (0.4 to 330 cfu/cm^2).

Our prevalence is in agreement with the 29% observed by Nesbakken et al. (2003), but in other studies hot carcasses contamination varies from 6.7% to 66% (Pearce et al., 2003 ; Sorensen et Christensen, 1997) ; differences in sampling and analytical methods may explain these results.

At cutting plants, 9,7% (95% CI : 6.6-13.4) of the refrigerated carcasses (8 sites) were contaminated. When calculated with the same sites than on the hot carcasses (2 sites), prevalence was 4,4 % (95% CI : 2.2-7.4). After further processing, primal cuts contamination was lower than 1%, *Campylobacter* being recovered from only 2 samples, and no positive sample was found on deboned cuts.

In a study conducted by the USDA on market hogs in 1995 and 1996 (USDA, 1996), *Campylobacter* could be enumerated from 20,5% of chilled carcasses, with an average contamination of 0,1 cfu/cm^2 (0.03 to 46 MNP/cm^2) by destructive method. Zerby et al. (1998) reported a prevalence of 7.9% using a 3 sites swabbing method. Sampling method (destructive or non destructive), carcass sites sampling (pooled or individual samples from, number and and size of sampled sites) and analytical methods (detection level and media) could explain the difference in the observed prevalence.

Some authors have previously reported a diminution of the prevalence during refrigeration process (Pearce et al., 2003 ; Gürtler et al., 2004), and the effect of different chilling systems have been studied (Oosterom et al., 1983 ; Chang et al., 2003 ; Laroche et al., 2004). Complex factors as humidity, ventilation, thermal stress, and oxidation are involved in Campylobacter survival during chilling and could explain these results.

A total of 1128 isolates were obtained from piglets to meat cuts. On the basis of identification with multiplex-PCR, no *C. jejuni* was recovered from the samples. *C. coli* was the only species identified with 91% (1028/1128) of the isolates, 9% (100/1128) being identified as campylobacter-like.

Conclusions

According to these results, *Campylobacter coli* appears to be specific to the French pork chain. Despite an early intestinal carriage at farms and a high faecal contamination levels of pigs at slaughter, carcass contamination is lower than it could be expected at the end of the slaughter line. If 23% of the carcasses are contaminated before chilling, the average contamination level is only about 2 cfu/cm^2, thanks to good hygiene procedures (GHP) during slaughtering, preventing evisceration accident and cross contamination.
After chilling, carcass prevalence droped to 4,4% (2 sites), *Campylobacter* survival being affected by industrial refrigeration conditions. During further processing, from primal cuts to deboned meat, contamination is reduced as reported for other pathogenic bacteria (Salmonella or STEC) due to skin removal and GHP limiting cross contamination.

From these data we concluded that *Campylobacter coli* carriage is high in French pork primary production, but efficient hygiene procedures (GHP, HACCP...) in slaughter and cutting plants, together with *Campylobacter* decrease during refrigeration, contribute to a very low contamination of meat cuts.
The link between *Campylobacter* porcine and human strains remains to be established, and their virulence for humans studied.

Acknowledgements: We would like to thank all farmers and industrial partners who collaborated on this study. This study was supported by grants from the French Ministry of Agriculture (Food General Directorate, AQS 2002/R0206)

References

Chang, VP, Mills, EW, Cutter, CN. 2003 Reduction of bacteria on pork carcasses associated with chilling method. *Journal of Food Protection*, 66(6),1019-1024.
Gürtler, M., Kasimir, S., Alter, K., Fehlhaber, K., 2004. Prevalences of *Yersinia enterocolitica* and *Campylobacter* spp – from piglets to pork. 18th *IPVS Congress*. Hamburg, Germany.
Laroche, M., Kaiser, J., Federighi M., Magras C., 2004. Survie de *Campylobacter jejuni* et *Campylobacter coli* sur des échantillons de couenne et de viande de porc stocké à 4°C. *10ème JSMTV*, 25-26 octobre, Rennes, France.
Magras, C., Garrec, N., Laroche, M., Rossero, A., Mircovich, C., Desmonts, M.H., Federighi, M., 2004. Sources of *Campylobacter* sp. – Contamination of piglet in farrowing units of farrow-to-finish farms : first results. *International Society for Animal Hygien*, France, 11-13 octobre, St Malo, France.
Nesbakken, T., Eckner, K., Hoidal, H. K., and Rotterud, O. J., 2003. Occurrence of *Yersinia enterocolitica* and *Campylobacter* spp. in slaughter pigs and consequences for meat inspection, slaughtering, and dressing procedures. *International Journal of Food Microbiology*, 80(3), 231-240.
OMS 2005. "Campylobacter". http://www.who.int/topics/campylobacter/fr/.
Oosterom, J., De Wilde, G.J.A, De Boer, E., De Blaauw, L. H., Karman, H., 1983. Survival of *Campylobacter jejuni* during poultry processing and pig slaughtering. *Journal of Food Protection*, 46(8), 702-706.
Payot, S., Dridi, S., Laroche, M., Federighi, M., Magras, C., 2004. Prevalence and antimicrobial resistance of *Campylobacter coli* isolated from fattening pigs in France. *Veterinary Microbiology*, 101(2), 91-99.

Pearce, R.A., Wallace, F.M., Call, J.E., Dudley, R.L., Oser, A., Yoder, L., Sheridan, J.J., Luchansky, J.B., 2003. Prevalence of Campylobacter within a swine slaughter and processing facility. *Journal of Food Protection*, 66(9), 1550-1556.

Sorensen, R., Christensen, H., 1997.: Campylobacter in pork – a problem? *Dansk Veterinaertidsskrift*, 80, 452-453.

USDA, 1996. Nationwide Pork Microbiological Baseline Data Collection Programm : Market Hogs. http://www.fsis.usda.gov/OPHS/baseline/contents.htm

Van de Giessen, A. W., Tilburg, J. J., Ritmeester, W. S., Van der Plas, J., 1998. Reduction of campylobacter infections in broiler flocks by application of hygiene measures. *Epidemiology and Infection*, 121(1), 57-66.

Weijtens, M.J.B.M., Reinders, R.D., Urlings, H.A.P., Van der Plas, J., 1999. Campylobacter infections in fattening pigs; excretion pattern and genetic diversity. *Journal of Applied Microbiology*, 86(1), 63-70.

Weijtens, M.J.B.M., Van der Plas, J., Bijker, P.G.H., Urlings, B.A.P., Koster, D., Van Logtestijn, J.G., Huis in't Veld, J.H.J., 1997. The transmission of campylobacter in piggeries; an epidemiological study. *Journal of Applied Microbiology*, 83(6), 693-698.

Young, C. R., Harvey, R., Anderson, R., Nisbet, D., and Stanker, L. H., 2000. Enteric colonisation following natural exposure to Campylobacter in pig. *Research in Veterinary Sciences*. 68(1), 75-78.

Zerby, H. N., Belk, K. E., Sofos, J. N., Schmidt, G. R., Smith, G. C., 1998. *Final report: Microbial sampling of hog carcasses*. Fort Collins : Colorado State University.

Topic n.2

The Enter-Vet Italian surveillance network: data on samples of pig origin from 2002 to 2005

Antonia Ricci (a), Veronica Cibin (a), *Marzia Mancin (b)**, Claudio Minorello (a),Cristina Saccardin(a), Lucia De Castelli (c), Silvia Tagliabue (d), Stefania Scuota (e), Monica Staffolani (e), Stefano Bilei (f), Elisabetta Di Giannatale (g), Maria Rosaria Carullo (h), Elisa Goffredo (i), Chiara Piraino (l), Antonio Vidili (m)

[a] Centro Nazionale di Referenza per le Salmonellosi,
[b] Centro Regionale di Epidemiologia Veterinaria - IZS delle Venezie, Istituto Zooprofilattico Sperimentale delle Venezie, Viale dell'Università 10, 35020 Legnaro (PD), Italy, Ph: 0039 049 8084282 Email: mmancin@regione.veneto.it
[c] IZS del Piemonte, Liguria, Valle d'Aosta,
[d] IZS della Lombardia e dell'Emilia-Romagna,
[e] IZS dell'Umbria e delle Marche,
[f] IZS del Lazio e della Toscana,
[g] IZS dell'Abruzzo e del Molise,
[h] IZS del Mezzogiorno,
[i] IZS della Puglia e Basilicata,
[l] IZS della Sicilia,
[m] IZS della Sardegna

Summary

The Enter-Vet net was established in 2002 in Italy, with the aim of collecting data at national level on Salmonella isolation from samples of animal origin. The Enter-Vet net consists of the laboratories of Istituti Zooprofilattici Sperimentali with the supervision of the National Reference Laboratory for Salmonella (NRL). The laboratories send to the NRL data on salmonella strains typed, together with Enteritidis and Typhimurium strains for phage typing. Data collected are sent to the Italian partner of Enter-Net (the European network for surveillance of human enteric infection) on a regular basis. A national database has been set up with the aim of collecting and organizing data and a report summarising the results is published annually (reports can be downloaded from the web site www.izsvenezie.it).
The data collected during these years allow to evaluate trends in serovars distribution and also trends in antimicrobial sensitivity as required also by the new UE legislation on zoonoses (Directive 99/2003/EC and Regulation 2160/2003/EC).
On average annually (considering the period from 2002 to 2005) the NRL has collected from the Enter-Vet laboratories data on 4572 strains isolated from samples of animal origin collected from animals, food and environment.
In this paper data on *Salmonella* surveillance in pigs and pork products from 2002 to 2005 are presented. Particularly the results of bacteriological investigation, serotyping, phage typing and antimicrobial susceptibility testing, performed on isolates of pig origin, are described and commented.

Introduction

This paper gives details on *Salmonella* strains isolated along the pig production chain by all the Enter-Vet network participants since 2002 to 2005. In these four years data regarding 18,304 swine *Salmonella* isolates were incorporated in the central database (4,550 isolates in 2002, 4,379 in 2003, 4,591 in 2004, 4,784 in 2005). These strains represent the 30% of the total amount of *Salmonella* strains collected by the participants of the network.

Methods

The Salmonella isolates identified by the Enter-vet laboratories were serotyped according to the Kauffman-White scheme and the S. Enteritidis or S. Typhimurium strains were sent to the National Reference Laboratory for Salmonellosis, where these isolates were phagetyped following the method provided by Health Protection Agency, Colindale, London.
Enter-vet participants tested the isolates for antimicrobial susceptibility against a panel of 16 antimicrobials (Na: Nalidixic acid; Am: Ampicillin; Ctx: Cefotaxime; Cip: Ciprofloxacin; C:

Chloramphenicol; Gm: Gentamicin; N: Neomycin; CL: Colistin; K: Kanamicyn; S: Streptomycin; S3: Sulfonamides; Te: Tetracycline; Sxt: Trimethoprim-Sulfamethoxazole; Amc: Amoxicillin-clavulanic acid, Enr: Enrofloxacin, Cf: Cephalothin) .

The data collected by the laboratories involved in the network were incorporated into a central database, periodically pooled and processed by the National Reference Laboratory for Salmonella in order to monitor trends of *Salmonella* and recognise unusual episodes.

The quality of the data is guaranteed by regular interlaboratory comparison studies within Enter-Vet participants.

Results

In figure 1 the distribution of swine samples considered in this paper is presented. The great majority of *Salmonella* strains were collected from foodstuffs (various types of fresh pig meat and pork products) and from animals (mainly samples of faeces, organs and tissues).

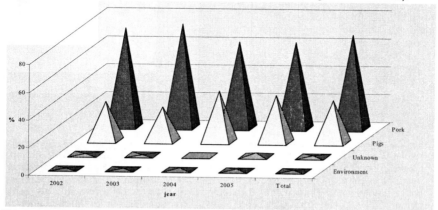

Figure 1 Distribution of samples of swine origin collected for the detection of *Salmonella* spp. by the Enter-Vet network from 2002 to 2005.

Serotyping

S. Typhimurium has been the predominant serovar isolated in pigs and pork products since 2002, followed by S. Derby and the monophasic strain 4,5:I:-. A clear tendency was not discernable in the trend of serotypes, except for the last year (2005) in which we noted a clear fall in the isolates of S. Typhimurium and an increase of the monophasic strains 4,5:I:- (figure 2).

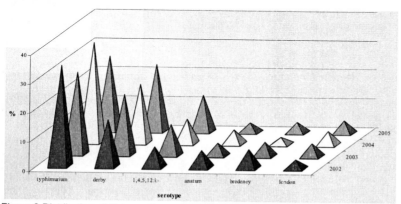

Figure 2 Distribution of *Salmonella* serovars of swine origin collected by the Enter-Vet network from 2002 to 2005.

Phage typing
Excluding nontypeable (NT) and RDNC isolates, the most frequent S. Typhimurium phage types in pigs and pork products were DT104, DT208, DT12 (figure 3). DT104 remained the dominating phagetype for the entire monitored period, even if its trend has not been constant (DT104 represented respectively 17.98%, 13.31%, 17.62%, 10.61% and 14.85% of S. Typhimurium strains collected in 2002, 2003, 2004 and 2005). As regards DT208, a high prevalence was detected in 2002, but a stead decrease of this phage type has been detected in the following years. In the fist year of the monitored period DT208 represented the 12.72% of the S. Typhimurium isolates while in the subsequent years the prevalence of this phagetype dropped (3.24% -2003-; 3.47% -2004-; 5.76% -2005-).

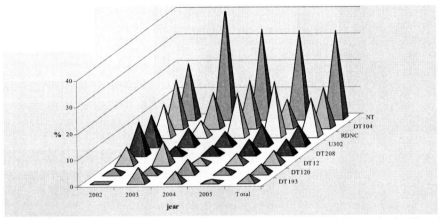

Figure 3 Distribution of phage types of S. Typhimurium of swine origin collected by the Enter-Vet network from 2002 to 2005.

Antimicrobial susceptibility tests
Data on the occurrence of antimicrobial resistance in swine *Salmonella* strains isolated by the Enter-Vet laboratories are given in table 1.

Jear	Na	Am	Ctx	Cip	C	Gm	N	Col	K	S	S3	Te	Sxt	Amc	Enr	Cf
2002	6,49	42,74	0,40	0,27	18,75	1,86	7,85	0,70	8,28	51,00	67,68	71,13	18,06	4,52	0,56	2,95
2003	7,45	36,75	0,76	0,00	13,46	2,43	7,77	1,31	11,07	43,66	54,27	58,43	16,95	2,62	0,19	1,33
2004	7,65	36,32	0,29	0,15	13,84	2,50	7,82	6,47	7,06	50,00	67,50	64,06	18,14	4,78	0,00	2,72
2005	11,21	32,45	3,24	0,15	15,58	4,27	13,49	4,19	8,70	44,33	51,11	62,39	23,86	6,06	0,30	3,41

Table 1 **Antimicrobial resistance profiles of swine *Salmonella* strains collected by the Enter-Vet network from 2002 to 2005.**

Resistance was widespread but a clear trend was not completely described. However, a continuous increase in the level of resistance to Nalidixic acid, Cefotaxime, Gentamicin, Neomycin and Trimethoprim-Sulfamethoxazole has been reported, whereas for Ampicillin, Streptomycin, Sulfonamides and Tetracycline prevalence of resistant isolates decreased progressively.
The most common pattern of antibiotic resistance was AmSS3Te -Ampicillin-Streptomycin-Sulfonamides- Tetracycline- (that accounted respectively for the 25% of Salmonella strains collected in 2002 and for the 16% of isolates tested in 2005), followed by the pattern AmCSS3Te (Ampicillin- Chloramphenicol- Streptomycin- Sulfonamides- Tetracycline, characterizing multidrug resistant strains of DT 104.
As showed in figure 4, the great majority of the multiresistant strains collected showed resistance to four or five antimicrobials. Considering the trend of antimicrobial resistance in swine isolates, during the 4-years monitored, a decrease in the prevalence of multiresitant strains has been

reported. The prevalence of isolates resistant to four or more antimicrobials was 47.9%, 40.8%, 41.1%, 39.7% and 42.4% respectively in 2002, 2003, 2004 and 2005. In addition to the increase of strains resistant to less than 4 agents (52% in 2002, 60% in 2005), also the growth of the number of isolates sensible to all antimicrobial agents has been reported in the four years (18% in 2002, 27% in 2005). However, even if the number of multiresistant strains collected has reduced steadily, an increase of isolates resistant to 6, 7 and also 8 different agents has been noted in the four years of the monitoring.

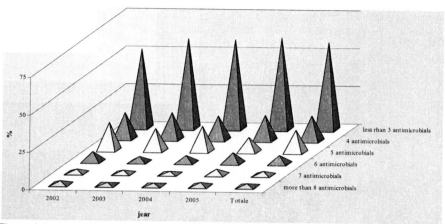

Figure 4 Antimicrobial resistance profiles of swine *Salmonella* strains collected by the Enter-Vet network from 2002 to 2005. Proportions of isolates resistant to less than three agents, resistant to four, five, six, seven or more than 8 different agents.

Conclusion

Salmonella strains of swine origin collected by Enter-Vet laboratories since 2002 to 2005 were represented mainly by foodstuffs (raw meat and pork products). During the 4 years considered in the paper, the most prevalent serotype identified in the samples of swine origin was *S.* Typhimurium followed by *S.* Derby. A great number of S. Typhimurium strains were DT104 presenting the characteristic profile of pentaresistance (AmCSS3Te). Multi-drug resistance was observed in a high percentage of the isolates and the dominant profile of resistance resulted to be AmSS3Te.

Salmonella enterica prevalence and serotype distribution in swine at slaughter

Rostagno, M.H.*[1], Hurd, H.S.[2], McKean, J.D.[2]

[1]USDA, ARS, Livestock Behavior Research Unit, West Lafayette, IN 47907, USA.
[2]Iowa State University, College of Veterinary Medicine, Ames, IA 50011, USA.

*corresponding author: rostagno@purdue.edu

Abstract

The objective of this cross-sectional study was to analyze data available from multiple studies conducted by our research team estimating the prevalence of *S. enterica*, and the serotype distribution in swine at slaughter, based on different sample types. A total of 1,110 pigs from three large capacity abattoirs located in the Midwestern U.S. were individually sampled at slaughter. Individually paired samples collected included: cecal contents and ileocecal lymph nodes. Samples were collected on multiple occasions in all three abattoirs, transported to the laboratory, and processed for the isolation and identification of *S. enterica*. The overall prevalence of *S. enterica*, based on cecal contents, mesenteric lymph nodes, and any of the samples (i.e., cecal contents and/or mesenteric lymph nodes) was 54.7%, 27.9%, and 62.6%, respectively. There was a significant difference (*P*<0.05) between prevalence estimates based on cecal contents and mesenteric lymph node samples in all three abattoirs, and overall. A variety of *S. enterica* serotypes was isolated in all abattoirs. The average number of serotypes isolated per group was 3.48. This study confirms that the *S. enterica* prevalence at slaughter in swine is high, requiring attention due to the associated risk of contamination of the abattoir environment. Moreover, our results demonstrate the common occurrence of a high diversity of serotypes in swine at slaughter. This study also shows that both cecal contents and mesenteric lymph nodes should be considered for a better estimate of *S. enterica* prevalence at slaughter.

Introduction

Salmonella enterica is recognized as an important foodborne pathogen with multiple potential sources. Although *S. enterica* constitutes a very heterogeneous group of bacteria, including more than 2,400 serotypes, only a limited number of serotypes are responsible for most outbreaks. Subclinical *Salmonella* infections in pigs constitute an important food safety problem as carrier animals pose a risk for pork product contamination. A variety of *S. enterica* serotypes have been recovered from pigs on-farm and at slaughter, with a much higher diversity of serotypes being found at slaughter. However, the current knowledge on the ecology of *S. enterica* serotypes, as well as the effect of different sample types on their frequency distributions is very limited. Unfortunately, the required large scale studies to investigate serotype ecology are cost prohibitive, and therefore, rarely conducted. With this limitation in mind, we decided to analyze data available from two previous studies (Rostagno et al.,2003; Hurd et al.,2005) conducted by our research team to determine the prevalence and distribution of *S. enterica* serotypes in swine at slaughter, based on different sample types.

Materials and Methods

A total of 1,110 pigs from three large capacity abattoirs (A, B, and C) located in the Midwestern U.S. were included in this study. Individually paired samples (cecal contents and mesenteric lymph nodes) were collected in multiple occasions in all three abattoirs, transported to the laboratory, and processed for the isolation and identification of *S. enterica* (Rostagno et al.,2003; Hurd et al.,2005). In each of abattoirs A and B, 12 groups of pigs were sampled in 3 different occasions, whereas in abattoir C, 21 groups were sampled in 7 different occasions. Results were organized in an electronic spreadsheet, and proportions were compared by Chi-square (*P*<0.05).

Results

The overall prevalence of *S. enterica*, based on cecal contents (CC), mesenteric lymph node (MLN), and any of the samples (CC and/or MLN) was 54.7%, 27.9%, and 62.6%, respectively. There was a significant difference ($P<0.05$) between prevalence estimates based on CC and MLN samples in all three abattoirs, and overall. The prevalence of *S. enterica*, based on any of the samples collected was: 57.1% in abattoir A, 48.3% in abattoir B, and 70.2% in abattoir C. All 45 groups of pigs sampled were positive for *S. enterica*. A variety of *S. enterica* serotypes was isolated in all abattoirs (16 in abattoir A, 16 in abattoir B, 9 in abattoir C, and 21 overall). The number of serotypes isolated from each group varied with an average of 3.48 serotypes per group (minimum of 1 and maximum of 6 serotypes per group). Although *S. enterica* serotype Typhimurium was the most frequently isolated (numerically), there was no statistical difference in comparison to the isolation frequency of serotype Derby (27% versus 21.8%, $P>0.05$). Other serotypes were isolated at a significantly ($P<0.05$) lower rate (Table 1).

Table 1. *Salmonella enterica* serotype distribution in swine at slaughter

Serotype	Cecal contents (CC)	Mesenteric lymph node (MLN)	Any sample (CC and/or MLN)
Typhimurium	19.8%	13.8%	27%
Derby	17.1%	7.8%	21.8%
Anatum	5.9%	1.5%	7.2%
Heidelberg	4.7%	2.5%	5.7%
Saint Paul	2.7%	1.6%	2.9%
Infantis	1.7%	0.2%	1.9%
Senftenberg	0.7%	0%	0.7%
Agona	0.4%	0.1%	0.5%
Newport	0.2%	0.3%	0.5%
Schwarzengrund	0.4%	0%	0.4%
Choleraesuis	0%	0.3%	0.3%
Ohio	0.2%	0%	0.2%
Mbandaka	0.2%	0%	0.2%
Hartford	0.1%	0.2%	0.2%
Worthington	0.1%	0.1%	0.2%
Muenchen	0%	0.2%	0.2%
Montivideo	0.1%	0%	0.1%
Babelsberg	0.1%	0%	0.1%
Molade	0%	0.1%	0.1%
Bovis-morbificans	0.1%	0%	0.1%
Cerro	0.1%	0%	0.1%
Untypable	0.5%	0.3%	0.7%

Discussion

This study shows that both cecal contents and mesenteric lymph node samples should be considered for a better estimate of *S. enterica* prevalence at slaughter. Our results corroborate a previous study conducted by our research team (Hurd et al.,2004) demonstrating that different sample types generate different prevalence estimates on-farm and at slaughter. Similarly, Swanenburg et al.(2001), studying *Salmonella* in slaughter pigs, also reported significant difference in the prevalence estimates based on different sample types. Davies et al.(2005) also reported similar results when analyzing the differential translocation of *S. enterica* serotypes Derby and Typhimurium to mesenteric lymph nodes in swine. This study shows that results of *S. enterica* isolation from pigs should always be carefully interpreted, with careful attention to the type of sample that has been collected. However, a critical question arises: Why are the results affected by the different sample types? We hypothesize that the combination of the invasiveness of the serotype(s) infecting the pigs prior to slaughter, and the period of time elapsed between infection and sampling will determine the prevalence estimate based on mesenteric lymph nodes. Probably, mesenteric lymph node samples reflect on-farm infections (as suggested by Bahnson et al.,2005) and, in the case of more invasive serotypes, rapid infections acquired from pre-slaughter contaminated environments (transport trailers and abattoir holding pens). In the other hand, cecal content samples reflect (mostly) rapid infections or contaminations of the gastrointestinal tract (i.e., passage of bacteria with no colonization or infection) after pigs leave the farm. However, further knowledge on the pathogenesis of *S. enterica* serotypes infection will allow refinement of this hypothesis.

Our results regarding serotype distribution are in agreement with a report from the USDA (Schlosser et al.,2000) on the *S. enterica* serotypes isolated from carcasses and ground pork. According to the report, a variety of serotypes was also commonly found, and *S. enterica* serotype Typhimurium was not the most common serotype isolated. Curiously, our results contrast with the reported distribution of *S. enterica* serotypes in pigs from Denmark (Nielsen et al.,2005) and the Netherlands (Van Duijkeren et al.,2002), where *S. enterica* serotype Typhimurium has been by far the most common serotype isolated with very low serotype diversity. However, it is difficult to compare results as the number of variables to be considered is overwhelming.

Conclusions

This study confirms that the *S. enterica* prevalence at slaughter in swine is frequently high requiring attention due to the associated risk of contamination of the abattoir environment, and consequently, of pork products. Moreover, our results demonstrate the common occurrence of a high diversity of serotypes in swine at slaughter. This study also shows that both cecal contents and mesenteric lymph nodes should be considered for a better estimate of *S. enterica* prevalence at slaughter.

References

BAHNSON, P.B., et al. 2005. Associations between on-farm and slaughter plant detection of *Salmonella* in market-weight pigs. *Journal of Food Protection*, 68:246-250.

DAVIES, P., et al. 2005. Differential translocation of *Salmonella* serovars to mesenteric lymph nodes of pigs. *In: Proceedings of the 6th International Symposium on the Epidemiology and Control of Foodborne Pathogens in Pork*; p.58-60.

HURD, H.S., et al. 2005. Variable abattoir conditions affect *Salmonella enterica* prevalence and meat quality in swine and pork. *Foodborne Pathogens Diseases*, 2:77-81.

HURD,H.S., et al. 2004. Estimation of the *Salmonella enterica* prevalence in finishing swine. *Epidemiology and Infection*, 132:127-135.

NIELSEN, B., et al. 2005. *Salmonella* serotype distribution in Danish swine herds and pork, 1998-2004. *In: Proceedings of the 6th International Symposium on the Epidemiology and Control of Foodborne Pathogens in Pork*; p.76-79.

ROSTAGNO, M.H., et al. 2003. Preslaughter holding environment in pork plants is highly contaminated with *Salmonella enterica*. *Applied and Environmental Microbiology*, 69:4489-4494.

SCHLOSSER, W., et al. 2000. Analysis of *Salmonella* serotypes from selected carcasses and raw ground products sampled prior to implementation of the pathogen reduction; Hazard Analysis and Critical Control Point Final Rule in the US. *International Journal of Food Microbiology*, 58:107-111.

SWANENBURG,M., et al. 2001. *Salmonella* in slaughter pigs: prevalence, serotypes and critical control points during slaughter in two slaughterhouses. *International Journal of Food Microbiology*, 70:243-254.

VAN DUIJKEREN, E., et al. 2002. Serotype and phage type distribution of *Salmonella* strains isolated from humans, cattle, pigs, and chicken in the Netherlands from 1984 to 2001. *Journal of Clinical Microbiology*, 40:3980-3985.

Session 2

Salmonella prevalence in "first pull" versus "close out" market pigs

Rostagno, M.H.*[1], Hurd, H.S.[2], McKean, J.D.[2]

[1]USDA, ARS, Livestock Behavior Research Unit, West Lafayette, IN 47907, USA.
[2]Iowa State University, College of Veterinary Medicine, Ames, IA 50011, USA.
*corresponding author: rostagno@purdue.edu

Abstract

Identifying potential risk factors to direct intervention strategies is fundamental to reduce the risk of pork contamination with *Salmonella*. This study was designed to compare the *Salmonella* prevalence in the first group of pigs selected for slaughter ("First pull") versus the last group of pigs selected for slaughter ("Close out") from typical commercial finishing barns containing 800 - 1,000 animals. Nine finishing barns from two production sites were included in the study (4 paired samplings from site A, and 5 paired samplings from site B). Each paired sampling consisted in matched groups of pigs from the same barn as the "first pull" and the "close out" with a 4-week interval between groups. From each group, individual fecal samples (n = 45) and meat samples (n = 50) were collected, on-farm and at slaughter, respectively. In the laboratory, fecal samples were selectively enriched, and analyzed for the presence of *Salmonella* by a commercially available antigen-capture ELISA. Meat samples were kept frozen, and thawed for processing. The resulting liquid ("meat juice") was collected and analyzed for the presence of antibodies against *Salmonella* by a commercially available ELISA. All lots of pigs housed in the finishing barns studied were *Salmonella*-positive, based on sampling from "first pull" and "close out". In 7/9 (77.8%) of the studied barns, an increase in *Salmonella* prevalence was observed, based on both bacteriologic and serologic analysis. Overall, there was an increase of 9.3% ($P<0.05$) in bacteriologic prevalence, and 25.1% ($P<0.05$) in serologic prevalence from "first pull" to "close out" groups. This study demonstrates that a significant increase of *Salmonella* prevalence occurs between the first and the last group of pigs from a finishing barn shipped to slaughter. In conclusion, "close out" groups of finishing pigs constitute a higher risk for *Salmonella* contamination of pork products.

Introduction

Subclinical *Salmonella* infections in pigs constitute an important food safety problem as carrier animals pose a risk for pork products contamination. Determining the *Salmonella* status of pig herds as part of a monitoring and intervention program to reduce the risk of pork contamination is fundamental. However, potential risk factors should first be identified and quantified. Although intervention strategies to assure food safety can be applied at all levels of the pork production chain, increased emphasis has been placed on the potential reduction of meat contamination by reducing contaminants at the pre-harvest level (i.e., on-farm). Theoretically, reducing the number of animals infected at the farm can decrease contamination of final products. However, the on-farm ecology and epidemiology of *Salmonella* is still not fully understood. A variety of potential risk factors have been identified over the last years, including; drinker type, feed form, hygiene and biosecurity measures, and others (Lo fo wong et al.,2004; Bahnson et al.,2006).

Due to the variation in body weight within groups of finishing pigs, it is common practice in many large swine production operations to remove animals for market over a period of time. Conventionally, the heaviest pigs would be removed first ("first pull") thus allowing more time for the lighter pigs to reach an acceptable market weight ("close out"). Research has shown that by removing up to 50% of the heaviest pigs from a pen, growth performance of the remaining animals is increased (Bates and Newcomb, 1997; Woodworth et al.,2000; DeDecker et al.,2006). Removing pigs from a pen results in an increase in floor and feeder space for the remaining animals, but also changes the social dynamics of the group. There is some concern that this marketing strategy may serve as a potential stressor to the remaining animals causing the reactivation of dormant infections and/or increased predisposition to new infections. Therefore, this study was designed to compare the *Salmonella enterica* prevalence in the first group of pigs selected for slaughter (i.e., "First-pull") versus the last group of pigs selected for slaughter (i.e., "Close-out"), under commercial conditions.

Materials and Methods

Two finishing production sites previously identified as being *Salmonella*-positive were visited multiple times to conduct group-paired samplings (4 paired samplings from one site, and 5 paired samplings from another site). Each paired sampling consisted in matched groups of pigs from the same barn as the "first-pull" (i.e., the first group of pigs selected to slaughter) and the "close-out" (i.e., the last group of pigs selected to slaughter). Each sampling consisted of 45 individual fecal samples collected directly from the rectum (2-3 pigs were sampled per pen, allowing the sampling of at least 10 different pens within a building group). At the abattoir, the same groups of pigs were followed and individual meat samples (diaphragm, 40-70g) were collected (n=50 samples per group). Each fecal sample (10g) was sequentially enriched in Tetrathionate and Rappaport-Vassiliadis broths. An aliquot (1mL) of the last enrichment was analyzed for the presence of *Salmonella* using a commercially available antigen-capture ELISA (Assurance® Gold EIA *Salmonella*, Biocontrol), previously evaluated in our laboratory (Rostagno et al.,2001). Meat samples were kept frozen until processed. Samples were then thawed, and the resulting fluid ("meat juice") was collected for each sample (1mL) and analyzed for the presence of anti-*Salmonella* antibodies using a commercially available indirect ELISA (HerdChek® Swine *Salmonella*, IDEXX), based on lipopolysaccharide antigens (Camitz et al.,2001). The cut-off value (S/P ratio) applied was 0.25. *Salmonella* bacteriologic and serologic prevalence and respective 95% confidence interval were estimated for each group sampled, and overall. Proportions were compared by Chi-square test, and the statistical significance level applied for inferences was $P<0.05$.

Results

All lots of pigs housed in the finishing barns studied were *Salmonella*-positive, based on sampling from "first pull" and "close out", both bacteriologically and serologically. Based on fecal samples, the overall *Salmonella* prevalence estimates were 10.6% (95% C.I. 6.03% − 15.2%) and 19.8% (95% C.I. 11.3% - 28.2%) for "first pull" and "close out" groups, respectively. Based on "meat juice" samples, the prevalence estimates were 18.9% (95% C.I. 12.7% - 25.1%) and 50.2% (95% C.I. 26.8% - 73.6%) for "first pull" and "close out" groups, respectively.

In 7/9 (77.8%) of the finishing lots studied, an increase in *Salmonella* prevalence was observed, based on both bacteriologic and serologic analysis. Overall, there was an increase of 9.2% ($P<0.05$) in bacteriologic prevalence, and 31.3% ($P<0.05$) in serologic prevalence from "first pull" to "close out" groups. A bacteriologic prevalence increase from "first pull" to "close out" occurred in 7/9 (77.8%), whereas in only 1 group (11.1%) the prevalence decreased, and in 1 group (11.1%) the prevalence was the same for both groups. A serologic prevalence increase from "first pull" to "close out" occurred in 7/9 (77.8%), whereas in 2 groups (22.2%) the prevalence decreased.

Discussion

Potential explanations for the increase in *Salmonella* prevalence between "first pulls" and "close outs" are; 1) the reactivation of dormant/latent infections and subsequent increased transmission, due to the stress caused by the social disruption consequent to the removal of the heaviest pigs from the pens, and 2) mechanical transmission (i.e., dissemination or spread) of the bacteria by the personnel entering the barns to remove the heaviest pigs from the pens. Although no definitive evidence exists, it may also be possible that a concentration of infected animals may have occurred, if the growth performance of *Salmonella*-infected pigs was detrimentally affected by the bacteria. However, based on the serological increase in prevalence observed, it is more likely that new infections occurred due to the transmission of the bacteria between the pigs and/or through the personnel involved in the selection and removal of the heaviest pigs.

Conclusions

Our study demonstrates that a significant increase of *Salmonella* prevalence occurs between the first and the last group of pigs from a finishing barn shipped to slaughter when applying a split marketing strategy. Therefore, it is concluded that "close out" groups of finishing (or market) pigs constitute a higher risk for *Salmonella* contamination of pork products.

References

BAHNSON, P.B., et al. 2006. Herd-level risk factors for *Salmonella enterica* subsp. *enterica* in U.S. market pigs. *Preventive Veterinary Medicine,* 76:249-262.

BATES, R.O., NEWCOMB, M.D. 1997. Removal of market ready pen mates improved growth rate of remaining pigs. *Journal of Animal Science,* 75(Suppl 1):441.

CAMITZ, A., et al. 2001. HerdChek *Salmonella* antibody ELISA for serological monitoring of *Salmonella* infection in swine. In: *Proceedings of the 4th International Symposium on the Epidemiology and Control of Foodborne Pathogens in Pork*; p.505-508.

DEDECKER, J.M., et al. 2005. Effects of proportion of pigs removed from a group and subsequent floor space on growth performance of finishing pigs. *Journal of Animal Science,* 83:449-454.

LO FO WONG, D., et al. 2004. Herd-level risk factors for subclinical *Salmonella* infection in European finshing-pig herds. *Preventive Veterinary Medicine,* 62:253-266.

ROSTAGNO, M.H., et al. 2001. Comparative evaluation of *Salmonella* detection assays in swine feces. In: *Proceedings of the 4th International Symposium on the Epidemiology and Control of Foodborne Pathogens in Pork*; p.531-533.

WOODWORTH, J.C., et al. 2000. Examination of the interactive effects of stocking density and marketing strategies in a commercial production environment. *Journal of Animal Science,* 78(Suppl 2):56.

Epidemiology of *Salmonella* infections in sow herds in the Czech Republic

Sisak, F.*[1], Havlickova, H.[1], Kolackova, R.[2], Karpiskova, I.[2]

[1]Veterinary Research Institute, Hudcova 70, 621 00, Brno, Czech Republic
[2]National Institute of Public Health, Centre for the Hygiene of Food Chains, Palackého 1-3, 612 42, Brno, Czech Republic
*corresponding autor: sisak@vri.cz

Abstract

Salmonella prevalence was assessed in six herds of sows by serological ELISA test and faecal culture. Blood and faecal samples were collected, prior to weaning of piglets, from 45 sows housed in separated pens in each group of a herd. Increased levels of specific antibodies were found in all six herds. Serologically positive samples averaged 41.85%. Faecal shedding of *Salmonella* from the carriers was found in four herds with the average of 7.8%. *Salmonella* prevalence, as assessed by serological testing and faecal culture, was 17.8% and 13.3% in herd I, 20.0% and 4.4% in herd II, 40.0% and 20.0% in herd III, 53.3% and 0% in herd IV, 86.7% and 8.9% in herd V, and 30.3% and 0% in herd VI. A total of 21 *Salmonella* spp. strains were isolated which were classified into the serotype Derby (n=17), London (n=2), Bredeney (n=1), and Goldcoast (n=1). All isolates were sensitive to the antibiotics used. No correlation was found between *Salmonella* seroprevalence in ELISA test and positive faecal culture in the examined herds of sows. The result of faecal culture was negative in two sow herds with high seroprevalence. Serological ELISA test is an efficient diagnostic tool for *Salmonella* detection in suspected herds. The results of our study showed association between the incidence of *S.* Derby in sows and slaughtered fattening pigs originated from the same farrow–to–finish herds.

Introduction

Swine herds are sources of human salmonellosis which is a very frequent alimentary disease in many countries. As a public health concern and food safety throughout the whole production chain, the European Commission has issued new legislations on monitoring and control of zoonoses and their causative agents (Anonymous, 2003). *Salmonella* infections in pigs are in most European countries including the Czech Republic predominantly caused by the serotype Typhimurium and Derby and occur very frequently in an asymptomatic form. No clinical symptoms can be seen in pigs following the infection; however, some of the pigs become permanent *Salmonella* carriers. Thus, a latent infection exists in a herd, which is difficult to detect due to intermittent *Salmonella* shedding via faeces. Therefore serological diagnosis of *Salmonella* infections in pigs has been introduced, using ELISA test (Nielsen et al., 1995) whose sensitivity and specificity was harmonised with the international standards (Van der Heijden, 2001). The carriers play an import role in *Salmonella* transmission. These are especially sows of the basic (breeding) herd or newly purchased animals which persistently shed *Salmonella* in faeces and thus keep the infection in a herd (Kranker et al., 2001). The objective of our study was to assess *Salmonella* prevalence by serological ELISA test and faecal culture in sow herds and evaluate the risk of Salmonella transmission to progeny.

Material and methods

Six herds of sows housed in the farrowing units were examined by serological ELISA test and cultivation over the period October 2005 – June 2006. *Salmonellas* were isolated from caecum contents and mesenteric lymph nodes (MLN) in slaughtered fattening pigs from four farrow-to-finish herds. *S.* Typhimurium, *S.* Derby and *S.* Infantis were isolated from sows of herd I., *S.* Typhimurium and *S.* Derby were isolated from herd II, III and IV. In these herds *Salmonella* seroprevalence ranged from 20 to 40%. Forty-five specimens of blood and faeces were collected from each farrowing unit prior to weaning of piglets. Serum samples were examined by the

Svanovir® *Salmonella* Covalent Mix-ELISA (Svanova, Sweden) kit and evaluated according to the manufacturer's instructions. Fresh faecal samles of 10g were collected from floor in individual pens and cultured using the method EN ISO 6579:2002 for *Salmonella* isolation. The isolated strains were typed with agglutination O and H antisera and classified into serotypes according to the Kaufmann-White scheme. After serotyping, the isolated strains were examined by the disc diffusion method (NCCLS, 2002) for sensitivity to antibiotics. The following antibiotics were used: Ampicillin (AMP 10 µg), Amoxycillin/Clavulanic acid (AMC 30 µg), Apramycin (APR 15 µg), Colistin (CT 10 µg), Sulphamethoxazole/Trimethoprim (SXT 25µg), Cefotaxime (CTX 30 µg), Enrofloxacin (ENR 5 µg), Gentamicin (CN 10 µg), Neomycin (N 30 µg), Streptomycin (S 10 µg), Tetracycline (TE 30 µg), Chloramphenicol (C 30 µg), Nalidixic acid (NA 30 µg), Sulfisoxazole (Su 300 µg), Kanamycin (K 30 µg).

Results

Salmonella status of sow herds estimated by serology and culture is provided in Table 1. Samples of blood and faeces taken from a total of 270 sow originated from six farrow-to-finish herds were examined. Increased antibody levels were detected in all six herds. The average *Salmonella* seroprevalence was 41.85%. *Salmonella* excretion in faeces of carriers was demonstrated in four herds. The percentage of ELISA and culture positive faecal samples was 17.8% and 13.3% in herd I, 20.0% and 4.4% in herd II, 40.0% and 20.0% in herd III, 53.3% and 0% in herd IV, 86.7% and 8.9% in herd V, and 30.3% and 0% in herd VI. A total of 21 *Salmonella* spp. strains were isolated. The most frequent serotype was Derby (n=17) which was isolated from herd I (n=2), II (n=2), III (n=9) and V (n=2). The serotype London (n=2) was only isolated from herd I. In herd V, serotypes Bredeney (n=1) and Goldcoast (n=1) were further isolated. All the isolates were sensitive to the antibiotics used (not shown).

Tab.1 *Salmonella* status in sow herds estimated by serology and culture

Herd	ELISA Number of positive/Number of examined samples*	Culture	*Salmonella* serotypes
I	8/45 (17.8 %)	6/45 (13.3 %)	Derby 4x, London 2x
II	9/45 (20.0 %)	2/45 (4.4 %)	Derby 2x
III	18/45 (40.0 %)	9/45 (20.0 %)	Derby 9x
IV	24/45 (53.3 %)	0/45 (0 %)	0
V	39/45 (86.7 %)	4/45 (8.9 %)	Derby 2x, Bredeney 1x, Goldcoast 1x
VI	15/45 (33.3 %)	0/45 (0 %)	0
Total	113/270 (41.9 %)	21/270 (7.8 %)	

*samples of blood and faeces

Figure 1 presents the comparison of *Salmonella* prevalence in sow herds as determined by serological ELISA test and faecal culture. No correlation was found between *Salmonella* seroprevalence tested by ELISA and positive faecal culture in sow herds under study. Negative faecal culture was found in herd IV and VI with high seroprevalence (53.3% and 30.3%).

Fig. 1 *Salmonella* prevalence in sow herds determined by serological ELISA test and faecal culture

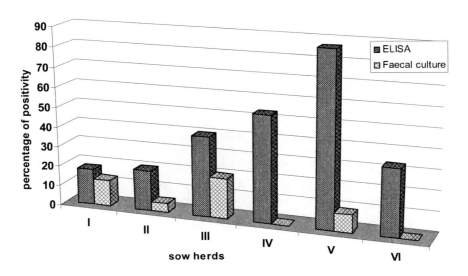

Discussion

The results of our study confirmed the data from other countries showing that sows are an important link in the epidemiology of *Salmonella* infections in farrow-to-finish herds of swine. Sows, as *salmonella* carriers, are the source of infection for piglets and can contaminate the stable environment. Through weaned piglets from infected litters, *Salmonellas* are transmitted to fattening pigs in the production chain, which may further cause contamination of swine carcasses and the slaughter line (Kranker et al., 2003; Beloeil et al., 2004; Nollet et al., 2005). High *Salmonella* prevalence demonstrated in our study by serological ELISA test and faecal culture made evidence of a widespread infection in six herds under study. No correlation was found in our study between *Salmonella* seroprevalence in ELISA test and positive faecal culture (Funk et al., 2005). In herd I, II, III and V seroprevalence was markedly higher compared to positive faecal culture. In spite of a high seroprevalence (53.3% and 30.3%) found in herd IV and VI, no *Salmonellas* were isolated from faecal samples. We assume the result of faecal culture to be false negative, because *S.* Derby and *S.* Typhimurium were isolated from slaughtered fattening pigs originated from herd IV. The results of our study indicate an indirect association between *S.* Derby isolation from sows and the slaughtered fattening pigs in identical farrow-to-finish swine herds. The results further show that efficient control of *Salmonella* infections in farrow-to-finish herds of swine should start on sow level.

Conclusions

High *Salmonella* prevalence in the investigated sow herds as determined by serological ELISA test and faecal culture gave evidence of a widespread infection within the sow herds. No correlation was found between *Salmonella* seroprevalence in ELISA test and faecal culture. Active shedders of the prevalent *Salmonella* serotype Derby in infected sow herds presented a high risk of transmission of the infection to piglets. Based on isolation of the above serotype from sows and slaughtered fattening pigs originated from the same farrow-to-finish herds, indirect transmission of the infection is suggested. Intensive *Salmonella* surveillance using serology and culture methods is crucial to effective *Salmonella* control in farrow-to-finish swine herds.

Acknowledgement

This study was supported by the Ministry of Education (Grant No. OC.NA001) and Ministry of Agriculture of the Czech Republic (Grant No. MZE0002716201).

References

ANONYMOUS, 2003. Directive 2003/99/EC of the European Parliament and of the Council of November 2003 on the monitoring of zoonoses and zoonotic agents, amending Council Decision 90/424/EEC and repealing Council Directive 92/117/EEC. Official Journal of the European Union, L325 31-40.

BELOEIL, P.A., FRAVALO, P., FABLET, C., JOLLY, J.P., EVENO, E., HASCOET, Y., CHAUVIN, C., SALVAT, G., MADEC, F., 2004. Risk factors for Salmonella enterica subsp. enterica shedding by market-age pigs in French farrow-to-finish herds. Prev Vet Med, 63 (1-2), 103-120.

FUNK, J.A., HARRIS, I.T., DAVIES, P.R., 2005. Comparison of fecal culture and Danish Mix-ELISA for determination of Salmonella enterica subsp. enterica prevalence in growing swine. Vet Microbiol, 107 (1-2), 115-126.

KRANKER, S., ALBAN, L., BOES, J., DAHL, J., 2003. Longitudinal study of Salmonella enterica serotype Typhimurium infection in three Danish farrow-to-finish swine herds. J Clin Microbiol, 41 (6), 2282-2288.

KRANKER, S., DAHL, J., WINGSTRAND, A., 2001. Bacteriological and serological examination and risk factor analysis of Salmonella occurrence in sow herds, including risk factors for high Salmonella seroprevalence in receiver finishing herds. Berl Munch Tierarztl Wochenschr, 114 (9-10), 350-352.

NCCLS, 2002. Performance Standards for Antimicrobial Disc and Dilution Susceptibility Tests for Bacteria Isolated from Animals. Approved Standard. 2nd ed. NCCLS document M31-A2. 81 pp. National Committee for Clinical Laboratory Standards Wayne, Pa.,

NIELSEN, B., BAGGESEN, D., BAGER, F., HAUGEGAARD, J., LIND, P., 1995. The serological response to Salmonella serovars Typhimurium and Infantis in experimentally infected pigs. The time course followed with an indirect anti-LPS ELISA and bacteriological examinations. Vet Microbiol, 47 (3-4), 205-218.

NOLLET, N., HOUF, K., DEWULF, J., DE, K.A., DE, Z.L., MAES, D., 2005. Salmonella in sows: a longitudinal study in farrow-to-finish pig herds. Vet Res, 36 (4), 645-656.

VAN DER HEIJDEN, H.M., 2001. First international ring trial of ELISAs for Salmonella-antibody detection in swine. Berl Munch Tierarztl Wochenschr, 114 (9-10), 389-392.

A pilot study on occurrence of *Yersinia enterocolitica* and *Yersinia pseudotuberculosis* in Latvian pigs at slaughtering

Terentjeva, M.*, Bērziņš, A., Liepiņš, E.

Institute of Food and Environmental Hygiene, Latvia University of Agriculture, Jelgava, Latvia
*corresponding author: Margarita.Terentjeva@llu.lv

Abstract

The aim of the study was to detect the distribution of presumptive pathogenic *Yersinia* species in pigs of Latvian origin. In total tonsils of 108 pigs were collected from 6 farms in two abattoirs situated in different parts of Latvia. Samples were investigated by using direct plating on the selective CIN media and cold enrichment technique for 2 weeks. All presumptive isolates were confirmed biochemically. During the direct plating only 58% of cultures of *Y.enterocolitica* and *Y.pseudotuberculosis* were recovered. *Y. enterocolitica* was isolated from the pig tonsil samples originated from all six farms. The distribution of positive samples among different farms varied from 15 to 45%. *Y.pseudotuberculosis* was recovered from 3 out of 6 herds studied ranging from 5 to 25% on each positive farm. The mean prevalence of *Y.enterocolitica* and *Y.pseudotuberculosis* in all six farms was 31% and 8% respectively. Results of study indicate that none of the investigated herds was free of potentially pathogenic *Yersinia*. The presence of *Yersinia* species in pigs indicates that a possibility for contamination with bacteria occurs during the offal removal of and meat inspection of carcasses. Further investigations on pathogenic properties and slaughtering techniques at the slaughterhouses involved in this study should be continued.

Introduction

Yersiniosis is one of the most actual human food-borne infections in the European Union (EU) caused by two *Yersinia* genus species- *Yersinia enterocolitica* and *Yersinia pseudotuberculosis*. Disease is characterized by gastro- intestinal disorders, sometimes with severe imunological sequelae. Yersiniosis is recognized in Latvia and at present a trend to increase is observed with average incidence of 2.3 cases per 100 000 inhabitants during 2001-2005 (2).

An important source of pathogenic *Yersinia* is suggested to be pigs. Healthy animals may harbour pathogenic microorganisms in their lymphatic tissues, especially in tonsils without any clinical signs. Thus, it is not possible to detect the presence of *Yersinia* in animals without additional laboratory tests at the routine ante-mortem inspection in abattoirs. During slaughtering and dressing of yersinia- positive pigs, the offal and carcass of animal easily become contaminated with pathogen if cross- contamination from the pig tonsils occurs (1). Thereby, it is important to estimate the prevalence of presumptive pathogenic microorganisms in pigs to prevent introduction of bacteria in the food chain. This is the first Latvian survey on occurrence of presumptive pathogenic *Yersinia* species in Latvian pig tonsils.

Material and methods

In total of 108 pig tonsil samples were collected from 6 different farms in two main Latvian slaughterhouses located in Zemgale and Vidzeme during January- March, 2006.

The samples of tonsils were directly plated out onto Cefsulodin- Irgasan- Novobiocin agar (CIN agar) (Oxoid, UK) and plates and incubated for 48 h at 30°C. The presumptive colonies with a typical "bull-eye" like appearance were tested for oxidase and urea reaction. Urea- positive and oxidase- negative isolates were confirmed with API 20E (BioMérieux, Marcy l'Etoile, France). *Yersinia* negative samples were cold enriched for 2 weeks at 4°C with plating out on 8th and after alkali treatment on 15th day of incubation with a subsequent confirmation.

Results

All the selected herds were presumptive pathogenic Yersinia spp. positive with the mean prevalence of 31% of Y.enterocolitica and 8% of Y.pseudotuberculosis. Y.enterocolitica was isolated from 6 herds, located in different parts of Latvia ranging from– 3/20(20%) on farm situated in North Zemgale to 6/20(45%) in herd located in North West Zemgale (Table 1). Y.pseudotuberculosis was recovered from 3 out of 6 herds.

Table 1. The prevalence of Y.enterocolitica and Y.pseudotuberculosis in different pig farms

Region	No. of positive samples/ No. of samples (%)	Y.enterocolitica positive samples (%)	Y.pseudotuberculosis positive samples (%)
North Zemgale	5/20 (25)	4	1
North West Zemgale	11/20 (55)	6	5
South Kurzeme	9/20 (45)	9	-
South East Latgale	6/20 (30)	5	2
South West Latgale	8/20 (40)	7	-
North Vidzeme	3/8 (38)	3	-

Discussion

None of randomly selected herds was *Yersinia* negative. Moreover on some farms the prevalence of presumptive pathogenic *Yersinia* was about 50% - in North West Zemgale and South West Latgale. *Y.enterocolitica* was isolated more frequently than *Y.pseudotuberculosis* from all six herds. The highest *Y.pseudotuberculosis* prevalence was found from the herd situated in North West Zemgale- 25%. Besides, 60% of *Y.pseudotuberculosis* isolates where recovered after direct plating during 1st week of incubation. This may indicate that the herd was heavily contaminated with *Y.pseudotuberculosis*. The results of the study may support evidence that *Yersinia* can establish a long-term reservoir within pig herds (3). Bacteria are easily spreading in a healthy pig population, or even contamination may occur at abattoirs from *Yersinia*- positive animals, so the animal became a carrier of bacteria before slaughtering (4). All the investigated herds were placed in the waiting pens, located in the same unit, where they stayed for 3-4 hours. This could be the additional factor for introduction of bacteria in negative herds, as the contact between animals is not completely excluded. Pigs usually harbour the human pathogenic *Y.enterocolitica* bioserovars, so transmission of bacteria within pig herds is unfavorable from the epidemiological point of view. During the dressing and *post- mortem* examination possibilities for introduction of bacteria to carcasses and by- products from pig tonsils is higher in herds heavily contaminated with *Yersinia*. It seems to be more difficult to avoid from cross-contamination with pathogen.
High prevalence of potentially pathogenic *Yersinia* (39%) shows evidence that Latvian pigs could be an important factor for transmission of pathogenic bacteria to consumers.

Conclusions

Latvian pigs can be an important source for raw meat and meat products contamination with pathogenic Yersinia.
Further epidemiological studies on Yersinia pathogenic properties and the role of slaughtering techniques in distribution of bacterium are needed to evaluate the significance of this pathogen in epidemiology of yersiniosis in Latvia.

References

1. Fredriksson –Ahomaa, M., Bucher, M., Hank, C., Stolle, A., Korkaela, H., 2001. High prevalence of *Yersinia enterocolitica* 4:O3 on pig offal in Southern Germany: a slaughtering technique problem. Systematic and Applied Microbiology. 24: 457-463

2. Public Health Agency, Latvia. www.sva.lv

3. Nesbakken, T., Iversen, T., Eckner K., Lium, B, 2006. Testing of pathogenic *Yersinia enterocolitica* in pig herds based on the natural dynamic of infection. International Journal of Food Microbiology, 111(2), 99- 104

4. Skjerve, E., Lium, B., Nielsen, B., Nesbakken, T., 1998. Control of *Yersinia enterocolitica* in pigs at herd level. International Journal of Food Microbiology. 45:195- 203

Session 2

Analysis of the cause for Salmonella spread from bacteriological sampling of stall surroundings

Battenberg, L., Elicker, S.*, Ritzmann, M., Heinritzi, K.

Clinic for Swine, Ludwig-Maximilians-University Munich, Sonnenstr. 16, D-85764 Oberschleissheim, Germany

*corresponding author: S.Elicker@med.vetmed.uni-muenchen.de

Abstract

The cause for Salmonella spread and reinfection was tried to be analysed and identified from bacteriological sampling of stall surroundings in 50 fattening farms and closed farms that had shown an increased prevalence of Salmonella detected by meat-juice-examination. In the bacteriological examination 388 samples of the stall surroundings were analysed. Only in 5 (3x rodent droppings, 1x stall dust and 1x animal feed) samples Salmonella Typhimurium was isolated. Generally, it was impossible to ascertain the reasons for Salmonella spread and reinfection in a farm with a positive meat-juice sample based on pathogen identification.

Introduction

Salmonellosis has become one of the most important food borne diseases in terms of both morbidity and economic cost with increasing incidence reported worldwide (BRYAN, 1988, NIELSEN, 2002, GARCÍA, 2004). While Salmonella contamination of beef and poultry products exceeds the contamination of pork, a lot of research has focused on risk factors of Salmonella prevalence in pig herds, with the general aim to identify possible measures to reduce the Salmonella prevalence in slaughter pigs and to guarantee safe pork. Salmonella reduction programs in swine are becoming commonplace and will continue to be a primary focus of food safety initiatives (MOUSING et al., 1996). In many projects, efforts are now being made at farm level to reduce the incidence of Salmonella infected live animals (DAHL et al., 1996). Since Salmonella can be found widely in the environment and animals can be infected by Salmonella introduced by chronic carriers, contaminated feed or rodents, control is difficult to achieve (STRAW et al., 2006).

The aim of this study was to analyse and identify the cause for Salmonella spread and reinfection in swine farms that had shown an increased prevalence of Salmonella detected by meat-juice-examination from bacteriological sampling of stall surroundings.

Material and methods

In this study investigations of 50 fattening farms and closed farms were carried out. The proportion of seropositive reagents was lower than 20% in 4 fattening farms and 2 closed farms, whereas values between 20% and 39% were observed in 8 fattening farms and 7 closed farms. In 17 fattening as well as 12 closed farms more than 40% of the pigs examined at the slaughterhouse were seropositive. Individual sampling profiles were developed for each farm since typical bavarian agricultural practice does not facilitate systematic sampling.

A total of 388 samples comprising of rodent droppings (n=43), faeces (canine, feline and bovine) (n=16), stall dust (n=30), insects (n=8), feed (n=226), drinking water (n=59) and ground impression smears (n=6) underwent bacteriological examination (Tab. 1).

Table 1: The number of samples taken from different stall surroundings ordered to different types of business

material	rodent droppings	feed	stall dust	drinking water	faeces	insects	ground impression smears
number of samples	43	226	30	59	16	8	6
closed farm	15	115	5	24	8	2	3
fattening farm	24	99	23	30	7	6	3
other farms	4	12	2	5	1	0	0

Results

Successful pathogen identification was rare despite the high percentage of farms with more than 40% positive reagents. *Salmonella* Typhimurium was isolated in only 5 (3x rodent droppings, 1x stall dust and 1x animal feed) of the 388 samples (Tab. 2).

Table 2: Results of bacterial examination from different stall surroundings

material	rodent droppings	feed	stall dust	drinking water	faeces	insects	ground impression smears	Total number of samples
number of samples	43	226	30	59	16	8	6	388
number of positive samples	3	1	1	0	0	0	0	5
positive samples (%)	7,0%	0,4%	3,3%	0%	0%	0%	0%	2,6%

A positive bacterial identification was achieved in one fattening farm and 3 closed farms. In the fattening farm 25% of the meat-juice samples taken at the slaughterhouse were tested positive. The positive fraction was 32%, 88% and 100% in the closed farms. The identification of a pathogen entry-point due to *Salmonella* isolation from a feed sample was successful in only one of the 50 farms. A correlation between a high percentage of seropositive animals based on meat-juice evaluation and *Salmonella* spp. identification in swine farms was not established.

Discussion

The identification of the entry-point for *Salmonella* based on bacteriological examination of the stall surroundings is very difficult, because of the low rate of positive findings in the samples (BOHM, 1993, QUANTE, 2000, MEYER, 2004, RINCÓN et al., 2006). Furthermore it is only safe to determine the entry-point, if *Salmonella* is detected in faeces and if serovars in faeces and stall surroundings are matching. None the less results are indicating stall surroundings as a possible source of an infection with *Salmonella*. Respectively BAGGESEN et al. (1996) are describing the distribution of *Salmonella* in the extra animal environment in *Salmonella* infected pig herds. In their opinion the environmental contamination may be enough to ensure the infection to newly introduced pigs. However only a repeated sampling and a sufficient large sample can make a statement on the presence of *Salmonella* in a herd.

Conclusions

Generally, it was impossible to ascertain the reasons for *Salmonella* spread and reinfection in a farm with a positive meat-juice sample based on pathogen identification.

References

BAGGESEN, D.L., et al., 1996. Critical control points (CCP) in relation to subclinical *Salmonella* infection. 14th International Pig Veterinary Society Congress, Bologna, Italy, 171.

BOHM, R., 1993. Verhalten ausgewählter Salmonellen in der Umwelt. Deutsche tierärztliche Wochenschrift, 100, 275-278.

BRYAN, F.L., 1988. Risks of practices, procedures and processes that lead to outbreaks of foodborne disease. Journal of food protection, 51, 663-667.

DAHL, J., et al., 1996. Salmonella reduction at the farm level. 14th International Pig Veterinary Society Congress, Bologna, Italy, 181.

GARCÍA, K., et al., 2004. 18th International Pig Veterinary Society Congress, Hamburg, Germany, Vol. 2, 672.

MEYER, C., 2004. Qualitative und quantitative Risikofaktoren für die Einschleppung und Verbreitung von Salmonellen in unterschiedlichen Produktionsverfahren beim Schwein. Thesis, Med. vet., Hannover.

MOUSING, J., et al., 1996. Concepts of the integrated *Salmonella Enterica* control programme in Danish pork. 14th International Pig Veterinary Society Congress, Bologna, Italy, 167.

NIELSEN, B., 2002. Pork safety - a world overview. 17th International Pig Veterinary Society Congress, Ames, Iowa, USA, Vol. 1, 121.

QUANTE, U., 2000. Untersuchungen zum Vorkommen von Salmonellen bei Zuchtschweinen. Thesis, Med. vet., Hannover.

RINCÓN, M.A., et al., 2006. 19th International Pig Veterinary Society Congress, Copenhagen, Denmark, Vol. 2, 362.

STRAW, B.E., et al., 2006. Diseases of swine 9th edition. Iowa: Blackwell Publishing.

The Dutch *Salmonella* monitoring programme for pigs and some recommendations for control plans in the future

Hanssen, E.J.M.[1], Swanenburg, M.[2], Maassen, C.B.M.[2]

[1]Product boards for Livestock, Meat and Eggs, P.O. Box 460, 2700 AL Zoetermeer, The Netherlands
[2]Animal Sciences Group, Division of Infectious Diseases, P.O. Box 65, 8200 AB, Lelystad, The Netherlands

corresponding author: e.j.m.hanssen@pve.agro.nl

Abstract

In The Netherlands, a monitoring programme for *Salmonella* in pigs started in 2005. Monitoring occurs at the farm level and at the slaughterhouse level. The results over 2006 show that 4% of the farms is in category 3, which means that they are advised to take measures against *Salmonella*. The prevalence of *Salmonella* on carcasses is low (0,8%). Research showed that the slaughterline is the most important contamination source for carcasses. This means that *Salmonella*-free pigs, delivered to the slaughterhouse, will only end up as *Salmonella*-free carcasses if contamination in lairage and during the slaughter process is not possible. Measures at farm level, to lower the *Salmonella* prevalence on pig farms, are more or less senseless if those conditions are not fulfilled. It should therefore be discussed if the actual EU regulations, concerning *Salmonella* in fattening pigs, will be effective to reach a lower prevalence of *Salmonella* on carcasses.

Introduction

During all phases of the pork production chain (farm-transport-lairage-slaughter-retail-consumer) *Salmonella* can be introduced into the chain, can be multiplied and spread to other animals or carcasses. It is evident that pigs from *Salmonella*-positive farms will carry *Salmonella* with them into the slaughterhouse. However, if the slaughter process is carried out properly (e.g. if the intestines are removed in a hygienic way), carcasses should not be contaminated with *Salmonella* after slaughter. So, in the ideal slaughterhouse, all carcasses would end up *Salmonella*-free, irrespective of their *Salmonella*-status before slaughter.

Although much effort has been spent on the prevention and control of *Salmonella* in the pork production chain, pork is not always free of *Salmonella* at this moment. Denmark was the first European country that started with a control plan to decrease *Salmonella* contamination of pork. The Danes have put a strong emphasis on the farm and logistic procedures in the supply chain in order to control *Salmonella* on pork. Danish control plans put most effort in decreasing the *Salmonella* infection level of farms, based on the idea that *Salmonella* contamination of carcasses after slaughter is caused by introduction of *Salmonella* infected pigs into the slaughterhouse, while the Dutch pork industry strengthened mainly the hygienic procedures during slaughter and further processing of pork. In The Netherlands a monitoring programme for *Salmonella* including the preharvest started in 2005.

To be able to take the right decisions when implementing a control plan, it is important to know which measures will lead to the best result. This paper describes the Dutch monitoring programme and the most important conclusions of the research that was carried out in The Netherlands on this subject during recent years. Furthermore, some recommendations will be given for future control plans in the pork supply chain..

The Dutch monitoring programme

The Dutch monitoring programme on *Salmonella* is an obligatory programme, which includes both herd level of fattening pigs (preharvest) and the slaughterhouse level. Herd level monitoring is based on testing blood samples for the presence of antibodies against *Salmonella*. From each farm that delivers more than 30 fattening pigs per year, 12 blood samples have to be collected per period of 4 months. Blood samples can be taken on the farm or in the slaughterhouse, and are tested by approved laboratories. Samples are tested in the Idexx ELISA, or comparable serological tests, with a cut off level of 40% OD.

When a total of 36 blood samples per farm is reached, this farm is classified into one of the three Salmonella categories. Category 1 means that a farm is not or low infected, category 3 means that a farm is heavy infected and is advised to take measures in order to control Salmonella.

All 36 samples have the same weight. The scores of the previous 12 months determine the Salmonella category.

Results per 4 months period (12 tests)	Score
≤20% positive	1
20-40% positive	2
≥40% positive	3

Results per 12 months period (36 tests)	Salmonella category
3 or 4	1
5, 6 or 7	2
8 or 9	3

Besides serological monitoring, bacteriological monitoring is performed on carcasses. Slaughterhouses that slaughter more than 150.000 pigs each year have to sample 5 carcasses per day (analysed in the laboratory as one pooled sample). Slaughterhouses that slaughter between 10.000 and 150.000 pigs each year have to sample 10 carcasses per week (individual samples). Slaughterhouses can choose between sampling with the destructive method (cork bore) or the sponge method. Samples are collected in the cooling room.

Results of the monitoring programme

Preharvest data over 2006 show that 73% of the herds were in category 1, 23% in category 2 and 4% of the herds were in category 3. At this moment, farms in category 3 are advised to take measures against Salmonella (e.g. acidification of feed or drinking water). At the end of 2007 it will be discussed if those farms will be obliged to take measures.

The average Salmonella contamination of the carcasses in the slaughterhouses was 0,8% (sponge method). Because the prevalence of contaminated carcasses was in all Dutch slaughterhouses below the EU standard of 10%, they are not obliged to take additional measures. However, slaughterhouses with a result that is above the mean prevalence of 0,8% are advised to take some actions to decrease the prevalence of Salmonella contaminated carcasses.

Recent research carried out in The Netherlands

Salinpork project (1996-2000):
The Salinpork project was carried out together in 5 European countries. In The Netherlands two large slaughterhouses were involved in the project. These slaughterhouses were sampled extensively during different slaughter days. Samples were also collected at the farms that delivered pigs to these slaughterhouses, and these pigs were followed along the chain.

In all slaughterhouses Salmonella could be isolated from slaughter equipment before onset of slaughter. The contamination of slaughter equipment existed during the whole slaughter day. In one slaughterhouse a specific Salmonella serotype was isolated from the carcass splitter on all different sampling days, and this Salmonella type was also isolated from the carcasses after slaughter. Salmonella could be isolated from carcasses when pigs were originating from Salmonella-free farms.

All isolated Salmonella strains were serotyped and genotyped. Salmonella types on the carcasses were compared to the Salmonella types isolated from related samples, and from samples taken from possible sources for the contamination of the pig sample (Swanenburg et al., 2001). It was concluded that the slaughterline (slaughter equipment) was the most important contamination source for carcasses and it was evident that *Salmonella* multiplicated substantially on the slaughterline. In fact, contamination in the slaughterline was responsible for about 80% of *Salmonella*-positive carcasses. This means that "farm *Salmonella's*" do not play such an important role in contaminating pork with *Salmonella* as is usually thought.

Feasibility of Salmonella control in pork meat, (2000-2002):
This Dutch project was carried out to get more insight into the possibilities to produce pork with low *Salmonella* contamination under Dutch practical circumstances. Selected herds, with low or zero *Salmonella* prevalence were slaughtered in a big Dutch slaughterhouse each week on the same day. The prevalence of *Salmonella* contaminated carcasses after slaughter of the low and zero *Salmonella* herds was compared to the prevalence of *Salmonella* contaminated carcasses, slaughtered on the "control" day in the week, when randomly selected herds were slaughtered (herds with average *Salmonella* prevalence).
The most important conclusion of this project was the fact that separate delivery of *Salmonella*-free herds did result in a lower infection pressure directly after arrival in the slaughterhouse, but did not result in less *Salmonella* contaminated carcasses, compared to the control herds. Like in the Salinpork project, also in this experiment *Salmonella* was isolated from the carcass splitter on almost every slaughter day, and the same *Salmonella* serotype was isolated from carcasses after slaughter. In this project it could also be concluded that again the slaughterline was the source of 80% of the *Salmonella* contaminated carcasses. If the *Salmonella* strain, that was found both on carcasses and carcass splitter, was left out of the results, then the prevalence of *Salmonella* contaminated carcasses from herds with low prevalence was significantly lower than the prevalence of contaminated carcasses from control herds. This result shows that separate slaughter of *Salmonella*-free pig herds can lead to low *Salmonella* prevalence of meat, but it has only relevance if carcasses do not get contaminated during slaughter.

Discussion and recommendations

In both research projects it was concluded that the slaughterline was the most important source of *Salmonella* contamination of carcasses. This was mainly caused by the existence of a so called "residential flora" on the slaughter equipment. Although the slaughterlines in our projects were cleaned and disinfected every day and according to legislation also between each carcass, some specific *Salmonella* strains managed to attach to the equipment and survive disinfecting.
This problem was also described by Sørensen (1999), who observed persistent *Salmonella* strains in the polishing machine and the splitting saw in two different slaughterhouses in Denmark. In both cases, intensive cleaning and disinfection were not sufficient to solve the problem.

Logistic slaughter (separate slaughter of *Salmonella*-free and *Salmonella*-infected herds) has often been mentioned as an effective measure to avoid contamination of pork with *Salmonella*. However, results of recent projects have shown that logistic slaughter will only be effective if no contamination of carcasses occurs during the slaughter process. Unfortunately it was concluded that many carcasses get contaminated during slaughter, and that current regular cleaning and disinfection procedures of the slaughterline are not sufficient to solve this problem. Therefore, most effort should be put into implementing measures that avoid contamination of carcasses during slaughter. Slaughterline equipment should be constructed in a way that it is easy to clean, and without the possibility for bacteria to attach and multiply on the equipment. Furtheron, it is important to avoid cross contamination of *Salmonella* between different herds in the lairage of the slaughterhouse.
If both conditions (lairage and slaughterline) are fulfilled, then the delivery of *Salmonella*-free herds to the slaughterhouse will result in *Salmonella*-free pork after slaughter. Farmers should then be stimulated to lower the *Salmonella* prevalence at their farm with specific measures.

The actual EU baseline study "fattening pigs" focuses on the primary production phase. Our results show that focusing on the slaughterhouse phase would be more effective in decreasing the prevalence of *Salmonella* on pork. It should be discussed if the actual regulations, concerning *Salmonella* in fattening pigs, will lead to a lower prevalence of *Salmonella* on carcasses.

Conclusions

- The results of the Dutch monitoring programme for Salmonella on pork show that the prevalence of Salmonella on pig carcasses in The Netherlands is low (0,8%).
- There is no (linear) relationship between the Salmonella level at pig farms and the Salmonella contamination level of carcasses after slaughter. Salmonella can be isolated from pig carcasses after slaughter, irrespective of the Salmonella status of the farms that delivered the pigs.
- The most important source for Salmonella on pig carcasses under Dutch circumstances (with a low prevalence of Salmonella on carcasses) is contamination during the slaughter process.
- Salmonella-free pigs, delivered to the slaughterhouse, will only end up as Salmonella-free carcasses if contamination in lairage and during the slaughter process is not possible.
- Measures at farm level, to lower the Salmonella prevalence on pig farms, are more or less senseless if above mentioned conditions are not fulfilled.
- It should be discussed if the actual regulations, concerning Salmonella in fattening pigs, will be effective to reach a lower prevalence of Salmonella on carcasses.

References

SØRENSEN, L.L., SØRENSEN, R., KLINT, K., NIELSEN, B. 1999. Persistent environmental strains of Salmonella Infantis at two Danish slaughterhouses, two case stories. Proceedings of the 3rd International Symposium on the Epidemiology and Control of Salmonella in Pork, Washington DC, 1999, 285-286.
LO FO WONG, D., HALD, T., Salmonella in pork (SALINPORK): pre-harvest and harvest control options based on epidemiologic, diagnostic and economic research. Final report, 2000.
SWANENBURG, M., BERENDS, B.R., URLINGS, H.A.P., SNIJDERS, J.M.A., VAN KNAPEN, F., 2001. Epidemiological investigations into the sources of Salmonella contamination of pork. Berl. Münch. Tierärztl. Wschr. 114, 356-359.
SWANENBURG, M., URLINGS, B., VAN DER WOLF, P., SNIJDERS, J., "Haalbaarheidsproject Salmonellabeheersing varkensvlees", Eindrapport. ID-Lelystad, Gezondheidsdienst voor Dieren, VVDO, oktober 2002.
PRODUCT BOARDS FOR LIVESTOCK, MEAT AND EGGS, 2007: Personal communication

Carry-over risks in fattening units for Campylobacter spp.

Wehebrink, T.[1], Kemper, N.[1]*, grosse Beilage, E.[2] , Krieter J.[1]

[1] Institut für Tierzucht und Tierhaltung der Christian-Albrechts-Universität, Olshausenstraße 40, 24098 Kiel, Germany
[2] Außenstelle für Epidemiologie der Tierärztlichen Hochschule Hannover, Buescheler Straße 9, 49456 Bakum, Germany

* corresponding author: nkemper@tierzucht.uni-kiel.de

Abstract

There is a lack of information about the prevalence of the important zoonotic pathogens *Campylobacter* spp. and *Yersinia* spp. at different stages in the pig production chain. The aim of this study was to determine these prevalence in a total of 1040 faecal samples and to gather further information about the sources of infection with *Campylobacter* spp. and their qualitative and quantitative importance in the pig production. During the slaughtering process, 122 pigs and their carcasses respectively, were sampled three times. *Campylobacter* spp. were isolated in sows (33.8%), piglets (80.9%), growing (89.2%) and finishing (64.7%) pigs. *Yersinia* spp. were detected in growing (15.2%) and finishing (13.3%) pigs only. For statistical analysis, bacteriological results for *Campylobacter* spp. were evaluated with questionnaire facts from four farrowing and twelve fattening units. In the production stage farrowing, a significant influence for the factors "number of sows" and "forage store cleaning" was detected by a generalized linear model. In the production stage fattening, following factors had a significant effect on the *Campylobacter* spp. prevalence: "number of fattening places", "mixed farm", "sampling time", "bottom", "forage", "antibacterial" and "anthelmintic prophylaxis".
During lairage, *Campylobacter* spp. were identified from faeces of pigs from all farms whereas *Yersinia* spp. were detected in pigs from just two herds. After twelve hours of chilling neither *Campylobacter* spp. nor *Yersinia* spp. were detected. Common slaughter techniques and hygiene procedures may be effective tools to reduce the risk of contamination and recontamination of meat products.

Introduction

Infections caused by *Campylobacter* spp. (C.) are prevalent worldwide. *Campylobacter* spp. are part of the normal gut microflora in many food-producing animal species, including chickens, turkeys, swine, cattle and sheep (BLASER 1997). Transmission to humans appears to occur primarily through the consumption of contaminated poultry products, unpasteurised milk products and meat products (EFFLER et al. 2001; FRIEDMAN et al. 2004). In addition to the consumption of undercooked meat, cross-contamination to other food products may play a significant role in the number of illnesses observed. The infective dose in humans can be very low as 800 colony-forming units of specific strains can lead to *Campylobacter* infection (BLACK 1988).

The farmer and the participating manufacturing industry in the food production have the main responsibility for food safety. Now and in future, this adds up to the demand for preventive measures in primary production following the principle "from the producer to the consumer". For these reasons, this study was conducted with the aim to determine the prevalence of *Campylobacter* spp. in farrowing and fattening units by the collection of faeces and rectal swabs. Further risk factors for the occurrence of *Campylobacter* spp. in farrowing and fattening units should be observed via environmental and feed samples from the checked herds and questionnaires in the corresponding pig farms.

Material and methods

Four farrowing and twelve fattening farms provided the basis for the present study. The sampling size on every farm was calculated according to the formula from NOORDHUIZEN et al. (1997). In total, 1.040 faecal or swab samples respectively from pigs of all ages from farrowing and fattening units were analysed. Additionally, 56 environmental and feed samples were collected. Cultural methods were used to test all samples for *Campylobacter* spp., including the differentiation of subspecies. The bacterial detection of *Campylobacter* spp. proceeds from ISO 10272 (1995) with following biochemical differentiation of C. coli and C. jejuni.

Calculation of the intraherd and animal prevalence and the 95%-confidence intervals within the production stage was performed with the PROC SURVEYMEANS procedure from SAS® (2002). On every farrowing and fattening farm, data collection was carried out with the aid of a questionnaire. Besides the general farm information, detailed data about the housing system, management, state of health and aspects of disease surveillance were acquired. In consideration of the bacteriological results, these data contributed to a hazard analysis to detect the origin and spread of *Campylobacter* spp. infections.

The statistical analysis was performed with a generalised linear model. At first the management-specific parameters were tested respectively with the χ2-test regarding the influence on the pathogen prevalence. Every parameter having a value p<0.3 in the χ2-test and an adequate distribution was included in the generalised linear model. The GENMOD procedure from the software package SAS® (2002) was reviewed for significance (p≤0.05). For the estimation, a binomial distribution and a logistic link function (i.e. logistic regression) were assumed. As a result of the small sample size in the farrowing unit, it was not possible to perform a risk analysis which yielded significant conclusions. From the fattening unit, the following fixed effects were considered in the model: sampling time (growing pigs, finishing pigs), herd organisation (number of fattening places, mixed farming, housing system and forage (floor space design, feed origin) and health (antibacterial and anthelmintic treatment). The estimates (ê) from the risk factors were transformed into odds ratios (OR=exp (ê)) and the 95%-confidence intervals were calculated. A low absolute frequency in the least sub classes from some factors did not allow a statistical analysis with logistic regression. For the factors having a p-value ≤0.05 in the χ2-test, the odds ratios and 95%-confidence intervals were calculated separately.

Results

Campylobacter (C.) spp. were isolated in 33.8% of the sows and in 80.9% of the piglets (Figure 1). Neither pathogen was isolated from the environmental and feed samples.

For the statistical risk factor analysis in the fattening unit, 716 results from the bacteriological examination were evaluated in context with the questionnaire data from the twelve fattening herds. Twenty factors were tested regarding their influence on the prevalence of *Campylobacter*. Significant effects were shown for the following factors: sampling time, number of fattening places, mixed farming, floor space design, feed origin, antibacterial and anthelmintic treatments.

Over the fattening period the *Campylobacter* spp. prevalence decreased. At the beginning the odds ratio increased by a factor of 4.46. he risk factor fattening places per herd was differentiated between farms size under 1000 pigs and alternatively over 1000 pigs. The bacteriological results show that pigs from farms with less than 1000 fattening places had a prevalence of 80.0% and those from larger farms a prevalence of 74.3%. The chance to isolate *Campylobacter* spp. from pigs from smaller herds increased by a factor of 1.44. Housing in separated stalls is another preventive influence. When the animals on mixed farms were kept in separated stalls the chance of a positive bacteriological result decreased (OR=0.61). Pigs which were kept on a plan floor without bedding had the highest prevalence in comparison to the other flooring systems. In this housing system, the chance of obtaining a positive result was highest. An antibacterial treatment at the beginning of the fattening period was implemented on seven herds. The following antibiotics were used for this treatment: Amoxicillin, Tetracycline and Sulfonamide. The chance of a positive finding decreased when the animals were treated with antibacterial substances during this time period (OR=0.66). On four herds, anthelmintics were used at the beginning of fattening period. The appliance of Ivermectin, Flubendazol and Levamisolhydrochlorid was adopted for deworming. The chance of obtaining a positive result rose by a factor of 1.99 when anthelmintics were administered.

Further risk factors "source of piglets", "feed consistency" and "blank dwell time" had an influence on the prevalence of *Campylobacter* spp., too. The chance of obtaining a positive result from the bacteriological investigation was smaller from fattening pigs in a closed herd system (OR=0.26).

Furthermore, the following cases were preventive: feeding meal (OR=0.63) instead of granule or pellets and blank dwell time under 10 days.

Discussion

The results from the present study prove that *Campylobacter* spp. are of increasing importance in farrowing and fattening units: high prevalence of *Campylobacter* spp. were found in suckling, growing and finishing pigs (WEHEBRINK 2006). Other studies also confirm these results (KASIMIR 2005; GAULL 2002).

The occurrence of *Campylobacter* spp. in subsequent samples of pigs and sows was often variable in this analysis. As known from further studies, *Campylobacter* spp. prevalence may vary because the physiological status of the animal and external factors can influence the intestinal flora. The ability of *Campylobacter* spp. to colonise the intestinal tract of pigs is probably subject to the various factors influencing the colonisation resistance of the gut (RUCKEBUSCH et al. 1991). In contrast to recent studies, risk factor analysis in the fattening unit demonstrated a significant influence on the *Campylobacter* spp. detection rate for the "number of fattening places". The chance of obtaining a positive *Campylobacter* spp. result is higher when animals are held in smaller herds (<1000 places). Separating the herds in "mixed farming" is a useful method to decrease pathogen transmission. In contrast to our study, BOES et al. (2005) could not assert this effect: investigation of the occurrence and diversity of *C. jejuni* infections in finisher pigs in herds with combined cattle or poultry production and herds only producing pigs showed no evidence of transmission of *C. jejuni* from cattle or poultry to pigs in mixed production herds. A lower *Campylobacter* spp. detection rate is not promoted by a plan floor without bedding and purchase forage. One reason for the higher prevalence in housing systems with plan floor is the intensive contact of the pigs with their faeces for a longer time. A further result from the questionnaire analysis was that an arranged antibacterial treatment but no anthelmintic treatment was preventive against *Campylobacter* spp. infections. This results must be questioned critically because it is not known first which health status in detail can be found in the different herds and, second, what the antimicrobial resistance of *Campylobacter* spp. is. Further studies will be needed to explain these two risk factors. Despite the fact that forage in granule form is heated during the manufacturing process, the chance of obtaining a positive *Campylobacter* spp. result rose by a factor of 1.23 in this form of forage feeding. SCHUPPERS et al. (2005) detected that important risk factors contributing to the prevalence of resistance strains were shortened tails, lameness, skin lesions, feed without whey, and *ad libitum* feeding. Multiple antimicrobial resistance was more likely in farms which only partially used an all-in-all-out system, or a continuous-flow system compared to a strict all-in-all-out animal-flow. Presence of lameness, ill-thrift, and scratches at the shoulder in the herd also increased the odds for multiple resistance. Thus, the results from SCHUPPERS et al. (2005) showed that on finishing farms which maintained a good herd health status and optimal farm management the prevalence of antimicrobial resistance was also more favourable.

Conclusions

Based on the zoonotic directive (Nr. 2160/2003), a monitoring for *Campylobacter* spp. is mandatory. It should take place at an adequate stage of the food chain. Control has to be directed primarily at the prevention of colonisation of farm animals by means of the implementation of Good Hygienic Practice (GHP), biosecurity measures and husbandry practices incorporating Hazard Analysis Critical Control Point (HACCP) based on risk management systems (WHYTE et al., 2002). Because of this, the objective of this study was to obtain more information about the risk factors influencing the prevalence of this pathogen. As a result of the small sample size in the farrowing unit, it was not possible to perform a risk analysis which yielded significant conclusions. In the fattening unit the attention was focused additionally on risk factors which do not reach the significant limitation of the 5% probability error because of the small sample size. Effects which exceeded the housing and management factors were not acquired in the questionnaire and could not consequently be regarded in the evaluation. Because of this the results should only be regarded as tendencies.

References

BLACK, R.E., LEVINE, M.M., CLEMENTS, M.L., HUGHES, T.P., BLASER, M.J., 1988. Experimental *Campylobacter jejuni* infection in humans. *Journal of Infectious Diseases*, 157 (3), 472-479.

BLASER, M.J., 19997. Epidemiologic and clinical features of *Campylobacter jejuni* infections. *Journal of Infectious Diseases*, 176 (Suppl. 2),103-105.

BOES, J., NERSTING, L., NIELSEN, E.M., KRANKER, S., ENØE, C., WACHMANN, H.C., EFFLER, P., IEONG, M.C., KIMURA, A., NAKATA, M. BURR, R., CREMER, E., 2001. Sporadic *Campylobacter jejuni* infections in Hawai: associations with prior antibiotic use and commercially prepared chicken. *Journal of Infectious Diseases*,183 (7),1152-1155.

FRIEDMAN, C.R., HOEKSTRA, R.M., SAMUEL, M., MARCUS, R., BENDER, J., SHIFERAW B., 2004. Risk factors for sporadic *Campylobacter* infections in the united states: a case-control studie in FoodNet sites. *Clinical Infectious Diseases*, 38 (Suppl. 3), 285-296.

GAULL, F., 2002. Vorkommen thermophiler *Campylobacter* spp. bei Schweinen im Betrieb und auf dem Schlachthof, auf Putenschlachttierkörpern und in Lebensmitteln tierischen Ursprungs – Typisierung der Isolate mit molekularbiologischen Fingerprintingmethoden und Vergleich der Isolate untereinander und mit humanen Isolaten. Leipzig, Veterinärmed. Fak., Dissertation.

INTERNATIONAL ORGANIZATION FOR STANDARDIZATION, 1995. International Standard 10272.

KASIMIR, S., 2005. Verlaufsuntersuchungen zum Vorkommen potentiell humanpathogener *Yersinia enterocolitica* und *Campylobacter* spp. in Schweinebeständen von der Geburt bis zur Schlachtung sowie Genotypisierung ausgewählter Isolate. Leipzig, Veterinärmed. Fak., Dissertation.

NOORDHUIZEN, M., FRANKENA, K., GRAAT, E., 1997. Animal health care and public health issues. In: World Congress on Food Hygiene, The Hague/Netherlands, Proceedings, 59.

RUCKEBUSCH, Y., PHANEUF, L.P., DUNLOP, R., 1991. Microflora and immunology of the digestive tract. In: Physiology of Small and Large Animals. Philadelphia: Becker.

SAS INSTITUTE INC., 2002. User's Guide (release 8.1.), Cary, NC, USA .

SCHUPPERS, M.E., STEPHAN, R., LEDERGERBER, U., DANUSER, J., BISSING-CHOISAT, B., STÄRK, K.D.C., REGULA, G., 2005. Clinical herd health, farm management and antimicrobial resistance in *Campylobacter coli* an finishing pig farms in Switzerland. *Preventive Veterinary Medicine* 69,189-202

VERORDNUNG (EG) NR. 2160/2003 des Europäischen Parlaments und des Rates vom 17. November 2003 zur Bekämpfung von Salmonellen und bestimmten anderen durch Lebensmittel übertragbaren Zoonoseerregern.

WEHEBRINK, T., KEMPER, N., GROSSE BEILAGE, E., KRIETER, J. Prevalence of *Campylobacter* spp. and *Yersinia* spp. in the pig production. *Preventive Veterinary Medicine* (submitted).

WHYTE, P., BOLTON , D., O'MAHONY, H., COLLINS, J.D., 2002: Development and Application of HACCP in Broiler Production and Slaughter, University College Dublin.

YOUNG, C.R., HARVEY, R., ANDERSON, R., NISBET, D., STANKER, L.H., 2000. Enteric colonisation following natural exposure to *Campylobacter* in pigs. *Research Veterinary Science* 68 (1), 75-78.

Isolation of *Escherichia coli* O157 in pigs at slaughter in Northern Italy

Gabriella Conedera*[1], Massimo Fabbi[2], Stefano Morabito[3], Denis Vio[1], Antonia Ricci[4], Alfredo Caprioli[3]

[1]Istituto Zooprofilattico Sperimentale (IZS) delle Venezie, Sezione territoriale di Pordenone, Via Bassa del Cuc 4, 33084 Cordenons (PN), Italy
[2] IZS della Lombardia e dell'Emilia-Romagna (IZS LER), Sezione di Pavia, Strada Campeggi 59/61, 27100 Pavia, Italy
[3] Istituto Superiore di Sanità, Dipartimento di Sanità alimentare animale, Viale Regina Elena 299, 00161 Roma, Italy
[4] IZS delle Venezie, viale dell'Università 10, 35020 Legnaro (PD), Italy

*Corresponding author: gconedera@izsvenezie.it

Abstract

A study of VTEC O157 intestinal carriage was performed in pigs at slaughter, carrying out surveys respectively in the Veneto and the Lombardia regions of Italy within a common research project. The study was conducted for 15 months, starting in June 2002. As a minimum, a sample size of 300 samples was defined for each survey, assuming an expected prevalence of 1%, C.I. 95%, accuracy 5%. One gram samples of intestinal content from the distal gut were tested for *E. coli* O157 using an isolation method based on immunomagnetic separation. In the survey performed in the Veneto region, all the 397 samples collected from pigs of 132 farms tested negative for VTEC O157, but one *E. coli* O157 harbouring the *eae* gene only was isolated. In the survey performed in the Lombardia region, VTEC O157 was detected in 3 (0.63%, 95% C.I. 0.12 – 1.81) of the 480 sampled pigs from 3 (2.80%, 95% C.I. 0.58 – 7.97) of the 107 farms of origin. Therefore in the study a total of 877 pigs were tested in 15 slaughters of two regions, with a prevalence of 0.34% (95% C.I. 0.07 – 0.99) of positive pigs from 1.26% (95% C.I. 0.25 – 3.62) of the herds. In one of the positive farms also cattle were reared with pigs, even if housed separately, and in a follow-up investigation VTEC O157 strains sharing more than 96% homology with the pig strain were found in cattle.

Introduction

Verocytotoxin-producing *Escherichia coli* (VTEC) and in particular *E. coli* O157 has emerged in the past two decades as a significant human pathogen that can cause a broad spectrum of diseases including severe illnesses such as haemorrhagic colitis and haemolytic uraemic sindrome.
Most human cases have been associated with consumption of contaminated food (in particular of bovine origin) or water, although direct contact with animals and person-to-person transmission have also been documented.
Cattle are considered to be the major reservoir of *E. coli* O157 but the organism has also been isolated from other ruminants and more occasionally from other animals. *E. coli* O157 has been reported from swine in different countries (Japan, The Netherlands, Sweden, Norway, Canada, United States), generally at a low prevalence (0.1-2.0%), while in South America a surprisingly high rate of carriage was found (8-10.0%) maybe due to differences in pig husbandry practices.
In Italy in a one-year survey, VTEC O157 was isolated from the intestinal content of one slaughtered pig (0.7%) and from one carcass (0.7%) of 150 randomly selected pigs. Since as only few data are available for swine, the aim of this study was to investigated more extensively the intestinal carriage of VTEC O157 in pigs at slaughter, collecting samples from several abattoirs of two regions of Northern Italy, in which swine productions has particular relevance.

Materials and methods

Sampling scheme

Two surveys (A and B) were carried out respectively in the Veneto and the Lombardia regions in Northern Italy during a 15 months period, from June 2002 to September 2003. Samples of distal intestinal content from fattening pigs were collected at slaughter, equally distributed in the period. One animal was sampled for each batch. A sample size of 300 samples was defined, assuming an expected prevalence of 1%, C.I. 95%, accuracy 5%. Samples were sent to the laboratory in refrigerated boxes and analyzed as individual samples within 48-72 hours after sampling. In both the surveys the sampled pigs originated from farms located in Northern Italy.

In "Survey A" samples were collected in 11 slaughterhouses of the Veneto region, having a capacity $\geq$ 3000 animals slaughtered per year. Samples were stratified according to the capacity of each slaughterhouse. Samples were sent for analysis to IZS delle Venezie – Laboratory of Pordenone.

"Survey B" was performed in 4 slaughterhouses of the Lombardia region having a capacity $\geq$ 5000 animals slaughtered per year. Samples were sent for analysis to IZS della Lombardia e dell' Emilia Romagna – Laboratory of Pavia.

A "Follow-up survey" with rectal samples collected from cattle was performed on the farm of origin of one VTEC O157 positive pig, in which both pigs and cattle were kept. This farm was divided in two subunits located at a distance of about 4 Km, both of them rearing pigs as well as cattle at different production stages, housed separately but with farmworkers and veterinarian in common.

Laboratory methods

In both the surveys the same laboratory methods were performed.

Isolation of E. coli O157

One gram faecal sample (distal gut contents) was added to 9 ml of Buffered Peptone Water (BPW, Oxoid), and incubated at $37\pm1°C$ for 6 hours. After incubation, Immunomagnetic Separation (IMS) was performed using Dynabeads anti-E. coli O157 (Dynal, Oslo); magnetic beads were inoculated onto Sorbitol MacConkey agar (Oxoid) supplemented with cefixime and tellurite (CT-SMAC) and incubated. at $37\pm1°C$ for 24 hours. Sorbitol non-fermenting colonies were tested for agglutination with O157-latex test (Oxoid) and positive isolates were confirmed biochemically as E. coli and further characterized.

Characterization of virulence factors

The presence of virulence genes was determined by polymerase chain reaction (PCR) amplification using the primer pairs KS7/KS8 for VT1, GK3/GK4 for VT2 and SK1/SK2 for the intimin-coding eae gene.

Pulsed field gel electrophoresis

Plugs were prepared as previously described (Morabito et al. 1999). Restriction endonuclease digestion was performed with 50 Uts of Xba I (Takara Biomedicals) at 37°C overnight. Electrophoresis was performed with a 1% agarose gel in the following conditions: 2.2 sec. initial switch time, 48.5 sec. final switch time, 6 V/cm for 20 hours in Tris-Borate-EDTA buffer 0.5 x at 14°C. Gels were stained with ethidium bromide (0.5 µg/ml) and analysed under UV light.

For analysis of genetic relatedness, PFGE profiles were analyzed by the BioNumerics Software (Applied Maths Belgium) using the UPGMA algorythm with Dice coefficient.

Results

Survey A

In survey A, 397 samples from pigs originating from 132 farms were tested. No VTEC O157 was isolated. Only one non-sorbitol fermenting E. coli O157 harbouring the eae gene but not the VT genes was detected.

Survey B

In survey B, VTEC O157 was detected in 3 (0.63%, 95% C.I. 0.12 – 1.81) out of 480 samples collected from pigs originating from 3 (2.80%, 95% C.I. 0.58 – 7.97) out of 107 farms. All the 3 isolates possessed the eae gene; two of them carried the VT1 and VT2 genes, one the VT2 gene only. PFGE analysis showed that the 3 strains had different profiles.

Follow-up survey

The follow-up survey showed that the positive pig was kept during the finishing period in one of the two farm subunits in which cows were reared, but had moved there approximately 2 months before from the other subunit were young heifers were kept. 60 rectal samples, 30 for each subunit were collected from cattle; eight of 30 (26.6%) sampled heifers tested positive for *E. coli* O157 carrying VT1 and VT2 genes, while all the 30 cows were negative.

The genetic relatedness among isolates was investigated by performing a cluster analysis on the PFGE profiles obtained from the isolates. All the bovine isolates were about 90-100% homologous and were closely related to the VTEC O157 strain from the positive pig, sharing more than 96% homology.

Discussion and conclusions

In this 15 months study on fattening pigs, VTEC O157 was isolated from 3 (0.63%) of the 480 sampled pigs from 3 (2.80%) of the 107 farms of origin in "survey B" conducted in slaughters of the Lombardia region and it was not detected in any of 397 pigs from 132 farms in "survey A" performed in slaughters of the Veneto region. Considering these data as a whole due to the similar criteria and period of the two surveys and the same laboratory methods used, in this study a total of 877 pig intestinal samples were tested in 15 slaughters of two regions, isolating VTEC O157 from 3 of them (0.34%, 95% C.I. 0.07 – 0.99). The positive pigs originated from 3 of 239 farms (1.26%, 95% C.I. 0.25 – 3.62). Our data confirm the very low prevalences found in studies carried out at slaughter in other European countries: a prevalence of 0.1% was reported in Norway (Johnsen et al., 2001), 0.08% in Sweden (Erikkson et al, 2003), 0.67% in The Netherlands (Heuvelink et al, 1999).

In Italy a survey performed in two slaughterhouses of the Emilia-Romagna region between December 1999 and December 2000 found VTEC O157 in one of 150 randomly sampled pigs with a prevalence of 0.7% (Bonardi et al., 2003); in a survey of the Piemonte region between May and October 2002, the organism was not detected in any of 504 pigs originating from 6 farms and tested at slaughter Decastelli et al., 2004).

In non European countries a prevalence of 2.0% was reported from USA (Feder et al, 2003). About the herd prevalence, a large study in The Netherlands (Schouten et al, 2005) with sampling performed on farms detected VTEC O157 in 0.4% of finishing pig herds.

Even though these prevalences can be considered low, the isolation of VTEC O157 from pig herds has raised concern. Studies in the USA have shown that pigs experimentally infected with *E. coli* O157 can shed the organism in their faeces for at least two months and that from magnitude and duration of shedding it cannot be excluded that swine could serve as a reservoir host under suitable conditions (Cornick et al., 2004).

Considering the risk of introduction in the pig herds, the results of other studies suggest that keeping pigs and cattle together on farms, with possibility of direct or indirect contact with one another, can be a risk factor for establishing VTEC O157 in pigs (Erikkson et al, 2003). An exposure could result from contamination of feedstuff or environment with ruminant manure; dogs, insects, rodents and bird could play a role in transmission of the organism in the farm environment as well as the man itself, in case of improper management or hygienic practices.

A follow-up investigation conducted in this study on the farm of origin of one positive pigs where both pigs and cattle where reared, showed that 26.6% of the heifers were harbouring VTEC O157; the analysis of PFGE profiles demonstrated that all the bovine isolates were 90-100 homologus, indicating that colonization with a prevalent clone had occurred. The VTEC O157 strain isolated from the positive pigs was closely related to the bovine strains, sharing more than 96% homology, suggesting that the same clone may have been spread crosswise to the two species.

The risk of introduction of this foodborne pathogen in the swine food chain should not be neglected and other surveys have shown that the contamination of pig carcasses by *E. coli* O157 at slaughter is possible.

So far pork meat or products containing pork meat only have not been definitely identified as a source of human outbreaks, although sausages containing beef and pork have been implicated in human infection and a family cluster of *E. coli* O157 infection microbiologically associated with consumption of salami that contained pork meat only, but stuffed in a natural casing of bovine origin (Conedera et al., 2007), has recently been described in Italy.

References

Bonardi, S., Brindani, F., Pizzin, G., Lucidi, L., D'Incau, M., Liebana, E., Morabito, S., 2003. Detection of *Salmonella* spp., *Yersinia enterocolitica* and verocytotoxin-producing *Escherichia coli* O157 in pigs at slaughter in Italy. *Int J Food Microbiol,* 85,101-110.

Conedera, G, Mattiazzi, E., Russo, F, Chiesa, E., Scorzato, I., Grandesso, S., Bessegato, A., Fioravanti,A., Caprioli, A., 2007. A family outbreak of *Escherichia coli* O157 haemorrhagic colitis caused by pork meat salami. *Epidemiol Infect,* 135, 311-314.

Cornick, N.A., Helgerson, A.F., 2004. Transmission and infectious dose of *Escherichia coli* O157:H7 in swine. *Appl Environ Microbiol,* 70, 5331-5335.

Decastelli, L., Ru, G., Brizio, G., Gentile, D., Gallina, S., Caprioli., 2004. Lack of isolation of *Escherichia coli* O157 from pigs fed with bovine whey. *Vet Rec,* 155, 337-338.

Feder, I., Wallace, F.M., Gray, J.T., Fratamico, P., Fedorka-Cray, P.J., Pearce, R.A., et al., 2003. Isolation of *Escherichia coli* O157 from intact colon faecal samples of swine. *Emerg Infect Dis,* 9, 380-3.

Heuvelink, A.E., Zwartkruis-Nahuis, J.T., Van Den Leeuwen, W.J., De Boer, E., 1999. Isolation and characterization of verocytotoxin-producing *Escherichia coli* O157 from slaughter pigs and poultry. *Int J Food Microbiol,* 52:67-75.

Johnsen, G., Wasteson, Y., Heir, E., Berget, O.I., Herikstad, H., 2001. *Escherichia coli* O157:H7 in faeces from cattle, sheep and pigs in the southwest part of Norway during 1998 and 1999. *Int J Food Microbiol.,* 65,193-200.

Morabito, S., Karch, H., Schmidt, H., Minelli F., Mariani Kurdjikian, P., Allerberger, F., Bettelheim, K. A., Caprioli., A., 1999. Molecular characterization of Verocytotoxin-producing *Escherichia coli* of serogrup O111 from different countries. *J Med Microbiol,* 48, 891-896.

Schouten, J.M., Van de Giessen, A.W., Frankena, K., De Jong, M.C.M., Graat, E.A.M., 2005. *Escherichia coli* O157 prevalence in Dutch poultry, pig finishing and veal herds and risk factors in Dutch veal herds. *Prev Vet Medicine,* 70, 1-15.

ORAL & POSTER

THIRD SESSION

**Viruses, parasites,
other pathogens**

Hepatitis E virus RNA in commercially available porcine livers in The Netherlands

Bouwknegt, M.[*][(1,2)], Lodder-Verschoor, F.[(1)], Van der Poel W.H.M.[(3)], Rutjes, S.A.[(1)], De Roda Husman, A.M.[(1)]

[(1)]Laboratory for Zoonoses and Environmental Microbiology, Centre for Infectious Disease Control Netherlands, National Institute for Public Health and the Environment, PO Box 1, 3720 BA Bilthoven, The Netherlands
[(2)]Quantitative Veterinary Epidemiology Group, Wageningen Institute of Animal Sciences, PO Box 338, 6700 AH Wageningen, The Netherlands
[(3)]Animal Sciences Group of Wageningen UR, Department of Infectious Diseases, PO Box 65, 8200 AB Lelystad, The Netherlands
[*]corresponding author: martijn.bouwknegt@rivm.nl

Abstract

Hepatitis E virus (HEV) infections caused by genotype 3 are increasingly observed in industrialized countries, without a distinct source. High similarity between human and swine strains of HEV strongly suggest possible zoonotic transmission. It was reported previously that in 55% of Dutch pig farms HEV-excreting fattening pigs were present. In the current study, presence of HEV RNA in commercially available porcine livers was shown. We examined 62 commercially available porcine livers for HEV contamination. Before examination of livers, the most sensitive combination of tissue disruption and RNA-extraction was chosen from four disruption and seven RNA-extraction methods. Four of 62 livers were shown to be positive for HEV RNA by RT-PCR and Southern blot hybridization, and three sequences were obtained. Phylogenetic analysis showed clustering of the sequences with previously published Dutch HEV genotype 3 sequences from humans and swine. To study infectivity of possible virus, three pigs were intravenously inoculated with suspensions from commercially available HEV positive livers. Two other pigs served as high-dose or low-dose controls. The low-dose control received a comparable viral count as animals receiving inocula from commercially available livers, the high dose control received a viral count that was known to generate infection. Faecal shedding of HEV was observed in the high-dose control, indicating that the control virus was infectious. No faecal shedding of HEV was observed for the low-dose control and the three pigs that were administered the commercially available livers extracts. In conclusion, HEV RNA was found in commercially available porcine livers. Inoculation of susceptible pigs with extracts from HEV-positive livers did not lead to infection, but this may be a dose-dependent effect. The risk for consumers should be investigated further.

Introduction

Hepatitis E virus (HEV) is an enterically transmitted RNA virus that causes liver inflammation in humans and belongs to the family *hepeviridae* (1). Hepatitis E virus is currently classified into four genotypes (named 1 to 4) (2). Genotype 1 and genotype 2 strains circulate in developing countries and are a major cause of outbreaks and sporadic cases of hepatitis E (3). Genotype 3 and genotype 4 strains circulate predominantly in Western countries and cause sporadic cases of locally acquired hepatitis E, which are increasingly observed in industrialized countries (4, 5). The source of HEV in these locally acquired cases is mostly unknown, but a possible role for swine has been suggested, based on high prevalence of HEV among pigs and high similarity between porcine and human HEV sequences from the same geographical region (6). One route that may lead to zoonotic transmission involves food. Foodborne transmission from wild boar and deer to humans has been observed in Japan (7, 8). Furthermore, Japanese studies suggested the possibility of HEV-transmission through contaminated un(der)cooked porcine liver or intestines (9). In the Netherlands, hepatitis E virus RNA was detected on 55% of 97 finishing pig farms in 2005 (10). This finding raises concern on possibility of foodborne transmission. The objective of this study was to quantify presence of HEV in commercially available porcine livers. Detected HEV RNA was sequenced and infectivity of possible virus present in livers was examined by experimental inoculation of pigs. Prior to detection of HEV in livers, four methods for tissue disruption and seven for RNA extraction were compared on RNA yield. The method yielding most RNA was used for screening of commercially available porcine livers.

Materials and Methods

In total, 62 livers were obtained from different butcher shops (n=56) and retail stores (n=6). The positive control liver was obtained from a pig after experimental infection. The negative control liver was purchased from a local butcher shop.

A standard method for mechanical disruption of tissues is extensive vibration in the presence of small beads. We examined the destructive capability of beads of 1 mm and 2 mm in diameter, vibrating twice at 4 m/s for 40 seconds in the presence or absence of proteinase K (0.35 mg/ml lysis buffer) for additional enzymatic disruption. The method with highest RNA yield in PCR detectable units (PDU) per gram was selected. Estimates of PDU/g were obtained as described (11).

For RNA extraction, seven methods were compared (Table 1). Method 1 was an in-house method based on Boom et al (12), all others were commercially available. The comparison study consisted of three parts. In part one, 150 mg of liver tissue was analyzed with all methods except Method 2, and the method with highest PDU/g was selected. Method 2 was not included, because of a maximum loading capacity of 50 mg. In part two, amount of liver tissue as input (50 mg, 150 mg or 250 mg) was examined for the best method from part one, and for Method 2 (50 mg) and Method 3 (250 mg). Method 3 was included because of a maximum loading capacity of 250 mg. In part three, the effect of a second elution of RNA compared to one elution was examined for Methods 1 and 2. To account for the varying volumes of elution buffer, samples were precipitated using ethanol and RNA was subsequently dissolved in 35 µl elution buffer. Subsequently, the method with highest estimated PDU/g was selected for analysis of commercially available livers.

Detection of HEV RNA was done with RT-PCR and Southern blot hybridization of RT-PCR products (11). For comparison of methods for tissue disruption and RNA extraction, RNA was diluted serially in sterile, RNAse-free water in 10-fold for part one of the comparison and in 5-fold for parts two and three of the comparison. For HEV detection in commercially available porcine livers, two serial 10-fold dilutions were included. Positive controls were included during extraction and RT-PCR, blanks were included after each dilution series in RT-PCR, and an internal RNA control was added at reverse transcription to examine inhibition (10). The HEV positive RT-PCR products were cloned for sequencing.

To examine infectivity of possible viral particles, three domestic pigs were intravenously inoculated with 3 ml – 4.5 ml of a liver suspension made from commercially available livers. The pigs had been used as untreated controls in another experiment and were about 7-8 weeks old. Prior to inoculation, faeces and sera were collected to examine HEV RNA or anti-HEV antibodies, respectively. One pig was inoculated with 3 ml of a low-dose control inoculum, and one pig with 2 ml of a high-dose control inoculum. The low-dose control contained a viral count equivalent to the inocula made from commercially available livers, as determined by endpoint dilution in RT-PCR. Faecal samples were taken on 0, 3, 7, 10, 14 and 16 dpi. Pigs were sacrificed at 21 dpi and liver, bile and faecal samples were collected. Hepatitis E virus RNA was extracted from a 10% faecal suspension and from undiluted bile using the QIAamp Viral RNA Mini Kit. Liver samples were subjected to the optimized protocol described in this paper.

Results

For beads of 1 mm and 2 mm in diameter, similar estimates for PDU/g of liver were obtained. Addition of proteinase K increased variation between duplicates and did not increase estimates of PDU/g compared to absence of proteinase K. Subsequently, liver tissue was disrupted with 1 mm beads without addition of proteinase K. Estimates of PDU/g for all RNA extraction methods are displayed in Table 1. In part one of the comparison, Method 1 and Method 6 gave highest estimates of PDU/g for 150 mg of liver as input. For Method 6, however, more aspecific RT-PCR-products were observed in undiluted samples and therefore Method 1 was selected for subsequent parts of the comparison. In part two, methods 1, 2 and 3 were further examined on input of liver. A higher input generated higher estimates of PDU/g for Method 1 and Method 3, without an increase of inhibition in RT-PCR. Method 2 was less sensitive than the other two methods. In part three, a second elution followed by ethanol precipitation was compared to a single elution step for Method

Table 1. *Estimated RNA yield in PCR detectable units per g of liver tissue (on a log-scale) for different RNA extraction methods, with various amount of porcine liver as input.*

Method Description	Reference	Input of liver tissue		
		150 mg	50 mg	250 mg
In house silica	Method 1	8.0	6.4	8.5
RNeasy® Mini kit	Method 2	nd	7.8	nd
RNeasy® Midi kit‡	Method 3	7.0	nd	8.5
NucliSens® Isolation	Method 4	7.0	nd	nd
NucliSens® Magnetic Extraction	Method 5	7.0	nd	nd
Trizol™	Method 6	8.0	nd	nd
Combination of Method 6 and Method 1	Method 7	6.0	nd	nd

nd: not determined; ‡ A second elution step was done always, followed by ethanol precipitation

1 and Method 2. A second elution step decreased estimated PDU/g for Method 1 with 0.7 log PDU/g for 150 mg and 250 mg of liver, and for Method 4 with 0.6 log PDU/g for 50 mg of liver.

Conclusively, Method 1 was used as optimized protocol in subsequent analyses of commercially available porcine liver, with an input of 250 mg of liver and a single elution of RNA.

Hepatitis E virus RNA was detected in four commercially available porcine livers with RT-PCR and Southern blot hybridization of the RT-PCR products, giving a prevalence estimate of 6.5% (95% exact confidence interval (CI): 1.8% – 15.7%). HEV RNA was detected in the undiluted samples only, yielding an estimated viral load of approximately 65 PDU/g of liver (95% CI: 3 – 580 PDU/g liver).

Sequences from three of four RT-PCR products were obtained and all three sequences clustered within different subgroups of genotype 3. Two of three sequences showed highest similarity to published Dutch swine sequences (94% and 97%), the other to a published UK swine sequence (92%). Comparison of sequences from liver with sequences from locally acquired hepatitis E cases in The Netherlands showed at most 93% similarity.

Pre-inoculation samples of all five pigs were free of anti-HEV antibodies in serum and free of HEV RNA in faeces. Experimental inoculation of pigs resulted in viral excretion by only the high-dose control from 7 dpi up to at least 16 dpi, but not on 21 dpi. No HEV RNA was observed in any of the liver and bile samples collected at 21 dpi.

Discussion

Hepatitis E virus RNA was present in four of 62 commercially available porcine livers in The Netherlands and three sequences were obtained. In Japan, 7 of 362 (1.9%) pig livers were shown to contain HEV RNA, with six of seven sequences classified as genotype 3 (13). The three viral strains identified in the current study were also classified as genotype 3, which is similar to strains causing locally acquired hepatitis E in humans in The Netherlands (6).

Experimental infection of pigs with an inoculum of commercially available porcine livers did not result in faecal excretion of HEV and a possible explanation is that HEV RNA originated from defective viral particles. Another hypothesis, however, might be that the administered dose was too low to cause infection. Absence of infection was also observed in the low-dose control pig, while this inoculum was a dilution of the infectious inoculum given to the high-dose control pig. Molecular examination of all inocula prior to administration showed presence of viral RNA only in the high-dose control inoculum. HEV RNA was likely to be present in the other inocula, but inside (aggregations of) hepatocytes, because a lysisbuffer was absent during liver disruption. This interferes with a homogenous distribution of virus in the inoculum and hence decreases the detection probability of HEV. In addition, only a small volume of inoculum was examined, further decreasing the detection probability. A dose dependency for HEV in pigs was demonstrated by Meng et al. (14), who observed no infection in pigs after dilution of an infectious HEV-pool. This observation favors the hypothesis that the dose administered to pigs in the current study was too low to establish infection.

Data from a national food consumption survey in 1997 and 1998 indicated that raw porcine liver is handled by consumers on roughly 900,000 occasions annually, but no data on condition of the livers at consumption were available. Effects of preparation methods on viral infectivity likely exist and will influence a possible foodborne risk. For instance, thermal stability of genotype 1 strains of HEV has been examined and the majority of HEV was inactivated at 60°C, although ~1% of the viral particles were still able to infect cells (15). If these results apply to genotype 3 strains, improper heating of porcine livers may not inactivate all possible viral particles and consumption of undercooked porcine liver may results in ingestion of infectious viral particles.

In conclusion, HEV RNA has been observed in commercially available porcine livers in The Netherlands. Observed sequences belonged to genotype 3, which is the genotype that is associated with locally acquired hepatitis E. A possible dose-dependent relationship for HEV in swine was observed, because the high-dose control inoculum only led to infection in a pig. The risk of foodborne HEV transmission is currently unknown and will be dependent on factors such as infectivity of HEV RNA, method of preparation of liver for consumption, and amount consumed.

References

1 PANDA, S. K., THAKRAL, D. and REHMAN, S., 2006. Hepatitis E virus. *Reviews in Medical Virology*, In press.

2 LU, L., LI, C. and HAGEDORN, C. H., 2006. Phylogenetic analysis of global hepatitis E virus sequences: genetic diversity, subtypes and zoonosis. *Reviews in Medical Virology*, 16 (1), 5-36

3 EMERSON, S. U. and PURCELL, R. H., 2003. Hepatitis E virus. *Reviews in Medical Virology*, 13 (3), 145-54

4 SCHLAUDER, G. G., DAWSON, G. J., ERKER, J. C., KWO, P. Y., KNIGGE, M. F., SMALLEY, D. L., ROSENBLATT, J. E., DESAI, S. M. and MUSHAHWAR, I. K., 1998. The sequence and phylogenetic analysis of a novel hepatitis E virus isolated from a patient with acute hepatitis reported in the United States. *Journal of General Virology*, 79 (Pt 3), 447-456

5 WIDDOWSON, M. A., JASPERS, W. J. M., VAN DER POEL, W. H. M., VERSCHOOR, F., DE RODA HUSMAN, A. M., WINTER, H. L. J., ZAAIJER, H. L. and KOOPMANS, M., 2003. Cluster of cases of acute hepatitis associated with hepatitis E virus infection acquired in the Netherlands. *Clinical Infectious Diseases*, 36 (1), 29-33

6 HERREMANS, M., VENNEMA, H., BAKKER, J., VAN DER VEER, B., DUIZER, E., BENNE, C. A., WAAR, K., HENDRIXKS, B., SCHNEEBERGER, P., BLAAUW, G., KOOIMAN, M. and KOOPMANS, M. P. G., 2007. Swine-like hepatitis E viruses are a cause of unexplained hepatitis in the Netherlands. *Journal of Viral Hepatitis*, 14 (2), 140-6

7 LI, T. C., CHIJIWA, K., SERA, N., ISHIBASHI, T., ETOH, Y., SHINOHARA, Y., KURATA, Y., ISHIDA, M., SAKAMOTO, S., TAKEDA, N. and MIYAMURA, T., 2005. Hepatitis E virus transmission from wild boar meat. *Emerging Infectious Diseases*, 11 (12), 1958-60

8 TEI, S., KITAJIMA, N., TAKAHASHI, K. and MISHIRO, S., 2003. Zoonotic transmission of hepatitis E virus from deer to human beings. *Lancet*, 362 (9381), 371-3

9 MATSUDA, H., OKADA, K., TAKAHASHI, K. and MISHIRO, S., 2003. Severe hepatitis E virus infection after ingestion of uncooked liver from a wild boar. *Journal of Infectious Diseases*, 188 (6), 944

10 RUTJES, S. A., LODDER, W., BOUWKNEGT, M. and DE RODA HUSMAN, A. M., In press. Increased hepatitis E virus prevalence on Dutch pig farms from 33% to 55% by using appropriate internal quality controls for RT-PCR. *Journal of Virological Methods*,

11 VAN DEN BERG, H., LODDER, W., VAN DER POEL, W. H. M., VENNEMA, H. and DE RODA HUSMAN, A. M., 2005. Genetic diversity of noroviruses in raw and treated sewage water. *Research in Microbiology*, 156 (4), 532-40

12 BOOM, R., SOL, C. J. A., SALIMANS, M. M. M., JANSEN, C. L., WERTHEIM-VAN DILLEN, P. M. and VAN DER NOORDAA, J., 1990. Rapid and simple method for purification of nucleic acids. *Journal of Clinical Microbiology*, 28 495-503

13 YAZAKI, Y., MIZUO, H., TAKAHASHI, M., NISHIZAWA, T., SASAKI, N., GOTANDA, Y. and OKAMOTO, H., 2003. Sporadic acute or fulminant hepatitis E in Hokkaido, Japan, may be food-borne, as suggested by the presence of hepatitis E virus in pig liver as food. *Journal of General Virology*, 84 (9), 2351-2357

14 MENG, X. J., HALBUR, P. G., SHAPIRO, M. S., GOVINDARAJAN, S., BRUNA, J. D., MUSHAHWAR, I. K., PURCELL, R. H. and EMERSON, S. U., 1998. Genetic and experimental evidence for cross-species infection by swine hepatitis E virus. *Journal of Virology*, 72 (12), 9714-21

15 EMERSON, S. U., ARANKALLE, V. A. and PURCELL, R. H., 2005. Thermal stability of hepatitis E virus. *Journal of Infectious Diseases*, 192 (5), 930-3

Risk-based surveillance for human health hazards: the example of *Trichinella*

Alban, L.*[1], Boes, J.[1], Kreiner, H.[2], Petersen, J.V.[1], Willeberg, P.[2]

[1]: Danish Meat Association, Vinkelvej 11, DK-8620 Kjellerup, Denmark
[2]: Danish Veterinary and Food Administration, Mørkhøj Bygade 19, DK-2860 Søborg, Denmark
* Lis Alban: lia@danishmeat.dk

Abstract

Increasing demands for cost-effectiveness in surveillance for human health hazards can be met by introducing risk-based principles. This implies targeting subpopulations with higher risk of infection compared to the whole population. We demonstrate how historical data from surveillance can be used to assess risk of infection. The model is called "Discounting historical evidence" and depends mainly on two variables: Annual risk of introduction PIntro and surveillance system sensitivity SSe (ability to detect infection if present). The model implies simulations that reiterate for a number of years, and for each year the output is updated with the confidence on absence of infection. *Trichinella spiralis* infection in pigs is used as an example. In Denmark, pigs at slaughter are tested (currently 23 million per year), and despite of >70 years of sampling no pigs have been found positive. Hence, we concluded that PIntro is low. SSe can be estimated from the maximum number of infected carcasses expected under the specified design prevalence, and the sensitivity of the test applied. According to the assessment, the prevalence of *Trichinella* in Danish pigs is negligible (<1 case/ million). Based on this, a risk-based surveillance programme for *Trichinella* is designed that targets all out-door reared pigs as well as all sows and boars (currently 610,000 per year). Compared to confined pigs, outdoor-reared pigs have higher risk of getting *Trichinella* because of their exposure to wildlife, which might harbour *Trichinella*. Sows and boars are at increased risk, because they live longer than finishers. Again, SSe and PIntro are estimated and the model is used to show how risk-based surveillance can be applied without jeopardizing human health. Finally, we incorporate wildlife surveys and test quality assurance in the programme. The model results are included in an application to the European Commission concerning Denmark's status as a region with negligible risk of *Trichinella*.

Introduction

Trichinella spiralis is a zoonotic infection that previously constituted a common risk in many parts of the world. In Denmark, the surveillance programme for *Trichinella* is based on individual sampling of all pigs delivered to an export authorised abattoir. An increasing number of pigs have been surveyed since 1930, initially by use of the compression method, and since the 1970s by the digestion method (currently 22 m corresponding to 99% of the annual production). No pigs have ever been found positive during the more than 70 years that the programme has been in place. The question is whether a more cost-effective surveillance can be designed without jeopardising human health. Such surveillance should be risk-based, i.e. it should target the sub-population(s) with the highest risk of *Trichinella* since the aim is to detect infection if present. The question is how a risk-based approach would affect the ability to detect infection.

The present analysis aimed to:

1) Demonstrate that Denmark as a region has a negligible risk of *Trichinella* infection in domestic pigs
2) Design a risk-based surveillance system that is able to identify *Trichinella* infection in the national pig herd if it were present at a level above the chosen design prevalence

Method

A model called "Discounting historical evidence" was used for the analyses. The model was developed in connection with an EpiLab Research Project in Copenhagen (Martin et al., in press). In the following, the model will be explained in more detail.

Two variables are of importance for the model:
1) the annual probability of introduction of *Trichinella* – PIntro
2) the sensitivity of the system (SSe) i.e. the surveillance system's capacity to identify *Trichinella* once the infection is present in the national pig herd above the level of the chosen design prevalence P^*

We have looked at two different scenarios:
1) Current surveillance, where we simulated surveillance for the previous 16 years; from 1990 to 2006. In this period we have sampled all pigs in the entire population of slaughtered pigs
2) Risk-based surveillance where we only sample outdoor-reared pigs as well as sows and boars being slaughtered (610,000 pigs, 2005 estimate)

In each scenario, 10,000 simulations were run using the software programme @Risk (Palisade Inc.).

The choice of parameters describing PIntro in the current surveillance was based on the fact that *Trichinella* has not been found in Denmark since 1930 (Maddox-Hyttel et al., 2003). The probability of infection next year (Pintro) can then be conservatively estimated as: 1 / (waiting time since last outbreak), corresponding to 1/76=1.3%. To account for variation in PIntro an interval of ± 25 years was used, corresponding to a probability range of 1.0% to 2.0%. This approach captures changes in risk during the 76-year period of surveillance (the risk of introduction may have varied over the years), but since the current system has prevented introduction for 76 years, an estimated annual risk varying between 1.0% and 2.0% is considered a conservative estimate.

In a risk-based surveillance programme for *Trichinella* for slaughter pigs, outdoor-reared pigs as well as sows and boars will be sampled. Outdoor-reared pigs harbour a higher risk of introduction because of the possibility of contact with wildlife. Sows and boars are at increased risk because they have a longer possible exposure period compared to finishers. Wildlife surveys conducted in Denmark in 1974-75 (Maddox-Hyttel et al., 2003), 1996-97 and 1998-99 (Enemark et al., 2000) all revealed a very low (<0.1%) *Trichinella* prevalence in red foxes. This suggests a stable situation in the sylvatic *Trichinella* cycle in Denmark. Raccoon dogs *Nyctereutes procyonoides* typically show a higher prevalence and larval burden of *Trichinella* than foxes. The raccoon dog is currently not established as a species in Denmark but it is expected to spread into Denmark in the future. The exact magnitude of the increased risk of introduction from wildlife to outdoor-reared pigs compared to indoor-kept pigs is unknown. We therefore chose to model the risk as an interval, where the lower bound of PIntro was set at twice the risk that we found for indoor-kept pigs: $PIntro_{outside} = 2 \times PIntro_{inside} = 2 \times 1/76$ years $= 1/38$ years $= 2.6\%$. As the upper bound of PIntro we used 3 $\times$ $PIntro_{inside}$ corresponding to 3.9%. Again, both bounds should be regarded as conservative estimates.

The surveillance system sensitivity (SSe) in the current surveillance can be estimated from the number of infected carcasses expected among the tested under the specified design prevalence, and the sensitivity of the test applied. We estimated that the prevalence of *Trichinella* in Denmark is negligible. According to EFSA (2005) this corresponds to less than one case per million individuals. Therefore, a design prevalence of 1/m was chosen. According to the literature, the test sensitivity might be as low as 40% in case only 1g of pig muscle is sampled, and only few encapsulated *Trichinella* larvae are present (3-5 larvae/g). If more larvae are present, or larger amounts of meat are digested, then the sensitivity is much higher than 40% (see Forbes & Gajadhar, 1999). To account for variability we assumed that the sensitivity of the individual test varied from 35% to 45%.

Based on the information about the expected number of infected animals and the sensitivity of the individual test, the system sensitivity in the present surveillance that includes all finishers was estimated to be 99.99% (Table 1). We assumed a design prevalence (P^*) of 1/m, implying that if *Trichinella* infection were present, the prevalence would be $\geq 1/m$. This implies that at least 23 infected pigs are expected within a population of 23 m pigs. Because of the epidemiology of *Trichinella*, we expect that the main part of the 23 infected pigs will be present among the outdoor-reared pigs as well as the sows and boars. We assumed that 2/3 of the infected pigs would be found here corresponding to 15 out of the 23 infected pigs. Using these assumptions, the risk-based surveillance system chosen will have an SSe of 99.95% (Table 2).

Table 1. Estimated surveillance system sensitivity (SSe) for *Trichinella* in Danish pig production in the current system that involves testing of almost all pigs (currently 99%)

SSe = Prob(identifying infection) = 1-Prob(overlooking infection) = $1-(1-Se)^D = 1-(1-0.4)^{23} = 0.9999$
Where: Se = Test sensitivity =0.40   D = Expected minimum number of diseased in population = $P^* \times N$ = (1/m) x23 m=23 pigs P^* = Estimated design prevalence = 1/1.000.000 = 1/m   N = Size of total population, here the entire national pig herd = 23.000.000 pigs   n = Sample size = 23.000.000 pigs

Table 2. Estimated surveillance system sensitivity (SSe) for *Trichinella* in Danish pig production in a risk-based surveillance including outdoor-reared pigs as well as sows and finishers

SSe = Prob(identifying infection) = 1-Prob(overlooking infection) = $1-(1-Se)^{D2} = 1-(1-0.4)^{15} = 0.9995$
Where   Se = Test sensitivity = 0.40 D_1 = Expected minimum number of diseased in population = $P^* \times N$ = (1/m) x23 m=23 pigs D_2 = Expected number of diseased in sample= Prop x D_1 = 0.67 x 23 = 15 infected pigs   Prop = Proportion between infected pigs found in risk populations (outdoor-reared pigs/sows and boars) and in indoor-reared pigs = assumed to be 2/3 = 67% P^* = Estimated design prevalence in national herd = 1/1.000.000 = 1/m   N = Size of population, the entire national herd =23m pigs   n = Sample size = finishers raised outdoor as well as sows and boars in 2005 = 610,000

The simulation model updates the probability of infection in the national herd every year based on a combination of the probability of infection at the end of last year with the probability of introduction during the specific year. In the first year (1990) we assume that we have no knowledge of the infection; it might be present or not, i.e. we set the probability of infection to 50%, which is a very conservative estimate, since no cases have been found in the preceding 60 years. In each of the following 16 years we survey the pigs and do not find any positive pigs; by doing so we increase our confidence that we do not have the infection in the national pig herd, including our outdoor pig population.

Results

According to the simulation model there is a probability of 98.6% that the national pig herd in Denmark currently is free from *Trichinella* (Probability of free adjusted 95% CI: 98.1%-99.0%). A high degree of confidence is obtained already after one year. This is mainly due to the large sample size. Hence, the risk is entirely driven by the annual risk of introduction PIntro, which is estimated to 1.3%. In a simulation of the effect of risk-based surveillance, the probability of freedom from infection is again set to 50% in the first year, to simulate a situation without prior knowledge. Because of annual sampling with no positive findings the probability that the national pig herd is free from *Trichinella* in a risk-based sampling scheme increases to 96.7% after one year and remains stable thereafter (95% CI: 96.1%-97.3%). This is a slightly lower probability than in the current system. Again, the risk is entirely driven by the annual risk of introduction PIntro, which

Session 3

is estimated at between 2.6 and 3.9% (mean 3.3%). As with the current system, the risk-based surveillance achieves a high level of sensitivity after just one year.

Discussion and conclusion

As pointed out by a previous risk assessment report (EFSA, 2005), the existence of true *Trichinella*-free areas/countries is very unlikely, because even though *Trichinella* may be absent in domestic pigs it may still be present in wildlife. What we can conclude from our simulations based on surveillance data from a 76-year period with increasing intensity is that the prevalence in domestic pigs in Denmark has been negligible and that Denmark is a low-risk area for *Trichinella in pigs for slaughter*. Therefore, risk-based sampling targeting sub-populations with higher risk is justified.

Sampling the entire population of 160,000 outdoor-reared pigs plus 450,000 sows and boars only gives a slightly lower confidence instead of sampling 23 m indoor-reared pigs. The negligible risk of infection among confined (i.e. indoor-reared) finishers is due to the strict biosecurity in place in Danish indoor pig herds. Hereby, outdoor-reared pigs will act as a sentinel for infection of *Trichinella* in the national herd. Similarly, testing of 450,000 sows and boars will act as an indicator of infection in individual herds in the event of infection in wildlife and biosecurity failing to prevent introduction of *Trichinella*. The sows and boars will be tested for *Trichinella* no matter if they are raised in confinement or outdoors, and no matter where they are slaughtered (export slaughterhouse or local butcher).

The model by Martin et al. (in press) assumed an "all other things equal" situation. For *Trichinella*, it may be argued that the advent of the raccoon dog means an increased risk of *Trichinella* transmission. If an infected raccoon dog harbours more *Trichinella* larvae than foxes (Oivanen et al., 2002), and if this results in a higher degree of exposure of outdoor pigs, then there is a higher likelihood that infection will be identified through the surveillance system in place. Moreover, the decreasing number of pig farms in Denmark will inevitably lead to larger indoor farms with better biosecurity.

The model results are included in an application to the European Commission concerning Denmark's status as a region with negligible risk of *Trichinella*. A decision is expected in 2007. The proposed risk-based surveillance programme for *Trichinella* in Denmark will also include annual wildlife surveys, pig traceability, contingency plans and test quality assurance.

References

EFSA, 2005. Opinion of the Scientific Panel on Biological Hazards on "Risk assessment of a revised inspection of slaughter animals in areas with low prevalence of *Trichinella*". The EFSA Journal 200: 1-411

ENEMARK, H.L., BJØRN, H., HENRIKSEN, S.A., NIELSEN, B., 2000. Screening for infection of *Trichinella* in red foxes (*Vulpes vulpes*) in Denmark. *Vet. Parasit.* 88: 229-237

FORBES, L. & GAJADHAR, A.A., 1999. A validated *Trichinella* digestion assay and an associated sampling and quality assurance system for use in testing pork and horse meat. *J. of Food Protect.* 62: 1308-1313

MADDOX-HYTTEL. C., ANDERSEN, J.S., BOES, J., DIETZ, H.H., KAPEL, C.M.O., ROSENQUIST, H., 2003. Risk assessment for *Trichinella* in Danish pork (in Danish with English summary). Report, Danish Veterinary Institute. Available online at: www.dfvf.dk/files/filer/om%20forskningen/risikovurdering_trikiner_2002-2003.pdf

MARTIN, P.A.J., CAMERON, A.R., GREINER, M. (in press). Demonstrating freedom from disease using multiple complex data sources: 1. A new methodology based on scenario trees. *Prev. Vet. Med.*

OIVANEN, I., KAPEL, C.M.O., POZIO, E., LA ROSA, G., MIKKONEN, T., SUKURA, A. 2002. Associations between *Trichinella* species and host species in Finland. *J. Parasitol.* 88: 84-88

A qualitative assessment of the probability of human exposure to *Trichinella* spp. in Switzerland

Schuppers, M.E.[1]*, Breidenbach E.[2], Frey, C.[3], Gottstein, B.[3], Kihm, U.[1], Stärk, K.D.C.[2]+

[1] SAFOSO, Bremgartenstrasse 109A, CH-3012, Bern, Switzerland
[2] Federal Veterinary Office, Schwarzenburgstrasse 155, CH-3003 Bern, Switzerland
[3] VetSuisse Faculty, University of Bern, Institute of Parasitology, Länggassstrasse 122, CH-3012 Bern, Switzerland
+ Current address: Royal Veterinary College, Department of Veterinary Clinical Science, Hawkshead Lane, North Mymms, Hertfordshire, AL9 7TA, England
* corresponding author: manon.schuppers@safoso.ch

Abstract

Trichinellosis is a zoonotic disease caused by *Trichinella* spp. Pork is a potential source of infection for humans. A qualitative assessment was conducted to assess the probability of human exposure to *Trichinella* spp. in Switzerland via the consumption of pork. For the assessment, both the wildlife cycle and the domestic cycle were taken into account. The probability of occurrence of *Trichinella* infections in domestic pigs was assessed negligible under controlled housing systems due to biosecurity measures. Free-range pigs were assessed to have a very low probability of being infected. Pork from free-range pigs that were not tested for *Trichinella* spp. was estimated to carry a very low probability for human exposure to *Trichinella* spp.

Introduction

Trichinellosis is a zoonotic disease caused by the nematode *Trichinella* spp. Infections occur in a wide range of animal species as well as in humans, but clinical disease is largely restricted to humans. Transmission of infection from host to host occurs via the oral intake of meat containing infectious larvae (OIE, 2006). Human trichinellosis has been attributed to a variety of meat sources, including pork (Pozio, 2000).

Since 1 January 2007, all pigs, horses, wild boar, bears, and nutrias are tested for *Trichinella* spp. at slaughter or at game handling establishments in Switzerland in order to comply with the EU regulation 2075/2005, although small slaughter plants may be exempted from testing of pigs (Anonymous, 2005). Before this date, testing for *Trichinella* spp. was only compulsory for game that was sold for commercial purposes.

Human cases of trichinellosis were not reported in Switzerland since more than two decades. Cases that were reported earlier in the 20th century were not attributed to pork, but were attributed either to meat from dogs, nutrias and lynxes, or the source of infection could not be identified (Hörning, 1976; Jakob et al., 1994).

The Swiss Federal Veterinary Office therefore considers the Swiss domestic pig population to be free from *Trichinella* infections. Under this assumption, the recent implementation of the testing program for pigs will lead to an increased use of resources, without leading to a significant improvement of public health.

A release assessment was conducted to assess the probability that *Trichinella* infections occur in the Swiss domestic pig population and to assess the probability that humans in Switzerland will be exposed to *Trichinella* spp. via the release of pork containing *Trichinella* larvae. The results from this assessment can be used to evaluate the efficacy of a large scale testing of domestic pigs for *Trichinella* spp. in Switzerland.

Hazard characterisation
Pathogen

Four *Trichinella* species are indigenous on the European continent, out of 11 species that have been recognized (OIE, 2006). In this assessment only three of these (*T. spiralis*, *T. britovi* and *T. pseudospiralis*) are considered, because the natural host animals of the fourth European species *T. nativa* – arctic and subarctic carnivores – do not occur naturally in Switzerland.

Transmission of all species occurs via the oral intake of infective larvae, which are localized in muscle tissue. After maturing and reproduction in the intestinal tract, newborn larvae migrate to striated muscles where they penetrate individual muscle cells and develop into the infective stage (OIE, 2006). Transmission via worms and larvae that were excreted via faeces (Pozio, 2000) was not considered in this assessment, because it is most likely that they are damaged or killed due to environmental impact before they reach the intestines of a new host where they could replicate (B. Gottstein, pers. comm.).

Release assessment

A risk pathway was developed to identify all possible routes that may lead to the exposure of humans in Switzerland to *Trichinella* spp. via the consumption of pork (figure 1).

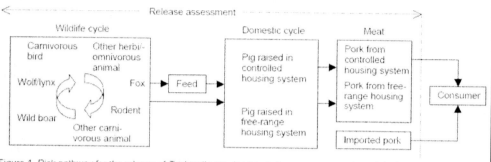

Figure 1. Risk pathway for the release of *Trichinella* spp. leading to human exposure via pork in Switzerland

Wildlife cycle

Trichinella infections were diagnosed in several wild animal species in Switzerland, but it should be noted that all larvae that were investigated were identified as *T. britovi*. The prevalence is considered to be highest in lynxes. There is a small lynx population of 30-40 lynxes, and of 53 animals that were investigated in 1999-2006, 15 were *Trichinella*-positive. Also, one of two wolves that were investigated in 2006 was positive for *T. britovi* (B. Gottstein and C. Frey, pers. comm.). The likelihood of occurrence of *Trichinella* infections in lynxes and wolves was assessed very high. The fox population is very large; annually approximately 50,000 animals are hunted or otherwise killed (BAFU, 2006). The most recent data about *Trichinella* infections in foxes date from a study conducted in 1992, when larvae were isolated from 1.3% of the tested foxes, and an antibody response against *Trichinella* spp. was detected in 12.6% of the investigated foxes (Jakob et al., 1994). The probability of occurrence of *Trichinella* infections in foxes was assessed medium.

The size of the wild boar population in Switzerland was estimated between 24,000 and 66,000 animals (Leuenberger, 2004), and according to hunting statistics 4,800 to 6,300 animals were hunted annually in 2002-2004 (BAFU, 2006). The number of wild boar that is tested annually does not exceed 2,700, but this number also includes many imported wild boar (BVET, 2006a; D. Bernet, pers. comm.). Despite this testing, since many years there are no reports about *Trichinella* infected wild boar. In neighbouring countries, *Trichinella* infections are known to occur in wild boar (Gari-Toussaint, M., 2005; Nöckler, 2005; ITRC, 2007). The probability of occurrence of *Trichinella* infections in wild boar was assessed low.

Birds, mainly carnivorous birds, are only susceptible to *T. pseudospiralis* (Pozio, 2005). This *Trichinella* species was never described in Switzerland, and also reports from neighbouring countries are absent or rare (Nöckler et al., 2006; ITRC, 2007). However, no birds were ever investigated for *Trichinella* spp. in Switzerland. The probability of occurrence of *Trichinella* infections in birds was assessed negligible.

There are no recent studies in Switzerland about the occurrence of *Trichinella* infections in other wildlife species. The probability of occurrence of *Trichinella* infections in other herbi- and omnivorous species was assessed negligible, because their exposure to *Trichinella* spp. was assessed negligible due to their feed pattern. The probability of occurrence of *Trichinella* infections in other carnivorous species was considered low and in rodents very low.

Feed

Commercial pig feed and kitchen waste that is processed in licensed companies was assessed to pose a negligible risk related to *Trichinella*, because the compulsory heat treatment steps in the production process will inactivate any infective *Trichinella* larvae if they were present. The probability that kitchen waste from private households or slaughter waste from home slaughter is fed to pigs was considered very low, but no data were available. It is unknown how well the compulsory heat treatment is applied in this situation. Closed feed storage prevents rodent access, and manual feed distribution by the farmer allows the farmer to detect rodents in the feed. There were no data available to assess the frequency with which feed containing rodents is eaten by pigs.

Domestic cycle

In Switzerland, animal-friendly production systems are widely implemented. Over 50% of all pigs have access to outdoor areas (BLW, 2005), but these systems are not equal to free-range, extensive housing systems where pigs for example have access to pasture areas. It was estimated that maximally 1-3% of all pigs are raised under such free-range conditions, but exact numbers were not available.

In addition to feed, cannibalism and the ingestion of synanthropic or sylvatic animals can lead to a *Trichinella* infection in domestic pigs (Pozio, 2000). Tail musculature can contain *Trichinella* larvae, and tail biting can contribute to maintaining an existing infection within an infected herd. This route of transmission was assessed to play a negligible role in Switzerland. Ingestion of a synanthropic or sylvatic animal could occur when an infected synanthropic or sylvatic animal died within reach of a domestic pig, or when a domestic pig chased and caught such an animal. Under controlled housing conditions, access of synanthropic or sylvatic animals to domestic pigs is restricted, but under free-range conditions access of synanthropic or sylvatic animals cannot be prevented.

Until the end of December 2006, testing for *Trichinella* was conducted on a voluntary base in a few slaughter plants. Between 2001 and 2005 the proportion of slaughtered pigs that was tested increased from 14.7% to 33.8% (BVET, 2006a). No positive results were found, which indicated that the maximum prevalence in the slaughter pig population did not exceed 0.0003% in 2005 (95% confidence).

In conclusion, the probability of occurrence of *Trichinella* infections in domestic pigs under controlled housing conditions was assessed negligible. The probability of occurrence of *Trichinella* infections in domestic pigs under free-range conditions was assessed very low.

Meat

Since 1 January 2007, all pigs are subject to testing for *Trichinella* at slaughter, however, small slaughter plants may be exempted from testing (Anonymous, 2005). Pigs from free-range housing systems can be slaughtered in both large and small slaughter plants, but no data were available to estimate the volume of each of these routes. Pork from free-range pigs that were tested negative for *Trichinella* spp. was assessed to carry a negligible probability for the exposure of humans to *Trichinella* spp. Pork from free-range pigs that were not tested was assessed to carry a very low probability for the exposure of humans to *Trichinella* spp.

Officially imported pork must be tested for *Trichinella* spp. (BVET, 2006b). Therefore, this pork was assessed to carry a negligible probability for the exposure of humans to *Trichinella* spp. Limited amounts of pork can legally be imported without import permit from Europe for private consumption (BVET, 2006c). Pork imported from EU member states was assessed to carry a negligible probability for the exposure of humans to *Trichinella* spp., but pork imported from non EU-member states was assessed to carry a low probability for the exposure of humans to *Trichinella* spp. However, no data were available to estimate the volume of each of these routes.

Discussion and conclusions

This assessment showed that free-range pigs in Switzerland have a very low probability of being infected with *Trichinella* spp. However, there is a lack of high quality data about *Trichinella* infections in free-range pigs in Switzerland. As well, part of the free-range pigs are excluded from *Trichinella* testing when they are slaughtered in small slaughter plants. Currently, a study including a serological survey is conducted that specifically targets free-range pigs to improve the knowledge base for this group of pigs.

A second category that needs special attention is the imported pork for private consumption. Pork from non-EU member states was considered to carry a low probability for human exposure to *Trichinella* spp. However, these imports are not under government control.

Other meat sources (for example game or horse meat) were not considered in this assessment. However, they should be considered as well in order to assess the overall likelihood for human exposure to *Trichinella* spp. in Switzerland.

This assessment showed that the large scale testing of pigs from controlled housing systems does not contribute significantly to the improvement of public health in Switzerland, since the probability of occurrence of *Trichinella* infections in these pigs was considered negligible. A risk based surveillance system that targets high risk animal categories, such as free-range pigs, could reduce the volume of the program without increasing the probability of human exposure to *Trichinella* spp.

References

ANONYMOUS, 2005. Verordnung über das Schlachten und die Fleischkontrolle (Stand am 5. Dezember 2006). SR-Nummer 817.190. www.bvet.admin.ch. Accessed 22 January 2007.

BUNDESAMT FÜR LANDWIRTSCHAFT (BLW), 2005. Agrarbericht 2005. www.blw.admin.ch. Accessed 23 January 2007.

BUNDESAMT FÜR UMWELT (BAFU), 2006. Eidgenössische Jagdstatistik. www.wild.unizh.ch/jagdst/. Accessed 23 January 2007.

BUNDESAMT FÜR VETERINÄRWESEN (BVET), 2006a. Schweizer Zoonosebericht 2005. BVET Magazin 3/2006. www.bvet.admin.ch. Accessed 23 January 2007.

BUNDESAMT FÜR VETERINÄRWESEN (BVET), 2006b. Technische Weisung über die *Trichinella*-Untersuchung von Schlachttierkörpern und Fleisch von Hausschweinen, Pferden, Wildschweinen, Nutrias, sowie weiteren empfindlichen Wildtierarten. www.bvet.admin.ch. Accessed 23 January 2007.

BUNDESAMT FÜR VETERINÄRWESEN (BVET), 2006c. Führen Sie Tiere oder Waren wie Fleisch, Kaviar, Elfenbein, Pelze, Reptilleder mit? Veterinär- und artenschutzrechtliche Vorschriften bei der Einreise in die Schweiz und Liechtenstein. Stand im Juni 2006. www.bvet.admin.ch. Accessed 22 January 2007.

GARI-TOUSSAINT, M., TIEULIÉ, N., BALDIN, J.L., DUPOUY-CAMET, J., DELAUNAY, P., FUZIBET, J.G., 2005. Human trichinellosis due to *Trichinella britovi* in Southern France after consumption of frozen wild boar meat. *Eurosurveillance*, 10 (4-6), 117-118.

HÖRNING, B., 1976. *Trichinella spiralis und Trichinellose in der Schweiz*. Bern: Hausdruckerei Institut für exakte Wissenschaften.

INTERNATIONAL TRICHINELLA REFERENCE CENTRE (ITRC), 2007. Database of *Trichinella* strains. www.iss.it/site/Trichinella/scripts/sear.asp. Accessed 23 January 2007.

JAKOB, H.P., ECKERT, J., JEMMI, T., GOTTSTEIN, B., 1994. Untersuchungen von Schlacht- und Wildtieren in der Schweiz auf Trichinellose mit der Verdauungsmethode und einem serologischen Verfahren (E/S ELISA). *Schweizer Archiv für Tierheilkunde*, 136, 298-308.

LEUENBERGER, R., 2004. *Surveillance of wild boar in Switzerland: prevalence of infections relevant to domestic pigs*. Inauguraldissertation zur Erlangung der Würde einer Doktorin der Philosophie. Basel: Universität Basel.

NÖCKLER, K., 2005. Vorkommen und Bedeutung von *Trichinella* spp. in Deutschland. *Wiener Tierärztliche Monatsschrift*, 92, 301-307.

NÖCKLER, K., RECKINGER, S., POZIO, E., 2006. *Trichinella spiralis* and *Trichinella pseudospiralis* mixed infection in a wild boar (*Sus scrofa*) of Germany. *Veterinary Parasitology*, 137, 364-368.

POZIO, E., 2000. Factors affecting the flow among domestic, synanthropic and sylvatic cycles of *Trichinella*. *Veterinary Parasitology*, 93, 241-262.

POZIO, E., 2005. The broad spectrum of *Trichinella* hosts: from cold- to warm-blooded animals. *Veterinary Parasitology*, 132, 3-11.

WORLD ORGANISATION FOR ANIMAL HEALTH (OIE), 2006. Manual of diagnostic tests and vaccines for terrestrial animals. Chapter 2.2.9 Trichinellosis. www.oie.int. Accessed 23 January 2007.

Risk assessment for *Toxoplasma gondii* in the Danish pig industry

Boes, J.*[1], Alban, L.[1], Sørensen, L.L.[2], Nersting, L.[3]

Danish Meat Association, [1]Vinkelvej 11, DK-8620 Kjellerup, [2]Axeltorv 3, DK-1609 Copenhagen, [3]Maglegårdsvej 2, DK-4000 Roskilde, DENMARK
* Jaap Boes: *jbo@danishmeat.dk*

Abstract
The parasite *Toxoplasma gondii* is capable of infecting most mammals including man. In humans, toxoplasmosis is usually asymptomatic but may have serious consequences for pregnant women or immuno-compromised patients. Contact with infected cats and cat litter, contaminated soil and infected meat are risk factors for toxoplasmosis. Although the prevalence of *Toxoplasma* in pig production has declined significantly during the past 30 years, it has recently been suggested that a large part of human cases of toxoplasmosis may be ascribed to meat, including pork and pork products. Moreover, perinatal screening of pregnant women and infants for *Toxoplasma* has proven to be of limited value. This has raised the question of how to survey for *Toxoplasma*: in humans or meat? Therefore, the role of meat, including pigs and pork, as a risk factor for human toxoplasmosis was assessed by the Danish Meat Association. The release assessment showed that outdoor-reared pigs as well as sows and boars were at higher risk of infection with *Toxoplasma*. With respect to exposure, consumption of mildly cured pork products and inadequately heat-treated pork were associated with increased risk. Knowledge on elimination or survival of *Toxoplasma* in cured pork products is sparse, which is unsatisfactory given current trends toward lower salt content and lower cooking temperatures. It was concluded that, aside from consumption of raw pork, which is rare in Denmark and not recommended for other reasons, certain mildly cured ready-to-eat pork products, that have not been heat-treated, may constitute a risk for toxoplasmosis, if not frozen prior to manufacturing. Information on the effects of curing on survival of *Toxoplasma* in meat is sparse and therefore deserves further research. However, most of the pork used for manufacturing in Denmark originates from pigs raised indoors and for logistic reasons it is frozen prior to processing, thereby reducing the risk for human toxoplasmosis.

Introduction
Toxoplasma gondii is a ubiquitous protozoan parasite that can infect most mammals, including man. The main sources of infection for humans are contact with infected cats or cat litter, contaminated soil or ingestion of undercooked infected meat. The prevalence of *Toxoplasma* in pig production has declined significantly during the past 30 years, and especially in finisher pigs raised indoors seroprevalences are now typically below 5% (see Tenter et al., 2000, for review). This decline is mainly attributed to more intensive housing systems especially in Europe and hence reduced exposure to *Toxoplasma* from cats and the environment (Tenter et al., 2000).

However, recently a European multi-centre study on *Toxoplasma* has suggested that 30-60% of human cases of toxoplasmosis may be ascribed to meat, including pork and pork products, albeit with substantial variation between centres as regards the type of meat involved (Cook et al., 2000). Other studies have also indicated an association between the risk of acquiring *Toxoplasma* and consumption of undercooked pork or certain cured pork products (e.g. Buffolano et al., 1996; Kapperud et al., 1996). However, the question remains: what is the role of meat, and in particular pork, for human toxoplasmosis?

To address this question, a risk assessment was conducted by the Danish Meat Association. The aim was to assess the risk for human toxoplasmosis associated with pork and pork products. The risk assessment followed the guidelines issued by Codex Alimentarius and OIE and contained the following steps:

- Hazard identification
- Release assessment
- Exposure assessment
- Consequence assessment
- Risk estimation

Finally, we provide some suggestions for risk management.

Hazard identification

Toxoplasma is, amongst others, a meat-borne infection that can cause serious disease in unborn children or immuno-suppressed patients. Like in many other European countries with intensive pig production, *Toxoplasma* is found at a low prevalence (3%) in Danish finisher pigs (Lind et al., 1994). However, it cannot be excluded that some cases of human toxoplasmosis in Denmark can be ascribed to pork. Therefore, *Toxoplasma* was considered a relevant hazard.

Release assessment

To date, serology is the quickest and most-often used method of testing pigs for *Toxoplasma*, being a good indicator for the burden of *Toxoplasma* in a pig (Dubey et al., 1995). *Toxoplasma* seroprevalence in pigs in Europe is generally low (i.e. ≤5%) in finisher pigs that are raised indoors. Higher prevalences have been found in outdoor-reared pigs (Fehlhaber et al., 2003; Kijlstra et al., 2004; Venturini et al., 2004), and the highest prevalences are found in sows and boars (Tenter et al., 2000).

Exposure assessment

Due to expensive bioassay methods and not yet validated DNA methods, only limited data exist on occurrence of *Toxoplasma* in raw, unprocessed pork. Evidence stems largely from human case-control studies showing that toxoplasmosis might be associated with, amongst others, consumption of raw pork (e.g. Cook et al., 2000). In a recent comprehensive study, Dubey et al. (2005) found *Toxoplasma* in 0.4% of 2,094 fresh pork samples purchased in retail outlets in the US.

Toxoplasma in pork will survive refrigeration at 4°C but not at 0°C (Hill et al., 2006). *Toxoplasma* does not multiply in fresh or refrigerated meat. Processing methods with a well-documented effect of eliminating *Toxoplasma* in meat are freezing and heat-treatment (cooking, frying). Freezing at − 12°C for 24 hours (e.g. Kotula et al., 1991; Smith, 1991), or heating to a core temperature of 61°C for at least 1 minute (e.g. Dubey et al., 1990; Dubey, 2000) will inactivate *Toxoplasma*. In addition, *Toxoplasma* tissue cysts can be eliminated using radiation techniques (Smith, 2001) or high-pressure processing (Lindsay et al., 2006).

In contrast, knowledge on elimination or survival of *Toxoplasma* in cured pork products (salted, smoked, dried or fermented meat) is sparse. This is unsatisfactory given current trends toward lower salt content and lower cooking temperatures. Among curing procedures, the effect of salting is best-documented. Salt concentrations of ≥6% eliminate *Toxoplasma* in pork, whereas *Toxoplasma* may survive at lower salt concentrations (Dubey, 1997). Curing of pork loins with 2% sodium chlorate or ≥1.4% potassium or sodium lactate for at least 8 hours prevented transmission to cats (Hill et al., 2004; Hill et al., 2006).

The very few studies that looked at survival of *Toxoplasma* in dried, smoked and/or fermented pork did not detect viable *Toxoplasma* (Sommer et al., 1965; Warnekulasuriya et al., 1998).

Consequence assessment

Seronegative pregnant women and immuno-compromised patients are the main risk groups for toxoplasmosis. Depending on the time of infection, congenital *Toxoplasma* infection may result in abortions or birth of infants with clinical signs (transmission during early pregnancy) or birth of infants with subclinical infections, resulting in nervous disorders or eye problems later in life (transmission during late pregnancy). Immuno-suppressed patients (e.g. AIDS patients) may show severe clinical symptoms such as encephalitis.

Risk estimation

Humans: Toxoplasmosis has serious consequences for pregnant women without immunity to *Toxoplasma*, because both foetus and newborn children may be affected. From 1992 to 1996, the incidence of congenital toxoplasmosis in Denmark was 3 per 10.000 newborn infants. The proportion of newly acquired *Toxoplasma* infections in pregnant women that can be ascribed to pork is unknown, as is the infective dose for congenital toxoplasmosis.

Pigs: In Denmark, the prevalence of *Toxoplasma* was 3% in finishers and 12% in sows (Lind et al., 1994). *Toxoplasma* prevalence in outdoor-reared pigs in Denmark is presently unknown, but other studies have shown a higher prevalence compared to indoor pig production. This suggests that sows and outdoor-reared pigs constitute a higher risk for human toxoplasmosis. On the other hand, the bulk of pork produced in Denmark originates from finishers, not sows, while pork from outdoor-reared pigs in Denmark constitutes less than 1% of the total production.

Pork: No data are available for *Toxoplasma* in fresh pork in Denmark. *Toxoplasma* in meat will remain infective during refrigeration. On the other hand, if pork is sufficiently frozen before/heated during preparation, then the probability of *Toxoplasma* infection is negligible (see Table 1).

Processing: Aside from consumption of raw or undercooked meat, possible risk products for *Toxoplasma* are certain ready-to-eat pork products that have not been heat-treated and/or contain low levels of salt. Examples are smoked filet, smoked ham and some naturally fermented fresh sausages, but not dry-cured sausages (Table 1). In theory, the risk for human toxoplasmosis will increase if risk products are produced using meat from sows or outdoor reared pigs. However, both production and consumption of risk products manufactured with e.g. meat from outdoor reared pigs is limited in Denmark, suggesting that this is of minor importance.

Table 1:
The effect of meat processing on survival of *Toxoplasma gondii* in pork and pork products

Product type	Effect on *Toxoplasma*	Risk product
Fresh pork Minced pork Raw sausage, marinated meat	Eliminated by heat treatment* or freezing	Insufficiently heat-treated meat
Bacon		Raw bacon
Cured meat products (salted, not heat treated, ready-to-eat)	May survive; no multiplication Elimination if the meat is frozen prior to processing	All mildly-cured products from meat that has not been frozen prior to processing
Fermented sausage, salami	Probably eliminated (high salt content)	Probably none
Pasteurised meat products Ready-to-eat products (heat treated) Conserves (canned meat)	Eliminated	None

* To a core temperature of at least 61°C for 1 min.

Risk management

Our assessment shows that occurrence of *Toxoplasma* in confined finishing pigs reared in modern industrialized farms is very low, and that most of the pork is processed in ways that will eliminate *Toxoplasma*. Therefore, from a cost-effectiveness point of view, risk management for *Toxoplasma* should not focus on release (pigs) but on exposure (pork).

There are several ways to reduce the risk of exposure to *Toxoplasma*. Firstly, proper processing by use of freezing, heat-treatment or effective curing will reduce exposure through meat. For example, it could be recommended not to use meat from sows or outdoor reared pigs for risk products, unless the meat has been frozen. Secondly, information campaigns directed at pregnant women can be a very effective means of focusing on ways to reduce exposure to sources of *Toxoplasma*. These campaigns should include advice on not only to avoid consumption of raw or undercooked meat, but also to avoid contact to cat litter and soil, as well as maintaining good kitchen hygiene. A third option, suggested by several authors, would be labelling of risk products, in line with the labelling of certain French soft cheeses that contain a message to pregnant women about the risk of *Listeria* infection.

Conclusions

It was concluded that, aside from consumption of raw pork, which is rare in Denmark and not recommended for other reasons, certain ready-to-eat pork products, that have not been heat-treated, may constitute a risk for toxoplasmosis, if not frozen prior to manufacturing. Information on the effects of curing on survival of *Toxoplasma* in meat is sparse and therefore deserves further research. However, most of the pork used for manufacturing in Denmark originates from pigs raised indoors and for logistic reasons it is frozen prior to processing, thereby reducing the risk for human toxoplasmosis.

References

BUFFOLANO, W., GILBERT, R.E., HOLLAND, F.J., FRATTA, D., PALUMBO, F., ADES, A.E., 1996. Risk factors for recent *Toxoplasma* infection in pregnant women in Naples. *Epidemiol. Inf.* 116, 347-351.

COOK, A.J.C., GILBERT, R.E., BUFFOLANO, W., ZUFFERY, J., PETERSEN, E., JENUM, P.A., FOULON, W., SEMPRINI, A.E., DUNN, D.T., 2000. Sources of *Toxoplasma* infection in pregnant women: European multicentre case-control study. *BMJ* 321, 42-47.

DUBEY, J.P., MURRELL, K.D., FAYER, R., SCHAD, G.A., 1986. Distribution of *Toxoplasma gondii* tissue cysts in commercial cuts of pork. *JAVMA* 188, 1035-1037.

DUBEY, J.P., KOTULA, A.W., SHARAR, A., ANDREWS, C.D., LINDSAY, D.S., 1990. Effect of high temperature on the infectivity of *Toxoplasma gondii* tissue cysts in pork. *J. Parasitol.* 76, 201-204.

DUBEY, J.P., THULLIEZ, P., POWELL, E.C., 1995. *Toxoplasma gondii* in Iowa sows: Comparison of antibody titers to isolation of T. gondii by bioassays in mice and cats. *J. Parasitol.* 81, 48-53.

DUBEY, J.P., 1997. Survival of *Toxoplasma gondii* tissue cysts in 0.85-6% NaCl solutions at 4-20°C. *J. Parasitol.* 83, 946-949.

DUBEY, J.P., 2000. The scientific basis for prevention of *Toxoplasma gondii* infection: studies on tissue cyst survival, risk factors and hygiene measures. In: P. AMBROISE-THOMAS & E. PETERSEN (Ed.). *Congenital toxoplasmosis: scientific background, clinical management and control.* Springer-Verlag, Paris.

DUBEY, J.P., HILL, D.E. et al., 2005. Prevalence of viable *Toxoplasma gondii* in beef, chicken and pork from retail meat stores in the United States: Risk assessment to consumers. *J. Parasitol.* 91, 1082-1093

FEHLHABER, K., HINTERSDORF, P., KRÜGER, G., 2003. Prävalenz von *Toxoplasma gondii*. Untersuchungen bei Schlachtschweinen aus verschiedenen Haltungsformen und in handelsüblichen Hackfleischproben. *Fleischwirtschaft* 2 (2003), 97-99.

HILL, D.E., SREEKUMAR, C., GAMBLE, H.R., DUBEY, J.P., 2004. Effect of commonly used enhancement solutions on the viability of *Toxoplasma gondii* tissue cysts in pork loin. *J. Food Prot.* 67, 2230-2233.

HILL, D.E., BENEDETTO, S.M.C., COSS, C., McCRARY, J.L., FOURNET, V.M., DUBEY, J.P., 2006. Effects of time and temperature on the viability of *Toxoplasma gondii* tissue cysts in enhanced pork loin. *J. Food Prot.* 69, 1961-1965.

KAPPERUD, G., JENUM, P.A., STRAY PEDERSEN, B., MELBY, K.K., ESKILD, A., 1996. Risk factors for *Toxoplasma gondii* infection in pregnancy. Results of a prospective case-control study in Norway. *Am. J. Epidemiol.* 144, 405-412.

KIJLSTRA, A., EISSEN, O.A., CORNELISSEN, J., MUNNIKSMA, K., EIJCK, I., KORTBEEK, T., 2004. *Toxoplasma gondii* infection in animal-friendly pig production systems. *Inv. Ophthal. Vis. Sc.* 45, 3165-3169.

KOTULA, A.W., DUBEY, J.P., SHARAR, A., ANDREWS, C.D., SHEN, S.K., LINDSAY, D.S., 1991. Effect of freezing on infectivity of *Toxoplasma gondii* tissue cysts in pork. *J. Food Prot.* 54, 687-690.

LIND, P., HAUGEGAARD, J., HEISEL, C., WINGSTRAND, A., HENRIKSEN, S.A., 1994. Seroprevalence studies of toxoplasmosis in Danish swine populations. In: *Proceedings of the Baltic-Scandinavian Symposium on Parasitic Zoonoses and Ecology of Parasites.* Vilnius, Lithuania, 7-8 September.

LINDSAY, D.S., COLLINS, M.V., HOLLIMAN, D., FLICK, G.J., DUBEY, J.P., 2006. Effects of high-pressure processing on *Toxoplasma gondii* tissue cysts in ground pork. *J. Parasitol.* 92, 195-196.

SMITH, J.L., 1991. Foodborne toxoplasmosis. *J. Food Safety* 12, 17-57.

TENTER, A.M., HECKEROTH, A.R., WEISS, L.M., 2000. *Toxoplasma gondii*: from animals to humans. *Int. J. Parasitol.* 30, 1217-1258.

VENTURINI, M.C., BACIGALUPE, D., VENTURINI, L., RAMBEAUD, M., BASSO, W., UNZAGA, J.M., PERFUME, C.J., 2004. Seroprevalence of *Toxoplasma gondii* in sows from slaughterhouses and in pigs from an indoor and an outdoor farm in Argentina. *Vet. Parasitol.* 124, 161-165.

WARNEKULASURIYA, M.R., JOHNSON, J.D., HOLLIMAN, R.E., 1998. Detection of *Toxoplasma gondii* in cured meats. *Int. J. Food Microbiol.* 45, 211-215.

Seroprevalence of *Toxoplasma gondii* in German swine herds

Ludewig, M.* [1], de Buhr, K. [1], Fehlhaber, K. [1]

[1]) Institute of Food Hygiene, University of Leipzig, An den Tierkliniken 1, 04103 Leipzig, Germany
* mludewig@vetmed.uni-leipzig.de

Abstract

The protozoan parasite *Toxoplasma (T.) gondii* is prevalent worldwide and is found in a wide range of warm-blooded hosts including humans. Raw and undercooked pork containing tissue cysts is an important cause of the *T. gondii*- Infection in humans. The aim of our study was to investigate the occurence of *T. gondii*-antibodies in German swine herds. Alltogether 4999 pigs including 38 sows were tested. 119 different farms of eight German Federal states were involved. An Enzyme-Linked-Immunosorbent Assay was used. In 4.1 % of the pigs including sows *T. gondii*-antibodies were detected. 3.9 % of the finishing pigs were seropositive. About 60 % of all investigated farms were seropositve. In this study in eight German states different *T. gondii*-seroprevalences between the states and between the farms were observed. Sows always showed higher prevalence rates than finishing pigs. These results show that Germany wide relative high *T. gondii* -seroprevalence rates in finishing herds exist.

Introduction

Toxoplasma (T.) gondii is a protozoan which can infect all warm-blooded hosts including humans. This parasite is transmitted by ingestion of mature oocysts or of raw and undercooked meat containing tissue cysts. It's well known, that pork is an important cause of the *T. gondii*-infection in humans. In Germany pork is the most popular meat compared with meat from other animals. In the past decades the *T. gondii*-prevalence in German finishing pig livestocks was changing from a high up to a very low level. In the last time the farming systems have been changed to nature-related management systems. Current prevalence data for finishing pigs are not available.

In a first study in Saxony-Anhalt (Halle/Wittenberg area) in all management systems including organic farms seropositive animals were detected (FEHLHABER et al., 2003). The objective of this study was to organise a Germany wide survey.

Material and methods

In total 4999 pigs including sows from 119 farms were investigated. Pigs from eight German Federal states and different management systems were tested (table 1). The blood samples were collected at the slaughterhouses. Serum was taken after storage over night at 4 °C.

Table 1: Distribution of serum sampling in German Federal states

Federal state	Number of investigated animals	
	Finishing pigs	Sows
Lower Saxony	1591 including 180 outdoor	1
North Rhine-Westphalia	791	-
Bavaria/Baden Württemberg	544	1
Brandenburg	160	-
Saxony-Anhalt	240	-
Saxony	981 including 60 organic	13
Thuringia	654	22

To determine the prevalence of antibodies to *T. gondii* in naturally infected pigs an Enzyme-Linked Immunosorbent Assay according to SEINEKE (1996) was used. The *T. gondii*-Antigen Tx12 RH (Statens Veterinaere Serumlaboratorium, Kopenhagen, DK) was applied. A cut-off OD % 20 was estimated as positive.

Results

In total 4.1 % of the investigated pigs were seropositive. Table 2 shows the *T. gondii*-seroprevalences in pigs in relation to the management system and the age. In sows high seroprevalences were detected. 3.9 % of the finishing pigs were seropositive.

Table 2: *T. gondii*-seroprevalence in German pigs including sows

	Number of investigated pigs	Seroprevalence		
		Number of positive pigs	%	
Finishing pigs - conventional	4721	183	3.8	
Finishing pigs - outdoor	180	5	2.8	3.9
Finishing pigs - organic	60	7	11.7	
Sows	38	12	31.6	

In seven states antibodies against *T. gondii* in finishing pigs were detected (figure 1). No *T.*-antibodies were found in pigs from Brandenburg. The highest prevalence was observed in Bavaria and Baden-Württemberg, followed by Saxony and North-Rhine-Westphalia. The lowest prevalence was found in Lower Saxony (1.6 %).

Figure 1: *T. gondii*-seroprevalence in finishing pigs - tested in eight German Federal states

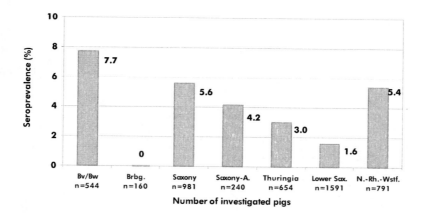

Session 3: Viruses, parasites, other pathogens

In 71 (59.7 %) farms pigs with *T. gondii*-antibodies were observed. The results of the German states will be summarised in table 3.

Table 3: Number of farms with *T. gondii*-seropositive pigs

Federal state	Number of investigated farms	*T. gondii*-seropositive farms
Lower Saxony	39	19
North Rhine-Westphalia	15	10
Bavaria/Baden Württemberg	36	22
Brandenburg	2	0
Saxony-Anhalt	2	2
Saxony	14	12
Thuringia	11	6
Total	*119*	71

The results between the farms within the states were partly extremely different. For example the results from Saxony: In one Saxony farm 28.3 % of 60 finishing pigs were *T. gondii*-seropositive. 11.7 % of the finishing pigs from organic farms were tested seropositive (figure 2).

Figure 2: *T. gondii*-seroprevalence in Saxonian farms

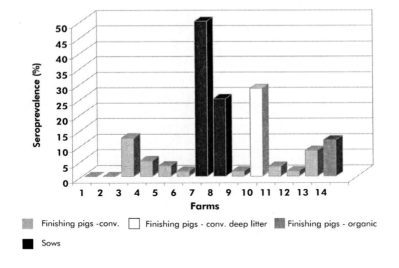

Discussion and Conclusion

For this study an ELISA was established. A commercial test for detecting antibodies in pigs is not available so far. The results can be compared with former findings from our group (FEHLHABER et al. 2003, SCHULZIG, FEHLHABER, 2005). Here average seroprevalences in finishing pigs from 5.6 up to 20.4 % were observed. In this current study in eight German Federal states different *T. gondii*-seroprevalences between the farms and between the states were found. This different *T. gondii*-seroprevalence-status between the farms was also observed in our former studies (FEHLHABER et al. 2003, SCHULZIG, FEHLHABER, 2005) and from other groups (WEIGEL et al., 1995; WYSS et al., 2000). Sows are often infected with *T. gondii* (ASSADI-RAD et al., 1995; WYSS et al., 2000). Our examinations confirmed that.

These current results show that there are partially high prevalences of *T. gondii*-antibodies in finishing pig herds. It seems that the prevalence of *Toxoplasma*-antibodies in finishing pigs is increased significantly compared with studies ten years before. The results indicate that there is a real risk for human *Toxoplasma*-infection caused by raw or undercooked pork. Pork is used for meat products which are processed with no further thermal treatment (fermented sausages, smoked products). From this point of view it is deemed necessary to assess the prevalence of *T.gondii*-infection in finnishing farms before the raw material is processed further. To protect the consumer effectively we need a working monitoring and hygiene system at all levels of the chain.

In the context of infection rates, the capability of *T.gondii* to survive under unfavourable conditions and remain infective for prolonged time periods is of special importance. Still, many questions regarding the tenability of *T.gondii* in different food remained unanswered so far. Further examinations in meat products to test the capability of survival of the tissue cysts are needed.

References

ASSADI-RAD, A. M., NEW, J. C., PATTON, S., 1995. Risk factors associated with transmission of *Toxoplasma gondii* to sows kept different management systems in Tennessee. Vet. Parasitol. 57, 289-297.

FEHLHABER, K., HINTERSDORF, P., KRÜGER, G., 2003. Prävalenz von *Toxoplasma gondii* - Untersuchungen bei Schlachtschweinen aus verschiedenen Haltungsformen und in handelsüblichen Hackfleischproben. Fleischwirtsch. 83 (2), 97-99.

SEINEKE, P., 1996. Seroprävalenz von Antikörpern gegen *Toxoplasma gondii* bei Schafen, Ziegen und Schweinen in Niedersachsen [Dissertation med. vet.] Hannover: Tierärztliche Hochschule Hannover.

SCHULZIG, H. S., FEHLHABER, K., 2005. Longitudinalstudie zur Seroprävalenz der *Toxoplasma gondii*-Infektionen in vier deutschen Schweineaufzucht- und Mast-betrieben. Berl Münch. Tierärztl. Wochenschr. 118, 399-403.

WEIGEL, R. M.; DUBEY, J. P., SIEGEL, A. M., KITRON, U. D., MANNELLI, A., MITCHELL, M. A., MATEUS-PINILLA, E., THULLIEZ, P., SHEN, S. K., KNOW, O. C., 1995. Risk factors for transmission of *Toxoplasma gondii* on swine farms in Illinois. J. Parasitol. 81, 736-741.

WYSS, R., SAGER, H., MÜLLER, N., INDERBITZIN, F., KÖNIG, M., AUDIGE´, L., GOTTSTEIN, B., 2000. Untersuchungen zum Vorkommen von *Toxoplasma gondii* und *Neospora caninum* unter fleischhygienischen Aspekten. Schweiz. Archiv Tierheilk. 142, 95-108

I.suis medication of piglets with Baycox° 5% against coccidiose and for stabilisation of the microflora against intestinal infections and reducing the application of antibiotica and vaccines against diarrhoea with E.coli and Clostridia

Busse,F.-W.[1], Westphal,B. *[2]

[1]Animal Health Service,LWK NDS,Am Schoelerberg 7,49082 Osnabrueck,Germany
[2]Bayer Health Care,Animal Health,51368 Leverkusen,Germany
*bernhard.westphal@bayerhealthcare.com

Abstract
After the oral treatment of all piglets 3 - 5 days after birth with Baycox° 5% we found a better intestine health in the suckling and in the flatdeck period.In this study there was a reduced diarrhoea during suckling and in the flatdeck.With the Baycox° therapeutic the vaccination program against E.coli and Clostridium perfringens Typ C and the application of antibiotica to the weaners could be decreased for nearly 40 % during the breeding period.All pigs got better health status with higher weight gain and uniformity.

Introduction
Endoparasits,enteric bacteria and viral infections have a economic impact on the profitability of pig production through reduction in daily weight gain and in higher drug costs by different therapeutic treatments for grower and finisher animals.In piggeries diarrhoea of piglets is a important disease during suckling,associated with coccidiose and bacterial infections by E.coli or Clostridiose.Coccidiosis in nursing piglets is a disease caused by Isospora suis and is found in all types of farrowing facilities and under all types of management systems (9).If I.suis has established in a farm it is maintained through piglet to piglet transmission,by infected suckling sows and by the contaminated farrowing floor.Reports about the piglets coccidiose caused by Isospora suis demonstrate a high farm prevalence of the disease in different European countries.Overall I.suis was found in 26% litters and in 69% farms (12).In the farms in our region with a high pig density we watch,that a coccidiose favoured the increasing of the pathogenity of enteric diseases in growing pigs and the prescription of drugs,as antibiotica or vaccines.The present study was carried out to investigate the relationship between the treatment with Baycox°5% against I.suis and for stabilation of the microflora against intestinal infections and reducing the application of antibiotica and vaccines against diarrhoea with E.coli and Clostridia for a higher health status in the production.

Material and methods
During the farm visits of the animal health service we look for the health status of the pigs in the different parts of the stables with sows, piglets, growers and finisher by clinical monitoring and obsevation and collect different samples for laboratory tests. During our visits together with the farmer we control the performance,the productivity and the consumption of drugs during the pig production.In our country 3 -5.days old piglets get a oral metaphylactic treatment with Baycox° 5% against I.suis.In many farms with diarrhoea,after a clinical diagnose and a laboratory test by the vet the pigs were treated with antibiotica or vaccinated against E.coli or Clostridiose.In this study we collected the different dates about productivity,intestinal infections and treatments against diarrhoea during the different periods.

Results
In the faecal samples of 86% from the litters with diarrhoea we found Oozysten of I.suis.In the samples from the younger piglets were more Oozysts (56%) than in the older once;in the litters with diarrhoea were 86 % Oozysts (Table 1).In the faecal samples from different farms,tested for bacterial,virus and parasitic colonisation,before the treatment against I.suis,we found more gaims than after the oral application of Baycox° (Table 2).In the autopsy material of suckling pigs before

the Baycox° treatment were more germs in the laboratory test kits than after (Table 3).With the oral dose of the therapeuticum Toltrazuril against I.suis the vaccination program against Clostridia perfringens and E.coli could be reduced (Table 4) and the feeding of antibiotic agents against E.coli infections could be mined by nearly 80% of the enteritic cases during suckling and 45% during weaning in the flatdeck.

Table 1   Clinical examination of farrows (N=94) and detection of Oocysts in fecal samples

parameter	detection of Ooysts (%)
piglets 7-14 days p.p.	56
piglets 15-28 days p.p.	48
litters with diarrhoea	86
litters without diarrhoea	24

Table 2   Results for the incidence of germs in fecal samples (N=281) of piglets (5-21 days p.p.) before and with Baycox° 5% therapie

probs (N=281)	without Baycox° treatment (%)	with Baycox° treatment (%)
Oozysts	89	6
E.coli	62	24
hä.E.coli	14	11
Cl.perfring.Typ A	81	12
Rotavirus	6	4

Table 3   Sectio results of piglets,age 6 - 28 days,(N=46) for germs before and after treatment with Baycox°5%

sectio results (N=46)	without Baycox° treatment (%)	with Baycox°treatment (%)
Ooysts	64	8
E.coli	83	29
hä.E.coli	48	12
Streptok.	34	20
Staphylok.	12	9
Cl.perfringens	56	24
Rotavirus	8	6
Endoparasits	14	12

Table 4   Vaccination of sows/pigs against infections with E.coli, Cl perfringens Typ C in farms (N=102),piglets diarrhoea before and after treatment with Baycox°5%

Vaccination sows/piglets (N=102)	without Baycox° treatment (%)	with Baycox°treatment (%)
E.coli	89	11
Cl.perfringens Typ C	77	4

Discussion

I.suis is a cause of diarrhoea on piglet-rearing farms.It is a primary pathogen and the occurence correlates positively with the occurence of diarrhoea at the age of 2 – 3 weeks (6). In the first weeks after birth different germs produce clinical problems with enteritis under the piglets.The reasons for diarrhoea are different germs after birth (Table 5).

Table 5
Reasons for enteritis and clinical symptoms during the suckling period

Germs	sickness symptoms
Rotavirus	apathie,vomiting,yellow-pasty enteritis
Coronavirus	vomiting,wasting,slight enteritis
TGE Virus	vomiting,grey-yellow,foul smelling enteritis
EVD Virus	grey-yellow enteritis
KSP Virus	fever >41°C,foul-smelling,bloody enteritis
E.coli	aques-yellow or dilute,brown enteritis
Cl.perfringens	fluid red brown enteritis, with blood
Coccidien	yellow pasting,fatty steatorrhoea

Blood and fecal samples were collected and in a laboratory tested for the different infections.The Oozysts of I.suis were found by a flotation medium with NaCl and sugar under UV-light of a flourescence-mikroskope (2).In piggeries affected by I.suis all piglets were treated with a single oral dose Baycox°5% with 20 mg Toltrazuril per kg live weight The "metaphylactic" treatment prevented the appearance of clinical signs, better immunity against different germs,a better intestinal morphologie allowing the developement of immunity.The pathomorphological examinations showed that on average the intestinal villi length was longer on days 10 and 14 in animals treated with Toltrazuril compared with the other groups (13).The link between Oocysts excretion and clinical signs seems to be precluded by interaction between parasites,animals,management and the enviroment (3). In commercial units with grower-finisher pigs in GB they found interactions between the level of dietary fibre and infestation with endoparasits and between infection with L.intracellularis and infestation with Trichuris suis in grower pigs (8). In our study the incidence of diarrhoea in the Baycox° treated group were more reduced than those of the control.In the farms the therapeutic programs could be stopped after the Baycox° medication,as the health status for the pigs was higher.

Intestinal picture (Bayer Animal Health,2003)

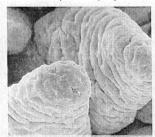  

intestinal villi obB	destructed intestinal villi 5 days post infectionem	destructed intestinal villi 7 days post infectionem

In the early Baycox° treated piggeries the piglets had a better weight gain,more uniformity,reduced diarrhoea and lower therapeutic costs in the suckling period.In our study we found,that in many farms with the Baycox° treatment of piglets the veterinariens and the farmers could reduce the therapie with antibiotika against E.coli and haemorrhagic enterotoxaemie.After the treatment against coccidiose in more than 80 % of the farms the medication with antibiotica and the vaccination against E.coli and/or Clostridia was stoppt by the farmers,as the piglets were saver than before. We summarize,by the "metaphylactic" use of Baycox° for the piglets,the drugs could be reduced and the pigs had a better health status.In Dutch herds with Toltrazuril treatment the piglet feed intake increased with a better health and on average 789 gramm per litter more than the control (5).In a german field study the mean average weight gain on six selected farms at the end of the suckling period was + 376.9g.The Baycox° treatment resulted in monetary benefits because of better weight gain to the tune of 0.93€ to 1.33€,depending on weight of animals (9 or 25 kg) (1).

Disinfection measures did not reduce the maximum incidence of Isosporosis,because the Oocysts are very resistant to commenly used disinfectans (4).A in vitro study with Neopredisan° 135-1 (Menno-Chemie,22850 Norderstedt) - concentration:2%,exposure time:2 hours - reduced 96.96% of the Oocysts by lysis (7). In a field study with two farms without I.suis therapie and normal disinfection before farrowing the floor was disinfected one and two weeks p.p. again with Neopredisan°135-1 (2%).Afterwards the excretion of Oozysts from the piglets was reduced for 43% (11).When the initial contamination of the pen with I.suis is high in poorly cleaned pens the majority of the piglets are infected almost soon after birth (10).In a Greece study there was a remarkable variation of the infestation incidences between untreated litters in a I.suis contaminated farm.This might be associated to pen related factors such as efficiency of cleaning and disinfection (10).

Conclusions

Coccidiosis represents a problem in nursing piglets,specially in countries with a intensive pig production.I.suis infected pigs excrete Oocysts and infect the hole pen.By the intestinal lesions of the micro villi the piglets are more infected with different germs and have a reduced protection against clinical diseases.The weight gain profile for Baycox° groups revealed consistently higher values than the untreated.The piglets have a better weight gain,are healthier without drugs therapia for reducing germs and diarrhoea.Coccidiosis is a disease,which has not only a negative consequence in the piggery but also during the fattening.With a Toltrazuril treatment in the first days p.p. the pig production costs are lower and the benefit is higher till the fattening.

References

(1)Boehne,I.et al.,2006,Coccidiose in suckling piglets,Proc.IPVS,275
(2)Daugschies,A.et al.,2001,Autofluo.microsc.for the detection of nematode eggs and protozoa, in particular I.suis in swine faeces,Parasit.Res.87,409 ff
(3)Castilo,J.et al.,1996,The effect of coccidiosis on pre-weaning and post-weaning groth of early-weaned piglets,Proc.IPVS,357
(4)Gevaert,D.et al.,2006,Prevalence of Isospor. in farms with a history darrhoe, Proc.IPVS,269
(5)Gevaert,D.et al.,2006,Influence of Toltrazuril treatment of Isosporose,Proc.IPVS,270
(6)Mundt,H.C.et al.,2000,Incidens,diagnosis and significance of I.suis coccidiosis on pig rearing farms, Proc.IPVS,79
(7)Nevermann,J.,2004,Desinfection gegen I.suis Oocysten,Proc.BpT,9
(8)Pearce,G.,1998,Interaction between dietary fibre,endoparasits and enteric bacteria in grower finisher pigs,Proc.IPVS,252
(9)Sotiraki,S.et al.,2004,The effect of pen contamination level on intra-litter spread of I.suis infection under on-farm farrowing conditions,Proc.IPVS,245
(10)Sotiraki,S.et.al.,2006,Effect of early blind treatment of isosporosis on the spread of I.suis under field conditions,Proc.IPVS,180
(11)Straberg,E.et al.,2003, Desinfection gegen I.suis,Proc.DVG,66
(12)Torres,A.et al.,2004, Prevalence survey of I.suis in twelve EU countries,Proc.IPVS,243
(13)Wüstenberg,S.et al.,2001,Studies on the efficacy of toltazuril,diclazuril and sulfadimidin against artificial infections with I.suis in suckling pigs, Proc.I.C.Vet.Parasit.,Stresa,I.,26ff

Prevalence of hepatitis E virus in Italian pig herds. Preliminary results

Di Bartolo, I. [1], Inglese, N. [1], Pourshaban, M. [1], Martelli, F. [2], Caprioli, A. [3], Ostanello, F. [2], Ruggeri, F. M. * [1]

[1] Dept. of Food Safety and Veterinary Public Health, Istituto Superiore di Sanità, Rome, Italy;
[2] Dept. of Veterinary Public Health and Animal Pathology, University of Bologna, Ozzano Emilia (BO), Italy;
[3] Direzione Generale Sicurezza Alimentare e Nutrizione, Ministry for Health, Rome, Italy
* corresponding author: franco.ruggeri@iss.it

Abstract

Hepatitis E virus (HEV) is the causative agent of hepatitis E, and is an unenveloped positive sense single-stranded RNA virus. Swine HEV strains are genetically closely related to human strains from the same area, suggesting the occurrence of zoonotic transmission. Recently, human cases of hepatitis E have been linked to the consumption of raw or undercooked meat or organs from deer, wild boars or pigs. The disease is now considered an emerging food-borne transmitted zoonosis. During 2006, a pilot investigation was performed to determine the prevalence of HEV in pig farms located in Northern Italy., 274 faecal samples were collected from healthy fattening animals (3-4 and 8-9 months of age) and from healthy breeding animals (gilts and sows) from 6 different farms, and analyzed using a Nested-RT-PCR targeting the open reading frame 2 (ORF2) region. Stool samples were suspended in water, and viral RNA extraction was performed using a commercial kit. Extracted viral RNA was subjected to RT-PCR amplification using degenerate primers conA1-conS1 for the first amplification, and degenerate primers conA2-conS2 for the nested PCR, yielding a final fragment of 145 bp. HEV RNA was detected in sixty-nine of the 274 (25.2%) examined samples. None of the six farms resulted negative and the prevalence within the farms ranged between 2% and 60.5% For the characterization of the strains, randomly selected positive samples were subjected to nucleotide sequencing, and aligned with those present in the NCBI Data Bank Sequence analysis showed that all strains were Swine Hepatitis E belonging to Genotype 3. These preliminary results confirm that swine HEV is widespread in Italian swine farms.

Introduction

Hepatitis E is a human viral disease with clinical and morphological features of acute hepatitis. Hepatitis E virus (HEV) is the etiological agent of hepatitis E, and is a small virus classified as Hepevirus genus within the *Hepeviridae* family. HEV isolates have been so far classified into four genotypes. The majority of infections occurring in Asia and Africa are caused by genotype 1, whereas genotype 2 prevails in Mexico and Nigeria. In industrialized countries, where until few years ago the infection was considered non-endemic, only strains belonging to genotype 3 and 4 have been detected (Emerson and Purcell 2003). Genotype 3 prevails in USA and Europe, while genotype 4 is mainly distributed in Asia (Hsieh et al., 1999; Banks et al., 2004; Zheng et al., 2006). Although hepatitis E is a sporadic disease, in countries with good health-care systems the seroprevalence rate among healthy individuals can nonetheless be high (Emerson and Purcell 2003). The first animal HEV strain was characterized in pigs in USA in 1997 (Meng et al., 1997). Since then, several other swine strains have been described worldwide. In particular genotype 3 and 4 isolates from swine and humans from the same geographic area are often genetically closely related, suggesting that swine can represent a reservoir for the virus and that zoonotic transmission of HEV may play a relevant role in industrialised countries (Meng et al., 1998; Zanetti et al., 1999; Van der Poel et al., 2001; Clemente-Casares et al., 2003; Buti et al., 2004). Furthermore, several studies have reported that in people who work in contact with swine such as pig farmers, veterinarians and slaughterhouse workers, the HEV seroprevalence rate can be higher than in normal control populations (Meng et al., 2002; Hsieh et al., 1999). Recently hepatitis E cases have been linked to the consumption of raw or undercooked meat from deer, wild boars or pigs, and the disease is now considered an emerging food-borne transmitted zoonosis (Matsuda et al., 2003; Tei et al., 2003; Yazaki et al., 2003). If the possibility of zoonotic transmission of the infection is accepted, it is clear that the higher the prevalence in animals, the greater the risk of transmission will be to humans. An evaluation of the prevalence and the genetic characterization of the HEV strains circulating in italian pig farms will be therefore necessary to perform a risk assessment of zoonotic transmission in Italy. In this regard, this study was performed as a pilot investigation to evaluate the prevalence of HEV infection within farms in Northern Italy.

Material and Methods

Between January to August 2006, 274 faecal samples were collected from randomly selected pigs of 3-4 months of age (weaners), 8-9 months of age (fatteners), gilts (0 parities), young sows (1-2 parities) and old sows (> 2 parities) belonging to 6 different farms (2 farrow-to-weaning and 4 farrow-to-finish) located in Northern Italy, area of the country with the highest concentrations of pigs. To an external examination all the pigs sampled appeared clinically healthy. Faecal samples were collected directly from the rectum and placed in sterile containers. From each farm, the faeces of at least 10 animals for each production category were collected. This scheme provides a systematic sampling of different pig classes present within the herds and can estimate, with a 95% probability, the prevalence of swine HEV-positive animals with an expected prevalence of 30% and an accepted error of 25%. In order to detect the HEV genome, a nested-RT-PCR targeting a region of the ORF2 (coding for the HEV capsid protein) was performed. Total viral RNA was extracted from a faecal suspension (10%) using a QIAamp Viral kit (Qiagen).First round amplification utilized primers HEV ORF2 con-S1 (GACAGAATTRATTTCGTCGGCTGG) and HEV ORF2 con-A1 (CTTGTTCRTGYTGGTTRTCATAATC) yielding a product of 197 nucleotides. Nested reactions used primers HEV ORF2 con-S2 (GTYGTCTCRGCCAATGGCGAGC) and HEV ORF2 con-A2 (GTTCRTGYTGGTTRTCATAATCCTG) to produce a 145 nucleotide product (Erker et al., 1999) (figure 1). For further characterization, randomly selected positive samples coming from 3 different farms were subjected to nucleotide sequencing using ABI PRISM BigDye Terminator Kit 2.0 (Applied Biosystems). The sequenced fragments were aligned with those present in the NCBI Data Bank and analyzed using DNASIS Max software (Hitachisoft).

Figure 1. Position of primers conA1-conS1 and conA2-conS2 within the HEV ORF2

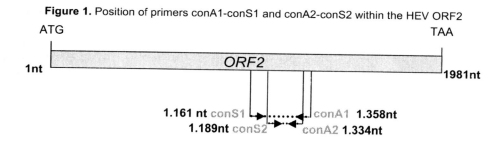

Results

HEV RNA was detected in 25.2% of the pigs sampled. None of the six farms resulted negative for HEV and the prevalence within the farms ranged between 2% and 60.5% (table 1). The 11 HEV strains considered for sequencing in this preliminary survey could be all placed within genotype 3 and shared 88.5 to 100% nucleotide sequence identity to each other. Sequence analysis showed that at least 6 different strains were circulating simultaneously in the farms considered. However, most of the nucleotide changes detected were found to represent silent mutations, and no differences at amino acid level were revealed.

Table 1. Prevalence of HEV infection in the 6 examined farms

Type of farm *	Farm n°	HEV positive/tested	(%)
F-F	1	1/50	2.0
F-W	2	6/40	15.0
F-F	3	12/48	25.0
F-F	4	6/47	12.8
F-F	5	21/51	41.6
F-W	6	23/38	60.5
All farms		69/274	25.2

* F-F= farrow-to-finish; F-W= farrow-to-weaning

Discussion

This investigation confirms that HEV is present in pigs in Italy (Caprioli et al., in press) and demonstrates that HEV is probably widely spread in Northern Italy swine farms. This study also demonstrates that not less than six distinct HEV Genotype 3 strains circulate in the country, suggesting that the repertoire of the swine HEV pool in Italy is probably as wide as described in other European countries (Van der Poel, 2001; Clemente-Casares et al., 2003; Banks et al., 2004; Buti et al., 2004). In this pilot investigation, none of the 6 examined farms resulted HEV free, and the mean prevalence observed was 25.6%, generally higher than the prevalence reported in other countries (Huang et al., 2002). Moreover, in our study, in contrast with previous works in which the infection was reported mainly to occur in animals of 3 to 5 months of age (Meng et al. 1997; Van der Poel, 2001; Banks et al., 2004), we found HEV positive animals distributed in all age classes. These findings, together with the observation that HEV infection is probably sub-clinical (all examined animals were apparently healthy) and was present also in pigs close to the slaughtering age, are of concern because of the risk of transmission of HEV to human beings by either contact with infected swine, infected carcasses or contaminated undercooked meat or organs (Yazaki et al., 2003). Moreover, the possibility of virus spread in the environment through manure from pig farms, with the consequent possible contamination of vegetables and drinking water, should also be taken into consideration. The finding of a widespread circulation of HEV in pig farms indicates the need of implementing surveillance systems and risk analysis programs to better clarify the role of swine as a HEV reservoir for human beings and the possible implications of this emerging zoonosis for public health in Italy.

References

BANKS, M., HEATH, G.S., GRIERSON, S.S., KING, D.P., GRESHAM, A., GIRONES, R., WIDEN, F., HARRISON., T.J., 2004. Evidence For The Presence Of Hepatitis E virus in pigs in the United Kingdom. *Veterinary Record*, 154, 223-227.

BUTI, M., CLEMENTE-CASARES, P., JARDI, R., FORMIGA-CRUZ, M., SCHAPER, M., VALDES, A., RODRIGUEZ-FRIAS, F., ESTEBAN, R., GIRONES, R., 2004. Sporadic cases of acute autochthonous hepatitis E in Spain. *Journal of Hepatology*, 41, 126-131.

CAPRIOLI, A., MARTELLI, F., OSTANELLO, F., DI BARTOLO, I., RUGGERI, F., DEL CHIARO, L., TOLARI F., 2007. Detection of Hepatitis E Virus (HEV) in Italian pig herd. *Veterinary Record (in press)*.

CLEMENTE-CASARES, P., PINA, S., BUTI, M., JARDI, R., MARTIN, M., BOFILL-MAS, S., GIRONES, R., 2003. Hepatitis E virus epidemiology in industrialized countries. *Emerging Infectious Disease*, 9, 448-454.

EMERSON, S.U., PURCELL, R.H., 2003. Hepatitis E virus. *Reviews in Medical Virology,* 13, 145-154.

ERKER, J.C., DESAI, S.M., SCHLAUDER, G.G., DAWSON, G.J., MUSHAHWAR, I.K., 1999. A hepatitis E virus variant from the United States: molecular characterization and transmission in cynomolgus macaques. *Journal of General Virology*, 80, 681-690.

HSIEH, S.Y., MENG, X.J., WU, Y.H., LIU, S.T., TAM, A.W., LIN, D.Y., LIAW, Y.F., 1999. Identity of a novel swine hepatitis E virus in Taiwan forming a monophyletic group with Taiwan isolates of human hepatitis E virus. *Journal of Clinical Microbiology*, 37, 3828-3834.

HUANG, F. F., G. HAQSHENAS, D.K. GUENETTE, P.G. HALBUR, S.K. SHOMMER, F.W. PIERSON, T.E. TOTH, MENG, X.J., 2002. Detection by reverse transcription-PCR and genetic characterization of field isolates of swine hepatitis E virus from pigs in different geographic regions of the United States. *Journal of Clinical Microbiology*, 40, 1326-1332.

Matsuda, H., Okada, K., Takahashi, K., Mishiro, S. (2003). Severe hepatitis E virus infection after ingestion of uncooked liver from a wild boar. *Journal of Infectious Disease*, 188, 944.

MENG, X.J., PURCELL, R.H., , HALBUR, P.G., LEHMAN, J.R., WEBB, D.M., TSAREVA, T.S., HAYNES, J.S., THACKER, B.J., EMERSON, S.U., 1997. A novel virus in swine is closely related to the human hepatitis E virus. *Proc. National Academy of Sciences of the USA*, 94, 9860-9865.

MENG, X.J., HALBUR, P.G., SHAPIRO, M.S., GOVINDARAJAN, S., BRUNA, J.D., MUSHAHWAR, I.K., PURCELL, R.H., EMERSON, S.U., 1998. Genetic and experimental evidence for cross-species infection by swine hepatitis E virus. *Journal of Virology*, 72, 9714-9721.

MENG, X.J., WISEMAN, B., ELVINGER, F., GUENETTE, D.K., TOTH, T.H., ENGLE, R.E., EMERSON, S.U., PURCELL, R.H., 2002. Prevalence of antibodies to hepatitis E virus in veterinarians working with swine and in normal blood donors in the United States and other countries. *Journal of Clinical Microbiology*, 40, 117-122.

TEI S., KITAJIMA N., TAKAHASHI K., MISHIRO S., 2003. Zoonotic transmission of hepatitis E virus from deer to human beings. *Lancet*, 362, 371-373.

VAN DER POEL, W.H., VERSCHOOR, F., VAN DER HEIDE, R., HERRERA, M.I., VIVO, A., KOOREMAN, M., DE RODA HUSMAN, A.M., 2001. Hepatitis E virus sequences in swine related to sequences in humans, The Netherlands. *Emerging Infectious Disease*, 7, 970-976.

YAZAKI, Y., MIZUO, H., TAKAHASHI, M., NISHIZAWA, T., SASAKI, N., GOTANDA, Y., OKAMOTO, H., 2003. Sporadic acute or fulminant hepatitis E in Hokkaido, Japan, may be food-borne, as suggested by the presence of hepatitis E virus in pig liver as food. *Journal of General Virology*, 84, 2351-2357.

ZANETTI, A. R., SCHLAUDER, G.G., ROMANÒ, L., TANZI, E., FABRIS, P., DAWSON, G.J., MUSHAHWAR, I.K., 1999. Identification of a novel variant of hepatitis E virus in Italy. *Journal of Medical Virology 57*, 356-360.

ZHENG, Y., SHENGXIANG, G., ZHANG, J., GUO, Q., HON NG, M., WANG, F., XIA, N., JIANG, Q., 2006. Swine as a principal reservoir of Hepatitis E virus that infects Humans in Eastern China. *Journal of Infectious Disease*, 193, 1643-1649.

Evaluation of serological tests for Trichinella infections in pigs

Maassen, C.[*][(1)], Achterberg, R.[(1)], Engel, B.[(1)],van der Giessen, J[(2)], Teunis, P[(2)], van der Heijden, H.[(3)], van der Wolf, P.[(3)], Haughey, S[(4)] Viviana Molina[(5)], E. Larrieu[(6)], J.L. Peralta[(7)], Döpfer, D.[(1)]

[(1)]Animal Sciences Group, Wageningen University and Research Centre, P.O. Box 65, 8200 AB Lelystad, The Netherlands.
[(2)] National Institute for Public Health and the Environment, P.O. Box 1, 3720 BA Bilthoven, The Netherlands
[(3)]Animal Health Service (GD), P.O. Box 9, 7400 AA Deventer, The Netherlands
[(4)]Xenosense Ltd, Queen's road, Queen's Island, Belfast BT3 9DT, Northern Ireland
[(5)]Department of Parasitology, Instituto Malbrán, Av. Velez Sarsfield 563, Buenos Aires, Argentina
[(6)]Secretaria de Estado de Salud, Laprida 240, 8500 Viedma, Argentina
[(7)]Universidad Litoral a Esperanza, Facultad de Ciencias Veterinarias, Kreder 2805, 3080 Esperanza, Santa Fé, Argentina
*corresponding author: kitty.maassen@wur.nl

Abstract

The Dutch slaughter pig population is practically free of Trichinella spiralis. However, at slaughter every pig is tested for presence of larvae using the digestion method for export certification. A new 2006 EU directive concerning meat inspection for Trichinella spp. offers new opportunities to monitor Trichinella at herd level instead. Also serological methods are allowed when approved by the Community Reference Laboratory (CRL). To evaluate the usefulness of serological tests for monitoring a virtually free population for Trichinella, Bayesian methodology was used to estimate the diagnostic test parameters sensitivity and specificity, in the absence of a Gold Standard test.

Introduction

Trichinella are nematodes (round worms) which live as intracellular parasites. The diseases they cause are collectively referred to as trichinellosis. The most prevalent human infections are caused by T. spiralis. Domestic pigs are the dominant reservoir host for T. spiralis, which is now considered endemic in Japan and China. Trichinellae infect nearly all mammal species, making it one of the world's most widely-distributed parasite groups. Infection occurs by ingesting contaminated raw or undercooked meat, which might cause severe symptoms, sometimes even death.

Trichinellosis is included in the EU white paper on food safety (EC Zoonosis Directive) and the costs for mandatory routine meat inspection of pigs, horses and game animals for Trichinella in the EU is estimated to be 570 million € annually. A new EU legislation concerning meat inspection for Trichinella spp., which came into force in 2006, offers new opportunities to monitor Trichinella-free herds using serological methods (EU 2075/2005). In The Netherlands, Trichinella is absent in industrialised pig farming, and the serological monitoring might replace individual carcass control for those herds fulfilling the criteria of Trichinella-free herds. In order to set up a surveillance system for population monitoring, information about the test parameters of available assays is necessary.

To evaluate the usefulness of serological tests applied to monitor a Trichinella free population, Bayesian methodology will be used to estimate the diagnostic test parameters: sensitivity and specificity, in the absence of a Gold Standard test. In the absence of positive Dutch serum samples for Trichinella, serum panels originating from regions with endemic Trichinellosis in Argentina and Croatia were used to estimate these test parameters.
The diagnostic test parameters from the imperfect serological tests under validation together with prior knowledge about the historically recorded infection status of farms will be used to set up a surveillance system in the future. The surveillance system has to guarantee freedom-of-infection to humans while using an imperfect test in a very low prevalence population.

Material and methods

Five serological assays were evaluated; 2 commercial ELISAs, 2 in-house ELISAs and a Biacore surface plasmon resonance (SPR) assay. All assays were based on ES-antigen. Cut-off values were used according to standard protocols.

One of the evaluated assays is based on the surface plasmon resonance phenomenon. Surface plasmon resonance (SPR) occurs at the surface of a gold film that is adhered to a glass plate (the sensor chip). Electrons on the surface of the gold film ripple around in waves (surface plasmons). When incident polarized light is directed to the gold film, energy is transferred to the surface plasmons and this causes a dip in intensity of the reflected light. A prerequisite for this to occur is that the incident light reaches the gold film at a certain angle (the resonance or SPR angle). The value of the reflected resonance angle changes when the refractive index at the sensor surface changes. Since the relation between the two is linear, the change in resonance angle can be used to measure changes in refractive index caused by a liquid (containing the analyte of interest) that is guided along the sensor chip surface. For instance, an antigen can be immobilized to the gold film of the sensor chip. A sample is injected into a flow channel that transports the sample to the sensor chip. The antigen captures the antibody (if present) from the liquid and this causes a mass change at the sensor chip surface resulting in a different refractive index at the sensor surface. In turn the value of the resonance angle of the reflected light is changed and measured. Events are displayed by a sensorgram on the screen of the computer that is interfaced to the Biacore apparatus. An advantage of this technology is that the surface can be regenerated and reused many times. Although Biacore technology is routinely used in many fields, it has not yet been used for the detection of antibodies directed against pathogenic microorganisms in animals in a routine setting. The serum sets included ~900 Dutch field sera from pigs that were digestion negative and sera from pigs infected with *Salmonella enterica* serotype Panama. In addition a total of 849 swine sera were collected during routine controls from 11 endemically infected regions in 6 provinces (Santiago del Estero, Santa Fé, 5 regions of Neuquén, 2 regions of Rio Negro, Chubut, and Tierra del Fuego) of Argentina on 18 different dates between 2000 and 2006. The pigs were older than 3 months of age and belonged to small subsidiary farmers. The animals were kept for local consumption in small groups of 1 to about 10 pigs in corals with wooden sheds. Also a small set of field sera from Croatia was tested by all assays.

The test results from the Dutch, Croatian and Argentinean field sera were analysed employing Bayesian statistics. Prevalence (separately per region for the sera from Argentina and for the Croatian sera), sensitivity, and specificity were estimated, in the absence of a gold standard test, with a latent class model. The model accounted for possible (conditional) dependence between tests. Calculations were performed with Markov chain Monte Carlo (MCMC), employing the Gibbs Sampler, as implemented in WinBUGS (Spiegelhalter *et al.*, 2000). For details about the model and the Bayesian inference we refer to Engel *et al.* (2006). Priors were set for prevalences to peak around 10% (Larrieu *et al.*,2004). Gamble *et al.* (2004) reported that the sensitivity of serological tests for Trichinella spp. was between 93.1 and 99.2%, while the specificity was between 90.6 and 99.4%. In this study, the priors for the sensitivity and the specificity were set to peak close to 100% with a large variance. Less informative priors were also employed and the impact of the priors on estimated values and Bayesian confidence intervals (credible intervals) was studied (and found to be small).

Results

The 5 evaluated assays did not show any positive responses in the tested Dutch field samples. Nor did any of the sera from animals infected with *S.* Panama, and which were positive in a Salmonella D-LPS ELISA, show up as positive. Those sera were tested because D serogroup Salmonella strains contain tyvelose in their LPS. Tyvelose is considered to be the most antigenic compound in ES-antigen. This possible cross-reactivity was investigated but has not been found. Within the Croatia serum set the exact same samples were found positive by all assays. Some differences between the assays were found when evaluating the Argentinean serum set, comprising of sera collected from 6 regions with different prevalences. The results of the Dutch, Croatian and Argentinean sera were used to estimate the test parameters and prevalences using Bayesian statistics. Predictably, the Dutch cohort had a marked impact on the specificity. The Argentinean

Session 3: Viruses, parasites, other pathogens

and Croatian cohorts primarily affected sensitivity, but specificity as well. The estimated sensitivity and specificity of the tests and the associated 95% credible intervals are shown in Table 1

Table 1: The diagnostic test parameters and the 95% credible intervals (CI) for the 5 assays, estimated in absence of a Gold Standard, using 849 Argentinean field sera, 889 Dutch slaughter sera and 39 Croatian field sera

Test	Estimated Sensitivity (post. median)	95% conf. int. (credible interval)		Estimated Specificity (post. median)	95% conf. int. (credible interval)	
A	0.93	0.78	0.98	0.997	0.993	0.999
B	0.78	0.65	0.87	0.997	0.994	0.999
C	0.75	0.62	0.85	0.998	0.995	0.999
D	0.64	0.53	0.75	0.981	0.969	0.991
E	0.92	0.83	0.97	0.985	0.976	0.994

Conclusions

In this study, 5 serological Trichinella assays were compared including a SPR assay. Unique serum panels from endemic regions were used to estimate test parameters in the absence of a Gold Standard by Bayesian statistics. All Dutch sera that were negative in the digestion assay, were also found negative by the serological assays. The estimated test parameters can be helpful to calculate the sample sizes and frequency of a surveillance system for *Trichinella spiralis*. If necessary, sensitivity can be enhanced (lowering specificity) or vice versa to adjust to a different expectation of the monitoring system.

Acknowlegdements

The Argentinean and Croatian field workers, farmers and laboratory technicians are dearly thanked for their contribution to this study.
Biacore is thanked for its generous support and advice
The authors thank the Ministry of Agriculture, Nature and Food quality for financially supporting this study.

References

SPIEGELHALTER D., THOMAS, A., and BEST, N., 2000. *WinBUGS Version 1.3.* MRC Biostatistics Unit, Institute of Public Health, Robinson Way, Cambridge CB2 2SR, UK

ENGEL, B., SWILDENS, B., STEGEMAN, A., BUIST, W. and DE JONG, M. 2006. Estimation of sensitivity and specificity of three conditionally dependent diagnostic tests in the absence of a gold standard. *Journal of Agricultural, Biological and Environmnetal statistics*, 11 (4), 360-380.

LARRIEU, E., MOLINA, V., ALBARRACIN, S, MANCINI, S., BIGATTI, R., LEDESMA, L., CHIOSSO, C., KRIVOKAPICH, S., HERRERO, E., and GUARNERA, E., 2004. Porcine and rodent infection with Trichinella, in the Sierra Grande area of Rio Negro province, Argentina. *Ann Trop Med Parasitol,* 98(7),725-31.

GAMBLE, H.R., POZIO, E., BRUSCHI, F., NOCKLER, C., KAPEL, C.M., GAJADHAR, A.A., 2004. International Commission on Trichinellosis: recommendations on the use of serological tests for the detection of Trichinella infection in animals and man. *Parasite,*11(1), 3-13.

Trichinae Certification in the UNITED STATES Pork Industry

*Pyburn, D.[1], Gamble, R.[2], Anderson, L.[1], Miller, L.[1]

[1]USDA APHIS, Riverdale, MD, USA
[2]National Academy of Sciences, Washington, DC, USA
*210 Walnut Street, Suite 891, 50309, Des Moines (IA), USA
e-mail : David.G.Pyburn@aphis.usda.gov; fax: 001-515-284-4191

Abstract

Objective: Control of *Trichinella* infection in U.S. pork has traditionally been accomplished by inspection of individual carcasses at slaughter or by post-slaughter processing. Declines in prevalence of this parasite in domestic swine during the last thirty years, coupled with improvements in pork production systems, allows pork safety to be documented at the farm level. We report here on a proposed on-farm Trichinae Certification Program.

Materials and Methods: Knowledge of risk factors for exposure of swine to *Trichinella spiralis* were used to develop an objective audit that could be applied to pork production sites. In a pilot study, 461 production site audits were performed by trained veterinary practitioners. Trichinae verification testing of swine raised on audited sites was subsequently performed using an ELISA test.

Results: The on-farm good production practices audit includes aspects of farm management, bio-security, feed and feed storage, rodent control programs, and general hygiene. In pilot studies, objective measures of these good production practices were obtained through review of production records and a site inspection. Of the 461 production site audits, 450 audits (97.6%) indicated adherence to good management practices and these sites were granted either entry into the program, or actual program certification. To remain in the program these sites will be audited regularly on a schedule established by the Trichinae Certification Program Standards. Verification testing of 11,713 swine from these sites verified that all swine from certified sites were negative for *Trichinella*.

Conclusions: The described trichinae certification mechanism will establish a process for ensuring the quality and safety of animal-derived food products from the farm through slaughter. Uniform standards stating the requirements of this program have been developed. Federal regulations in support of the program are currently being developed.

Introduction

Prevention of human trichinellosis is a public health goal and there are numerous international standards for testing and treating pork to prevent human infection. Individual carcass testing has been an effective method for preventing clinical trichinellosis in humans in many countries, but the cost of testing is substantial (Pozio, 1998). In developed countries, modern pork production systems have all but eliminated trichinellosis as a food safety risk. In recognition of this, alternatives to individual carcass testing are now being explored for documentation of pork safety. Groups including the International Commission on Trichinellosis (ICT), the Office Internationale des Epizooties (OIE) and the European Union Veterinary Working Group are considering these alternatives. It is with this background that the United States Department of Agriculture (USDA) and the U.S. pork industry are developing the U.S. Trichinae Certification Program.

Food safety is a high priority for the U.S. government and the U.S. pork industry. In an effort to ensure the safety of U.S. pork, research projects have been ongoing over the last ten plus years to identify and control the risk factors for trichinae at the farm level. The USDA has worked with the National Pork Board and the pork processing industry to utilize knowledge from this research to develop a federal regulatory program, the U.S. Trichinae Certification Program. The U.S. Trichinae Certification Program is a pork safety program that provides documentation of pork production management practices that minimize the risk of exposure of pigs to *Trichinella spiralis*. It is an alternative to individual carcass testing that can be used when pigs are raised in production systems where risk of exposure to *T. spiralis* has been eliminated.

Materials and methods

Knowledge of risk factors for exposure of swine to *Trichinella spiralis* were used to develop an objective audit of on-farm production practices that could be applied to pork production sites (Gamble and Bush 1999, Gamble et al. 2000, and van Knapen 2000). The on-farm audit includes aspects of farm management, bio-security, feed and feed storage, rodent control programs, and general hygiene. In a pilot study, objective measures of these good production practices were obtained through review of production records and an inspection of the production site. 461 production site audits were performed by veterinary practitioners. These veterinarians had previously been trained on auditing procedures, *Trichinella* risk factor identification, and *Trichinella* Good Production Practices (Pyburn 2002, Trichinae Certification Pilot Program Standards 2001 and Trichinae Certification Pilot Program Auditor Handbook 2001). Site specific trichinae certification was granted or denied each of the pork production sites dependent upon the outcome of the audit. Program sites will be audited on a regular schedule as established by the Trichinae Certification Pilot Program Pilot Program Standards. In the same pilot study, verification testing of swine raised on certified sites was subsequently performed at slaughter using an ELISA test. Verification testing is random testing of a statistically valid sample of swine from Trichinae Certified production sites. This testing is performed to verify that the swine coming from Trichinae Certified production sites are free of *Trichinella*. Verification testing of swine from audited production sites was performed by trained laboratory technicians at the slaughter plant.

The Good Production Practices that are employed and audited in the Trichinae Certification Program:

1. All non-breeding swine entering the site have either originated from certified pork production sites or, in the case of swine less than 5 weeks old, have originated from either a certified or non-certified pork production site. The source herd Trichinae Identification Number (TIN) must be documented in an animal movement record.
2. Sources of feed or feed ingredients meet Good Manufacturing Practices, as defined in this program or quality assurance standards recognized by the feed industry and documentation to this effect is maintained at the site.
3. Swine feed supplies at the site must be prepared, maintained and handled in a manner such that the feed is protected from possible exposure or contamination by rodents or wildlife. An up-to-date rodent control logbook documenting these practices is maintained at the site.
4. Exclusion and control of rodents and wildlife at the site are to a level such that fresh signs of activity of these animals are not observed in the swine production or feed preparation and storage areas. The producer maintains at the site an up-to-date rodent control logbook with a site diagram, or maintains comparable records from a Pest Control Operator. All records are updated on at least a monthly basis.
5. Wildlife carcasses are not intentionally fed to swine. Swine shall not have access to wildlife harborage or carcasses on the site. This harborage limitation includes wood lots and other natural wildlife access areas.
6. If meat-containing waste is fed to swine, the pork production site must hold a State license to feed such waste. Cooking times and temperatures must be consistent with State and Federal regulations and up-to-date records of waste feeding and cooking practices must be maintained at the site. Cooked waste products that are stored prior to feeding must not be contaminated with uncooked material. Uncooked household waste must not be fed to swine.
7. Procedures are in place and are carried out that call for the prompt removal and proper disposal of swine carcasses found in pens in order to eliminate the opportunity for cannibalism, as well as to prevent attraction of rodents or wildlife.
8. General hygiene and sanitation of the production site is maintained at all times such that rodents and wildlife are not attracted.
   - Solid waste (facility refuse) must be contained in covered receptacles and regularly removed from the site to prevent rodent and wildlife access and attraction.

- Spilled feed must be regularly removed and properly disposed of.
9. Animal arrivals and departures from the site must be documented in an animal movement record and take place in a manner that ensures that swine can be traced to/from that particular certified production site.
10. All records required under the Trichinae Certification Program must be up to date and must be readily available for inspection at the enrolled or certified pork production facility. (Trichinae Certification Pilot Program Standards, 2001)

In the program, pork production sites are audited by USDA qualified and accredited veterinarians. The purpose of these audits is to observe and collect information about the production site, pig sources, feed sources, feed storage methods, rodent and wildlife control, carcass disposal procedures, and facility hygiene. Information is collected on USDA approved official program audit forms. The USDA regulates the audits to ensure that the program standards are met and certifies that the specified Good Production Practices are in place and are maintained on the audited pork production sites. USDA maintains a database containing program records for each certified site. USDA also maintains oversight of the auditing process by qualifying program auditors and by conducting random spot audits. Spot audits are intended to verify that the program's Good Production Practices are maintained between scheduled audits and to assure that the audit process is conducted with integrity and in a consistent manner across the program.

In the program, in order for pigs originating from certified sites to be sold into commerce, the swine slaughter facility must have in place a procedure by which pigs from certified sites and edible pork products derived from pigs from certified sites are segregated from pigs and edible pork products originating from non-certified sites. This process is verified by the USDA Food Safety and Inspection Service. Swine slaughter facilities processing pigs from certified sites are responsible for conducting verification testing to confirm the trichinae-free status of those pigs originating from certified production sites. On a regular basis, statistically valid samples of pigs from certified herds are tested at slaughter to verify that on-farm trichinae-infection risk reduction practices are working. This process verification testing is performed using a USDA approved tissue or blood-based post-mortem test, and is regulated by the USDA Agricultural Marketing Service.

Results
Of the 461 production site audits, 450 audits (97.6%) indicated compliance with the good production practices as defined in the program, and these sites were granted status in the program ("enrolled" or "certified"). Random verification testing of 11,713 swine from farms in the pilot certification program resulted in 11,712 negatives and one positive by ELISA. The one positive ELISA result was determined to be a false-positive when a five gram sample of diaphragm from the carcass was tested by artificial digestion.

Discussion
Trichinella spiralis is a parasitic nematode affecting animals and people. The disease, trichinellosis, is acquired by consuming encysted larvae of Trichinella spiralis in muscle tissue from an infected animal. Consumption of undercooked pork has traditionally been a common source of trichinellosis in humans worldwide. In the U.S. the prevalence of this organism in pork has dropped sharply due to changes in swine management practices within the U.S. pork industry. In 1900, greater than 2.5% of the pigs tested were found to be infected with Trichinella. The infection prevalence declined to 0.95% in the 1930's, 0.63% in 1952, 0.16% in 1965, and 0.12% in 1970. The USDA National Animal Health Monitoring System's National Swine Survey in 1995 showed an infection rate of 0.013% (Gamble & Bush 1998). The same survey in 2000 demonstrated that the infection rate in U.S. swine had fallen to 0.007% (Bush 2002).

In the mid 1980s, the convergence of three factors provided a powerful rationale for the development of industry supported programs to improve food safety in the U.S. First, the prevalence of Trichinella in U.S. swine reached such a low level that disease free status could be envisioned. Second, there was recognition by U.S. pork industry leaders that international markets were closed to U.S producers and U.S. pork products because of the now inaccurate perception that U.S. produced pork had a comparatively high risk of being infected with Trichinella. Finally, the development of a rapid, ELISA based diagnostic test provided a relatively inexpensive tool, which could be utilized in a control program.

The U.S. Trichinae Certification Program is a developing USDA program based on scientific knowledge of the epidemiology of *Trichinella spiralis* and numerous studies demonstrating how specific GPPs can prevent exposure of pigs to this zoonotic parasite. This program is a model program for on-farm assurance of product safety. The International Commission on Trichinellosis in their publication, <u>Recommendations on Methods for the Control of *Trichinella* in Domestic and Wild Animals Intended for Human Consumption</u>, states that, "Modern swine production systems reduce or eliminate risks of swine infection with *Trichinella* and testing of individual animals raised under these conditions could be eliminated." (Gamble et al., 2000). This publication continues with details of the requirements of such production systems. The Trichinae Certification Program meets these standards in all respects.

The U.S. Trichinae Certification Program is regulated by the USDA. Collaborative efforts between the Animal and Plant Health Inspection Service (APHIS), the Food Safety Inspection Service (FSIS), and the Agricultural Marketing Service (AMS) verify that certified pork production sites manage and produce pigs according to the requirements of the program's GPPs and verify the identity of pork from the certified production site through slaughter and processing.

Conclusions
The described Trichinae Certification Program will establish a process for ensuring the quality and safety of animal-derived food products from the farm through slaughter. Uniform standards stating the requirements of this program have been developed. Federal regulations in support of the program are currently being developed.

References
Benson, A.S., 1990. Control of Communicable Diseases in Man. Washington: American Public Health Assoc.

Bush, E., 2002. Veterinary Epidemiologist and Swine Specialist with the USDA Center for Animal Health Monitoring. Personal Communication.

Gamble, H.R., Bessonov, A.S., Cuperlovic, K., Gajadhar, A.A., Knapen, F. van, Noeckler, K., Schenone, H. & Zhu, X., 2000. International Commission on Trichinellosis: Recommendations on Methods for the Control of *Trichinella* in Domestic and Wild Animals Intended for Human Consumption. *Veterinary Parasitology* 93, 393-408.

Gamble, H.R., Bush, E., 1998. Seroprevalence of *Trichinella* Infection in Domestic Swine Based on the National Animal Health Monitoring System's 1990 and 1995 Swine Surveys. *Veterinary Parasitology* 80, 303-310.

Pozio, E. 1998. Trichinellosis in the European Union: Epidemiology, ecology and economic impact. *Parasitology Today* 14, 35-38.

Pyburn, D.G., Gamble, H.R., Anderson, L.A. and Miller, L.E., 2002. Verification of Good Production Practices Which Reduce the Risk of Exposure of Pigs to *Trichinella*. *The Professional Animal Scientist* 18, 13-17.

Pyburn, D., 2002. *Trichinella* Certification in the U.S. Pork Industry. *Proceedings of the 17th International Pig Veterinary Society Congress*. Volume 1: 267.

Trichinae Certification Pilot Program Standards. 2001. Copyrighted Publication of USDA and the National Pork Board.

Van Knapen, F., 2000. Control of trichinellosis by inspection and farm management practices. *Veterinary Parasitology*. 93, 385-392.

Cellular immune responses in porcine reproductive and respiratory syndrome virus (PRRSV) vaccinated weaned piglets challenged with a virulent strain of PRRSV

David Trubiano[1], Renée Larochelle[2], Ronald Magar[2] , and Lucie Lamontagne[1]

[1]Dépt. Sciences Biologiques, Université du Québec à Montréal, C.P. 8888, Succ. Centre-Ville, Montréal, Qué. Canada H3C 3P8
[2]Laboratoire d'hygiène vétérinaire et alimentaire, Agence canadienne d'inspection des aliments, St-Hyacinthe, Québec, Canada.

corresponding author : lamontagne.lucie@uqam.ca

Abstract

The porcine reproductive and respiratory syndrome (PRRS) is an important viral infection of swine that can persist in lymphoid organs of infected pigs despite the induction of specific immune responses, suggesting an immune evasion mechanism. Vaccination has been shown to prevent clinical signs but remains ineffective against viral persistence. Our objective was to investigate the immunological disorders related to vaccination and subsequent challenge by a virulent strain. Groups of piglets were vaccinated with RespPRRS vaccine (Boehringer-Ingelheim) and challenged 4 weeks later with the virulent LHVA-93-3 strain of the PRRS virus. Animals were sacrificed at various times after vaccination and the lungs and lymphoid organs were collected. Lymphoid cell subsets were analysed and viral persistency was determined by RT-PCR. No modifications were observed in the percentages of CD2+CD4+ and CD2+CD8[high] T cells in PRRSV-vaccinated animals, whereas these cells decreased in spleen, tonsils and lymph nodes in vaccinated-challenged piglets. Similarly, specific antibody secreting-B cells were increased after vaccination, but decreased following challenge with the virulent virus. Persistent viral RNA was found in lungs, blood, tonsils, and lymph nodes up to 24 days either in vaccinated or vaccinated-challenged pigs. Taken together, these results indicate that vaccination favours a decrease in CD4+ and CD8 cells and antibody producing-B cells in blood and lymphoid organs and viral persistency in animals challenged with a virulent virus, suggesting a failure in the immune processes.

Introduction

Porcine reproductive and respiratory syndrome virus (PRRSV) represents a widespread viral infection which remains uncontrolled in many countries despite the use of attenuated vaccines. These vaccines decrease the lesions in lungs and significantly improve reproductive performance of the sow (1). However, different vaccinal strains express different immunological properties, thus conferring different levels of protection in pigs (2). In this respect, the clinical protection and the immune responsiveness to PRRSV infections varies considerably between farms and sows within farms (3) The PRRSV is known to persist during several weeks in lungs and lymphoid organs (4). We have previously demonstrated that, in spite of a transient polyclonal activation of B cells, the metabolic activity of lymphoid cells from blood and spleen decreased up to 60 days p.i., while specific anti-PRRSV-secreting B cells occurred later in blood and lymphoid organs (5). In addition, the percentages of the CD2+CD8[high] cell subset increased in spleen and blood of experimentally-PRRSV-infected pigs up to 45 days while they did not increase in mediastinal lymph nodes (MLN) and tonsils (6). However, lymphoid T cells isolated from the blood or lymphoid organs of PRRSV persistently-infected pigs were hyporesponsive to mitogens, an effect correlating with viral replication (6).

Recently, Diaz et al. (2) confirmed the absence of neutralizing antibodies and low frequencies of virus-specific IFN-□ secreting cells in pigs vaccinated with two European-type modified live strains. These observations suggest that attenuated live vaccines can induce immunodisorders favouring viral persistence in absence of clinical signs.

In this work, we report that vaccination with an attenuated PRRSV strain does not prevent viral persistence and correlates with decreased numbers of in CD4+ and CD8[high] cells and of antibody producing-B cells in blood and lymphoid organs from animals challenged with a virulent virus variant.

Materials and methods

Virus and experimental infection in pigs: Forty young pigs were vaccinated with RespPRRS vaccine (Boehringer-Ingelheim) and challenged, 4 weeks later with the virulent strain LHVA-93-3 of the PRRS virus. At various times after vaccination (p.v.) or challenge (p.c.) animals were sacrificed and lungs and lymphoid organs were collected.

Lymphoid cells: The lymphocytes were isolated from blood, spleen, mediastinal lymph nodes (MLN) and tonsils as previously described (5). Lymphoid cells were incubated with anti-CD2 mAb (Cedarlane; Hornby, Ontario, Canada) and anti-CD4 mAb (VMRD Inc. Pullman, WA) or anti-CD8 mAb (Cedarlane) and then with secondary antibodies: phycoerythrine (PE)-conjugated anti-rat IgG2a; (Cedarlane) and fluorescein isothiocyanate (FITC)-conjugated anti-mouse IgG2a (Cedarlane). Flow cytometric analysis was done using a FACScan (Becton-Dickinson, Mountain View, CA) and a Cell Quest software (Becton-Dickinson). Ten thousand events were analyzed per sample and the percentages of CD2+CD4+, CD2+CD8[high], and cell subsets were determined by multiparametric analysis (6). Specific antibody-secreting B cells were evaluated by an ELISPOT assay, and virus detection by done by RT-PCR as reported previously (5).

Statistical analysis:
The difference in the percentages of cell subsets measured by flow cytometric in unvaccinated and PRRSV-vaccinated animals or vaccinated-challenged animals at each time p.i. were evaluated using a Student's t test. A probability level of $P < 0.05$ was considered significant.

Results

Viral RNA was detected in tonsils, spleen and MLN as soon as three days p.i. while it was detected after 10 days in lungs of most of vaccinated animals and persisted up to 24 days in lungs and lymphoid organs. Following challenge with a virulent PRRSV strain, viral RNA increase at three days p.c. and persisted up to 24 days in most animals (Table 1).

To verify the relationship between lymphoid T cell subsets and viral persistence in lymphoid organs, the percentages of CD2+CD4+ and CD2+CD8[high] T cell populations were studied in blood, spleen, MLN and tonsils of PRRSV-vaccinated and vaccinated-challenged weaned pigs at various times. As shown in figure 1A , the percentages of CD2+CD4+ T cells were not altered in blood, spleen, tonsils and MLN in vaccinated pigs (except in tonsils at 24 days p.v.) (p< 0.05). However CD2+CD4+ cells decreased in the blood and lymphoid organs three days after challenge, and two weeks later in blood and MLN. In addition, the percentages of CD2+CD8[high] decreased 10 days pi in blood and MLN after vaccinated-challenged pigs (p< 0.05) (Fig. 1B).

The production of specific antibody secreting-B cells in blood was stimulated in vaccinated animals at 10 days p.v. and later in lymphoid organs (Fig. 2). Surprisingly, the number of secreting-B cells decreased two weeks after challenge with virulent PRRSV in blood, spleen and MLN. It was not possible to evaluate the number of specific antibody secreting-B cells in tonsils since bacterial infections occurred 10 days after the challenge.

Discussion

The use of live vaccine against PRRSV infection in weaned pigs induced no abnormalities in CD4+ and CD8[high] T cells and stimulated the production of B-secreting antiviral antibodies. However, following challenge with a virulent PRRSV strain the percentages of CD4+ cells and CD8[high] T cells, and specific B-secreting cells decreased while viral RNA persisted in the lungs and lymphoid organs of most animals.

Organs	Vaccinated (days post vaccination)				Vaccinated-challenged (days post challenge)			
	3	10	17	24	3	10	17	24
Lungs	0/4	3/4	3/4	3/4	3/4	3/4	4/4	3/4
Tonsils	3/4	3/4	3/4	3/4	4/4	4/4	4/4	4/4
MLN	3/4	3/4	2/4	2/4	3/4	4/4	4/4	3/4
Spleen	3/4	2/4	2/4	2/4	3/4	3/4	3/4	2/4

Table 1: Detection of viral RNA in lungs and lymphoid organs from vaccinated and vaccinated-challenged pigs. Viral RNA was detected by a RT-PCR method.

A) CD2+CD4+   B) CD2+CD8high

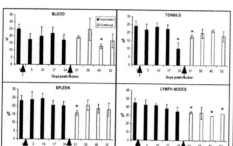
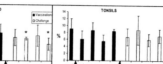

Figure 1: Percentages of CD2+CD4+ (A) and CD2+CD8 high (B) in blood, spleen, tonsils and mediastinal lymph nodes from PRRSV vaccinated and vaccinated-challenged pigs.* p≤0.05

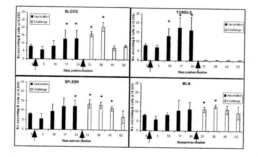

Figure 2: Specific anti-PRRSV antibody secreting-B cells in tonsils, spleen, mediastinal lymph nodes, and blood from vaccinated and vaccinated-challenged pigs.* p≤0.05

These observations are in accordance with previous studies which have reported no significant changes in CD4 and CD8 cells subsets in pigs vaccinated with a modified live virus (7). The decreased percentages in CD4+ and CD8+ T cells and in specific antibody secreting-B cells in blood, spleen and MLN observed in vaccinated-challenged animals suggests that a generalized immunosuppression may occur, or that CD4+, CD8high and B cells are recruited to infected tonsils or lungs. The simultaneous decrease of T and B cell subsets and persistence of viral RNA in lungs and lymphoid organs observed in vaccinated-challenged pigs support the first hypothesis. However, we have previously shown that the virulent PRRSV strain used for the challenge did not significantly modify the percentages of CD4+ cells in spleen, MLN or tonsils in the first days p.i. suggesting that the cell immunosuppression does not directly result from the effects of challenging virus (6). Kiss *et al.* (8) have observed that new variant PRRS viruses might originate from interaction with virulent and vaccine viral strains in vaccinated herds showing recurrence of the disease. Recent works also suggest that PRRSV infection increased the production of suppressive cytokines, such as IL-10 (9). We can propose that the virus used for challenge or new generated variants may exacerbate the production of immunosuppressive cytokines in vaccinated animal due to the viral persistence in macrophages from lungs and lymphoid organs. The second hypothesis concerning a viral-induced recruitment of antiviral T and B cells in infected organs is not supported by our results, since no significant increase in lymphoid cells were taken place in the tonsils in spite of the fact that lymphoid cells in the lungs were not included in this study. In addition, viral RNA was present in spleen and MLN.

Taken together, these results indicate that vaccination does not prevent viral persistence but rather favours a decrease in CD4+ and CD8 T cells and in antibody producing-B cells in blood and lymphoid organs when animals are subsequently infected with a virulent virus, suggesting a failure in the immune processes.

References

1. PAPATSIROS, V.G. *et al.* 2006. Long-term administration of a commercial reproductive and respiratory syndrome virus (PRRSV)-inactivated vaccine in PRRSV-endemically infected sows. Journal of Veterinary Medicine B Infectious Diseases Veterinary Public Health 53(6), 266-272.
2. DIAZ, I., *et al.* 2006. Different European-type vaccines against porcine reproductive and respiratory syndrome virus have different immunological properties and confer different protection to pigs. Virology 351(2), 249-259.
3. LOWE, J.E. *et al.* 2005. Correlation of cell-mediated immunity against porcine reproductive syndrome virus with protection against reproductive failure in sows outbreaks of porcine reproductive and respiratory syndrome in commercial herds. Journal of American Veterinary Medical Association 226 (10), 1707-1711.
4. ALLENDE, R. *et al.* 2000. Porcine reproductive and respiratory syndrome virus: description of persistence in individual pigs upon experimental infection. Journal of Virology 74, 10834-10837.
5. LAMONTAGNE, L. *et al.* 2001. Polyclonal activation of B cells in occurs in lymphoid organs from porcine reproductive and respiratory syndrome virus (PRRSV)-infected Veterinary Immunology and Immunopathology 82 :165-182.
6. LAMONTAGNE, L. *et al.* 2003. Porcine reproductive and respiratory syndrome virus persistence in blood, spleen, lymph nodes, and tonsils of experimentally infected pigs depends on the level of CD8high T cells. Viral Immunology 16(3),395-406.
7. SIPOS, W. et al. 2003. Parameters of humoral and cellular immunity following vaccination of pigs with a European modified-live strain of porcine reproductive and respiratory syndrome (PRRSV). Viral Immunology 16(3),335-346.
8. KISS, I., *et al.* 2006. Genetic variation of the prevailing porcine respiratory and reproductive syndrome viruses occurring on a pig farm upon vaccination. Archives of Virology 151(11),2269-2276.
9. DIAZ, I., *et al.* 2005. Immune responses of pigs after experimental infection with a European strain of porcine reproductive and respiratory syndrome virus. The Journal of General Virology 86, 1943-1951

Session 3

Reducing liver lesion incidence in the Dutch pork supply chain

Van Wagenberg, C.P.A.*[1], Urlings, H.A.P.[2], Van der Vorst, J.G.A.J.[3], Backus, G.B.C.[1]

[1] Agricultural Economics Research Institute LEI, Wageningen University and Research Centre, Burgemeester Patijnlaan 19, 2585 BE, Den Haag, the Netherlands.
[2] VION N.V., p.o. box 380, 5680 AJ, Best, the Netherlands and Animal Nutrition Group, Wageningen University and Research Centre, Marijkeweg 40, 6709 PG, Wageningen, the Netherlands
[3] Operations Research and Logistics Group, Wageningen University and Research Centre, Hollandseweg 1, 6706 KN, Wageningen, the Netherlands
* Corresponding author: coen.vanwagenberg@wur.nl

Abstract

Livers with lesions are an important quality aspect among slaughter pig producers and slaughterhouses. Total losses of non-marketable livers with lesions, lower growth and higher feed intake of pigs in the Netherlands in 2003 were estimated at €3.5 million. The major cause of liver lesions is the roundworm Ascaris suum. Worm treatment on the farm can be effective in reducing liver lesions. Before July 2004 an insurance with a fixed premium for each slaughtered pig was in place in the Netherlands to compensate slaughterhouses for pathological lesions. Individual pig producers had low incentives to take control measures. In July 2004 a new incentive mechanism was introduced: a reduction in the payment of €1 for each pig with a liver lesion. This placed the financial burden of livers with lesions on the producer, thereby increasing incentives to treat roundworm infections. We analysed the data of 1,104 farms with 55,802 deliveries from 2003 to 2006. The mean liver lesion incidence decreased from 8% in 2003 when a collective insurance was in place to 5% in 2006, after the change to the price reduction. Of the producers, 68% reduced liver lesion incidence. Of the producers with an increased incidence, 83% showed a low increase (less than 5%). We conclude that the price reduction was effective in reducing the mean incidence of liver lesions, although large differences between individual producers exist. Further research is needed to determine what causes these large differences.

Introduction

Livers with lesions are an important quality aspect among pig producers and slaughterhouses. Since the late 1990s the mean liver lesion incidence in slaughter pigs in the Netherlands was high, fluctuating between 8 and 12%. The majority of liver defections are caused by an infection with the roundworm Ascaris suum. Application of anthelmentica (worm medicines) on group level through injection, feed or water is generally sufficient to reduce the incidence to 2-4%, although effectiveness depends on the active ingredient and the extent of implementation of the treatment in the producers' management. Treatment costs are around €0.85 per delivered pig when medicine is applied three times. Since pathologically deformed livers are unfit for human consumption, slaughterhouses must dispose of livers with lesions. Further financial losses include a lower growth, higher feed intake, and lower meat percentage as a result of an infection with Ascaris suum. Loss estimates vary from €0.85 to €4.50 for an infected pig, depending on the infection level. Total losses in the Netherlands in 2003 were estimated at €3.5 million (Bondt et al. 2004).
EU legislation (EG/854/2004) prescribes that all pigs delivered for slaughter must be assessed individually for pathological lesions directly after slaughter. This was already prescribed by Dutch legislation. The procedure is documented in the handbook for IKB-encoding developed by the National Inspection Service for Livestock and Meat (RVV) in the early 1990s. The inspection of the carcasses is conducted by official assistants, under the supervision of veterinarians from the Food and Consumer Product Safety Authority (VWA). This guarantees the independency of the assessment. The assessment of livers is based on the degree of infection with the roundworm Ascaris suum. When larvae have migrated through the liver the immune response leads to inflammatory tissue in the liver that shows as white spots. A liver has minor lesions if it has one or

two white spots on the front side of the liver and declared unfit for human consumption - and consequently rejected - if it has three or more white spots.

To compensate slaughterhouses for the resulting economic losses of slaughter lesions a mandatory collective insurance was in place. A pig producer paid a fixed insurance premium per pig delivered to a Dutch slaughterhouse. Until July 2004 rejected livers were part of the insurance. Since a lower rejected liver incidence did not directly result in a lower premium - and thus in lower costs - insufficient incentives for an individual producer existed to implement control measures to reduce liver lesion incidence.

To reduce the financial losses caused by liver lesions, in 2004 the Dutch pig sector created a new financial incentive mechanism to induce individual pig producers to control liver lesion incidence. Such incentives are commonly used in agricultural supply chains to induce growers to provide processors with the correct amount of raw materials of the desired quality at the correct time (e.g. Hueth and Ligon 2002; Martinez and Zering 2004). According to incentive theory increasing the financial consequences of production risks should induce producers to take action to control the risks (Prendergast 1999). On 5 July 2004 - the first Monday in July - a new incentive mechanism was introduced in the Netherlands aimed at putting the costs where they originate: a direct price reduction in the payment to a pig producer of €1 for each delivered pig with a liver lesion. This price reduction places the financial consequences of liver lesions on the producers, theoretically increasing the incentives for them to treat roundworm infections. This paper describes the effect of the introduction of the price reduction on liver lesion incidence.

Material and methods

To show the effects of the change from the insurance to the price reduction we used a dataset with slaughter data of individual pigs of a pig slaughter company with multiple locations in the Netherlands. In the analysis we used livers with lesions, the sum of rejected livers and livers with minor lesions, as 1) both are caused by *Ascaris suum* and 2) coding problems made it impossible to identify rejected livers from livers with minor lesions in time.

The data included 213,398 deliveries of herds of 7,532 different producers from January 2003 to September 2006, including internal deliveries and imports. Deliveries from the analysis that could not be traced directly to a specific producer, such as internal deliveries and imports, were excluded. We also excluded small producers (less than 500 slaughter pigs a year), since often pigs are a - possibly less commercial - side activity on these farms and these producers might therefore be influenced less by a financial incentive. This resulted in 1,104 producers with 55,802 deliveries to be used in the analysis. We tested if the distribution of liver lesion incidence over producers in the sample correctly represented the whole dataset. A Kolmogorov-Smirnov test-statistic of 0.05 indicated that his indeed is the case.

We estimated the effects of the price reduction by comparing the weighted mean of the liver lesion incidence before with the weighted mean after 5 July 2004. The unit of analysis was a delivery and weighing factors were the delivery size. Because pig producers in the Netherlands are free to choose between slaughter companies, a decrease in the mean incidence of livers with lesions measured at a slaughterhouse could be caused by producers switching slaughterhouses. Therefore we used producers that that did not change slaughterhouses and delivered before and after the change. The literature is not clear on whether the current intensive pig husbandry systems as used in the Netherlands have a seasonal influence on liver lesion incidence. By using the same period before and after the change we overcame possible seasonal influences. We defined 1 July 1 2003 to 30 June 2004 as the insurance period (sample X1) and 1 July 2005 to 30 June 2006 as the price reduction period (sample X2). To determine the impact of the price reduction we tested if the weighted mean liver lesion incidence in the insurance period was significantly higher than in the price reduction period using the paired data from X1 and X2. The null hypothesis was H0: $\mu(X2–X1) \geq 0$, with $\mu(X2-X1)$ the weighted mean of X2-X1. The data were analysed with SAS 9.1.

Results

Figure 1 provides the development of weighted (with delivery size) mean of liver lesion incidence from 2003 to 2006 for the 1,104 selected producers. The bold line marks 5 July 2004, the introduction date of the price reduction. The intervals marked by the dashed lines indicate the insurance period X1 and the price reduction period X2. The incidence of livers with lesions in the insurance period was around 7-9% with a standard deviation (not in figure 1) of 8-10%. The incidence remained at this level until April 2005. Then the incidence of livers with lesions decreased in a few months to 4-5% in August 2005, where it remained. The standard deviation decreased to around 5-6%. The decline in liver lesion incidence started ten months after the introduction of the price reduction. This can be explained by producers only starting to apply worm treatment in new groups after 5 July 2004 and by the time it takes for the treatment to become effective. After implementation of the treatment it takes 6 to 18 months to sufficiently decrease infection pressure in the housing to actually reduce liver lesion incidence.

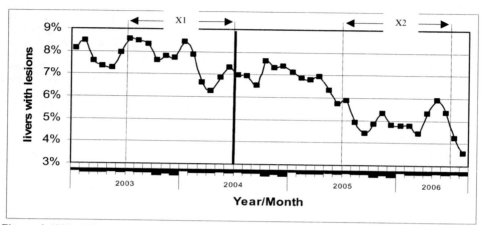

Figure 1: With delivery size weighted calculated mean liver lesion incidence in 2003-2006

Table 2 gives basic with delivery size weighted statistics of the liver lesion incidence in the two periods. The mean decreased from 7.5 to 5.1% and the 95% percentile decreased from 26.8 to 15.5%. The differences between producers reduced as indicated by the decreased standard deviation from 8.5% in period 1 to 5.5% in period 2. We tested H0: $\mu(X2-X1) \geq 0$. Because X2-X1 was not distributed normally - Kolmogorov-Smirnov test statistic for goodness of fit for a normal distribution equals 0.19 - we used bootstrapping (1,000 iterations with seed 0) to test for this difference. The results showed that the difference was significantly different from 0 at P < 0.001. Alternatively, interpreting the data as a time series, we performed a prediction test. We forecast liver lesion incidence in the period of the price reduction using the data of the insurance period on a weekly basis. The actual observed weekly incidences from July 2005 onwards lay outside the 95% confidence interval of the forecast, indicating a significant decrease at the 5% level.

Table 2: With delivery size weighted statistics of liver lesion incidence in period 1 and 2

Period	P5[1]	Mean	P95[1]	Standard deviation
Insurance period 1	0.017	0.075	0.268	0.085
Price reduction period 2	0.012	0.051	0.155	0.055

[1] P5: 5% percentile and P95: 95% percentile

We observed differences between individual producer's liver lesion incidence developments from the insurance period to the price reduction period. Table 3 gives weighted (with delivery size) statistics of the distribution of producer developments. The mean development was -2.4% and the median development -0.9%. The standard deviation was 7.3%, indicating a spread between the developments of individual producers. Of the 1,104 producers 753 showed a decrease in liver lesion incidence ranging from 0% to -46.1%. Of the 352 producers with an increase 295 showed an increase less than 5.0%. The maximum increase was 30.9%.

Table3: Weighted statistics of the distribution of producer developments (X2-X1) of liver lesion incidence

Number of farms used in analysis	1,104	Mean development	- 0.024
- with μ(X2–X1) < 0	753	Median development	- 0.009
- with 0 ≤ μ(X2–X1)	352	St. dev development	0.073
- with 0 ≤ μ(X2–X1) ≤ 5.0%	295	Minimum development	- 0.461
		Maximum development	0.309

Discussion

Because of the use of empirical data, non-observed external factors such as climate, housing or the assessment procedure could have contributed to the decrease in liver lesion incidence. Available data from a German slaughterhouse showed that the liver lesion incidence remained around 9% from 2001 to 2006. This suggests that housing systems and climate did not cause the decrease seen in these Dutch slaughterhouses. As the meat inspection assessment procedure did not change since 2003 it is not expected that this caused the decrease.

A specialised pig veterinarian indicated in an interview that, although communication towards pig producers about the financial consequences of roundworm infections started before 2004, pig producers started to actually take control measures only after the introduction of the price reduction. He argued that the direct negative financial consequences for the producers lead to them taking control measures to reduce liver lesion incidence.

Increased efforts to control liver lesions should show through an increase in the amount of purchased and used anthelmentica. LEI's Farm Accountancy Data Network dataset includes the medicine use of around 70 individual pig producers in the Netherlands. These data showed that the amount of anthelmentica bought increased with 15% from 2004 to 2005. This indicated that Dutch pig producers were more inclined to administer a worm treatment in 2005, confirming our hypothesis of the price reduction effect.

This research showed the effect of a change in incentive mechanism. It did not show why producers changed their management and therefore cannot indicate what leads to different reactions between farmers. To better understand farm decision making and to more effectively design new incentive mechanisms on an individual producer level we need an understanding of the reasons why individual producers reacted the way they did to this change.

Conclusion and further research

The introduction of an individual financial incentive mechanism for livers with lesions, a price reduction in the payment to pig producers, effectively put the financial burden on individual producers, leading to increased activities to control the causes. The mean liver lesion incidence decreased from 8% in 2003 - when a collective insurance was in place - to 5% in 2006, after the change to the price reduction. Of the producers, 68% reduced liver lesion incidence. Of the producers with an increase 83% showed only a low increase (less than 5%). We conclude that the price reduction of €1 was effective in reducing the mean liver lesion incidence, although large differences between individual producers exist. Further research is needed to determine what causes these differences.

References

Bondt, N., et al., 2004. *Reduction of slaughter lesions in the pork supply chain.* The Hague, the Netherlands, Agricultural Economics Research Institute LEI (in Dutch).

Hueth, B. and E. Ligon, 2002. Estimation of an efficient tomato contract. *European Review of Agricultural Economics* 29 (2), 237-253.

Martinez, S. W. and K. Zering, 2004. *Pork quality and the role of market organization.* Agricultural Economic Report No. 835, United States Department of Agriculture.

Prendergast, C., 1999. The provision of incentives in firms. *Journal of Economic Literature* 37 (1), 7-63.

Seroprevalence of *Toxoplasma gondii* in swine slaughtered in Sicily

Vesco G.*, Liga F., Vella A., Lo Cascio G., Villari S.

Istituto Zooprofilattico Sperimentale della Sicilia, Italy

*Corresponding author: gesualdo.vesco@izssicilia.it

Introduction

Several studies showed that the consumption of raw or undercooked meat containing *Toxoplasma gondii* tissue cysts from infected animals is one of the most important sources of human toxoplasmosis. Foods of animal origin most frequently contaminated are pork and small ruminants' meat.

In order to investigate the seroprevalence of Toxoplasmosis in Sicilian pig farms, 1063 swine sera were collected during the slaughtering from locally born and bred animals and 1312 from imported ones (from France and Spain). The local animals came from 154 farms distributed along Sicily, representing pigs of all ages; the others came from lairages.

Materials and methods

The samples were collected by jugular puncture immediately before the slaughtering, and sent to the laboratory under cold conditions. Sera were separated after centrifugation and stored at -20°C until tested.

A commercial kit (ELISA *Toxoplasma gondii* serum screening – Institute Pourquier) has been used. Briefly, according to the manufacturer instructions, 200 µl. of the sera (positive and negative controls and samples) at the dilution of 1/20 were dispensed in a microtiter plates coated with Toxoplasma antigen. The microplate was incubated for 1hour (±5 min.) at 37°C. (±3°C.); after 3 times washing with the solution included in the kit, 100 µl. of Protein G labelled with HRPO were added and incubated for 30 min. (±3 min.) at 37°C. (±3°C.). The conjugate will bind, if present, to the immune-complex. Finally each well has received 100 µl. peroxidase substrate. After incubation at room temperature (21 ± 5°C) for 20 min. away from the light, the reaction was stopped with 100 µl. stop solution. The optical density (OD) of each well was measured using a photometer at a wavelength of 450 nm. The S/P% was calculated. S/P% = (OD_{450} value of the sample - OD_{450} value of the negative control) / (mean OD_{450} value of the positive control - OD_{450} value of the negative control) x 100.

Any sample with a S/P% $\leq$ 40% was considered negative.
Any sample with a 40% < S/P% < 50% was considered borderline.
Any sample with a 50% $\leq$ S/P% $\leq$ 200% was considered coming from an infected animal.
Any sample with a S/P% $\geq$ 200% was considered coming from an affected animal.

Results

The overall seroprevalence of *Toxoplasma*-specific IgG-antibodies was 20.04% (213/1063) in sicilian pigs and 0.99% (13/1312) in imported ones. The 46.75% (72/154) of the farms had at least one *Toxoplasma*-positive animal. The increasing age of the animals and a small farm size (considered as pigs' number) were significantly associated with presence of *T. gondii* infection in the farm ($p \leq 0.001; X^2 = 45.63$ and 36.54, respectively).

Cats' presence in farm and farming method were not found as significant risk factors.

Conclusions and Discussion

The high seroprevalence found for local animals in our research (higher than in other European studies) is partially due to the Sicilian habit to eat imported pigs as fresh meat and slaughter the local ones at the end of their reproductive career for transformed products; thus, considering the increased risk of developing toxoplasmosis with the age, can explain our results, together with the worse developed and less hygienically controlled management conditions. *T. gondii* is usually killed through freezing, heating and salting; nevertheless, in some Sicilian areas still exists the habit to eat raw sausages, and this could represent a risk for human infection. In fact,

Toxoplasmosis can't be controlled without a good health education, to increase the knowledge on infection risk factors, sanitary strategies and food habits to reduce them.

References

VESCO G., POURQUIER J., VILLARI S., CHEBANIER S., LIGA F., ALFANO M., LO CASCIO G., BILLÈ A., GRADINARU D., 2006. Evaluation of a commercial ELISA kit compared to IFAT for the detection of toxoplasmosis in pigs. Proceedings "Toxo&Food" Congress, p. 102.

VILLARI S., PAGANO V., ALFANO M., FIORENTINO G., SCIACCA C., SCHEMBRI P., 2006. Some considerations about sicilian pigs and sheep farms' management. Proceedings "Toxo&Food" Congress, p. 104.

VESCO G., VILLARI S., CHIANCA A., CARACAPPA S., PETERSEN E., BUFFOLANO W., 2006. Eating unprocessed pork meat is a risk factor for human Toxoplasmosis is Sicily. COST Action 854 Final Conference, Proceedings, p. 19.

HILL D.E., CHIRUKANDOTH S., DUBEY J.P., LUNNEY J.K., GAMBLE H.R. 2006. Comparison of detection methods for Toxoplasma gondii in naturally and experimentally infected swine. Vet Parasitol.Oct10;141(1-2):9-17.

GAMBLE H.R., DUBEY J.P., LAMBILLOTTE D.N., 2005. Comparison of a commercial ELISA with the modified agglutination test for detection of Toxoplasma infection in the domestic pig. Vet Parasitol. Mar 31;128(3-4):177-81.

EDELHOFER R., 1994. Prevalence of antibodies against Toxoplasma gondii in pigs in Austria. Parasitol Res. 80(8):642-4.

Trichinellosis in Switzerland

Zeeh, F.[*][(1)], Frey, C.[(2)], Schuppers, M.E.[(3)], Müller, N. [(2)], Zimmermann, W.[(1)], Gottstein, B.[(2)]

[(1)]Swine Clinic, University of Bern, Bremgartenstrasse 109a, POB 8466, 3001, Bern, Switzerland
[(2)]Institute for Parasitology, University of Bern, Länggass-Strasse 122, 3012 Bern, Switzerland
[(3)]SAFOSO, Bremgartenstrasse 109a, 3012 Bern, Switzerland
*corresponding author: friederike.zeeh@knp.unibe.ch

Abstract

Human trichinellosis is a food-borne zoonosis exhibiting significant health and economical problems predominantly in countries with high pork consumption. During the past ten years the number of human outbreaks around the world has increased in certain areas. In Europe, more than 20,000 human cases have been detected between the year 1991 and 2000. Conversely, Trichinella infection has not been reported for many decades among Swiss domestic pigs. The last autochthonous cases of human trichinellosis in Switzerland date to a time period prior to the first half of the last century. Nevertheless, Trichinella occurs in a sylvatic cycle in Switzerland. Molecular and genotyping investigations on the taxonomy of present Swiss Trichinella isolates always yielded T. britovi as a species. In an earlier study, foxes had been tested using the artificial digestion method with a prevalence finding of 1.3%. Similar investigations in Swiss lynxes yielded a parasitological prevalence of 27%. Based upon this epidemiological background, a risk based surveillance project is presently running under the sponsorship of the Swiss Federal Veterinary Office, including a detailed parasitological and serological (E/S-ELISA and Westernblot) investigation of representative populations of domestic pigs, wild boars, foxes, lynxes and other wild carnivores. In order to obtain reference laboratory specimens for the standardization of parasitological and serological tests, experimental infections in pigs were carried out with T. spiralis, T. britovi and T. pseudospiralis. Seroconversion occurred on day 21 p.i. for T. spiralis and on day 28 p.i. for T. britovi and T. pseudospiralis. As expected, all sera of the three species cross-reacted with the T. spiralis E/S-antigen, thus indicating that this kind of antigen will be suitable to catch hold of all three species by serological means. All three Trichinella species yielded an appropriate muscle-stage larval infection intensity in order to provide positive reference muscle samples for Swiss diagnostic laboratories involved in the diagnosis of animal Trichinella infection.

Introduction

Trichinella sp. range among the porcine parasites which cause food-borne zoonosis in humans. These nematodes are the causative agents of trichinellosis in man, a disease that rarely affects animals. The transmission of the parasites occurs via oral intake of tissue containing infective larvae. Humans become infected by consumption of uncooked or improperly heated meat containing infectious larvae. During the past ten years the number of human outbreaks around the world has increased in certain areas. In countries with high pork consumption, health and economical problems are noteworthy. Human trichinellosis is characterised by abdominal problems, oedema in the head region, fever, muscle pain or skin reactions. In Europe, more than 20,000 human cases have been detected between the year 1991 and 2000. Conversely, Trichinella infection has not been reported for many decades among Swiss domestic pigs or wild boars (Gottstein et al., 1997). The last autochthonous cases of human trichinellosis in Switzerland date to a time period prior to the first half of the last century. Between 1935 and1968 4 outbreaks occurred after the - in Switzerland uncommon - consumption of infected dog meat (Rehsteiner 1939; Käppeli, 1955; Hörning, 1976).
Nevertheless, Trichinella occurs in a sylvatic cycle in Switzerland. Wild carnivores as lynxes and foxes play an important role. Molecular and genotyping investigations on the taxonomy of present

Swiss *Trichinella* isolates always yielded *T. britovi* as a species (Gottstein et al., 1997; Gottstein et al., 2006; Müller et al., 2006). In an earlier study, foxes had been tested using the artificial digestion method with a prevalence finding of 1.3% (Jakob et al., 1994). Similar investigations in Swiss lynxes yielded a parasitological prevalence of 27% (B. Gottstein, pers. communication). With the pig keeping structures in Switzerland, where outdoor ranging or pasturing is becoming more common, contact with infected wild animals can not be excluded. Especially foxes are known to look for food near pig stables.

Additionally, in the course of the implementation of EU legislation regarding *Trichinella* monitoring in pork, the Swiss abattoirs have to test every slaughtered pig since 2007. In the sight of these requests and the assumed very low prevalence or freedom of *Trichinella* in Swiss domestic pigs, testing would lead to an enormous increase in costs and labour. Based upon the epidemiological and lawful background, a risk based surveillance project is presently running under the sponsorship of the Swiss Federal Veterinary Office, including investigation of representative populations of domestic pigs, wild boars, foxes, lynxes and other wild carnivores in Switzerland. Detailed parasitological and serological (E/S-ELISA and Westernblot) research will be undertaken. The aim of this project is the determination of the actual prevalence of *Trichinella* sp. in Switzerland, and based upon these findings a risk adapted control program for *Trichinella* sp. could be developed.

In order to obtain reference laboratory specimens to standardize parasitological and serological tests, experimental infections in pigs were carried out with *T. spiralis*, *T. britovi* and *T. pseudospiralis* at the Vetsuisse Faculty Bern.

Materials and methods

Three healthy fattening pigs weighing between 30 and 37 kg at day 0 of the trial were orally infected with infectious muscle-stage larvae 1 of three different species of *Trichinella*. Larvae were obtained by artificial digestion of experimentally infected mice. The three *Trichinella* species are thus routinely kept by serial passage in Balb/c-mice in the frame of the Swiss reference laboratory for trichinellosis. Pig no.1 received 30,400 L1 of *T. spiralis*, pig No.2 60,000 L1 of *T. pseudospiralis* and pig no. 3 60,000 L1 of *T. britovi*. Prior to inoculation, control blood and faeces were sampled for standard laboratory and parasitological investigations. Serum samples were tested for the demonstration of the absence of anti-*Trichinella* antibodies, and specimens underwent conventional parasitological examination (flotation and sedimentation technique). The three pigs were separately housed for 2 weeks. They were daily monitored upon conventional clinical examination and blood was collected at day 7, 14, 21, 28, 35, 42, 49, and 57 p.i. by puncturing the jugular vein. Clotted blood samples were sedimented for obtaining appropriate serum specimens. Sera were stored at -20°C. Serological investigation was carried out by a *Trichinella*-E/S ELISA as previously described by Gottstein et al. (1997). At day 61 of the trial, the three pigs were euthanised, and 2 litres blood and 25 to 35 kilograms muscle per animal were collected, respectively. Samples of 5 grams isolated from different striated muscles were quantitatively tested for the presence of *Trichinella* larvae by a standardized artificial digestion method, and sera were assessed for their anti-*Trichinella* antibody concentration by a standardized *T. spiralis* E/S-antigen-ELISA. Once laboratory testing had yielded the appropriate results, all meat and serum samples were aliquoted and stored frozen at -30°C for being further used as standard reference material in the frame of epidemiological surveys or of quality control trials for Swiss veterinary diagnostic laboratories.

Results

Prior to experimental infection, two of the three pigs were coprologically positive for *Trichuris suis* and *Ascaris suum*. Consequently, all three animals were conventionally treated with flubendazole, treatment efficacy being demonstrated coproscopically. Subsequently, the three animals were orally infected with the *Trichinella* larvae. The pigs showed no signs of illness. Body temperature, digestion and muscular system were inconspicuous during the whole trial. All preinfection sera tested negative for *Trichinella* sp. by E/S-ELISA. Seroconversion occurred on day 21 p.i. for *T. spiralis* and on days 28 p.i. for *T. britovi* and *T. pseudospiralis*, respectively (Fig. 1). Thus, all sera of the three species significantly cross-reacted with the *T. spiralis* E/S-antigen.

Fig. 1: Time course of anti-*Trichinella*-antibody development in experimentally infected pigs. S8192: *T. spiralis*; S0952: *T. pseudospiralis*; S0946: *T. britovi*. The red arrow indicates the infection onset (22.06.2005).

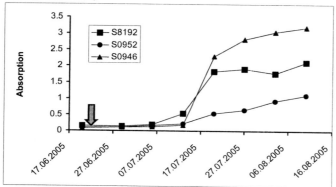

The calculated densities of larvae recovered in the muscle samples are presented in Table 1.

Table 1: Infection doses and larvae burden at end of the trial in three experimentally infected pigs (average obtained from different samples).

	Pig infected with *T. spiralis*	Pig infected with *T. pseudospiralis*	Pig infected with *T. britovi*
Infection dose	30.400 larvae per os	60.000 larvae per os	60.000 larvae per os
Calculated larvae density in diaphragm	330 larvae/g	75 larvae/g	1.65 larvae/g
Calculated larvae density in the masseter	490 larvae/g	13 larvae/g	3.35 larvae/g

Discussion

Trichinella sp. are of importance in Switzerland. Beside legislative demands, the epidemiological background of the sylvatic circle and its possible connection with outdoor pigs require an appropriate monitoring. The assumed absence of *Trichinella* sp. in the Swiss domestic pigs population and the comparable low number of slaughtered pigs per year prompted Switzerland to look for alternatives instead of the testing each individual pig with direct detection methods. Serological testing such as the well described E/S-ELISA appear particularly suitable to carry out risk-based surveillance or monitoring programs. In order to provide standardized test procedures, sufficient amounts of positive and negative reference test materials (sera or meat juice) are required. Such sera and meat juice were now generated and obtained by experimental infection of three pigs with L1 of three *Trichinella* species. Testing the sera of the pig infected with *T. spiralis* larvae showed that seroconversion occurred after 21 days p.i.. In the two other pigs infected with *T. pseudospiralis* and *T. britovi*, respectively, first detectable antibodies became apparent 7 days later. The rise of the antibody concentration against *T. pseudospiralis* was relatively weak when compared to *T. britovi*. Nevertheless, the use of *T. spiralis* E/S-antigen proved to be suitable to detect antibodies by ELISA against all three *Trichinella* species addressed in this study, thus a major cross-reactivity can be concluded from these findings.

With regard to the infection intensity determined by the quantitative artificial digestion method, the pig infected with *T. spiralis* yielded 330 larvae per gram diaphragm muscle and 490 L/g cheek muscle. A much lower infection intensity was anticipated and finally also demonstrated for *T. pseudospiralis* and especially *T. britovi*. This confirmed the much lower susceptibility of the domestic pig as a host for these latter two species, however without affecting the potential to develop an appropriate humoral immunity that sufficiently cross-reacts with *T. spiralis* E/S-antigen, thus allowing an adequate immunodiagnosis by the respective ELISA.

To summarise, *Trichinella* infection is a contemporary topic in Switzerland. Diagnosis of the parasitic nematodes, especially in the surroundings of safe pork production, requires efforts and adequate methods. Serology appears to suitably contribute to this approach.

Conclusion

The sera and meat juice as well as muscle specimens obtained in the present study can now be provided to Swiss veterinary diagnostic laboratories interested in the diagnosis of *Trichinella* infections.

References

GOTTSTEIN, B., POZIO, E., CONOLLY, B., GAMBLE, H.R., ECKERT, J., JAKOB, H.-P., 1997. Epidemiological investigation of trichinellosis in Switzerland. *Veterinary Parasitology*, 72 (1997) 201-207.

GOTTSTEIN, B., SAGER, H., MÜLLER, N., 2006. *Trichinella britovi* in wolves, Switzerland. *ProMED-Id:* 20060427.1219

HÖRNING, B., 1976. *Trichinella spiralis* und Trichinellose in der Schweiz. *Schweizerische Hausdruckerei Institut für exakte Wissenschaften, Bern.*

JAKOB, H.-P., ECKERT, J., JEMMI, T., GOTTSTEIN, B., 1994. Untersuchungen von Schlacht- und Wildtieren in der Schweiz auf Trichinellose mit der Verdauungsmethode und einem serologischen Verfahren (E/S-ELISA). *Schweizer Archiv für Tierheilkunde*, 136 (9), 298-308.

KÄPPELI, F., 1955. Beobachtungen über Trichinose bei Mensch und Tier in Biasca. Oral presentation, Jahresversammlung der Gesellschaft Schweizer Tierärzte, Lugano. 24th of September 1955.

MÜLLER, N., SAGER, H., SCHUPPERS, M., GOTTSTEIN, B., 2006. Methoden zur Untersuchung von *Trichinella*- Infektionen bei Haus- und Wildtieren. *Schweizer Archiv für Tierheilkunde*, 148 (9), 463-471.

REHSTEINER, 1939. Trichinose nach dem Genuss von Hundefleisch. *Schweizer Archiv für Tierheilkunde*. 81, 155-156.

Study on the virulence and cross-neutralization capability of recent porcine parvovirus field isolates and vaccine viruses in experimentally infected pregnant gilts

Zeeuw, E.[(1)], Leinecker, N.[(1)], Herwig, V.[(2)], Selbitz, H.-J.[(2)], Manteufel, J.[(1)], Truyen, U.*[(1)]

(1) Institute for Animal Hygiene and Veterinary Public Health, Faculty of Veterinary Medicine, University of Leipzig, An den Tierkliniken 1, D-04103 Leipzig, Germany
(2) Impfstoffwerke Dessau-Tornau GmbH, PF 400214, 06855 Rosslau, Germany

corresponding author: truyen@vetmed.uni-leipzig.de

Abstract

The pathogenicity of two recent German field isolates of *Porcine parvovirus* (PPV-27a and PPV 143a) and two vaccine viruses [PPV-NADL-2 and PPV-IDT (MSV)], which are used for the production of inactivated vaccines, was investigated by inoculation of pregnant sows at day 40 of gestation. Post-infection sera of these sows as well as antisera prepared in rabbits by immunization with the four above-mentioned PPV isolates and with the virulent strain PPV-Challenge (Engl.) were tested for their homologous and heterologous neutralization activities. All antisera had high neutralization activities against the vaccine viruses, the PPV-Challenge (Engl.) and PPV-143a, but much lower activity against PPV-27a. These results suggest that PPV-27a represents a new antigenic variant or type of PPV and vaccines based on the established vaccine viruses may not be fully protective against this field isolate. PPV-27a has been characterized based on the amino acid sequences of the capsid protein as a member of a new and distinct PPV cluster. Interestingly, the homologous neutralizing antibody titres of the sera of all three pigs and both rabbits inoculated or immunized with PPV-27a were 100- to 1000-fold lower than the heterologous titres against any of the other viruses. The low homologous neutralizing antibody titres suggest a possible, yet undefined, immune escape mechanism of this PPV isolate.

Introduction

Porcine parvovirus (PPV) is a member of the family *Parvoviridae*. PPV is widespread in swine herds, despite vaccination. The virulent strains cause reproductive failures in swine, represented by stillbirth, embryonic death, infertility (SMEDI-syndrome) and delayed return to oestrus. The manifestation of clinical disease depends on the pathogenicity of the virus and on the stage of gestation. Fetuses infected before day 70 of gestation usually die, whereas fetuses infected at a later time point develop antibodies against PPV, eliminate the virus and survive the infection.

PPV strains can be distinguished by their different pathogenicity. Substitution of only a few residues in the VP2 capsid protein is thought to be responsible for distinct biological properties.

Phylogenetic analysis of the VP1/VP2 protein gene revealed that there is a relatively weak sequence similarity between PPV-NADL-2 and recent field isolates from Germany.
The aim of the study was to examine two of these recent field isolates, one from each cluster, under experimental conditions for their pathogenicity (*in vivo*) and antigenicity (*in vitro*), particularly in comparison to the vaccine viruses PPV-NADL-2 and PPV-IDT (MSV).

Material and methods

Animal experiment. Twelve specific-pathogen-free Pietrain x Large White sows, 11 months of age, were randomly assigned to four groups. Groups were kept separately throughout the experiment. At day 40 of gestation the sows were inoculated with the respective viruses by both the intranasal (i.n.) and intramuscular (i.m.) route. Clinical signs (general performance, respiratory activity, food and water intake, and rectal temperature) were recorded daily for 50 days postinoculation. Blood samples were taken in intervals and analysed for antibodies against PPV. At day 90, about three weeks before term, all gilts were euthanized and the fetuses were aseptically delivered via Caesarean and euthanized. Blood and tissue samples were collected from the sows and all fetuses.

Polyclonal sera. To prepare virus-specific sera for cross-neutralization tests with the selected field isolates, vaccines viruses and PPV-Challenge (engl.), rabbits were immunized with CsCl-density-purified virus. The resulting sera were heat-inavtivated and stored frozen at -20°C.

Serology. Hemagglutination inhibition test for detection of PPV-specific antibodies and serum neutralization test for checking cross-neutralization activity are described in detail in Zeeuw, E. J. et al. (2007).

Virus detection. SPEV cells were used for virus reisolation from lung and kidney of the fetuses. Viral DNA was detected by real-time PCR as described by Wilhelm, S. et al. (2006).

Results

Clinic. All sows remained clinically healthy. Fetal mummification was significantly ($P < 0.05$) higher in the gilts infected with PPV-27a as compared to the other groups (85% vs. 5-18%). Almost all fetuses of the gilts of the group 2 infected with PPV-27a showed various ranges of fetal mummification. In contrast, only single mummified fetuses were found in litters of the gilts of groups 1 (PPV-143a), 3 (PPV-IDT [MSV]), or 4 (PPV-NADL-2).

Serology. Gilts infected with PPV-143a, PPV-27a and PPV-NADL-2 developed a significant ($p < 0.05$) higher serological response at 2 weeks p.inf. compared to PPV-IDT (MSV). Umbilical cord blood of the non-mummified fetuses from all groups revealed HI antibody titer (Table 2), indicating transplacental infection of all PPV-isolates examined. Neutralizing antibody titers were determined in the post infection sera of the sows and rabbit sera raised against the various PPV-isolates. The neutralizating antibody titer in sera raised against PPV-143a, PPV-IDT (MSV), PPV-NADL-2 and PPV-Challenge (Engl.) against the PPV-Isolate 27a were generally very low, with SN titers ranging from 0.5–0.69, but high against PPV-143a, PPV-IDT (MSV), PPV-NADL-2 and PPV-Challenge (Engl.). Sera raised against PPV-27a neutralized all heterologous PPV-isolates with high titers ranging from 2.99-3.99 (overall geometric mean titer), the homologous virus, however, was less efficiently neutralized (0,69-1,19, see table 4).
Virtually identical results were obtained with rabbit sera raised against the PPV isolates, with SN titers of antisera raised against PPV-27a ranging from 2.29-3.99 against all heterologous viruses, but only titers of 0.69-1.39 against the homologous virus.

Virus detection. After two passages, no evidence for virus replication was observed in the fetuses of group 1 (PPV-143a), group 3 (PPV-IDT [MSV]) and group 4 (PPV-NADL-2). . In contrast, virus could be readily isolated from fetuses of group 2 (PPV-27a). Viral DNA could be detected by PCR in virtually all mummified and non-mummified fetuses of the PPV-27a inoculated sows, and in single non-mummified piglets of the other groups. However the viral loads differed dramatically (by a factor of 10^9) between PPV 27a piglets and those of the other groups.

Discussion

The fact that in this study antibody and viral DNA could be detected in fetuses of all four groups provides indirect evidence for transplacental infection of both the PPV isolates and the vaccine viruses PPV-IDT (MSV) and PPV-NADL-2. This is in contrast to previous reports where it was postulated that PPV-NADL-2 is not able to cross the placental barrier. But the direct proof for tranplacental transmission, the virus reisolation of infectious virus is still missing.

Session 3

A difference in virulence of PPV-27a to members of the other cluster (PPV-143a, PPV-IDT [MSV], PPV-NADL-2) was indicated by the high mortality of the fetuses. PPV spreads inside the uterus from fetus to fetus. Virus spread was probably more slowly between the fetuses of the groups PPV-143a, PPV-IDT (MSV) and PPV-NADL-2 than between those of the group PPV-27a.

In the present study we investigated in two independent cross-neutralization tests post infection sera of pigs and antisera of rabbits immunized with the respective viruses. Cross-neutralization of the sera raised against the vaccine viruses PPV-NADL-2 and PPV-IDT [MSV], against the field isolates PPV-143a and PPV-27a as well as against the PPV-Challenge (Engl.) revealed low neutralization activity (0.5-0.69) against PPV-27a, indicating an incomplete protection. Therefore, if PPV-27a is representative for current PPV-isolates in the population, this indicates that vaccines, which are used since 30 years, may no longer be fully protective.

The phylogenetic cluster containing the German isolate PPV-27a is defined by three amino acid substitutions (Q228→E, E419→Q and S436→T) in VP2 (Simpson, A. A. et al., 2002b ; Soares, R. M. et al., 2003 ; Zimmermann, P. et al., 2006)). All three residues are located in accessible regions on the capsid's surface and position 228 was identified to be part of one of the nine known linear epitopes on VP2 (Kamstrup, S. et al., 1998 ; Simpson, A. A. et al., 2002a). To what extent the capsid structure will be altered by changing amino acid 228 from Gln to Glu and amino acid 419 from Glu to Gln, and whether they are even involved in the apparent immune escape, needs to be further investigated.

Conclusions

In conclusion, our results indicate that possible antigenic variation represented by PPV-27a may influence the effective vaccination against PPV. Further studies and animal inoculation experiments using PPV-27a mutants will be required to address this important issue.

References

KAMSTRUP, S., LANGEVELD, J. et al., 1998. Mapping the antigenic structure of porcine parvovirus at the level of peptides. *Virus Res*, 53 (2), 163-173.

SIMPSON, A. A., HEBERT, B. et al., 2002a. The structure of porcine parvovirus: comparison with related viruses. *J Mol Biol*, 315 (5), 1189-1198.

SIMPSON, A. A., HEBERT, B. et al., 2002b. The structure of porcine parvovirus: comparison with related viruses. *J Mol Biol*, 315 (5), 1189-1198.

SOARES, R. M., CORTEZ, A. et al., 2003. Genetic variability of porcine parvovirus isolates revealed by analysis of partial sequences of the structural coding gene VP2. *Journal of General Virology*, 84

WILHELM, S., ZIMMERMANN, P. et al., 2006. Real-time PCR protocol for the detection of porcine parvovirus in field samples. *J Virol Methods*, 134 (1-2), 257-260.

ZEEUW, E. J., LEINECKER, N. et al., 2007. Study of the virulence and cross-neutralization capability of recent porcine parvovirus field isolates and vaccine viruses in experimentally infected pregnant gilts. *J Gen Virol*, 88 (Pt 2), 420-427.

ZIMMERMANN, P., RITZMANN, M. et al., 2006. VP1-sequences of German porcine parvovirus isolates define two genetic lineages. *J Gen Virol*, 87   295-301.

ORAL & POSTER

FOURTH SESSION

Control strategies

The use of a *Salmonella* Typhimurium live vaccine to control *Salmonella* Typhimurium in fattening pigs in field and effects on serological surveillance

Lindner,T*., Springer, S., Selbitz. H.-J.

Impfstoffwerk Dessau Tornau (IDT) GmbH, Streetzer Weg 15 a, D-06862 Rodleben, Germany, Phone: +49 34901 885 435 Fax: +49 34901 885 327

*corresponding author: thomas.lindner@idt-direct.de

Abstract
This field study was designed to evaluate the use of a live-attenuated *Salmonella* Typhimurium vaccine in pigs in respect of efficacy against *S.* Typhimurium at time of slaughter and the effect on serological herd monitoring using a commercial mixed LPS-ELISA.
About 1289 slaughtered pigs (805 of non vaccinated groups and 484 of vaccinated groups) were investigated by bacteriological and serological examination (1149 pigs).
The study showed the efficacy of an oral vaccination with a live-attenuated *Salmonella* Typhimurium vaccine in reducing the number of *Salmonella* carrying pigs at slaughter without a detectable interference with the serological monitoring of *Salmonella* (using a cut off at 40% OD level).

Introduction
The work carried out in this study was designed to evaluate efficacy of a live Salmonella Typhimurium vaccine in a pig population with low prevalence of Salmonella Typhimurium and no clinical signs of salmonellosis. Furthermore the impact of the vaccination on the monitoring of the herd with a commercial ELISA kit test was investigated.

Material and Methods
The study was conducted as sequential trial in a commercial pig herd with no signs of clinical salmonellosis but subclinical infection with Salmonella Typhimurium.
The swine population was a fattening one with piglet production and rearing under "all-in-all-out"-management. During the first period of this study 805 nonvaccinated pigs were sampled at slaughter. At the same time sows and their offspring were vaccinated. Thereafter 484 vaccinated pigs were examined in the same way.
The vaccine used was a commercial available live Salmonella Typhimurium vaccine (SALMOPORC®) and was based on a double-attenuated strain of S. Typhimurium, phage type DT 9, containing the serotype-specific plasmid of 60 MDa. This strain can be distinguished from field strains of the same serotype on the basis of its auxotrophy (ade- and his-), using a rapid test (Salmonella Diagnostic Kit from IDT GmbH) and molecular biology methods (Schwarz et al., 1995). As far as possible all sows were given one dose of the vaccine ($\geq$ 5 x 108 cfu) at 6 and again at 3 weeks ante partum by the subcutaneous route. All viable piglets of the vaccinated sows were given a single dose by the oral route on day 21 and 42 post partum.
Culturing of ileocaecal lymph nodes was done to demonstrate the presence of Salmonella (qualitative) using standard microbiological culturing. Bacteriological culture carried out by 18 hours pre-enrichment at 37o C Buffered Peptone Water (BPW: Merck), 48 hours selective enrichment at 37o C in RVS medium (Merck), with subculturing on to Rambach and XLT4 agar (Merck) plates after 24 and 48 hours culture. The plates were incubated for 24 hours at 37o C and suspect colonies confirmed by standard biochemical and serological tests (SIFIN, Berlin). The wild-type strain distinguished from the vaccine strain using the IDT Salmonella Diagnostic Kit.
Blood samples were examined by a Mixed-LPS-ELISA (SALMOTYPE®, Labor Diagnostik, Leipzig) using a cut off at 40% OD level.

Results
In the bacteriological examination 64 of 805 non-vaccinated pigs showed Salmonella Typhimurium at slaughter whereas 10 of 484 of vaccinated pigs did so (Table 1). All isolates of the vaccinated

pigs have been wild strains. The Odd Ratio for being tested positive in bacteriological examination for non vaccinated pigs was 4.09 (ci95%: 2.05 – 9.03, p=3.38E-6). The risk factor was not being vaccinated. The result suggested that vaccination reduced the number of Salmonella carrying pigs at slaughter.

The serological examination of blood samples taken at slaughter revealed 127 of 802 pigs tested positive among the non-vaccinated groups and 55 of 347 pigs tested positive of the vaccinated groups. The OR for being tested positive in ELISA at 40% OD level was 1.0 (ci95%: 0.70 – 1.44, p=1.0). The results of the serological examination showed that the oral vaccination didn't increase the number of pigs tested positive by ELISA.

Table 1: Bacteriological and Serological results among vaccinated and not vaccinated pigs

Date	Group	No Lymph nodes tested	tested positiv	Rate (%) of pos. lymph node samples	No Serum samples	No positiv samples (40%OD)	Rate (%) of pos. serum samples
2407	non-vaccinated	165	10	6.06	160	45	28.13
2108	non-vaccinated	100	3	3.00	92	26	28.26
2011	non-vaccinated	69	3	4.35	100	7	7.00
0412	non-vaccinated	118	1	0.85	100	16	16.00
1112	non-vaccinated	88	5	5.68	70	19	27.14
0502	non-vaccinated	135	16	11.85	-	-	-
1202	non-vaccinated	109	15	13.76	93	6	6.45
0904	non-vaccinated	83	0	0.00	90	5	5.56
3004	non-vaccinated	103	21	20.39	97	3	3.09
0907	vaccinated	95	0	0.00	98	12	12.24
2307	vaccinated	150	4	2.67	50	7	14.00
3007	vaccinated	124	2	1.61	100	15	15.00
0608	vaccinated	115	4	3.48	99	21	21.21
	non vaccinated (Total)	**805**	**64**	**7.95**	**802**	**127**	**15.84**
	vaccinated (Total)	**484**	**10**	**2.07**	**347**	**55**	**15.85**

Considering lower cut off levels (%OD) than 40% resulted in a rising rate of pigs tested positive among the vaccinated group than in the control group (Figure 1). That trend increases with lowering of the cut off level.

Figure 1: The influence of the cut off level (%OD) that has chosen in the Salmonella ELISA on the rate of pigs tested positive at slaughter in vaccinated and non vaccinated pigs.

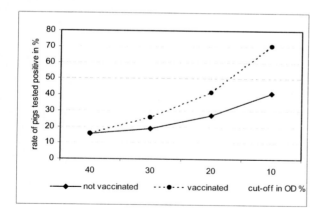

Discussion

This study demonstrates that the vaccination of pig with a live attenuated Salmonella Typhimurium vaccine (SALMOPORC®) was efficacious in reducing the number of Salmonella Typhimurium positive pigs at slaughter when used in a herd with low level of prevalence of Salmonella. This result corresponds to other trials using that Salmonella live vaccine in herds with high prevalence of Salmonella Typhimurium (LINDNER, 2001). The serological control of both groups (ELISA with cut off level 40% OD) showed nearly a similar overall rate of pigs tested positive whereas the bacteriological examination revealed lower rate of Salmonella Typhimurium carrying pigs among the vaccinated animals. But both methods show a low prevalence of the herd. Using lower cut off levels to be more stringent in the control of Salmonella may cause a change the category of vaccinated herds earlier than in non-vaccinated herds. That may be seen as an effect of the vaccination itself or of a different immune response of vaccinated pigs compared to non-vaccinated pigs to Salmonella present in the environment during fattening period.

Conclusions

The vaccination in a herd with low level of prevalence of Salmonella following that scheme proposed for the vaccine will be efficacious in reducing Salmonella Typhimurium in fattening pigs and will not have an adverse impact on the classification into risk categories as long as Salmonella ELISA are used at the 40% OD level. When using cut off levels lower 40% OD there may be an influence on to the classification into risk categories. In situations were a bacteriological monitoring is used there will be no influence. This has to be considered when preparing control programs based on serological surveillance of pig herds.

References

LINDNER, T., SPRINGER, S., STEINBACH, G.,SELBITZ, H.-J., 2001. Immunoprophylaxis as a method to help to reduce the incidence of Salmonella infection in swine. Proceedings of the 4th International Symposium on the Epidemiology and Control of Salmonella and other food borne pathogens in Pork, 89-91

SCHWARZ, S., et. al., 1995. Die komplexe Charakterisierung von Salmonella-Stämmen für Lebendimpfstoffe – dargestellt am Beispiel einer auxotrophen S. Typhimurium Mutante. Tieraerztliche Umschau, 50, 832-834.

Session 4

Protection of pigs against experimental *Salmonella* Typhimurium infection by use of a single dose subunit slow delivery vaccine.

Quessy, S.[1]*, Desautels A.[1], Prud'homme, R.E.[2], Letellier, A[1].

[1] Research chair in meat safety, GREMIP, Faculté de Médecine Vétérinaire de l'Université de Montréal, 3200 Sicotte, J2S 7C6, St-Hyacinthe, Canada.
[2] Département de biochimie, Faculté de médecine, Université de Montréal, Montréal, Canada.
*corresponding author : sylvain.quessy@umontreal.ca

Abstract

Infections caused by septicemic strains of *Salmonella* are significant animal health as well as food safety concerns for the North American swine industry. Among the various strategies to control these infections at the herd level, development of vaccines are attractive alternatives. In this study, based on previous studies of immune response to various proteins following natural and experimental infections of pigs by *Salmonella*, we designed a subunit slow delivery vaccine and tested it in an experimental model of infection. The selected immunogenic protein was cloned and purified by chromatography. The purified protein was then incorporated in PLGA (a polymer that is slowly degraded within the animal's gastro intestinal system) microspheres and given orally once to groups of pigs (n=8) while control animals (n=8) received only PBS. Animals were challenged orally 4 weeks after the vaccination with 10^8 cells of a virulent strains of *Salmonella* Typhimurium. Animals were examined twice a day and clinical signs evaluated using a predetermined scoring grid. Pigs were sacrificed 12 days later and bacterial cultures of various organs, electron microscopy and evaluation of IgA response by ELISA were performed. No significant difference was found at bacteriology and ELISA but marked differences in clinical signs were observed between vaccinated and non vaccinated animals. None of vaccinated animals showed fever exceeding 40°C while it was observed in 5 out of 8 non vaccinated. Only one of vaccinated pigs showed mild diarrhea while severe diarrhea was observed in all control animals. Different sizes of microspheres were observed in intestinal crypts of vaccinated animals at electron microscopy. We concluded that this vaccine can protect pigs against clinical signs associated with experimental infection by *Salmonella* Typhimurium.

Introduction

Although Salmonella is, in pigs, most often associated with sub-clinical infections, the Typhimurium serovar can cause severe clinical signs such as septicaemia and may as well result in mortalities that can have significant economical impacts in affected herds. This serovar is often among the most important serovar recovered from humans and it is therefore critical to reduce the number of affected animals. When herds are affected by clinical outbreaks of S. Typhimurium, it was shown that the bacteria is present in most animals/pens and environmental samples (Letellier and al 1999), increasing the likelihood of meat contamination. It is therefore important to control these infections at the herd level both for productivity and food safety point of views. Since the host-adapted serovar Choleraesuis was in the past, and is still, associated with similar clinical signs, most vaccines, live or autogenous, were developed to protect pigs against this serovar. Nevertheless, a few live vaccines were proposed to reduce S Typhimurium clinical signs (Roesler et al, 2004). In this study, we report the development of a sub-unit slow delivery vaccine against S. Typhimurium in pigs and results of a pre-clinical protection trial using an experimental model of infection.

Material and Methods

Selection of immunogenic proteins. The protein to be included in vaccine was selected by western blots using various strains of S. Typhimurium as antigens and antisera. Bacteria were grown in different conditions (low and high osmolarity, low iron, low pH, …) to ensure that the targeted protein would be expressed in various phases of infection. The antisera used to detect immunogenic proteins were recovered from over a hundred of animals that survived episodes clinical salmonellosis in various herds. The selected protein (p 37) was recognized by all antisera and was expressed in al types of growth conditions.

Purification of protein. The selected protein was sequenced and cloned into E. coli M15 using pCR®2.1::gapAREZ as vector. Using the histidine tail the protein was purified by affinity chromatography (FPLC).

Microspheres production. The selected matrix was a co-polymer of (poly (DL-lactic-co-glycolic) acid) (PLGA), a non toxic, non teratogenic, FDA approved molecule. The delivery rates are controlled by the relative proportion of copolymers. The end products of this polymer are CO_2 H_2O. Moreover, it is known that 11 µm and less microspheres are well absorbed by intestinal cells at Payers patches level (Tabata et al., 1996). This compound also possesses adjuvant properties (Igartua et al., 1998). The P37 protein was incorporated into PLGA in a pre-determined ratio with co-incorporation of albumin to improve P37 incorporation rates. The resulting microspheres were lyophilized until the protection trials.

Protection trial. Groups of 8 cross-bred Salmonella negative pigs were administered orally 2 cc of microspheres or PBS (control pigs) at 3 weeks of age. At 7 weeks of age, animals were given orally 10 8 cells of a virulent Salmonella Typhimurium DT 104 strains. Pigs were examined twice a day for 12 days using a pre-determined evaluation grid (the sum of clinical signs scores and diarrhea scores (on 4 levels of severity each) and then sacrificed. At necropsy, bacterial cultures and Salmonella counts in feces and internal organs were performed. Washes of intestinal mucus were also performed and IgA production was assessed using an ELISA, adapted from a previously described procedures (Côté et al, 2004). Finally, electron microscopy was done on small intestines of necropsied animals to check for the presence of microspheres in intestinal crypts.

Results

Animals that received the microsphere vaccine had clearly less clinical signs compared to the control group (figure 1). Only one of vaccinated animals showed a mild diarrhea while diarrhea, often severe, was observed in all control animals. None of vaccinated animals had temperature over 40° C while it was observed in 5 out of 8 control pigs. Although a trend to higher IgA levels was observed in vaccinated pigs, no statistical diffence was observed between to groups of animals. Electron microscopy revealed the presence of microspheres in intestinal crypts and palatine tonsils 2 days after immunization (data not shown) and 12 days after the experimental challenge (figure 2), more than 5 weeks after vaccination. It was not possible to observe statistically significant reduction of bacterial counts in tissues of both groups of animals.

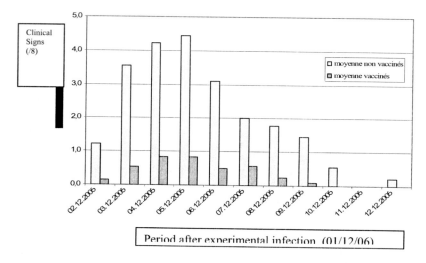

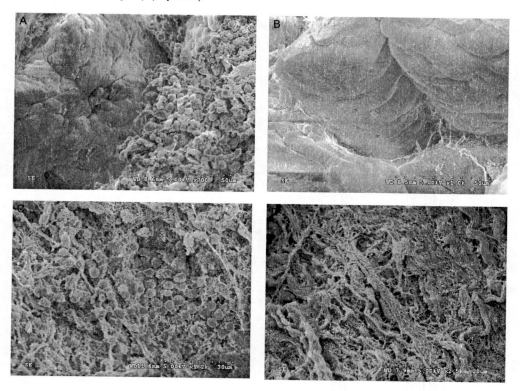

Figure 1. : Mean scores of clinical signs observed in pigs vaccinated (green) with P37 incorporated PLGA microspheres following a challenge with *Salmonella* Typhimurium DT104 strain compared to control group (in yellow).

Figure 2. Electron microscopy of intestinal crypts (A) and palatine tonsils (C) of vaccinated and control pigs (B,D)

Discussion

Use of sub-unit vaccines can be beneficial to avoid undesirable effects seldom seen with live vaccine. In addition, when the selected antigen is embedded within an appropriate matrix, it may be delivered into the host gradually, avoiding repetitive vaccine administrations. Results obtained in this study suggest that co-polymer of PLGA can be use to protect immunogenic proteins in swine and to slowly deliver the antigens within the intestinal tract. Indeed, even 5 weeks after vaccine administration, it was possible to observe microspheres in the intestinal tract of pigs suggesting that the vaccine will be efficiently delivered for a prolonged period of time. Moreover, the fact that the end products of this compounds are non toxic would eliminate any concern related to food safety.

Since relatively high dosages of bacteria were used to ensure reproduction of clinical signs and given the low numbers of animals that were used, it was not unexpected to not observe significant difference in bacterial counts in various organs. Further studies with different experimental designs will have to be conducted to assess the ability of this vaccine to reduce shedding of *Salmonella* or to assess cross protection against other serovar.

Conclusion

Use of a subunit slow delivery vaccine composed of the P37 protein embedded within PLGA microspheres succeeded in protecting animals against an experimental infection by *Salmonella* Typhimurium. It is suggested to conduct further research to assess the efficacy of this vaccine to protect animals against the disease in field conditions or to reduce the carriage in sub-clinical infections.

References

COTÉ, S., LETELLIER, A., LESSARD, L., QUESSY, S. 2004. Distribution of Salmonella in tissues following natural and experimental infection in pigs. Canadian Journal of Veterinary Research. Oct;68(4):241-8

IGARTUA, M., HERNANDEZ, R.M., ESQUISABEL, A.,GASCON, A.R., CALYO, M.B., PEDRAZ, J.L. 1998. Enhanced immune response after subcutaneous and oral immunization with biodegradable PLGA microspheres. J Control Release. Dec 4;56(1-3):63-73

LETELLIER, A, MESSIER, S., PARÉ, J., MÉNARD, J, QUESSY, S. 1999. Distribution of Salmonella in swine herds in Quebec. Veterinary Microbiology. Jul 1;67(4):299-306.

ROESLER,U., MARG,H., SCHRODER, I., MAUER, S., ARNOLD, T., LEHMAN, J., TRUYEN, U., HENSEL, A. 2004 . Oral vaccination of pigs with an invasive gyrA-cpxA-rpoB Salmonella Typhimurium mutant. Vaccine16;23(5):595-603.

NAKAOKA, R., INOUE, Y., TABATA, Y. IKADA, Y. 1996. Size effect on the antibody production induced by biodegradable microspheres containing antigen Vaccine Sep;14(13):1251-6.

Use of toll-like receptor agonists to reduce *Salmonella* colonization in neonatal swine[tt]

Genovese, K.J.[*], He H., Nisbet, D. J., Kogut M.H.

USDA-ARS, FFSRU SPARC 2881 F & B Road College Station, TX 77845, USA
corresponding author: *genovese@ffsru.usda.gov
[tt]This research was sponsored in part by a grant from the National Pork Board, #06-003.

Abstract

Toll-like receptors (TLR) are members of a highly conserved group of receptors which recognize conserved molecular aspects of microbes. The purpose of these experiments were to ascertain the effects of the administration of the TLR 9 agonist, CpG, on the colonization of neonatal swine with *Salmonella*. Piglets were treated within 24 hr after birth (Day 0) with CpG via oral gavage. On day 5 post-treatment, piglets were challenged with *Salmonella* orally. Daily rectal swabs were taken until day 10 post-treatment. On day 10, piglets were euthanized and gut contents and tissues were cultured for the presence of *Salmonella*. Piglets in the CpG group had a one log reduction of *Salmonella* in cecal and colon contents, and no *Salmonella* was detected in rectal contents in this group compared with *Salmonella* infected control pigs. Rectal swabs showed a reduction in fecal shedding of *Salmonella* on days 7-10 in CpG treated pigs. No *Salmonella* was detected in any pigs treated with CpG in the spleen or rectum. Reductions in the number of pigs positive for *Salmonella* were found in the lymph nodes, colon and cecum. The data show that CpG may be an effective tool in reducing *Salmonella* colonization and shedding in neonatal pigs and supports previous data in weaned pigs where CpG had similar effects on *Salmonella* colonization.

Introduction

Salmonella is an important food-borne pathogen in humans (Voetsch *et al.*, 2004). Poultry, swine, and cattle are known carriers of *Salmonella* and are important vectors of transmission of *Salmonella* to humans (Patrick *et al.*, 2004). Initial interactions between cells of the host innate immune system and pathogens, such as *Salmonella,* depends on the host's recognition of evolutionarily conserved molecules unique to a certain class of microbes called pathogen-associated molecular patterns (PAMPs) (Fearon & Locksley, 1996; Akira, 2001; Janeway & Medzhitov, 2002). These PAMPs are recognized by the cells of the innate system via pattern recognition receptors (PRRs), such as the Toll-like receptors (TLR), and this recognition initiates signaling pathways within the cell that result in the production and release of cytokines, chemokines, and activation of the cell itself (Imler & Hoffman 2001; Janeway & Medzhitov 2002, Kopp & Medzhitov 2003). The recognition and subsequent release of cytokines aids in the direction of the acquired arm of the immune system, leading the response towards either a T_H1, cell-mediated response or a T_H2, antibody-mediated response (Medzhitov & Janeway 1997a,b; Romagnani 1992).
Bacterial DNA contains unmethylated portions of its sequence that are conserved regions called CpG DNA. CpG DNA is recognized by the mammalian innate immune system through TLR 9 (Hemmi et al, 2000; Bauer et al, 2001). Previous studies have indicated that CpG DNA can stimulate neutrophils of weaned pigs and protect weaned pigs against a laboratory challenge with *Salmonella choleraesuis* (Genovese et al., Safe Pork 2005). In addition, CpG DNA have been found to stimulate the avian immune system and show protective effects against *Salmonella* challenge (He et al., 2005).
The purpose of the present studies was to observe the effects of the TLR9 agonist, CpG DNA, in a laboratory challenge model of *Salmonella choleraesuis* (SC) infection.

Materials and metods

The sequence of the CpG DNA was as follows:
pD19 - G*G*T*G*C*A*T*C*G*A*T*G*C*A*G*G*G*G*G.
Piglets in the CpG group received 1.0 mg CpG DNA in 2ml of phosphate-buffered saline (PBS) by oral gavage. Pigs in the SC infected control group received an oral dose of 2ml PBS. Piglets were weighed, ear-tagged, and given their respective treatment within 24 hours after birth. The day the treatment was administered was designated day 0. On day 5 post-treatment, all piglets were weighed; piglets in infected groups were orally administered 2 ml of phosphate-buffered saline solution (PBS) containing 10^9 colony-forming units (cfu) of *Salmonella choleraesuis* (SC). Daily rectal swabs were taken from all groups and cultured for the presence of SC following established procedures. On day 10 post-treatment, pigs were weighed, then euthanized and sections of the gut and lymph nodes were cultured for the presence of SC. The cecum, colon, and rectum tissues and the luminal contents were cultured for the presence and enumeration of SC, respectively. In addition, the liver, spleen, and ileocecal lymph nodes were cultured for the presence of SC.

Results

Results of the SC enumeration studies are presented in Table 1. Treatment of neonatal swine with CpG within 24 hr after birth reduced the number of SC recovered from all three areas of the gut sampled and enumerated. In both the colon and the cecum, SC cfu were reduced by at least one log 10. No SC was recovered from the rectum during enumeration studies in the pigs treated with CpG (a 3 log10 reduction).
Results of enriched samples of the gut and tissues are presented in Figure 1. In the spleen, lymph nodes, colon, cecum, and rectum, the number of pigs positive for SC upon enrichment was reduced in the CpG treatment group compared to the SC control group. Again, pigs in the CpG group showed no recovery of SC in the rectum samples.
Daily rectal swab data are presented in Figure 2. On the first day of sampling (Day 6), pigs in the CpG group had 40% SC positive rectal swabs compared to 20% in the SC control group. However, on Day 7, 8, 9, and 10 the CpG group had greatly reduced recovery of SC in rectal swab samples compared to the SC control group.

Table 1: Enumeration of *Salmonella*/gram of gut contents

Group	Colon	Cecum	Rectum
CpG	1.0×10^4 cfu/g[†]	1.1×10^4 cfu/g	0.00 cfu/g
SC control	3.85×10^5 cfu/g	1.67×10^5 cfu/g	3.0×10^3 cfu/g

† cfu = colony forming units

Figure 1: *Salmonella* isolated from tissues treated with CpG DNA at birth and challenged with SC 24 hr after treatment

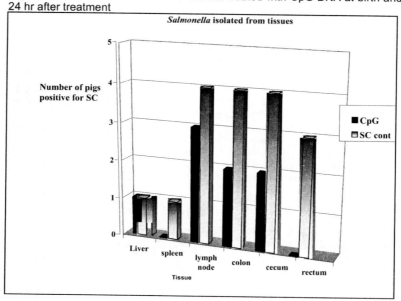

Figure 2: Daily Rectal swab data from pigs treated with CpG DNA and challenged 24hr later with SC

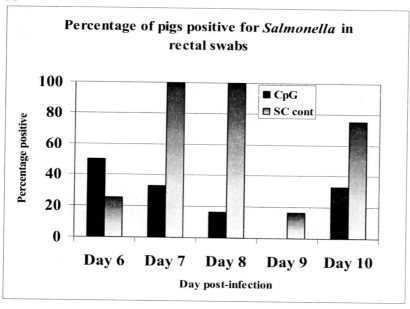

Discussion

In this study, CpG DNA reduced fecal shedding and gut and tissue colonization by *Salmonella choleraesuis* in neonatal pigs. These results are similar to previous studies of CpG DNA treatment and reductions in *Salmonella* colonization in weaned pigs (Genovese et al., Safe Pork 2005). Although preliminary, these results indicate that CpG DNA could be effective in reducing *Salmonella* colonization of the swine gut and perhaps reduce the load of *Salmonella* moving through swine during later stages of production. However, more research is needed to form any conclusions on the effectiveness of CpG DNA treatment in neonatal pigs and subsequent effects on *Salmonella* carriage in later production stages. CpG DNA has been shown as a potent stimulator of the innate immune system in poultry and in mammals (He et al., 2005; Genovese et al., SafePork 2005). The use of TLR agonists on their own or in combination with vaccines as adjuvants may provide effective agents for reducing both foodborne and animal disease pathogens in food animals.

Conclusions

The results of these studies provide a basis for further characterization of TLR agonists effects against pathogens in swine. CpG DNA treatment of neonatal pigs within 24 hr after birth reduced the levels of Salmonella choleraesuis in the cecum, colon, and rectum by at least one log10 and reduced the number of pigs positive for Salmonella choleraesuis after enrichment in the spleen and lymph nodes. Treatment of neonatal pigs with CpG DNA also reduced the number of pigs shedding Salmonella choleraesuis in their feces. Further studies are needed to determine the overall effectiveness of CpG DNA administration to neonatal pigs in reducing Salmonella colonization of the gut and of tissues and its effects throughout later stages of swine production.

References

Akira S. 2001 Toll-like receptors and innate immunity. *Advances in Immunology* 78: 1-56.

Bauer, S., et al., 2001. Human TLR9 confers responsiveness to bacterial DNA via species-specific CpG motif recognition. *Proc Natl Acad Sci* USA98:9237-9242

Fearon, D.T. & Locksley, R.M. 1996. The instructive role of innate immunity in the acquired immune response. *Science, 272, 50-54.*

He, H., et al., 2005. In vitro activation of chicken leukocytes and in vivo protection against *Salmonella enteritidis* organ invasion and peritoneal *S. enteritidis* infection-induced mortality in neonatal chickens by immunostimulatory CpG oligodeoxynucleotide. *FEMS Immunol Med Microbiol* 43:81-89.

Hemmi, H, et al., 2000. A toll-like receptor recognizes bacterial DNA. *Nature* 408:740-745.

Imler, J.-L. & Hoffman, J.A. 2001. Toll receptors in innate immunity. *Trends in Cell Biology, 11, 304-311.*

Janeway Jr. CA, Medzhitov R. 2002. Innate immune recognition. *Annual Review of Immunology* 20: 197-216.

Kopp, E. & Medzhitov, R. 2003. Recognition of microbial infection by Toll-like receptors. *Current Opinions in Immunology, 15, 396-401.*

Medzhitov, R. & Janeway Jr., C.A. 1997a. Innate immunity: impact on the adaptive immune response. *Current Opinion in Immunology, 9, 4-9.*

Medzhitov, R. & Janeway Jr., C.A. 1997b. Innate immunity: the virtues of a nonclonal system of recognition. *Cell, 91, 295-298.*

Patrick ME, et al., 2004. *Salmonella enteritidis* infections, United States, 1985-1999. *Emerging Infectious Diseases* 10:1-7.

Romagnani, S. 1992. Induction of Th1 and Th2 responses: a key role for the "natural" immune response? *Immunology Today, 13, 379-381.*

Voetsch AC, et al., FoodNet estimate of the burden of illness caused by nontyphoidal *Salmonella* infections in the United States. *Clinical Infectious Diseases* 38:S3:s127-134.

Session 4

Breeding for genetic resistance to Salmonella in pigs

Velander, H.I.[1], Boes, J.*[2], Nielsen, Bj.[1], Nielsen, B.[3]

Danish Pig Production, [1]Axeltorv 3, DK-1609 Copenhagen, [2]Vinkelvej 11, DK-8620 Kjellerup, [3] Danish Meat Association, Axeltorv 3, DK-1609, Copenhagen, Denmark
* *Jaap Boes:* jbo@danishmeat.dk

Summary

Previous experimental Salmonella infection studies in Denmark have shown that some pigs remain faecal culture negative and seronegative despite oral inoculation with 10^8 c.f.u. S. Typhimurium and housing in highly contaminated pens, suggesting that some pigs are genetically resistant to Salmonella. Our study tested the following hypothesis: The Salmonella-negative status in certain pigs is due to genetic resistance, related to a single gene. The resistance gene was supposed to have a low frequency and to be recessive and that full resistance only would appear if both alleles were recessive. A challenge study was conducted to test this hypothesis. The pigs used were three bred crosses of Duroc boars and LY-dams. We infected 600 Salmonella-negative pigs with approximately 10^9 S. Typhimurium via the feed at 15-20 kg live weight. On day 15, 22 and 29 post inoculation, pigs were blood sampled and the sera were examined for Salmonella antibodies using the Danish Mix-ELISA. From seronegative pigs and pigs with low antibody levels individual faecal samples were cultured qualitatively for Salmonella. In total, 7% of the 600 pigs developed no or very low antibody levels, indicating genetic resistance; those pigs were selected for the next study phase. In phase two, 22 resistant female pigs were mated with 17 resistant males. Their second-generation offspring comprised 183 pigs, which were challenge infected as described above. The results showed that 7% of second-generation pigs had low antibody levels. Heritability was estimated to be 0.13. Our study shows that resistance to Salmonella has a genetic background and is most probably ruled by several genes.

Introduction

Salmonella infection studies in Denmark have shown that some pigs remain faecal culture negative and seronegative despite oral inoculation (Nielsen et al., 1995). This suggests that these pigs are resistant to Salmonella infection and that this resistance could have a genetic background. This resistance could be located on a single gene where the allele is recessive with a low frequency and resistance will only appear if both alleles are recessive. Therefore a carrier of one allele is predicted as being sensitive to the disease. For example, in E.coli-149 F4 infection in pigs a single recessive gene is found to cause diarrhoea in piglets (Jørgensen et al., 2003). Salmonella challenge studies in chicken and in lamb indicate that resistance exhibited a genetic background and that selection for reduced carrier state is possible (Beaumont et al., 2006; Moreno et al., 2003).The mechanism proposed for genetic resistance to Salmonella in the gut is that bacteria will not adhere to the epithelial cells of the intestine and thereby not colonize the host. This means that the bacteria will not cause infection in resistant animals, characterised by animals remaining seronegative and culture-negative upon challenge with Salmonella infection. Genetic resistance to Salmonella in e.g. pigs and poultry will have a potential impact on food safety.

A challenge experiment was carried out in two consecutive generations of pigs to investigate if genetic resistance to Salmonella Typhimurium existed in Danish pig breeds. The aim was to investigate the genetic background to resistance and to test the feasibility of genetic improvement. The hypothesis was that Salmonella seronegative status in pigs is related to a single recessive gene.

Materials and methods

In a multiplying herd 66 Landrace*Yorkshire (LY) crossbred sows were inseminated with semen from 66 Duroc (D) boars. The herd had been seronegative for Salmonella for 4 years as shown by monthly blood sampling as part of the Salmonella control program in Danish breeding herds. The sows selected were 1st, 2nd and 3rd parity sows. The piglets were weaned at 7 kg live weight (approx. 28 days) and moved to a Salmonella-free research facility in 6 groups of about 100 animals per batch. Each group of animals was housed in a separate unit and inoculated on the same day. Upon arrival, it was ensured that pigs were negative for Salmonella by examining pooled faecal samples.

Pigs were orally inoculated via the feed with approximately 10^9 cfu S. Typhimurium at a live weight of 15-20 kg. On day 15 post inoculation (p.i.) all pigs were blood sampled and sera were examined for antibodies against Salmonella using the Danish mix-ELISA (Nielsen et al., 1995). The trait analyzed was Antibody response, measured as optical density (OD%). OD% <27 was considered indicative of resistance to Salmonella. On day 22 and 29 p.i. pigs with negative or low antibody response in the first blood sample (at an empirical cut-off <27 OD%) were re-tested serologically. A control group of pigs with OD% >26 at first sampling were also re-tested at least once. Seronegative pigs and pigs with antibody levels <27 OD% were also examined for Salmonella by standard bacteriological methods using 3 consecutive faecal samples collected at day 20-22 and 27-29.

In the second phase of the study, the seronegative pigs remaining from phase 1 were mated and their offspring was subjected to the same inoculation and testing protocol as described above. In both parts of the study, pigs that tested positive for Salmonella both serologically (OD% >26) and/or bacteriological were excluded from the study and necropsied.

Contingency tables were used to estimate the expected number of animals within the three different genotypes, and chi-square tests were used to test for homogeneity between litters and for testing the hypothesis of a single gene. Data of the first generation was analysed by a linear mixed repeatability model with random effects:

$$g(OD_{ij}) = s_i + g_i + d_i + b_1 x_i + b_2 (x_i)^2 + L_i + e_i + \varepsilon_{ij}$$

In the model, $g(OD_{ij})$ is the transformed response of OD_{ij} recorder by animal i on measurement j using function g to stabilize the variance between animals, $e_i \sim N(0, \sigma_e^2)$ and the variance between repeated measurements within the same animal, $\varepsilon_{ij} \sim N(0, \sigma_\varepsilon^2)$. For each animal i s_i is a two level sex effect, g_i is a group effect of six levels, $L_i \sim N(0, \sigma_L^2)$ is the random effect of litters with variance σ_L^2, and b_1 and b_2 are regression coefficients of the first and second order value of age at first inoculation time x_i. To estimate genetic variance an animal model was used:

$$g(OD_{ij}) = s_i + g_i + d_i + b_1 x_i + b_2 (x_i)^2 + L_i + a_i + e_i + \varepsilon_{ij}$$

In this model, $a_i \sim N(0, \sigma_a^2 A)$ is the genetic component of animal i with genetic variance σ_a^2 and A is the relationship matrix.

Results
In the 1st generation (phase 1) 606 pigs were inoculated with Salmonella as desribed above. Out of the 606 pigs, 87 were tested again on day 22 and on day 29 p.i. In total 62 pigs in the 1st generation had an OD% <27 at the first test (Table 1 and Figure 1). A total of 42 pigs (6.9%) remained seronegative until 30 days p.i. Three pigs were culled for other reasons and thus 39 pigs were included in the second part of the study. A randomly selected control group of 25 pigs with higher values at the first test were re-examined at least once.

Table 1: Antibody response in pigs inoculated with Salmonella Typhimurium (1st generation)

Grouping	No. of pigs	% of all pigs	Mean OD% (±SD) 15 days p.i.	22 days p.i.	29 days p.i.
1st blood test, all pigs	606	100	77 (40)	-	-
Low response 1st test (<27 OD%)	62	10.2	14 (7.1)	22 (13.4)	21 (14.8)
Low response all tests (<27 OD%)	42	6.9	13 (7.3)	15 (7.8)	14.7 (7.0)
High response 1st test (>26 OD%)(control group)	25	4.1	85 (41.9)	73 (39.4)	86 (30.4)

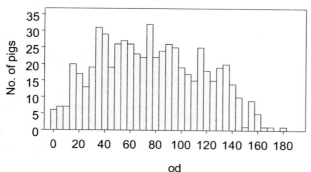

Figure 1: Antibody response (individual OD%) in pigs inoculated with Salmonella Typhimurium 15 days p.i. (1st generation).

In phase 2 of the experiment the second generation of 22 seronegative sows and 17 seronegative boars were mated with each other, which resulted in 21 litters with a total amount of 203 pigs, of which 183 were included in the inoculation study. The second-generation pigs originated from 30 different 1st generation litters. Three full-sibs were selected from each of three litters, 2 full-sibs from each of 6 litters and from 21 litters one pig/litter was selected. Assuming that antibody response is connected to resistance, 45.3% of the litters thus had one or more resistant pig and 13.5% of the litters had two or more resistant full sibs/litter.

In total 6.6% of the pigs showed a low antibody response to Salmonella compared to 6.9% of the pigs in the first generation (see Table 2 and Figure 2). The standard deviation of the antibody response was decreasing in the 2nd generation.

Table 2: Antibody response in pigs inoculated with Salmonella Typhimurium (2nd generation)

	No. of pigs	% of all pigs	Mean OD% (±SD)	
			15 days p.i.	22 days p.i.
First blood test , all pigs	183	100	73 (29.3)	-
Low response 1st test (OD%<27)	18	9.8	14 (7.8)	8 (9.0)
Low response all tests (OD%<27)	12	6.6	12 (7.9)	8 (8.1)
High response 1st test (control group)	38	Control	80 (22.4)	63 (23.8)

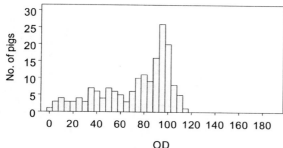

Figure 2: Antibody response in pigs (individual OD%) inoculated with Salmonella Typhimurium 15 days p.i. (2nd generation).

From pigs re-tested for antibody response faecal samples were collected and cultured individually day 20-22 and day 27-29 p.i. The results of the culture analysis were analyzed as a binomial trait (presence/absence). In total 25 (31.6%) were tested negative and 18 pigs (22.8 %) were positive in all repeated culture tests in the 1st generation. There was no significant relationship between antibody response and bacteriological results, neither in the 1st nor the 2nd generation.

As 7% of the offspring in first generation had a low antibody response, the genotype frequency of the resistant allele was assumed to be 7%. To express resistance both parents have to be heterozygous or homozygous for the recessive allele. Testing the hypothesis for homogeneity (H_0) with Chisquare test showed that the hypothesis could not be rejected. Hence, homogeneity between litters was assumed, i.e. the recessive genotype (rr) was equally distributed in all litters. The expected and actual gene and genotype frequencies are presented in Table 3. Based on Chisquare testing the segregation found was significantly different from the expected segregation of genotypes where a single recessive gene was assumed to cause resistance to Salmonella. The hypothesis of a single gene was therefore rejected.

Table 3: Gene and genotype frequencies, expected and actual no. of litters, 1st generation

Genotype parents[1)	Freq. of offspring with rr	Genotype offspring	Freq. of genotypes	Expected no. of litters	Actual no. of litters	Chisquare contribution
rr*rr	1.0	0.07	0.0049	0.3	0	0.3
rr*rS	0.5	0.38	0.0270	1.8	30	28.62
rS*rS	0.25		0.1513	9.9		
SS*(rS,rr,SS)	0	0.55	0.8168	54	36	6.0
□		1.00	1.000	66	66	34.92

1) r = recessive gene causing resistance, S = non resistant gene

Analyzing first generation a mixed repeatability model showed significant differences for group, day of blood sampling and for age. There were no significant sex differences (p-values and variances not shown). Furthermore, an animal model including relatives was performed and heritability for antibody response was calculated to be 0.13.

Discussion and Conclusion
Genetic control of resistance depends on several factors such as the Salmonella strain, inoculation dose and time interval from inoculation to blood testing p.i. This underlines the importance of precision in measurements and the choice of measured traits due to the complexity of genetic resistance. Selection to improve resistance to Salmonella in practice would be very difficult, as it requires experimental infections under controlled environmental conditions combined with a large group of pigs with known genetic background. This could be done in special designed reference herds but would be both expensive and complicated. The heritability found in our study indicates that several genes are interacting in the process of antibody response but the mechanism is not known. Furthermore, apart from genetic resistance, low levels of antibodies could also be due to pigs being unable to mount an effective immune response to Salmonella, or to differences in pathogenicity between Salmonella species. In addition, the relationship between genetic resistance and antibody levels is not known. In conclusion, selecting for resistance to e.g. Salmonella primary in a breeding scheme, without having found the actual gene or genes, is not practically possible. Identification of the responsible gene or genes would improve the possibility for selection under practical conditions.

References
Beaumont, J., Marly, J., Protais J., Protais, M., Chapuis, H., Le Bihan-Duval, E., Trotereau, J., Sellier, N., Velge, P., Salvat, G. 2006. Selection for increased resistance to Salmonella carrier-state. Proc. 8th WCGALP, Communication 15-12
Jørgensen, B.C., Cirera, S., Anderson S.I. Raudsepp,T., Chowdhary, B., Edfors-Lilja, I., Andersson, L., Fredholm, M. 2003. Linkage and comparative mapping of the locus controlling susceptibility towards E. coli F4 ab/ac diarrhea in pigs. Cytogenet. Genome Res. 102:157-162

Session 4

Moreno, C.R., Lantier, F., Berthon, P., Gautier-Bouchardon, A.V., Boivin, R., Lantier, I., Brunel, J.C., Weisbecker, J.C., François, D., Bouix, J., Elsen, J.M. 2003. Genetic parameters for resistance to the Salmonella abortusovis vaccinal strain Rv6 in sheep. Genet. Sel. Evol. 35:199-217

Nielsen, B., Baggesen, D.L., Bager, F., Haugegaard, J., Lind, P., 1995. The serological response to Salmonella serovars Typhimurium and Infantis in experimentally infected pigs. The time course followed with an indirect anti-LPS ELISA and bacteriological examinations. Vet. Microbiol. 47: 205-218

An investigation into the efficacy of washing trucks following the transportation of pigs - a *Salmonella* perspective

C. Mannion[1*], Egan, J.[2], P. B. Lynch[3] and F.C. Leonard[1]

[1]School of Agriculture, Food Safety and Veterinary Medicine, UCD, Dublin 4, Ireland, [2]Central Veterinary Research Laboratory, Backweston, Celbridge, Ireland and [3]Pig Production Department, Moorepark Research Centre, Teagasc, Fermoy, Co. Cork, Ireland.

*corresponding author: celine.mannion@ucd.ie

Abstract

A National *Salmonella* Control Programme is in place in the Republic of Ireland, which requires the categorisation of all pigs according to their *Salmonella* status. Herds in Categories 1, 2 and 3 have a serological prevalence of infection with *Salmonella* serotypes of ≤10%, >10-≤50% and >50-≤100%, respectively. Transport of animals constitutes a stress which may induce shedding of salmonellae by carrier pigs. Although washing of trucks before leaving the abattoir is mandatory in the Republic of Ireland, little is known about the efficacy of the cleaning methods in use on trucks following the transportation of live pigs.

The main objective of this study was to determine the efficacy of washing trucks transporting live pigs from Category 1 and Category 3 herds. In total, six Category 3 and three Category 1 herds supplying three separate abattoirs were investigated. *Salmonella* organisms in samples collected from farm pens and from trucks preload, postload and after washing were quantified and compared using serotyping and phage typing. *Enterobacteriaceae* counts were also evaluated to indicate the level of contamination of the pigs' environment with enteric bacteria.

Preliminary results suggest that washing of trucks is not effective at reducing levels of *Enterobacteriaceae* regardless of category. Of the 108 samples taken from trucks transporting Category 3 herds, 6% were positive for *Salmonella* preload, 17% postload and 18% after washing. In contrast, of the 54 samples taken from trucks transporting the three Category 1 herds, 11% were positive for Salmonella preload, 11% postload and 6% after washing. These results demonstrate the need for better cleaning of trucks after each load, particularly when transporting pigs from high-risk herds.

Introduction

A National Salmonella Control Programme for pork is in place in the Republic of Ireland, which requires the categorisation of all pig herds according to their *Salmonella* status. Herds in Categories 1, 2 and 3 have a serological prevalence of infection with *Salmonella* serotypes of ≤10%, >10-≤50% and >50-≤100%, respectively.

Pigs are subjected to many stress factors during transportation and these stresses may induce *Salmonella*-carrier pigs to shed the bacterium at a higher rate and increase the susceptibility of *Salmonella*-free pigs to infection. *Salmonella*-contaminated trucks may infect farms, abattoirs and animals if the trucks are not cleaned and the bedding material is not removed and replaced between trips. Previous research has shown that pigs can acquire this pathogen as soon as 2 hours after exposure to such a contaminated environment (Hurd *et al.*, 2001) and Rajkowski *et al.* (1998) confirmed the contamination of truck floors and bedding material with *Salmonella* spp. after the transportation of pigs.

This study formed part of a major project examining *Salmonella* levels in pigs and pork on the island of Ireland. The main objectives of the study were 1) to investigate the role of transport and the efficacy of truck washing as potential factors in the dissemination of *Salmonella* spp. and 2) to compare *Salmonella* isolates identified from the farm and truck environment.

Materials and methods
Herd and animal selection.

Farms that participated in the study were selected on the basis of their *Salmonella* categorisation. A total of three Category 1 and six Category 3 production units were selected, from each of which sixteen to twenty finishing pigs were followed from the farm, through transport, to the lairage. Herd sizes averaged 400 sows and on all farms, finishing pigs were reared under similar husbandry and feed conditions.

Sample collection.

One week before the scheduled depopulation environmental swabs of the dunging area in the relevant pens were taken by vigorous swabbing of $1.0 \, m^2$ surface area using a large gauze surgical swab (Robinson Healthcare, Chesterfield, UK: No.5345), which had been autoclaved and premoistened with 10 ml of buffered peptone water (BPW, Lab M). On the Category 3 units sixteen to twenty pigs from the pen with the greatest number of positive samples were randomly selected and followed to the abattoir the following week. In contrast to this, pigs from Category 1 units were selected from a pen that tested negative for *Salmonella* spp.

Swabs from the trucks were collected at three stages: on the farm before the pigs were loaded (preload), at the processing plant immediately after the transported pigs had been moved into the lairage (postload) and after the trucks had been cleaned at the processing plant (post-washing). At each of these three stages six environmental samples were taken using a large gauze surgical swab, with each swab covering a surface area of $0.5-1m^2$, thus ensuring the entire surface of the compartment transporting the relevant pigs was sampled. All trucks were immediately cleaned following unloading and a cold power-wash was used on site in all incidences. In order to prevent external contamination of samples, aseptic measures were taken at all times.

Microbiological analysis.

Each swab was suspended in 90 ml of BPW. All samples were shaken vigorously in a stomacher before analysis.

Salmonella isolation and enumeration procedures were performed on the basis of BS EN 12824; 1998 as described previously (Boughton *et al.*, 2004) with a slight modification of the volumes used in the enumeration method. All *Salmonella* Typhimurium strains were phage typed by the Health Protection Agency (Centre for Infections, Colindale, London, U.K.).

Enterobacteriaceae counts were obtained by preparing violet red bile glucose agar (VRBGA; Oxoid) pour plates using 1 ml of the BPW containing the swabs or derived 1:10 dilutions in BPW. Plates were over-poured with VRBGA to create a semi-anaerobic environment, incubated at $37°C$ for 24 h and examined. The *Enterobacteriaceae* enumeration method had a minimum detection limit of -2.0 $\log_{10}$ CFU cm^{-2}.

Statistical analysis

Salmonella prevalence was reported as the number of samples that tested positive. Differences in prevalence at each sampling stage were compared by Fischer's exact test. Due to the wide range and skewed nature of the data, the effect of washing the trucks and the transportation of pigs on *Enterobacteriaceae* and *Salmonella* levels was investigated by calculating the median count, preload, postload and after washing on each truck followed by analyses using the Wilcoxon signed rank test. All statistically significant differences are reported at the $P < 0.05$ level.

Results

Table 1 shows the recovery of *Salmonella* spp. on farms and on trucks, preload, postload and after washing. There was a significant increase in the number of samples positive for *Salmonella* spp. on the trucks transporting Category 3 pigs, from 19% (7/36) preload to 50% (18/36) postload (p<0.05). Following washing of the trucks there was no significant change with the number of samples positive for *Salmonella* spp. increasing to 53% (19/36). On the trucks transporting the Category 1 farms, the *Salmonella* isolation rates preload, postload and after washing were 33% (6/18), 33% (6/18) and 17%, (3/18) respectively and did not differ significantly (p<0.05).

Although the trucks transporting the Category 1 farms had a significantly higher isolation rate of *Salmonella* than those transporting the Category 3 farms preload (p<0.05), this could be attributed to a single Category 1 unit. There was no significant difference between the categories postload, however, the number of samples positive for *Salmonella* spp. after washing was significantly higher on the trucks transporting the Category 3 herds (p<0.05). Numbers of *Salmonella* organisms did not differ significantly between categories preload, postload or after washing. Overall levels of contamination with *Enterobacteriaceae* did not differ significantly preload and postload (p>0.05). Similarly the results postload and after washing did not differ significantly (p>0.05).

Table 1. The recovery of *Salmonella* spp. from trucks before (preload) and after (postload) transporting pigs to slaughter and after washing (post-washing)

Farm[a]	Journey (hr)	Location[b]	Positive Samples / Samples Tested (n)	Min - Max Count[c]	Serovars and Phage Types (n)
A	3	F_2	3/3	>110	Typhimurium DT104 (3)
		Preload	6/6	0.94 - >110	**Typhimurium PTU288 (5)**, Derby (1)
		Postload	6/6	1.1 - >110	Typhimurium DT104 (6)
		Post-washing	6/6	9.3 - >110	Typhimurium DT104 (6)
B	2.5	F2	6/6	0.92 - >110	Derby (6)
		Preload	0/6	-	-
		Postload	6/6	0.3 - 2.3	Derby (1), **Goldcoast (5)**
		Post-washing	5/6	0.36 - 46	Derby (5)
C	2	F2	1/3	<0.3	Typhimurium DT104b (1)
		Preload	0/6	-	-
		Postload	1/6	<0.3	Typhimurium DT104b (1)
		Post-washing	0/6	-	-
[d]D	3.5	F2	0/3	-	-
		Preload	0/6	-	-
		Postload	2/6	0.3 - 0.92	Typhimurium DT193 (2)
		Post-washing	6/6	<0.3 - >110	Typhimurium DT193 (6)
E	3.5	F2	1/6	<0.3	Typhimurium DT104b (1)
		Preload	0/6	-	-
		Postload	3/6	3.8 - 16	Typhimurium DT104b (3)
		Post-washing	2/6	21 - >110	Typhimurium DT104b (2)
F	1	F2	1/3	0.92	Typhimurium PTU302 (1)
		Preload	1/6	2	Typhimurium PTU302 (1)
		Postload	0/6	-	-
		Post-washing	0/6	-	-
G	4.5	F2	0/6	-	-
		Preload	0/6	-	-
		Postload	0/6	-	-
		Post-washing	0/6	-	-
H	0.5	F2	0/6	-	-
		Preload	6/6	<0.3 - >110	Kimuenza (6)
		Postload	6/6	<0.3 - 21	Kimuenza (6)
		Post-washing	3/6	<0.3 - 0.74	Kimuenza (3)
I	2.5	F2	0/7	-	-
		Preload	0/6	-	-
		Postload	0/6	-	-
		Post-washing	0/6	-	-

Session 4

[a]Category 3 (A-F) and Category 1 (G-I) farms.
[b]F_2, farm samples day of transport; Preload, truck before pigs; Postload, truck after pigs; Post-washing, truck after washing. Bold type indicates most frequently isolated serovars for each set of samples.
[c]$cfu/1000cm^2$; detection limit, $0.3cfu/1000cm^2$.
[d]1 of 4 samples collected a week before transport was positive

Discussion

Although preliminary, the results of this study indicate that there are particular problems with the washing of trucks following the transport of pigs especially from high-risk herds in the Republic of Ireland. Both the results for *Salmonella* serotypes and for levels of *Enterobacteriaceae* suggest that washing of trucks as carried out in Irish abattoirs is ineffective in reducing contamination with these organisms. These findings support those of previous research, which has shown that 80% of trucks transporting pigs were contaminated with *Salmonella* spp. before transportation, despite drivers being asked to clean and disinfect their trucks thoroughly before loading the pigs (Swanenburg *et al.*, 2001). Dorr *et al.* (2005) showed a reduction in contamination levels from pre to post wash, however, trucks still remained a potential source of *Salmonella* spp. Despite this, correct cleaning procedures after animal unloading have been shown to significantly reduce the incidence of *Salmonella* spp. and *E. coli* found in trucks (Rajkowski *et al.*, 1998).

It is believed that the stress of transport alters the excretion pattern of *Salmonella* spp. Williams *et al.* (1970) found that a greater percentage of pigs were shedding *Salmonella* spp. after a 'joyride' of over 3 hours than those transported for only 20 minutes. In addition to this Isaacson *et al.* (1999) showed that the stress of transport increased the proportion of carrier pigs positive for *Salmonella* spp. only when feed was not withheld. In the study reported here transport lasted on average 2.6 hours and we know this to be sufficient for pigs to acquire infection (Hurd *et al.*, 2001)

In summary, this study showed that transport increases the *Salmonella* isolation rate regardless of category and that better cleaning of trucks is necessary especially when transporting pigs from high-risk herds so as to reduce the potential for contamination during the slaughter process.

Acknowledgements

This project is funded by *safefood* and the Food Institutional Research Measure of the Department of Agriculture and Food under the National Development Plan. The authors gratefully acknowledge the assistance of participating farmers, truck drivers and abattoir staff.

References

BOUGHTON, C., LEONARD, F.C., EGAN, J., KELLY, G., O'MAHONY, P., MARKEY, B.K., GRIFFIN, M., 2004. Prevalence and number of Salmonella in Irish retail pork sausages. *Journal of Food Protection* 67, 1834-9.

DORR, P. M., LOWMAN, H. and GEBREYES, W., 2005. The role of truck wash practices in dissemination of *Salmonella* and Campylobacter in commercial swine production. In: Proceedings of the 6th International Symposium on the Epidemiology and Control of Salmonella in Pork, California 161-163.

HURD, H. S., GAILEY, J. K., McKEAN, J. D. and ROSTAGNO, M. H., 2001. Rapid infection in market-weight swine following exposure to a *Salmonella* Typhimurium-contaminated environment. *American Journal of Veterinary Research* 62, 1194-1197.

ISAACSON, R. E., FIRKINS, L. D., WEIGEL, R. M., ZUCKERMANN, F. A. and DIPIETRO, J. A., 1999. Effect of transportation and feed withdrawal on shedding of *Salmonella* Typhimurium among experimentally infected pigs. *American Journal of Veterinary Research* 60, 1155-1158.

RAJKOWSKI, K. T., EBLEN, S. and LAUBACH, C., 1998. Efficacy of washing and sanitizing trailers used for swine transport in reduction of *Salmonella* and *Escherichia coli*. *Journal of Food Protection* 61, 31-35.

SWANENBURG, M., VAN DER WOLF, P. J., URLINGS, H. A. P., SNIJDERS, J. M. A. and VAN KNAPEN, F., 2001. *Salmonella* in slaughter pigs: the effect of logistic slaughter procedures of pigs on the prevalence of *Salmonella* in pork. *International Journal of Food Microbiology* 70, 231-242.

WILLIAMS, L. P. and NEWELL, K. W., 1970. Salmonella excretion in joy-riding pigs. *American Journal of Public Health* 60, 926-929.

Changes in carcass microbial distribution and water conditions during the scalding and dehairing of pig carcasses

Wilkin, C.-A. [1], Purnell, G. [2], James, S. J. *[2], Howell, M. [3], James, C. [2]

[1] Division of Farm Animal Science (DFAS), University of Bristol, Langford, BS40 5DU, UK.
[2] Food Refrigeration and Process Engineering Research Centre (FRPERC), University of Bristol, Langford, BS40 5DU, UK.
[3] Food Standards Agency (FSA), Aviation House, 125 Kingsway, London, WC2B 6NH, UK.
*corresponding author: steve.james@bristol.ac.uk

Abstract

Salmonella contamination is of major concern in the production of pork. As part of a UK Food Standards Agency project looking at reducing salmonella contamination, a survey of current processing conditions in UK pig slaughterhouses and a review of published data identified pork scalding and dehairing systems as a likely major source of salmonella contamination during pork processing.

The aim of this study was to evaluate the factors that may have an influence on the levels of Salmonella spp. on the surface of pigs during the scalding and dehairing process. The scald tank temperature, scalding time and changes in the condition of the scald tank water were analysed during the processing of two batches of pigs in a small EU licensed abattoir. In each trial the levels of Enterobacteriaceae (indicative of faecal and hence possible Salmonella contamination) at 8 different sites on three carcasses, both before and after the scalding and dehairing process, were determined.

Introduction

The treatment of pigs differs from that of sheep and cattle in that the skin is not usually removed during slaughter. The hair is removed by scalding and dehairing, usually followed by singeing and polishing. Traditionally carcasses are passed through a trough of hot water – the scalding tank. The water is kept at approximately 60-65°C and the period of immersion can last for up to 10 minutes. This softens the attachment of the hair roots to the skin facilitating the removal of the bristles with the minimum of force. Following scalding the carcass passes to a dehairing machine, where it is rapidly rotated horizontally while being scraped by metal tipped rubber fingers or protrusions that run at high speed and have the action of flails. There are some systems that combine scalding and dehairing in a single piece of equipment. Dehairing systems are not always completely effective, and in many abattoirs there may be a manual scraping stage after dehairing (and before singeing) to remove any stubborn hairs.

Very few studies have investigated the effect of scalding temperatures on carcass temperatures. Van der Wal et al. (1993) found that scalding at 60°C for as long as 12 min results in an increase in temperature just below the skin of more than 10°C and in the muscle temperature of 1°C. Scalding (in a combined scalder/dehairer) for 5.5 to 7.5 min gave satisfactory results (though "autumn hair" required 9 min). Maribo et al. (1998) measured a 1.0 and 0.4°C rise in the temperature of the m. longissimus dorsi (at 40 mm depth between the 2nd and 4th lumber vertebra) and m. biceps femoris after scalding (60°C, 7 min). Since the skin of pigs is frequently dirty, the water in the tanks can become contaminated with protein, blood, urine and faeces building up in the tank. Studies have shown that large numbers of thermophilic bacilli capable of growing at high temperature can be found in tank scalding water (Sörqvist & Danielsson-Tham, 1987). However, they conclude that although the exterior surfaces of carcasses may become contaminated with Bacillus spp. they are not a problem regarding health or spoilage. Adjustment of the pH by adding lime has been reported to reduce counts in the scald water but fail to reduce contamination on the skin (Mackey & Roberts, 1991). A study on the survival of Salmonella spp. in samples of commercial scald tank water at 50, 55 and 60°C showed that a time-temperature combination of 1.4 min at 60°C is required to achieve a 1 log reduction in salmonella in scald tank water (Bolton et al., 2003).

Materials and methods

Batches (n=23 and n=15) of pigs were slaughtered and bled in the normal manner in the EU licensed abattoir at Langford on separate days.

Physical analysis: For each pig processed the residence time in the scalding tank and the dehairer was measured, as well as the surface temperature of each carcass before and after scalding/dehairing using infrared thermometry (trial 1: Minolta Land Cyclops Compac 3; trial 2: Digitron D202AFCF). The water temperature in the scald tank, at a height of 1 and 33 cm from the base, was logged throughout the process (Comark Diligence EV N2014) and water samples removed at the start and after pigs 6, 10, 17 and 23 in the first batch and at the start and after each pig in the second batch. The Redox potential, pH, conductivity, turbidity, free chlorine and total chlorine in each sample were determined (Hanna 4 in 1 water tester; Hanna C114 meter).

Microbiological analysis: Before scalding seven 50 cm^2 sites (randomising between left and right) of 3 animals (first, last and one in the middle of the batch) were sampled using a wetted sponge swab and the inside of the mouth was swabbed using jumbo swabs. The pigs were then scalded and dehaired using the normal practice at the abattoir. After this process the pigs were sampled at positions adjacent to those previously sampled. Swabs were also taken on surfaces in the dehairer and gambrelling table at the beginning and end of each trial. All samples were enumerated for Enterobacteriaceae.

Results and discussion

Manually controlled processing times were found to be very variable (Figure 1) with extremes from 3.6 to 7.5 minutes for scalding and 0.48 to 1.67 minutes for dehairing in trial 1 and 2.77 to 6.47 minutes for scalding and 0.87 to 2.13 minutes for dehairing in trial 2. Overall, carcasses were on average scalded for 4.93 (SD 1.32) minutes and dehaired for 0.97 (SD 0.40) minutes.

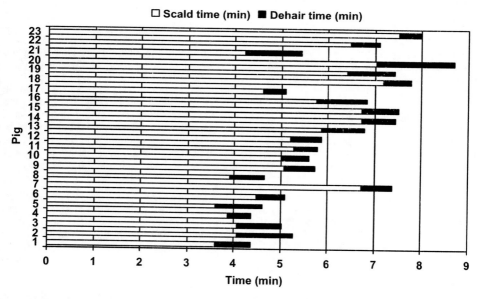

Figure 1. Time spent by each pig in the scald tank and in the dehairing machine in trial 1.

No significant temperature stratification was measured in the scald tank during each trial with the difference between the two temperatures being within measurement errors. In trial 1 the mean scald tank temperature was approximately 60°C with fluctuations between 58 and 64°C. In trial 2 the mean scald tank temperature was again approximately 60°C with fluctuations between 59 and 62°C.

There was a marked change in all the measured water quality parameters during each trial (Table 1). The pH dropped to 7.3 by the time the last carcass had been treated in each trial whilst the conductivity and turbidity continued to rise as each pig was scalded and did not appear to have reached a peak or steady value by the end of each trial.

Table 1. Changes in water quality in scalding tank during use.

	Pig no.	Redox (mv)	pH	Conductivity (mS)	Turbidity (NTU)	Free Chlorine (mg/l)	Total Chlorine (mg/l)
Trial 1	0	153	8.1	0.413	22.7	0.23	0.02
	6	162.5	7.5	0.463	97.3	0.21	0.015
	10	132.5	7.5	0.501	150	0.1	0.005
	17	104.5	7.4	0.560	248	0.04	0.005
	23	50.5	7.3	0.590	379	0.03	0.005
Trial 2	0	236	7.9	398	10.4	0.67	0.01
	2	232	7.7	424	21.4	0.34	0.01
	3	225	7.5	436	36.4	0.22	0.01
	5	215	7.4	440	67.8	0.29	0.01
	6	184	7.4	450	88.2	0.11	0.01
	7	175	7.4	453	89.7	0.07	0.00
	8	170	7.4	462	113	0.04	0.00
	9	153	7.3	474	138	0.01	0.00
	10	141	7.3	480	169	0.17	0.00
	11	135	7.3	482	136	0.56	0.00
	12	134	7.3	497	209	0.87	0.00
	13	125	7.3	505	191	0.10	0.00
	14	142	7.3	519	247	0.96	0.00
	15	124	7.3	525	326	0.07	0.00

Carcass surface temperatures before scalding ranged from 26.7 to 37.1°C and after dehairing from 27 to 44°C (Figure 2). Mean surface temperature pre-scald and post-dehair in trial 1 were 33.8 and 39.2°C respectively whilst comparable values in trial 2 were 29 and 31.6°C. A different instrument was used to measure temperatures in the second trial and this is the likely reason for the difference in results. Further trials indicate that the temperatures measured in trial 1 are more likely to reflect the actual surface temperatures.

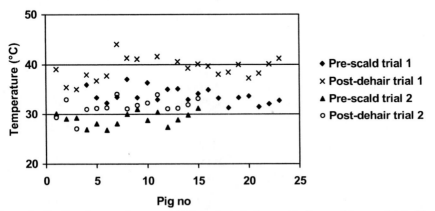

Figure 2. Surface temperatures on pig carcasses before and after scalding and dehairing.

The overall counts of Enterobacteriaceae did not show any clear trend for the carcasses processed later through the tanks and dehairer to become more contaminated. In general scalding and dehairing tended to reduce bacterial levels by between 1.6 and 3.7 log_{10} CFU cm^2 (Figure 3).

However, on three sites in trial 1 (anus, back and mouth), numbers increased. One possible explanation for these increases is voiding of faecal and stomach liquids from some pigs in trial 1. Further trials are ongoing to look at the effect of different types of bunging and clipping during these processes. The average level of Enterobacteriaceae contamination of the surfaces in the dehairing unit increased by 2.5, 3.6 and 3.6 $\log_{10}$ CFU cm^{-2} on the paddle, curtain and roof. While a smaller increase of 1.6 $\log_{10}$ CFU cm^{-2} was measured on the surface of the table.

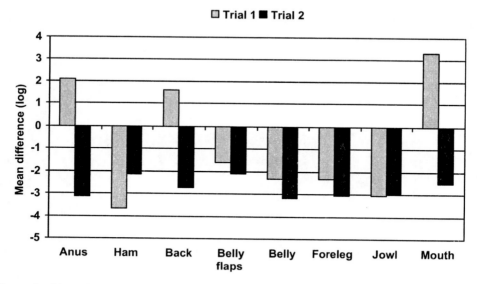

Figure 3. Mean (3 replicates) changes in Enterobacteriaceae numbers ($\log_{10}$ CFU cm^{-2}) during scalding and dehairing at different poistions on carcass.

Conclusions

Manual operated scalding and dehairing systems result in very variable processing times. During operation little change was recorded in the scalding tank temperature but marked changes in water quality were observed. At present these changes to water quality through the day do not appear to have a marked influence on the number of Enterobacteriaceae at the sites examined on the carcasses processed. Further investigations are ongoing into the effect of bunging before scalding and on pre-scald washing.

References

BOLTON, D.J., PEARCE, R., SHERIDAN, J.J., MCDOWELL, D.A., BLAIR, I.S., 2003. Decontamination of pork carcasses during scalding and the prevention of salmonella cross-contamination. *Journal of Applied Microbiology*, 94 (6), 1036-1042.

MACKEY, B.M., ROBERTS, T.A., 1991. Hazard analysis and critical control point programmes in relation to slaughter hygiene. *Proceedings of the 37th International Congress of Meat Science and Technology (ICoMST 91), Kulmbach, Germany*, 3, 1303-1313.

MARIBO, H., OLSEN, E.V., BARTON-GADE, P., MØLLER, A.J., 1998. Comparison of dehiding versus scalding and singeing: Effect on temperature, pH and meat quality in pigs. *Meat Science*, 50 (2), 175-189.

SÖRQVIST, S., DANIELSSON-THAM, M.-L., 1987. Investigations into the growth of thermophilic bacilli in water used at vat scalding of pig carcasses. *Fleischwirtschaft*, 2, 198-190.

WAL, P.G. VAN DER, BEEK, G. VAN, VEERKAMP, C.H.J., WIJNGAARDS, G., 1993. The effect of scalding on subcutaneous and ham temperatures and ultimate pork quality. *Meat Science*, 34, 395-402.

Pasteurization profiles of cured meats products with respect to safety

Genigeorgis, C [1]*., Dalezios, I[1]. and Panoulis, Ch.[2]

[1] Creta Farm ABEE, Rethymno, 74100, Greece
[2] Laboratory of Clinical Microbiology, Medical School, University of Crete, Heraklion, 71409, Greece
*Corresponding author:cgenigeorgis@ucdavis.edu

Abstract

A total of 162 heat penetration sets were collected during commercial pasteurization of 9 types of cured meats. Calculated FP_{70}–values (with z=10 C) ranged from 45 to 391 min. For L.monocytogenes (D_{70} =0.27 min) such FP_{70} represented at least 167 to 1448 decimal reductions (DR) to the initial population of the pathogen. Lack of heating uniformity in lots of the same product and samples in the same chamber was detected. Maximum core temperatures and FP_{70} values could vary by up to 6.4 C and up to 345 min respectively. Observed FP_{70} may affect product nutritional value, yield decrease and energy waste. In hundreds of samples of cooked in casing product no Salmonella spp, L.monocytogenes and E.coli were detected immediately after processing. During 2003-5 no Salmonella spp was detected in 404 in retail samples of sliced or pealed meats produced by 8 companies. L.monocytogenes incidence was 7.9%. Incidence per company for sliced and pealed products ranged from 2.5-40% and 0-20% respectively. Incidence decreased with age since production day. Commercial thermal processing of meat products is more than sufficient to assure safety from non-sporoforming pathogens. Cross contaminations lead to isolations of pathogens from cooked and later sliced and repackaged products.

Introduction

The canning industry routinely uses heat penetration data and calculates F_0 values (minutes at 121.1 C as a reference temperature) to meet legal requirements. The collection of heat penetration data and the calculation of F-values at a particular reference temperature (usually 70 C known also as FP_{70}) are rarely applied to pasteurized meat products. The usual practice is to bring the core temperature to a certain level and maintain it for a predetermined time. Such practices do not allow comparisons of processing schedules for meat products and estimation of risk from non sporoforming and mild heat resistant sporoforming pathogens like the non proteolytic C.botulinum types E, B and F. Determination of FP_{70} values allows also the estimation of the number of DR of the initial numbers of pathogenic or spoilage bacteria based on available literature with respect to D- and z-values and optimization of thermal processes. The present study expands previous local studies concerning pasteurized meats (Sergelidis et al 1995) by determining initial microbial loads in meat formulations, heat penetration data, estimation of FP_{70}, number of DR, and potential survival of non-sporoforming pathogens. In addition we have been collecting data on the microbiological quality of pasteurised meat products available to the Greek consumer through the food chain. This has been considered important in order to verify that the overall processes by the meat industry including thermal processes are providing product safety.

Material and methods

The Ellab CTF 9008 (Denmark) automatic temperature recorder having 8 temperature probes was used to measure the heat penetration and the environmental temperature in the cooking chamber during processing. Six probes were placed in the geometric centre of six meat samples and two probes were placed in two locations in the chamber. Calculation of FP_{70} values for each heat penetration curve was done automatically using a z-value of 10 C. Microbial detection and counting was based on ISO methods.

Session 4

Results

Thermal processing: A total of 9 products were evaluated in triplicate using six probes for each replication during a period of 6 months in 2004. A total of 162 heat penetration curves were derived and the corresponding FP_{70} values were calculated. Tables 1 presents the maximum core temperatures recorded by 7 probes (1-7) inserted in 7 sausages during the processing of three lots Turkey Roll. A difference of 6.4 C among probes in lot B was recorded.

Table 1. Maximum temperatures recorded by 8 probes during the processing of three lots of Turkey Roll.

Probes	1	2	3	4	5	6	7	8 (chamber)
Lot A	75.3	76.3	75.7	77.1	75.8	77	76.2	79.9
Lot B	71.3	72.8	73.4	77	71.8	70.6	72.8	79.9
Lot C	74.7	72.8	73.4	74.8	73.4	75	74	79.5

Table 2 presents an example of the FP_{70} for the heating and cooling phases and total process of 3 lots of Ham Snack. The cooling phase contribution to the total FP_{70} ranged from 8.4 min to 64.2 min. The FP_{70} for the 27 lots of the 9 products studied ranged from 45 to 391 min with a difference among the 18 probes representing 3 lots of the same product as much as 85 to 345 min. This lack of uniformity in processing may have a serious impact on product quality and cost. The longest reported D_{70} for L.monocytogenes is 0.27 min. (ICMSF, 1996). Therefore cooking for the equivalent of 45 to 391 min will cause at least 167 to 1448 DR to the initial L.monocytogenes population in the paste. Killing all bacterial cells/spores in a cm^3 (estimated at 10^{12}) will require 13 DR. Therefore processes resulting in 167 to 1448 DR reflect an over kill of no importance to safety from non sporoforming pathogens but with a potential impact on product quality, yield and energy cost. Process optimisation to meet organoleptic properties apart from safety is needed.

Microbial ecology of pastes and retail products: In 48 paste samples before and after stuffing the $\log_{10}$ median (range)/g for total plate counts (TPC), lactic acid bacteria (LAB), coliforms and E.coli were 4.43 (3.39-5.93), 4.69 (3.39-6.04), 2.44 (1-3.87), and 1.23 (<0.69-3.09) respectively. Salmonella spp was not detected. L.monocytogenes (Lm) was present in 22.9% at levels of <10 cells/g (in 15 samples), 20 and 80 cells/g. Other Listeria were present in 35.4% of samples at levels of <10 cells/g. In 54 additional paste samples the $\log_{10}$ median (range)/g for TPC, LAB, coliforms and E.coli were 4.54 (3.57-5.91), 4.54 (2.69-5.87), 2.25 (<0.69-4.04), <0.69 (<0.69-3.61) respectively. Salmonella spp was present in 7.4% of the samples, L.monocytogenes in 25.9% (all <10 cells/g) and other Listeria spp in 20.4% (all <10 cells/g).

Table 2. Estimated FP_{70} for the heating (H), cooling (C) phases and total FP_{70} during the commercial cooking of three lots of Ham Snack as recorded and calculated by 6 probes.

Lot	Probe	1	2	3	4	5	6
A	FP_{70} H	125.8	111.7	125	208	106.8	130.1
	FP_{70} C	20.2	58.4	34	64.2	23.3	25.7
	FP_{70} Total	146	170.1	163	272	130.1	155.8
B	FP_{70} H	105.4	112.1	99.6	94.4	59.6	101.1
	FP_{70} C	57.1	36.6	30.6	27.1	22.1	40.1
	FP_{70} Total	162.5	148.7	130	121	81.7	141.2
C	FP_{70} H	90.4	247.8	124	63	61.4	125
	FP_{70} C	54.2	8.4	31.3	30	27.5	51
	FP_{70} Total	144.6	256.2	155	93	88.9	176

Table 3 presents selected data concerning the impact of delays in processing on potential microbial growth. Coliforms, E.coli and L.monocytogenes were below detectable levels after cooking, indicating process effectiveness. Delays increased LAB counts but not L.monocytogenes, counts. Cold water cooling increased systematically LAB counts as compared to their numbers immediately after cooking. Product cross contaminations from the cooling water, slow cooling with potential growth of bacteria surviving inside the product or both might be contributing factors.
During 2003-5 we analyzed (Tables 4, 5) 404 packaged sliced and pealed type meats manufactured by 8 Greek companies and collected from supermarkets, hotel storage rooms,

catering facilities, restaurants, taverns and military cold storage facilities. The number of samples collected (and % incidence for L.monocytogenes) for slices of hams, shoulders, pick nicks, bacon and Frankfurter, Wieners and Farmers sausages were 40 (10), 57 (8.8), 69 (8.7), 43 (2.3), 100 (9), 54 (7.4) and 42 (4.8) respectively. Company incidence (Table 4) for sliced and pealed products was 2.5-40% and 0-20% respectively. In all categories of products the incidence of L.monocytogenes declined with the aging of the products which also coincided with the increase in the numbers of LAB within the packages (Table 5). Listeria spp incidence declined also from 7.44, to 3.1, to 2.06, and 1.18% for the four age groups of table 5.

Table 3. Microbial ecology (log$_{10}$ cfu/g of emulsion type sausage pastes before or after stuffing. immediately after cooking or after cooking and chilling

Product	Processing stage	Time (hrs)	LAB	Colif	E.coli	Lm
Frankfurter A	Paste	+4	6.04	4.32	2.44	2.41
	Paste	+52	6.60	NT	NT	3.11
	Paste	+60	5.60	2.99	3.14	1.84
	After cooking	0	2.87	<0.69	<0.69	-
	after cooking and chilling	+8	3.17	<0.69	<0.69	-
Frankfurter B	After cooking	0	<2.69	<0.69	<0.69	--
	After cooking and chilling	+8	4.09	<0.69	<0.69	-
Frankfurter C	After cooking	0	3.65	<0.69	<0.69	-
	After cooking and chilling	+8	4.19	<0.69	<0.69	-
Turkey A	Paste	0	4.65	NT	NT	-
	After chopping	+1	5.65	NT	NT	1.30
	Before stuffing	+16	5.64	1.90	1.77	1.69
Turkey B	Paste	0	4.44	3.50	4.04	-
	After chopping	+1	5.65	NT	NT	1.30
	Before stuffing	+16	5.39	NT	NT	<1
Turkey C	Paste	0	4.47	NT	NT	-
	After chopping	+1	4.90	NT	NT	1
	Before stuffing	+16	5.31	NT	NT	1

Table 4. Incidence (%) of L.monocytogenes in 240 sliced and 165 pealed and packaged meats, manufactured by 8 Greek companies and collected from various outlets in 2003-5

Product type	Company							
	1	2	3	4	5	6	7	8
Sliced	2.5	6.25	6.7	11.1	17.9	12.5	24	40
Peeled	0	9.1	18.8	12.5	4.8	5	9	20
Total	0.7	7.4	10.9	11.6	13.3	9.6	16	30

Table 5. Samples (% Incidence of L.monocytogenes) (Lm) and LAB, log$_{10}$ cfu/g) in 405 meat products manufactured by 8 Greek companies and collected from various outlets (2003-5)

Product	Product age since production (days)							
	1-15		16-30		31-45		46-60	
	LAB	Lm*	LAB	Lm	LAB	Lm	LAB	Lm
Ham	5.1-6.1	8(12.5)	6.2-7.3	19(10.5)	6.9-8.0	7(14.3	6.3-8.9	6(0)
Shoulde	4.7-6.4	11(18.2)	5.7-6.8	16(12.5)	7.0-7.7	17(5.9	6.9-8.9	13(0)
Picknic	4.7-5.9	13(15.4)	6.1-7.4	19(10.5)	7.0-7.8	19(5.3	7.87-8.9	18(5.6
Bacon	2.4-4.0	10(0)	4.7-5.3	12(8)	5.4-6.8	12(0)	5.7-6.8	9(0)
Frankfs	3.9-5.8	21(19.1)	5.7-6.7	39(7.7)	6.7-7.9	20(5)	7.2-8.0	20(5)
Wieners	3.6-5.8	19(10.5)	5.4-7.1	14(14.3)	6.7-7.4	14(0)	6.9-9.0	7(0)
Farmers	4.1-6.1	12(0)	5.6-6.8	10(10)	6.9-7.4	8(12.5	6.7-8.2	12(0)
Total(%)		94(11.7)		129(10.1)		97(5.2		85(2.4

Discussion

Delays in product preparation, stuffing and cooking may support microbial growth requiring adjustments to cooking to assure predictable safety and shelf life. L.monocytogenes and other Listeria spp were present in 22.9-25.9% and 35.4-20.4% respectively of raw sausage pastes before and after stuffing. Cell concentrations were <10cells/g in most samples. Calculated FP_{70} values of 9 meat products in triplicate lots and six samples per lot ranged from 45 to 391 min theoretically causing 167 to 1448 DR to L.monocytogenes initial population in meat pastes. Significant variability in FP_{70} values even among the 6 probes monitoring 6 samples in the same heating chamber was observed. While this variation could not affect the safety of the products with respect to non sporoforming bacteria, effects on quality attributes are possible due to overheating. Similar data from two meat companies were reported before (Sergelidis et al, 1995). The European Chilled Foods Federation recommends that pasteurised minimally processed foods should be heated to an FP_{70} of at least 2 min. (Anonymous, 1996). Sergelidis (2000) found that in order to cause at least 6 DR of initial L.monocytogenes, Salmonella spp and E.coli O157:H7 in emulsion type sausages the required FP_{70} was 2.54; 1.95 and 1.29 min for Pariza and 2.28; 1.76; and 1.76 min for Frankfurter type sausages respectively.

Recent analysis of hundreds of cooked in casing and marketed as such meat products did not indicate survival of Listeria spp, Salmonella spp or E.coli. This is in agreement with a previous study (Sergelidis et al, 2002). The FP_{70} values reported in this and a previous study (Sergelidis et al 1996) should be responsible for such an effective thermal process. On the contrary isolations from sliced or pealed and packaged products are not unusual as the data of tables 4 and 5 show, thus demonstrating the significance of cross contaminations. The probable cause of the decline of L.monocytogenes and other Listeria spp with the aging of the product might be attributed to the competition effect by the gradually increasing LAB flora which increased from a range of $\log_{10}$ cfu/g of 2.44-6.41 in 0-15 day old products to $\log_{10}$ cfu/g of 5.73-8.96 in products of 46-60 days old. This might be due to death and decreasing numbers of L.monocytogenes cells or failure of enrichments to encourage L.monocytogenes growth in the presence of high numbers of competing spoilage bacteria. Garayzabal and Genigeorgis (1989) reported that the probability of growth initiation in enrichment broths is affected by the number of cells in the sample. Sampling at a particular time without taking into account the age of the products may lead to erroneous conclusions with respect to the true incidence of L.monocytogenes. Angelidis and Koutsoumanis (2006) reported increased prevalence with increased level of cutting of retail meats.

Conclusions

The study demonstrated that commercial thermal processing of meat products is more than sufficient to assure safety from non-sporoforming pathogens. Observed lack of uniformity in heat penetrations and possible overheating may have and impact of product quality attributes. Lack of effective sanitation during product pealing or cutting for later packaging contributed to a significant prevalence of L.monocytogenes in retail meat products.

References

ANGELIDIS, A. KOUTSOUMANIS, K. 2006. Prevalence and concentration of Listeria monocytogenes in sliced ready-to-eat meat products in the Hellenic retail market. Journal of Food Protection, 69, 938-942.
ANONYMOUS. 1996. Guidelines for the hygienic manufacturing of chilled foods. European Chilled Food Federation, (ECFF) London
ICMSF.1996. Microorganisms in foods. Microbiological specifications of food pathogens pp 155-164. Blackie Academic & Professional.
SERGELIDIS D. 2000. Investigation of selected CCP`s during the manufacturing of cooked sausages which have implications to their safety. PhD Thesis. Aristotle University. Thessaloniki.
SERGELIDIS,D, AMIN, A. GENIGEORGIS, C.1995. Fate of L.monocytogenes, E.coli O157:H7 and Salmonella spp. during commercial thermal processing of cured cooked meat products in Greece with or without sodium lactate. Proceedings 41st Inter. Congress Meat Science and Technology. San Antonio, Texas. Pp.284-285.
SERGELIDIS, D. AMIN,A. A. SARIMBVEI,A. GENIGEORGIS, C. 2002. Microbial hazards at several stages of production and distribution of cooked sausages. J Hellenic Vet Soc, 53:201-218.

Pig herds free from pathogenic *Y. enterocolitica* – dream or reality?

Nesbakken, T.*[1], Iversen, T.[2], Lium, B.[3]

[1] Norwegian School of Veterinary Science, Dept. of Food Safety and Infection Biology, P.O. Box 8146 Dep., N-0033 Oslo, Norway
[2] Nortura, P.O. Box 360 Økern, N-0513 Oslo, Norway
[3] Norwegian Pig Health Service, Animalia, P.O.Box 8156 Dep., 0033 Oslo, Norway
*corresponding author: truls.nesbakken@veths.no

Abstract

The results indicate that 15 of the 16 SPF (specific pathogen free) herds examined may be free from *Y. enterocolitica* O:3. In a broad perspective this investigation indicates that it is possible to establish cluster of pig herds free from *Y. enterocolitica* O:3, and to keep the herds free from the bacteria for many years. According to serological testing, the basic herd at the top of this SPF pyramid seem to have been free from this pathogenic variant since 1996. A total of 14 herds are confirmed negative also by culture.
By a systematic work it should be possible to market pork from pigs reared in herds documented free from *Y. enterocolitica* O:3.

Introduction

Yersinia enterocolitica serotype O:3 is the most common cause of yersiniosis in man in Europe (Nesbakken, 1992). In a case-control study, raw or undercooked pork have been identified as the main source of this infection in Norway (Ostroff et al., 1994). Based on serological surveys *Y. enterocolitica* O:3 seems to be common in the Norwegian pig population (Skjerve at al., 1998).
The aim of this study was to investigate the possibility of establishing and maintaining a cluster of pig herds free from *Y. enterocolitica* O:3.

Material and methods

Herds: In 1996 a specific-pathogen-free (SPF) nucleus herd (herd 1) was established by hysterectomi, and the piglets were reared without contact with other pigs. In 1999 a second nucleus SPF herd (herd 2) was established with gilts recruited from herd 1. Afterwards these two herds have been totally isolated from pigs in other herds, except for the use of semen from Norsvins AI-station.
Since 1997 another 17 conventional SPF herds have been established with gilts recruited from one or both of the above-mentioned SPF nucleus herds. The conventional herds have since they were established either been closed or they have bought replacement gilts from one of the two SPF nucleus herds.

The basis for the methods used and the time for collection of samples is presented in the study of Nesbakken et al. (2006) presented in Figure 1.
Blood samples: Since 1996, blood samples from 30 to 60 pigs in herd 1 have been taken every year and tested for antibodies against *Y. enterocolitica* O:3, whilst blood samples from 30 pigs in herd 2 have been collected and tested yearly since 2001. In 2004 and 2005 blood samples from 20 to 60 pigs from 14 of the conventional SPF herds have been tested. The majority of the blood samples have been from 4- to 6-month-old fatteners or gilts, while some samples from the two nucleus herds have been from sows.

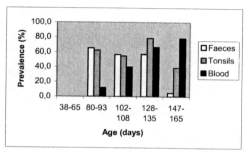

Figure 1. The basis for collection of samples and methods used in this study. Occurrence of *Y. enterocolitica* O:3 in samples from faeces and tonsils, and occurrence of antibodies against *Y. enterocolitica* in blood samples from different age groups of pigs (Nesbakken et al., 2006)

Serology: The *sera* were analysed for antibodies against *Y. enterocolitica* O:3 by a LPS-ELISA (Nielsen et al., 1996). A basic cut-off of optical density (OD%) 20 was used. The analyses were performed at the Danish Institute for Food and Veterinary Research.

Bacteriology: The bacteriological examination of faeces from 20 animals from each of 14 herds in 2005 or 2006 was performed according to International Organization for Standardization (1994) method (ISO 10273) with modifications (Nesbakken et al., 2006).

Results

The serological results are summarized in Table 1. During the first five years 10 of 174 blood samples from pigs in herd 1 had a low level of antibodies against *Y. enterocolitica* O:3 (OD%: <30). None of the 163 blood samples taken from pigs in this herd from 2002 to 2005 have tested positive. Only one of the 16 herds examined (herd 14) has been classified as serologically positive for antibodies against *Y. enterocolitica* O:3, This is the only herd which was positive by culture.

Discussion

The serological investigation indicates that 15 of the 16 SPF herds examined may be free from *Y. enterocolitica* O:3. The low positive reactions in some blood samples from pigs in herd 1 during the first five years may have been unspecific reaction because many of these samples were from old sows which may have more serological interference. At the moment we have no explanation of why herd 14 has been infected with *Y. enterocolitica* O:3.

This investigation indicates that it is possible to establish cluster of pig herds free from *Y. enterocolitica* O:3, and to keep the herds free from the bacteria for many years. The serological results are supported by bacteriological investigation of faeces. Fourteen herds have already been confirmed negative by culture in 2005 or 2006.

Table 1. Results of testing for antibodies against *Y. enterocolitica* O:3 in blood samples from pigs in a closed system of 15 SPF herds in Norway. **Herds in "bold" are confirmed negative by culture for *Y. enterocolitica* in 2005 or 2006.**

Herd no. (year establishment)	Serology of no. pos/no. tested
1 (1996)	**10[1]/337**
2 (1999)	**0/120**
3 (1997)	**1/61**
4 (1997)	**0/19**
5 (1998)	0/30[2]
6 (1999)	**0/34**
7 (1999)	**0/20**
8 (2000)	**0/60**
9[3] (2001)	0/30
10 (2002)	**1/61**
11 (2002)	**0/20**
12 (2003)	**0/30**
13 (2003)	**0/41**
14 (2004)	**15/30[4]**
15 (2004)	**0/20**
16 (2004)	**0/30**

[1] All these samples had OD% < 30
[2] Not investigated by culture
[3] Not a SPF–herd anymore
[4] 11 of 24 faecal samples positive for *Y. enterocolitica* O:3 by culture

Conclusions

By a systematic work it should be possible to market pork from pigs reared in herds documented free from *Y. enterocolitica* O:3. That means that the whole breeding pyramid has to be free from pathogenic *Y. enterocolitica*. In this context, our preliminary results are promising.

References

INTERNATIONAL ORGANIZATION FOR STANDARDIZATION, 1994. Microbiology - General Guidance for the Detection of Presumptive Pathogenic *Yersinia enterocolitica (ISO 10273). International Organization for Standardization,* Genève, Switzerland, 16 pp.

NESBAKKEN, T.: *Epidemiological and food hygienic aspects of* Yersinia enterocolitica *with special reference to the pig as a suspected source of infection.* Thesis for the degree of *Doctor Medicinae Veterinariae (Ph D).* Norwegian College of Veterinary Medicine, Oslo, 1992, 114 pp.

NESBAKKEN, T., IVERSEN, T., ECKNER, LIUM, B., 2006. Testing of pathogenic Yersinia enterocolitica in pig herds based on the natural dynamic of infection. *International Journal of Food Microbiology*, 111, 99-104.

NIELSEN, B., HEISEL, C., WINGSTRAND, A., 1996. Time course of the serological response to *Yersinia enterocolitica* O:3 in experimentally infected pigs. *Veterinary Microbiology*, 48, 293-303.

OSTROFF, S.M., KAPPERUD, G., HUTWAGNER, L.C., NESBAKKEN, T., BEAN, N.H., LASSEN, J., TAUXE, R.V., 1994. Sources of *Yersinia enterocolitica* infections in Norway: a prospective case-control study. Epidemiology and Infection, 112, 133-141.

SKJERVE, E., LIUM, B., NIELSEN, B., NESBAKKEN, T., 1998. Control of *Yersinia enterocolitica* in pigs at herd level. *International Jounal of Food Microbiology*, 1998, 45, 195-203.

The effect of cereal type and micronisation on the concentration of lactic acid in the production of fermented liquid feed for pigs.

*Doridant S, Niba A. T. and Beal J. D.

School of Biological Sciences University of Plymouth, Plymouth, UK
*Corresponding author: School of biological sciences, University of Plymouth, Plymouth UK
PL4 8AA e.mail* jbeal@plymouth.ac.uk.

Introduction

The use of fermented liquid feeds (FLF) is gaining popularity in Europe as a means of improving the gut health of pigs and improving the stability and safety of liquid feed in *ad libitum* feeding systems. With modern liquid feeding systems it is often advantageous to ferment the cereal component of the diet and use this as a base to which other components are added to formulate a range of diets for the whole unit. The exception to this may be diets for newly weaned pigs where it is normal (in the UK) for processed cereals to be used.

Liquid feed provides an ideal medium for the growth of a range of micro-organisms which compete for nutrients. If left alone spontaneous lactic acid fermentation normally occurs and as lactic acid concentrations increase pH is reduced and competing organisms die out or suffer a marked reduction in growth rates, a process similar to that which occurs in forage silages. High lactic acid concentrations and low pH contribute to the stability of the feed and prevent the growth of undesirable organisms such as *Salmonella* spp. In addition to these benefits in feed safety FLF has beneficial effects on gut health. Van Winsen (2001) showed that the numbers of *Enterobacteriaceae* in the contents of the stomach, ileum, cecum, colon, and rectum of pigs fed fermented feed were significantly lower than the contents of the stomach, ileum, caecum, colon, and rectum of pigs fed dry feed.

Salmonella can persist in FLF containing less that 75 mmol/L lactic acid (Beal *et al.* 2002). If the goal of fermentation is to achieve lactic acid concentrations greater than 75 mmol/L at the point of delivery to the pig, this in essence means achieving > ca 110 mmol/L lactic acid in a fermented cereal base. Whilst these levels of lactic acid are rarely achievable in spontaneously fermented cereals (Beal *et al.* 2005), they can be readily achieved with the use of starter cultures. However, most commercial starter cultures have been developed for use in dairy products or for the production of silage. None have been developed for the specific purpose of fermenting liquid feed for pigs. In this study the effect of substrate in the form of four different cereals, barley, wheat, oats and maize, on the production of lactic acid by four different starter cultures was investigated. In the UK heat treated cereals are commonly used in diets for newly weaned pigs. Therefore, in addition to the unprocessed cereals the effect of micronization on lactic acid production was investigated.

Methods

The study was conducted as a three factor factorial, Factor 1 was cereal processing (raw or micronised. Factor 2 was cereal type (wheat, barley, oats or maize) and Factor 3 was lactic acid bacteria inoculant (*Pediococcus acidilactici* (PA), *Lactobacillus farciminis* (LF), *Lactobacillus plantarum* (LP) or *Lactobacillus salivarius* (LS)). Raw cereals were ground in a disc mill (Skiold2500 Danagri Bridgnorth UK) using a setting of 0 and along with the micronised cereals were sterilized by irradiation (25kG □ radiation from ^{60}Co). Sterile liquid cereals were prepared by mixing 100g cereal with 250 ml sterile distilled water. Triplicate samples of each cereal were inoculated with a 0.01% (v/v) of a 24h broth culture (de Mann rogosa Sharpe Broth (Oxoid Basingstoke UK)) of each LAB and incubated at 30°C for 30h. Samples taken at 0, 4, 8, 24 and 30h after the commencement of fermentation were analysed for lactic acid by HPLC using the method of Niven *et al* (2004).

The results were analysed by analysis of variance using a general linear model (Minitab release 14)

Results

In all liquid grains lactic acid levels started to increase between the 4 h and 8 h sampling point and thereafter increased linearly for a further 16h after which the rate of lactic acid production decreased in some samples. All fermentations followed a similar pattern, data for *Lb salivarius* (LS) is shown in Figure 1.

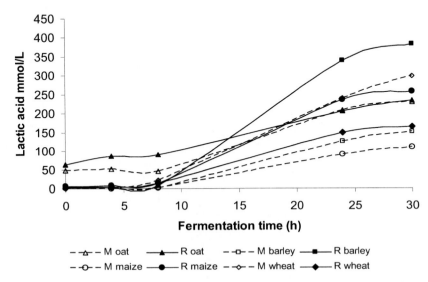

Figure 1 Lactic acid production in raw (R) or micronised (M) liquid cereals fermented for 30 h at 30°C with *Lb salivarius*.

The lactic acid concentration in the cereals prior to fermentation was variable and ranged from 2.5 mmol L^{-1} in wheat to 63 mmol L^{-1} in oats. Therefore the efficacy of fermentation was evaluated by taking the rate of lactic acid production between 8 and 24h fermentation (Table 1) rather than the total lactic acid produced. There was a significantly higher (P >0.001) rate of lactic acid production in raw barley with all LAB than there was from any other cereal.

Table 1 Rate of Lactic acid produced (mmol L^{-1} h^{-1}) in raw (R) or micronised (M) liquid cereal (1 cereal:2.5 water) fermented with *P. acidilactici* (PA), *Lb. farciminis* (LF), *Lb. plantarum* (LP) or *Lb. salivarius* (LS)

Fermenting organism	Wheat		Barley		Oats		Maize	
	R	M	R	M	R	M	R	M
PA	5.28[a1]	9.75[b1]	18.48[1]	5.24[a1]	6.44[a12]	1.47	9.47[b1]	4.28[a1]
LF	6.11[a1]	10.85[b1]	20.48[12]	6.39[a12]	5.61[a1]	5.82[a1]	9.01[b1]	4.14[a1]
LP	8.64[a2]	15.72[b2]	21.33[2]	9.55[a3]	8.65[a2]	7.82[a1]	16.97[b2]	6.14[a1]
LS	8.51[ac2]	13.64[d2]	20.79[12]	7.77[abc23]	7.23[ab12]	10.09[c]	13.95[d2]	5.55[b1]

[abcd] means in the same row with the same superscript are not significantly different (P >0.05)
[123] means in the same column are not significantly different (P>0.05)
s.e.m = 0.4512

For barley and maize all four lactic acid bacteria produced significantly more lactic acid from the raw cereal compared with the micronised cereal. The opposite was seen with wheat where the rate of lactic acid production was significantly higher (P<0.001) in micronised wheat compared with raw wheat for all four lactic acid bacteria. In oats the picture was more variable with *P. acidilactici* the rate of lactic acid production was significantly higher (P <0.001) in raw oats, whereas with *Lb. salivarius* the rate of production was significantly higher (P<0.05) in micronised oats. There was no significant difference (P>0.05) in the rate of lactic acid produced in raw or micronised oats fermented with *Lb. farciminis* or *Lb. plantarum*.

The goal of fermentation was to achieve 110 mmol L^{-1} lactic acid. After 24 h this was achieved in the most of the raw cereals, the exceptions being raw wheat fermented with *P. acidilactici* and *Lb. farciminis*. After 30 h fermentation the all raw cereals contained at least 110 mmol L^{-1} lactic acid (Figure 2).

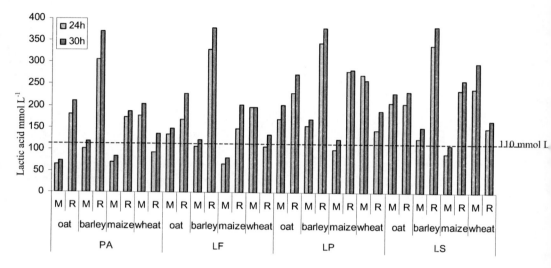

Figure 2   Lactic acid concentration in fermented liquid cereals fermented for 24 and 30 h with *P. acidicalctici* (PA), *Lb. farciminis* (LF), *Lb. plantarum* (LP) or *Lb. salivarius* (LS)

In contrast micronised maize was poorly fermented by all four LAB with none reaching target lactic acid levels in 24 h and only that fermented with *Lb. plantarum* reaching over 110mmol L^{-1} lactic acid after 30 h. Micronised oats and barley were poorly fermented by *P acidilactici*.

Discussion

The results of this study demonstrated that cereals are not equally well fermented by lactic acid bacteria.   Apart form wheat, raw cereals were fermented to a greater degree than micronised cereals.   This was possibly due to breakdown of complex carbohydrate in the grains to simpler oligosaccharides and sugars by endogenous enzyme action. These simpler sugars would be fermented more efficiently by the lactic acid bacteria.   The process of micronisation destroys endogenous enzymes and breakdown of complex carbohydrate would be limited to that of microbial enzyme action. This was reflected in reduced rates of lactic acid production in barley, maize and to a large extent oats.   The picture with wheat was the opposite, with all four organisms fermenting micronised wheat much more efficiently than raw wheat.   The reasons for this are unclear and further investigations are being undertaken.

All four organisms produced by far the most lactic acid in raw barley, *ca* 100 mmol L^{-1} in excess of any other substrate.   The reasons for this are unclear but it may be that the endogenous enzymes in barley efficiently breakdown storage polysaccharides and release simple sugars such as glucose and fructose for use by LAB.

In practice micronised cereals are only used to formulate diets for newly weaned pigs and the practice of fermenting feed for very young pigs is limited to a small number of producers. However, the results here suggest that producers following this practice would achieve the best results in terms of feed stability and safety if the majority of the cereal in the feed was wheat. Most producers practicing fermentation use raw cereals. In this case by far the best results in terms of feed stability and safety would be produced with barley. If fermented barley containing lactic acid levels of 350 mmol L^{-1} is used to make up a complete feed then that feed would contain approximately 240 mmL^{-1} lactic acid at the point of delivery to the pig. It is unlikely that this level of lactic acid would affect feed intake, but it would be sufficient to prevent the proliferation of any enteropathogenic organism that might contaminate the feed in the trough.

Acnowledgements

The authors would like to thank Becton and Dickinson (Plymouth UK) for irradiating the cereals.

*Sandrine Doridant conducted this study whilst on placement from Institut National des Sciences Appliquées Toulouse France

References

BEAL, J. D., NIVEN, S. J., BROOKS, P. H. and GILL, B. P. 2005. Variation in short chain fatty acid and ethanol concentration resulting from the natural fermentation of wheat and barley for inclusion in liquid diets for pigs. *Journal of the Science of Food and Agriculture*, 85, (3) 433-440.

BEAL, J. D., NIVEN, S. J., CAMPBELL, A. and BROOKS, P. H. 2002. The effect of temperature on the growth and persistence of salmonella in fermented liquid pig feed. *International Journal of Food Microbiology*, 79, (1-2) 99-104.

NIVEN, S. J., BEAL, J. D. and BROOKS, P. H. 2004. The simultaneous determination of short chain fatty acid, monosaccharides and ethanol in fermented liquid pig diets. *Animal Feed Science and Technology*, 117, (3-4) 339-345.

VAN WINSEN, R. L., URLINGS, B. A. P., LIPMAN, L. J. A., SNIJDERS, J. M. A., KEUZENKAMP, D., VERHEIJDEN, J. H. M. and VAN KNAPEN, F. 2001. Effect of fermented feed on the microbial population of the gastrointestinal tracts of pigs. *Applied and Environmental Microbiology*, 67, (7) 3071-3076.

Session 4

Evaluation of the tolerability of the Salmonella Typhimurium live vaccine Salmoporc® for oral administration in three day old piglets

Eddicks, M.[1], Palzer, A.[1], Ritzmann, M.[1], Hörmannsdorfer, S.[2], Heinritzi, K.*[1]

[1]Clinic for Swine, Ludwig-Maximilians-University Munich, Sonnenstr. 16, D-85764 Oberschleissheim, Germany
[2]Bavarian Health and Food Safety Authority, Veterinaerstr. 2, D-85764 Oberschleissheim, Germany
*corresponding author: sekretariat.heinritzi@med.vetmed.uni-muenchen.de

Abstract

Vaccination against *Salmonella* is a measure to reduce salmonella disease in pigs. In this study a *S. Typhimurium* live vaccine (Salmoporc®, Impfstoffwerk Dessau-Tornau, Rosslau, Germany) was applied to 3 day old conventional piglets in order to investigate safety and persistence of the vaccine strain in different tissues. The results indicate that an early vaccination against *Salmonella* shall be deemed to be safe.

Introduction

Salmonellosis is one of the most important food-associated zoonosis and pork is an important source of *S. Typhimurium* infections for humans (HAESEBROUCK et al., 2004). Since Salmonella is widely distributed in the environment, control is difficult to achieve (LETELLIER et al., 2000). Vaccination against Salmonella in pigs appears to merely reduce the infection pressure and is effective especially in addition to other measures taken at farm level (HAESEBROUCK et al., 2004). The aim of this study was to examine a *S. Typhimurium* live vaccine for its safety in 3 days old piglets applicated by the oral route.

Material and methods

Salmonella negative piglets (n=32) were vaccinated orally twice with a *S. Typhimurium* live vaccine Salmoporc® (Impfstoffwerk Dessau-Tornau, Rosslau, Germany) when the piglets were 3 and 21 days of age. The faeces consistence, body temperature, suckling frequency, and general health status were evaluated in a period of time comprising 8 hours after vaccination. Control of body weight was done weekly. The immunological response to this early vaccination was measured and the spread and persistence of the vaccine strain in different tissues was investigated by an bacteriological examination. Physiological NaCl solution was administered to the control group (n=28) orally.

Results

The piglets vaccinated twice with the single dose showed a significant higher mean body weight at weaning with an age of 4 weeks (7,63 kg) compared to the unvaccinated pigs (6,47 kg) (p<0,05). The vaccine strain was detected in faeces until day 7 after the second vaccination. The colonization of the internal tissues with the vaccine strain was timely restricted until six weeks after the second immunization, as a sample of the ileum and the colon have been found to be positive (Tab. 1). The vaccine strain was isolated in decreasing amounts from samples of the ileoceacal lymph nodes, the ileum, caecum content, colon, lung, liver and skeletal- and heart muscle. Samples from the kidney were not found to be positive at any time. Salmonella field strains could be detected neither in the control nor in the vaccinated group in any time during this study. A serological response in answer to the vaccination on day 3 and 21 could be seen from day 7 after the second vaccination (Fig. 1). The maximum of the mean antibody titre concentration was measured on day 49 after the second vaccination.

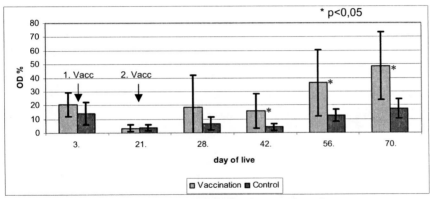

Figure 1: Mean antibody titre in the vaccinated and unvaccinated group

Table 1: Number of Salmonella vaccine positive tissues samples post vaccination in the vaccinated group from 2 piglets per day

Tissue	3. p. I	7. p. I	3. p. II	7. p. II	14. p. II	21. p. II	28. p. II	35. p. II	42. p. II	56. p. II	Total
small intestine	2	1	0	0	1	0	1	1	1	0	7
Colon	1	1	0	0	0	0	0	0	1	0	3
Caecum	2	0	1	2	0	0	0	0	0	0	5
Lnn.	2	2	2	0	1	1	0	0	0	0	8
Lung	2	0	0	0	0	0	0	0	0	0	2
Liver	1	0	0	0	0	0	0	0	0	0	1
Skelet. muscle	1	0	0	0	0	0	0	0	0	0	1
Heart	1	0	0	0	0	0	0	0	0	0	1
Kidney	0	0	0	0	0	0	0	0	0	0	0
Total	12	4	3	2	1	1	1	0	2	0	28

3.p.I – 7.p.I: 3. and 7. day after 1. vaccination
3.p.II – 56.p.II: 3. and 56. day after 2. vaccination

Discussion

In Western Europe, *S. Typhimurium* accounts for most of the cases of clinical salmonellosis (HAESEBROUCK et al., 2004). It is not possible to prevent an infection with Salmonella or to eradicate Salmonella on the farm level by antibiotics. Furthermore the therapy for long times is not effective in preventing the shedding and infection with Salmonella (ROESLER et al., 2005). For these reasons the prophylaxis by vaccination is very important strategy in farms with Salmonella problems. After experimentally infections Salmonella can be isolated in samples from the liver, spleen, lung, kidney and skeletal muscles (COTÉ et al., 2004). The highest isolation rate results in the investigation of tonsil samples, followed by samples of the jejunum and caecum (WOOD et al., 1989). In the presented study the colonisation of the tissues are similar as described by other authors. This is important to assume a sufficient immune reaction of the organism (HAESEBROUK et al., 2004; SELBITZ, 2001). The duration of the persistence is in this study sufficient to stimulate the cellular immunity. A contamination of carcasses or organs in the abattoir can be excluded, because the colonization of the internal tissues with the vaccine strain was timely restricted until six weeks after the second immunization, as a sample of the ileum and the colon have been found to be positive. When piglets are vaccinated with the considered doses at the 3 and 21 day of live an introduction of the vaccine strain in fatting units is unlikely. Therefore a serological reaction of unvaccinated fattening pigs is not possible. It was not possible to detect a serological response after the first vaccination at day 3. An interaction with maternal antibodies can not be excluded.

Therefore a serological response was detected after the second vaccination on day 21. Perhaps it is possible to vaccinate sows and to vaccinate their piglets on day 21.

Conclusions

Vaccination of 3 day old piglets with a *S. Typhimurium* live vaccine seems to be safe. For reasons of practicability the application of the vaccine is more considered in 3 and 21 day old piglets, compared to licensed application in 3 and 6 week old piglets.

References

COTÉ, N., et al., 2004. Distribution of Salmonella in tissues following natural and experimental infections in pigs. *The Canadian Journal of Veterinary Research* 68, 241-248.
HAESEBROUCK, F., et al., 2004. Efficacy of vaccines against bacterial diseases in swine: what can we expect? *Veterinary Microbiology* 100, 255-268.
LETELLIER, A., et al., 2000. Assessment of various treatments to reduce carriage of Samonella in swine. *The Canadian Journal of Veterinary Research* 64 (1), 27-31.
WOOD, M.W., et al., 1989. Distribution of persistent Salmonella Typhimurium infection in internal organs of swine. *American Journal of Veterinary Research* 50, 1015-1021.
ROESLER, U., et al., 2005. Effects of Flourequinolone of Salmonella Typhimurium DT104 in an Intergrated Pig Breeding Herd. *Journal of Veterinary Medicine* 52, 69-74.
SELBITZ, H.J., 2001. Grundsätzliche Sicherheitsanforderungen beim Einsatz von Lebendimpfstoffen bei Lebensmittelliefernden Tieren. *Berliner und Münchener Tierärztliche Wochenschrift* 114, 428-432.

Isolation of *Salmonella* spp. and bacteriophage active against *Salmonella* spp. from commercial swine.

Callaway, T.[1]*, Edrington, T.[1], Brabban, A.[2], Kutter, E.[2], Karriker, L.[3], Stahl, C.[3], Wagstrom, L.[4], Anderson, R.[1], Genovese, K.[1], McReynolds, J.[1], Harvey, R. [1] and Nisbet, D. [1]

[1] USDA/ARS, Food and Feed Safety Research Unit, College Station, TX, USA
[2] Evergreen State College, Olympia, WA, USA
[3] Iowa State University, Ames, IA, USA
[4] National Pork Board, Des Moines, IA, USA
*corresponding author, callaway@ffsru.tamu.edu

Abstract

Bacteriophage are viruses that prey on bacteria and may be a potential strategy to reduce foodborne pathogenic bacteria in the gastrointestinal tract of food animals. Phages are fairly common in the gastrointestinal microbial ecosystem of mammals, but the incidence is unknown. If phage are to be an intervention strategy, we must understand their role in the microbial ecology of the gut. From a regulatory perspective, knowing incidence of phage is crucial. Therefore the current study was designed to determine the incidence of phage active against *Salmonella* spp. in the feces of commercial finishing swine in the United States. Fecal samples (n=60) were collected from each of six commercial swine finishing operations. Samples were collected from 10 randomly selected pens throughout each operation. Total number of fecal samples collected in this study was n=360. *Salmonella* spp. were found in 6.6% of the fecal samples. *Salmonella* spp. were isolated from only 2 farms and the serotypes represented were Schwarzengrund, Anatum, Ohio and Heidelberg. Bacteriophages were isolated from fecal sample through 2 parallel methods, 1) initial enrichment in *Salmonella* Typhimurium, or 2) initial enrichment in *E. coli* B (a strain very sensitive to phages); followed by direct spot-testing against *Salmonella* Typhimurium. Bacteriophages active against *Salmonella* Typhimurium were isolated from 1.1% (4/360) of the individual fecal samples when initially enriched in *Salmonella* Typhimurium, but *E. coli* B-killing phages were isolated from 43.8% (158/360) of the fecal samples but only 2 of these isolates were capable of killing *Salmonella* Typhimurium. Our results indicate that bacteriophage capable of killing *Salmonella* Typhimurium are fairly widespread across commercial swine production facilities but may be present at relatively low populations. These results indicate that phage (predator) populations may vary along with *Salmonella* (prey) populations and that phage could potentially be used as a food safety pathogen reduction strategy.

Introduction

Food-borne *Salmonella* infections in the United States are estimated to cost the economy $2.4 billion annually (ERS/USDA, 2001). Approximately 6-9% of human salmonellosis is associated with the consumption of pork products (Frenzen et al., 1999). *Salmonella* is relatively common on swine farms and has been isolated from all stages of the pork production chain (Davies et al., 1999; Fedorka-Cray et al., 1997; Rostagno et al., 2003). *Salmonella* is a threat to the pork industry not only from a food-safety perspective as a public health concern, but some *Salmonella* serotypes can cause clinical illnesses in swine, negatively impacting production efficiency and profitability (Schwartz, 1991).

Bacteriophage are viruses that specifically infect bacteria and reproduce within them, killing the host bacterium through cellular lysis caused by the release of daughter phages. Phage were widely used in eastern Europe in place of antibiotics and have been called an "infectious cure for infectious disease" (Barrow, 2001). Due to increasing concerns about antibiotic resistance linkage to animal agriculture, considerable research has been focused on finding alternatives to antibiotics to reduce pathogens in food animals. Because phage exhibit a high degree of specificity for target bacteria it has been suggested that bacteriophage be used as a "designer antimicrobial" to eliminate specific pathogens from the gastrointestinal microbial population, including *Salmonella*,

Campylobacter, Listeria and E. coli O157:H7 (Alisky et al., 1998; Loc Carrillo et al., 2005; Smith and Huggins, 1983).

Bacteriophage have been long known to be members of the intestinal microbial consortium. But the role they play in the ecology of the gut has been unclear; theories have abounded about preventing overgrowth to a role in diurnal variation to a role in nutrient cycling. However the exact incidence of these bacterial predators has never been fully investigated. Most research involving phages in the intestinal tract of animals has been exclusively qualitative in nature; incidence rates were determined using less than 20 animals of various species (Dhillon et al., 1976). Therefore this study was conducted to determine the incidence of phage in swine, by examining two separate issues, 1) what is the incidence of phage that kills Salmonella Typhimurium (one of the most important human illness serotypes in the United States), and 2) what is the overall incidence of bacteriophage in commercial swine.

Materials and Methods

Fresh fecal samples (approximately 100 g from a single source; n = 6 samples per pen) were collected from each of 10 finishing pens per commercial swine farm (n = 10 pens/farm; n = 60 fecal samples/farm). Total number of fecal samples collected in this study was n=360.All samples were collected within a 45 min period immediately after the morning feeding. Immediately upon collection, samples were individually bagged in sealed whirl-pak bags after collection and kept on ice during transport prior to analysis (for approximately 24 h).

To qualitatively enrich for Salmonella populations, 3 g of feces were added to tubes containing 27 mL of tetrathionate broth (Difco Laboratories) and incubated at 37 °C for 24 h. After this incubation, 200 µL of the tetrathionate enrichment were added to 5 mL Rapport-Vassilidis R10 broth and incubated an additional 24 h at 42 °C before being streak-plated onto brilliant green agar (BGA) supplemented with novobiocin (25 µg/mL). The BGA$_{Nov}$ plates were incubated for 24 h at 37 °C; colonies that exhibited typical Salmonella morphology were individually picked for further physiological characterization and were inoculated onto Triple Sugar Iron (TSI) agar slants and Lysine Iron agar (LIA) slants (Difco, Inc.). Each slant was incubated at 35 °C for 24 h. Salmonella-positive samples were confirmed by slide agglutination using SM-O antiserum poly A-I and V-I, and group C1 factors. Salmonella isolates were stored in glycerol and TSB at -80 °C until confirmatory serotyping was performed by the National Veterinary Services Laboratory (NVSL) in Ames, IA.

Bacteriophage enrichment and isolation, Fecal samples were screened for the presence of Salmonella Typhimurium bacteriophage. Feces (1 g) were mixed in sterile conical tubes containing 9 ml of phosphate buffered saline (pH 6.8). Chloroform (0.5 ml) was added to each tube and tubes were thoroughly mixed before being allowed to stand at 24 °C for 2 h. The top layer from this tube was removed and placed in a new sterile tube containing 0.5 ml chloroform. Portions (0.3 ml) of the chloroform-free top layer were mixed with 1.2 ml volumes of early-log-phase (< 0.2 OD) S. Typhimurium or E. coli B (10^8 CFU/ml, grown at 39 °C) and were incubated in anoxic TSB broth in sealed Hungate tubes overnight at 39 °C. E. coli B was used in this study as an initial propogation strain because, 1) it is susceptible to bacteriophage of several types, and 2) use of this strain to propagate natural bacteriophage allows us to detect a broader range of phage in an initial bacteriophage activity screening. Samples (1.5 ml) were collected and added to tubes containing 0.2 ml of chloroform for 30 min. These samples were subsequently centrifuged at 19,000 x g in a microcentrifuge for 10 min. The top layer of the supernatant was removed, and stored in a fresh sterile tube following sterilization by filtration through a 0.2 mm filter. Samples were subjected to a plaque assay (Sambrook and Russell, 2001) using S. Typhimurium or E. coli strain B as the propagation host and grown on TSB plates incubated anaerobically. Plates were incubated overnight at 39 °C.

Spectrum of bacteriophage activity, All bacteriophage plaques purified from the S. Typhimurium and E. coli B plates (3 plaques/sample) were assessed for their ability to form plaques on a range of intestinal bacteria. E. coli F18 and K88 were obtained from the FFSRU culture collection. Other bacterial species tested for bacteriophage activity included Salmonella derby, S. typhimurium, S. dublin, S. enteriditis, S. cholerasuis, S. montevideo, S. mbandaka, Enterococcus faecalis, Entero. faecium and E. coli O157:H7 from the FFSRU culture collection. Each bacterial strain was grown on TSB plates incubated anaerobically and were exposed to an equal amount of bacteriophage plaque forming units (PFU) of each bacteriophage isolate. The bacteriophage that were isolated in this study are currently being genetically and physiologically characterized and further characteristics of the bacteriophage will be reported in future studies.

Data Analysis,   Point prevalence of *Salmonella* and bacteriophage shedding was calculated individually by dividing the number of pathogen culture-positive fecal samples by the total of samples collected per farm (n = 60 per farm, 360 total samples).   Correlations of prevalence were using Epi Info 6.0, but due to the relatively low numbers of pens and incidences in this study, no correlations were found. Length of time spent in pen or farm were not included in the models because the record-keeping was not complete or available to the researchers.

Results

Salmonella Enterica serotypes were found in 6.6% of the fecal samples (24/360). *Salmonella* spp. were isolated from only 3 of the 6 farms and the serotypes represented were Schwarzengrund, Anatum, Derby, Ohio and Heidelberg (Table 1).

Table 1. *Salmonella enterica* serotype, serogroup, phage active against *Salmonella* Typhimurium, and phage active against *E. coli* strain B isolated from commercial finishing swine in the central United States.

Farm	Serotype (number)	Serogroup	Phage + on *S.* Typh	Phage + on *E. coli* B
A	Anatum (1)	E1	0	0
	Derby (1)	B		
B	None		3	18
C	None		0	13
D	None		1	7
E	Ohio (3)	C1	2 (after B enriched)	60
	Heidelberg (1)	B		
F	Schwarzengrund (14)	B	0	60
	Anatum (4)	E1		
Total	24/360		6/360	158/360

Bacteriophages were isolated from each fecal sample through 2 parallel methods, 1) initial enrichment in *Salmonella* Typhimurium, or 2) initial enrichment in *E. coli* B (a strain very sensitive to phages) followed by direct spot-testing against *Salmonella* Typhimurium. Bacteriophages active against *Salmonella* Typhimurium were isolated from 1.6% (6/360) of the total individual fecal samples, but *E. coli* B-killing phages were isolated from 43.8% (158/360) of the fecal samples. Only 2 of the *Salmonella*-killing phage were isolated from samples that were first enriched in *E. coli* B.   All of these phages created clearing zones when plated onto *S.* Typhimurium and were characterized by their pattern against other *Salmonella* serotypes (data not shown). However, the spectrum of Salmonella-killing activity was very narrow, with only one of the phage killing another *Salmonella* serotype than Typhimurium (Derby).

Discussion

Salmonella spp. and other foodborne pathogenic bacteria can live in the gut of mammals, including swine. A wide variety of *Salmonella* serotypes have been isolated from swine around the world. The present study indicates that Salmonella are present in commercial finishing operations in the U.S. at a relatively low incidence that is comparable to other published surveys (Davies et al., 1999; Morrow et al., 1999). However, the fact that *Salmonella* are isolated from apparently healthy finishing swine has serious implications for pork safety; yet of the serotypes isolated in this study, only Anatum is found in the most common human isolates of the CDC.   It is important to note that less than 7% of the fecal samples were positive for *Salmonella* spp., and these were limited to 3 of the 6 farms surveyed, indicating that herd health measures have indeed been effective in reducing the incidence of *Salmonella* in finishing swine.

Phages are normal members of the microbial ecosystem of the gastrointestinal tract of animals and humans, and are commonly isolated from community wastewater streams. In spite of understanding that phage are widespread in nature, no research has been performed to estimate the incidence of phage in food animals until recently, and never before in commercial swine. The

Session 4

widespread nature of phage that were active against *E. coli* B was surprising, but the incidence varied between farms, from being ubiquitous on 2 farms to completely absent on one farm.

Phage that killed *Salmonella* Typhimurium were not as widespread on farms; only 6 out of the 360 samples tested positive for phage active against *S.* Typhimurium. Phage active against S. Typhimurium had a very narrow activity spectrum, and did not affect a variety of other *Salmonella* serotypes. Phage specific to *S.* Typhimurium were not widespread on these farms, likely because *S.* Typhimurium is not widespread on the farms for a *S.* Typhimurium phage to prey upon. These data suggest that in order to utilize phage to reduce *Salmonella* in swine, that a specific phage or phages be isolated for each specific serotype or group of related serotypes.

Phage have been suggested as a mechanism to reduce *Salmonella* spp. contamination in swine as an animal health adjunct, or as a potential preharvest intervention strategy. It appears that this strategy may be more difficult than previously considered due to the relatively narrow spectra of phage activity against *Salmonella* serotypes. In order to reduce *Salmonella* in the U.S. swine population, *Salmonella*-killing phage that affect the serotypes of interest must be isolated from several swine sources to reduce the possibility of resistance development and to ensure that the phage are effective against all strains of the serotypes of interest.

Conclusions

Our results indicate that bacteriophage are fairly widespread across commercial swine production facilities, but they may be present at relatively low populations. Phage capable of killing *Salmonella* Typhimurium are found in commercial swine, but were not found at a high incidence. This is potentially due to a predator/prey cycle between the phage (predator) and *Salmonella* (prey) populations. These results suggest that because this cycle naturally exists in the commercial environment, that phage could potentially be used as a food safety pathogen reduction strategy. However, further research is needed to understand the spectrum of activity of each phage type, and to specifically isolate phages active against the *Salmonella* spp. that most directly affect swine production efficiency, animal morbidity/mortality, and food-borne illness.

References

ALISKY, J., ICZKOWSKI, K., TROITSKY, N. 1998. Bacteriophages show promise as antibacterial agents. Journal of Infection 36, 5-15.

BARROW, P. 2001. The use of bacteriophages for treatment and prevention of bacterial disease in animals and animal models of human infection. Journal of Chemistry Technology and Biotechnology. 76, 677-682.

DAVIES, P. FUNK, J., MORROW, M. 1999. Fecal shedding of *Salmonella* by a cohort of finishing pigs in north carolina. Swine Health and Production 7, 231-234.

DHILLON, T., DHILLON, E., CHAU, H., LI, W., TSANG, A. 1976. Studies on bacteriophage distribution: Virulent and temperate bacteriophage content of mammalian feces. Applied and Environmental Microbiology 32, 68-74.

ERS/USDA. 2001. ERS estimates foodborne disease costs at $6.9 billion per year No. 2004. Economic Research Service/United States Department of Agriculture. http://www.ers.usda.gov/Emphases/SafeFood/features.htm

FEDORKA-CRAY, P., HOGG, A., GRAY, J., LORENZEN, K., VELASQUEZ, J., VON BEHREN, P. 1997. Feed and feed trucks as sources of *Salmonella* contamination in swine. Journal of Swine Health Production 5, 189-193.

FRENZEN, P., BUZBY, J., ROBERTS, T. 1999. An updated estimate of the economic costs of human illness due to foodborne *Salmonella* in the United States. In, 3rd Int. Symp. on the Epidemiology and Control of *Salmonella* in Pork, Washington, DC. p 215-218.

LOC CARILLO, C., ATTERBURY, R., EL-SHIBINY, A., CONNERTON, P., DILLON, E., SCOTT, A., CONNERTON, I. 2005. Bacteriophage therapy to reduce *Campylobacter jejuni* colonization of broiler chickens. Applied and Environmental Microbiology 71, 6554-6563.

MORROW, W., DAVIES, P., SEE, T., EISEMANN, J., ZERING, K., KIHLSTROM, S., KARLI, K. 1999. Prevalence of *Salmonella* spp. In the feces on farm and ceca at slaughter for a cohort of finishing pigs. In, 3rd Int. Symp. Epidemiol. Control of *Salmonella* in Pork, Washington, D. C. p 155-157.

ROSTAGNO, M., HURD, H., MCKEAN, J., ZIEMER, C., GAILEY, J., LEITE, R. 2003. Preslaughter holding environment in pork plants is highly contaminated with *Salmonella enterica*. Applied and Environmental Microbiology 69, 4489-4494.

SCHWARTZ, K. 1991. Salmonellosis in swine. In: The compendium on continuing education for the practicing veterinarian No. 13. p 139-147.

SMITH, H., HUGGINS, R. 1983. Effectiveness of phages in treating experimental *Escherichia coli* diarrhoea in calves, piglets and lambs. Journal of General Microbiology 129, 2659-2675.

Session 4

Effect of the use of organic acids in drinking water during the last two weeks prior to slaughter on *salmonella* shedding

E.V. De Busser[1,2*], J. Dewulf[1], N. Nollet[4], K. Houf[2], K. Schwarzer[5], L. De Sadeleer[3], L. De Zutter[2], D. Maes[1]

[1] Department of Reproduction Obstetrics and Herd Health, Faculty of Veterinary Medicine, Ghent University, Belgium
[2] Department of Veterinary Public Health and Food Safety, Faculty of Veterinary Medicine, Ghent University, Belgium
[3] Animal Management, Ghent Highschool, Belgium
[4] INVE België NV, Oeverstraat 7, 9200 Baasrode, Belgium
[5] Nutri-Ad International NV, Kloosterstraat 1/7, 2460 Kasterlee, Belgium
*Corresponding author: Emily.DeBusser@UGent.be

Abstract

In this study we investigated the effect of adding organic acids to the drinking water of finishing pigs two weeks prior to slaughter on the shedding and prevalence rate of *Salmonella* at slaughter. One hundred animals from 4 Belgian pig herds infected with *Salmonella* were included. Fifty of these animals received drinking water supplemented with a mixture of different organic acids during 14 days prior to slaughter. Non-treated animals served as controls. Different samples were taken: contents of ileum and rectum, mesenteric lymph nodes and carcass swabs. All samples were submitted to *Salmonella* isolation using standard procedures. The results could not reveal a significant difference between both groups. This may be due to the limited power of the study (only 50 animals sampled in each group) or due to the fact that the treatment duration was insufficient to prove the benefit of the used organic acids.

Introduction

Salmonella is known as one of the most important zoonotic pathogens and the consumption of pork meat is a major source of infection. Seventy-five percent of all pig farms in Belgium are infected and it is known that the amount of animals shedding *Salmonella* increases at times of stress (Nollet et al., 2004). Transport to the slaughterhouse and waiting in the lairage room is a stress moment for the pigs (Berends et al., 1996). Acidifying the feed and/or drinking water during a long period seems to be useful to control *Salmonella* (Van der Wolf et al., 1997; Van der Wolf et al., 1998). In this study we assessed the effect of the addition of organic acids to the drinking water in finisher pigs for two weeks prior to slaughter to specifically target the expected increase of shedding during transport and lairage.

Materials and Methods

This study was conducted in 5 groups of fattening pigs on 4 different Belgian pig farms with a high *Salmonella* infection status as determined by serology in the *Salmonella* Surveillance Programme (Animal Health Care Flanders, personal communication, 2006). The farmers had not taken any *Salmonella* reducing measures before.
Two weeks prior to the expected slaughter date, the pigs were randomly divided into two groups (treatment and control group) each containing on average fifty animals. The treatment group received from this day onwards acidified drinking water. A mixture of different organic acids were added until a pH of 4 was achieved. The control group received the normal, untreated drinking water. Housing and feeding were identical in both groups. At the time of loading, the animals of each group were held separated during transport and in the lairage room. Ten randomly selected pigs of each group were sampled in the slaughterhouse. After evisceration, contents of ileum and rectum, as well as samples of the mesenteric lymph nodes and swabs of the carcasses were collected.
All samples were submitted to *Salmonella* isolation using standard procedures.

Results

Table 1 shows the pH of the drinking water in the treatment and control groups of the different herds.

The results of this study are summarized in Table 2. In herd B, no *Salmonella* organisms were detected despite of the fact that the serological screening results suggested a high *Salmonella* infection level in the herd. For some pigs there was not enough content of ileum or rectum, so isolation of *Salmonella* was not possible.

In the herds where *Salmonella* was isolated (herd A, C, D and E), the differences between the treatment and control groups were variable and small (Fisher's Exact Test, p>0.1). No significant differences in the number of *Salmonella* positive samples were found between the treatment and control groups.

Table 2: pH values of the drinking water in treatment and control groups of the different herds

Study Group	Herd	pH	
		Treatment group	Control group
1	A	3.9	8.4
2	B	4.0	8.5
3	C	3.8	7.8
4	D	3.6	8.4
5	A	3.7	8.4

Table 3: Number of *Salmonella* positive samples in the treatment and control groups of the different herds

Study Group	Herd	Group	IL	R	LN	CS	Total*
1	A	Treatm	2/10	0/10	3/10	3/10	6/10
		Contr	4/10	1/10	5/10	0/10	6/10
2	B	Treatm	0/10	0/10	0/10	0/10	0/10
		Contr	0/10	0/10	0/10	0/10	0/10
3	C	Treatm	1/10	2/10	1/10	1/10	3/10
		Contr	2/9	0/8	3/10	0/10	4/10
4	D	Treatm	3/10	1/10	1/10	0/10	3/10
		Contr	2/10	0/9	1/10	0/10	3/10
5	A	Treatm	2/10	4/10	6/10	0/10	8/10
		Contr	3/10	2/10	5/10	0/8	8/10
	Total	Treatm	8/50	7/50	11/50	4/50	20/50
		Contr	11/49	3/47	14/50	0/48	21/50

IL: content of ileum (12g)
R: content of rectum (10g)
LN: mesenteric lymph nodes (10g)
CS: carcass swabs
Total*: amount of animals tested positive in at least one sample / amount of animals tested

Session 4

Discussion

Different studies (Van der Wolf et al., 1997; Van der Wolf et al., 1998) revealed the benefit of acidifying feed and/or drinking water during a long period in the reduction of the *Salmonella* prevalence. However, it is not yet known whether the strategically administration of acidified drinking water during a limited period of time is also able to reduce the *Salmonella* prevalence. To reduce the costs for the farmer, it might be enough to acidify the drinking water only the last 14 days before slaughter.

The present study could not demonstrate a significant reduction of *Salmonella* positive samples in finishing pigs receiving acidified drinking water. This may be due to the fact that only 100 animals (50 per group) from 4 different herds were examined in the present study. This number might not be enough to demonstrate the benefit of the used organic acids in the drinking water.

It has been proven before that acidifying the drinking water is a useful tool to reduce the number of *Salmonella* shedding animals at herd level (Van der Wolf et al., 2001). However, one of the problems in the control of *Salmonella* is the existence of carriers, hiding the pathogen in the mesenteric lymph nodes (Schwartz, 1999). Organic acids are killing bacteria in the intestinal lumen (Van Immerseel et al., 2006), but can probably not reach the mesenteric lymph nodes. When these *Salmonella* carriers are transported to the slaughterhouse, shedding is reactivated due to stress, leading to the equal number of positive samples in the treatment and the control group.

Further research is necessary to investigate the optimal strategies to control *Salmonella*.

References

Berends, B.R., Urlings, H.A., Snijders, J.M., et al., 1996. Identification and quantification of risk factors in animal managment and transport regarding *Salmonella* spp. in pigs. International Journal of Food Microbiology 30, 37-53

Nollet, N., Maes, D.,.De Zutter, L., et al., 2004. Risk factors for the herd-level bacteriologic prevalence of *Salmonella* in Belgian slaughter pigs. Preventive Veterinary Medicine 65, 63-75.

Schwartz, K.J., 1999. Salmonellosis. In Straw B.E. et al. (Ed.), Diseases of Swine, Iowa State University Press, Ames, Iowa, USA, 535-551

Van der Wolf, P.J., Wolbers, W.B., Elbers, A.R.W., et al.,1997. Blood sampling at two slaughterhouses and serological screening of *Salmonella* infections in swine using an indirect ELISA. 2nd International Symposium on Epidemiology and Control of Salmonella in Pork, Copenhagen, Denmark, 199-202.

Van der Wolf, P.J., Elbers, A.R.W., Wolbers, W.B., et al., 1998. Risk factors for *Salmonella* in slaughter-pigs in the Netherlands. 15th IPVS Congres, Birmingham, England, 98.

Van der Wolf, P.J., van Schie, F.W., Elbers, A.R.W., et al., 2001. Administration of acidified drinking water to finishing pigs in order to prevent *Salmonella* infections. The Veterinary Quarterly 23, 121-125

Van Immerseel, F;, Russell, J.B., Flythe, M.D., et al., 2006. The use of organic acids to combat *Salmonella* in poultry: a mechanistic explanation of the efficacy. Avian Pathology 35, 182-188

Vaccination against *Salmonella* and the association with measures of *Salmonella* prevalence in live and slaughtered swine - A systematic review.

Denagamage, T.[1], O'Connor, A.*[1], Sargeant, J.[2], Rajic, A.[3] and McKean, J.[1]

[1]Department of Veterinary Diagnostic and Production Animal Medicine, College of Veterinary Medicine, Iowa State University, Ames, 50011, IA, USA.
[2]Department of Clinical Epidemiology and Biostatistics, McMaster University, 1200 Main St. W., Hamilton, L8N 3Z5, ON, Canada.
[3]Laboratory for Foodborne Zoonoses, Public Health Agency of Canada, 110 Stone Road W., Guelph, N1G 3W4, ON, Canada.
corresponding author: oconnor@iastate.edu

Abstract

A systematic review was conducted to evaluate the effectiveness of vaccination to reduce *Salmonella* prevalence in market weight finisher swine. To identify relevant studies, online databases and selected conference proceedings were searched. Two reviewers independently assessed the relevance screening and methodological quality of studies. Data of characteristics of study population, intervention, outcome, statistical analysis, and results were extracted. Four clinical trials and 21 challenge studies were identified for the final review as they described vaccination to reduce *Salmonella* in swine. Present evidence suggests that vaccination is associated with reduced *Salmonella* prevalence in swine.

Introduction

Salmonella is considered one of the major foodborne pathogens transmitted by pork and pork products. Vaccination is considered one method of reducing pre-harvest *Salmonella* prevalence in swine. The aim of this systematic review was to appraise and synthesize studies describing vaccination as a method of reducing *Salmonella* prevalence in market weight finisher swine (Cook et al., 1997; Sargeant et al., 2005).

Materials and Methods

The review question was "What is the association between *Salmonella* prevalence in the ante-mortem or post-mortem animal and vaccination against *Salmonella* in market weight finisher swine?". A comprehensive literature search was conducted on online bibliographic databases. Three major conference proceedings were searched by hand. No language or publication restrictions for the searches were imposed. Inclusion criteria for relevance screening were 1) primary research in English, 2) Ph.D. theses in English, 3) citations from conference proceedings, 4) described evaluation of vaccination against *Salmonella* in swine in a challenge trial or clinical trial, and 5) reported ante-mortem or post-mortem presence of *Salmonella* in swine. The methodological quality of all relevant studies was independently assessed by two reviewers using checklists to assess challenge trials and clinical trials. Methodological grades of low/high were assigned based on the quality criteria. Components of the quality assessment included objectives and study population, intervention, withdrawals and loss to follow-up, outcome assessment, and data analysis. Data extraction included the characteristics of population, intervention and level of allocation to treatment groups, outcome, and results. Only outcomes describing ante-mortem or post-mortem culture of *Salmonella* post-vaccination were extracted.

Session 4

Results

Four clinical trials and 21 challenge studies that reported vaccination against *Salmonella* in swine were identified for the final review. (Baum et al., 1997; Charles et al., 1999; Charles et al., 2000a; Charles et al., 2000b; Coe et al., 1992; Draayer, 1986; Foster et al., 2003; Gibson et al., 1999; Groninga et al., 2000; Hanna et al., 1979; Kennedy et al., 1999; Kern, 1994; Kolb et al., 2001; Kolb et al., 2002; Kramer et al., 1987; Kramer et al., 1992; Letellier et al., 2000; Lumsden et al., 1991; Maes et al., 2001; Neubauer and Roof, 2005; Roesler et al., 2004b; Roesler et al., 2004a; Roof and Doitchinoff, 1995; Springer et al., 2001). Out of 25 studies, 18 and two studies were conducted in the USA and Canada, respectively, and five studies were conducted in Europe. All four clinical trials reported isolation of *Salmonella* in market weight finisher swine, though received a low methodological quality grade. All the challenge studies were conducted on age less than 15-week-old pigs while four of them received a high methodological quality grade.

Discussion

The majority of studies reported a reduction in *Salmonella* associated with vaccination using a variety of outcomes such as number of *Salmonella* positive pigs or number of *Salmonella* positive environmental samples. Some studies did not provide any data on the outcome effect other than a p value. Most of the studies did not report study features which reduce bias and increase internal validity, i.e. random allocation of treatment units or blinding at outcome assessment. Not all the studies tested for *Salmonella* status prior to the intervention.

Conclusion

The present evidence suggests that vaccination against *Salmonella* is associated with reduced level of *Salmonella* prevalence in finisher swine. However, many of the studies in the review did not to include information that would have increased the evidentiary value of the papers in answering the review question.

References

Baum DH, Harris DL, Roof MB, Nielsen B, Holck JT, Polson DP, and Baik J. 1997. Use of SC54 for the reduction of *Salmonella* in swine. In: Proceedings of the Second International Symposium on Epidemiology and Control of *Salmonella* in Pork, Copenhagen, Denmark. p 215-220.

Charles S, Trigo E, Settje T, Abraham A, and Johnson P. 1999. Evaluation of a Δ cya Δ(crp-cdt) *Salmonella choleraesuis* commercial vaccine to protect against clinical signs caused by and reduce shedding of *Salmonella typhimurium* in pigs. In: Proceedings of the 3rd International Symposium on the Epidemiology and Control of *Salmonella* in Pork, Washington, DC. p 293-295.

Charles SD, Abraham AS, Trigo ET, Jones GF, and Settje TL. 2000a. Reduced shedding and clinical signs of *Salmonella typhimurium* in nursery pigs vaccinated with a *Salmonella choleraesuis* vaccine. Swine Health Pro 8:107-112.

Charles S, Trigo E, Settje T, Blaha T, Gibson K, and Frank R. 2000b. Evaluation of cross protection afforded by a cya Δ(crp-cdt) *Salmonella choleraesuis* commercial vaccine against *Salmonella typhimurium* infection in pigs. In: Proceedings of 31st Annual Meeting of American Association of Swine Practitioners, Indianapolis, Indiana, USA. p 105-106.

Coe NE, Frank DE, Wood RL, and Roth JA. 1992. Alteration of neutrophil function in BCG-treated and non-treated swine after exposure to *Salmonella typhimurium*. Vet Immunol Immunopathol 33:37-50.

Cook DJ, Mulrow CD, and Haynes RB. 1997. Systematic reviews: synthesis of best evidence for clinical decisions. Ann Intern Med 126:376-380.

Draayer HA. 1986. Protecting weanling pigs against salmonellosis. Vet Med776-777.

Foster N, Lovell MA, Marston KL, Hulme SD, Frost AJ, Bland P, and Barrow PA. 2003. Rapid protection of gnotobiotic pigs against experimental salmonellosis following induction of polymorphonuclear leukocytes by avirulent *Salmonella enterica*. Infect Immun 71:2182-2191.

Gibson KJ, Blaha T, Frank RK, Charles SD, and Trigo E. 1999. Investigation into the capability of a *Salmonella cholerasuis* live vaccine to reduce the shedding of *Salmonella typhimurium* in swine. In: Bahson PB, editor. Proceedings of the 3rd International Symposium on the Epidemiology and Control of Salmonella in Pork. p 302-304.

Groninga KJ, Springer E, Braunschmidt M, and Pankratz D. 2000. *Salmonella derby* cross-protection study. Vet Ther 1:59-63.

Hanna J, McCracken R, and O'Brien JJ. 1979. Evaluation of a live *Salmonella choleraesuis* vaccine by intranasal challenge. Res Vet Sci 26:216-219.

Kennedy MJ, Yancey RJ, Jr., Sanchez MS, Rzepkowski RA, Kelly SM, and Curtiss RI. 1999. Attenuation and immunogenicity of Deltacya Deltacrp derivatives of *Salmonella choleraesuis* in pigs. Infect Immun 67:4628-4636.

Kern D. 1994. Duration of immunity to *Salmonella chorereasuis* using SC-54. In: Proceedings of 25th American Association of Swine Practitioners, Chicago, Illinois, USA. p 29-33.

Kolb J, Roof M, and Burkhart K. 2001. Reduction of *Salmonella cholerasuis* contamination in pork carcasses by vaccination. In: Proceedings of 5th International Symposium on the Epidemiology and Control of Foodborne Pathogens in Pork, Heraklion-Crete, Greece. p 210-212.

Kolb J, Roof M, and Burkhart K. 2002. Reduction of *Salmonella* in carcasses using Enterisol SC-54 vaccination. In: Proceedings of 17th International Pig Veterinary Society Congress, Ames, Iowa, USA. p 14.

Kramer TT, Pardon P, Marly J, and Bernard S. 1987. Conjunctival and intramuscular vaccination of pigs with a live avirulent strain of *Salmonella choleraesuis*. Am J Vet Res 48:1072-1076.

Kramer TT, Roof MB, and Matheson RR. 1992. Safety and efficacy of an attenuated strain of *Salmonella choleraesuis* for vaccination of swine. Am J Vet Res 53:444-448.

Letellier A, Messier S, Lessard L, and Quessy S. 2000. Assessment of various treatments to reduce carriage of *Salmonella* in swine. Can J Vet Res 64:27-31.

Lumsden JS, Wilkie BN, and Clarke RC. 1991. Resistance to fecal shedding of salmonellae in pigs and chickens vaccinated with an aromatic-dependent mutant of *Salmonella typhimurium*. Am J Vet Res 52:1784-1787.

Maes D, Gibson K, Trigo E, Saszak A, Grass J, Carlson A, and Blaha T. 2001. Evaluation of cross-protection afforded by a *Salmonella choleraesuis* vaccine against *Salmonella* infections in pigs under field conditions. Berl Munch Tierarztl Wschr 114:339-341.

Neubauer A, and Roof MB. 2005. Enterisol SC-54 cross-protection against a virulent *S. typhimurium* strain. In: Proceedings of American Association of Swine Veterinarian, Kansas City, Missouri, USA. p 245-248.

Roesler U, Heller P, Altrock T, Arnold T, Lehmann J, Waldmann KH, Truyen U, and Hansel A. 2004a. Reduction of *Salmonella* by vaccination of sows using herd-specific inactivated vaccines but not by antibiotic treatment. In: Proceedings of 18th International Pig Veterinary Society Congress, Hamberg, Germany. p 666.

Roesler U, Marg H, Schroder I, Mauer S, Arnold T, Lehmann J, Truyen U, and Hensel A. 2004b. Oral vaccination of pigs with an invasive gyrA-cpxA-rpoB *Salmonella typhimurium* mutant. Vaccine 23:595-603.

Roof MB, and Doitchinoff DD. 1995. Safety, Efficacy, and Duration of Immunity Induced in Swine by Use of An Avirulent Live *Salmonella choleraesuis*-Containing Vaccine. Am J Vet Res 56:39-44.

Sargeant JM, Rajic A, Amezcua MDR, and Waddell L. 2005. A guide to conducting systematic reviews in agri-food public health. In: http://www.fsrrn.net.

Springer S, Lindner T, Steinbach G, and Selbitz HJ. 2001. Investigation of the efficacy of a genetically-stabile live *Salmonella typhimurium* vaccine for use in swine. Berl Munch Tierarztl Wschr 114:342-345.

CEVA Matrix Technology™ : A new alternative for pig medicated premixes

Domps P.*, Zanichelli C., Crambert G.

CEVA Santé Animale, BP 126, 33501, Libourne, France

*corresponding author: pierre.domps@ceva.com

Abstract

Specific problems are posed by medicated premixes : stability of the active ingredient, homogeneity of the medicated premix distribution in the feed and cross-contamination due to dust emission. These problems can have two major consequences: a treatment failure and a risk for human health with selection of resistant strains. CEVA Matrix Technology™, an exclusive CEVA Santé Animale manufacturing process, matches all expectations of an effective and modern medicated premix. CEVA Matrix Technology™ consists of an innovative protective granulation technology. Most non-protected medicated premixes available in the market do not provide good stability and may not reach efficient concentration as the active ingredient is not protected enough. First, the CEVA Matrix Technology™ guarantees that the active ingredient is protected during manufacture (pelleting) and storage of the medicated feed without altering its bioavailability. Secondly, the particle size of CEVA Matrix Technology™ premixes is similar to the feed in which it is to be blended. Therefore the active ingredient is mixed homogeneously into the feed and remains homogeneous even after transportation and storage. This perfect mixability ensures the right active ingredient concentration and dosage in feed every time. Consequently, treatment failure resulting from unequal dosage distribution of the active ingredient in the feed is considerably limited. Thirdly, CEVA Matrix Technology™ guarantees that the premix does not release dust. Therefore, it reduces risks such as cross contamination between two medicated feed batches in mills and inhalation of antimicrobial by users. It protects the workforce and reduces the risk of selecting resistant strains. This article validates all these points by comparing a tiamulin medicated premix manufactured with the CEVA Matrix Technology™ and some non-protected tiamulin.

Introduction

CEVA Matrix Technology™, an innovative protective granulation technology, brings a solution to the specific problems posed by medicated premixes : stability of the active ingredient, homogeneity of the medicated premix distribution in the feed and cross-contamination due to dust emission. The objectives of this study are to compare stability, homogeneity and dust emission of a tiamulin premix (Tiamvet®) manufactured with Matrix Technology™ to others.

Materials and methods

Stability of the active ingredient:
An HPLC method was developed and validated for determination of tiamulin in creep and pelleted feed. The equipment used for the validation was an HPLC system Shimadzu LC-10 AD VP, with a diode array detector. Through a reverse phase column and a mixture of the appropriate solvent, it is possible to separate the substance from the other components present in the feed and make the quantitative determination by comparing the peak area of the sample with the peak area of a reference solution with a known content of Tiamulin hydrogen fumarate. The chromatographic conditions are listed below:

- Column: Hypersil ODS, 250 x 4 mm, 5 µm.
- Mobile phase: (MeOH/ACN/1% ammonium carbonate) (50/30/20) (V/V/V)
     Control pH at 8.9 ± 0.1
- Flow rate: 1.0 ml/min
- U.V. detection: 250 nm
- Injected volume: 20 µl

Granulometry :
In order to evaluate the "in feed homogeneity" the particle size of three different medicated premixes was measured. The equipment used was an Octagon test sieve shaker.

The method is described below :

   - Weigh about 100 g of the product under test and transfer above a series of nine sieves with different aperture sizes. Start sieving with Octagon test sieve shaker.
   - Operative condition :
Accommodate the selected sieves (n° 9) of 200 mm diameter and the receiver on the centre of shaker location and stack them on the top of the receiver.

Place the clamp plate on the top of the sieve located the two holes over an hexagonal rods.

Tighten with two handles firmly.

Start shaker vibration for 10 minutes.

   - Results:
After the test, collect and weigh the amount settled on each sieve and calculated the % of the total deposited amount.

Dust emission
The total powders are determined through dust meter Heubach of specific type II for the fine powder tenor (fraction deposited on the filter less than 10 µm) in granular powders.
   - Principle of the method
The test simulates the conditions that are taken place in the course of the production of feeds (weighing, mixing, transport, handling) and represents an objective method for the measurement of fine powders in granular powders. The product (100 g) is placed in the stress room that turns at 30 r.p.m. and it is stirred from a set of rotary shovels. In the same room, air is introduced, generated from a calibrated vacuum pump (standard flow 20 litre/minute for 5 minutes) and the produced powders are spread along the system. The particles of greater dimensions are separated to level of the first elbow and the subsequent rooms of separation, while those finer (under to the 10 µm) are deposited on the terminal filter in glass fibre ($\varnothing$ 50 mm).
   - Calculation
The total powders are calculated according to the following formula:
 mg/filter = weight of the filter in mg (after test) – weight of the filter in mg (time zero)
The formula expresses the mg/filter for 100 g of product.

Results and Discussion
Stability study
The two products performed differently in pelleted feed (Figure 1). After three months of storage, active ingredient concentration for the tiamulin without Matrix Technology™ is 60 % of the initial

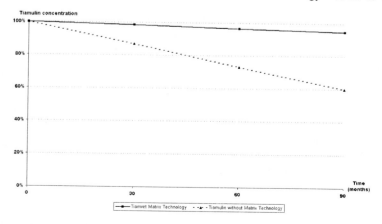

Figure 1 Stability of tiamulin in pelleted feed (t° 25°C / RM 60 %)

active ingredient concentration. With the protection of the Matrix Technology™, the active ingredient concentration remains stable even after three months of storage (95 % of the initial value).

Homogeneity study
In order to ensure a good homogenisation, the main criterion is the granulometry of medicated premixes. Actually, the simplest solution to ensure effective homogenisation of the active ingredient in the feed and to avoid demixing is to use a medicated premix whose particles are the same size as those of the swine feed. A previous study, conducted by CEVA Santé Animale on fifteen batches of swine feed from seven different countries has shown that more than 70% of the swine feed consists of grains whose size is higher than 300 μm with an average grain size of 700 to 900 μm. On the three tiamulin premixes tested, the tiamulin premix with Matrix Technology™ is the only one with a huge percentage of grains whose size is higher than 300 μm (Table 1).

Grain size (μm)	< 45	45-63	63-90	90-100	100-150	150-300	> 300
Tiamvet®	0%	0%	0%	0%	0%	1%	**99%**
Product A	10%	36.4%	22.1%	13.4%	5.6%	8.4%	**4.1%**
Product B	0.3%	4.5%	6%	10.9%	19.5%	46%	**12.8%**

Table 1 Granulometry of three tiamulin premixes

A second granulometry study with higher grain size tested has be done on the tiamulin premix with Matrix Technology™. The results show that the grain size of a tiamulin premix with Matrix Technology™ is consistent with the specific granulometry of swine feed (Figure 2). We can therefore conclude that this medicated premix will have a good homogenisation in swine feed.

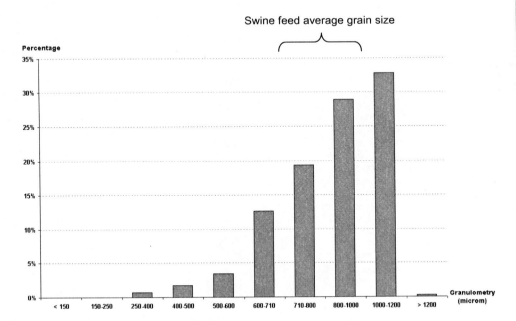

Figure 2 Granulometry of a tiamulin premix with Matrix Technology™

Dust emission study

The dust emission of the three tiamulin premixes is radically different (Figure 3). The tiamulin premix with Matrix Technology™ emits 0.1 mg of dust for 100 g of product, making it a medicated premix with a very low level of dust emission. The two other products tested emit respectively 4326 and 9276 more dust, making them a medicated premix with a very high level of dust emission and with the inherent risks of cross-contamination and of inhalation of active ingredient by the operators.

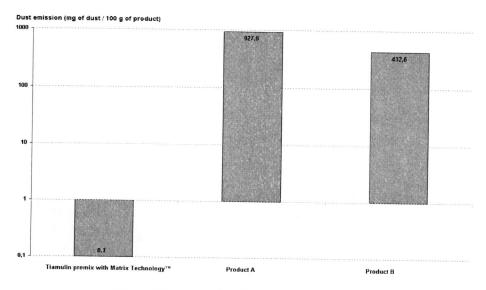

Figure 3 Dust emission of three tiamulin premixes

Conclusion

CEVA Matrix Technology™ is a global solution to answer all the problems posed by medicated premixes :

- very good stability of the active ingredient during manufacture (pelleting) and storage of the medicated feed (without altering the bioavailability)
- particle size similar to the feed in which it is to be blended allowing a perfect mixability
- very low dust level emission (< 2 mg / 100 g of product)

Consequently, CEVA Matrix Technology™ enables to :

- avoid treatment failure due to incorrect active ingredient concentration
- limit the risk of selecting resistant strains due to low active ingredient concentration
- protect the workforce (no dust emission)
- avoid cross-contamination of batches

Interaction of *Bifidobacterium animalis* Subspecies *lactis* (Bb12) and *Salmonella typhimurium* in Continuous-Flow Chemostatic Culture

Harvey, R.[1][*], Genovese, K.[1], Droleskey, R.[1], Andrews, K.[1], Solano-Aguilar, G.[2]

[1]Food and Feed Safety Research Unit, SPARC, ARS, USDA, 2881 F&B Road, College Station, TX 77845 USA, [2]Beltsville Human Nutrition Research Center, ARS, USDA, Beltsville, MD 20705 USA, *Corresponding author: harvey@ffsru.tamu.edu

Abstract

A commercially available probiotic, *Bifidobacterium animalis* subspecies *lactis* (Bb12) was adapted to and maintained in a continuous-flow chemostat culture. We evaluated the growth characteristics and interactive effects of Bb12 and *Salmonella typhimurium* (St) when cultivated singly or together. When the continuous-flow culture of Bb12 was challenged with 10^4 to 10^7 CFU/ml of St, the St was eliminated within 24 h. This was replicated 3 times. Because the pH of the Bb12 was 4.5, it appeared that St elimination was due to the reduced pH. In a second study, St was grown in pure culture and the pH reduced to 4.5. Although still present, St concentrations dropped to unculturable levels within 28 h. In a third study, the pH of the Bb12 culture was maintained at pH 5.6 by means of a continuous drip of NaOH and challenged with St. Although at reduced concentrations (10^3 CFU/ml), the St remained in the chemostat until day 9 when the drip was discontinued. By day 14, the St was eliminated. It is apparent in these *in vitro* studies that Bb12 has antagonistic properties against St and it is possible that there could be some *in vivo* applications of Bb12 against St.

Introduction

Probiotics have been defined as live microorganisms that may beneficially affect the host (following ingestion) by improving the balance of the intestinal microflora. Some of the most commonly used probiotics contain lactic-acid-producing bacteria such as *Lactobacillus* and *Bifidobacterium* species (Lin, 2003). Among other effects, probiotics are purported to normalize the intestinal microflora, to reduce gut colonization by potential pathogens, to treat or prevent various types of diarrhea, to decrease the symptoms of irritable bowel syndrome and inflammatory bowel disease, and to modulate immune function (Lin, 2003).

Bifidobacterium are some of the earliest colonizers of the gastrointestinal (GI) tract of human infants and play an important role in the development of the permanent microflora. Many species of *Bifidobacterium* have been touted for health benefits, but *B. lactis* is probably the most commonly used. *B. lactis* conferred resistance to single or multiple oral challenges with virulent *Salmonella typhimurium* (St) in mice (Shu et al., 2000). The authors have viewed probiotics and mixtures of commensal bacteria as potential intervention strategies to increase immune function and as alternatives to antibiotics to control disease associated with enteropathogens such as *Salmonella* and enterotoxigenic *Escherichia coli* in swine (Harvey et al., 2002; Harvey et al., 2005). On the basis of the above-mentioned results of *B lactis* against St in mice (Shu et al., 2000), we hypothesized that a commercial probiotic of *Bifidobacterium animalis* subspecies *lactis* (Bb 12) might have antagonistic properties against *Salmonella* colonization in pigs. To test the potential of *in vivo* application, we decided that we must determine the *in vitro* effects of Bb12 against a swine isolate of St. The purpose of the present study was to evaluate the growth characteristics and the interactive effects of Bb12 and St when cultivated singly or together in an *in vitro* continuous-flow chemostatic model.

Materials and methods

B. animalis subspecies *lactis*. This strain of bacteria is commercially available as a probiotic (Bb12) and was obtained from Chr. Hansen, Inc. (Milwaukee, WI). A continuous-flow culture of Bb12 was adapted to Modified Reinforced Clostridia Media (MRCM), the culture established in a BioFlo 110 Fermentor (New Brunswick Scientific, Edison, NJ) using a 500 ml culture vessel with an exchange rate of 500 ml/day under anaerobic conditions. The MRCM consisted of pancreatic digest of casein (Casitone, 5.0 g/l), proteose peptone No. 3 (5.0 g/l), beef extract (10.0 g/l), yeast extract (3.0 g/l), dextrose (5.0 g/l), NaCl (5.0 g/l), soluble starch (1.0 g/l), cysteine HCl (0.5 g/l), and sodium acetate (3.0 g/l).

Salmonella typhimurium (St). A primary porcine isolate of St, obtained from the National Veterinary Service Laboratories, Ames, IA, resistant to 20 µg/ml nalidixic acid (nal) and 25 µg/ml novobiocin (nov), was selected in our laboratory as the *Salmonella* challenge strain. For the continuous culture establishment of St control cultures, a 500 ml chemostat, filled with the MRCM was inoculated with St and grown under anaerobic conditions to achieve a final concentration of approximately 1×10^5 CFU/ml. The CFU of St were determined by serial dilution in phosphate buffered saline (PBS) and spread plating on BGA that contained 20 µg/ml nal and 25 µg/ml nov and incubated at 37° C for 24 h.

CFU determination of Bb12/St following challenge.

When Bb12 and St were grown in combination, a chemostat with an established steady-state culture of Bb12 would be inoculated (challenged) with an overnight culture of St. CFU of St were determined at 30 m, 4 h, 8 h, 24 h, and 48 h after St challenge. The procedures for CFU determination were described in the previous section. If BGA plates were negative for St growth, then 2.0 ml of the chemostat medium was added to tetrathionate enrichment broth and incubated at 37° C for 48 h. No growth after 48 h was considered a negative sample.

The CFU for Bb12 were determined by anaerobic serial dilution in PBS and spread plating on PRAS Bifido Selective Agar (Anaerobe Systems, Morgan Hill, CA) followed by incubation at 37° C for 24 h in a Bactron IV Anaerobic Chamber (Sheldon Manufacturing, Inc., Cornelius, OR). Samples for Bb12 CFU determination were collected at 30 m after St inoculation and every 24 h thereafter according to the serial dilution procedures outlined above.

Experimental design.

Study A. Challenge Bb12 with St
  Replicate 1; challenge with 1×10^4 CFU/ml
  Replicate 2; challenge with 1×10^5 CFU/ml, monitor pH at challenge and 24 h post-challenge
  Replicate 3; challenge with 1×10^7 CFU/ml, monitor pH at 4, 8, and 24 h post-challenge

Study B. Effects of decreased pH on St growth.

To determine the effects of reduced pH on St growth, a chemostat that had reached a steady-state St concentration of 1×10^5 CFU/ml had concentrated HCl added every 2 h until a pH of 4.5 was reached. Serially diluted samples were streaked onto BGA, and if necessary, were enriched with tetrathionate broth. As mentioned above, a negative sample was one that was negative on BGA and had no growth after 48 h incubation in tetrathionate broth.

Study C. Effects of increased pH on St challenge of Bb12.

We hypothesized that increased pH in the chemostat could favor the colonization of St when grown in combination with Bb12. Following St challenge of an established culture of Bb12, we maintained a pH of 5.6 to 5.8 by the addition of sterile anaerobic NaOH (0.48 M) by continuous drip at a rate of approximately 82.0 ml/24 h (0.5%).

Results and Discussion

In study A, there was no growth of St on Brilliant Green Agar (BGA, Oxoid Ltd., Basingstoke, UK) at 24 h, 48 h, and 24 h post-challenge in replicates 1, 2, and 3, respectively, and were negative following enrichment. The pH of the Bb12 culture at challenge ranged from 4.42 to 4.50, before, during, and 24 h post-challenge in replicates 2 and 3.

Within 24 h in study B, St decreased from 10^6 CFU/ml at pH 5.6 to 10^3 CFU/ml at pH 4.5. By 28 h, the BGA plates were negative for St growth and continued to be negative though day 13. We continued to add hydrochloric acid (HCl) throughout 168 h (d 7), but at 192 h (d 8) we discontinued. The pH then slowly returned to 5.6 by day 13. Although BGA plates continued to be negative during this study, the tetrathionate-broth-enriched samples were consistently positive throughout day 13 when we terminated the study.

In study C, by 24 h post-challenge, St concentrations were 10^4 CFU/ml whereas Bb12 was at 10^8 CFU/ml. By day 9 when we turned off the continuous drip of sodium hydroxide (NaOH), the counts were 10^3 CFU/ml for St and 10^5 CFU/ml for Bb12. The pH went from 5.7 on day 9 to 4.7 on day 10 while the counts were 10^1 CFU/ml for St and 10^4 CFU/ml for Bb12. Beginning on day 11 and continuing through day 13, the sample for St was negative on BGA plates, but positive in tetrathionate broth. On day 14, the tetrathionate-enriched samples were negative for St, the pH was at 4.4, and the Bb12 was 10^7 CFU/ml (See Figure). The study was terminated.

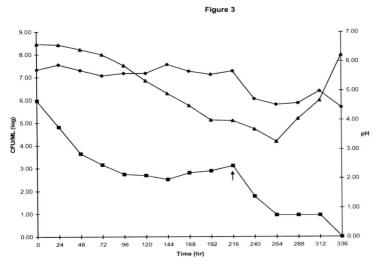

Figure 3

Figure. Study C: Interaction of Bb12 (▲) and St (■) when grown simultaneously in continuous -flow culture with pH (♦) at 5.6 to 5.8. pH was adjusted by continuous drip of NaOH. At 216 h (see arrow), the drip was discontinued.

In study A, Bb12 produced dramatic reductions of St in the chemostat. Because Bb12 produces lactic acid and the culture consistently maintained the pH at 4.42 to 4.50, we assumed that the elimination of St was due to the lowered pH. To test this hypothesis, we then conducted study B with St alone in a reduced pH environment. While the decrease in pH slowed the growth and reduced the CFU to a non-culturable level, pH alone did not sterilize the chemostat. Although pH appeared to have a great influence on St colonization, the results from this study showed that it is not the only factor in elimination. Hence, we designed study C in which increased pH should favor the growth of St and offset the acid-producing properties of Bb12. Study C suggested that Bb12 had some bacteriostatic properties against St because at 24 h post-challenge, St was 10^4 CFU/ml and by day 9 the CFU was 10^3. During that same time frame, Bb12 concentrations were also decreasing. Following the removal of the NaOH drip, Bb12 concentrations went up to 10^7 CFU/ml and St was eliminated from the chemostat.

While not conclusive, these results suggest that Bb12 may have some antagonistic properties against St. Our results are similar to another *in vitro* study (Bielecka et al., 1998) in which *B. animalis* was bactericidal to *S. enteritidis*. *B. lactis* has been shown to enhance resistance to oral challenge of mice with *S. typhimurium*, including a ten-fold survival rate in treated mice (Shu et al., 2000).

While the authors are not suggesting that *in vitro* data can be directly applied to *in vivo* conclusions, there are *in vivo* studies that show *B. lactis* (Bb12) added to infant formula had ameliorating effects on GI tract disease (Weizman, 2005), that consumption of *B. bifidum* (Bb12) increases leukocyte phagocytosis in human subjects (Schiffrin et al., 1995), that ingestion of *B. lactis* can enhance natural immunity in elderly human subjects (Arunachalam et al., 2000), and that probiotics such as *Bifidobacterium* have a major impact on the development and maintenance of immune function (Isolauri et al., 2001).

We do not know the mechanism of action for the antagonism of Bb12 on St, but it is known that early colonization of the GI tract by commensal bacteria can competitively exclude enteropathogens such as *Salmonella* and *Escherichia coli*. It has been said that commensals reduce pathogen colonization by competition for nutrients, competition for receptor sites, stimulation of the immune system, and production of bacteriocidal products such as bacteriocins (Harvey et al., 2005).

We conclude that Bb12 can eliminate St in a continuous-flow chemostat culture and although it appears primarily due to reduced pH that inhibits St replication, our results suggest that other factors may play a role in St reduction. It is possible that there may be *in vivo* applications of Bb12 against St.

References

Arunachalam, K., et al., 2000. Enhancement of natural immune function by dietary consumption of *Bifidobacterium lactis* (HN019). *European Journal of Clinical Nutrition*, 54, 262-267.

Bielecka, M., et al., 1998. Interaction of *Bididobacterium* and *Salmonella* during associated growth. *International Journal of Food Microbiology*, 45, 151-155.

Harvey, R., et al., 2005. Use of competitive exclusion to control enterotoxigenic strains of *Escherichia coli* in weaned pigs. *Journal of Animal Science*, 83(E Suppl), E44-E47.

Harvey, R., et al., 2002. In vitro inhibition of *Salmonella enterica* serovars Choleraesuis and Typhimurium, *Escherichia coli* F-18, and *Escherichia coli* O157:H7 by a recombined porcine continuous-flow competitive exclusion culture. *Current Microbiology* 45, 226-229.

Isolauri, R., et al., 2001. Probiotics: Effects on immunity. *American Journal of Clinical Nutrition*, 73(Suppl), 444S-450S.

Lin, D.C. (2003). Probiotics as functional foods. Nutrition in Clinical Practice, 18, 497-506.

Schiffrin, E., et al., 1995. Immunomodulation of human blood cells following the ingestion of lactic acid bacteria. *Journal of Dairy Science*, 78, 491-497.

Shu, Q., et al., 2000. Dietary *Bifidobacterium lactis* (HN019) enhances resistance to oral *Salmonella typhimurium* infection in mice. *Microbiology and Immunology*, 44, 213-222.

Weizman, Z., et al., 2005. Effect of a probiotic infant formula on infections in child care centers: Comparison of two probiotic agents. *Pediatrics*, 115, 5-9.

Sources of salmonella contamination in pig processing

James, S. J. *[1], Purnell, G. [1], Wilkin, C.-A. [2], Howell, M. [3], James, C. [1]

[1] Food Refrigeration and Process Engineering Research Centre (FRPERC), University of Bristol, Churchill Building, Langford, BS40 5DU, UK.
[2] Division of Farm Animal Science (DFAS), University of Bristol, Churchill Building, Langford, BS40 5DU, UK.
[3] Food Standards Agency (FSA), Aviation House, 125 Kingsway, London, WC2B 6NH, UK.
* corresponding author: steve.james@bristol.ac.uk

Abstract

The quantification of current state of the art on alternative/novel pig slaughtering and processing procedures and pork decontamination was the initial aim of a project to reduce salmonella in pig processing for the UK Foods Standards Agency. To achieve these aims a survey of current commercial processing conditions was carried out, the published literature reviewed, and a review performed of technology from other sectors.

The main consensus of industrial opinion gleaned from the plant visits suggests that contamination comes from the live animals and the main cross-contamination issues in the abattoir are in the lairage, some scald tanks and polishers. The main cross-contamination issues in the evisceration line are considered to be in handling and inadvertent gut rupture.

In the published data there is general agreement that the main source of bacterial contamination on a meat carcass is from the animals themselves. There are comments in the literature that 70% of carcasses contaminated with salmonella are derived from carrier pigs and the remaining 30% are from cross-contamination from other sources. The main sources of cross-contamination are the skin and hooves of the animal; faeces voided by the animals; bacteria derived from the opened gut; and soil, dust, etc., carried to the killing-floor. Some researchers, however, believe that a degree of the initial contamination may be airborne. There is conflicting evidence as to the role and importance of different processing steps.

The results from all these studies have been analysed and a number of brainstorming sessions carried out to identify

1. The processes that are the main source of salmonellae contamination, and;
2. Areas where further work is likely to have the largest impact.

Survey of literature

In the published data there is general agreement that the main source of bacterial contamination on a meat carcass is from the animals themselves. At the point of slaughter, the musculature of the animal is effectively sterile and initial contamination occurs on the exposed surface. There are comments in the literature that 70% of carcasses contaminated with salmonella were derived from carrier pigs and the remaining 30% were from cross-contamination. The main sources of cross-contamination are the skin and hooves of the animal; faeces voided by the animals; bacteria derived from the opened gut; and soil, dust, etc., carried to the killing-floor. Two main routes of contamination have been identified:

1. Deposition of bacteria scattered in the air and splashing with contaminated faeces, etc.
2. Contact with dirty instruments, hands, clothes, etc.

Most authorities consider contact to be the primary route. Some, however, believe that a degree of the initial contamination may be airborne.

The difficulty of identifying the importance of different processing stages on contamination of specific bacteria, such as salmonella, may be illustrated by the study reported by Thorberg & Engvall (2001). Five Swedish pig abattoirs were visited six times, and sampling was done repeatedly at specific points in the slaughter line during the day. Both sampling of pork carcasses and the slaughterhouse environment was carried out. During the study, a total of 3,388 samples from the five slaughterhouses were collected and cultured for Salmonella. All of the samples were culture negative for Salmonella.

A number of authors recommend the separation of incoming pigs from salmonella-positive and -negative herds, and separate slaughtering, preferably on separate days (Wong *et al.*, 2002). Animals can become clearly become contaminated externally and infection spread during transport to the abattoir and during lairage. Many authors recommend withholding feed for 3-6 hours before transport to reduce faecal excretion, and limiting the time in transit and lairage to reduce spread of entero-pathogens (e.g. salmonella) (Galland, 1998).

It is clear that the sides and floor of the killing area can accumulate dirt, faeces and body fluids. Immediately after stunning carcasses are allowed to fall onto the floor or into a chute. The floor or sides of the chute may act as a means of transferring contamination. Few actual studies on pork have identified how important this contamination may be. One of the few (Bolton *et al.*, 2002) showed it to be the most significant stage of production in relation to the incidence of salmonella spp.

The speed and efficiency of stunning and bleeding may effect the contamination of pig carcasses. The more rapid and efficient it is, the quicker the blood circulation will stop and thus potentially there will be less risk for the scald water entering the system, via the cut, to reach all the tissues (Troeger, 1994).

Washing animals before scalding to reduce soiling of scald water has been recommended by a number of authors, but studied by surprisingly few. The dehairing process, whatever range of steps it uses, currently has been solely designed from a non-microbial product quality standpoint. Process steps and conditions are designed to facilitate the removal of hair and produce a rind with the required organoleptical properties. Plugging or bagging the anus to prevent the escape of faeces into scalding water, or during dehairing, scraping or polishing, has been recommended in a number of reports (Richmond, 1991; Wong *et al.*, 2002). Similarly tying the oesophagus to prevent spillage from the rumen would appear to be a potential method of reducing contamination during these processes. Neither of these operations have been widely studied. In general, a reduction in bacteria counts is achieved during the scalding operation. However, the subsequent dehairing operation often leads to recontamination and higher bacteria numbers. This appears to be due to faeces and gut fluid voided from the carcass during the operation and by cross-contamination of this detritus as it accumulates and is recirculated in the machine (Gill & Bryant, 1993; Korsak *et al.*, 2003). It has been recommended that the water in dehairing machinery should be at 60-62°C to reduce carcass contamination (ICMSF, 1998). However, it has also been reported that using water at about 60°C in the dehairing machines may cause the skins of carcasses to become flaccid and prone to being torn by the dehairing flails (Gill & Bryant, 1993). Chemically treating the water has also been recommended by some to reduce bacterial build up in the water.

Singeing has been identified by many studies as the most important operation for reducing microbial contamination, including salmonella. It is the last operation, after scalding, that actually reduces contamination. However, the exact effects of the operating conditions (temperature, treatment, duration etc.) on bacterial reduction appear to be unknown. There appears to be evidence that bacteria may be protected in folds, orifices or hair follicles and be spread in the subsequent polishing operation, but this is not clear. In contrast polishing has been identified by many reports as the most important operation for the recontamination of pork carcasses following the reduction that occurs during singeing. However, is it not clear whether it has a particularly important role in salmonella recontamination. Polishing systems are very hard to clean and by the end of the day they can be transferring large numbers of bacteria to the surface of the carcass.

Pre-evisceration washing with hot water appears to be successful at reducing microbial contamination. A 20 s deluge wash at 85°C has been reported to reduce the levels of spoilage organisms and *E. coli* on pork carcasses by 2.5 log_{10} cfu cm^{-2} (Gill *et al.*, 1995). It is not clear what proportion of salmonella contamination on a carcass are from surface bacteria that have survived on the surface since polishing and what proportion arise during evisceration. Some authors have stated that evisceration is the single most important source of contamination. Published data appears to indicate that evisceration does not have a significant effect on total aerobic bacterial numbers. However, it does appear to have a significant effect on Enterobacteriaceae and salmonella numbers. In reviewing evisceration, Berends *et al.* (1996, 1997) concluded that approximately 60-90% of the total carcass contamination with *Salmonella* spp. occurs during evisceration, while splitting, fat trimming and meat inspection together may contribute between 5-35%. However, other authors contend that provided the correct precautions are taken – the anus and oesophagus are closed and the gut is not punctured – evisceration will cause little contamination.

Berends *et al.* (1998) came to the conclusion that the "most efficient and cost-effective way of reducing the 'Salmonella problem' entailed by the consumption of pork would be to decontaminate carcasses" pre-chilling providing "the entire production chain strictly adheres to GMP principles". Although chilling is not usually considered a method of decontamination, it does have an important role in reducing bacterial multiplication. In many cases, intervention treatments are believed to extend the lag phase of the bacteria of interest. If the surface temperature of the meat is then cooled to below the organism's minimum growth temperature before the lag phase expires, then bacterial growth will not occur.

Key areas for further work
In parallel to the literature review a large survey current practices and operations in UK pig abattoirs was carried out. Some details of the results of the industrial survey are presented in this symposium (Tinker *et al.*, 2007). However, in addition at all the abattoirs visited the operators were asked which of their current operations they felt were an important source of salmonella distribution and required further research or development. They were asked to rank them as of high, medium or low importance. A similar exercise was carried out on data from the literature review and a composite table produced to guide the next stage of the investigations (Table 4).

Table 4.   Rating (H = High, M = medium and L = low) of importance of an operation as a contamination route and worthy of further research.

	Are the following an important contamination route and/or worthy of more research?	Literature	Industry
1	Current lairage design and operation	H	H
2	Escape of faeces	H	H
3	Current polishing processes	H	H
4	Existing evisceration processes	H	H
5	Dehairing processes	M	M
6	Lack of decontamination interventions pre-evisceration	M	M
7	Current late removal of pigs head	H	L
8	Lack of decontamination interventions pre-chill	M	M
9	Current operation of derinder	M	M
10	Lack of pre-scald wash	M	M
11	Cleanliness of grambling tables	H	L
12	Current scalding operations	M	L
13	Current sticking operations	M	L
14	Current chilling operations	M	L

Work required
All the data gathered was analysed at a number of brainstorming sessions and the following areas in chronological order of processing that were felt to have the most potential identified:

Scheduling:
        A rapid method of identifying salmonella-positive herds is required so that +ive and –ive groups can be separated.
Lairage:
        Develop an automatic lairage floor scrubber, tactilely guided by walls.
Scalding, singeing and polishing:
        Investigate 100°C steam scald which would use full latent heat potential of steam.
        Investigate ultrasonic water baths for a combined dehair and scald.

Develop a non-damaging and easy to implement anus bunging systems.
Investigate faeces sucking to clear rectal passage before scald.
Investigate application of alternative dehairing concepts abrasion, epilation, etc.
Investigate a full singe dehairing process.
Investigate replacing flail/whip type wet polisher with high pressure water jets.
Evisceration:
Development of a non-damage and easy to implement throat bunging system.
Develop local washing/cleaning techniques for pertinent areas on the carcass surface (such as belly opening cut line, or around anus, etc).
Interventions:
Develop heat based pasteurization methods for eviscerated, split carcasses.
Investigate final toast on outer surface immediately prior to chilling.

Work is now ongoing in many of the areas identified both in the laboratory and with industrial producers to minimise salmonella contamination of pig carcasses and subsequent food poisoning.

References

BERENDS, B.R., URLINGS, H.A.P., SNIJDERS, J.M.A., VAN KNAPEN, F., 1996. Identification and quantification of risk factors in animal management and transport regarding *Salmonella* spp. in pigs. *International Journal of Food Microbiology*, 30, 37-53.

BERENDS, B.R., VAN KNAPEN, F., SNIJDERS, J.M.A., MOSSEL, D.A.A., 1997. Identification and quantification of risk factors regarding *Salmonella* spp. on pork carcasses. *International Journal of Food Microbiology*, 36 (2-3), 199-206.

BERENDS, B.R., VAN KNAPEN, F., MOSSEL, D.A.A., BURT, S.A., SNIJDERS, J.M.A., 1998. Impact on human health of Salmonella spp. on pork in The Netherlands and the anticipated effects of some currently proposed control strategies. *International Journal of Food Microbiology*, 44, 219-229.

BOLTON, D.J., PEARCE, R.A., SHERIDAN, J.J, BLAIR, I.S., MCDOWELL, D.A., HARRINGTON, D., 2002. Washing and chilling as critical control points in pork slaughter hazard analysis and critical control point (HACCP) systems. *Journal of Applied Microbiology*, 92, 893-902.

GALLAND, J.C., 1998. Prevention of contamination during slaughter. *Revue Scientifique et Technique de l'Office Internationale des Epizooties*, 16 (2), 395-402.

GILL, C.O., BRYANT, J. ,1993. The presence of Escherichia coli, Salmonella and Campylobacter in pig carcass dehairing equipment. *Food Microbiology*, 10 (4) 337-344.

GILL, C.O., MCGINNIS, D.S., BRYANT, J., CHABOT, B., 1995. Decontamination of commercial, polished pig carcasses with hot water. *Food Microbiology*, 12(2) 143-149.

ICMSF, 1998. *Microorganisms in Foods 6: Microbial Ecology of Food Commodities*. Blackie Academic and Professional, London.

THORBERG, B.M., ENGVALL, A., 2001. Incidence of salmonella in five Swedish slaughterhouses. *Journal of Food Protection*, 64 (4), 542-545.

TINKER, D.B., DODD, C.E.R., RICHARDS, P., JAMES, S.J., JAMES, C., WILKIN, C-A., BURFOOT, D., HOWELL, M., PURNELL, G., 2007. Assessment of processes and operating conditions in UK pork abattoirs. *Proceedings of Safepork*.

RICHMOND, M., 1991. *The Microbiological safety of food - Part II*. Report of the Committee on the Microbiological Safety of Food, HMSO, London.

TROEGER, K., 1994. Evaluating hygiene risks during slaughtering. *Fleischwirtschaft*, 74 (6), 624-626.

WONG, D., HALD, T., VAN DER WOLF, P.J., SWANENBURG, M., 2002. Epidemiology and control measures for salmonella in pigs and pork. *Livestock Production Science*, 76 (3), 215-222.

Effect of mash feed on swine intestinal microflora and non-specific immune response.

Letellier A. [1]*, Collazos J.A[2]., Ménard J[3]., Quessy S[1].

[1]Faculté de Médecine Vétérinaire de l'Université de Montréal, 3200 Sicotte, J2S 7C6, St-Hyacinthe, Canada.
[2] University of Léon, 24071 León,Spain
[3] F. Ménard Inc., 251 route 235, Ange-Gardien, Québec, J0E 1E0, Canada.
*corresponding author : ann.letellier@umontreal.ca

Abstract

Pelleting of feed was recommended in the past to reduce the risk of introduction of *Salmonella* in swine herds. However it was shown more recently that consumption of pelleted feed was associated with an increased probability of seropositivity. Furthermore, several studies showed that the prevalence of *Salmonella* is decreased when mash feed is used. The objective of this study was to evaluate the effect of mash feed as a pre-harvest intervention strategy to prevent *Salmonella* colonization, to modify of intestinal microflora and to stimulate of the immune system in swine. Two experimental groups of 45 and 43 piglets were given respectively conventional corn-based pelleted feed or mash feed from 10 weeks of age to slaughter. Rectal swabs and blood samples were taken periodically from each pig. Fecal swabs were cultured for the presence of *Salmonella* while a semi-quantitative evaluation of various fecal bacterial populations was also done. Phagocytosis rates of FITC marked *Salmonella* using whole blood of both groups of animals were evaluated by flow cytometry as an indirect measurement of non-specific immune response. At slaughter, mesenteric lymph nodes (MLN) were collected and cultured for *Salmonella* and an evaluation of presence of stomach ulcera or hyperkerotasis was done for each group. Although prevalence of *Salmonella* in both groups was to low to observe difference in prevalence, our results indicated that mash feed promoted some gram positive bacterial populations in comparison to pelleted feed group. The percentages of phagocytosis by PMN in the mash feed group was higher than in the pelleted feed group. In the mash feed fed group, all stomach were normal while in the pelleted fed group, only 40% of pig stomachs were normal. These results suggest that mash feed influence bacterial content of intestine by promoting protective microbial flora; it positively affect the stomach mucosal integrity as well as it may stimulate non specific immune system of pigs.

Introduction

Salmonella infections can cause clinical and sub-clinical diseases in pig that may result in contamination of pork products. Feed had already been considered as a significant source of *Salmonella* infections in swine and can therefore potentially spread *Salmonella* to a large number of farms. For this reason, the pelleting of feed was recommended to reduce the introduction of *Salmonella* in farms during decades (Edel et al., 1974). However, it was shown more recently that pelleting of feed was associated with an increased risk of seropositivity for *Salmonella* at slaughter (Leontides et al, 2003; Lo Fo Wong et al, 2004). Jørgensen et al., 2002 showed that prevalence of *Salmonella* is decreased when coarse feeds rather than fine feeds are fed, suggesting that the stomach acts as a barrier that decreases the occurrence of pathogenic bacteria (Mikkelsen et al., 2004). Moreover, nonpelleted diets change the level of mucin secretion in the small intestine, creating conditions that decrease binding of *Salmonella* (Hedemann et al, 2005). The objective of this study was to evaluate the effect of mash feed as a pre-harvest intervention strategy to prevent *Salmonella* colonization, to modify of intestinal microflora and to stimulate of the immune system in swine

Session 4

Material and methods

Animals: Two groups (45 and 43 piglets) from six pens in the nursery unit were randomly selected (three pens each group) and the animals were identified individually. Piglets were then moved to the fattening unit and each group was located in two different fattening units. Piglets (20-25 kg, approximately 10 weeks of age) of each group were placed randomly in three pens. The fist sampling was performed in the nursery and all piglets were tested in bacteriology individually. The next samplings were done in the fattening units. Randomly, 80 fecal samples (40 each group) and 40 blood samples (20 each group) were taken. The fecal samples were taken by rectal swabs. Two different blood samples were taken by animal: with heparin to test phagocytosis rates and without anticoagulant to obtain serum. In the nursery, animals were feed with the same feed, while in the fattening units one group received commercial pelleted feed (PF) and the other group received commercial mash feed (MF) (most of particles had a size larger than 1000 μm). Management and housing conditions were the same for each group of pigs.

Bacteriological culture: Rectal swabs and MLN were incubated in 9 ml (BWP) at 37°C for 24h. 0,1ml of culture of pre-enrichment was transferred to 9, 9 ml of RV broth and incubated at 41,5°C for 24h. Then, 10 μl of the selective enrichment media was inoculated on BGS containing novobiocin at 20μg/ml and incubated for 24 h at 37°C. Pooled fecal samples from pens (25g) was placed into 225ml de BWP and for feed samples, 100g were put on 900ml BWP, and also incubated for 24 h at 37°C. The selective enrichment was done with two selective media (TBG and RV broth); 1ml was transferred to TBG and 0,1 ml to RV and incubated at 41,5°C for 24h. Finally, 10 μl were plated into BGS with 20μg/ml at 37°C for 24h. Three suspected colonies by plate were tested for urease production and for typical reaction on Triple sugar iron media, and the typical colonies were tested by slide agglutination with polyvalent O-antiserum (Poly A1-Vi, Difco).

Serological status: Salmonella seroprevalence was evaluated with the Diakit Salmonella-ELISA test (Maxivet Inc, Québec, Canada) on 40 sera, 20 from each group, on first sampling and last sampling.

Ulcera and Hyperketarosis evaluation: For each slaughtered pig, the stomach was evaluated and signs of hyperketarosis and ulcera were noted (normal stomach, hyperkeratosis mild or severe and light, mild or severe ulcera).

Fecal flora evaluation: The evaluation of fecal bacterial populations was done by smearing rectal swabs on glass slide with subsequent Gram staining. A total of four groups of bacterial population were evaluated depending of shape and gram stain: coccoid gram positive, coccoid gram negative, rods gram positive and rods gram negative. The evaluation was done on 5 fields at 1000 x magnification.

Phagocytosis evaluation: One ml of whole blood was incubated with a suspension (100μl) of S. Typhimurium (1-5 10^8 ufc/ml) labeled with FITC, for 1h at 37°C o at 4°C for the control. Phagocytosis was stopped by addition of ice-cold PBS. The samples were read in the flow cytometer, and the ratio of phagocytosis were obtained by subtracting the percentage of phagocytosis at 4°C from the percentage of phagocytosis obtained at 37°C. The different populations of cells were identified by their forward- scatter and side-scatter characteristics, always considering that the normal percentage of PMN was 25-40% and monocytes were 5-8%.

Results and discussion

Bacteriological and serological prevalence of salmonella: In both groups the prevalence of Salmonella (bacteriology and serology) was very low (<2,5%). In MF group, the same animal was found positive to Salmonella (group E) in the sampling 1 and 3. In PF group, Salmonella (group B) was found. All feed and pooled fecal samples from pens were negative to Salmonella. At slaughter, the prevalence of Salmonella in MLN was 0% in MF group and 20% in PF group (Salmonella group B).

Ulcera and Hyperketarosis evaluation: In the MF group, all stomachs were normal while in the PF group, only 40% of pig stomach were normal: 20% were noted as having hyperkeratosis signs and 40% of pig stomach had ulcera, indicating that the MF positively affect the stomach mucosal integrity.

Fecal flora evaluation: There were differences observed between groups. In the MF, the populations of Gram positive bacteria are higher than in the PF group. The populations of Gram negative bacteria increased through samplings 1 to 4 while the populations of Gram negative bacteria decreased. In the MF group, changes were observed in different subgroups of bacteria. The populations of Gram positive coccoids were very important in the first sampling, but decreased in the next sampling. Overall, the populations of Gram positive rods generally increased over time with the different samplings in MF group. This effect was not apparent in the PF group. The populations of Gram-negative rods in both groups were stable through different sampling. While the populations of Gram negative coccoids decreased slightly.

Figure 1. Evaluation of bacterial microflora in feces of swine fed with different diets (**MF: mash feed** or **PF: pelleted feed**).

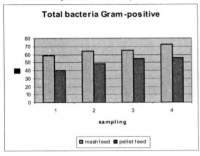 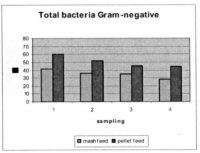

Similar results were obtained by Miskkelsen et al, 2004. They studied the effect of different diets on the populations of acid lactic bacteria and coliform bacteria. The population of acid lactic bacteria of the animals fed with a coarse feed (MF) was higher than the population of the pigs fed with a PF. On other hand, the number of coliforms in pigs fed with coarse feed (MF) was lower than in pigs fed with PF, the population of Gram positive bacteria in the group of MF was higher and the population of Gram negative bacteria was lower than the PF group. Letellier et al, 2000 also found that prebiotics and probiotics induced changes in the microflora and a predominantly Gram positive bacterial flora was noted in pigs supplemented with these products.

Table 1. Phagocytosis of FITC-*Salmonella Typhimurium* by swine whole-blood phagocytes

% Phagocytosis by polymorphonuclears (PMN)

sampling	Pellet feed group			Mash feed group		
	4°C	37°C	Difference	4°C	37°C	Difference
1	6,0	31,6	25,6	8,7	38,0	29,3
2	7,8	19,6	11,8	7,9	21,0	13,0
3	8,4	15,8	7,4	12,2	29,2	17,0
4	12,3	24,8	13,1	11,2	30,1	18,9

The percentage of phagocytosis by PMN in the MF group was higher than in the PF group. Neutrophils or PMN play an important role in the first step of immune and inflammatory response. Stabel et al, 2002 showed that swine infected with *S. choleraesuis*, the phagocytosis by neutrophils was increased 2 days post inoculation. Therefore, this may contribute to the establishment of a carrier status or to clinical infection in swine.

Conclusion

These results suggest that mash feed influence bacterial content of intestine by promoting protective microbial flora; it positively affect the stomach mucosal integrity as well as it may stimulate non specific immune system of pigs.

Reference

DAVIES P.R., et al. 2000. Comparison of methods for isolating Salmonella bacteria from faeces of naturally infected pigs. *Journal of Applied Microbiology.* 89 ,169.

EDEL W., et al. 1974. Salmonella in pigs on farms feeding pellets and on farms feeding meal. *Zentralbl. Bakteriol.* 226(3):314-323.

HEDEMANN MS, et al. 2005. Effect of feed particle size and feed processing on morphological characteristics in the small and large intestine of pigs and on adhesion of Salmonella enterica serovar Typhimurium DT12 in the ileum in vitro. *J Anim Sci* 83, 1554–1562

JORGENSEN, L., et al. 2002. Particle size in meal feed to slaughter pigs. Effect on productivity, Salmonella prevalence, and the gastrointestinal ecosystem. *Publication No. 580. The Natl. Comm. for Pig Prod.,* Copenhagen, Denmark.

LEONTIDES, L.S., et al. 2003. Factors associated with the serological prevalence of Salmonella entericaSalmonella enterica in Greek finishing swineherds. *Epidemiol. Infect.* 131:599-606.

LETELLIER A, et al. 2000. Assessment of various treatments to reduce carriage of Salmonella in swine. *Can J Vet Res.* 64(1):27–31

LO F.W.et al. 2004. Herd-level risk factors for subclinical Salmonella infection in European finishing-pig herds. *Prev. Vet. Med.* 62(4):253-66.

MIKKELSEN, L.L., 2004. Effects of physical properties of feed on microbial ecology and survival of Salmonella enterica serovar Typhimurium in the pig gastrointestinal tract. *Appl. Environ. Microbiol.* 70:3485–3492

STABEL T.J., et al. 2002 Neutrophil Phagocytosis Following Inoculation of *Salmonella choleraesuis* into Swine, *Veterinary Research Communications,* 26 (2), 103 - 109

Critical review of interventions against *Salmonella* in the farm-to-processing pork production continuum

Mounchili, A.[1], Rajić, A.[2], Fazil, A.[2], Sargeant J.[3], Friendship R.[1], McEwen, S.[*1]

[1]Department of Population Medicine, University of Guelph, Ontario N1G 2W1
[2]Laboratory for Foodborne Zoonoses, Public Health Agency of Canada, Guelph, Ontario N1G 3W4
[3] Department of Clinical Epidemiology and Biostatistics, McMaster University, Canada, 1200 Main St. West Hamilton, Ontario, Canada L8N 3Z5

The purpose of this study was to identify, evaluate and summarize the available scientific literature on the effectiveness of interventions against *Salmonella*, in the farm-to-processing pork production continuum, following the principles of systematic review methodology. A comprehensive computerized and hand literature search was conducted using pre-determined search terms. Publication abstracts were screened for relevance, and those retained were assessed for quality using pre-determined inclusion/exclusion criteria. Data were extracted from the publications using a structured protocol. Among 1,126 potentially relevant references, 173 were found relevant and 76 met necessary quality criteria. On-farm interventions included vaccinations, antibiotics, sodium chlorate, probiotics/competitive exclusion, acidification of feed or water, management related strategies, feed-related control, and novel strategies, e.g. bacteriophages. Eight intervention categories were identified at the transport, lairage and slaughter levels. A large heterogeneity among the studies was observed for all intervention categories precluding pooled analyses of data from individual studies. More consistent, beneficial effects in controlling *Salmonella* in swine were observed for vaccines, feeding coarse mash feeds, acidification of feed, carcass treatment with lactic acid, water, chlorine and chilling. For fermented liquid feed, antibiotics, sodium chlorate, competitive exclusion, the results were less consistent. This review also revealed the lack of studies on the effectiveness of certain bio-security practices that have been identified in observational studies as potential interventions for *Salmonella* in swine and are often recommended to swine producers, e.g. limiting visitors to the farm, changing clothes and boots for visitors. Further investigations are needed in these areas and in those that showed promising results in controlling *Salmonella*, e.g. prebiotics, probiotics, and bacteriophages. Systematic review approach provided transparent, structured and replicable format for identifying effective interventions, gaps in the current knowledge and future research needs. Furthermore, evidence-based inputs were generated for a complementary risk assessment.

*Department of Population Medicine
Ontario Veterinary College, University of Guelph
Guelph, ON, N1G 2W1, Canada
e-mail: amounchili@uoguelph.ca

Session 4

Interventions associated with feeding management practices and feed characteristics, and measures of *Salmonella* prevalence in live and slaughtered swine: A systematic review and summation of evidence

O'Connor, A.M. *[1], Denagamage, T., [1] Sargeant, J.,[2] Rajic, A[3]. McKean,. J.,[1]

[1]Department of Veterinary Diagnostic and Production Animal Medicine, College of Veterinary Medicine, Iowa State University, Ames, 50011, IA, USA.
[2]Department of Clinical Epidemiology and Biostatistics, McMaster University, 1200 Main St. W., Hamilton, L8N 3Z5, ON, Canada.
[3] Public Health Agency of Canada and University of Guelph, Canada
*corresponding author: oconnor@iastate.edu

Abstract

The aim of this review is to evaluate and summarize the evidence for associations between feeding management practices and feed characteristics, and *Salmonella* prevalence in swine, which may represent opportunities for interventions. *Salmonella* prevalence in the reviewed literature was measured either by culture or by the presence of antibodies. A systematic review of the area was conducted, the goal being to minimize the impact of bias. Systematic reviews include an assessment of the quality of studies and exclusion of studies that fail to meet standards for published material. The review evaluated evidence for an association between feed withdrawal from swine prior to slaughter, acidification of feed, heat treatment of feed, pellet vs. mash, course vs. fine grind, and wet vs. dry. A large number of intervention studies were excluded from the review because they failed to report design features designed to limit the introduction of bias such as randomization and blinding. The majority of studies included were cross sectional studies, however these failed to provide strong evidence of an association because of the potential for confounding and the failure to document a temporal association between exposure to the risk factor and the outcome. The review concluded that the strongest body of work was available for pelleted feed and dry feed, however there was still uncertainty about the situations were this association may be effective. The conclusion was that there should be a *low level of comfort* among qualified scientists that the claimed association/relationship is scientifically valid. This ranking is primarily based on moderate to low quality studies, or insufficient numbers of tested individuals or herds, resulting in a low degree of confidence that results could be extrapolated to the target population.

Zoonoses Action Plan for Salmonella in slaughter-age pigs: how will changes in sampling methods influence estimates of Salmonella?

O'Reilly, K. M.*, Hill, A., Miller, A., Snary, E., Cook, A.

Centre for Epidemiology and Risk Analysis, Veterinary Laboratories Agency – Weybridge, New Haw, Addlestone, Surrey, KT15 3NB, United Kingdom.

*corresponding author: k.o'reilly@vla.defra.gsi.gov.uk

Abstract

In June 2002 the British Pig Executive introduced the Zoonoses Action Plan (ZAP) *Salmonella* Monitoring Programme with the aim of reducing the prevalence of *Salmonella* infection in British pigs. A serological screening programme was developed where meat juice samples were collected from pigs at slaughter and tested using a mix-ELISA and herds were assigned a ZAP score from low to high on the basis of these results. We posed several questions concerning the predictive value of a ZAP score and how this may change if the frequency of sample collection were changed.

A statistical model was developed which described the different sampling strategies and the resultant ZAP score was estimated for each of the modelled farms. The model was used to assess how changing the sampling frequency would affect the ability to assign a correct ZAP score given an assumed true within-farm prevalence and how the ZAP scores may be used to predict the likely prevalence of *Salmonella* at a farm level.

The model predicted that reducing the number of samples tested had a large effect on correctly assigning herds with a medium (50-75%) meat juice prevalence but little effect on herds with a low (50%) or high (>75%) prevalence. A change in an individual farm's prevalence of infection between sampling periods is unlikely to be detected. At a national and regional level the estimated prevalence had small confidence intervals and a change of approximately 2% is likely to be detected.

Currently the ZAP scheme requires that farms in the medium or high ZAP level must act to reduce the herd ZAP score to low within a specified time or face eventual loss of their quality assured status. Thus correct ZAP classification is important. As the herd ZAP level is assigned using a rolling 3 month average, incorrect classification is less likely than if monthly ZAP scores were calculated. The requirement for a farm to stay at a high level for 11 months before incurring the penalty is a further safeguard.

Introduction

The ZAP programme involves use of a meat juice mix-ELISA (MJE) system to detect antibodies to group B and C_1 *Salmonella* in pigs (Nielsen *et al.* 1998), through surveillance of pigs sent to assured abattoirs in Great Britain. The optical density (OD) of the test is calculated using standard methods. A ratio between test and control samples of 0.25 is used to define a positive test result.

The ZAP scheme was developed to act as a tool to monitor the prevalence of *Salmonella* in pigs at slaughter in Great Britain, and to drive a reduction in prevalence (*www.bpex.org*), with the ultimate aim of providing safer meat to the consumer. For a holding to have a ZAP score, fifteen samples must be submitted for analysis per quarter. Currently a minimum of three pigs are sampled per batch, and the minimum number of batches per holding submitted for each quarter is five. A ZAP score is calculated using the MJE prevalence on a three-month rolling average and the score is assigned as follows; ZAP 1; ≤50% positive samples, ZAP 2; 50-75% positive samples, ZAP 3; ≥75% positive samples. Holdings assigned a ZAP score of 2 or 3 are required to adopt an action plan to reduce the level of *Salmonella*. If a holding is assigned to ZAP 3 for more than 11 consecutive months their assured status could be suspended. This will have a significant financial impact on the farm and it is therefore important that holdings are not incorrectly assigned a ZAP 3 score.

The objectives of this study were to explore how varying the frequency of sampling would affect the estimate of *Salmonella* prevalence. Specifically, the following questions were phrased. If the number of samples submitted from each herd per quarter were reduced;

A. What would be the impact on the likelihood that a herd were assigned the correct ZAP score?
B. What would be the predictive value of a given ZAP score – ie. if it were stated as ZAP 1, then how likely is it that the herd truly had a prevalence of <50%?
C. What would be the impact on the likelihood of detecting a reduction in prevalence within Great Britain, nationally (England, Scotland and Northern Ireland), and at a herd level?

Materials and methodology

The methodology for each objective is addressed in turn;

Objective A. A model developed by Snary *et al.* (2004) was modified. For the purposes of this paper, the estimated proportion of test positive pigs, $P_{+,i}$, was extrapolated from the known prevalence (P_H), test sensitivity and test specificity of the MJE used in the ZAP scheme, which was reported to be 0.92 and 0.93 respectively (Nielsen *et al.* (1998) and Proux *et al.* (2000)). When a batch of pigs arrives to the abattoir with a *Salmonella* prevalence (P_B), a sample (S_B) of these pigs is tested using the MJE. Multiple batches of pigs will arrive from a pig herd to an abattoir over a three-month period, where the number of pigs in each batch is denoted as $n_{B,i}$ and the total number of pigs in all batches is denoted by N_B (where $N_B = \sum n_{B,i}$). The number of these pigs with a positive MJE ($n_{+,i}$) is assumed to be binomially distributed with the number of samples corresponding to $n_{B,i}$ and the probability set as the proportion of test positive pigs $P_{+,i}$. The number of positive pigs in each batch was distributed assuming a hypergeometric distribution (Vose 2000), which accounts for sampling without replacement. From these assumptions the prevalence of MJE is assumed to be;

$$P_{MJE} = \frac{\sum_{i=1}^{N_B} Hypergeometric(S_B, n_{+,i}, n_{B,i})}{S_B N_B} \qquad (1)$$

Given that not all pigs are sampled in the ZAP sampling scheme, and the imperfect test sensitivity and test specificity, the true herd prevalence is not known. However, P_{MJE} was simulated for a range of P_H values (i.e. from P_H = 0 to P_H = 1, in steps of 0.01). For each estimate of P_{MJE} a ZAP score, $\hat{Z}$, was assigned according to the definitions described in the introduction. The values of S_B and N_B were varied to observe the change in P_{MJE} and hence $\hat{Z}$. For each incremental value of P_H, there is a corresponding true ZAP score, Z, which can be compared to the estimated ZAP score, $\hat{Z}$. The probability of assigning the correct ZAP score, P(Z= $\hat{Z}$), was estimated:

$$P(Z = \hat{Z}) = \frac{\# \text{ of iterations where } Z = \hat{Z}}{\text{total } \# \text{ of iterations for } P_H \text{ value}} \qquad (2)$$

Given a ZAP score of 1, 2 or 3, the probability that the true herd prevalence (P_H) lies within the range of each ZAP score is the sum of the number of correctly assigned ZAP scores for that range of prevalence over all iterations used in the model.

Objective B Using the same simulations described above, the ZAP scores for all iterations are stored for each value of P_H. For all simulations, the predictive value of each ZAP score is calculated by counting the number of correctly allocated ZAP scores divided by the number of iterations assigned that ZAP score.

Objective C National prevalence is defined as the proportion of positive samples submitted, irrespective of batch or holding, and gives an indication of what proportion of pigs being sent to slaughter are MJE-positive (and hence an indication of the proportion of *Salmonella*-positive pigs). The observed national MJE prevalence for a quarter (3-months) was used to estimate the national *Salmonella* prevalence. The data used were from January-March 2006 where 37961 samples were submitted, of which 8571 (23%) were positive.

To estimate the *Salmonella* prevalence of all pigs sent to the abattoir, a beta distribution (with uniform priors) was used to account for the uncertainty due to the sample size (Vose 2000), and test sensitivity and specificity were also included in the estimate. This results in the estimated *Salmonella* prevalence being symmetrically distributed. If the number of samples submitted were reduced, the estimate of prevalence may differ. Therefore, a two-sample *t*-test (Petrie and Watson 1999) was used to test the null hypothesis that reducing the number of samples tested would not significantly (P<0.05) change the estimated *Salmonella* prevalence. The prevalence within each country (England, Scotland, and Northern Ireland) was investigated in the same way.

Similar methods as described above were used to examine the estimate of herd prevalence. However the *Salmonella* prevalence estimate per holding was positively skewed as there were fewer samples submitted. Consequently a *t*-test could not be used to compare distributions and 5th and 95th percentiles of each distribution were used to estimate *Salmonella* prevalence.

Results

Objective A Simulations are shown assuming that five batches were sampled per quarter. The probability of being assigned the correct ZAP score, $P(Z = \hat{Z})$, was reasonably high (>0.75) when the prevalence was less than 0.40 (Figure 1). As the herd prevalence of *Salmonella*, P_H, approached the boundaries of a ZAP score (i.e. when P_H was 0.5 or 0.75) the probability of assigning a correct ZAP score reduced in value. When P_H was between 0.50 and 0.75 (which was equivalent to a ZAP 2 score) $P(Z = \hat{Z})$ varied from 0.4-0.75: many scores were either ZAP 1 or ZAP 3. Assuming that there was one pig sampled per batch resulted in the value of $P(Z = \hat{Z})$ being less than 0.50 for many values of P_H. As the number of pigs sampled per batch increased, the ability to estimate the correct ZAP score increased. The main difference between sampling either three or two pigs per batch was that the estimate of $P(Z = \hat{Z})$ improved at low values of P_H when three pigs were sampled per batch.

Objective B When a ZAP score of 1 was assigned, the predictive value of a ZAP score was always above 0.90 irrespective of the number of batches sampled per quarter (Figure 1). The predictive value of a ZAP 2 score was comparatively low; when 2 pigs were sampled per quarter the predictive value was 0.45. The predictive value of the ZAP score had reduced to 0.40 when 1 pig was sampled per batch: more holdings were incorrectly assigned a ZAP 2 score than correctly assigned. The predictive value of a ZAP 3 score performed better and varied from 0.75-0.80

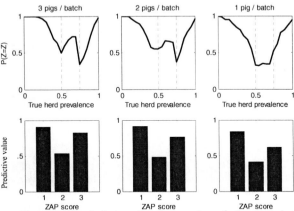

Figure 1 Effect of changing the number of pigs sampled per batch on the probability of assigning the correct ZAP score, $P(Z = \hat{Z})$ and the predictive value of the ZAP score. Five batches per quarter were assumed in the simulations.

according to the number of samples submitted.

Objective C-National level Reducing the number of pigs sampled per batch will reduce the number of submitted samples at a national and regional level by up to 33%. Reducing the number of samples submitted by 33% will not significantly ($P<0.05$) change the crude estimate of national *Salmonella* prevalence, which for January-March 2006 was 18%. A change of 2% will be detected at a national level. The *Salmonella* prevalence was estimated for each region, and 24% of samples from England were positive, 1% of samples from Scotland were positive and 5% of samples from Northern Ireland were positive. Even when considering a reduction in sample size of 33% a change in prevalence of 2% would be detected by the ZAP scheme.

Objective C-Herd level Assuming 15 pigs per quarter were sampled; a wide range in the estimated prevalence was estimated for each value of P_{MJE}. For example the 5th and 95th percentiles were 0.07 and 0.45 respectively when the true prevalence was 0.2, and 0.54 and 0.93 respectively when the true prevalence was 0.80. Therefore only a large change in prevalence, e.g. from 0.2 to 0.8, would be detected using the current minimum sampling. Using the same method, the minimum increase in MJE-prevalence that can be detected from 0.20 would be 0.70. By reducing the minimum number of pigs sampled to 10 samples per quarter, a statistically significant ($P<0.05$) change in P_H would not be detected if a holding were to submit the minimum number of samples.

Discussion

Simulations have been used to show that reducing the minimum number of pigs sampled per quarter to a minimum of five pigs had a varied effect on the probability of correctly assigning a ZAP score and the predictive value of the ZAP score, as a result of testing less samples per batch. Hence, sampling two pigs per batch, rather than three, should not have a major effect on the predictive abilities of the ZAP scheme. It should be noted that the batch prevalence when two pigs are sampled will be either 0, 0.5 or 1.0. Therefore it is important that a sufficient number of batches (ie. greater than five) are sampled per quarter in order to provide a good estimate of MJE prevalence, and hence the ability of the ZAP scheme to correctly allocate a ZAP score.

The high number of samples collected in the ZAP scheme resulted in accurate estimates of *Salmonella* prevalence at a national level; simulations suggest that a change in prevalence of 2% will be detected. At a herd level, the minimum number of samples collected to be allocated a ZAP score, currently set at 15 pigs per quarter, results in a wide estimate of true *Salmonella* prevalence. Therefore changing the sampling methods will influence the estimated holding prevalence. In practice, a majority of holdings submit more than 15 samples per quarter and therefore in these herds the estimate of *Salmonella* has small confidence intervals.

The current sampling scheme is not a sensitive method of detecting true changes in herd prevalence, and reducing the number of samples submitted would reduce this ability further. Using a rolling average of samples collected per quarter improves the sensitivity of the current sampling scheme, but herds with a prevalence close to each ZAP score cut-off are likely to change ZAP score from one month to the next without any true underlying change in *Salmonella* prevalence. However, the ZAP scheme is intended to identify those farms with persistently high levels of infection, and taking 2 rather than 3 samples per batch would not change the conclusion that herds with a ZAP 3 score for 11 consecutive months are likely to have a high MJE prevalence.

References

NIELSEN, B., EKEROTH, L., BAGER, F. and LIND, P. 1998. Use of muscle fluid as a source of antibodies for serologic detection of *Salmonella* infection in slaughter pig herds. *Journal of Veterinary Diagnostic Investigation*, 10, 158-163.

PETRIE, A. and WATSON, P. 1999. *Statistics for Veterinary and Animal Science*. Oxford: Blackwell Publishing.

SNARY, E. L., MUNDAY, D., ARNOLD, M. and COOK, A. 2004. Zap *Salmonella:* an investigation of the sampling protocol. FZ2014: Use of routine data to investigate risk factors for *Salmonella* in pigs. Report to Defra.

VOSE, D. 2000. *Risk analysis: a quantitative guide*. New York: John Wiley & Sons.

Aspects of metabolic disorders in pigs fed exclusively with barley

Dr. Rădoi Ion [1], Dr. Tudoran Cristina* [2]

[1]Veterinary Medicine University, 050557, Bucharest, Romania
[2]Institute of Diagnosis and Animal Health,050557, Bucharest, Romania
*Corresponding author: tudoran.cristina@idah.ro

Abstract
Nutritional surveillance on pig herds, represents the main way to increase the pig production and eventually to obtain a high quality meat production.
Alimentary stress caused in pigs fed exclusively with barley, induce serious health problems , affecting productive performance , such as daily consume, daily average output, conversion rate.
Our research establish the variation of some biochemichal and hematological values such as erythrocytes and leukocytes number, albumins, total globulins, glucose, total cholesterol, total lipids, gamma globulins, ser iron, ceruloplasmine, CPK, A and E vitamins, PT, Hemoglobin, HCT, MCHC..
The stress produced in pigs fed exclusively with barley, increase the level of metabolic disorders, the values obtained showing progressive hypoglycemia, a lack of vitamin A and E, leukocytosis,, hyperlipemia and hypercholesterolemia progressive, enzymatic disorders(hypoceruloplasminemia, hypercreatine phosphokinazemia),in anemia context.

Introduction
This research emphasizes the main aspects of the metabolic profile in pigs fed exclusively with barley, in order to ensure the most efficient monitoring of the pig populations in farms and to avoid nutritional/metabolic disorders induced by the alimentary stress.
The results of this research are intended to help in several areas: establishing the therapeutic and prophylactic measures necessary to obtain high quality pork, leveraging the fodder reserves with an average daily gain, etc.

Materials and methods
The research is conducted in a pig farm during July – August 2005, on two groups of animals with 25 members each and with the same age, one fed with mixed fodder and the other experimentally fed only with barley.
The experimental group comprises 25 pigs, age 90 days, fed exclusively with barley ground for 20 days, the whole experiment period.
The control group comprises 25 pigs, age 90 days, fed with mixed fodder, recipe 02, for 20 days with the following ingredients: barley 32.6%, wheat 36%, soybean groats 24%, meat and bone flour 3.8%, mineral and vitamin supplements 3.6%.

Results
Blood samples taken at the moments T0, T1 (after 10 days), and T2 (after 20 days) from the piglets in both groups, are analyzed statistically (the average and the standard deviation) and compared with the reference values for the species and the category, as systematized in the table below:

Investigated parameters	Measuring unit	Barley diet group at T1	Barley diet group at T2	Control group at T1	Control group at T2	Reference Values	Momentary values
Total lipids	mg/dl	401±24,9	287±34,9	199±27.9	236±19,9	235±19,9	257±34,8
Total globulins	g/dl	3,70±0,82	3,03±0,41	3,08±1,1	3,10±0,15	3±0,4	2,92±0,6
Total protein	g/dl	5,50±0,60	4,53±,0,27	5,75±0,7	5,60±0,4	5,40±0,4	5,45±0,8
Albumins	g/dl	1,60±0,01	1,44±0,06	2,8±0,70	2,30±0,12	3,2±0,6	2,75±0,4

Glucose	mg/dl	57,7±11,9	51,7±9,6	84,26±11,9	70±11,4	80,0±85,0	83±8,7
Cholesterol	mg/dl	118,5±1	127±20	75,7±3,5	85±1		83,35±1,5
Gamma globulins	g/dl	0,87±0,45	0,731±0,26	1,70±1	2,06±0,54	1,34±0,61	1,97±0,6
Iron	µg/dl	107,82±19,4	98,2±47,1	127,7±14,5	127,1±27,5	121±20	131±22,5
Leukocyte #	Mil	30,20±3,2	39,70±2,9	21,80±2	22,5±1,7	18±5	19,75±1
Erythrocyte #	Mil	5,34±1,22	4,70±1,02	5,90±1,7	5,80±1,38	5,4±1,2	5,5±1,1
HCT	%	30,0±5,80	27,90±5,90	36,4±6	33,1±5,8	38±3	30,4±5,1
Hemoglobin	g/dl	7,94±1,60	7,73±2,05	9,90±1,8	9,47±2,3	11,6±0,8	11,3±2
MCHC	g/dl	27,70±4,20	30,16±3,80	30,20±3	30,13±4,2	-	29,94±4
Vitamin E	UI/dl	13,34±10,85	14,38±10,81	80,30±22	74,38±18,1	40±150	98.8±20
Vitamin A	UI/dl	37,11±20,3	37±20,60	95,40±35	87,1±26,60	78±84	90,4±24,4
CPK	UI/l	122,9±29,3	112,3±17,95	45,10±9,3	64,1±0	40±80	51±4,5
Ceruloplasmin	mg/dl	99,9±13,5	77±9,8	189,9±14,5	175,5±34,9	220±20	190,5±15

Discussion

The main biochemical blood parameters are analyzed (total globulins, gamma globulins, total proteins, albumins, total lipids, total cholesterol, serum iron, ceruloplasmin, creatine phosphokinase, vitamin A, vitamin E), as well as the main hematological parameters (hemoglobin, hematocrit, mean corpuscular hemoglobin concentration, number of erythrocytes and leukocytes).

The number of leukocytes at T1 and T2 in pigs fed only with barley is significantly higher than the reference values and the values of the control group. These increased values draw an ascending curve, implying that high leukocyte numbers are a hematological stress reaction, accentuated in pigs fed exclusively with barley.

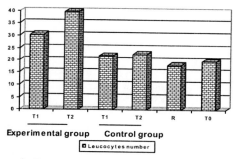

Figure 1. The increase of leukocytes number in experimental group compared with the reference, momentary and control group values

In the experimental group, the values of gamma globulins and albumins at T2 are much lower than the values of the control group and the reference values, showing a severe disorder of the protein metabolism, closely related with the iron deficiency confirmed in pigs fed exclusively with barley.

The energetic deficiency of the exclusive barley diet induces severe hypoglycemia in the pigs in the experimental group, unlike the control group and the references values.

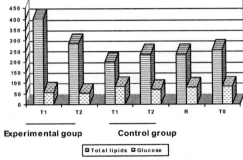

Figure 2. Compared aspects of lipids and glucose values in the two groups of pigs

The total cholesterol values are significantly higher at T1 and T2 in relation to T0, for the pigs fed with barley, as compared with the references values and the values of the control group. These results, together with the increased level of total lipids for this group, show not only a hepatic disorder, but also a mobilization of stored lipids, a typical aspect for stress situations.

The decrease of the iron levels in pigs fed with barley, as compared with the reference values and the control group values, explains the subsequent anemia, closely related with the low values of ceruloplasmin, the enzyme responsible for the oxidation of ferrous iron.

The increase values of creatine phosphokinase in pigs fed with barley illustrate the effect of stress on the muscular mass. These values correlate with the aggressive behavior present during certain stages of the stress syndrome (characteristic for starvation).

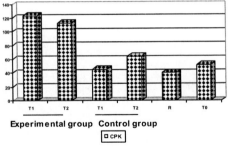

Figure 3. The increased values of creatine phosphokinase in experimental group compared with the reference , momentary and control group values

Determining the creatine phosphokinase values is essential since, together with GOT values, they are important factors in monitoring the pork quality.

In pigs fed only with barley ground, the lower ceruloplasmin levels and the higher creatine phosphokinase levels induce a stress syndrome, expressed by tissue autophagy, poor administration of energy resources or their poor conversion.

The significantly low values of vitamin A and E, caused by the low supply of retinol and tocopherol, together with the high values of creatine phosphokinase, induce a myopathy distinguished by the low pork quality.

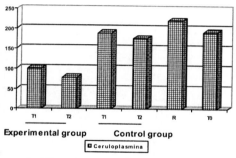

Figure 4. The decreased ceruloplasmin values in experimental group compared with the reference , momentary and control group values

Conclusions

The conclusions obtained in the end of this experiment are the following:

1. An exclusive barley diet in pigs induces severe metabolic disorders that can lead to severe illness, since the immune system is also impaired.

2. Enzymatic disorders lead to low quality pork with stress muscular mass (PSE), because of the subsequent anemia and the lack of antioxidants (vitamin A and E).

3. Starvation stress induced by an unhealthy and uneconomic diet (barley ground only) leads to severe energy disorders caused by the low blood values of lipids and glucose and the high cholesterol value.

4. The high leukocyte values in pigs fed exclusively with barley ground shows that this type of feeding is an alimentary stress, inducing nutritional anemia as well as vitamin, mineral and protein deficiency.

References

1. AVRAM N., TĂNĂSESCU V., BARAT A., FAUR., BUCUL E., -*The vitamin E and selenium deficiency in pigs*, Vet. Med., INMV Pasteur, vol. 1, Bucharest, 1992.
2. BÂRZĂ H., M. MARINESCU- *Adaptation pathology in swine*, IANB, vol.XXXII, 1989.
3. COTRUȚ M., MARCU E., BREZELEANU I., BANTU V., - *Obsevations of some metabolic disorders in piglets*, vol.10, 44-47, Vet Med. Bucharest, 1989.
4. COTRUȚ M., MARCU E., IVAȘ E., HUȚANU E., AXENTE D., - *Aspects regarding the variation of some metabolic parameters in swine.*, RRMV, vol 4, Bucharest 1991.
5. RĂDOI ION, LEAU FELICIA, - *Guide book for metabolic and nutritional diseases* , Ed. Printech, Bucharest 2004.
6. RĂDOI ION, LEAU S., BONCEA I., -Animals *metabolism, nutrition and adaptation diseases*, Ed. Printech, Bucharest., 2003

Salmonella contamination of pork carcasses: UK baseline culture-based data determined by sponge sampling during 2006

Richards, P.[1] Tinker, D.[2], Howell, M.[3], Dodd, C. E. R.*[1]

[1] University of Nottingham, Sutton Bonington, UK; [2] David Tinker & Associates Ltd, Bedfordshire, UK; [3]Food Standards Agency, London, UK
*Corresponding author: christine.dodd@nottingham.ac.uk

Abstract

During 2006-7, microbiological baseline data on the frequency and distribution of Salmonella contamination of pig carcasses in UK slaughterhouses were collected. Data were generated from four separate abattoirs which were determined as having practices representative of the UK slaughter industry. Studies were designed to provide estimates of the prevalence and levels of Salmonella contamination of the UK pork industry. Results allowed a comparison of variations in process to be assessed, including differences in methods of slaughter, scalding, dehairing, singeing, polishing and dressing practices. Salmonella were rarely isolated from the process after the scalding stage and never from the final carcasses. The use of E. coli counts as a means of evaluating process control was a more consistent marker for examining enteric pathogen cross-contamination.

Introduction

Pork and pork products are recognised as one of the sources for human salmonellosis. The importance of focusing control at the slaughterhouse, once controls have been established at the farm level, has been demonstrated by Alban et al. (2005). They demonstrated, through modelling the procedures in Danish slaughterhouses, that it is economically advantageous to achieve a reduction in the contamination of pork post-slaughter through minimum modification of the existing slaughter process. None of the current processes which exert control over contamination levels on the carcass were introduced specifically for this purpose. In the UK this project, funded by the Food Standards Agency, is attempting to determine which of the currently used processing practices can be modified or, where not routinely used, inserted into a pork line to reduce the contamination of pig carcasses by Salmonella.

Materials and methods

Following an assessment study of processes and operating conditions in UK pork abattoirs (Tinker et al., 2007), four abattoirs were chosen as following practices representative of those of the UK industry. Differences in practice which were encompassed were differences in scalding (hot water tank scald; injected/sprayed hot water scalding), dehairing (integral scald/dehairer; separate dehairer) and singeing (multi-flame open unit; enclosed style with a main flame at the base). Microbiological sampling of carcasses for Salmonella was carried out by the Food Standards Agency recommended swab-sampling method for carcass sampling in abattoirs (Anon, 2006), so that contamination rates obtained would reflect the levels routinely determined by UK abattoirs. Individual carcasses were sampled following each key stage of processing (after bleeding, scalding, dehairing, singeing, polishing, evisceration and splitting) with ten carcasses evaluated on each slaughter house visit. In some instances sources of cross contamination such as scald water and fomites were also sampled. Salmonella was determined as presence/absence by standard enrichment techniques and levels of the organism were estimated by a semi-quantitative approach. As well as sampling for Salmonella, other microbiological contamination levels (Escherichia coli, Enterobacteriaceae and total aerobic bacteria) were enumerated throughout the slaughtering process to allow effective decontamination/cross contamination stages to be readily identified.

Results

Viable count data

Total aerobic counts (TAC), Enterobacteriaceae and *E. coli* counts and prevalence of *Salmonella* were obtained for all four slaughterhouses. Figure 1 shows a comparison of mean total aerobic counts from ten pig carcasses at each stage of processing at four of the slaughterhouses which showed differing processing procedures. These are expressed as log cfu cm^{-2} with the standard deviation (SD) adjacently plotted. Slaughterhouses A and D had an integral hot water tank scald and dehairing system and so no counts could be obtained post scalding due to lack of access. Slaughterhouses B and E had an injected/sprayed scald system (condensation scalding). At slaughterhouse E there was also a small carcass washer unit (flails and sprayed water) immediately before, and integrated into, the scalder. B had an enclosed style singer giving a heavy (bacon) singe and produced primarily bacon; the rest had open singers and produced primarily pork; no post-singe samples were available from Slaughterhouses D or E due to lack of accessibility.

As expected, scalding and singeing (where measurable) reduced the total aerobic counts significantly, but subsequent stages recontaminated the carcasses. This was particularly evident post-scalding in E where counts increased 4 log cfu cm^{-2} at the dehairing stage. In this plant dehairing was a particularly vigorous process and escape of faecal material from the carcasses was noticeable. This is also reflected in the Enterobacteriaceae and *E. coli* counts at this stage (Figure 2). Scalding in slaughterhouse E was much more effective than in slaughterhouse B despite both slaughterhouses using condensation scalding. A more detailed study of this is presented in Richards et al. (2007). In slaughterhouse A singeing significantly reduced the total aerobic counts by 5 log cfu cm^{-2} but levels of reduction in B & E were much less despite the much harder singe given in B. The final TAC on the carcasses ranged from 1-3 log cfu cm^{-2} although *E. coli* and Enterobacteriaceae were not significant components of these.

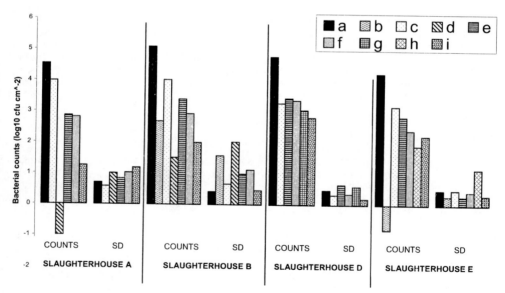

Figure 1: Total aerobic counts on pork carcasses after (a) bleeding; (b) scalding; (c) dehairing; (d) singeing; (e) polishing; (f) evisceration; (g) halving and prior to (h) washing and (i) chilling. SD; standard deviation.

The level of variation in TAC seen between carcasses, as demonstrated by the standard deviation, was generally low (0.5 log cfu cm^{-2}); this suggests the processes produced pigs of a consistent microbiological standard. However, one exception was slaughterhouse B where the standard deviation for TAC was between 0.5 and 2 log cfu cm^{-2}. In particular it is noticeable that the two potential control procedures, scalding and singeing, produced a variation in counts of 1.5-2 log cfu cm^{-2} variation in this slaughterhouse. This shows a greater level of pig-pig variation and thus the potential for some pigs to show good count levels and some much poorer ones. This level of variation was also evident in the E. coli counts (Figure 2).

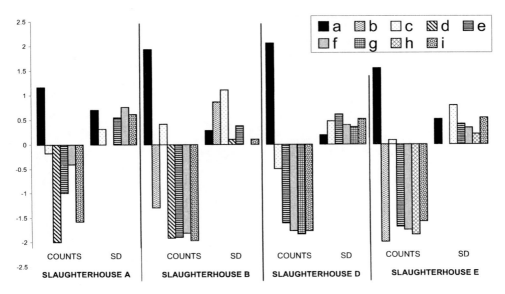

Figure 2: *Escherichia coli* counts on pork carcasses after (a) bleeding; (b) scalding; (c) dehairing; (d) singeing; (e) polishing; (f) evisceration; (g) halving and prior to (h) washing and (i) chilling. SD; standard deviation.

Distribution of Salmonella

At Slaughterhouse A, 10% (1 pig) of carcasses were found to be positive at the bleeding stage and at the dehairing stage but the organism was not found at any other stage. The gambrelling table was shown to be positive for *Salmonella* prior to isolation of the organism from the dehaired pig and so may represent a source of cross contamination. At Slaughterhouse B, 40% of the carcasses were found to be positive post bleeding; one of these was later positive following evisceration but no *Salmonella* were detected in the interim stages. At Slaughterhouse D, 80% of carcasses were found to be positive post-bleeding but the organism was not found at any of the stages thereafter, although *Salmonella* was again isolated from the gambrelling table. At Slaughterhouse E 70% surface carriage of *Salmonella* was isolated post bleed but no isolations were made thereafter. All these results would suggest that surface contamination is removed by the scald process and subsequent recontamination may be as a result of rectal leakage reintroducing the organism onto the surface of the carcass directly or through cross contamination of fomites.

The intermittent isolation of *Salmonella* is typical of what is found in examining the cross contamination events occurring in slaughterhouses and demonstrates the difficulties found in understanding where control processes need to be focussed.

Discussion

These studies have provided a set of base-line data for abattoirs processing pigs in the UK. The process in general reduces total aerobic counts on the carcass surface by 2-3 log cfu cm^{-2} with individual processing stages such as singeing reducing counts by 5 log cfu cm^{-2} in some plants. However the effectiveness of such stages varied and this level of reduction was not consistently seen in all plants. Plants operating the same type of scald systems showed significant variation in their level of effectiveness, being important control points in some plants and giving only minor control of the flora levels in others. However, following both scalding and singeing processes, subsequent operations always increased the levels of the flora. Control of numbers of Enterobacteriaceae and *E. coli* were effective with very low levels (10^{-1} to 10^{-2} log cfu cm^{-2}) seen on the final carcasses. *E. coli* was a more consistent marker for examining enteric pathogen cross-contamination than isolation of *Salmonella* which was infrequent and sporadic in its isolation after the scalding stage. Although *Salmonella* was found on 10-80% of pigs at the start, it was never found on the final carcasses.

References

Alban, L. & Stärk, K.D.C. 2005. Where should the effort be put to reduce the *Salmonella* prevalence in the slaughtered swine carcass effectively? *Preventative Veterinary Medicine* 68(1), 63-79.

Anon. 2006. Red carcass sampling. Food Standards Agency. London, UK. *http://www.ukmeat.org/RedSampling.htm*

Tinker, D., et al., 2007. Assessment of processes and operating conditions in UK pork abattoirs. *Ibid*

Richards, P. et al., 2007. Assessment of the influence of condensation scalding on microbial contamination of pork carcasses. *Ibid*

Assessment of the influence of condensation scalding on microbial contamination of pork carcasses

Richards, P.[1] Tinker, D.[2], Dodd, C. E. R.*[1]

[1] University of Nottingham, Sutton Bonington, UK; [2] David Tinker & Associates Ltd, Bedfordshire, UK *Corresponding author: christine.dodd@nottingham.ac.uk

Abstract

Scalding has been identified as one of the measures which can control microbial contamination of pork carcasses. In this Food Standards Agency funded study the effectiveness of condensation scalding on levels of microbial contamination on pork carcasses was investigated by examining the changes in total aerobic populations at two slaughterhouses where condensation scalding was in routine use. Sampling was by the Food Standards Agency recommended sponge swab-sampling method for carcass sampling in abattoirs and carcasses were sampled before and after scalding and on entry to the chiller. Following scalding, a 1-2 $\log_{10}$ cfu/cm^2 difference in reduction of the mean total aerobic counts was observed, with the lower temperature scald proving more effective. However, at chilling no difference was seen in contamination levels and there was no evidence that condensation scalding increased bacterial adhesion to scalded meat surfaces. The differing results of these two nominally similar vertical scalding systems indicates that there are other factors involved which need to be investigated further in order to understand how to obtain the best reduction of microbiological contamination.

Introduction

Hot water scalding has been demonstrated to remove a substantial proportion of the skin microflora (Borch et al. 1996; Berends et al. 1997). However, there are reports of increases in total aerobic count following hot water tank scalding (Warriner et al. 2002) and of *Salmonella* being isolated from scalding tank water (Swanenburg et al. 2001; Hald et al. 2003). It has been hypothesised that a reduction in water temperature to below 60°C and/or a build up in the amount of organic material suspended in the scald tank could facilitate bacterial survival and increase the chances of cross-contamination at this stage (Dickson et al. 2003; Hald et al. 2003). Condensation scalding (vertical scalding), although not a new development in the dressing of pork carcasses, has become more widespread, but little has been published on the efficacy of the method in reducing microbial contamination. Such systems, which inject and/or spray hot water, are advantageous over hot water tank systems in that carcasses are only in contact with fresh water, they are easy to ventilate during emergency stops, no damage to carcass surfaces occurs and water consumption is vastly reduced as water vapour is required for operation.

Materials and methods

Two abattoirs which used condensation scalding were visited during 2006-7. Microbiological sampling of carcasses for *Salmonella* was carried out by the Food Standards Agency recommended swab-sampling method for carcass sampling in abattoirs, so that contamination rates obtained would reflect the levels routinely determined by UK abattoirs (Anon, 2006). Individual carcasses were sampled after bleeding, after scalding and pre-chill. Thirty five carcasses were sampled over two visits at Slaughterhouse B and ten carcasses evaluated at Slaughterhouse E. In some instances sources of cross contamination such as scald water and fomites were also sampled. *Salmonella* was determined as presence/absence by standard enrichment techniques and levels of the organism were estimated by a semi-quantitative approach. As well as sampling for *Salmonella,* total aerobic bacterial contamination was enumerated.

Results

A Slaughterhouse B

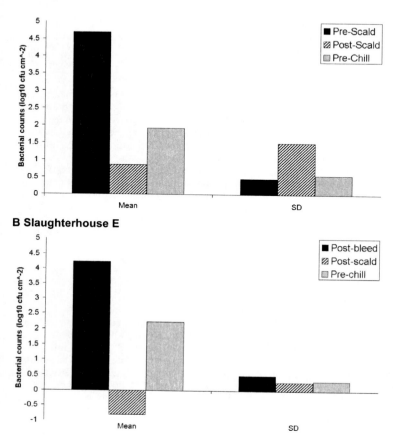

B Slaughterhouse E

Figure 1 Total aerobic counts of pork carcasses after the bleeding and scalding processes and prior to chilling. SD; standard deviation.

The total aerobic counts from the two slaughterhouses are shown in Figures 1A and 1B. Similar initial counts were present on the carcasses prior to scalding, however, after scalding there was a difference of 1-2 $\log_{10}$ cfu/cm^2 in the mean count, with slaughterhouse E showing the lower counts. This was surprising as the scald procedure in slaughterhouse B was carried out at an indicated temperature of 65.8°C for 8 min and so would be expected to be more effective than that at slaughterhouse E which ran at 63.7°C for 4.5 min. However there are differences between the two scalders. The scalder at slaughterhouse B was considerably older (installed in earlier 1990s) and was a straight through line with no pre-scald washing of the carcasses. The scalder in slaughterhouse E was about 10 years newer, was serpentine in operation and, in particular, had an integrated pre-scald washing unit. The additional pre-scald wash procedure may be important in helping to reduce surface contamination by, for example, helping to remove large amounts of organic debris or freeing matted hair.

Another notable difference was the level of variation carcass to carcass at each slaughterhouse. In slaughterhouse B there was a much greater variation in counts post scalding (as evidenced by the standard deviation values), despite the results being on a larger sample size. This slaughterhouse was visited on two occasions and this may mean there was a difference in the running conditions between each visit which could account for this effect. Despite this difference post scalding, the final carcasses at chilling showed similar counts of ~ 2 $\log_{10}$ cfu/cm^2, demonstrating the significance of other processes in controlling the final flora level of the carcasses.

Discussion

Although condensation scalding offers many advantages to the processor as carcasses always come into contact with clean water and the volume of water used is reduced, some data have suggested that this method of scalding increases the potential for bacterial attachment by changing the surface of the carcass (Warriner et al., 2001). Comparison of data from slaughterhouses using condensation scalding with slightly varying parameters has shown that although the levels of bacteria are different following scalding under the two conditions, the counts on the final carcasses were similar and not substantially different from those produced by slaughterhouses using conventional methods (Richards et al. 2007). As the more stringent scald parameters produced a lower reduction in counts by condensation scalding, it suggests that the control of microbial loads by the method relies on factors other than time-temperature parameters. The effectiveness of the pre-scald washer used in combination with scalding may be an important feature which improves the microbial load seen after scalding in Slaughterhouse E.

References

Anon. 2006. Red carcass sampling. Food Standards Agency. London, UK. *http://www.ukmeat.org/RedSampling.htm*

Berends, B. R., Van Knapen, F., Snijders, J. M. A. and Mossel, D. A. A. 1997. Identification and quantification of risk factors regarding Salmonella spp. on pork carcasses. *International Journal of Food Microbiology* 36(2-3), 199-206.

Borch, E., Nesbakken, T. and Christensen, H. 1996. Hazard identification in swine slaughter with respect to foodborne bacteria. *International Journal of Food Microbiology* 30(1-2), 9-25.

Dickson, J. S., Hurd, H. S. and Rostagno, M. H. 2003. Salmonella in the pork production chain. *Pork Checkoff* (Review). 1-12. National Pork Board. Des Moines, Iowa, USA.

Hald, T., Wingstrand, A., Swanenburg, M., von Altrock, A. and Thorberg, B.-M. 2003. The occurrence and epidemiology of Salmonella in European pig slaughterhouses. *Epidemiology and Infection* 131(3), 1187-1203.

Richards et al. 2007. *Salmonella* contamination of pork carcasses: UK baseline culture-based data determined by sponge sampling during 2006. *ibid*

Swanenburg, M., Urlings, H. A. P., Snijders, J. M. A., Keuzenkamp, D. A. and Van Knapen, F. 2001. Salmonella in slaughter pigs: prevalence, serotypes and critical control points during slaughter in two slaughterhouses. *International Journal of Food Microbiology* 70(3), 243-254.

Warriner, K., Aldsworth, T. G. and Dodd, C. E. R. 2002. Establishment of critical control points for enteric pathogens in pork production. FSA Final Report. Food Standards Agency. London, UK.

Warriner, K., Eveleigh, K., Goodman, J., Betts, G., Gonzales, M. and Waites, W.M. 2001. Attachment of bacteria to beef from steam-pasteurized carcasses. *Journal of Food Protection* 64(4), 493-7.

Routes of salmonellae contamination in pig lairages and the development and evaluation of simple cleaning methods

Small, A. [(1)], Purnell, G. [(2)], James, S. J. [(2)], James, C. *[(2)]

[(1)] Division of Farm Animal Science (DFAS), University of Bristol, Churchill Building, Langford, BS40 5DU, UK.

[(2)] Food Refrigeration and Process Engineering Research Centre (FRPERC), University of Bristol, Churchill Building, Langford, BS40 5DU, UK.

* corresponding author: chris.james@bristol.ac.uk

Abstract

The aim of this project was to identify, and validate, the best "lairage-to-stunning" practices to reduce cross-contamination, and to assess the general status of the lairage hygiene and lairage cleaning effectiveness in UK abattoirs.

A survey of a large number of UK abattoirs was conducted via a questionnaire designed to obtain information on lairage construction and operation. A representative group of abattoirs was selected on the basis of the responses to the questionnaire and the lairage at these plants investigated through enumeration of *Escherichia coli* remaining after routine cleansing operations. The results of these visits showed that the *E. coli* indicator was not completely removed from abattoir lairages by standard cleaning practices. Follow up work indicated that routine cleansing measures in commercial abattoirs are insufficient to remove Salmonella contamination from the lairage environment, and the incidence of *Salmonella* spp. on pig carcasses is quite high.

Based on the results of the abattoir survey, an experimental study was conducted to evaluate the efficacy of different cleaning regimes. Concrete tiles were artificially contaminated with field strains of *E. coli* and *Salmonella Kedougou*, with and without the presence of bovine faecal matter. This simulated visually clean and visually dirty surfaces respectively. They were then cleaned using a specially designed mechanical rig. Cleaning was carried out using: 1) water at mains pressure, 2) water under pressure, 3) water under pressure with a proprietary sanitising agent, 4) steam under pressure and combinations of 5) mains water followed by steam under pressure, or 6) water under pressure followed by steam under pressure.

Introduction

Recent studies, funded by the UK Food Standards Agency and conducted at the University of Bristol, as well as recent studies abroad, have indicated that significant environment-to-animal microbial cross-contamination takes place in the lairage-to-stunning areas in abattoirs. The results also indicate that routine cleaning regimes in commercial abattoirs are very variable and often appear inadequate to reduce/prevent that cross-contamination.

Relatively high prevalence of foodborne pathogens (particularly *E. coli* O157) on animal coats post-stunning has been demonstrated, and a high risk of coat-to-carcass transfer of these pathogens during dressing exists. However, the work had concentrated on sheep and cattle slaughtering and less data appeared to be available on pork slaughtering. Therefore the aim of this project was to identify, and validate, the best "lairage-to-stunning" practices to reduce cross-contamination of animal coats during that phase and to assess the general status of the lairage hygiene and lairage cleaning effectiveness in UK abattoirs and at the same time extend the study to cover pork slaughtering operations.

Literature review

A comprehensive review of relevant information from previous studies, published papers and other sources was conducted on various pre-lairage factors potentially affecting contamination of lairages and also data on contamination in the lairage itself.

The lairage is the delivery and final point where the animal is penned before slaughter. Following arrival at the abattoir, animals are placed in the lairage for a holding period. This holding period serves a number of purposes; it allows animals to recover (to a certain extent) from the stresses associated with marketing and transport; it provides the opportunity for animals to clean up and/or dry out if required; and it is reported that 'resting' pigs in lairage for at least 12 hours leads to better bleeding, a reduction of endogenous contamination, a restoration of glycogen content and a reduction of intestinal bacterial load with the intake of plenty of water (Yadava, 2002). Rostagno *et al.* (2003) demonstrated that pig lairage pens became highly contaminated with salmonella, and the water source was also found to be contaminated. This was identified as the critical source of infection because pigs that were negative following transport subsequently became positive after penning.

The survey data provided the UK-wide, basic, information needed for rational design and optimising, of the experimental and validation work in subsequent objectives.

Postal survey of UK abattoirs

A survey of a large number of UK abattoirs was conducted via a questionnaire designed to obtain information on:

1. Throughput and species slaughtered.
2. Construction materials used.
3. Use and type of bedding.
4. Details of cleaning/sanitation regimes.

Twenty three of the responding abattoirs processed pigs and a detailed analysis of the data obtained can be found in Small *et al.* (2006).

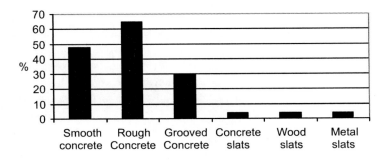

Figure 4. Flooring types in pig lairages.

The materials used and the type of construction varied between abattoirs however the floor of lairages was predominantly concrete, but it could be smooth, rough or grooved (Figure 4). Cleansing practices in the premises surveyed were very variable. Small premises were more likely to thoroughly wash and disinfect the lairage after each working day. This may be a function of the fact that these premises operate on one day each week, and have more time available to thoroughly clean the premises. On the whole, holding pens were washed out on a daily basis, and the race, stun box and roll-out ramp at each break. Chemical agents tended to be used daily in the stun box and roll-out areas, which are more likely to be considered as part of the slaughter hall, and weekly in the race and holding pens, if they were used at all.

Site visits

A representative group of abattoirs were selected on the basis of the responses to the questionnaire and the lairage at these plants investigated through enumeration of *E. coli* remaining after routine cleansing operations. In pig abattoirs the floors of the holding pens tended to be more highly contaminated than the walls (Table 5). A detailed analysis of the data obtained can be found in Small *et al.* (2007a).

Table 5. Mean *E. coli* counts ($\log_{10}$ cfu cm^{-2}) in holding pens.

| Abattoir | Site | | | | | | |
	Holding Floor	Pen	Holding Wall	Pen	Holding Edge	Pen	Holding Corner	Pen
A	0.4^b (1.7)		$-1.7^{d,e}$ (0.8)		1.0^f (0.9)		$0.3^{g,h}$ (2.5)	
B	0.8^b (1.9)		$-1.3^{c,d,e}$ (1.1)		1.2^f (2.0)		$1.3^{g,h}$ (1.9)	

Standard deviations shown in parenthesis, Values sharing similar superscripts are not statistically different.

The results of these visits showed that the *E. coli* indicator was not completely removed from abattoir lairages by standard cleaning practices. Thus lairages may allow a risk of transfer of contamination from one processing day to the next. Potentially, bacteria such as salmonella may be transferred to the outer surfaces of animals held in the lairage facilities, and the skin or hide is a significant source of microbial contamination on the red meat carcasses subsequently produced. To determine if this was the case, a second round of plant visits collected samples (n=556) from lairages and red meat carcasses (n=1050) in commercial abattoirs in the South-West of England. The samples were tested for the presence of *Salmonella* spp. 6.5% of lairage samples were positive, containing estimated numbers of up to 104 Salmonellae per sample. Of carcass samples, *Salmonella* spp. was found on 31% of pig carcasses. These results indicate that routine cleansing measures in commercial abattoirs are insufficient to remove Salmonella contamination from the lairage environment, and the incidence of *Salmonella* spp. on red meat carcasses is quite high, although the implications of residual lairage contamination on carcass meat microbiology are not clear from this study.

Experimental cleaning

Based on the results of the abattoir survey, an experimental study was conducted to evaluate the efficacy of different cleaning regimes.

Initially it was thought that the experiments could be carried out in two stages.

1. Systems that were most effective at producing a visually clean surface would be identified.
2. The microbial reductions achieved by the best visual systems would then be evaluated and their performance optimised.

A search was carried out to identify a method of physically contaminating a surface, that would: a) be repeatable; b) be similar to that occurring in an abattoir; and c) allow the effect of different systems to be quantified. A number of possible visible contaminants, i.e. shaving foam, butter, honey, powder paint, grease, etc, were identified. However, in initial trials none were found to even approach the performance required. With some, it was difficult to produce a repeatable application on a concrete surface. With others, all the cleaning methods of interest either removed all traces of the contaminant very quickly or failed to remove them at all. Initial trials with typical (faecal) lairage contamination showed that in practice most rudimentary cleaning systems could produce a visually clean surface relatively quickly.

A decision was therefore made to concentrate on the microbial reductions that could be achieved. Concrete tiles were artificially contaminated with field strains of *E. coli* and *S. Kedougou*, with and without the presence of bovine faecal matter. This simulated visually clean (but contaminated) and visually dirty surfaces respectively. They were then cleaned using a mechanical rig that was designed to produce a repeatable treatment. Cleaning was carried out using: 1) water at mains pressure, 2) water under pressure, 3) water under pressure with a proprietary sanitising agent, 4) steam under pressure, and combinations of 5) mains water followed by steam under pressure or 6) water under pressure followed by steam under pressure. Thirty replicates of each of visually clean and visually dirty concrete surfaces were cleaned using each method.

The results showed that where there was no faecal matter, the use of a proprietary sanitiser at the maximum recommended concentration, or the application of steam under pressure gave greater reductions in microbial contamination than the use of mains or a pressure wash. Where the surface was visually contaminated with the faecal material, the use of a pressure wash followed by immediate steam application gave reductions in microbial contamination comparable with the use of a proprietary sanitiser at maximum recommended concentration. The use of steam alone on a visually dirty surface was not an effective means of reducing microbial contamination. A small pilot trial under commercial conditions ranked the efficacy of cleaning treatments as follows:

1. Pressure washing followed immediately by steam application.
2. Use of a sanitising agent at the greatest concentration recommended by the manufacturer, and then by pressure washing alone.
3. Pressure washing followed by a delayed steam application appeared to give a poor final result on the surface.

A full analysis of the data obtained can be found in Small et al. (2007b). It was concluded that further work is required to explore the interactions between the angle of application, pressure of jet, and temperature of cleaning fluid, all of which may impact upon the effectiveness of the cleaning procedure. Similarly, alternative proprietary chemical cleaning agents may have effects dissimilar from the Janitol sanitiser used in this study. There may be a significant impact of climatic or environmental conditions on the change in microbial contamination of a surface during the drying phase.

Conclusions

Overall the study has shown that at present microbial contamination, including Salmonella, often remains in UK lairage holding pens after routine cleaning operations. It would appear that there are significant differences in the effectiveness of lairage cleaning programmes at commercial abattoirs, and that the stuning-roll-out areas are often cleaned to a better standard than the holding areas. As a result, there is a possible the risk of foodborne pathogens persisting in the environment and potentially contaminating animals and carcasses processed on subsequent days. Slaughterhouse operators should take steps to reduce the level of contamination both in their premises and on their carcasses. Pressure washing followed immediately by steam application appears the best method of cleaning a holding pen floor, followed by use of a sanitising agent at the greatest concentration recommended by the manufacturer.

The results of this work provided the Food Standards Agency with a scientific base to derive related guidelines for the meat industry, which will ultimately contribute to improved meat safety.

References

ROSTAGNO, M.H., HURD, H.S., MCKEAN, J.D., ZIEMER, C.J., GAILEY, J.K., LEITE, R. C., 2003. Preslaughter holding environment in pork plants is highly contaminated with salmonella enterica. Applied and Environmental Microbiology, 69, 4489-4494.

SMALL, A, JAMES, C., JAMES, S., DAVIES, R., HOWELL, M., HUTCHINSON, M., BUNCIC, S., 2006. Construction, management and cleanliness of red meat abattoir lairages in the UK. Meat Science, 75, 523-532.

SMALL, A., JAMES, C., JAMES, S., DAVIES, R., HOWELL, M., HUTCHISON, M., BUNCIC, S., 2007a. Presence of Salmonella spp. in the red meat abattoir lairage after routine cleansing and disinfection, and on carcasses. Journal of Food Protection, 69 (10), 2342-2351.

SMALL, A., JAMES, C., PURNELL, G., LOSITO, P. JAMES, S., BUNCIC, S., 2007b. An evaluation of simple cleaning methods that may be used in red meat abattoir lairages. Meat Science, 75, 220-228.

YADAVA, R., 2002. Pre-abattoir and pre-slaughter status of pigs affecting salmonella contamination of pork. Journal of Research, 14, 141-144.

Cost reductions in the Danish Salmonella surveillance program

Sørensen, L.L[1]., Møgelmose, V. [*][1], Enøe, C. [1], Goldbach, S. G.[2],

[1]Danish Meat Association, Axeltorv 3, DK-1609 Copenhagen V, Denmark
[2] Copenhagen Economics, Nyropsgade 13, 1, DK-1602 Copenhagen V, Denmark

*Vibeke Møgelmose: vim@danishmeat.dk

Abstract

In 1993 Denmark implemented a surveillance program for Salmonella in pigs and pork. Since then the program has been adjusted several times leading to a reduction of the associated cost. The program has been optimized in breeder and multiplier herds as well as for fattening pig herds and at the slaughterhouses. All in all, optimizations of the program have reduced the over-all costs from 0.65 € to 0.15 € per fattening pig produced. This has been achieved without jeopardizing the food safety which can be seen from the numbers of human Salmonella infections attributed to pork. From 1993 to 2005, the number of human cases has decreased from app. 1,100 to around 100-200 per year.

Introduction

In 1993, the Danish authorities launched a program for surveillance of Salmonella in pork (Mousing et al, 1996). The surveillance program was comprehensive and expensive, and the financial burden was shared between producers, industry and the authorities. Over the years, the program has been adjusted several times. The industry's need for ensuring a cost-effective program has been an important part of the motivation for changing the program. The adjustments have been approved by the authorities because the industry has been able to demonstrate that the changes did not jeopardize food safety. Only the major and more important changes are mentioned in this proceeding.

The surveillance in breeder and multiplier herds is based on detection of antibodies in serum. In 1996, the number of samples collected from each herd was reduced from 20 to 10 per month.

In fattening herds, Salmonella specific antibodies are detected in meat juice samples collected at slaughter. Based on the seroprevalence, herds are classified as level 1, 2 or 3, indicating a low, intermediate or high risk, respectively. Initially, 70,000 samples were collected and examined each month. In 2001, the criterion for classification of herds was changed – reducing the number of samples to 50,000 per month (Alban et al. 2001). The meat-juice ELISA-test was also simplified. Before 2001 each sample was examined by a doublet test. From 2001 and onwards a single analysis is used. Analyses showed that this did not alter the ability of the program to correctly classify herds (Alban et al. 2001). By this change in procedure the cost associated with serology was reduced. In 2005, a risk-based approach was applied in fattening herds (Enøe et al. 2005). In herds with no positive samples, sampling was reduced to one sample per month, hereby reducing the total number of samples per month to 21,000.

In fattening herds assigned to level 2 or 3, pen faecal samples are collected. In 2003, the procedure was changed from analyzing individual samples to pooled pen samples. Typically 20 samples are collected in a herd and instead of analyzing these as 20 individual samples, the laboratories now pool the individual samples by 4 to 5 pooled samples (Enøe et al, 2003). Furthermore, the number of sero and phage typing was reduced to only one isolate from each herd unless specific resistance patterns were found. These initiatives reduced the associated cost by 60%.

Up till 2001, the surveillance at the abattoir was based on examination of 27,000 samples of different cuts of pork. This was changed to a surveillance based on pooled swab samples from 5 carcasses per day (Sørensen et al. 2001), reducing the associated cost with 60%.

Pigs from level 3 herds are slaughtered under special hygienic precautions. Slaughter hygiene is measured by microbiological testing and if the number of positive samples exceeds a predefined limit, the carcasses included in the batch are heat-treated causing considerable loss in carcass value. This regulation is still in force, but in 2001 the authorities approved, that carcasses from level 3 herds are showered with hot water (81°C), which has a well documented reducing effect on *Salmonella* (Jensen et al. 2001). This process too is monitored by microbiological testing, but very seldom batches of carcasses are found positive for *Salmonella* leading to heat treatment. This change in processing carcasses from level 3 herds has reduced the costs with 90%.

Materials and methods

The expenses to the Danish *Salmonella* surveillance are published every year (Anonymous 1998 – 2005). From the information in these reports the expenses for the *Salmonella* surveillance can be calculated per fattening pig produced. Unfortunately accounts for the years 2001 and 2005 are not available. In the calculations the increase in number of slaughter pigs produced in Denmark has been taken into consideration and costs have been converted to the price level to 2006.

Results

As seen from table 1 and figure 1 (With adjustments), adjustments and optimizations of the surveillance program has led to considerable reductions in the costs per fattening pig produced.

	Costs per fattening pig produced, in €, price level 2006						
Year	1998	1999	2000	2002	2003	2004	2006
Costs	0,65	0,67	0,50	0,32	0,20	0,19	0,15

Table 1. Account of expenses for the *Salmonella* surveillance. The expenses are presented per slaughter pig produced. Calculation was not done for the years 2001 and 2005 due to lack of data.

It has also been looked upon what the cost of the program would have been today had there been no optimizations of the surveillance. As above, all figures were transformed to 2006-prices. The results are shown in fig. 1 (Without adjustments).

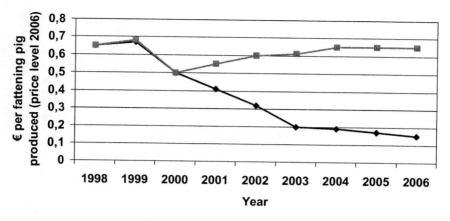

Fig 1. Expenses for the *Salmonella* surveillance with and without cost-effective adjustments. The results for the years 2001 and 2005 are interpolated.

Discussion

Adjustments of the Danish *Salmonella* surveillance program has led to a reduction of the over-all cost associated with the program from 0.65 € to 0.15 € per fattening pig. The adjustments and optimizations have been approved by the authorities, because the industry has been able to demonstrate that the changes could be carried out without jeopardizing the food safety. This is supported by the number of human cases of *Salmonella* infection attributed to pork. From 1993 to 2005 the number of human cases has decreased from app. 1,100 till around 100-200 per year (Anonymous 2, 1998-2005).

References

Alban, L., Stege, H., Dahl, J., 2002. The new classifications system for slaughter-pig herds in the Danish *Salmonella* surveillance-and-control- program. Prev. Vet. Med. 53, 133-146.

Anonymous, 1998 – 2005. Overvågning og kontrol af *Salmonella* i svinebesætninger og svinekødsproduktion. Teknikergruppen for svin, Status 1998, Status 1999, Status 2000, Status 2001, Status 2002, Status 2003, Status 2004, Status 2005.

Anonymous 2, 1998-2005. *http://www.dfvf.dk/Default.aspx?ID=9202*

Enøe, C., Boes, J., Dahl, J., Svensmark, B., 2003. Sensitivity of cultivation of *Salmonella enterica* in pooled samples of pig faeces. In: Proceedings of the Fifth International Symposium on the Epidemiology and Control of Food borne Pathogens in Pork, Crete, Greece, October 1-4, 34-35.

Enøe, C., Wachmann, H., Boes, J., 2005. Surveillance of *Salmonella* in low prevalence swine herds in Denmark. In: Proceedings of the 6th International Symposium on the Epidemiology and Control of Food borne Pathogens in Pork, California, USA, September 6-9, 97-99.

Jensen, T., Christensen, H., 2001. Decontamination of Pig Carcasses with hot water. In: Proceedings of the 4th International Symposium on the Epidemiology and Control of *Salmonella* and other food borne pathogens in Pork, Leipzig Germany, 2-5 September 2001, 127-129.

Mousing, J., Thode Jensen, P., Halgaard, C., Bager, F., Feld, N., Nielsen, B., Nielsen, J.P., Bech-Nielsen, S., 1997. Nation-wide *Salmonella* enterica surveillance and control in Danish slaughter swine herds. Prev. Vet. Med. 29, 247-261.

Sørensen, Wachmann, H., Dahl, J., Nielsen, B., 2001. The new Danish Salmonella surveillance on fresh pig carcasses base don pooled swab samples including compatibility with levels of the former system. In: Proceedings of the 4th International Symposium on the Epidemiology and Control of *Salmonella* and other food borne pathogens in Pork, Leipzig Germany, 2-5 September 2001, 30-32.

Session 4

Running the farrowing rate fluctuations in order to prevent diseases of pigs, farmers, neighbours and the pork consumers

Sviben, M.[1]

[1]Freelance consultant (retired University Professor), Siget 22B, HR-10020 Zagreb, Croatia

Abstract

Recently, at the 19th I.P.V.S. Congress, it was reported what the farrowing rate fluctuations had been during unfavourable conditions for the pig production in Bosnia and Herzegovina. Observed results were compared to the situation when the farmers had tried and succeeded to achieve the improvement in Croatia, knowing that continuous and even number of farrowings through the year is the presumption of good health status of pigs and worth results of the pig farming. It was exposed that farrowing rates fluctuated regularly when the farmers tried to improve the conditions and during unfavourable circumstances for the pig production. After the Congress held in Copenhagen, Denmark, it has been found that farrowing rate fluctuations from the beginning of autumn till the end of summer were expressible with the trend of II° or more often with the trend of III° not only in the northern hemisphere but in southern hemisphere too. Considering the necessity of organizing the pig production on large scale during the era of globalization, the SAFE PIG PRODUCTION SYSTEM has been established as the strategic way of prevention not only of pig diseases but the human diseases of pig producers and their neighbours as well as the zoonoses risky for the pork consumers.

Introduction

Recently, at the 19th International Pig Veterinary Society Congress, it was reported what the farrowing rate fluctuations had been during unfavourable conditions for the pig production caused by the war in Bosnia and Herzegovina. Results observed by Sviben and Pavlovski (2006) were compared to the situation when the farmers had tried and succeeded to achieve the improvement in Croatia, as it had been reported by Herak and Sviben (1974). Producers and consultants were conscious that continuous and even number of farrowings through the year, from month to month, shift by shift, is the presumption of worth economic results of the pig farming which can be achieved only if the health status of pigs is good. Even piglet production was not achieved because the farrowing rate fluctuated. It was of great importance the cognition that the sows' farrowing rate altered lawfully depending on the time of covering and the suggestion the piglet producers to use the formula: number of needed matings = desired number of farrowings / farrowing rate of the month. The equation was proposed by Sviben, Herak and Vuković (1974) and at the same time the following farrowing rates of months of coverings were suggested to be used: September 0.66, October 0.74, November 0.78, December 0.80, January 0.80, February 0.78, March 0.74, April 0.70, May 0.66, June 0.61, July 0.59 and August 0.55. The annual mean farrowing rate of sows was accordingly 0.70 and so it was 32 years later at the I.P.V.S. Congress in Copenhagen where Carr, Nelson and Olson (2006) exposed that piglet producers need to take the seasonal effect into account when calculating the number of females to breed in order to achieve the required number of farrow per batch on such a way that the farrowing rates are 75% only in November and December and 80% in all other months. Aforementioned authors did not expose the farrowing rate fluctuations in USA or Western Australia with any equation of trend. During the autumn 2006, till November 9th, the normal farrowing rate curve exposed in 1974 and in 2006 again was reestablished and presented with the equation for the time of covering sows and gilts from the beginning of autumn till the end of summer as it follows: $Yc = 80.518 - 3.822\ Xc - 0.463\ Xc^2 + 0.120\ Xc^3$ (the origin between winter and spring; the unit of Xc is 1, corresponding to a month). The annual mean farrowing rate of females was accordingly 75%, for sows 80% (being a = 85.518), for gilts 65% (being a = 70.518 - Potočnjak, 1987). The equations of normalcy of the expression of the farrowing ability of sows and gilts served us to find out the numbers of farrowings expected during the year after the same number of coverings as it had been suggested by Marjušin (1980) and

Chatenet et al. (2004). We tried to show how to get continuous and even, through the year equal number of farrowings appreciating the farrowing rate fluctuations and we are reporting on it.

Material and Methods

In any case desired number of farrowings was equal to 1.0000 or 100.00% of the farrowing rates to be used at particular time. The data exposed by Marjušin (1980) that 1.0 sow can give suck to piglets from 1.1 farrowed female have shown that 90.91% of farrowed sows could be weaned and covered after weaning. The farrowing rate trend for sows was expressed with the equation $Y_c = 85.518 - 3.822\ X_c - 0.463\ X_c^2 + 0.120\ X_c^3$ (the origin between winter and spring; the unit of X_c is 1 corresponding to a month). The annual mean repeating rate of sows was equal to 20%. According to Marjušin (1980) it was necessary 20% of gilts to be covered per every batch. The farrowing rate trend for gilts was expressed with the equation $Y_c = 70.518 - 3.822\ X_c - 0.463\ X_c^2 + 0.120\ X_c^3$ (the origin between winter and spring; the unit of X_c is 1 corresponding to a month). Using the aforementioned data the numbers of farrowings of sows covered after weaning or as repeaters as well as the numbers of the 1st farrowings were figured out. On the same way the numbers of farrowings in twelve months were found using the data exposed by Chatenet at al. (2004) and supposing 79% of farrowed sows to be covered after weaning having the repeating rate equal to 18%. Culling of females was presumed on the 3rd repeat. It was taken that 22.50% (the mean between 20% and 25%) gilts should be incorporated per group of covered females. The farrowing rate trend was expressed for sows with the equation $Y_c = 87.518 - 3.822\ X_c - 0.463\ X_c^2 + 0.120\ X_c^3$ and for gilts with the equation $Y_c = 72.518 - 3.822\ X_c - 0.463 X_c^2 + 0.120\ X_c^3$ (the origin between winter and spring; the unit of X_c is 1 corresponding to a month). In order to find out how to get continuously even numbers of farrowings 82% of farrowed sows were supposed to be covered in 24 days after weaning according to Šalehar, Sviben and Herak (1970). Since the method of reproducing swine S.S.P. (Sustainable Swine Production – Sviben, 2001) had been described, the annual mean repeating rate of sows equal to 13% was taken into account. The farrowing rate trends were expressed for sows with the equation $Y_c = 92.518 - 3.822\ X_c - 0.463\ X_c^2 + 0.120\ X_c^3$ and for gilts with the equation $Y_c = 77.518 - 3.822\ X_c - 0.463\ X_c^2 + 0.120\ X_c^3$. Sows were supposed to be covered after weaning, during the 1st repeat from January till December, during the 2nd repeat from June till October in northern hemisphere or from December till April in southern hemisphere and during the 3rd repeat from July till October in northern hemisphere or from January till April in southern hemisphere. Since the numbers of farrowing of covered sows were figured out, required numbers of coverings of gilts were calculated using the formulas exposed by Sviben (1989). Gilts were supposed to be covered after taking, during the 1st repeat from May till October in northern hemisphere or from November till April in southern hemisphere and during the 2nd repeat from June till October in northern hemisphere or from December till April in southern hemisphere.

Results

Results of calculating are exposed in Table 1. Numbers of farrowing expected after the same number of coverings as it was suggested by Marjušin (1980) or Chatenet et al. (2004), appreciating during this research work the normal farrowing rate trend – vary being over desired number of farrowings from February or January till June or May in northern hemisphere and from August or July till December or November in southern hemisphere. During other periods of the year numbers of farrowings are under desired number. Suchlike figure is equal 1.0000 from month to month after the appreciation of normal farrowing rate curve covering different numbers of sows and gilts in different periods of year.

Table 1. Numbers of farrowings expected after the same number of coverings (Marjušin, 1980; Chatenet et al., 2004) and after different numbers of coverings appreciating the normal farrowing rate curve

| Month of farrowing in northern hemisphere | Number of farrowings | | | Month of farrowing in southern hemisphere |
	After Marjušin (1980)	After Chatenet et al. (2004)	With different numbers of coverings	
January	0.9697	1.0127	1.0000	July
February	1.0895	1.1254	1.0000	August
March	1.0877	1.0958	1.0000	September
April	1.0694	1.0436	1.0000	October
May	1.0452	1.0083	1.0000	November
June	1.0191	0.9827	1.0000	December
July	0.9927	0.9625	1.0000	January
August	0.9665	0.9478	1.0000	February
September	0.9432	0.9395	1.0000	March
October	0.9273	0.9399	1.0000	April
November	0.9255	0.9535	1.0000	May
December	0.9443	0.9838	1.0000	June

Discussion

Negative deviations of numbers of farrowings from desired number of dropped litters have bad consenquences for economic efficiency of pig producers. Farmers having constant number of farrowing rates are not able to get any advantage from positive deviations of numbers of farrowings from desired number of piglets to be born. Different diseases happen in overcrowded farrowing rooms, nurseries and raising rooms. The rate of technological runts is on the increase as losses of pigs for fattening are too. Feeders have not enough time till best paid live weight. As continuous as even number of farrowings through the year is obvious presumption of good health status of pigs and worth results of the pig farming. Butchers and the pork manufacturers can always get animals and the raw materials of standard high quality from the suppliers producing pigs continuously and evenly. It has been shown that achieved numbers of farrowings at the Pig Farm Nova Topola during months in 1978 and 1979 deviated from hyogenotechnologically projected and expected i.e. desired number of 386.8 farrowings per month positively from 0.5% till 3.15% and negatively from 0.46% till 3.05% what was proven to be insignificant (Sviben, 1983). The test was made with data from a large pig farm in Bosnia and Herzegovina but during the era of globalization there is the necessity of organizing the pig production of large scales (Sviben, 1995). To ensure even number of farrowings through the year is only the first step in attempts to prevent not only the pig diseases but the human diseases of pig producers and their neighbours as well as the zoonoses risky for the pork consumers. As the strategic way to suchlike prevention HEALTHY SWINE PRODUCTION SYSTEM > 75,000 S.S.A. was designed by Sviben till March 5th 1990 (Sviben, 2000) and the SAFE PIG PRODUCTION SYSTEM was conceived at the end of 2006.

Conclusions

Considering the normal farrowing rate trend expressible all over the world lawfully from the beginning of autumn till the end of summer it is not possible to get even number of farrowings from month to month covering the same, equal number of sows and gilts shift by shift. Continuous and even numbers of farrowings through the year can be achieved covering different numbers of sows and required numbers of gilts in accordance to desired number of farrowings and appreciating the normal farrowing rate trend. Even numbers of farrowings through the year should be achieved as the first step in the way of prevention not only of the pig diseases but the human diseases of pig producers and their neighbours as well as the zoonoses risky for the pork consumers.

References

CARR, J., L. NELSON, S. OLSON, 2006. Consistent pig flow-setting appropriate breeding targets. Proceedings of the 19th IPVS Congress. Vol. 2,517 Copenhagen: IPVS2006 Secretariat DMA

CHATENET, X., P. EVIAN, P. GARRES, J-M. GUILLAME, V. MULLER, F. PELENC, B. ROBINE, C. SOYER, 2004. How to run a successful piggery. Ancenis: Coophavet.

HERAK, M., M. SVIBEN, 1974. Trends in the farrowing rate of sows covered in different months 1965-1968. 3rd International Congress (I.P.V.S.), G 6, 1-5. Lyon: International Pig Veterinary Society.

MARJUŠIN, V.D., 1980. Vosproizvodstvo stada. Spravočnik po promišlennomu proizvodstvu svinini. Str. 67-73. Moskva: Rosseljhozizdat.

POTOČNJAK, M., 1987. Zabilježeno, očekivano i kontrolirano kretanje stope oprasivosti u istočno slavonskom svinjogojstvu. Radovi centra JAZU Vinkovci 6, 153-183.

SVIBEN, M., 1983. Hiotehnološki projektiran i očekivan te u praksi Svinjogojske farme Nova Topola po mjesecima ostvaren broj prasenja. Stočarstvo, 37 (5-6), 181-192.

SVIBEN, M., 1989: Svinjogojstvo. Veterinarski priručnik. IV obnovljeno i dopunjeno izdanje. Str. 1044-1062. Zagreb: Jugoslavenska medicinska naklada.

SVIBEN, M., 1995. Perspectives of the pig meat production regarding design. Zbornik Biotehniške fakultete Univerze v Ljubljani. Suplement 22. Kmetijstvo (Zootehnika). Str. 207-218. Ljubljana: Biotehniška fakulteta Univerze v Ljubljani.

SVIBEN, M., 2000. Proizvodnja svinjetine na početku 21. stoljeća. Agronomski glasnik 62 (5-6), 297-317.

SVIBEN, M., 2001. Izgledi za ekonomičniju proizvodnju svinjetine. Agronomski glasnik 63 (3), 89-124.

SVIBEN, M., V. PAVLOVSKI, 2006. Farrowing rate fluctuations during unfavourable conditions for the pig production. Proceedings of the 19th IPVS Congress. Vol. 2, 519. Copenhagen: IPVS2006 Secretariat DMA

SVIBEN, M., M. HERAK, I. VUKOVIĆ, 1974. Changes in the farrowing rate of sows mated during the individual months of the year and the calculation of the needed number of matings for a constant number of farrows. 3rd International Congress (I.P.V.S.), G 3, 1-8. Lyon: International Pig Veterinary Society.

ŠALEHAR, A., M. SVIBEN, M. HERAK, 1970. Trajanje odmora krmača nakon odbića legla različite uzastopnosti. Stočarstvo 24, 247-256.

Effect of fumonisins and *Salmonella* on digestive flora profiles assessed using a molecular tool (CE-SSCP).

Maël Tanguy (1)*, Marilyne Queguiner (1), Isabelle P Oswald (2), Philippe Guerre (4), François Grosjean (3), Roland Cariolet (1), Christine Burel (1), Philippe Fravalo (1)

(1) French Food Safety Agency, Zoopôle des Côtes d'Armor, BP 53, 22440 Ploufragan, France
(2) INRA , Pharmacology-Toxicology Laboratory, BP3, 31931 Toulouse Cedex
(3) ARVALIS, Institut du Végétal, 27 rue de la Vistule 75013 Paris
(4) Veterinary School of Toulouse, 23 chemin des Capelles 31076 Toulouse cedex France
corresponding author: *m.tanguy@afssa.fr

Abstract

Fumonisins (FB) are mycotoxins frequently found in vegetal feedstuffs, especially in maize used for pig feeding. Among fumonisins, FB_1 was the better described toxin. It caused pulmonary and hepatic damages as well as immune response disorders in pigs that were recognised as especially sensitive to FB intoxication. The FB_1 immunosuppressor induced a higher susceptibility of pigs to gut pathogens such as *E coli*. Effects on *Salmonella* have poorly been studied despite the frequent asymptomatic carriage in pigs and the presumptive role of flora equilibrium on prevention of *Salmonella* excretion or re-excretion. To determine the influence of *Salmonella* carriage, fumonisins or both on digestive flora equilibrium, the use of a molecular technique : CE-SSCP (Capillary-Electrophoresis Single Strand Conformation Polymorphism) appeared a good complement to the conventional bacteriological techniques. The objective was to assess the perturbation of flora associated with co-exposition in experimental conditions in absence of clinical sign.

Forty eight piglets were clustered following a 2x2 "factorial scheme" in order to analyse on faecal flora, the effect of a feeding naturally contaminated with FB (8.5 ppm of FB_1 and 2.8 ppm of FB_2) associated with an asymtomatic carriage of *Salmonella* Typhimurium. The effect of FB and *Salmonella* has been investigated onto 10 week old piglets and during 9 weeks. Faeces of the pigs were taken regularly. Bacteriological numeration of total aerobic flora was conducted. DNA of each sample was extracted using the QIAmp DNA Stool Minikit. The extracted DNA were pooled, the PCR amplification of the rDNA 16S V3 region was carried out. Then the PCR products were analysed by CE-SSCP. Profiles were classified via dendrograms using the BioNumerics software and the Jaccard coefficient for similarity determination.

In this study, 5.10^4 CFU *Salmonella* per pig induced infections and asymptomatic carriages that didn't affect the faecal flora profiles. Intoxication of the pigs by the contaminated feed has been confirmed by the increase of the sphinganine/sphingosine ratio. The 8.5 ppm concentration of FB_1 did not induce any effect on the animal health indicators, but it affected transiently the digestive flora equilibrium. In case of co-infection with FB and *Salmonella*, the flora profiles were rapidly and strongly modified as soon as 48h post *Salmonella* infection. Therefore under our experimental conditions, exposure to a medium concentration of FB in naturally contaminated food had no effect on the pig health but can affected the digestive flora equilibrium, the *Salmonella* exposure amplifying this phenomenon.

Introduction

The contamination of pig herds by the ubiquitous *Salmonella* may lead to subclinical infection in pigs (Humbert, 1997). Then contaminations of carcasses by this pathogen constitute a threat to human health. Ingestion of contaminated pork meat may lead to food-borne illness. Therefore, decrease of the *Salmonella* contamination level throughout food-chain appeared to be crucial for human health (Giovannacci, et al., 2001).. Epidemiological studies identified risk factors associated with *Salmonella* excretion (Beloeil, et al., 2004): implementation of hygiene measures and preservation of digestive ecology equilibrium (Fravalo, et al., 2002) would reduce *Salmonella* prevalence.

Fumonisins (FB) are mycotoxins, secondary metabolites of fungi (*Fusarium moniliforme* and *Fusarium proliferatum*), which may contaminate animal and human feeds. Their global occurrence is considered as an important risk for human and animal health, as up to 25% of the world crops production may be contaminated with mycotoxins. In pig, a chronic exposure to FB1 are associated with alteration of sphingolipid metabolism and hepatotoxicity. In this specie, FB1 is a predisposing factor for gut infectious disease by local immunosuppressor effect (Oswald, et al., 2003).

The impact of Fumonisin contaminated feed on salmonella excretion intensity in a herd containing asymptomatic carrier pigs has, until now, never been investigated. To determine the influence of *Salmonella*, fumonisins or both on digestive flora equilibrium, the use of a molecular technique of CE-SSCP (Capillary-Electrophoresis Single Strand Conformation Polymorphism) appeared a good complement to the conventional bacteriological techniques (Tanguy, et al., 2007). The objective of the present study was to assess the perturbation of flora of SPF pig's groups in relation to co-exposition (FB or/and *Salmonella*) in experimental conditions.

Material and methods

Forty eight piglets were clustered following a 2x2 "factorial scheme" after randomisation the day of weaning:

> ➢ 12 piglets FB(-)-*Salmo*(-)
> ➢ 12 piglets FB(+)-*Salmo*(-)
> ➢ 12 piglets FB(-)-*Salmo*(+)
> ➢ 12 piglets FB(+)-*Salmo*(+)

FB(+)-*Salmo* (+) and FB(+)-*Salmo* (+) piglets fed a diet containing 8.5 ppm FB1 and 2.8 ppm FB2 (incorporation of 15% of naturally contaminated maize) since week 7 of age. FB(-)-*Salmo*(+)and FB(+)-*Salmo*(+) piglets were inoculated at 8 weeks of age by 5.10^4 UFC *Salmonella* /pig.

Sa/So determination

Free sphinganine and free sphingosine were determined in pig serum, liver, and kidney by HPLC according to Riley et al. (1993) with minors modifications (Riley, et al., 1993;Tran, et al., 2003). Determination of Sa/So ratio is used to test the intoxication of the pigs following the ingestion of naturally contaminated food.

Salmonella enumeration

The detetction and quantitative assesment for *Salmonella* were carried out in the faeces according to the methods described by Fravalo (Fravalo, et al., 2003a;Fravalo, et al., 2003b).

Total aerobic numeration

Fecal bacteriological numeration (total aerobic flora) was conducted for each pig at each sampling date by dilution plating on PCA (incubated 48h/30°C)..

DNA extraction/amplification

Fecal samples DNA extractions were performed using a QIAamp DNA Stool Minikit (Qiagen) (McOrist, et al., 2002). One grams of fresh feces were homogeneised with 7 mL of lysis buffer, then 1.6 mL suspensions were used for DNA extraction.. DNA coding for the V3 region of the 16S rDNA was amplified from 1 µL of the DNA solution, using the w49 (AGGTCCAGACTCCTACGGG)-w104* (*TTACCGCGGCTGCTGGCAC) primer couple. PCR conditions were as follows: 2' at 94°C, and then 25 cycles of 30'' at 94°C, 30'' at 61°C, 30'' at 72°C and a final elongation of 10' at 72°C.

Migration of PCR products

CE-SSCP consisted in the migration of DNA single strands into the 50-cm capillaries of the four-capillary AbiPrism Genetic Analyser 3100 Avent sequencer (Applied Biosystems, France). After a 1:5 dilution of the amplification products obtained, one µL was dispensed per well and a mixture of 18.5 µl formamide (Applied Biosystems) and 0.5 µl of Genescan-standard-HD-400-rox internal Standard (Applied Biosystems) were then added. The amplification products were heat-denatured (5 minutes/90°C), then cooled for ten minutes in ice added with water. Migrations took place in a polymer (6.22 g CAP polymer (Applied Biosystems), 1 g Glycerol (In Vitrogen), 1 mL 10X buffer (Applied Biosystems) and water for injection (Cooper) q.s. 10 mL), at 32°C under a power of 15 kV.

Result analysis

Profile analyses were performed with the GeneMapper (Applied Biosystems) and Bionumerics (Applied Maths) software. The GeneMapper software was used to align the profiles obtained based on the migration internal standard. Similarity of the profiles was studied by analyzing the presence/absence of bands from profile to profile using Bionumerics software. The Jaccard index (Legendre and Legendre, 1998) was selected during this project for studying profile similarity.

Results

The chronic effect of the FB1 on the Sa/So ratio after the 9 weeks of treatment is presented in table 1. A significant increase of the Sa/So ratio, in the kidney, the liver or the serum, was observed during the test, comparing the batches fed with FB1 contaminated food with the control batches .

Table 1 - Sa/So ratio increase in the FB1 exposed pigs batches (FB1(+)-*Salmo*(- or +)) compared to non exposed batches (FB1(-)-*Salmo* (- or +) in the kidney, the liver, and the serum, according to time.

Day before or after inoculation	kidney	liver	Serum
D-5	ND	ND	+6%
D+2	+19%*	+50%*	+45%*
D+56	+54%*	+60%*	+149%*

* significant increases compared with the control animals (batches FB1(-)) (ANOVA and test of Tuckey) ND: Non determinated

The *Salmonella* inoculation conducted to a contaminated batch, the majority of the pigs shedding *Salmonella* (Table 2). The proportion of shedding pigs did not vary during the test depending on FB1 presence. Nevertheless, only 3 of the 12 pigs had a countable excretion in batch FB1(-)-*Salmo*(+) against 9 out of 12 in the batch FB1(+)-*Salmo*(+) two days post inoculation, but this difference is not significant and disappeared as of 7 days post inoculation. *Salmonella* was countable on 75-100 % of the excretory pigs along the growth period.

Table 2 Search for *Salmonella* Typhimurium in faeces of pigs of the batches FB(-)-*Salmo*(+) and FB(+)-*Salmo*(+) during 49 days after the inoculation.

		Time (reference *Salmonella* infection)								
		D-6	D+2	D+7	D+14	D+21	D+28	D+35	D+42	D+49
Salmonella	FB1(-)Salmo(+)	0	8/12	7/8	7/7	7/8	7/8	7/8	7/8	2/4
shedding pigs	FB1(+)Salmo(+)	0	11/12	5/8	4/8	4/8	4/8	4/8	4/8	2/4

No effects of FB1 or *Salmonella* were observed on aerobic flora during the study (Figure 1). The aerobic was comprised between 10^7 to 10^8 bacter/gr of faeces without significantly differences.

Figure 1: Numeration of mesophile aerobic flora in faeces of batches FB(-)-*Salmo*(-), FB(+)-*Salmo*(-), FB(-)-*Salmo*(+) and FB(+)-*Salmo*(+) during 49 days after the inoculation.

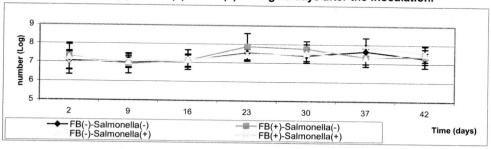

Bacteriological analyses were completed by fecal flora profile comparison using CE-SSCP. IResults were expressed as similarity percentage (Jaccard index) using FB1(-)-*Salmo*(-) as references. The similarity of FB1(-)-*Salmo*(+) batches did not vary significantly during the study (90% of similarities, figure 2). A transient reduction for batch FB1 (+)-*Salmo*(-) was observed : the similarity between the two batches decreased from 95,2% to 80,1% between D-6 to D+22, then reached the control value at D+49. In addition, a transient but marked reduction in the similarity percentage was observed between control and FB1 (+)-*Salmo* (+) (Figure 2). Indeed, the similarity of the profiles between these two batches decreases from 89,2% to 74,2% in values, between D-6 to D+2, stabilized between D+2 to D+7 then increased back to high similarity value at D+49.

Figure 2: profile similarities of batches FB(+)-*Salmo*(-), FB(-)-*Salmo*(+) and FB(+)-*Salmo*(+) compared to batch FB(-)-*Salmo*(-) during 49 days after the inoculation used to Jaccard coefficient and UPGMA average

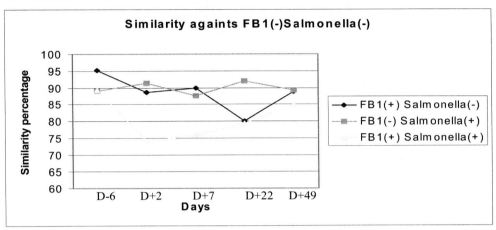

Discussion

The statistically significant increase in the Sa/So ratio during our study confirmed the fumonisin intoxination of the pigs. This increase confirmed the impact of the 8,5 ppm of FB1 contamination on the sphingolipid metabolism in the kidney, in the liver or in the serum of the pigs after several weeks of exposure. These results agreed with studies showing that the sphingolipid presence increased in the serum from pigs receiving a food containing of low dose of FB1 (higher or equal to 5 ppm) (Riley, et al., 1993).

This study was a first step to approach the influence of a food naturally contaminated by fumonisins on the excretion of *Salmonella* as it focused on the infectious context (a few days after the inoculation) but also on the finishing pigs. Our experimental conditions showed that a food containing 8,5 ppm FB1 and 2,5 ppm of FB2 did not generate significant effect on the asymptomatic carriage of *Salmonella* but the observed difference in shedding pig proportion and intensity need to be further investigated in conventional herd condition..

However, a major but also transitory reduction on the similarity of the profiles of the batch exposed to the fumonisins and contaminated by *Salmonella* was observed compared to the other batches during the acute phase of the *Salmonella* infection. Therefore, a food containing 8,5 ppm FB1 and 2,5 ppm of FB2 accompanied by an asymptomatic infection with *Salmonella* would transitory induce deterioration of the digestive balance. This should be add to the immunosupressor effect of FB1 (Bouhet et al., 2006) to take into account the effect of presence of FB in pig feed.

Conclusion

In conclusion, under our experimental conditions, an oral exposure of the pigs to chronic exposure during all the fattening of 8,5 ppm of FB1 in naturally contaminated food induce a transitory deterioration of the digestive flora profiles during the acute phase of the *Salmonella* infection.

Bibliography

Beloeil, P. A., et al. 2004. Risk factors for Salmonella enterica subsp. enterica shedding by market-age pigs in French farrow-to-finish herds. *Prev Vet Med*, 63, 103-20.

Fravalo, P., et al. 2002. Risk factors of Salmonella excretion by finishing pigs. *Salmonella and Salmonellosis*, 282-289.

Fravalo, P., et al. 2003a. le portage asymptomatique de Salmonella enterica par des porcs : résultats issus de la constitution d'un modèle en conditions expérimentales. *Journées Rech. Porcine*, 35, 393-400.

Fravalo, P., et al. 2003b. Convenient method for rapid and quantitative assessment of Salmonella enterica contamination : The MINI-MSRV MPN technique. *J. rapid Methods Automation Microbiology*, 11, 81-88.

Giovannacci, I., et al. 2001. Tracing of Salmonella spp. in two pork slaughter and cutting plants using serotyping and macrorestriction genotyping. *J Appl Microbiol.*, 90(1):, 131-47.

Humbert, F. 1997. Les salmonelles. *Manuel de bactériologie alimentaire*, 27-52.

McOrist, A., et al. 2002. A comparison of five methods for extraction of bacterial DNA from human faecal samples. *J Microbiol Methods.*, 50(2), 131-9.

Oswald, I. P., et al. 2003. Mycotoxin fumonisin B1 increases intestinal colonization by pathogenic Escherichia coli in pigs. *Appl Environ Microbiol*, 69, 5870-4.

Bouhet S, et al.. Mycotoxin fumonisin B1 selectively down-regulates the basal IL-8 expression in pig intestine: in vivo and in vitro studies. Food Chem Toxicol. 2006 Oct;44(10):1768-73. Epub 2006 Jun 7.

Riley, R. T., et al. 1993. Alteration of tissue and serum sphinganine to sphingosine ratio: an early biomarker of exposure to fumonisin-containing feeds in pigs. *Toxicol Appl Pharmacol*, 118, 105-12.

Tanguy, M., et al. 2007. Effect of fumonisins and Salmonella on digestive flora profiles assessed using a molecular tool (CE-SSCP). *Safepork*.

Tran, S. T., et al. 2003. Sphinganine to sphingosine ratio and predictive biochemical markers of fumonisin B1 exposure in ducks. *Chem Biol Interact*, 146, 61-72.

Assessment of processes and operating conditions in UK pork abattoirs.

Tinker, D. B.*[1], Dodd, C. E. R.[2], Richards, P.[2], James, S. J.[3], James, C.[3], Wilkin, C-A.[3], Burfoot, D.[4], Howell, M.[5], Purnell, G.[3].

[1] David Tinker & Associates Ltd, Bedfordshire, UK; [2] University of Nottingham, Sutton Bonington, UK; [3] University of Bristol, Langford, UK; [4] Campden and Chorleywood Food Research Association, Gloucestershire, UK; [5] Food Standards Agency, London, UK
*Corresponding author: d.tinker@ntlworld.com

Abstract

In order to determine typical and atypical operations in the slaughtering and dressing of pigs for pork and bacon practices and operations were recorded at eight pig abattoirs. Data included physical parameters such as temperatures and durations. The results indicate that plants are reasonably similar if processing pigs mainly for pork, but those processing mainly for bacon had more aggressive singeing and polishing (black scraper) arrangements. The plants visited used either hot water (tank) or vertical (sprayed hot water) scalding systems prior to dehairing.

This study was carried out to establish a microbiological and physical process baseline which would then enable effective existing practices to be identified, as well as identifying those existing, and also novel, practices which have the potential to be developed in order to reduce carcass contamination by *Salmonella*.

Introduction

Although great strides have been made in trying to reduce the incidence of pigs with salmonella it is logical that efforts should be made in the abattoir to further reduce the contamination of pork by *Salmonella*. Alban et al (2005) indicated that effort applied in Danish slaughterhouses would be more effective at reducing salmonella than further effort on the farms.

The processes, and operating conditions, at the slaughterhouse have an important impact on the microbiological load of the carcasses. Two related projects, funded by the UK's Food Standards Agency (FSA), are attempting to determine which processes can be modified or inserted into a pork line to reduce the contamination of pig carcasses by salmonella. One project, led by the University of Nottingham, is focussing on modifying existing practices that can be shown to have a worthwhile impact on salmonella contamination. The other project, led by the University of Bristol, is investigating novel practices that may be more effective but are likely to require major equipment changes or be included in new plants.

Both projects require a sound understanding of existing practices used in UK pork plants and how these practices impact on carcass contamination. Equipment used for meat plants always has to be reliable, both in the consistency of processing carcasses and also in avoiding mechanical breakdown. The additional impact of equipment design on carcass hygiene is increasingly important.

These two research projects aim to show how current UK pork lines can make best use of existing equipment and practices to reduce salmonella contamination and how, either additions or alterations to the current slaughtering and dressing protocols could reduce the contamination, or cross-contamination, of carcasses by *Salmonella*..

Session 4

Materials and methods

An initial phase, and relevant to both projects, has been to determine what processes and operating conditions are found in pigmeat plants in the UK.

A checklist was prepared covering 50 general points and 27 processes on which operating parameters would be collected. Visits were made, during spring 2006, to eight plants with nominal throughputs of 150-390 pigs per hour. A diagram of each plant was made and measurements taken for certain process durations and conditions. The information was used to determine a) which plants offer typical processes and operating conditions, b) which plants offer atypical processes for further investigation, c) how the processes interrelate, d) what processes, current or novel, might be expected to control or reduce *Salmonella* contamination and e) to give the researchers a sound understanding of how and why these current practices have evolved.

Results
General
All the plants surveyed slaughtered, dressed, chilled, cut and packed pigmeat. The majority of plants killed in the range 5,000-8,000 pigs per week but two plants killed over 12,000 pig per week. Pigs were typically 70-78 kg (the range was 55-110 kg overall). Across all plants the throughput ranged from 50 pigs per hour to 390 pigs per hour; the mean being 270 pigs per hour.

Three plants specialised in producing bacon while the others produced carcasses mainly for pork with some bacon. All plants supply UK supermarkets, with two plants having close ties with one supermarket and the others supplying several supermarkets and niche outlets.

All plants have made minor process changes and refurbished existing equipment since the original plant construction. Recent changes have been in stunning and scalding equipment for perceived improvements to welfare, water use, effluent costs or microbiology. Many changes were under consideration to tackle specific processing issues; common ones being introduction of CO_2 stunning and steam scalding equipment.

Plants had 30-100 abattoir staff, including those in the lairage. The transit time from kill to chill was between 30 mins and 60 mins; the mean was 38 mins. Every plant processed carcasses identically, whether for pork or bacon, as the final products were not known until grading.

Microbiology
All plants stated that they produced a safe product. Reasons for this confidence included the bacterial kill potential of the singeing operation, and that all products would be cooked before consumption. If microbiological results on the final product are good then it is often assumed the production process must be hygienic.

Generally plants are content with current microbial information but most would find microbiological profiles along the line interesting, although these have not been carried out by the plants themselves. The majority of plants perform shelf life microbiology on the finished product.

All plants specify visually clean animals from supplier farms. Excessively dirty pigs are commonly washed with the sprinklers in the lairage (if air temperature is warm enough). Producers of habitually dirty animals are typically dropped from supplier lists.

The majority of plants use the UK Meat Hygiene Service Inspectors to record contamination incidents, but a few make their own records. Typically the incident type (gut rupture, machine damage, trimming/cutting errors, etc) is notified by a coloured tag or band. Corrective actions for all but the most serious problems take place on the line for lower speed plants while higher speed plants have a detain rail for corrective action. Some plants feed information back to the farm regarding diseases or defects found, and to dressing staff for gut spillage incidents.

The majority of plants are not considering carcass decontamination measures as final product microbiology results are good and cooking will occur before consumption. However one plant would use a chlorine-based carcass wash if it were legal and two plants were considering steam pasteurisation units and one a hot water decontamination unit for the final carcass. As a principle, processors attempt to keep the carcass as dry as possible.

Robotics and automation technologies are seen as the only major processing development in the last 10 years, but the expensive commitment is not currently financially prudent for the UK pork industry.

Slaughterline and Dressing Operations

Figure 1 shows schematically the main stages of a bacon plant. Table 1 provides a summary of UK pigmeat production processes seen across the plants surveyed.

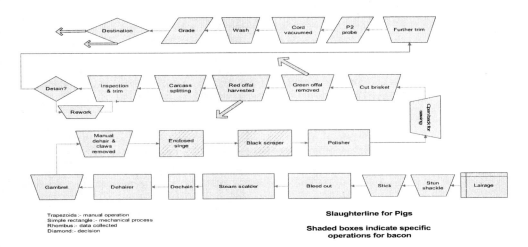

Trapezoids :- manual operation
Simple rectangle :- mechanical process
Rhombus :- data collected
Diamond :- decision

Slaughterline for Pigs

Shaded boxes indicate specific operations for bacon

Figure 1 Slaughterline and main dressing operations for a bacon plant.

Table 1. Summary of UK pigmeat production processes.

Abattoir Process	Notes
1. Lairage	All plants had similar lairages.
2. Stunning	Six plants used electrical stunning. Two had CO_2 stunning.
3. Sticking	Similar in all plants
4. Bleeding	Similar in all plants
5. Scalding	Six plants used hot water scalding. Two had vertical scalding units. Scald tank designs included pull, push, and "waterwheel" types (both continuous and intermittent). Scalding temperatures and durations were between 58-64°C and 4-6.75min respectively. Carcass surface temperatures at scalder outlet, measured across all plants, ranged between 48.6 and 63°C. The mean was 57.8°C.
6. Dehairing	Spiral type dehairers were the most common. A few plants used 2-stage horizontal flail types and one used a single stage horizontal flail type. Carcass surface temperatures at dehairer outlet, measured across all plants, ranged between 33.5 and 53.7°C. The mean was 43.4°C.
7. Gambrelling	Similar in all plants
8. Dry polishing	All dry polishers used combinations of rotary whip flails on vertical and horizontal axes. Polisher length was generally around 2m. Two plants did not have a dry polish operation and a third used a dry scraper instead.

9. Singeing	Vertical, intermittent gas flame singe units predominated with a few plants (specifically those specialising in bacon) using an enclosed unit that enclosed the carcass and had a single flame from the base.
	Measured singe durations ranged from 5s to 16s with a mean of 8.75s.
	Carcass surface temperatures at singe outlet measured across all plants ranged between 58 and 109.1°C. The mean surface temperature was 78.3°C. Where measured, the temperature varied by at least 20°C over the length of the carcass.
10. Wet polishing	The most popular type of wet polisher consisted of various numbers and combinations of vertical and horizontal rotary whip flails. The mean length of these types of polisher was 3.3m.
	Three plants, specifically those specialising in bacon, used black scrapers rather than polishers which had metal-tipped compliant scrapers on moving belts, and additional brushing and scraping components. The mean length of these types of polisher was 17.5m.
	Carcass surface temperatures at outlet measured across all plants ranged between 15.8 and 40.2°C. The mean surface temperature was 34.5°C.

For evisceration and final dressing all plants followed the same general sequence of rectum loosening, ventral opening, viscera removal, splitting, inspection, grading and chilling. However there were substantial differences in trimming, washing, additional cutting, etc. These variations are too numerous to describe in this document.

Discussion

Each plant had some aspect that was substantially different. The major difference between the eight plants was whether they were dedicated bacon plants, with a more severe, enclosed, singe and different scraping and polishing procedures, or whether they were plants producing mainly pork. The type of scalder used, whether it was a hot water tank or vertical spray, was another difference expected to have a major impact on carcass contamination. Processes such as evisceration, splitting, inspection and grading were broadly similar in all plants.

A further microbiological baseline study along with information from literature will be used to focus research effort on operations most likely to offer major reductions in *Salmonella* contamination.

This information, together with the baseline data, could be used in mathematical models to help determine operations most likely to have a major impact on the final carcass contamination levels.

Conclusions

All plants exhibit generally similar processes and encounter the same problems.

The differences between plants, particularly in type of scalder and singe unit (and associated polishing system), has indicated where to take further baseline microbiological measurements.

However because of practical and safety reasons it will prove difficult to directly compare all stages between all plants. Many operations are enclosed or guarded at one or both ends, forcing swabbing of carcasses to be undertaken away from the target operation.

Certain plants are more suitable for further measurements based on equipment in place and accessibility of line for sampling.

References

Alban, L. and Stärk, K., 2005. Where should the effort be put to reduce the *Salmonella* prevalence in the slaughtered swine carcass effectively? *Preventative Veterinary Medicine* 68 (1), 63-79.

Salmonella immunization confers cross protection without confounding pre-harvest serologic monitoring

Husa, J.*[1], Edler, R.[1], Saltzman, R.[2], Holck, JT.[1], Walter, D.[1]

[1] Boehringer Ingelheim Vetmedica, Inc., Ames, IA, USA. [2] Veterinary Resources, Inc., Ames, IA, USA.
*Husa, J: jhusa@bi-vetmedica.com

Abstract

Food borne *Salmonella* Typhimurium is a valid concern for the global pork industry. An attenuated oral swine *Salmonella* Choleraesuis vaccine has proven to be an effective tool for the pre-harvest reduction of carrier rates for multiple *Salmonella spp*. Serum antibody assays are available to monitor exposure to wild-type *Salmonella* infection. This clinical study assessed protection induced by an attenuated oral *Salmonella* Choleraesuis vaccine against challenge infection with S. Typhimurium in swine. A serologic antibody assay was concurrently evaluated for its ability to differentiate vaccinated pigs from those challenged with *Salmonella* Typhimurium. Vaccination significantly improved clinical scores, pyrexia, and enteric lesion prevalence, while numerically improving average daily weight gain, and group body weight variation in comparison to unvaccinated/challenged pigs. Vaccination, while protecting pigs against disease, did not generate detectable serum antibodies prior to challenge. No vaccinated animals became seropositive prior to challenge, indicating that conventional ELISA tests could be used in vaccinated pigs to monitor wild-type exposure. Following challenge, there was no detectable difference between vaccinated/challenged and non-vaccinated/challenged animals. All strict control pigs remained serum antibody negative. These findings support the use of this vaccine to protect swine against S. Typhimurium, without confounding pre-harvest *Salmonella* serologic monitoring programs.

Introduction

Salmonella Typhimurium infection in swine reduces growth performance and presents a food safety risk to humans. (Flores *et al*, 2002. CDC, 2005) A commercial swine vaccine has been shown to reduce the carrier rate of pigs infected with various *Salmonella spp* including S. Typhimurium. (Neubauer *et al*, 2005. Kolb *et al*, 2002. Letellier *et al*, 2001. Baum *et al*, 1998.) Various pre-slaughter diagnostic tools can aid in the appropriate implementation of vaccination and

FLORES, J., DUFRESNE, L., KOLB, J., 2002. Effect of Enterisol® SC-54 vaccination on pig growth performance. *Proceedings 17th International Pig Veterinary Society Congress*, (2),151.
CENTERS FOR DISEASE CONTROL AND PREVENTION (CDC), 2005. *Salmonella Surveillance: Annual Summary*. 2004: http://www.cdc.gov/ncidod/dbmd/offices.htm.
NEUBAUER, A., ROOF, M., KOLB, J., 2005. Vaccine efficacy in swine challenged with a highly virulent S. Typhimurium. *Proceedings 6th Intl Symposium of Epidemiology and Control of Food-borne Pathogens in Pork*:124-125.
KOLB, J., ROOF, M., BURKHART, K., 2002. Reduction of *Salmonella* in carcasses using Enterisol® SC-54 vaccination. *Proceedings 17th International Pig Veterinary Society Congress*, (2), 14.
LETELLIER, A., MESSIER, S., LESSARD, L., CHENIER, S., QUESSY, S., 2001. Host response to various treatments to reduce *Salmonella* infections in swine. *Canadian Journal of Veterinary Research*. (65):168-172.
BAUM, D., HARRIS, D., ROOF, M., NIELSEN, B., HOLCK, J., POLSON, D., BAIK, J., 1998. Use of SC-54 for the reduction of *Salmonella* in swine. *Proceedings 15th International Pig Veterinary Society Congress*, 124.

assessment of the infection status of farms. (Schwartz et al, 2006) Serum antibody tests would be most useful if they did not detect antibodies due to vaccination, while still detecting antibody generated by infection with wild-type Salmonella. This clinical study evaluated heterologous protection and the serum antibody response of pigs vaccinated with attenuated-live S. Choleraesuis vaccine, followed by challenge with virulent S. Typhimurium.

Materials and Methods

Sixty weaned pigs, approximately 3 weeks of age, were confirmed to be Salmonella serum antibody and fecal culture negative. They were blocked by weight and sex and randomly assigned to 3 treatment groups (n=20/group, Table 1). Group 1 (Infected Control) pigs were non-vaccinated and then challenged with virulent Salmonella Typhimurium on Day 43. Group 2 pigs (Vaccinates) were vaccinated on Day 0 (Enterisol® SC-54, Boehringer Ingelheim Vetmedica, Inc., St Joseph, MO, USA) according to the manufacturer's label instructions, and then followed by challenge on Day 43. Group 3 (Strict Control) pigs were non-vaccinated and non-challenged. To achieve blinding, the person performing observations or necropsies was not present during treatment administration. Serum samples were collected from all pigs on Days 0, 7, 14, 21, 28, 35, 43, 52, 57, 64 and 70, and tested for anti-Salmonella antibodies (IDEXX HerdChek® Swine Salmonella Antibody Test Kit, IDEXX Laboratories Inc., Westbrook, ME, USA). Rectal temperatures were measured on Days -2, -1, 0, daily from Day 1 through 21, 28, and daily from Day 43 through 58. Individual pig weights were recorded on Days -5, 0, 2, 7, 14, 21, 28, 35, 43, 50, 57, 64, and 71. Clinical observations were recorded on Days -2 through 7, 14, 21, 28, 35, daily from Day 43 through 58, 61, 63, 65, 68, and 70 using a qualitative scoring system. On Day 43, virulent Salmonella Typhimurium was administered intranasally to Groups 1 and 2 as described in previous studies. (Neubauer et al, 2005) On Day 57, half of the pigs in each treatment group were randomly selected for euthanasia. The remaining animals were euthanized on Day 71. Necropsy observations were recorded for all animals. Statistical analysis of pyrexia, average daily gain (ADG), and clinical score data was performed using Two-sample t-test, and enteric lesion statistical analysis used a Fishers Exact Test. Significantly different means were determined using the Tukey-Kramer multiple comparisons method with a confidence level of 95% (JMP v5.1, SAS Institute, Inc., Cary, NC, USA).

Table 1. Treatment Groups Events Timeline

	Day 0	Day 43	Day 57	Day 71
Group 1 (infected control)	-	C	N_1	N_2
Group 2 (vaccinates)	V	C	N_1	N_2
Group 3 (strict control)	-	-	N_1	N_2

V = Vaccination with Enterisol® SC-54
C = Challenge with S. Typhimurium
N_1 = Necropsy one-half of pigs in each treatment group
N_2 = Necropsy remaining pigs in each treatment group

Results

The number of days with elevated rectal temperatures following challenge was significantly less for the Vaccinated group than the Infected Control group on 3 of 16 measurement days (P<0.05). Mean clinical observation scores were significantly reduced in the Vaccinates compared to the Infected Controls on 3 of 20 observation days after challenge (P<0.05). Additionally, Vaccinates had numeric improvement of clinical scores compared to Infected Controls on 9 of 20 days, equivalent clinical scores on 7 of 20 days, and numerically higher clinical scores on only a single

SCHWARTZ, P., BOROWSKY, L., WALBER, E., KUNRATH, C., BARCELLOS, D., CARDOSO, M., 2006. Use of an attenuated vaccine for control of Salmonella enterica infection in a swine herd in southern Brazil. Proceedings 19th International Pig Veterinary Society Congress, (2):377.

day. Enteric lesion prevalence at necropsy was significantly reduced in Vaccinates compared to the Infected Controls with 3 of 20, and 9 of 19 pigs respectively showing lesions suggestive of *S.* Typhimurium infection (*P*<0.05). Vaccinates tended to have reduced post-challenge variability in average daily weight gain (ADG) (Day 43 through 57) compared to Infected Control pigs, with coefficient of variation (CV) values of 28.1% and 31.4% respectively. This trend continued from Day 57 through Day 71 with CV values of 11.3% and 16.6% respectively (Table 2). Only 1 of 140 serum samples from Vaccinates was ELISA positive from Day 0 through Day 43 (post-vaccination/pre-challenge). This singleton reactor was interpreted as a probable false positive consistent with published diagnostic kit specificity performance. (Rossi, Ballagi, 2006) Seroconversion of all Vaccinates and Infected Controls was observed by 9 days following challenge infection (study Day 52). Internal biosecurity measures utilized during the study were validated by the lack of *Salmonella* seroconversion in all Strict Control pigs (Figure 1).

Table 2. Clinical, Pathologic and Productivity Effects Due to Vaccination

	Group 1 Infected Controls	Group 2 Vaccinates	P Value
Days With Rectal Temperature (Pyrexia) Improved Versus Infected Controls: Day 43-58	NA	3/16	<0.001
ADG: Day 43-57	1.07 lbs	1.35 lbs	0.018
ADG Coefficient of Variation: Day 43-57	31.4%	28.1%	NA
ADG: Day 57-71	1.98 lbs	2.01 lbs	0.804
ADG Coefficient of Variation: Day 57-71	16.6%	11.3%	NA
Days With Clinical Scores Improved Versus Infected Controls: Day 44-70	NA	3/20	<0.01
Enteric Lesion Prevalence	9/19	3/20	0.04

Figure 1. Percent *Salmonella* Seropositive Pigs

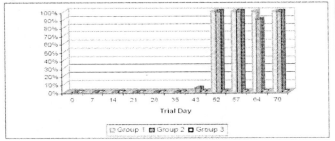

Discussion

Following *S.* Typhimurium challenge, pigs vaccinated with Enterisol® SC-54 had significant reductions in pyrexia, clinical signs, enteric lesion prevalence and significant improvement in ADG from Day 43 through 57. Vaccinates also demonstrated numeric improvements in ADG from Day 57 through 71 and reduced group weight variation compared to nonvaccinated pigs. These findings confirm the ability of this vaccine to provide heterologous protection. Vaccination did not result in a significant incidence of seroconversion. However, all pigs challenged with virulent *Salmonella* Typhimurium, regardless of vaccination status, seroconverted within 9 days of challenge. Lack of seroconversion in response to vaccination indicates that this assay is not suitable as a vaccination compliance tool or as an indicator of protective immunity. Rapid seroconversion following infection demonstrates the ability of this assay to differentiate *Salmonella*-exposed pigs from non-exposed pigs regardless of vaccination status. The findings from this study support the use of this vaccine to clinically protect pigs from heterologous *Salmonella* infection, while preserving the ability to use the serologic tool to assess exposure status to wild-type *Salmonella* infection. Other studies have

ROSSI, A., BALLAGI, A., 2006. Serological monitoring of Salmonella in slaughter pigs using the IDEXX HerdChek swine Salmonella antibody ELISA. *Proceedings 19th International Pig Veterinary Society Congress*, (2):381.

demonstrated the ability of this vaccine to reduce the carrier rate of multiple *Salmonella spp* (Neubauer *et al*, 2005. Kolb *et al*, 2002. Letellier *et al*, 2001. Baum *et al*, 1998.), thereby potentially improving the food safety profile of pork from vaccinated pigs. The collective effects reported from this and other referenced studies support broader use of this vaccine, both as a clinical and productivity tool in swine production, as well as a potential pre-harvest food safety improvement measure.

Conclusions

The results of this clinical trial indicate:

- Vaccination of swine with Enterisol® SC-54 provides heterologous protection against *Salmonella* Typhimurium infection; a common cause of food borne *Salmonella* illness.
- The IDEXX HerdChek® Swine *Salmonella* ELISA does not detect a serologic response to Enterisol® SC-54 vaccination, but will detect antibodies to wild-type *S.* Typhimurium infection regardless of vaccination status. This allows for vaccination without compromising serologic *Salmonella* monitoring programs using this assay.

Evaluation of subtherapeutic use of apramycin on reducing *Salmonella enterica* carriage by fattening pigs.

Martelli, P. *[(1)], Terreni, M.[(2)], Salmi, F.[(1)], Riboldi, E.[(1)], Bonardi, S.[(1)]

Department of Animal Health, Faculty of Veterinary Medicine, University of Parma , Via del Taglio, 8, 43100, Parma, Italy
Veterinary Practitioner – Vigevano (Italy)
* *corresponding author:* paolo.martelli@unipr.it

Abstract

Salmonella enterica is one of the major causes of foodborne diseases in humans and pigs. Pork meat is an important source of human salmonellosis. In order to reduce pig carcass contamination at slaughterhouse, a very effective measure could be the identification of *Salmonella* contaminated livestock farms and the reduction of *Salmonella* in carrier pigs.
The aim of the study was the control of *Salmonella* shedding in pigs by the use of apramycin (200 ppm) in feed medication in fatteners. After one week of treatment, grower pigs had been fed for three months with a mixture of formic acid (21%) and lactic acid (26%) (1000g/ 100 kg of feed). A group of un treated pigs was left as control. The two groups of pigs were tested for *Salmonella* faecal carriage both at the beginning, and in the middle of the trial period by means of pooled faecal samples. Prior to slaughter, each animal was tested by a single rectal swab. Microbiological examination of the two groups showed no differences in *Salmonella* shedding between the two groups.

Introduction

Salmonella has long been recognised as an important pathogen of economic significance in animals and humans. The ongoing increase in human outbreaks of salmonellosis originating from infections in animals contaminating eggs, carcasses, meat products, milk and other foodstuffs (food-born infections/diseases) need concern to be focused on the prevention and control of *Salmonella* in animal production by WHO (WHO, 1993) and the EU (Dir 92/117/EEC). The control of salmonellosis in breeding animals was primarily devoted to poultry production, but the need to control *Salmonella* in swine production is increasingly focused nowadays.
This study aims at evaluating the use of chemical agents (apramycin plus acids) in reducing the faecal carriage of *Salmonella* by fattening pigs, thus reducing the hazard of microbiological contamination of pig carcasses, environment and equipments at slaughter.

Material and methods

Fattener pigs reared in a farrow to finish 2000-sow herd located in Piedmont region, Northern Italy, were fed with apramycin (200 ppm) in feed. After one week of treatment, the grower pigs had been fed for three months with a mixture of formic acid (21%) and lactic acid (26%) (1000g/ 100 kg of feed). The selected pigs were divided into two groups (80 animals per group). A group of pigs was kept untreated and served as "control" group. The pigs were reared in four boxes of 40 animals each. Treated and control pigs did not share contact for the entire trial period.
The two groups of pigs were tested for *Salmonella* faecal carriage both at the beginning, and in the middle of the trial period by means of pooled faecal samples. Prior to slaughter, animals were individually tested by a single rectal swab. Samples were kept at 4°C and transported to the laboratory the day of collection.
For *Salmonella* detection, the ISO 6597:2002 method was followed. A 10-g aliquot of faecal material was diluted 1:10 in Buffered Peptone Water (BPW) and rectal swabs were transferred in tubes containing 10 mL of BPW. After incubation at 37 °C $\pm$ 1 °C for 18 $\pm$ 2 h, 1 mL of the pre-enrichment cultures was transferred into 10 mL of Muller-Kauffmann tetrathionate/novobiocin broth (MKTT) and 0.1 mL into 10 mL of Rappaport Vassiliadis broth with soya (RVS broth). Enrichment broths were incubated at 37 °C $\pm$ 1 °C and 41.5 °C $\pm$ 1 °C for 24 $\pm$ 3 h, respectively. Thereafter,

10-μl aliquots of the broth-cultures were plated onto Xylose Lysine Deoxycholate agar (XLD) and Brilliant Green Agar (BGA) selective media. The selective plates were incubated at 37°C °C for 24 ± 3 h and examined for suspect colonies. Negative plates were re-incubated for additional 18-24 h. *Salmonella* suspect colonies were picked up and subjected to biochemical (TSI, LIA, urease) and serological tests (*Salmonella* O-omnivalent serum). For *Salmonella* genus identification, the API 20 E ® (bioMérieux, Marcy l'Etoile, France) system was employed. *Salmonella* strains were serotyped by the Istituto Zooprofilattico Sperimentale della Lombardia e dell'Emilia Romagna, Brescia, Italy.

Results and conclusions

The microbiological findings showed no differences in *Salmonella* shedding between the "antimicrobial plus acids" treated pigs and the "controls". The results are shown in table 1. The only *Salmonella* serovar detected in the faecal matter of the two groups of pigs was *S. Rissen*, that is rather common in pigs and cattle in Italy (Enter-Vet, 2005).

	1st sampling (farm) (faecal pools)	2nd sampling (farm) (faecal pools)	3rd sampling at slaughterhouse (individual swabs) *
Treated group	Negative	Positive	5%
Control group	Positive	Positive	5%

* prevalence of Salmonella positive faecal swabs

On our opinion, more studies on *Salmonella* carriage reduction by pigs should be encouraged, together with the control of the introduction of infected-carrier pigs in livestock farms.

References

Enter-VET 2005. *Annual report.* Eds. Ricci A., Mancin M., Cibin V. Padua: Centro Referenza Nazionale Salmonellosi (CNRS), Istituto Zooprofilattico Sperimentale delle Venezie.
WHO (1993). *Report of the WHO Consultation on Control of Salmonella Infections in Animals. Prevention of Food-borne Salmonella infections in Man.* Jena, Germany, 21-26 November.

Reduction of antimicrobials by use of vaccination
- the ileitis experience -

Voets, H.

Boehringer Ingelheim Animal Health GmbH, Ingelheim, Bingerstrasse 173, 55216 Ingelheim, Germany. E-mail: *Harm.Voets@ing.boehringer-ingelheim.com*

Abstract

Porcine Enteropathy also known as ileitis in pigs, caused by *Lawsonia intracellularis,* is regarded as one of the major gut related health issues in pork production. Recent reports from national institutes for pharmaceutical products show that the annual amount of antibiotics against enteric diseases has increased over the last few years. Despite the ban of antimicrobial growth promoters in Europe since January 2006, the total amount of antibiotics used in pigs does not seem to be significantly reduced. This is contradictory to the demands of the consumers for a reduction in antibiotic use and the efforts to reduce the risk of antibiotic resistance. Recently several field studies have demonstrated that the use of Enterisol® ileitis (Boehringer Ingelheim), a vaccine against ileitis can reduce the amount of antibiotics needed to prevent this disease. Additionally, vaccination can contribute to the overall reduction in use of antimicrobials on farms due to the higher health status of the farms. This oral vaccine is therefore a better alternative compared to antibiotics to prevent ileitis.

Introduction

In the past few years, the political situation on antimicrobial use in agriculture has changed. According to Wagstrom (2006), "the issue of antimicrobial use in food animals has in many ways moved out of the arena of scientific debate, and into the arena of consumer activism". This statement is based on the increasing presence of consumer groups on the internet and other open sources which question the way food producing animals are kept and raised. In Europe the ban on antimicrobial growth promoters (AGP) was started in Sweden and Denmark. The results were a drastic reduction in the overall tonnage in preventive antimicrobials, with a shift to more therapeutic use of antimicrobials especially against enteric diseases. Since then, an increase in overall antibiotic usage has been reported in Denmark (Danmap 2005). New problems have arisen with the link between Methicillin resistant Staphylococcus Aureus bacteria and swine production (Voss et al. 2005). This problem has recently led to media coverage on national television in the Netherlands (Zembla 2006).

The use of vaccines in swine production has demonstrated over the years to be a good alternative for antibiotics for many diseases. In the year 2000 Boehringer Ingelheim introduced Enterisol® ileitis, the first and only vaccine against ileitis caused by *Lawsonia intracellularis,* in the United States market. Since then, this vaccine has obtained marketing authorisation in most of the major pig producing countries throughout the world. In multiple trials the potential of Enterisol® ileitis for the reduction of antibiotics is investigated.

Study 1 - Mexico
Materials and methods

This study was performed in northern Mexico. The production system was a multiple-site farm with 4000 sows. A total of 11 weekly production batches were evaluated; 7 control groups and 4 vaccinated groups. Production parameters were evaluated using standard statistical process control methods. Criteria evaluated included: Average daily weight gain (ADWG), Feed efficiency (FE), Age at market, Weight at market, and Percent Culls.

Treatment procedures for each group were as follows:

Group 1: The control group used a pulse feed medication program during the entire finishing phase (body weight in parenthases):

- Tylosin 110 ppm/carbadox 55 ppm (12-25Kg).
- Tylosin 88 ppm/carbadox 27.5 ppm (25-40kg)
- Tylosin 40 ppm/salinomycin 60 ppm (40-60kg)

Group 2: Pigs were given a live vaccine against *Lawsonia intracellularis* (Enterisol® Ileitis), vaccinated at 5 weeks of age in the nursery by oral administration. Additionally a reduced pulse medication program was implemented:

- Tylosin 88 ppm/carbadox 55 ppm (25-40 kg)
- Salinomycin 60 ppm (40-60 kg).

Results

Vaccinated pigs grew nearly 15% faster than conventionally medicated pigs (Table 1).

Table 1: Production Parameters and % Improvement

	Control	Vx EI	Dif	%
Number of pigs (n)	14,752	8,145		
ADWG (g)	758	863	+ 105	+ 14
FC (kg/kg)	2.65	2.60	- 0.05	- 2
Market Weight (kg)	87.88	98.33	+ 10.45	+ 12
Market age (d)	143.91	139.05	- 4.86	- 3
Mortality site 3 (%)	4.54	3.56	- 0.98	- 22
Culls (%)	7.16	3.79	- 3.37	- 47

Other parameters showing improvement include mortality, market weight and age, and cull rates. Feed efficiency remained unchanged even with total antimicrobial use reduced by 35% in vaccinated pigs.

Figure 1: Statistical Process Control (SPC) chart of ADWG pre and post vaccination.

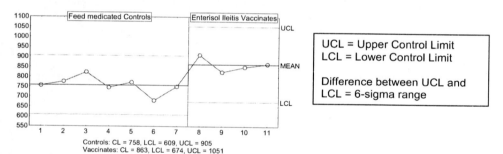

Controls: CL = 758, LCL = 609, UCL = 905
Vaccinates: CL = 863, LCL = 674, UCL = 1051

UCL = Upper Control Limit
LCL = Lower Control Limit

Difference between UCL and LCL = 6-sigma range

Study 2 - USA
Materials and methods

A production system, typical for the Midwestern U.S, raises approximately 2.5 M pigs per year, out of a total US production of 100 M pigs. The average sow farm size is 4000 sows, with approximately 1500 new gilts per farm per year. Nursery and finishers are housed separately off site (multi-site production). Most finishing barns have deep pig manure storage over slatted floors, though 20% are shallow pits with "pull plug" systems. In this large a production system, health controls, like any management programs, must be standardized, simple and repeatable to apply, and deliver consistent results, with little added treatments needed.

The history of enteric disease in the pigs included all common pathogens seen in commercial pig production - feed induced diarrhoea, gastric ulcers, Salmonellosis, PCV-2, nonspecific colitis, hemorrhagic bowel syndrome, torsions and endemic TGE (transmissible gastroenteritis virus). These conditions were diagnosed by routine pathology and histopathology. Both the chronic/Proliferative Intestinal Adenomatosis (PIA) form and acute/Porcine Haemorrhagic Enteropathy (PHE) form are present in the system. Chronic diarrhoea historically began in commercial pigs from 70 kg/150 lb to market, in the finishing barn. Hemorrhagic ileitis would occur in some groups of pigs around the first marketing cut, and in replacement gilts after placement into sow farms, at around 33 weeks of age.

Control of *Lawsonia intracellularis* and other enteric diseases was attempted with feed grade medications. In nursery pigs, a system of carbadox, tiamulin/chlortetracycline and chlortetracycline alone was used. This continues today for its broad spectrum respiratory and enteric benefit. Control of *Lawsonia intracellularis* in finishing was based on several combinations of tylosin, either at 100 ppm followed by 40 ppm, or 40 ppm continuously from 35 to 60 kg. Breaks on this medication program occurred frequently, at an average of 70 or more enteric cases per month. Water soluble tylosin was used as the first treatment option. When cases would not respond, water therapy was changed to tiamulin.

The goal for use of Enterisol® Ileitis was to reduce overall in-feed and water medication use, and, with similar cost, improve clinical control of disease in both high value replacement gilts and finishing pigs. Replacement gilts were the first target for vaccination given their cost and the poor response to treatment of PHE cases. Vaccination of these animals began in 2001. Following success in these animals, vaccine was tested in finishing pigs in 2002, with pigs vaccinated at 12-14 weeks of age, just following placement into finishing.

Results
Vaccination has dramatically altered the feed medication program in finishing pigs and replacement gilts. Routine use of both in-feed tylosin as well as growth promoting antibiotics has dropped to zero (see figure 2). The numbers of groups needing treatment for diarrhoea of any kind has been reduced over 75% (<15 cases/month now) even with the removal of all in-feed medications (100 % reduction). This has made health management much simpler at the field supervisor level, as well as in the feed mill.

Figure 2: Effect of Enterisol ileitis vaccination on the use of feed grade tylosin.

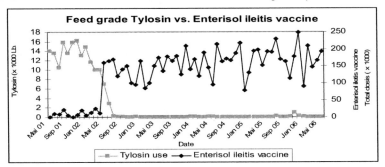

Study 3 - Germany
Materials and Methods
This longitudinal study was executed in a farrow-to-finish farm of 1,600 sows and 10.000 fattening places. The control group consisted of 16,032 pigs out of 32 fattening groups that were slaughtered between November 2004 and July 2005. The 13,848 slaughtered, Enterisol® ileitis vaccinated pigs belonged to 27 groups. They reached slaughter between May and November 2005. All pigs were housed under identical conditions. The monitored parameters for the fattening period were ADWG (average daily weight gain), FC (Feed conversion ratio), mortality, and amount of antibiotic used against enteric diseases (AB use). The gross margin (GM) indicates the possible economical benefit of the vaccination based on prior performance parameters.

Results

Table 2 summarizes the results, which showed significant improvement in all parameters.
Not only a reduction of the overall level of antibiotic use is shown, but additionally to table 2 an increased level of control in pig production in this farm is seen since vaccination started. Furthermore, an economic benefit, expressed as Gross Margin of € 6.37 was generated.

Table 2: Average growth performances, antibiotic use and Gross Margin (GM) in vaccinated pigs versus non-vaccinated controls.

	Control	*Vaccinated*	*Diff.*
ADWG g/day	738	766	+ 28 ***
FCR g/g	3.16	2.98	- 0.18 ***
Mortality %	4	2.8	- 1.2 ***
AB use Kg/group *	2.23	1.03	- 53% ***
Av. GM / pig (€) **	25.34	31.71	+6.37

* AB use for therapeutic treatment of enteric diseases
**Assumptions: Feed price 170 €/T; Piglet price 57 € or 1.93 €/ Kg if < 30 Kg; Pig price 1.44 €/Kg
*** Significantly different with a p-value < 0,001

Conclusion

The results show a broad improvement in groups of vaccinated pigs. Even with a reduction of antimicrobial use, pigs grew faster and more consistently.

These studies demonstrated that producers may have the option of eliminating finishing dietary antimicrobial use while reducing input costs and maintaining performance similar to or better than continuously medicated, non-vaccinated pigs. An overall reduction of 35 to 100 percent of in-feed antibiotics was realized.

As restrictions on antimicrobial use continue to increase, pork producers will need more options for controlling diseases like ileitis which have traditionally accounted for much of the need for antimicrobial use. Use of Enterisol® ileitis to control ileitis is a biologically feasible, environmentally responsible and economically attractive alternative to continuous feeding of antimicrobials.

Acknowledgments

Edgar Diaz, Jean Claude Chevez, Andy Holtkanp, Ricarda Steinheuer, Christoph Keller, Matthias Adam and Kirsten Klien

References

Wagstrom, L., 2006. The political situation surrounding antimicrobial use in agriculture. *Alan D. Leman Swine Conference 2006; 139 -141*

Danmap 2005 – July 2006. *Statens Serum Institut, Danish Veterinary and Food administration, Danish Medicines Agency, Danish Institute for Food and Veterinary Research.* ISSN 1600-2032

Voss A, et al., 2005. Methicillin-resistant *Staphylococcus aureus* in pig farming. *Emerg Infect Dis. 2005 Dec.* http://www.cdc.gov/ncidod/EID/vol11no12/05-0428.htm

ZEMBLA 2006. 'Ziekenhuisbacterie in de varkensstal', zondag 17 december 2006 om 22.15 uur bij de VARA/NPS op Nederland 3.
http://omroep.vara.nl/Nieuws_detail_Zembla.1536.0.html?&tx_ttnews[tt_news]=795&tx_ttnew s[backPid]=1303&cHash=6abd769c29

ORAL & POSTER

FIFTH SESSION

**Laboratory methods:
(pathogenesis,
detection, typing)**

A ring trial for testing the comparability of the laboratory results of three commercial Salmonella antibody ELISA tests in Germany, Denmark and The Netherlands

Blaha, T.[*(1)], Bode, K.[(1)], Merle, R.[(2)], Schneider, B.[(3)], Kreienbrock, L.[(2,3)]

[1]Field Station for Epidemiology, University of Veterinary Medicine Hannover, Buescheler Str. 9, 49456 Bakum, Germany.
[2]WHO Collaborating Centre for Research and Training in Veterinary Public Health, University of Veterinary Medicine Hannover, Buenteweg 2, 30559 Hannover, Germany.
[3]Department of Biometry, Epidemiology and Information Processing, University of Veterinary Medicine Hannover, Buenteweg 2, 30559 Hannover, Germany
[*]*corresponding author:* thomas.blaha@tiho-bakum.de

Abstract

Three commercial and one non-commercial ELISA test kits for detecting Salmonella antibodies in meat juice of pigs were tested in an international ring test. All test kits proved to produce highly comparable results. The result has relevance for the upcoming Salmonella control strategy in the EU, if the national Salmonella reduction measures are planned to be based on a serological risk categorisation of pig herds.

Introduction

Since 2002, a serological Salmonella monitoring programme has been carried out in all German finishing pig herds that participate in the "QS-System", a voluntary national quality management system approving the correctness of the production procedures for food resulting in the control stamp "QS". This monitoring aims at categorising the participating herds (40% of all German herds representing 75% of the German pork production) according to the risk of introducing Salmonella into the pork chain via infected slaughter pigs into three categories (I = low, II = middle, III = high). The classification into the categories is calculated quarterly based on the percentage of Salmonella antibody positive meat juice samples within a random sample of 60 per year for each farm. All data generated within the monitoring are entered into the central database Qualiproof® (Qualitype AG, Dresden), which provides automatically the categorisation every quarter of a year and suggest the daily sample size at slaughter for every herd participating (ANONYMOUS, 2007).

For the acceptance of the results obtained by using three commercial and additionally "QS-approved" ELISA test systems in "QS-approved" laboratories, it is extremely important to make sure that the results of all three tests in all laboratories are comparable. Therefore, every laboratory that wants to serve the QS-system has to take part in the yearly ring trial for maintaining their "QS-approval" valid.

Material and methods

From a multitude of pre-tested single meat juice samples, forty mixed meat juice samples à 50 ml were pooled in a way that 10 of these samples were adjusted to be highly positive (> 80 OD%), 10 to be highly negative (< 10 OD%), and 20 were adjusted to have OD% values around the cut-off value of 40 OD% (30 – 50 OD%).

These pooled meat juice samples were aliquoted into 1640 single test samples. These test samples were enumerated using a random generator, lyophilised and sent to 43 laboratories (4 Dutch, 1 Danish and 38 German labs) taking part in the 2006 ring trial. The samples were, of course, absolutely unknown to all laboratories.

The lyophilisation was chosen to minimise any thinkable influence of different treatment of the samples before using them in the ring trial such as failures in the freezing/cooling chain, multiple freezing and thawing procedures of the same sample and the like. Every laboratory was asked to apply its routinely used method and test system according to the test producer's instructions. The three commercial and "QS-approved" tests that were included into the ring trial used in the German laboratories and in the Dutch laboratories were: SALMOTYPE® Pig Screen (Labor Diagnostik Leipzig, Leipzig), HerdCheck® (IDEXX), and Enterisol® (Boehringer Ingelheim). The Danish laboratory used its own, non-commercial, but well established "Danish mixed ELISA".

Results

Two laboratories were excluded from the evaluation of the ring trial, since their results were completely non-congruent with the expected outcome. Both laboratories (No. 13 and 16) had only applied for the QS-approval and had used the test kits for the first time - they did not get the QS-approval.

All other participating laboratories showed a satisfying degree of congruity compared to the results of the Danish laboratory (the results of which were used as reference values). All laboratories detected the highly positive samples as "high positive" and all highly negative samples as "high negative" (see Figure 1a and 1b).

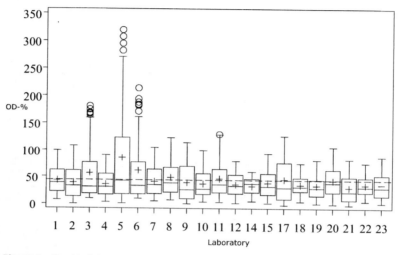

Figure 1a. Graphical demonstration of the results of all laboratories in OD% for all samples

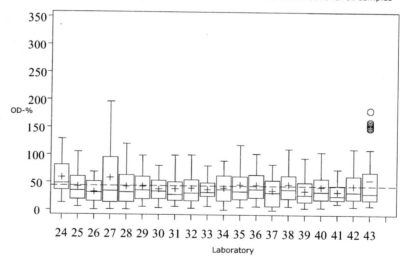

The results of the accuracy of the tests and the laboratories in terms of assigning a sample to "positive" or "negative" can be seen in Figure 2.

Figure 2. Dichtomised results of all samples and laboratories sorted according the median of the OD% values over all laboratories (0 = "negative", < 30 OD%; 1 = "around the cut-off", 30 – 50 OD%; 2 = "positive", > 50 OD%; L = Laboratory)

The ring test results show that there are some differences between the tests, but again mainly in the "very high positive" samples. However, if the assignment of the samples to "positive" and "negative" is taken into consideration, only samples "around the cut-off" differ from test to test (see Figure 3)

Session 5

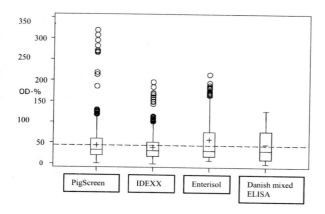

Figure 3. Graphical demonstration of the results sorted by test kit

Discussion and conclusion

There are huge differences in the positive values between the laboratories. These differences are due to the fact that some laboratories capped the positive values at 100 OD%, whereas others did not (the highest positive value measured was 319.7 OD%).

Since, however, the categorisation of the monitoring programme is based on the percentage of Salmonella "positive" animals in the random sample of 60, only the accuracy of the dichtomised decision ("positive" or "negative") is of importance for the accuracy of the monitoring. The fact that the group of "around the cut-off" samples show a lower degree of congruity, is "natural", since a sample measured with 39.9 OD% in one laboratory (or with one test) is "negative", and measured with 40.1 OD% in another laboratory (or another test) is "positive", although both laboratories (or tests) were very accurate. However, taking into consideration that only 10% to 15% of the samples in the field are around this cut-off (and not 50% as in the artificial test sample collection), and that the categorisation is always based on 60 samples, it becomes obvious that the few samples around the cut-off value in the 60 sample do not really influence the categorisation.

Summarising the results of the presented ring trial it can be said: the tested three commercial Salmonella antibody ELISA tests are highly comparable with the original Danish mixed ELISA, they are robust in terms of their repeatability and usability in various laboratories. These two characteristics of the tested tests is very important in the light of the EU Directive 99/2003/EC and the EU Regulation (EC) 2160/2003, since the harmonisation of Salmonella antibody ELISA tests for the categorisation of pig herds according to their risk of introducing Salmonella into the food chain is a prerequisite for the comparability of the Salmonella surveillance and reduction programmes in the EU member states (VAN DER HEIJDEN, 2001; VAN DER WOLF et al., 2001).

References

ANONYMOUS, 2007. Guidelines for the Salmonella monitoring and reduction programme within the QS-System. *www.q-s.info*

VAN DER WOLF P.J., ELBERS A.R., VAN DER HEIJDEN H.M., VAN SCHIE F.W., HUNNEMAN W.A., TIELEN M.J., 2001. *Salmonella* seroprevalence at the population and herd level in pigs in The Netherlands. *Vet. Microbiol.* 80, 171-184.

VAN DER HEIJDEN H.M., 2001. First international ring trial of ELISAs for *Salmonella*-antibody detection in swine. *Berl Munch.Tierarztl.Wochenschr.* 114, 389-392.

Comparative examination and validation of ELISA test systems for Salmonella diagnosis of slaughtering pigs

Szabó, I.*, Scherer, K., Nöckler, K., Appel, B., and Hensel, A.

Federal Institute for Risk Assessment (BfR), Berlin, Germany

Introduction

Infections with *Salmonella* enterica are one of the most important sources of human gastroenteritis. The consumption of contaminated pork products was found to be associated with 20% of human salmonellosis in Germany, whereas *S.* Typhimurium, especially phagetype DT 104, is the most frequently isolated *Salmonella* serotype from pork (Steinbach and Kroell, 1999).

Salmonella infection can be directly diagnosed in the abattoir or at farm level by serodiagnosis using anti-LPS ELISA (Nielsen et al., 1995, Mousing et al., 1997). Serological results are used to classify swine herds in three categories for assessing the hygienic status of farm in regard to *Salmonella* infection in pigs. In this context, reliable ELISA test systems are required for the categorisation of swine herds.

The object of our study was to monitor antibody response and faecal shedding in sixteen weaned pigs experimentally infected with *Salmonella* Typhimurium DT 104. For evaluation of serological results, four ELISA tests approved in Germany were used. Three tests were directed at IgG isotype and one test discriminated between antibody classes IgA, IgM and IgG.

Material and methods

Swine and experimental design

Sixteen 6 weeks old *Salmonella*-free piglets were orally exposed to *S.* Typhimurium DT 104 and followed by clinical examination, blood and faecal sampling until day 130 post inoculation (p.i.). Faecal samples of pigs were tested negative for *Salmonella* at day of arrival. A porcine isolate of multiresistant *Salmonella* Typhimurium strain (BB 440) obtained from a herd of swine with acute salmonellosis was used for infection of pigs. The strain was additionally provided with a nalidixic acid resistance in the National Reference Laboratory for Salmonella. Each pig was infected with 4.4×10^9 cfu DT 104 by intragastric application using a nasal stomach tube. Prior infection animals were sedated with $1.0 - 2.0$ mg/kg azaperon, i.m. Animals were fed with a commercial antibiotic-free feed and provided water ad libitum. Feed was withdrawn 20 h before infection.

Blood samples were taken from the cranial vena cava on the first and second day p.i., until 30 days p.i. twice a week and then at weekly intervals until slaughter. Prevalence of *Salmonella* in faeces was determined daily within the first eleven days p.i., until 30 days p.i. in intervals of 3 days and then once a week until slaughter at day 130 p.i.

Bacteriological examination

Faecal samples of approximately 10 g were inoculated in 1 % Buffered Peptone Water (1.12535, Merck) (1:10), homogenised using a Stomacher 400 (Seward, London, UK) for 2 min at high speed and incubated at 37°C for 24h. Afterwards 0.1 ml was inoculated on MSRV (modified semisolid Rappaport-Vassiliadis, CM 900100; SR161E, Oxoid) agar plates and incubated at 42°C for 24h.

Serological examination

Blood samples were coagulated for 20 h at 4°C and centrifuged for 10 min at 3500 g. Serum was collected and stored at −20°C until analysis. Swine sera were analysed for the presence of antibodies against *Salmonella* according to producers instructions using following kits:

- Salmotype® Pig Screen (LDL Leipzig, Germany),
- HerdChek® Swine Salmonella Antibody (IDEXX Laboratories, Wörrstadt, Germany),
- Enterisol® Salmonellen-Diagnostikum (Boehringer Ingelheim, Germany)
- Salmotype® Pig STM-WCE (LDL Leipzig, Germany)

Results

Clinical findings

During the first week p.i., 31% of pigs suffered from semi-liquid diarrhoea for 1-2 days. Only one pig showed anorexia, vomiting and diarrhoea until the 6th week p.i., thereafter it became convalescent. 69% of pigs had elevated body temperature up to 41.6°C within 24h to 48h p.i. that became normal within 9 days p.i. Weight increased continuously, at day 130 p.i. (age 24.5 weeks) the average weight was 121 kg per pig.

Faecal shedding of S. Typhimurium

S. Typhimurium was isolated from faeces of all 16 infected pigs after one day p.i. All animals excreted Salmonella in faeces until day 16 p.i. Thereafter shedding was intermittent until slaughter except one animal which remained Salmonella-negative (Figure 1).

Serological results

Figure 1 shows the results for percentage of Salmonella-positive animals over the study period for ELISA tests 1-3. In ELISA test 1, individual seroconversion in pigs was observed between day 13 and 67 p.i., whereas the majority of pigs (88%) was positive for Salmonella antibodies between day 28 and 47 p.i. Apart from one pig which became negative for Salmonella at day 130 p.i., all animals remained seropositive. ELISA test 2 detected seroconversion among pigs between day 16 and 47 p.i. However, the majority of pigs (94%) seroconverted between day 22 and 39 p.i. Afterwards, all pigs were tested positive for Salmonella antibodies until slaughter except one pig which became seronegative at day 88 p.i. By use of ELISA test 3, three pigs seroconverted from day 13 p.i. whereas the latest was positive for Salmonella antibodies from day 39 p.i. All animals remained seropositive until the end of experiment.

Results for ELISA test 4 are presented in Figure 2 as mean ELISA units for the different antibody classes IgG, IgM and IgA over the entire study period. Apparently, individual ELISA units varied within all antibody classes especially for anti-Salmonella-IgG. Almost 56% and 94% of infected pigs were already detected 7 and 13 days p.i., respectively by dominant IgM antibodies. Seroconversion of IgA and IgG was observed later whereas majority of animals yielded a positive result from day 22 (75%) and 25 (69%) p.i., respectively. All 16 pigs remained positive for all three immunoglobulin isotypes until day 130 p.i. except one pig which became negative for IgA at day 88 p.i. and another one which did not develop any anti-Salmonella-IgA.

Discussion

In the present study, all 16 animals excreted Salmonella within two weeks p.i., thereafter shedding rate declined and remained intermittent. Similar results were obtained in a study of experimental infections by Nielsen et al. (1995) where 80% of pigs excreted Salmonella Typhimurium during the first week p.i., thereafter excretion decreased and intermittent excretion could be observed. Although primary infection of pigs was induced by experimental inoculation of Salmonella via stomach tube, a spontaneous re-infection of animals due to Salmonella contaminated faeces even during the intermittent shedding stage is most likely.

According to results of serological examination by use of ELISA tests 1-3 and bacteriological findings, the majority of pigs developed no anti-*Salmonella* IgG within the third week in spite of high *Salmonella* excretion in faeces. It is known that the peak of *Salmonella* excretion in faeces is followed by an immune response after 1-2 weeks because it takes time to develop a detectable serological response (Nielsen et al. 1995). Own results confirm the problem of "diagnostic window" in the early stage of infection that may cause false-negative results during serological testing.

In the longitudinal study on detection of *Salmonella* infection in fattening pigs, ELISA tests 1-3 varied in regard to sensitivity. Dependent on the test applied, at least 50% of infected animals were tested positive for *Salmonella* antibodies from day 22 (test 3), day 25 (test 2), and 39 p.i. (test 1), respectively. The highest sensitivity was observed 39, 47, and 67 days p.i. (with test 3, 2, and 1, respectively) when all infected animals were serologically tested positive. This observation may be explained by the fact that the sensitivity to detect *Salmonella* antibodies mainly depends on the respective cut-off recommended for the specific test. Apparently, test 3 revealed the highest sensitivity due to the lowest cut-off. However, ELISA tests with a higher sensitivity likely lack in specificity what was not investigated in this study.

During the chronic stage of infection which covers the main part of life span of a fattening pig, animals showed a higher rate of seropositive reactors by use of all three ELISA tests compared to a lower rate of pigs shedding *Salmonella* in faeces. Considering the probability to find *Salmonella*-positive animals in a farm, antibody detection by ELISA will surpass the bacteriological examination of faeces. However, a conclusion from a seropositive result to the status of *Salmonella* infection (acute *vs.* chronic stage) is not possible. Therefore, ELISA tests directed at IgG are used as screening tests on herd level, but they are not suitable for individual pig testing confirming results from other studies (Nollet et al, 2005).

Meanwhile, novel ELISA systems have been developed, which besides IgG, additionally detect antibody classes IgM and IgA in order to distinct between an early and older infection on individual level (Lehmann, 2004, Ehlers et al., 2006). Own results obtained with ELISA test 4 confirm the usefulness to detect pigs in the early stage of infection better than ELISA tests 1-3. The higher sensitivity of ELISA test 4 is mainly due to the ability to detect antibodies of the early class IgM and finally, contributes to avoid false-negative results. However, this test is more labour intensive, needs a special software for evaluating results and should be considered from the financial point of view. Further investigations on ELISA test 4 are planned on distinction between an early and older infection with special regard to identification of *Salmonella* shedding pigs.

References

Ehlers, J., Alt, M., Trepnau, D., Lehmann, J. 2006. Use of new immunoglobulin isotype-specific ELISA-systems to detect *Salmonella* infections in pigs (German). Berl. Münch. Tierarztl. Wochenschr. 119, 461-466.

Lehmann, J., Lindner, T., Naumann, M., Kramer, T., Steinbach, G., Blaha, T., Ehlers, J., Selbitz, H.-J., Gabert, J., and Roesler, U. 2004. Application of a novel pig immunoglobulin-isotype-specific enzyme-linked immunosorbent assay for detection of *Salmonella enterica* serovar Typhimurium antibodies in serum and meat juice. Proceedings of the 18th International Pig Veterinary Society World Congress, Hamburg. Vol. 1, 383.

Mousing, J., Jensen, P.T., Halgaard, C., Bager, F., Feld, N., Nielsen, B., Nielsen, J.P., and Bech-Nielsen, S. 1997. Nation wide *Salmonella* enterica surveillance and control in Danish slaughter swineherds. Prev Vet med. 29, 247-261.

Nielsen, B., Baggesen, D., Bager, F., Haugegaard, J., and Lind, P. 1995. The serological response to *Salmonella* serovar Typhimurium and Infantis in experimentally infected pigs. The time course followed with an indirect anti-LPS-ELISA and bacteriological examinations. Vet. Microbiol. 47, 205-218.

Nollet, N., Maes, D., Duchateau, L., Hautekiet, V., Houf, K., Van Hoof, J., De Zuttera, L., De Kruif, A., Geers, R. 2005. Discrepancies between the isolation of *Salmonella* from mesenteric lymph nodes and the results of serological screening in slaughter pigs. Vet Res. 36:545-555.

Steinbach, G., und Kroell, U., 1999. Salmonella infections in swine herds – epidemiology and importance for human illness (German). Dtsch. Tierärztl. Wschr. 106, 269-308.

Session 5

Figures

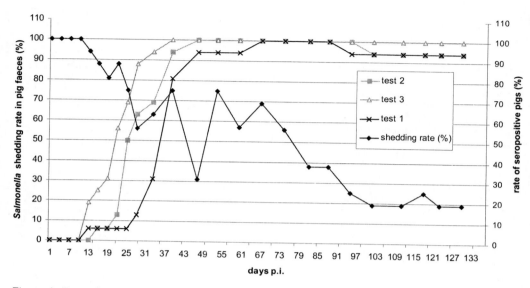

Figure 1: Rate of seropositive pigs (%) detected by ELISA tests 1-3 compared with shedding rate in faeces of pigs (16) infected with *S.* Typhimurium (day 1 to 130 p.i.)

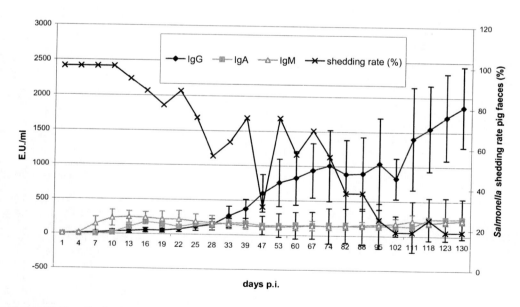

Figure 2: Results for ELISA test 4 (E.U./ml) for antibody classes IgM, IgA, IgG compared with shedding rate in faeces of pigs (16) infected with *S.* Typhimurium (day 1 to 130)

Assessment of a molecular tool (CE-SSCP) to study balance of caecal flora of SPF piglet's groups

Maël Tanguy (1)*, Christine Pissavin-Castillo (1), Marilyne Queguiner (1), Yves Desdevises (2), Roland Cariolet (1), Gérald le Diguerher (1), Christine Burel (1), Philippe Fravalo (1)

(1) French Food Safety Agency (AFSSA), Zoopôle des Côtes d'Armor, BP 53, 22440 Ploufragan, France
(2) Pierre et Marie Curie University, UMR CNRS 7628, BP 44, 66651 Banyuls-sur-Mer Cedex, France
corresponding author: *m.tanguy@afssa.fr*

Abstract

The aims of this study were to test the ability of CE-SSCP in describing the variability of the digestive contents flora of SPF (Specified Pathogenic Free) pigs from our experimental husbandry and to reach, by mixing individual samples, the concept of a digestive flora's profile characteristic of a batch of pigs. The faeces of six SPF sows were sampled and extracted DNA were mixed to constitute more and more composite samples. In addition, the caecal contents of 12 SPF piglets, issued from a single sow, were collected after slaughter at 28, 56 and 84 days postpartum and individually or after pooling tested. The DNA of each sample was extracted using the QIAamp DNA Stool Minikit. The PCR for amplifying the rDNA 16S V3 region was carried out on the individual DNAs and the mixed DNAs corresponding to each date of slaughtering. Then the PCR products were analysed by CE-SSCP. The reproducibility of the method has been tested first, and then the analysis of the profiles obtained from the faeces of the swine was conducted. It described a within-individual variability of about 40% when comparing SPF sows. When we mixed samples, variability between the profiles decreases with increasing number of faeces constituting the pool of DNA. Concerning the piglets, for each date of sampling, the pool of caecal contents DNA defined a characteristic group profile. Moreover, this profile varied with the age of the piglets. These results confirmed the use of CE SSCP as a tool for the description of the of digestive flora balances and their evolution at the batch level. This will be of particular interest in both animal health or food hygiene contexts associated with digestive flora perturbation.

Introduction

There are many issues regarding the composition, structure and stability of the digestive ecosystem. Until recently, only bacteriological techniques allowed us to describe the intestinal flora in a group of pigs reared and fed equivalently. The study of the intestinal microflora from a fecal matrix using classic bacteriological culture techniques thus revealed a wide microbial diversity (Moore et al., 1987). The bacterial population in intestinal contents is estimated between 10^{10} and 10^{11} bacteria per gram of contents. However, a major limitation is related to the cultivability of the species studied. According to the results of 16S ribosomal DNA sequences analysis after PCR amplification on feces 80% to 90% of the bacteria present in feces cannot be cultivated because of their unknown metabolic requirements) (Zoetendal et al., 1998).(Simpson et al., 1999). CE-SSCP (Capillary Electrophoresis-Single Strand Conformation Polymorphism) which targets the 16S-rDNA V3 region, allows detection of bacteria whatever their physiological and metabolic status. Applied on digestive content analysis, it could enlarge the field of investigation compared to conventional bacteriological techniques concerning complex microbial ecosystems. (Dabert et al., 2005).

Maintaining the balance in the digestive flora appeared as a factor of prevention as well for product hygiene (e.g. Salmonella excretion, Beloeil et al., 2004) as in animal health (e.g; weaning pigs transition Simpson et al., 2000) perspectives. However, before determining favorable or unfavorable balances, the within-individualvariability of animals needs to be assessed (Simpson et al., 2000), and then its influence should be minimized. Mixing the feces of animals from the same group and use of the CE-SSCP technique could then make it possible to characterize the balance of the digestive ecosystem of groups of pigs.

The objective of this study is to obtain a description of microbial composition of high-sanitary status pigs feces using CE-SSCP, then to measure the variability of SPF pig digestive contents, and to determine using a mixing sample approach to limit this variability, the ability to reach the notion of flora profiles of pig batches.

Materials and methods

The feces of six SPF sows (identified from number one to six) of different ages, parity numbers and fed with different diets were sampled in order to test the usefulness of the CE-SSCP method in describing flora (repeatability, within-individualand inter-group variability were checked). .

Twelve SPF piglets from AFSSA's experimental piggeries, born from the same sow were also used in this study in order to determinate the profiles of their cecal flora and to investigate their evolution over time. The piglets were randomized to three groups of 4 piglets on weaning day and slaughtered the same day for the first group to collect cecal contents. Ceaecal content were identified with number 1, 2, 3 and 4. The second group (pigs identified 5, 6, 7 and 8) and third (pin number 9, 10, 11 and 12) were sacrified at 28 and 56 days post-weaning, respectively. A starter feed was given to the piglets from the first week of age in the maternity until two weeks after weaning (21% protein). The transition feed was provided at 42 days of age (for a transition period of about 2 weeks, 18% protein). The grower feed started from 56 days of age until the end of the trial (16% protein).

DNA extraction from the samples was performed using a QIAamp DNA Stool Minikit (Qiagen) (McOrist et al., 2002). DNAs in the feces of sows 1, 2, 3, 4, 5, 6 were extracted and mixed as follows: DNAs 1-2-3, 4-5-6, 1-2-3-4, 1-2-3-4-5 and 1-2-3-4-5-6. DNAs in piglet cecal contents were extracted and the following mixs were carried out: 1-2, 3-4, 1-2-3-4, 5-6, 7-8, 5-6-7-8, 9-10, 11-12, 9-10-11-12. Gene amplification of DNAs and DNA pools was performed according to the methods described by Tanguy et al. (2007). CE-SSCP consisted in the migration of DNA single strands into the 50-cm capillaries of the four-capillary AbiPrism Genetic Analyser 3100 Avent sequencer (AppliedBiosystem, France). Profiles were classified via dendrograms built using the BioNumerics software (Applied-maths, France) and the Jaccard coefficient for similarity determination according to Tanguy et al (2007)

Results

SSCP profiles were obtained from sows fecal samples. Each profile included 50 to 60 peaks (Figure 1). The total reproducibility of the method was observed after comparison of several profiles of the same sample subjected to different protocols. The peaks number and position were identical. Results showed by CE-SSCP analysis were reproducible as early as DNA extraction and allowed to generate flora profiles from sows composite fecal samples.

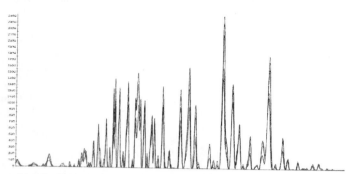

Figure n°1: Profile representations of two DNA extractions were carried out in parallel from the same pool of feces of 6 sows and profiles of two PCR of an individual DNA extraction from the feces of the 6 sows and the DNAs mixed after extraction

The SPF sows included in this study did not have any pathology, had not received any medication and were given two diets based on their physiological stage (gestation or lactation). Analysis of the profiles obtained from these sows feces showed low similarity of individual profiles composition (Jaccard coefficient ranging between 59% and 75%).

DNA mix samples revealed an increase in profile similarity, proportional to the increase in the number of individuals included in the pool. Thus, profile similarity comparing pools 1-2-3 and 4-5-6 was 81%, while it reached, and even exceeded 90% for mix 1-2-3-4, 1-2-3-4-5 and 1-2-3-4-5-6 (Figure 2).

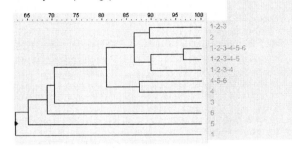

Figure 2: profile similarities of individuals or mix of 6 sows feces (Jaccard coefficient and UPGMA average)

The analysis of the profiles obtained from piglet cecal flora, presented in Figure 3, described three distinct clusters grouping the piglet according to their age. Inside each cluster, the within-individualvariability is low. , The minimal similarity between individuals being at least 68.8%, 81.3% and 88.6% for the 28 days aged piglets (in groups 1 to 4) , 56 d aged (5 to 8) and 82 d aged (9 to 12), respectively (Figure 3). In our confined piggeries the similarities of the caecal profile in a pig batch increase with the time.

In these conditions, we wanted to precise the place of the mix profiles in the dendrogramm. This analysis confirmed that each composite samples integrated the cluster characteristic of the piglet group at each slaughter date .. Profiles 1-2, 3-4 and 1-2-3-4 are thus representative of the group associating piglets 1 to 4 slaughtered at d28, profiles 5-6, 7-8 and 5-6-7-8 are characteristic of the piglets in group 5 to 8 slaughtered at d56 and profiles 9-10, 11-12 and 9-10-11-12 are representative of the profiles of individuals 9 to 12 slaughtered at d84. In addition, the similarity evolution, according to piglet age observed over time, is reinforced when the analysis is carried out on pools. Group 1-2-3-4 similarity is thus evaluated at 58% compared to groups 5-6-7-8 and 9-10-11-12, respectively, a 64% similarity being found between groups 5-6-7-8 and 9-10-11-12. These results showed that we can analyse the evolution of the pig group ceaecal flora profiles with composite samples inside a batch.

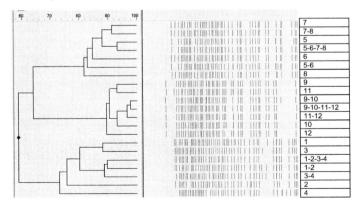

Figure 3: Analyse of profile similarities of individuals or pools of 12 piglets cecal floras using Jaccard coefficient and UPGMA average (slaughter date: 28 days (piglets 1, 2, 3, 4), 56 days (piglets 5, 6, 7, 8) and 84 days (piglets 9, 10, 11, 12))

Discussion

The CE-SSCP method, used for studying pig digestive microflora, provides reproducible profile even for separate sample DNA extractions. However, we observed that if we decided to pool samples within a study, the mix must be operated in a standardized way. For example it is to be decided once for all whether to pool samples, before or after DNA extractions.

The sow digestive flora profile analysis revealed within-individual variability between healthy high-sanitary-status sows (59%-75% similarity). Two sows were changed diet ten days prior to the study (gestation feed replaced by a lactation feed), but the change did not significantly affect their individual flora profiles. Mixing DNAs made it possible to ignore the variability between sows, and showed that it was possible to tend toward a digestive flora profile characteristic of a pig or sow herd (similarity higher than 90% with a feces mixture from at least 4 sows).

The analysis of all piglet cecal content profiles described a distribution in three clusters according to piglet age. Evolution with time of gastro intestinal microbiota contents in piglet was previously described using molecular approach (Simpson et al 2000). Analysis with CE-SSCP (at least 50 peaks) per profile would allow describing smaller variation than dgge (maximum 35 bands) (Loisel et al. 2006). Profile similarity (68.8%) within the weaning piglet cluster (d28) further increased with time to reach 90% similarity. The diet of pre-weaned piglets does not exclusively consist of the sow's milk, but also of starter feed to which piglets have free access. The diet, and hence the development of the flora in piglets, could thus be determined according to the piglets' interest in the starter feed, and could therefore account for the lower similarity between the profiles of the animals at this age. The mix profiles of the 3 groups integrate within the clusters of piglets treated individually; they are therefore representative of the piglets in these clusters. Thus, the results show that cecal flora profiles have a strong within-individual similarity between piglets of the same age which evolves identically with piglet age within the group.

Conclusion

In conclusion, capillary SSCP is a method that allows to describe digestive contents of sows and piglets qualify their variability. Using this method we described the evolution of piglet groups profiles over time (from the post-weaning through grower phases). The strategy of mixing intestinal contents in a way to enforce similarity between individuals digestive flora was validated. It provides a tool for studying digestive flora balances and their breakdown. This will be of particular interest in both animal health or food hygiene contexts associated with digestive flora perturbation.

Acknowledgements

Authors thank Patrick Dabert (Cemagref-Rennes) for its technical councils, Tom Sanderson for its English improvement and the 'Region Bretagne' for its financial support

Bibliography

Beloeil, P. A., Fravalo, P., Fablet, C., Jolly, J. P., Eveno, E., Hascoet, Y., Chauvin, C., Salvat, G. and Madec, F. (2004). Risk factors for Salmonella enterica subsp. enterica shedding by market-age pigs in French farrow-to-finish herds. *Prev Vet Med* 63, 103-20.

Dabert, P., Delgenes, J. P. and Godon, J. J. (2005). Monitoring the impact of bioaugmentation on the start up of biological phosphorus removal in a laboratory scale activated sludge ecosystem. *Appl Microbiol Biotechnol* 66, 575-88.

Loisel P, Harmand J, Zemb O, Latrille E, Lobry C, Delgenes JP, Godon JJ. Denaturing gradient electrophoresis (DGE) and single-strand conformation polymorphism (SSCP) molecular fingerprintings revisited by simulation and used as a tool to measure microbial diversity. Environ Microbiol. 2006 Apr;8(4):720-31

McOrist, A., Jackson, M. and Bird, A. (2002). A comparison of five methods for extraction of bacterial DNA from human faecal samples. *J Microbiol Methods.* 50(2), 131-9.

Moore, W., Moore, L., Cato, E., Wilkins, T. and Kornegay, E. (1987). Effect of high-fiber and high-oil diets on the fecal flora of swine. *Appl Environ Microbiol.* 53(7), 1638-44.

Simpson, J., McCracken, V., Gaskins, H. and Mackie, R. (2000). Denaturing gradient gel electrophoresis analysis of 16S ribosomal DNA amplicons to monitor changes in fecal bacterial populations of weaning pigs after introduction of Lactobacillus reuteri strain MM53. *Appl Environ Microbiol.* 66(11), 4705-14.

Simpson, J., McCracken, V., White, B., Gaskins, H. and Mackie, R. (1999). Application of denaturant gradient gel electrophoresis for the analysis of the porcine gastrointestinal microbiota. *J Microbiol Methods.* 36(3), 167-79.

Zoetendal, E., Akkermans, A. and De Vos, W. (1998). Temperature gradient gel electrophoresis analysis of 16S rRNA from human fecal samples reveals stable and host-specific communities of active bacteria. *Appl Environ Microbiol.* 64(10), 3854-9.

Development of a Microarray system for the Rapid and Simultaneous Detection of Bacterial and Viral Foodborne Pathogens

Gebreyes, W.A. *(1), Thakur, S. (2), Zhao S (2), McDermott, P. (2), White, D.G. (2), Harbottle, H. (2)

(1) Department of Veterinary Preventive Medicine, College of Veterinary Medicine, The Ohio State University, 1920 Coffey Road, 43210, Columbus, Ohio, USA
(2) Division of Animal and Food Microbiology, Office of Research, Center for Veterinary Medicine, U. S. Food and Drug Administration, 20708, Laurel, Maryland, USA

* corresponding author: gebreyes.1@osu.edu

Abstract:
Foodborne diseases are increasingly recognized as a significant global public health problem despite major advances and improvements in the quality of food, water, sanitation and hygiene. However, detection and characterization of foodborne pathogens during outbreak scenarios remains a laborious and time-consuming task. The aim of this work was to develop an oligonucleotide microarray for rapid detection and characterization of the most important infectious bacterial (*Campylobacter, Salmonella* and *Yersinia*) and viral (Noroviruses) pathogens found in swine and associated pork products. A total of 272 target regions and genes were identified that were specific for pathogen identification and characterization of specific antimicrobial resistance and virulence determinants. We designed multiple probes (up to three) per gene to increase the sensitivity and specificity of the microarray. After BLAST analysis, a total of 562 probes were finally selected to be printed on to glass slides. Appropriate control strains that were previously characterized in our laboratories by PCR were selected to test the developed arrays. Preliminary results indicated that the designed probes were highly specific and sensitive for identification of tested pathogens and known resistance and virulence genes present in the selected control strains.

Introduction:
Salmonella enterica serovars and *Campylobacter spp.* are two of the leading causes of bacterial foodborne illnesses in the United States (MMWR, 2006). It is estimated that the annual economic costs due to foodborne bacterial infections is $6.9 billion nationwide. Non-typhoidal *Salmonella* serovars are also important reservoirs for antimicrobial resistance factors. Emergence and spread of multi-drug resistance (MDR) in *Salmonella* has become a major concern among public health officials and the general public worldwide. *Yersinia enterocolitica* is another important foodborne bacterial pathogen, which causes an estimated 96,000 humans to become ill every year in the U.S. and has been listed as one of the top six priority foodborne pathogens. Pigs have been shown to be the primary reservoir for this pathogen and over 28% of the herds have been shown to carry the pathogenic species of *Y. enterocolitica* (Funk et al., 1998). With regards to viral pathogens, noroviruses (NoV) cause an estimated 23 million cases of acute, epidemic gastroenteritis in the U.S. annually.

Current standard protocols for the isolation and detection of these pathogens are laborious and have very low sensitivity. Further characterization to the species or strain level is also time consuming and costly. Therefore, development of a very sensitive, time-efficient, low cost simultaneous method that also enables detection of multiple antimicrobial resistance genes and other important determinants (e.g. virulence mechanisms) is essential. We proposed to achieve this by developing a multi-pathogen microarray system. This proposed research will benefit the swine industry by allowing the rapid and sensitive characterization of important foodborne bacterial and viral pathogenic strains in a short period of time thereby enabling development of efficient monitoring and tracking systems.

Materials and Methods:

After an exhaustive review of the available scientific literature, we selected a total of 272 genes/regions that were suitable for the purpose of identifying *Salmonella* spp. and characterizing known antimicrobial resistance genes and virulence determinants. In addition, we also selected six regions specific to the important *Salmonella* phage types of animal and human health significance. Probes were designed using the Allele ID software (Version 4.0, Premier Biosoft International, CA). We designed up to three probes per/gene. A total of 562 probes were finally selected after BLAST analysis to be printed on to glass slides. The average length of the probes selected under this method was approximately 68 base pairs and a melting temperature of around 73°C. The spots were printed using the Omnigrid Accent printer (Genomic Solutions, MI). We designed a 2x2 array with two sub arrays within an array. Therefore, every probe was spotted eight times on the glass slide. The two arrays were at a distance of 400 nanometers both horizontally and vertically. We selected two *Salmonella* and two *Campylobacter* control strains for testing and standardization of the microarray experiment as shown below. The *Salmonella* isolates were tested for the presence of β-lactamase genes (*bla*) using a Polymerase Chain Reaction (PCR) previously (Gebreyes and Altier, 2002).

Control Strains used include:

- *S.* Typhimurium DT 193 (UT 30)
  - AKSSuT antimicrobial resistance profile
  - *bla*$_{TEM-1}$ positive
  - *bla*$_{PSE-1}$ negative

    S. Typhimurium DT 104 (UT 8)
    -ACSSuT antimicrobial resistance

    -*bla*$_{TEM-1}$ negative
    -*bla*$_{PSE-1}$ positive

- *Campylobacter jejuni* (ID: 17858) and *Campylobacter coli* (ID: 11129)

Antimicrobial abbreviations: A: Ampicillin; C: Chloramphenicol; K: Kanamycin; S: Streptomycin; Su: Sulfamethoxazole and T: Tetracycline.

DNA from the control strains was purified using the Purelink Genomic DNA Isolation kit (Invitrogen Corporation, CA) following manufacturers instructions. The purified DNA was then labeled and purified with either Alexafluor dye 535 or 647 using the Bioprime comparative genomic hybridization kit following the manufacturer's instructions (Invitrogen Corporation, CA). Hybridization was done using the Pronto universal microarray system (Corning Incorporated, MI). Images were captured under the appropriate fluorescence wavelength in the Gene Pix Pro array machine (Molecular Devices Corporation, MA). Preliminary analysis of the results was done using the Excel program available in Microsoft. For analysis, we used the fluorescence reading at 535 wavelength minus the background at the same wavelength. All the values greater than 500 were considered as positive and value less than that was considered as negative.

Results:

Hybridization of the labeled DNA with the immobilized probe on the glass surface is influenced by different experimental parameters of which the hybridization temperature is the most important. Different hybridization temperatures were tested including 42°C, 55°C and 65°C to determine the ideal complementary strand binding conditions. After multiple experiments, we decided to use 42°C as the hybridization temperature since the results observed at this temperature were ideal after analysis. Slides were baked at 80°C for 30 minutes prior to cross linking at 600 MJ. Preliminary testing was conducted using the *Salmonella* and *Campylobacter* control strains. The initial focus was on the pathogen identification probes. We observed specific signal intensity with values greater than 500 generated by the binding of the labeled target with specific *Salmonella* and *Campylobacter* identification probes as shown in Figure 1. No cross hybridization signals were observed between the probe and non specific target DNA indicating the high sensitivity and specificity of the identification probes. We observed specific signal intensity with values greater than 500 generated by the binding of the labeled target with specific *Salmonella* and *Campylobacter* identification probes. Microarray analysis also identified multiple identification genes, antimicrobial resistance genes, integrons, plasmid sequences and multidrug resistant efflux pumps in the tested control strains which were further corroborated by PCR testing.

Salmonella identification probes

Campylobacter identification probes

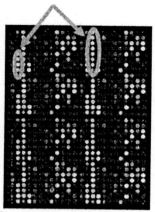
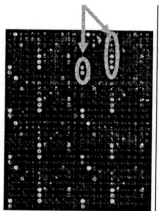

Figure1. Hybridization results showing the bright green pathogen identification probes after binding with the Alexafluor 535 labeled target DNA.

Preliminary data for characterizing select antimicrobial resistance genes using the control *Salmonella* strains was very encouraging. The β-lactamases genes coding for resistance against β-Lactam antimicrobials, including ampicillin, had been characterized by PCR previously in our laboratory. Microarray analysis of the scanned image corroborated the PCR results as shown in figures 2 and 3 for phage type *S.* Typhimurium DT 104 and DT 193, respectively. The Y-axis shows fluorescence on the graphs.

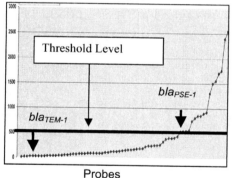

Figure 2. Fluorescence profile for *S.* Typhimurium DT 104

Figure 3. Fluorescence profile for *S.* Typhimurium DT 193

In addition to the pathogen identification and β-lactamase genes that are highlighted on the graph, additional identification genes, antimicrobial resistance genes, integrons, plasmid sequences and multidrug resistant efflux pumps were identified in the tested control strains. The list of genes/target regions that have been shown to be present are shown in Table 1. Further testing for detection of Noroviruses and *Yersinia* species as well as additional virulence and antimicrobial resistance genes is currently underway.

Table1. Pathogen identification & Antimicrobial resistance genes for *Campylobacter* and *Salmonella*

Target Gene/Region	Fluorescence 535-Background
Acinetobacter calcoaceticus class A beta-lactamase blaCARB-5 (blaCARB-5) gene, complete cds. **(Negative Control)**	36.875
Campylobacter coli GlyA (*glyA*) gene, partial cds.	1013
Campylobacter jejuni GlyA (*glyA*) gene, partial cds.	1900.167
Salmonella Typhimurium LT2, section 138 of 220 genome	960.75
Salmonella Typhimurium LT2, section 182 of 220 genome	1390.25
Salmonella Typhimurium LT2, section 91 of 220 genome	1555.125
Campylobacter jejuni strain 81-176 cmeR (*cmeR*),cmeABC	600.5
Campylobacter jejuni plasmid pCjA13 tetracycline resistance	1233.083
Citrobacter amalonaticus β-lactamase CTX-M-8 (*bla*$_{CTX-M-8}$)	942.625

Discussion:

The preliminary findings from this study have shown that the developed oligonucleotide microarray can both identify a wide range of bacterial pathogens and specific antimicrobial resistant and virulence genes present. DNA microarrays or gene chips represent the latest advance in molecular technology and offers a fast, high-throughput alternative for the parallel detection of hundreds to thousands of genes of interest simultaneously. The application potential spreads across most sectors of life sciences, including environmental microbiology and microbial ecology; human, veterinary, food and plant diagnostic, water quality control, and industrial microbiology (Bodrossy and Sessitsch, 2004). Samples were labeled with dyes that fluoresced on binding to the appropriate probe thereby generating a signal that was captured by the imager and recorded. This way, we were able to identify test probes that were not only specific for identifying different bacterial foodborne pathogens but also antimicrobial resistance and virulence genes present. In our study, we generated 562 probes from 272 target genes/ regions. The preliminary data is very encouraging and we were able to differentiate between different pathogens on the basis of the target identification probes that gave us specific signal based on the pathogen tested. Microarray technology is being increasingly used in numerous scientific disciplines including drug discovery and evaluation, cancer research, bacterial pathogenesis, antimicrobial resistance, as well as genomic "fingerprinting" and detecting genetic polymorphisms of microorganisms (Call et al., 2003; Chizikov et al., 2001; Hu et al., 2002; Kato-Maeda et al., 2001).

Sensitivity and specificity of the probes are important criteria that need to be addressed whenever a new microarray chip is developed. For this purpose, we specifically selected multiple probes and then spotted the same probes multiple times (up to eight) on the glass slide in a systematic manner. The fluorescence signal strength for the probes was uniform across the slide. To further confirm the microarray results, we are in the process of designing appropriate PCR primers. For the next step we will amplify all the genes by PCR that were shown to be positive by the microarray. We are currently also comparing the results from the two different microarray methods employed in this study. This high throughput oligonucleotide microarray designed in this study will benefit the swine industry as well as interested researchers in successfully identifying and characterizing common pathogens found in swine on farm, at slaughter and retail in an efficient, cheap and quick manner.

Conclusions:

The development of rapid and accurate detection methods for pathogen detection are needed as current culture based methods are time consuming and costly. The preliminary findings of this study have shown that the oligonucleotide microarray developed can identify a wide range of bacterial pathogens as well as specific antimicrobial resistance and virulence genes simultaneously. The microarray system developed in this study enables identification of specific

Session 5

strains in less than two days starting from the sample collection to the final analysis. This will enable us to monitor the presence of foodborne pathogens as well as associated antimicrobial resistance and virulence genes in animals, foods, humans and the environment.

References:

BODROSSY, L., and SESSITSCH, A., 2004. Oligonucleotide microarrays in microbial diagnostics. Current Opinions in Microbiology 7(3):245-254.

CALL, D. R., et al., 2003. Identifying antimicrobial resistance genes with DNA microarrays. Antimicrobial Agents and Chemotherapy, 47(10):3290-3295.

CENTERS FOR DISEASE CONTROL AND PREVENTION (CDC), 2006. Preliminary FoodNet Data on the Incidence of Infection with Pathogens Transmitted Commonly Through Food-10 States, United States, 2005. Morbidity and Mortality Weekly Report, 55(14), 392-395.

CHIZIKOV, V., et al., 2001. Microarray analysis of microbial virulence factors. Applied Environmental Microbiology, 67(7):3258-63.

enterocolitica in groups of swine at slaughter. : J Food Prot. 61(6):677-682

FUNK, J.A., et al.,1998. Prevalence of pathogenic *Yersinia enterocolitica* in groups of swine at slaughter. Journal of Food Protection, 61(6):677-682

GEBREYES, W.A. and ALTIER, C., 2002. Molecular characterization of antimicrobial resistance genes among multi-drug resistant *Salmonella*. Journal of Clinical Microbiology, 40(8), 2813-2822.

HU, H., et al., 2002. Fluorescent amplified fragment length polymorphism analysis of *Salmonella* enterica serovar Typhimurium reveals phage-type- specific markers and potential for microarray typing. Journal of Clinical Microbiology, 40(9):3406-3415.

KATO-MAEDA, M., et al., 2001. Microarray analysis of pathogens and their interaction with hosts. Cellular Microbiology, 3(11):713-719.

Evaluation of the relative sensitivity of carcase swabbing against belly strip excision for TVC, *E. coli* and *Salmonella* isolation

Hamilton, D.R*., Holds, G., Kiermeier, A., Pointon, A.M.

Food Safety Research, South Australian Research and Development Institute, 33 Flemington Street, Glenside, SA 5065, Australia.
*Corresponding author: hamilton.david@saugov.sa.gov.au

Abstract

The standard US method of swabbing pig carcases (3x 100cm^2) for determination of *E. coli* and *Salmonella* contamination was compared with a belly strip excision method (approx. 120cm^2). Swabbing for *Salmonella* and *E. coli* detection was found to have a relative sensitivity equal to $^1/_7$ and $^1/_2$ respectively, of the belly strip technique. Furthermore, swab sampling isolated 2 *Salmonella* serovars compared with 9 serovars by the belly strip technique. For studies on the effectiveness of carcase decontamination interventions or undertaking abattoir "flow-through" studies it is recommended that belly strip excision sampling be employed. This study also compared the use of a semisolid culture medium (MSRV) for *Salmonella* isolation developed for faecal samples with standard media. MSRV gave a result 24 hours faster but was not as sensitive as the standard medium (RV). Therefore, MSRV medium is not recommended for the isolation of *Salmonella* from carcases for regulatory purposes.

Introduction

The present ESAM (*E. coli* and *Salmonella* Monitoring) sampling regime and methodology used in Australia for monitoring the microbiological status of pig carcases is stipulated by the USDA, and involves swabbing (with a sponge) 1 in 5,000 carcases for *Salmonella* and 1 in 1,000 carcases for *E. coli* (Anon 2003). Although some may view ESAM more as a trade facilitation activity rather than a truly effective process control/food safety measure, processors and regulators are using results as an indicator of potential *Salmonella* contamination problems. The low sampling rate and relative insensitivity of swabbing raises concerns that low positive ESAM findings may lull the industry into a false sense of security if taken as a reliable measure of contamination prevalence. In turn, this may adversely influence Risk Management decisions. A preliminary study in the Netherlands (Swanenberg *et al* 2003) compared carcase swabbing with a new method of sampling, involving directly stomaching a thin strip of meat excised from the belly. They reported a significant (x3.5) increase in sensitivity compared with the swabbing method. In addition, van de Giesson *et al* (2003) found the use of a semi-solid *Salmonella* selective enrichment medium (MSRV) doubled the number of positive samples from pig faeces. This Australian study compared the sensitivity of standard carcase swabbing with the belly strip excision technique on carcases using both standard and semi-solid MSRV culture media.

Materials and Methods

Two farms of known (high) *Salmonella* status were selected by preliminary pen faecal sampling with a total of 9 different serovars being isolated (Table 2). A total of 298 finisher pigs from the two farms (n=150 and n=148) were sampled at slaughter over five days to minimise any day-of-kill effect. Pigs were held for 24 hours prior to slaughter on solid concrete floors in the abattoir lairage and killed late in the day to maximise the potential for *Salmonella* cross-contamination from other herds (i.e. a worst case scenario to maximise the potential of positive carcases). Routine ESAM *E. coli* and *Salmonella* data recorded at the participating abattoir over a 10-month period spanning the trial demonstrated an ongoing high standard of conformance with the Australian regulatory Microbiological Guidelines (Anon 2003).

Session 5

Pig carcases were sampled by both the belly strip (Swanenberg *et al* 2003; Hamilton *et al* 2004) and the ESAM swabbing technique (Anon 2003) following 8 hours of chilling. The two techniques were conducted concurrently on opposite sides of the same carcase, alternating sides with each succeeding carcase to avoid bias.

The belly strip technique entailed the removal of a thin strip (0.5 cm wide) of belly skin and muscle from the edge of the evisceration opening, from the xiphoid cartilage to the inguinal region. The strip was excised to avoid the superficial inguinal lymph node, thereby avoiding a possible confounding source of *Salmonella*. The total average area (that excludes the sampling incision) was calculated to be approximately 120 cm^2. The individually identified belly strips were collected aseptically from carcases in the chillers and dropped into sterile stomacher bags. After overnight storage at 4°C, buffered peptone water (BPW) was added and the belly strips stomached and cultured in the abattoir laboratory. The ESAM sampling involved swabbing the standard pig carcase monitoring sites (total 300cm^2 area from belly, rump and jowl) as per USDA requirements (Anon 2003). To ensure the technique reflected normal practice, abattoir QA personnel who routinely conducted this function took the samples under supervision.

Laboratory Methods

Samples were transported to the laboratory in a chilled state on the day of collection and either cultured on the same day or maintained at 4°C until processed. Faecal samples were homogenised and 25 gm samples were added to 225 mL buffered Peptone water (BPW) for pre-enrichment to maximise sensitivity (Funk *et al* 2000). Belly strip samples were all enriched in 250 mL of BPW irrespective of sample size.

Salmonella culture methods followed the Australian Standard (AS1766.2.5-1991(mod)) with enrichment in Rappaport Vassiliadis (RV) and Mannitol Selenite Cystine (MS) broth and plating on Xylose Lysine Desoxycholate (XLD) and Brilliant Green (BG) plates. In addition three separate drops of the BPW enrichment (totalling 0.1mL) were inoculated onto the surface of a Modified Semisolid Rappaport Vassiliadis Medium (MSRV) (van de Giesson *et al* 2003). Confirmation was by latex agglutination using Serobact™ *Salmonella*. Colonies that were latex agglutination negative were checked by biochemistry (MICROBACT™ 24E). To increase the potential to establish the presence of multiple serovars, up to 15 isolates (i.e. 3 colony picks from the 5 enrichment/media combinations) per carcase sample presumptively identified as *Salmonella* were forwarded for serotyping to the Australian *Salmonella* Reference Laboratory at the Institute of Medical and Veterinary Science, Adelaide

For *E. coli*, aliquots (1 mL) from each dilution of swabs (300 cm^2) and belly strips (120 cm^2) were spread on *E. coli* Petrifilm (3M) and incubated at 37°C for 2 days. Colonies were identified and counted according to the manufacturer's instructions.

Statistical Methods

Since belly strip excisions and ESAM swab samples were taken from the same carcase it follows that the data on *E. coli* and *Salmonella* isolation were in the form of matched pairs. Consequently, McNemar's Chi-squared test was used to assess the data.

Results

298 carcases were sampled by both belly strip excision and ESAM swab samples over five days. A summary of the sample results for *E. coli* and *Salmonella* are given in Table 1.

Table 1. Comparative *E. coli* and *Salmonella* isolation rates for belly strip and ESAM using standard media.

	E. coli (P-value < 0.0001)		Salmonella (P-value < 0.0001)	
	Belly strip neg	Belly strip pos	Belly strip neg	Belly strip pos
ESAM Swab negative	219	51	267	27
ESAM Swab positive	16	12	2	2

For *Salmonella* there was a significant difference in the proportion of samples that tested positive (P-value<0.0001) using belly strip excision (29/298=9.7%) compared with ESAM swab samples (4/298=1.3%). The semi-solid media (MSRV) gave 2 false negative results when compared with the traditional method (positive n=31), both being ESAM carcase swab samples (data not shown).

Similarly, for *E. coli*, significantly more samples tested positive (P-value<0.0001) using belly strip excision (63/298=21.1%) compared with ESAM swabs (28/298=9.4%).

For belly strips there was an association between *Salmonella* and *E. coli* contamination with significantly more *Salmonella* positives (p value <0.0001) found in samples also contaminated with *E. coli* (9/63=14.29%) compared with samples with no *E. coli* isolations (20/235=8.51%).

Serovars recovered from the carcases and faecal pen samples are shown in Table 2. Two carcases were positive by both sampling methods (*S*. Johannesburg was isolated from both sites on both pigs). A third carcase had *S*. Derby and Johannesburg isolated from 1 belly strip sample. Six of the 9 on-farm serovars were isolated from belly strip samples compared with 2 serovars from the ESAM samples. Further if the 2 rough belly strip isolates rough:r:1,5 and rough:d:1,2 are in fact degenerated organisms of *S*. Infantis and *S*. Stanley respectively, 8/9 farm serovars would have been detected on the carcases.

Table 2. Number of isolates of each *Salmonella* serovar isolated from carcases and the serovars isolated from farm pen faecal samples

Salmonella serovars	Sampling method		
	Pen faecal	Belly Strip	ESAM
Anatum	+ve	4	1
Johannesburg	+ve	10	3
Subsp 1 4,12:d:-	+ve	1	
Ohio	+ve	1	
London	+ve	6	
Derby	+ve	5*	
Worthington		1	
rough:r:1,5		1	
rough:d:1.2		1	
Infantis	+ve		
Stanley	+ve		
Agona	+ve		

Discussion

The comparison of the sampling methods found the *Salmonella* isolation rate from porcine belly strip samples to be approximately 7 times that from ESAM sites at the observed prevalences. This finding verifies those of Swanenberg *et al* (2003) and Hamilton *et al* (2004) who found rates of 3.5 and 5 times, respectively. Consequently, Australian and international ESAM based survey data may represent a substantial underestimate of the true prevalence of overall carcase contamination with *Salmonella*.

These data also demonstrate that hygiene indicators (i.e. ESAM swabbing) do not predict belly site contamination with *Salmonella* in an abattoir demonstrating a high standard of conformance with the regulatory microbiological standards, as observed by Hamilton *et al* (2004). These observations, therefore, point to the need to validate a decontamination procedure for sites prone to substantial contamination. To this end, hot water decontamination cabinets that have been in regular use in beef abattoirs in the US and Australia for some years are being investigated for use with pigs. In addition, SANOVA™ (acidified sodium chlorite), which has been registered for use in Australia as a potential final carcase rinse, is undergoing evaluation.

The association between *E. coli* and *Salmonella* from the same belly strip sample indicates localised faecal contamination. An explanation of these findings may be that the ingesta-contaminated arms of evisceration workers, or removal of contaminated viscera or anus, caused contamination of the belly strip. Contaminated arms could quite conceivably lead to a string of sequentially contaminated carcases after a contamination event. In a study of five pig slaughterhouses (Botteldoorn *et al* 2003), cross-contamination was estimated to account for 29% of positive carcases. In contrast to belly strips either side of the abdominal incision, other carcase sites that are handled less during processing could be expected to have a lower prevalence of faecal contamination.

Van de Giesson *et al* (2003) found that use of a semi-solid *Salmonella* selective enrichment medium (MSRV) doubled the number of positive samples with pig faeces compared to standard media. This result was not repeated in this study of carcase samples. The MSRV media failed to detect *Salmonella* in 2 of 33 samples found positive by the standard procedure (AS1766.2.5-1991(mod)). Similarly, in an earlier *Salmonella* farm-to-carcase "flow-through" study, of the 71/365 positive carcases that were cultured by both methods, 70/71 were detected by the standard RV medium but only 64/71 by the MSRV (Hamilton 2004 unpublished data). It is concluded that the standard method should be used in further studies involving carcase samples taken for regulatory purposes.

Conclusions

For international trade, the US standard method for sampling pig carcases for *Salmonella* and *E. coli* contamination (ESAM) by swabbing provides a useful international benchmark. However, this study verifies that for *Salmonella* epidemiological investigations or the validation of the effectiveness of carcase decontamination technologies, the belly strip sampling technique may provide a more practical and cost-effective approach due to the increased detection of. While MSRV media is useful for faecal culture and in cases where a more rapid estimate of *Salmonella* contamination is required, it is concluded that the standard culture methods should be used in further studies involving carcase samples taken for regulatory purposes.

References

ANON, 2003. Revised ESAM Program – Australian Quarantine and Inspection Service (AQIS) Notice Number Meat 2003/06.

BOTTELDOORN, N., HEYNDRICKX, M., RIJPENS, N., GRIJSPEEDT, K., HERMAN, L., 2003. *Salmonella* on pig carcasses: positive pigs and cross contamination in the slaughterhouse. *Journal of Applied Microbiology.* 95, 891-903.

FUNK, J.A., DAVIES, P.R., NICHOLS, M.A., 2000. The effect of fecal sample weight on detection of *Salmonella enterica* in swine feces. *J. Vet. Diagn. Invest.* 12, 412-418.

HAMILTON, D.R., HOLDS, G., BOBBITT, J., KIERMEIER, A., HOLYOAKE, P., FAHY, T., DAVOS, D., HEUZENROEDER, M., LESTER, S., POINTON, A., 2004. Ecology of *Salmonella* Infection across Australian Pig Rearing Production Systems. APL Final Report Project No. 1836. SARDI. August 2004.

SWANENBURG, M., VAN DER WOLF, P.J., URLINGS, H.A.P., SNIJDERS, J.M.A., 2003. Comparison of an excision and a sponge sampling method for measuring *Salmonella* contamination of pig carcasses. In: Proceedings of the 5th International Symposium on the Epidemiology and Control of Foodborne Pathogens in Pork. Crete. 1-4 October, 2003. pp 255-257.

VAN DE GIESSEN, A.W., BOUWKNEG, M., DAM-DEISZ, W.D.C., WANNET, W.J.B., NIEUWENHUIS, M., GRAAT, E.A.M., VISSER, G., 2003. Surveillance of zoonotic bacteria in finishing pigs in The Netherlands. In Proceedings of the 5th International Symposium on the Epidemiology and Control of Foodborne Pathogens in Pork, pp. 36-39, Crete.

Session 5

Quantification of *Campylobacter* carriage in pigs using a real-time PCR assay

Leblanc Maridor, M.[*(1)], Denis, M.[(2)], Lalande, F.[(2)], Beaurepaire, B.[(2)], Cariolet, R.[(2)], Fravalo, P.[(2)], Seegers, H.[(1)], Belloc, C.[(1)]

[(1)] ENVN-INRA, UMR 708 GSA, La chantrerie-Atlanpole BP 40706, 44307, Nantes, France
[(2)] AFSSA, Unité HQPAP, BP53, 22440, Ploufragan, France
*corresponding author : leblanc@vet-nantes.fr

Abstract

Campylobacter species are the major agent of bacterial gastroenteritis. *C. jejuni* and *C. coli* together are responsible for more than 95% of all cases of *Campylobacter* induced diarrheal disease in developped countries. Risk analysis shows consumption of foods of animal origin to be a major source of human infection. Pigs are known to be frequently infected with *Campylobacter* and to exhibit high counts of this pathogen in their faeces.

The study describes a rapid, sensitive, and specific real-time polymerase chain reaction (PCR) assay capable of detecting and quantifying *Campylobacter sp.*, *C. jejuni* and *C. coli* directly from faecal samples. The description of excretion of *Campylobacter* was carried out by inoculating pigs with three different strains of *Campylobacter*: one *C. coli* of porcine origin, one *C. coli* and one *C. jejuni* of poultry origin, alone or in a mix. The number of *Campylobacter* excreted in faeces was determined by numeration on Karmali plates and by the real time PCR assay.

The quantitative PCR results were consistent with data obtained by the bacteriological method. Two days after the inoculation, the inoculated pigs excreted from 10^4 to 10^6 CFU of *Campylobacter* per gramme of faeces. These levels of excretion were similar to those observed in the fattening pigs after spontaneous infection. Moreover, the real time PCR allowed species-specific detection of *Campylobacter*. Indeed, when pigs were infected with a mix of the three strains, the PCR showed that *C. coli* was predominant.

Introduction

Thermophilic *Campylobacter* are the major cause of bacterial gastroenteritis in humans in industrialized countries (Megraud *et al.*, 2004). The high incidence of clinical disease associated with this organism and its potentially serious complications confirm its importance as a significant public health hazard (Tauxe, 2002). The species involved is mainly *C. jejuni* (80%), followed by *C. coli* (10 to 15%) and *C. fetus* (5 to 10%). *Campylobacter* lives in the intestinal tract of a wide range of birds and mammals, including domestic animals used for food production without causing clinical signs. The dominance of *C. jejuni* is found in most healthy carrier animals, especially broiler chickens (Nielsen *et al.*, 1997). In contrast, pigs are known to be frequently infected with *C. coli* and to excrete high counts of this pathogen in their faeces (Weijtens *et al.*, 1999).

As food safety has become an increasing concern for consumers, there is a growing need for fast and sensitive methods for specific detection and identification of zoonotic microorganisms. Conventional methods for the detection and confirmation of *Campylobacter* in food or in stools requires 4-5 days and involve selective enrichment followed by isolation from selective agar and confirmation by biochemical and serological tests (On, 1996). While selective media are very efficient for the initial isolation of *Campylobacter*, biochemical methods may give ambiguous results. Therefore, molecular genotype-based methods represent an alternative for the identification of *Campylobacter*. Over the last decade, the Polymerase Chain Reaction (PCR) has become a basic tool for the identification of bacterial pathogens such as *Campylobacter* (On, 1996). The recent development of real-time, closed-tube PCR methods remove the need to manipulate PCR products after amplification, thereby reducing the risk of false positive results caused by cross-contamination between amplicons and test samples. Real-time PCR assays, beyond their rapidity, sensitivity and good reproducibility, allow a precise quantification of the target DNA copy number.

The aim of the present study is to describe real time PCR (rt-PCR) assays able to detect and quantify *Campylobacter sp.*, *C. jejuni* and *C. coli* directly from faecal samples and to compare results with conventional microaerobic bacterial cultivation.

Material and Methods

Bacterial strains, faecal samples and bacterial culture
The PCR assays were developed using differents strains of *C. jejuni* (NCTC 11168, wild strains isolated from chicken) and *C. coli* (ATCC 33559, CIP 7081, wild strains isolated from pigs faeces). The specificity was assessed using *C. lari*, *C. upsaliensis*, *C. fetus*, *Salmonella typhimurium*, *Listeria monocytogenes*, *Listeria innocua*, *Escherichia coli* and *Enterococcus faecalis*.

Faecal samples were collected individually from specific-pathogen-free (SPF) piglets either inoculated by oral way with 5.10^7 CFU of *C. coli* (two different strains) and *C. jejuni*, alone or mixed, or non inoculated (« control » pigs). Two hundred and fifty milligrams of fresh faecal material were used for rt-PCR and ten grams were cultivated according to the protocol described by Denis *et al.* (1999). Furthermore, for numeration, 100µL of 10-fold serial dilution (10^{-1} to 10^{-5}) were directly plated on Karmali plates and incubated for 72h.

Isolation of DNA from faecal samples and bacterial cultures
Double stranded DNA of all bacteria from the bacterial culture and from faecal samples (250mg) was extracted using the Nucleospin® Tissue mini-kit (Macherey Nagel, Hoerdt, France) according to the manufacturer's instructions. The DNA preparations were stored at −20°C prior to use.

PCR primers and probes
To detect *Campylobacter sp.*, we have used the primer-probe set described by Lund *et al.* (2004), which is based on the 16S rRNA sequence. The other primers and probes are based on the single-copy *hipO* and *glyA* genes for *C jejuni* and *C coli* respectively. Primers and probes were selected with Primer express version 2.O (Applied Biosystems, Foster city, CA, USA) and their homologies with unrelated sequences were checked with the BLAST program (NCBI).

The Taqman probes, labeled with a fluorescent reporter at the 5' end and conjugated to a minor groove binder (MGB) at the 3'end, and the primers were synthetized by Applied Biosystems. The primers selected for detection of *C. jejuni* were *hipO*-F 5'-CTTGCGGTCATGATGGACATAC-3' and *hipO*-R 5'-TTAGCACCACCCAAACCCTCTTCA-3', and the TaqMan probe was *hipO*-P 5'-VIC-ATTGCTTGCTGCAAAGT-MGB-3'. For detection of *C. coli*, the primers selected were *glyA*-F 5'-AAACCAAAGCTTATCGTGTGC-3', *glyA*-R 5'-AGTCCAGCAATGTGTGCAATG-3' and the TaqMan probe was *glyA*-P 5'-FAM-CAACTTCATCCGCAAT-MGB-3'. For detection of *Campylobacter sp.*, we used the primer-probe set described by Lund *et al.* (2004) with a VIC signal for the probe.

Evaluation of analytical performance of the real-time PCR assays
The analytical specificity of each rt-PCR assay was assessed with purified genomic DNA preparations of different bacterial strains (see above). To evaluate the analytical sensitivity of the rt-PCR, two standard curves were prepared : one with purified genomic DNA from *C. jejuni* NCTC 11168 and *C. coli* ATCC 33559 and the other with *Campylobacter*-negative faecal samples spiked with serial 10-fold dilutions from a broth of the two reference strains.

Quantitative real-time PCR amplification
The rt-PCR was performed in a ABI PRISM® 7300 Sequence Detection System (Applied Biosystems) and the data were analyzed with the appropriate sequence detector software. The 25µL PCR mixture for one reaction contained 12.5µL of 1X Taqman Universal PCR Mastermix (containing AmpliTaq Gold™ DNA polymerase, dNTPs, Passive reference 1 (ROX) and optimised buffer components including 5mM MgCl2), 400nM of each primers, 100nM probe and 5µL of template DNA. The thermal cycle protocol used was the following: activation of the Taq DNA polymerase at 95°C for 10 min and 40 cycles of 95°C for 15s and 60°C for 1 min. All reactions were carried out alongside a non template control containing sterile water and a positive control containing DNA from reference strains *C. jejuni* and *C. coli*.

A total of 68 samples were evaluated in parallel using the rt-PCR assays and the microbiological method. Sensitivity and specificity of rt-PCR were determined comparatively to the microaerobic cultivation and the agreement between the methods was measured using the kappa-statistic (Fleiss, 1981).

Results

Specifity and sensitivity of PCR primers and TaqMan probes
The specificity of the three primer-probes sets was optimized and tested against differents strains of other *Campylobacter sp.* as well as several bacteria, genetically related or not, all of which were found to be negative. We also observed that quantification of DNA from each *Campylobacter* target was not affected when DNA from a variety of other species was present in the PCR mixture.

The standard curves spanned six to eight orders of magnitude and showed linearity over the entire quantitation range, providing an accurate measurement over a large variety of starting target amounts (R^2 values were all equal or above to 0.99). The detection limits of the rt-PCRs were of 1 genome copies/reaction PCR and 100 CFU/g of faeces and was similar to the bacteriological method.

Analysis of the faecal samples of pigs experimentally infected with *Campylobacter*
Two days after the inoculation, pigs infected with *C. coli* alone or *C. coli* and *C. jejuni* excreted from 10^4 to 10^6 CFU of *Campylobacter* per gramme of faeces. The excretion of pigs inoculated with *C. jejuni* alone was lower (up to 10^3 CFU/g of faeces).

Validation of the real time PCR assays for analysis of faecal samples
The numbers of positive and negative samples determined by both detection methods for each assay are summarized in table 1.

Table 1 : Comparison between culture and rt-PCR for detection of *C. sp.*, *C. coli* and *C. jejuni*

		Microaerophilic culture								
		C. coli			*C. jejuni*			*C. sp.*		
		+	-	Total	+	-	Total	+	-	Total
rt-PCR	+	26	1	27	10	1	11	14	0	14
	-	0	5	5	1	6	7	1	3	4
	Total	26	6	32	11	7	18	15	3	18

C. coli: Sensitivity Se=100%, Specificity Sp=83%, Kappa K=0.89 ; *C. jejuni*: Se=91%, Sp=86%, K=0.77 ; *C. sp.*: Se=93%, Sp=100%, K=0.82

There was an excellent correlation between all positive and negative results by both techniques. Indeed for *C. coli*, all the culture-positive samples appeared to be positive by the rt-PCR assay (Se=100%). However, one culture-negative sample was positive by rt-PCR leading to a specificity of 83%. For *C. sp.*, results were similar: only one culture-positive sample was negative by rt-PCR. The k values equalled to 0.89 and 0.83, respectively, indicated an excellent agreement between the two methods. Finally, for *C. jejuni*, even if 2 out of 18 tested samples differed between the two methods, the k value (0.77) underlines a good agreement. The amount of CFU of *Campylobacter* in each faecal sample determined by the rt-PCR was calculated and compared to the results obtained by quantitative bacteriological method. Among the PCR-culture positive samples, 67% of the samples had a difference in cell number of less than 1 log, 27% less than 2 logs and 6% less than 3 logs.

Discussion

We found a high correlation between the positive and negative results obtained by rt-PCR and culture for all samples. Interestingly, in two samples culture didn't detect any *Campylobacter* cells, even after an enrichment step, while the rt-PCR detected them (10^3 CFU/g). This difference may be attributable to the presence of viable but not culturable (VNC) or dead *Campylobacter sp.*. Two samples were negative by rt-PCR and positive by culture: few colonies were observed after enrichment for the first one and 10^5 CFU/g of faeces for the second one. Different hypothesis can explain this discrepant result. First, the enrichment of *C. jejuni* in pig faecal samples can be difficult due to overgrowth by the more numerous *C. coli* and a high background flora (Madden *et al.*, 2000). Secondly, PCR inhibitors may occur in faeces that provide false-negative results with PCR methods (Wilson, 1997).

Moreover, in our trial, there is a good correlation between the techniques at the quantitative level and the discrepancies between the concentrations found by both methods could be attributed partly to the non viable cells resulting in higher concentrations with the real-time quantitative PCR. The observed variability might be due to dilution factors used for quantitative culture, to an insufficient homogenization of the samples, factors affecting the growth of different isolates, or possibly, the presence of antagonistic bacterial species.

Consequently, the use of PCR-based detection methods is very attractive because the *Campylobacter* specific rt-PCR assays allow (i) identification and discrimination of *C. coli* and *C. jejuni* without need of isolation, enrichment and/or biochemical tests, often difficult to interpret, (ii) a direct quantification of each target even if several species are present in the sample.

In conclusion, the rt-PCR developed in this study provide new tools to study the epidemiology of *Campylobacter*. Indeed, it could be applied to further epidemiological surveys to investigate the carriage and the excretion of *Campylobacter* by conventionnal pigs.

References

DENIS, M., SOUMET, C., RIVOAL, K., ERMEL, G., BLIVET, D., SALVAT, G., COLIN, P., 1999. Development of a m-PCR assay for simultaneous identification *Campylobacter jejuni* and *Campylobacter coli*. *Letters Applied Microbiology*, 29, 406-410.

FLEISS,J.L. 1981. *The measurement of interrater agreement*. In Fleiss, J.L. *Statistical methods for rates and proportions*, John Wiley & Sons, New York.

LUND, M., NORDENTOFT, S., PEDERSEN, K., MADSEN, M., 2004. Detection of *Campylobacter sp.* in chicken fecal samples by rt-PCR. *Journal of Clinical Microbiology*, 42 (11), 5125-5132.

MADDEN, R.H., MORAN, L., SCATES, P., 2000. Optimising recovery of Campylobacter spp. from the lower porcine gastrointestinal tract. *Journal of Microbiological Methods*, 42(2), 115-119.

MÉGRAUD, F., DENIS, J.B., ERMEL, G., FÉDÉRIGHI, M., GALLAY, A., KEMPF, I., LECLERQ, A., WEBER, P., 2004. Appréciation des risques alimentaires liés aux *Campylobacter*. Application au couple poulet/*C. jejuni*. *1ère edition Rapport technique de l'AFSSA (Agence Française de Sécurité Sanitaire des Aliments)*, Maisons-Alfort (France).

NIELSEN, E.M., ENGBERG, J., MADSEN, M., 1997. Distribution of serotypes of *Campylobacter jejuni* and *C. coli* from Danish patients, poultry, cattle and swine. *FEMS Immunology and Medical Microbiology*, 19(1), 47-56.

ON, S.L.W., 1996. Identification methods for *Campylobacters, Helicobacters*, and related Organisms. *Clinical Microbiology Reviews*, 9, 405-422.

TAUXE, R.V., 2002. Enering foodborne pathogens. *International Journal of Food Microbiology*, 78, 31-41.

WEIJTENS, M.J.B.M., REINDERS, R.D., URLINGS, H.A.P., VAN DER PLAS, J., 1999. *Campylobacter* infections in fattening pigs ; excretion pattern and genetic diversity. *Journal of Applied Microbiology*, 86, 63-70.

WILSON, C.J., 1997. Inhibition and facilitation of nucleic amplification. *Journal of Applied Microbiology*, 26, 9-11.

Session 5

Characterization of Salmonella enterica serovar Typhimurium isolates associated with septicaemia in swine

Bergeron, N.[1], Letellier, A. [1] , Daigle, F. [2], Quessy, S [1]*.

[1] Research Chair in Meat Safety, GREMIP, Faculty of veterinary medicine, Université de Montreal, Québec, Canada.
[2] Department of microbiology and immunology, Faculty of Medicine, Université de Montréal, Québec, Canada
* Corresponding author: sylvain.quessy@umontreal.ca

Abstract

In this study we characterized, using genotyping and phenotyping methods, isolates (n=33) from septicaemia outbreaks in swine herds as well as isolates (n=33) recovered from healthy animals at slaughter. We determined the antimicrobial agents resistance profiles using 24 different antimicrobial agents by the disk diffusion on agar method, the phage type, the plasmid profiles and the PFGE profiles using XbaI and SpeI as restriction enzymes for each isolates. Resistance to as much as 10 antimicrobial agents was found in both categories of isolates. A greater number of PFGE genotypes was observed in isolates from septicaemia. Various phage types were identified in both groups of isolates. Among the DT104 phage type, many genetic clusters were identified. Analysis of plasmid profiles indicated that septicemic strains possess higher molecular weight plasmids than asymptomatic isolates. These results indicated that strains associated with septicaemia belong to various genetic lineages and suggest that virulence traits are associated with plasmid profiles of strains. Our results also suggest that the genetic diversity of Salmonella DT 104 might be higher in North America if we consider results of similar studies in Europe.

Introduction

Infections caused by septicemic strains of *Salmonella* Typhimurium can be associated with significant mortality in mature pigs. Since previous studies showed persistence of strains in various tissues for many days following the infection, the presence of these strains represent as well a food safety concern. It is thus important to better characterize these isolates in order to understand pathogenesis of infection and develop appropriate control measures. The aim of this study was to characterize, using phenotypic and genotypic methods, isolates of *S. enterica* serovar Typhimurium associated with septicaemia in swine and to compare them to isolates recovered from clinically healthy pigs.

Material and Methods

Bacterial strains *Salmonella* isolates recovered from diarrheic and/or septicemic pigs and submitted for a necropsy were obtained from Dr. S. Messier (Faculté de médecine vétérinaire, Université de Montréal, St-Hyacinthe, QC), while those from clinically healthy pigs originated from previous studies in our laboratory (Letellier et al., 1999a; Rheault and Quessy, 2001). Isolates were serotyped at the MAPAQ (Minitère de l'Agriculture, des Pêcheries et de l'Alimentation du Québec) laboratory and phagetyped at the Health Canada Laboratory in Guelph (Ontario). The *S. enterica* serovar Typhimurium strain SL1344, previously described as highly invasive in *in vitro* invasion assays and fully virulent for mice, was provided by Dr. F. Daigle, Faculté de médecine, Université de Montréal, Montréal, QC. The *Escherichia coli* avirulent strain 862B (provided by Dr. J. M. Fairbrother, Faculté de médecine vétérinaire, Université de Montréal, St-Hyacinthe, QC) was used as negative control. In addition to clinical signs, virulence of strains was also established according to their invasion rates on intestinal cells lines (Int-407).

Antimicrobial susceptibility testing. Susceptibility of the isolates to antimicrobial agents was determined by disk diffusion test on Muller-Hinton agar. Antibiotic tested were nalidixic acid 30 µg, amikacin 30 µg, amoxicillin-clavulanic acid 30 µg, ampicillin 10 µg, cefoxitin 30 µg, ceftiofur 30 µg, ceftriaxone 30 µg, cephalothin 30 µg, chloramphenicol 30 µg, ciprofloxacin 5 µg, gentamycin 10 µg, kanamycin 30 µg, streptomycin 25 µg, sulfamethoxazol 25 µg, tetracyclin 30 µg, trimethoprime-sulfa 25 µg, apramycin 15 µg, bacitracin 10 IU, enrofloxacin 5 µg, erythromycin 15 µg, clindamycin 2 µg, neomycin 30 µg, quinupristin/dalfopristin 15 µg and vancomycin 30 µg. Results were interpreted according to the NCCLS guidelines for gram-negative enteric organisms.

Pulsed-field gel electrophoresis (PFGE). Chromosomal DNA plugs from an overnight bacterial culture on LB agar was digested with XbaI (recognition sequence TCTAGA) and SpeI (recognition sequence ACTAGT) (Invitrogen, Life Technology). PFGE performed on a horizontal agarose 1% gel for 13 h at 200 V, pulse time of 4-13,6 sec, at 14°C . Gels were stained with ethidium brmide and photograph on an UV transilluminator.The restriction endonuclease digest patterns were interpreted by considering migration distance and intensity of all visible bands

Plamids profiles. Bacterial culture were carried out at 37°C during 12 hours with agitation and low molecular weigh plasmid profiles on 0.7% agarose gels were determined using QIAprep[R].spin kit (Qiagen inc, Missisauga, Ontario, Canada) according to manufacturer's guidelines.

Results

Serotyping and phagetyping.. A total of 33 isolates of *S.* Typhimurium, the only serotype we have found so far in diseased animals, were recovered from septicemic pigs. When isolates were phagetyped, it was found that 33% (11/33) belonged to DT104 while the others belonged to various phage types. For the 33 isolates from clinically healthy pigs, the proportion belonging to DT104 was however similar.

Antimicrobials susceptibility testing. All isolates were resistant to at least 5 of the 22 tested antimicrobial agents. Resistance to as much as 10 antimicrobial agents were observed. Overall, there was no significant difference in antimicrobial resistance profiles in both group of isolates.

Pulsed-field gel electrophoresis (PFGE) A total of 15 different profiles were found with XbaI and 10 profiles with SpeI. Using XbaI, 11 different profiles were observed for strains from diseased animals compared to 7 for strains from healthy animals. Using SpeI, 9 profiles were identified in isolates from diseased animals while only 5 from isolates from healthy animals. Among the 11 S. Typhimurium DT 104 isolates from diseased animals, 6 different genotypes were observed.

Plasmid isolation and profiles. A higher number of low molecular weigh (< 10 000 bp) plasmids (average of 2.4 vs 1.3) was found in isolates from diseased animals. As much of 11 plasmids were observed on isolates from septicemic animals while a maximum of 3 bands were found in isolates from healthy pigs.

Discussion

In this study, different procedures were used in order to discriminate *S.* Typhimurium isolates recovered from septicemic animals to those from healthy pigs. Overall, as observed by other authors (Foley et al, 2006), a poor correlation was observed between the various typing methods. While it was not possible to find any differences between both groups of isolates regarding the antibiotic resistance profiles, we observed, with the convenient sampling scheme used in this study, a high genetic diversity in isolates from sick animals, suggesting that multiple genetic lineages are responsible for clinical outbreaks in swine herds. However, in a recent study (Perron et al, 2007) on the comparison, within the herds, of genetic variability of both groups of isolates, we observed a significantly higher genetic diversity in strains from asymptomatic animals, suggesting that once a virulent strains is established within a herd, this genetic lineage persist for a prolonged period. This high diversity was also observed in the S. Typhimurium DT 104 group of isolates, although it is generally accepted that isolates from this phage type are generally closely related (Baggesen et al, 2000).

When plasmid profiles of both groups of strains were compared, a higher number of low molecular weigh plasmids was observed in isolates from septicemic pigs, suggesting that some virulence attributes may be linked to low molecular weight (< 10 000 bp) plasmids. It is well known that higher molecular weight plasmids are carrying some virulence factors of Salmonella (Bäumler et al, 2000). The elucidation of the exact role of these low molecular weight plasmids will need further works. We are currently characterizing these plasmids.

Conclusion

Salmonella Typhimurium isolates from from septicemic pigs are genetically diversified and often multiresistant to antimicrobial agents. Results obtained in this study suggest that these isolates possess virulence attributes located on low molecular weight plasmids.

References

BAGESSEN, DL, SANDVANG, D, AARESTRUP, FM. 2000. Characterization of Salmonella enterica serovar typhymurium DT 104 isolated from Denmark and comparison with isolates from Europe and the United States.. Journal of Clinical Microbiology 38 (4); 1581-86.

BAÜMLER, AJ, TSOLIS, RM, HEFFRON, F. 2000. Virulence Mechanisms of Salmonella and their Genetic Basis. In Salmonella in domestic animals: Wray and Wray editors, CABI publishing.

FOLEY, SL, WHITE, DG, MCDERMOTT, PF, WALKER, RD, RHODES, B, FEDORKA-CRAY, PJ, SIMJEE, S, ZHAO, S. 2006. Comparison of subtyping methods for differentiating Salmonella enterica serovar Typhymurium isolates obtained from food animal sources. Journal of Clinical Microbiology., 44(10); 3569-77.

PERRON, GG, QUESSY, S, LETELLIER, A, BELL G. 2007. Genotypic diversity and antimicrobial resistance in asymptomatic Salmonella enterica serotype Typhimurium DT 104. Infection Genetic Evolution 7(2):223-8.

Porcine associated *Salmonella* Typhimuirum DT120: use of PFGE and MLVA in a putative outbreak investigation.

Best E..[1,2*], Hampton M.[1], Ethelberg S.[3], Liebana E.[2], Clifton-Hadley F.A.[2], Davies R.[2], Threlfall J.[1]

[1]Laboratory of Enteric Pathogens, Health Protection Agency, London. UK

[2]Department of Food and Environmental Safety, Veterinary Laboratories Agency, Addlestone, Surrey UK

[3]Statens Serum Institut, Department of Bacteriology, Mycology and Parasitology, Copenhagen, Denmark

*Corresponding author Emma.best@hpa.org.uk

Abstract

In November 2006 a cluster of *Salmonella* Typhimurium DT120 in the North East of England was putatively associated with the consumption of pork. At the same time cases of illness in Denmark were associated with this *Salmonella* type, and a EU alert was issued to determine the type of *S.* Typhimurium DT120 identified. Isolates from the UK and Denmark were compared on the basis of antibiogram, Pulsed Field Gel Electrophoresis (PFGE) and Multi-Locus-Variable number tandem repeat Analysis (MLVA or VNTR) to identify the *S.* Typhimurium DT 120 type and results were compared electronically. Isolates from England had the resistance profile ApSSuT (ampicillin, streptomycin, sulfamethoxazole and tetracycline), VNTR profile (171-244-316-0-487) and with the distinct PFGE type (STYMXB.0083). Isolates from Denmark were resistant to Ap (ampicillin) only, had the VNTR type (171-270-324-0-490) and a PFGE type distinct from England (STYMXB.0010). It was therefore possible to confirm that the isolates from England and Denmark were not identical. These results have verified the significance of VNTR in outbreak investigations for *S.* Typhimurium and have demonstrated how new molecular strategies may be used to supplement existing methods such as PFGE to enable the accurate and rapid comparison of isolates from different countries.

Introduction

Salmonella Typhimurium is a common cause of food borne gastroenteritis in England and Wales with 1418 cases reported to the Health Protection Agency (HPA) in 2006 (HPA data). *S.* Typhimurium is primarily a pathogen of cattle but other species including pigs, can become colonised and may pose a major risk factor for human infection through the handling or consumption of contaminated meat (Davies 2001). *S.* Typhimurium infection in pigs can be problematic for detection as it does not commonly result in clinical symptoms and such animals can be an important food safety problem because of the transmission route of the organism through the food chain to humans.

The current "gold standard" method of choice for molecular typing of *Salmonella* and other food borne pathogens as a means for outbreak identification and source identification is Pulsed Field Gel Electrophoresis (PFGE)(Liebana *et al.* 2002). This has good discriminatory power but can be labour intensive and within certain phage types e.g. definitive phage type (DT) 104 it has been unable to discriminate effectively, leading to problems in outbreak investigations and tracing of strains.

The method of VNTR as described by Lindstedt *et al.* (Lindstedt *et al.* 2004) exploits the repeated units within the *S.* Typhimurium genome, which evolve rapidly allowing an array of different alleles in different isolates. Preliminary results using VNTR for *S.* Typhimurium have demonstrated improved discrimination within certain groups e.g. DT104, suggesting it may be of benefit to epidemiological studies (Lindstedt *et al.* 2004) and be a useful tool in outbreak investigations.

Session 5

A putative outbreak was discovered in November 2006 in the North East of England where a cluster of S. Typhimurium of the rare phage type DT120 was identified and putatively associated with the consumption of pork. Interestingly at the same time, some cases of illness in Denmark were associated with this *Salmonella* type, and a EU alert was issued to determine the type of S. Typhimurium DT120 identified. Our aims here were to investigate the two outbreaks to see if they were linked on the basis of antibiogram, PFGE and VNTR. Additionally, we compared the PFGE, VNTR and antibiogram results from Denmark and England to a number of additional S. Typhimurium DT 120 obtained from pigs and other animals in the UK. These DT120 strains had been isolated before and up to November 2006, we aimed to investigate if the same PFGE and VNTR type had been seen in animals prior to its identification in humans.

Materials and Methods
PFGE
Pulsed Field Gel Electrophoresis (PFGE) was carried out by standardised methods using the laboratory protocol for molecular subtyping of nontyphoidal Salmonella by PFGE (Pulsenet, Centres for Disease Control and Prevention, Atlanta, Georgia). Macro restriction patterns were compared by the use of Bionumerics (version 3.5, Applied Maths, Belgium), and PFGE types were assigned based on the Salmgene PFGE naming system (Peters et al. 2003).

VNTR PCR
The VNTR loci were as described previously (Lindstedt *et al.* 2004) and the method utilising 5 VNTR loci suitable for accurate sizing on an automated capillary sequencer was used. A PCR reaction was set up incorporating all primers in one 25µl multiplex reaction, which comprised, 10pmol of each primer pair STTR5 and STTR3, 5pmol of each primer pair STTR9 and STTR6 and 15pmol of each primer pair STTR5 using WellRed oligos (Proligo, France) for the five labelled primers and standard unmodified HPSF purified oligos (MWG Biotech) for the remainder, with the Qiagen PCR multiplex kit and 1µl DNA per reaction. Cycling conditions were as follows 95° C for 15 min, then 25 cycles of 94° C for 30 s, 61°C for 90 s, and 72°C for 90 s with a final hold at 72°C for 10 min.

Fragment Analysis

Each PCR product (1µl) was added to 20µl deionised formamide including 0.5µl 600bp size standard per reaction, loaded onto the sequencer then denatured at 90°C for 120 seconds, with injection time of 30 seconds at 2.0 kV and separation time of 35 min at 7.5KV. Each fragment was identified by peak size (bp) and dye label.

Results
Thirteen DT120 isolates from England had the resistance profile ApSSuT (ampicillin, streptomycin, sulfamethoxazole and tetracycline), VNTR profile (171-244-316-0-487) and with the distinct PFGE type (STYMXB.0083) (Fig 1). One isolate from Denmark was resistant to Ap (ampicillin) only, had the VNTR type (171-270-324-0-490) and a PFGE type distinct from England (STYMXB.0010) (Fig 2). The VNTR profiles from England and Denmark differed at two loci (STTR5 and STTR6), which confirmed that the isolates from England and Denmark were not identical.

When the PFGE and VNTR results from England and Denmark were compared with other S. Typhimurium DT 120 animal isolates, one isolate from a pig matched the Denmark PFGE profile, however the VNTR profile differed at two loci (STTR5 and STTR3). No isolates from the UK outbreak were found to match the PFGE or VNTR profiles of the animal isolates (Table1). However investigation by VNTR locus revealed a number of similarities in all the DT120 isolates tested, all had similar sized fragments at the STTR9 loci (within the range 172-173bp) and the majority of isolates were missing the locus STTR10 (plasmid located).

Discussion

By using two different molecular typing methods we were able to confirm that the increases in the rare phage type DT120 in England and Denmark were unrelated. However we were able to prove the utility of VNTR for identifying outbreak isolates and demonstrate that it can be used as a complementary method to PFGE. In order to trace the source of an outbreak obtained from a food source such as pork it would be expected that the same *S.* Typhimurium would be found in the animal population six months or more prior to the cases in the human population. The *S.* Typhimurium DT120 type was found in the animal population tested and a number of similar alleles were present in all the isolates; this suggesting that alleles of this size may be specific to DT120 isolates. Further investigation would be needed to confirm the source of the UK outbreak, either the DT120 did not come from a porcine source or that it was not detected in the limited sample set tested.

These results have verified the significance of using VNTR in outbreak investigations for *S.* Typhimurium and have demonstrated how new molecular strategies may be used to supplement existing methods such as PFGE to enable the accurate and rapid comparison of isolates electronically between different countries. VNTR has potential advantages over existing molecular typing schemes including a high degree of strain discrimination, good strain coverage and rapidity. The extension of VNTR methods to other *Salmonella* serotypes would contribute significantly to outbreak investigation for *Salmonella*.

Figure 1
Isolates from England
Lanes 1, 9 & 17 standard
Lanes 3-8 and 10-15 DT120
isolates

Figure 2
Isolates from Denmark
Lanes 1 & 4 standard
Lanes 2 & 3 DT120
isolates

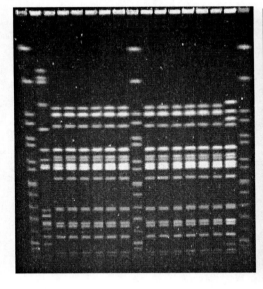
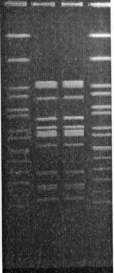

Session 5

Table 1 Human outbreak isolates from the UK and Denmark showing antibiogram, PFGE and VNTR type (shaded boxes indicated the similar strain type obtained from Denmark and a UK pig isolate)

Species	Antibiogram	Country	PFGE TYPE	STTR9	STTR5	STTR6	STTR10	STTR3
human	ApSSuT	UK	STYMXB.0083	172	244	316	0	486
human	ApSSuT	UK	STYMXB.0083	172	241	317	0	486
human	ApSSuT	UK	STYMXB.0083	172	244	321	0	485
human	ApSSuT	UK	STYMXB.0083	171	245	0	0	485
human	ApSSuT	UK	STYMXB.0083	171	244	315	0	485
human	ApSSuT	UK	STYMXB.0083	171	244	316	0	484
human	ApSSuT	UK	STYMXB.0083	172	244	316	0	488
human	ApSSuT	UK	STYMXB.0083	171	244	315	0	485
human	ApSSuT	UK	STYMXB.0083	172	244	316	0	488
human	ApSSuT	UK	STYMXB.0083	171	244	315	0	486
human	ApSSuT	UK	STYMXB.0083	172	244	316	0	487
human	ApSSuT	UK	STYMXB.0083	172	244	315	0	487
human	ApSSuT	UK	STYMXB.0083	172	244	339	0	487
human	Ap	Denmark	STYMXB.0010	171	270	324	0	490
cattle	N/A	UK	STYMXB.0061	150	199	302	366	0
cattle	N/A	UK	STYMXB.0061	172	258	341	407	513
cattle	T,AM,C,S,SU	UK	STYMXB.0061	171	268	346	457	461
pig	T,AM,S,SU	UK	STYMXB.0287	172	258	312	0	489
cattle	T,AM,C,S,SU	UK	STYMXB.0291	172	264	353	457	461
pig	T,AM,S,SU	UK	STYMXB.0061	172	258	312	0	488
pig	T,AM,S,SU	UK	STYMXB.0287	173	258	312	0	0
pig	T,AM,S,SU	UK	STYMXB.0287	172	258	311	0	487
cattle	N/A	UK	STYMXB.0061	172	269	353	0	462
pig	T, AM,C,S,SU	UK	STYMXB.0058	173	270	347	0	514
pig	T, AM,C,S,SU	UK	STYMXB.0292	173	270	347	0	514
pig	T, AM,C,S,SU	UK	STYMXB.0058	173	270	347	0	514
turkey	NA,T,AMC,S,SU	UK	STYMXB.0298	173	276	341	420	515
dog	T,AM,S,SU	UK	STYMXB.0061	173	246	324	0	487
pig	T,AM,S,SU	UK	STYMXB.0010	173	246	324	0	488
pig	T,AM,S,SU	UK	STYMXB.0287	171	258	311	0	488

References

Davies,R.H. (2001) *Salmonella* Typhimurium DT104:has it had its day? *In Practice* 23, 342-351.

Liebana,E., Garcia-Migura,L., Clouting,C., Clifton-Hadley,F.A., Lindsay,E., Threlfall,E.J., McDowell,S.W. and Davies,R.H. (2002) Multiple genetic typing of *Salmonella* enterica serotype typhimurium isolates of different phage types (DT104, U302, DT204b, and DT49) from animals and humans in England, Wales, and Northern Ireland. *J Clin Microbiol.* 40, 4450-4456.

Lindstedt,B.A., Vardund,T., Aas,L. and Kapperud,G. (2004) Multiple-locus variable-number tandem-repeats analysis of *Salmonella* enterica subsp. enterica serovar Typhimurium using PCR multiplexing and multicolor capillary electrophoresis. *J Microbiol. Methods* 59, 163-172.

Peters,T.M., Maguire,C., Threlfall,E.J., Fisher,I.S., Gill,N. and Gatto,A.J. (2003) The Salm-gene project - a European collaboration for DNA fingerprinting for. *Euro. Surveill.* 8, 46-50

ORAL & POSTER

SIXTH SESSION

Antimicrobial resistance

Salmonella (sero)types and their resistance patterns isolated from pig faecal and post-mortem samples in 2000 – 2003.

P.J. van der Wolf

Animal Health Service, Pig Health Dept., P.O.Box 9, 7400 AA Deventer, The Netherlands.
Corresponding author: p.vd.wolf@gddeventer.com

Abstract

The purpose of this survey was to describe the porcine Salmonella isolates derived from faecal samples and post-mortem material (PMM) during years 2000 – 2003. Salmonella was isolated by direct inoculation on BGANO-plates (faeces, intestinal content) or sheep blood agar (organs). Antimicrobial susceptibility was tested by the agar diffusion method. Salmonella was isolated in 3.2% of all porcine submissions received at the Animal Health Service. A total of 960 salmonellae were isolated from a total of 589 submissions from 488 different herds. S. Typhimurium was the most frequently isolated serotype (N= 808, 92.6% of 873 isolates typed), and Salmonella Typhimurium DT104 was the most frequently determined phagetype (N=98, 29.6% of 333 S. Typhimurium typed). Resistance to antimicrobials occurred in 52.5% of all isolates, mainly in the multiresistant phagetype DT104. In less than half of the submissions (44%), other pathogens were isolated as well. In cases of clinical diarrhoea, multiple pathogens and pathogens with multiple antimicrobial resistance may be involved and therapy and preventive measures should be adjusted accordingly.

Introduction

Results from continuous monitoring of prevalent Salmonella serotypes and the antimicrobial resistance patterns of Salmonellae isolated from faecal samples and from material for post-mortem examination from pigs can be used in various ways. First of all it helps veterinarians in choosing an effective treatment of clinical cases. Secondly, Salmonella monitoring results can be used to asses the risk for the human population of salmonellae circulating in the pig population, also because multiresistant strains can complicate the therapy of human salmonellosis. Finally, there is a possibility the resistance is transferred to other bacteriae in the human gut flora. Using this information, it should be kept in mind that these data are not based on a random sampling of the pig population and that extrapolation of these data to the general pig population is therefore hazardous. Purpose of this paper is to review the sero- and phagetypes and resistance patterns of Salmonellae that were isolated from pig faeces and post-mortems at the laboratory of the Animal Health Service in the period 2000 - 2003. Comparable data have been collected over the period 1996 – 1999 as described previously (1).

Material and Methods

Faecal samples and dead pigs were submitted to the laboratories by pig owners or their veterinarians for diagnostic investigation into the cause of the disease or the cause of death. Faecal samples were cultured for Salmonella if Salmonella isolation or general bacteriological investigation was requested at submission. In case of a post-mortem examination, bacteriological examination of the intestines always included direct culturing for Salmonella. Culturing of faeces and intestinal contents is done by direct inoculation onto a brilliantgreen agar plate containing 5 mg/L novobiocin, a selective medium for Salmonella isolation. Material from organs was inoculated on sheep blood agar. Suspect colonies were agglutinated with polyvalent anti-Salmonella serum, sero-group A to G or A to S. Positives were tested by sero-group specific O-antisera. Isolates belonging to sero-groups B and D were tested with H-antisera. Each isolate was tested in triple sugar iron, sulphide indol motility, urea and lysinedecarboxylase agar tube. Isolates were sent to the National Salmonella Reference Laboratory for serotyping and in case of Salmonella Typhimurium phagetyping. Enteropathogenic Escherichia coli were isolated by aerobic culturing on sheep blood agar and MacConkey agar. Suspect colonies were agglutinated with polyvalent antiserum and if applicable with monovalent antiserum. The presence of Brachyspira spp. was tested by Immuno-Fluorescence Test (IFT). PRRS was tested by either body fluid in an ELISA or by PCR. Porcine Circo-virus-2 was tested either by histology or PCR. Antimicrobial susceptibility testing of Salmonella isolates was done by the agar diffusion method, using Isosensitestagar and Neosensitabs. Salmonella-isolates were considered sensitive to antimicrobials if the inhibition zones were equal or larger than 28 mm for ampicillin and the combination of amoxicillin with clavulanic acid, Kana- Neomycin (22 mm), Spectinomycin (22 mm), Colistin (polymyxin E) (22 mm), trimethoprim-sulfamethoxazole (28 mm), and equal or larger than 24 mm for flumequin.

Results

From a total of 589 Salmonella positive submissions from 488 different herds, 960 Salmonella isolates were detected. Of these, 261 submissions consisted of one or more faecal samples (max. 40) and 324 consisted of one to a maximum of 9 carcasses. Four submissions were intestines only. Out of a total of 488 herds, 414 herds (84,8%) submitted material only once in those four years. 56 herds submitted material twice, 12 herds three times. 3 herds 4 times and 3 herds 5 times during these years. These 488 herds were about 5% of all pig herds in The Netherlands in that period. On average, Salmonellae were isolated in 14.6 percent of all submissions of pig faecal samples. An average of 2.7% of all PMM submissions was positive for Salmonellae (Table 1).

Table 1. Total number of submissions of faecal material and post mortem material and number and percentage of submissions positive for Salmonella and total number of samples of faecal material and PMM and number and percentage of samples positive for Salmonella in the period 2000 – 2003 inclusive.

Faecal material	Total submissions	Positive submissions	Percent positive	Total samples	Positive samples	Percent positive
2000	684	98	14.3	2362	214	9.1
2001	339	55	16.2	1061	112	10.6
2002	375	71	18.9	1175	137	11.7
2003	387	37	9.6	1440	71	4.9
Total	1785	261	14.6	6038	534	8.8

PMM	Total submissions	Positive submissions	Percent positive	Total samples	Positive samples	Percent positive
2000	4470	107	2.4	9212	142	1.5%
2001	2820	87	3.1	6431	112	1.7%
2002	2429	71	2.9	4677	92	2.0%
2003	2067	59	2.9	4065	80	2.0%
Total	11786	324	2.7	24385	426	1.7%

In 333 Salmonella-positive faecal samples, also isolation of pathogenic E. coli was attempted. In 23 faecal samples (6.9%) pathogenic E. coli was found. In 428 Salmonella-positive faecal samples Brachyspira spp. detection attempts were made by Immuno-Fluorescence Test. Brachyspira spp. were detected 162 (37.9%) times. Of a total of 422 Salmonella-positive post-mortem examinations, salmonellosis was the only diagnosis given in 181 cases (42.9%). In 20 cases (4.7%), Salmonella was an incidental finding and the mortality was due to other reasons or lesions e.g. hernia or torsion of (part of) the intestines, cardiac defects or mortality as a result of stress. In respectively 35.3%, 13% and 3.8% one, two or three additional causes of death were given.

Table 2. Number and percentage of the different symptoms / pathogens that were diagnosed besides *Salmonella* during post-mortem examinations from pigs.

symptom / pathogen	Number tested	Number positive	Percentage positive of tested
Brachyspira spp.	222	81	36.5%
Porcine Circo virus 2	217	58	26.7%
Enteropathogenic *E. coli*	277	40	14.4%
PRRS	25	12	48.0%
Lawsonia intracellularis	12	4	33.3%
Pneumonia	422	75	17.8%
Streptococci infection	422	28	6.6%
Organ systems*	422	43	10.2%

*Organ systems included hernia or torsion of (part of) the intestines, cardiac defects, gastric ulcers, mortality as a result of stress, etc.

In table 2 the number and percentage of the different symptoms or pathogens that were diagnosed during post-mortem examinations from pigs are presented. When comparing the submissions where only Salmonella was found to cause the symptoms with the submissions where also other causes were found, a significantly higher percentage of the samples within a submission were positive in the "only Salmonella"-group than in the "also other infections"-group (P<0.000, two samples t-test, 65.2% versus 53.5% respectively, see also table 3).

Table 3. Comparison between the submissions with only Salmonella as diagnosis and those with also other pathogens/pathology for the number of samples / carcasses that was positive for Salmonella.

Only salmonella	More than 1 sample	faeces	PMM
Yes	Yes	69% positive samples	59% positive samples
No	Yes	60% positive samples	50% positive samples
P-value		0.057	0.02

In those cases where Salmonella was found to be the single cause of the clinical symptoms and where more than one sample or carcass was submitted within a submission on average only 69% of the faecal samples and only 59% of the carcasses were positive for Salmonella. Clinical symptoms were reported on 505 of 589 submission forms (85.7%), in 215 cases for faecal material and in 290 cases for PMM. Varying from 1 to 6 different symptoms were given but mostly (55%) only one for faeces (diarrhoea) or one or two for PMM. Death, poor growth / runts, poor appetite or inappetence and other symptoms were significantly more often reported for PMM then for faecal samples. Diarrhoea and fever were reported significantly (P<0.05) more often for faecal samples then for PMM.

In PPM different materials were cultured for detection of Salmonella. These were colon (299 pos. out of 323 tested 92.6%), jejunum (288/269=84.8%), lungs (23/136=16.9%), brains (6/76=7.9%), spleen (23/73=31.5%), kidney (15/42=35.7%), joints (3/14=21.4%), hart (2/14=14.3%), serous membranes (4/9=44.4%), stomach (7/8=87.5%), mesenteric lymphnodes (5/8=62.5%), caecum (5/5=100%), liver (4/5=80%) nose (0/4), and uterus (0/2). During post-mortem examination mostly

Session 6

2 organs were cultured (39.7%) up to a maximum of 6 per carcass (1.1%). Mostly one culture was positive for Salmonella (61%) but up to a maximum of 5 per carcass (0.2%).

Table 4. Serovars of Salmonella found in faeces and post-mortem material.

serovar	Faeces Freq	%	PMM Freq	%
Typhimurium	471	93.3	337	91.6
Derby	7	1.4	11	3.0
Brandenburg	6	1.2	4	1.1
London	6	1.2	2	0.5
Livingstone	5	1.0	1	0.3
Bovismorbificans	3	0.6	2	0.5
Goldcoast	2	0.4	1	0.3
Panama	0	0.0	2	0.5
Falkensee	1	0.2	0	0.0
Kedougou	1	0.2	0	0.0
Infantis	1	0.2	4	1.1
Dublin	1	0.2	0	0.0
Ohio	0	0.0	1	0.3
enterica	1	0.2	3	0.8
Total	505	99.1	368	100.0

In table 4 the different serovars of Salmonella that were found are presented. S. Typhimurium was the most frequently isolated serotype (N= 808, 92.6% of 873 isolates typed), and Salmonella Typhimurium DT104 was the most frequently determined phagetype (N=98, 29.4% of 333 S. Typhimurium typed). Over the years the percentage of DT104 phagetype increases significantly from 21.5% in 2000 to 37.3% in 2003 (Table 5.)

Table 5. Number and percentage of Salmonella Typhimurium DT104 isolated per year for the periode 2000 – 2003.

Year	Salmonella Typhimurium	DT104	%	P<0.05*
2000	93	20	21.5	a
2001	95	25	26.3	ab
2002	86	31	36.1	b
2003	59	22	37.3	b

* Number of DT104 per year with different letters differ significantly at the given level

Next to DT104, corresponding to the Dutch phagetypes 506 and 401, 37 other Dutch phagetypes were identified (N=235). Main phagetypes were 507 (N=30), 1 (N=28), 510 (N=27), 350 (N=17), 296 (N=16), 353 (N=13), 80 (N=12), and 655 (N=11). Resistance to antimicrobials was found in 52.5% of all isolates that were tested (N=592). The number of antimicrobials that isolates were resistant to varied from 1 to 4, with respectively 21%, 20%, 9% and 2% for 1 through 4 resistances. Ampicillin was resistant in 37.4% of all tested isolates (223/597=37.4%), amoxicillin with clavulanic acid in 10.7% mostly intermediate resistant (64/597=10.7%), kana-/neomycin in 0.2% intermediate resistant (1/594=0.2%), spectinomycin in 25.3% resistant (150/593=25.3%), colistin in 0.3% intermediate resistant (2/593=0.3%), trimethoprim sulfa combination in 22.8% resistant (136/597=22.8%) and flumequin in 0.5% intermediate resistant (3/592=0.5%). Resistance for ampicillin, amoxicillin with clavulanic acid, spectinomycin and TMPS increased over the years (table 6).

Table 6. Frequency of resistant strains over the years for ampicillin, amoxicillin, spectinomycin and Trimethoprim sulfa combination (TMPS).

	2000 N = 209	2001 N = 144	2002 N = 145	2003 N = 99
Ampicillin	27.8^a	31.9^a	44.1^b	45.5^b
Amoxicillin	6.7^a	2.8^a	11.0^b	29.3^c
Spectinomyci n	18.7^a	22.5^{ab}	29.9^b	27.6^{ab}
TMPS	22.5^a	20.1^a	20.0^a	30.3^b

Different superscripts indicate a significant difference (P<0.05)

Discussion

These data show that *Salmonella* is found in a small minority of the faecal samples and the post-mortem material that is submitted to the Animal Health Service for diagnostic purposes. Most of the isolated *Salmonella*'s are *Salmonella* Typhimurium and within *Salmonella* Typhimurium the phagetype DT104 shows a growing prevalence over the years. Clinical symptoms reported at submission are almost exclusively diarrhoea for faecal samples but more divers symptoms are reported for post-mortem material like death, diarrhoea, poor growth / runt, and other symptoms like lameness of nervous symptoms. When more than one faecal sample or carcass is submitted not all samples are positive for *Salmonella*. This means that submitting only 1 sample or carcass is a waste of money and effort in respectively 30 or 40% of the cases just as a result of chance because even though Salmonella appears to be the cause of the symptoms not all samples are positive. This also means that the prevalence of Salmonella in clinical samples is underestimated because in many cases only one sample or carcass is submitted. About two thirds of all isolated *Salmonella*'s were resistant to at least one antimicrobial but with a maximum of resistance to 4 antimicrobials. Resistance was found mainly for ampicillin, TMPS, spectinomycin and amoxicillin with clavulanic acid. Resistance to these antimicrobials appears to be increasing over the years. This increase is partly due to the increasing number of phagetype DT104 of *Salmonella* Typhimurium but the increase in resistance to TMPS is a result of an increase of resistance in other serovars because DT104 is hardly resistant to TMPS.

Acknowledgements

The author wishes to thank Jan Lommerse for his contribution in entering the data, the National Reference Centre for Salmonella for typing the Salmonella isolates, and the Animal Health Service for the opportunity to write this article.

Reference

(1) van der Wolf PJ, Peperkamp NHMT. *Salmonella* (sero)types and their resistance patterns isolated from pig faecal and post-mortem samples. Vet Q 2001; 23(4):175-181.

Session 6

Prevalence and antimicrobial resistance profile of *Campylobacter* isolated from conventional and antibiotic free swine farms in three geographic locations

Daniel A. Tadesse[1], Julie A. Funk[2], Peter B. Bahnson[3], W. E. Morgan Morrow[4], Siddhartha Thakur[5] and Wondwossen A. Gebreyes[1*]

[1]Dept. of Veterinary Preventive Medicine, College of Veterinary Medicine, Ohio State University, 1920 Coffey Road, Columbus OH, USA
[2]National Food Safety and Toxicology Centre, College of Veterinary Medicine, Michigan State University
[3]Dept. of Medical Sciences, School of Veterinary Medicine, University of Wisconsin-Madison
[4]North Carolina State University - Department of Animal Science, [5]Food and Drug Administration, Center for Veterinary Medicine

* Corresponding author:gebreyes.1@osu.edu

Abstract

Background: The prevalence and antimicrobial resistance of *Campylobacter* were examined from swine reared in conventional and antimicrobial-free (ABF) production systems in three geographical locations: North Carolina (NC), Ohio (OH) and Wisconsin (WI).
Methods: A total of 1500 pigs and 1930 carcass swab samples were evaluated for the prevalence of *Campylobacter*. Fecal samples from 662 pigs from NC (370 conventional farms and 292 ABF farms), 379 from OH (268 conventional and 111 ABF) and 459 from WI (160 conventional and 299 ABF) were included. Antimicrobial susceptibility testing was performed using agar dilution method against a panel of six antimicrobials.
Results: *Campylobacter* was commonly found in swine herds in all the three states with a prevalence of 54.2% (NC), 54.1% (OH) and 58.2% (WI). The prevalence of *Campylobacter* in conventional farms (56.1%) was not significantly different from ABF farms (54.6%) (p > 0.05). However, the prevalence of *Campylobacter* in WI farms was higher in conventional farms (70.6%) than ABF (51.5%) (p<0.05). *Campylobacter* isolates showed resistance to all the six antimicrobials with different frequency. Tetracycline resistance was the most common followed by erythromycin in all the three states. Frequency of resistance to ciprofloxacin (MIC of >4 mg/L) was higher among OH and WI isolates than NC. Erythromycin and tetracycline resistance was significantly higher in conventional farms than ABF Farms (p<0.05). Ciprofloxacin and Nalidixic acid resistance was more common in ABF farms (p<0.05). The predominant resistance patterns were erythromycin-tetracycline (Ery-Tet) and tetracycline only (Tet).
Discussion: This study showed high prevalence of *Campylobacter* among swine herds in the three states with no significant difference by geographical locations and production systems (regardless of the antimicrobial use status). The high proportion of ciprofloxacin resistant isolates from ABF herds may have important implications on the potential role of risk factors other than mere antimicrobial use for production purposes and probably producer compliance.

Introduction

Campylobacter is one of the leading causes of foodborne bacterial infection worldwide and an estimated more than 2 million cases of *Campylobacter*iosis occur each year in the United States (Mead et al., 1999). The overall incidence rate of laboratory-confirmed *Campylobacter* infection in 2005 in the United States was 12.72 cases per 100,000 populations (CDC, 2006). Most *Campylobacter* infections in human are self-limited and do not require antimicrobial therapy unless there is some complication. The drugs of choice in such conditions are erythromycin and fluoroquinolones. There are reports of an increase resistance to tetracycline, erythromycin and fluoroquinolones (Prats et al., 2000; Engberg et al., 2001; Gupta et al., 2004; Thakur and Gebreyes, 2005). There are concerns over the transfer of antimicrobial resistance from food animals to human population as animal products can serve as a source of foodborne infection and important link between animals and humans. The use of antimicrobials for growth promotion and prophylaxis in animal industry exacerbate the conditions. The present study investigated the prevalence and antimicrobial resistance of *Campylobacter* recovered from swine reared under conventional and antibiotic free (ABF) production systems at farm and slaughter from three different geographic locations.

Materials and Methods

Samples were collected from 55 farm-slaughter pairs from conventional and antibiotic free (ABF) swine farms and slaughter plants from three geographic locations: 20 from North Carolina (10 conventional and 10 antimicrobial free farms (ABF)), 16 sites from Ohio (9 conventional and 7 ABF) and 19 sites from Wisconsin (6 conventional and 13 ABF). A total of 1500 fecal and 1930 carcass samples were examined for the presence of *Campylobacter* from North Carolina (662 fecal and 757 carcass swabs), Wisconsin (459 fecal and 680 carcass swabs) and Ohio (379 fecal and 493 carcass swabs). In conventional production system, antimicrobials were used for treatment and growth promotion purposes. In the antibiotic free swine rearing system, antimicrobials were not used after weaning age either for treatment or growth promotion purposes.

Fecal samples were collected from the rectum of live swine and directly plated on campy-cefex selective plates at 42°C for 48 hrs under microaerophilic conditions (10% C_2O, 5% O_2 and 85% N_2). Putative colonies were transferred to Muller Hinton agar (Remel, USA) and tested by catalase (Becton Dickinson, USA) and oxidase tests (Becton Dickinson, USA). Carcass swabs were collected from slaughter plants at different stage of processing pre- and post-evisceration and chill stages using multiple swipe (USDA) and single swipe carcass swabbing methods. Then carcass swabs were enriched in 30 ml Bolton broth (Oxoid, Hampshire, UK) and incubated at 42°C for 48 hrs in microaerophilic conditions. A loopful of the enriched sample were streaked onto campy-cefex and processed similar to fecal samples. Catalase and oxidase positive isolates were tested for antimicrobial susceptibility using agar dilution method against six antimicrobials following the recommendation of the Clinical and Laboratory Standard Institute (CLSI). The antimicrobials and break points used were chloramphenicol (Ch: 0.25 to 128 mg/liter, 32 mg/liter), erythromycin (Ery: 0.06 to 32 mg/liter, 8 mg/liter), gentamicin (Gen: 0.06 to 32 mg/liter, 16 mg/liter), ciprofloxacin (Cip: 0.008 to 4 mg/liter, 4 mg/liter), nalidixic acid (Nal: 0.25 to 128 mg/liter, 32 mg/liter) and tetracycline (Tet: 0.06 to 32 mg/liter, 16 mg/liter). The CLSI break points were used for all the antimicrobials except erythromycin. For the erythromycin, the National Antimicrobials Resistance Monitoring System (NARMS) break point was used.

Results

Prevalence of *Campylobacter*

The overall prevalence of *Campylobacter* in conventionally raised swine was 56.1%, while 54.6% in antibiotic free farms Table 1. Although a higher frequency of *Campylobacter* detected in conventional farms than ABF, this difference was not statistically significant (p>0.05). The pig level *Campylobacter* prevalence in the three states was 54.2%, 54.1%, and 58.17% in North Carolina, Ohio and Wisconsin, respectively. There was no significant difference in the prevalence of *Campylobacter* between the two production system in North Carolina (53% for conventional and 55.8% for ABF) and Ohio (51.9% for conventional and 59.5% for ABF) (p > 0.05). However, in Wisconsin significantly higher prevalence of *Campylobacter* was observed in conventional (70.6%) than ABF (51.5%) (p<0.05).

At slaughter, there was significantly higher recovery of *Campylobacter* at post-evisceration stage than pre-evisceration in both production systems. At the post evisceration stage, there was significantly higher recovery rate of *Campylobacter* from carcasses raised in conventional production (42.4%) than ABF (26.6%). The recovery was significantly reduced after chilling stage regardless of the method used (USDA or single swipe carcass swabbing method). The recovery rate of *Campylobacter* in the post chill stage was 3.4% and 3% using the USDA and single swipe methods, respectively.

Antimicrobial resistance

A total of 2360 *Campylobacter* isolates (1181 from conventional and 1179 from slaughter) were tested for susceptibility using six antimicrobials. At the farm level, resistance to all the six antimicrobials was observed with different frequency in both production systems. Frequency of resistance to tetracycline and erythromycin was significantly higher in conventional farms (72.1% for tetracycline and 69.5% for erythromycin) than ABF farms (60.2% for tetracycline and 37.5% for erythromycin) (p<0.05). Sixteen out of 849 from conventional and 83 out of 841 *Campylobacter*

Session 6

isolates from ABF were resistant to ciprofloxacin. We have found higher frequency of resistance to ciprofloxacin and Nalidixic acid in ABF farms (p<0.05) Table 1. Resistance to gentamicin was not observed at the farm level in both conventional and ABF farms from North Carolina. At slaughter, however, resistance to gentamicin was observed at post evisceration and post chill stage. Multidrug-resistant *Campylobacter* strains were detected in both conventional and ABF herds. Twenty four percent of the *Campylobacter* isolates from North Carolina, 25% from Ohio and 20% from Wisconsin were pansusceptible. In North Carolina and Ohio isolates, the predominant resistance pattern observed was erythromycin–tetracycline followed by tetracycline. On the other hand, tetracycline was the predominant resistance pattern (23.5%) followed by erythromycin– tetracycline (16.6%) Fig 1.

	Production Stage	Production System	Pig/Carcass % Tested	Prevalence	# of Isolates Tested	Resistance profile Chl (%)	Ery (%)	Gen (%)	NA (%)	Cip (%)	Tet (%)
Farm	Finishing	Conventional	798	56.1	849	15 (1.8)	590 (69.5)	17 (2.0)	104 (12.3)	16 (1.9)	612 (72.1)
		ABF	702	54.6	841	14 (1.7)	315 (37.5)	21 (2.5)	191 (22.7)	43 (5.1)	506 (60.2)
	Pre-Evisceration	Conventional	245	19.6	111	4 (3.6)	85 (77)	0 (0)	5 (4.5)	0 (0)	66 (59.5)
		ABF	251	21.9	143	21 (14.7)	50 (35)	0 (0)	26 (18.2)	4 (2.8)	64 (44.8)
Slaughter	Post-Evisceration	Conventional	231	42.4	199	7 (3.5)	112 (56.3)	1 (0.5)	3 (1.5)	1 (0.5)	151 (75.9)
		ABF	259	26.6	165	14 (8.5)	79 (47.9)	2 (1.2)	13 (7.9)	2 (1.2)	106 (64.24)
	Post-Chill (USDA)	Conventional	244	3.7	11	0 (0)	6 (54.5)	0 (0)	0 (0)	0 (0)	6 (54.5)
		ABF	228	3.1	15	0 (0)	6 (40)	0 (0)	0 (0)	0 (0)	6 (40)
	Post-Chill	Conventional	245	2.4	11	1 (9.1)	10 (90.9)	1 (9.1)	0 (0)	0 (0)	7 (63.6)
		ABF	227	3.5	15	3 (20)	2 (13.3)	0 (0)	0 (0)	0 (0)	7 (46.7)

Tabel1. Prevalence and antimicrobial resistance profile of *Campylobacter* from different production systems and stages.

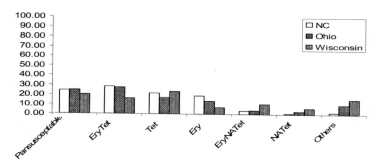

Fig1. The predominant *Campylobacter* resistance pattern observed among the three states

Discussion

The present study revealed that *Campylobacter* is prevalent in both conventional and antibiotic free swine farms. A *Campylobacter* prevalence of 56.1% was observed in conventional swineherds and previous reports indicated a prevalence ranging from 57.8 to 100% (Saez et al., 2000; Thakur and Gebreyes, 2005). However the prevalence was not significantly different from Antibiotic free farms (54.6%). There are limited information regarding the prevalence and antimicrobial resistance of *Campylobacter* in ABF swine farms. Luangtongkum and colleagues in 2006 compared the effect of production system on *Campylobacter* prevalence and antimicrobial resistance in poultry farms and showed high prevalence of *Campylobacter* in both conventional and organic poultry farms. There was no significant difference in the prevalence of *Campylobacter* among the three states. Higher recovery of *Campylobacter* at post evisceration stages could be due to cross-contamination during slaughtering. Chilling resulted in significant reduction in carcass *Campylobacter* load. In our study antimicrobial resistance to erythromycin and tetracycline were common. Different study in different part of the world showed higher *Campylobacter* resistance to tetracycline and erythromycin from pig isolates (Guévremont et al., 2006; Mayrhofer et al., 2004; Bywater et al., 2004). The current finding indicated that higher frequency of resistance to ciprofloxacin and Nalidixic acid in ABF farms than conventional. The finding of resistance to erythromycin and ciprofloxacin is a concern to public health as these drugs are the drugs of choice in severe and complicated cases. This study highlights the high prevalence of antimicrobial-resistant *Campylobacter* in both conventional and ABF pig production systems.

References

1. Bywater R, H. Deluyker, E. Deroover, A. de Jong, H. Marion, M. McConville, T. Rowan, T. Shryock, D. Shuster, V. Thomas, M. Valle, and J. Walters. 2004. A European survey of antimicrobial susceptibility among zoonotic and commensal bacteria isolated from food-producing animals. *J Antimicrob Chemother*. 54(4):744-54.
2. Centers for Disease Control and Prevention. 2006. Preliminary FoodNet data on the incidence of infection with pathogens transmited commonly through food—10 states, United States,2005. *MMWR* 55(14);392-395
3. Engberg J, F.M. Aarestrup, D.E. Taylor, P. Gerner-Smidt, and I. Nachamkin. 2001. Quinolone and macrolide resistance in Campylobacter jejuni and C. coli: resistance mechanisms and trends in human isolates. *Emerg Infect Dis*. 7:24–34.
4. Guévremont E., E. Nadeau, M. Sirois, and S. Quessy. 2006. Antimicrobial susceptibilities of thermophilic Campylobacter from humans, swine, and chicken broilers. *Can J Vet Res*. 70(2):81-6.
5. Gupta A., J.M. Nelson, and T.J. Barrett. 2004. Antimicrobial resistance among Campylobacter strains, United states, 1997–2001. *Emerg Infect Dis* 10:1102–9.
6. Luangtongkum T., T.Y. Morishita, A.J. Ison, S. Huang, P.F. McDermott, and Q. Zhang. 2006. Effect of conventional and organic production practices on the prevalence and antimicrobial resistance of Campylobacter spp. in poultry. *Appl Environ Microbiol*. 72(5):3600-7.
7. Mayrhofer S, P. Paulsen, F.J. Smulders, and F. Hilbert. 2004. Antimicrobial resistance profile of five major food-borne pathogens isolated from beef, pork and poultry. *Int J Food Microbiol*. 97(1):23-9.
8. Mead P.S., L. Slutsker, V. Dietz, L.F. McCaig, J.S. Bresee, C. Shapiro, P.M. Griffin, and R.V. Tauxe. 1999. Food-related illness and death in the United States. *Emerg Infect Dis*. 5(5):607-25.
9. National Committee for Clinical Laboratory Standards. 2002. Performance standards for antimicrobial disc and dilution susceptibility tests for bacteria isolated from animals; approved standard, 2nd ed., M31-A2. National Committee for Clinical Laboratory Standards, Wayne, Pa.
10. Prats G, B. Mirelis, T. Llovet, C. Munoz, E. Miro, F. Navarro. 2000. Antibiotic resistance trends in enteropathogenic bacteria isolated in 1985–1987 and 1995–1998 in Barcelona. *Antimicrob Agents Chemother*. 44:1140–1145.
11. Saenz Y., M. Zarazaga, M. Lantero, M.J. Gastanares, F. Baquero, and C. Torres. 2000. Antibiotic resistance in Campylobacter strains isolated from animals, foods, and humans in Spain in 1997–1998. *Antimicrob Agents Chemother*. 44:267–71.
12. Thakur S. and W.A. Gebreyes. 2005. Prevalence and antimicrobial resistance of Campylobacter in antimicrobial-free and conventional pig production systems. *J Food Prot*. 68(11):2402-10.

Session 6

Low prevalence of non-typable Methicillin-resistant *Staphylococcus aureus* in meat products in The Netherlands

Diederen, B.M.W.[1], van Loo, I.H.M. [1], Savelkoul, P[2], Woudenberg, J.H.C.[2], Roosendaal, R[2], Verhulst, C[3], van Keulen, P.H.J.[3], Kluytmans, J.A.J.W.*[2,3]

[1] Laboratory of Medical Microbiology, St Elisabeth Hospital, Tilburg, The Netherlands
[2] Medical Microbiology and Infection Control, Vumc Amsterdam, The Netherlands
[3] Laboratory for Microbiology and Infection Control, Amphia Hospital, Breda[1], The Netherlands
* Corresponding author: jankluytmans@gmail.com

Abstract

Recently, a new clone of methicillin resistant *Staphylococcus* (*S.*) *aureus* (MRSA) emerged in the Netherlands that was related to pigfarming. A survey in pigs showed that nearly 40% carried this new clone. This new type is characterised by being untypable with pulsed field gel electrophoresis (PFGE). This study was undertaken to determine the prevalence and genetic relationship of *S.aureus* and MRSA in meat products.

Samples were collected between February and May 2006. A total of 79 raw pork and cow meat products were randomly collected from 31 different shops (butcheries n=5, supermarkets n=26) in the South of The Netherlands. The samples were cultured using three procedures. Identification of the strains as *S. aureus* and methicillin resistance were determined by Martineau PCR assay for species identification and PCR for the presence of the *mecA* gene. Susceptibility to cefoxitin and doxycyclin was determined using disk diffusion according to CLSI standards. All isolated *S. aureus* strains were genotyped by amplified fragment gel electrophoresis (AFLP).

Direct inoculation of plates yielded no MRSA positive isolates. The first enrichment broth yielded 30 *S. aureus* isolates. One *S. aureus* isolate in pork meat was identified as MRSA. With the addition of the double-enrichment broth culture system another 6 *S. aureus* were detected, one of which was methicillin resistant. Combining the results of both enrichment broth culture procedures, in total 36 *S. aureus* isolates were obtained from 34 samples. Two isolates from pork meat (2.5% of total samples) were found to be methicillin resistant. A total of 19 shops (61%) were found to be positive for *S. aureus* in at least one meat sample. AFLP typing showed 8 genetic lineages, covering 81% (29/36) of the isolated strains, and a smaller number of unique sporadic isolates (20% (7/36) of isolated strains (figure 2). In 5 out of 6 shops (83%), in which more than one *S. aureus* isolate was found, there was evidence of clonal relationship between the strains of particular shops. PFGE typing of the MRSA isolates showed that 1 MRSA isolate was nontypable using *smaI* digestion and identical to isolates found in pigs. The other MRSA isolate was identical to the USA 300 clone.

In conclusion, this is the first report of MRSA prevalence that is available for meat products in the Netherlands. 2,5% of the meat contained MRSA. Furthermore, *S. aureus* is found regularly in low amounts in meat. Considering the low amounts of contamination these findings suggest that under normal conditions meat consumption is very unlikely to be a hazard to consumers for the acquisition of MRSA.

Introduction

In 2003 a new clone of methicillin resistant *Staphylococcus aureus* (MRSA) emerged in the Netherlands that was related to pig and cattle farming [1,2]. A survey in pigs showed that nearly 40% carried this clone [2]. The detection of this strain was relatively easy since it is non-typable (NT) with Pulsed Field Gel Electrophoresis (PFGE), the method that is used for surveillance of MRSA at the National Reference Centre for MRSA (National Institute of Public Health and the Environmental, Bilthoven, The Netherlands). Further typing of NT-MRSA showed that almost all strains belonged to one MLST cluster, ST 398. This study was undertaken to determine to what extend *S. aureus* and more specific MRSA was present in Dutch meat products.

Materials and methods

Samples of various meat products from pigs and cattle, obtained from local supermarkets and butcheries, were examined for contamination with methicillin susceptible *S. aureus* (MSSA) and MRSA. A total of 79 raw meat products (pork n=64 and beef n=15) were collected from 31 different shops (butcheries n=5, supermarkets n=26) in the period February - May 2006. From 14 shops 1 sample was investigated, from 6 shops 2 samples, from 4 shops 3 samples, from 3 shops 4 samples, from 2 shops 5 samples, from 1 shop 9 samples and from 1 shop 10 samples. A small portion of the meat products (mean 7.9 g +/- sd 3.97) was plated directly on a chromogenic screening medium for the detection of MRSA (MRSA ID; bioMérieux, La Balme Les Grottes, France) and put into 5 ml enrichment broth, containing Mueller Hinton broth with 6,5% NaCl. After 24 h incubation at 35°C the enrichment broth was subcultured on Columbia agar plates with 5% sheep blood (CA), an MRSA-ID plate and 1 ml of the enrichment broth was put into a second enrichment broth containing phenolred mannitol broth with ceftizoxim (5 µg/ml) and aztreonam (7.5 µg/ml) (Regional Public Health laboratory, Groningen, The Netherlands). The second enrichment broth was subcultured on CA and MRSA-ID. All plates were incubated 48 h at 35°C. Presumptive *S. aureus* colonies were confirmed with a latex agglutination test (Staphaurex Plus; Murex Diagnostics Ltd., Dartford, England), a tube coagulase test with rabbit plasma and DNase (DNase agar; Oxoid Ltd., Basingstoke, England). Species identification was confirmed by Martineau PCR. Confirmation of methicillin resistance was performed with *mecA* gene PCR. Susceptibility to cefoxitin and doxycyclin was determined using disk diffusion according to CLSI (formerly NCCLS) standards [3]. All isolated *S. aureus* strains (MSSA and MRSA) were genotyped by Amplified Fragment Gel Electrophoresis (AFLP).

Results

Direct inoculation of plates yielded no MRSA positive isolates (table 1). The first enrichment broth yielded 30 *S. aureus* isolates, 25 of which were detected in pork meat and 5 in beef meat. In one pork sample 2 phenotypically different *S. aureus* isolates were found. One *S. aureus* isolate in pork meat was identified as MRSA. With the addition of the double-enrichment broth culture system another 6 *S. aureus* were detected, one of which was methicillin resistant. Combining the results of both enrichment broth culture procedures, in total 36 *S. aureus* isolates were obtained from 34 samples (table 1). Twenty-seven (42,2%) pork samples and 5 (33.3%) beef samples harboured *S. aureus*. Two pork samples yielded 2 phenotypically different *S. aureus* isolates. Two isolates from pork meat (2.5% of total samples) were found to be methicillin resistant. A total of 19 shops (61%) were found to be positive for *S. aureus* in at least one meat sample. The range of *S. aureus* positive samples for each store is shown in figure 1.

AFLP typing showed 8 genetic lineages, covering 81% (29/36) of the isolated strains, and a smaller number of unique sporadic isolates (20% (7/36) of isolated strains. From the 2 samples that contained 2 phenotypically different strains, the 2 strains from 1 sample (number 31-1 en 31-2) belonged to the same lineage and the other sample contained 2 strains (number 17-1 en 17-2) belonging to 2 different genetic lineages. In 5 out of 6 shops (83%), in which more than one *S. aureus* isolate was found, there was evidence of clonal relationship between the strains of particular shops. PFGE typing of the MRSA isolates showed that 1 MRSA isolate was nontypable using *sma*l digestion and identical to isolates found in pigs. The other MRSA isolate was identical to the USA 300 clone.

Discussion

This is the first survey investigating the presence of MSSA and MRSA in meat products in the Netherlands. Two meat samples (2.5%) contained MRSA. Furthermore, *S. aureus* is found regularly in low amounts in meat as it is sold to consumers. The prevalence of *S. aureus* in meat products was found to be 4%, 22.7% and 65% in 3 other studies performed in Egypt , Switserland and Japan, respectively [4-6].

Contamination of the meat products could be traced back to certain abattoirs in Switserland and poor hygienic and sanitary conditions in Egypt. The high rate of clonal relatedness of different strains within particular shops indicates cross-contamination of the meat at some point during processing. Therefore, the strain in the sample is not necessarily indicative of the strain that was carried by the animal at the source.

Session 6

This study demonstrates that MRSA has entered the food-chain. As the amounts were very low it is not likely to cause disease, especially if meat is properly prepared before consumption. However, contamination of food products may be a potential threat for the acquisition of MRSA by the person who handles the meat and, even worse, foodborne illness by MRSA. Both events have been previously described. Foodborne disease caused by contamination of pork meat with MRSA was caused by a food handler who was carrier of MRSA with the same PFGE pattern as several cases [7]. Contamination of food products was the transmission route for an MRSA outbreak on a hospital ward in Erasmus MC in Rotterdam, The Netherlands [8]. A dietary worker carried MRSA in his throat and transmitted MRSA via food to patients. One immunocompromised patient was likely infected this way, developed a severe sepsis and died.

All reports of MRSA in meat-products described before dealt with MRSA from human origin that was contaminating the meat. In this report the NT-MRSA in the meat is from animal origin. Although in this study the pig-related MRSA strain was found in only one product and in very low amounts, it does show that MRSA has made its way into the food chain.

References

1. VOS, A., et al. 2005. Methicillin-resistant *Staphylococcus aureus* in pig farming. *Emerg Infect* Dis, 11(12), 1965-1966.
2. HUIJSDENS, X.W., et al. 2006. Community-acquired MRSA and pig-farming. *Ann Clin Microbiol Antimicrob*, 10 (5), 26.
3. National Committee for Clinical Laboratory Standards. 2006. Performance standards for antimicrobial susceptibility testing. National Committee for Clinical Laboratory Standards.Wayne, Pa.
4. BAKR, W.M., et al. 2004. Detection of coagulase positive staphylococci in meat products sold in Alexandria using two different media. *J Egypt Public Health Assoc*, 79 (1-2): 31-42.
5. SCHRAFT, H., et al. 1992. Contamination of pig hindquarters with *Staphylococcus aureus*. *Int J Food Microbiol*, 15 (1-2): 191-194.
6. KITAI, S., et al. 2005. Prevalence and characterization of *Staphylococcus aureus* and enterotoxigenic *Staphylococcus aureus* in retail raw chicken meat throughout Japan. *J Vet Med Sci*, 67 (3): 269-274.
7. JONES, T.F., et al. 2002. An outbreak of community-acquired foodborne illness caused by methicillin-resistant *Staphylococcus aureus*. *Emerg Infect Dis*, 8 (1): 82-84.
8. KLUYTMANS, J., et al. 1995. Food-initiated outbreak of methicillin-resistant *Staphylococcus aureus* analyzed by pheno- and genotyping. *J Clin Microbiol*, 33 (5): 1121-1128.

Table 1. Number of MSSA and MRSA in pork and beef meat, separated for the different culture systems.

	Direct culture				Single enrichment broth				Single and double enrichtment broth			
	Total no. of samples	MSSA strains	MRSA strains	No of positive samples	MSSA strains	MRSA strains	No of positive samples	MSSA strains	MRSA strains	No of positive samples
Pork	64	0	0	0	24	1	24	29	2	29
Beef	15	0	0	0	5	0	5	5	0	5
Total	79	0	0	0	29	1	29	34	2	34

Figure 1. Number of positive samples per shop.

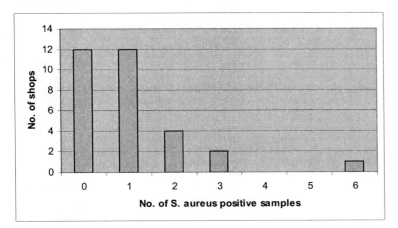

Take Care – Use Antibiotics Responsibly Swine Practitioner Project

Wagstrom, E.*[1], Bane, D.[2], Lassiter, A[3], Lehman, J[4], Perez, L.[3]

[1]. National Pork Board, 1776 NW 114th Street, Des Moines, IA, USA 50325
[2]. Research and Consulting Services, Sidney, IL, USA
[3]. Minnesota State University, Mankato, MN, USA
[4]. Health and Management Solutions, Sullivan, IL, USA

Corresponding Author: LWagstrom@pork.org

Abstract

The Take Care – Use Antibiotics Responsibly® program is an antimicrobial resistance and use education and awareness program for pork producers. The program is based on principles and guidelines intended to minimize the development of antimicrobial resistance while maximizing animal health. The program was developed by the National Pork Board, but veterinarians are key in the delivery of the program on farm. Since there are many factors that contribute to the amounts and types of antimicrobials used on farm it was decided that the best way to measure program effectiveness was through measurement of changes in the attitude and behaviors of program participants.

Ten veterinary clinics were selected to participate in the Take Care swine practitioners' pilot project. The practitioners were trained by the project managers and Pork Board staff and were provided brochures and PowerPoint presentations to use with their clients. They formally delivered education about the program and worked to implement it on farm with three clients (treatment group). Additionally they selected two other clients who did not receive the training (control group) to survey. Surveys were developed by industrial psychologists to objectively measure attitudes and behaviors related to antimicrobial use on farm. The surveys were administered to all producers at the beginning and end of the project. The treatment group was also surveyed shortly after going through the education and training. Analysis of the survey data is underway and results will be given in the oral presentation at SafePork 2007.

Introduction

The Take Care – Use Antimicrobials Responsibly program was developed by the National Pork Board with input from veterinary, allied industry, regulatory agencies, and public health agencies. The goal of the program is to educate pork producers on the importance of using antimicrobials responsibly and to provide them with principles and guidelines for antimicrobial use that will allow them to protect public health while maximizing animal health and welfare. The basis for using antimicrobials responsibly during pork production involves evaluating their use to protect animal health, optimize effectiveness, and minimize the risk of developing antimicrobial resistance, thereby protecting public health. Swine practitioners are vital in delivery and implementation of the program on farms.

Because there are not adequate surveillance programs within the pork industry in the United States to provide data regarding the amounts of antimicrobials used it was decided that the effectiveness of the program could best be determined by attempting to measure changes in attitudes and behaviors of pork producers participating in the Take Care program. Since the education about the program is largely delivered by the veterinary practitioner a pilot project with swine veterinarians was initiated. The objectives of the Take Care swine practitioners' project were: Provide training to veterinary clinics on the Take Care program and provide support so that these clinics could help their clients implement the program, to develop a statistically valid instrument that measured attitudes and behaviors about antimicrobial use on farm, and to summarize the clinics' reports, analyze the data and make recommendations for wider implementation of the Take Care program

Materials and Methods

A team of industrial psychologists developed a survey instrument to objectively measure attitudes and behaviors regarding antimicrobial use and resistance. The survey also collected data on the job responsibilities of the production workers surveyed. Answers were ranked on a scale, rather than as yes or no, to provide more measurements. Questions included information on: Swine herd health, response to health problems, knowledge of animal health products, knowledge and beliefs concerning antimicrobial resistance, factors used to decide on antimicrobial use, feed grade antimicrobial use, water delivered antimicrobial use, injectable antimicrobial use, and antimicrobial inventory. Completed questionnaires were returned to the industrial psychology program for data input and analysis.

Ten swine practitioners in five Midwestern states were selected to participate in the program. They underwent a training session with the project managers and National Pork Board staff about the program elements. They were provided with manuals, brochures, and a PowerPoint presentation for use in their producer training sessions. Additionally, they were encouraged to develop clinic or farm specific materials if they felt that would be beneficial. Each practitioner then presented the Take Care program to three producers (treatment group). A survey was given to the treatment group producers prior to, and following their training on the program. Additionally, prior to the end of the pilot project the practitioners were encouraged to refer to the Take Care principles and guidelines during the interactions with their clients regarding antimicrobial use. Two additional producers (control group) within the practice clientele were surveyed but not provided individualized training on the program. Follow-up surveys of both treatment and control group producers were administered approximately nine months following the initial survey.

Results

Nine of the ten practitioners completed the entire project. The number of farms completing surveys is listed in Table 1, however all Time 3 surveys were not completed at the time this paper was submitted. The number of individual surveys is presented in Table 2. The reduction in numbers of farms surveyed between Time 1 and Time 2 was largely due to the withdrawal of one practitioner from the project. The number of individuals surveyed was also reduced due to the withdrawal of the one practitioner, as well as employee turnover on some of the farms. Results of the analysis of the surveys will be presented during the oral presentation at the SafePork 2007.

Table 1: Number ff participating farms responding to surveys

	Time 1	Time 2	Time 3 (Not complete at time of publication)
Control	29	25	15
Treatment	30	29	20

Table 2: Number of surveys (individuals)

	Time 1	Time 2	Time 3 (Not complete at time of publication)
Control	80	73	47
Treatment	136	125	23

A video DVD of interviews with the swine practitioners has been developed to help demonstrate to other veterinary practitioners the value of participation in the Take Care program. Resource materials that the practitioners have developed during their implementation of the program on farm will be made available to all practitioners interested in delivery of the program to their clientele. Concerns or comments expressed by the practitioners will be considered for incorporation into subsequent versions of the program.

Session 6

Discussion

With the current US regulatory structure it is difficult to accurately measure antimicrobial use on swine farms. In addition, factors other than attitude about antimicrobial use, such as changes in animal health status, impact the amounts and types of antimicrobials used by pork producers. Because of this, it was decided that program effectiveness of an education and awareness program is best measured by measuring changes in attitude and behavior. Measurements at different time intervals can help measure the permanence of any observed attitude changes. By involving the discipline of industrial psychology we were able to develop a survey instrument that will objectively measure those attitudes and behaviors. Information learned by analysis of these trends will be presented during the oral presentation.

Having veterinarians champion the program was helpful in providing credibility to the program from the producer's viewpoint, as well as providing the practitioners a platform upon which to base their recommendations. As an example, by providing an overview of the extra-label drug use regulations as part of the Take Care program the practitioners were able to demonstrate to their clients that their instructions were founded not only on science but also under regulatory oversight. Participation in the project generally helped the practitioner to better understand the program and see value to their business and to their clients from participation with the Take Care program. It is expected that they will convey that attitude and information to their peers in swine veterinary medicine.

Conclusions

The Take Care swine practitioner program provided a format to judge the effectiveness of the awareness and education provided by the Take Care – Use Antibiotics Responsibly program. It did not measure changes in antimicrobial use on farm, nor in antimicrobial sensitivity patterns of bacteria isolated from the farms. However, the project did provide an objective measurement of producer attitudes and behaviors regarding antimicrobial resistance and use. By involving influential practitioners in the project it is expected that their participation will encourage other veterinarians to become more involved in program delivery on farm.

Cryopreservation of *Salmonella enterica* in porcine fecal samples

Bahnson, P. B.,* West, S. E. H., Sekorski A. and Verstoppen, J.

School of Veterinary Medicine, University of Wisconsin-Madison, Madison, Wisconsin, U.S.A.

*corresponding author: pbbahnson@wisc.edu

Abstract

Fecal samples are normally tested for *Salmonella* soon after collection because storage at any temperature, including refrigeration or freezing, can reduce detection. To evaluate several cryopreservation techniques, autoclaved porcine feces with and without additives were inoculated with 10^3 CFU S. Derby (UW -9)/g with autoclaved feces prior to freezing. The mixtures and % of the CFU inoculum that was recovered was as follows: Feces only, 11%; 50% feces plus 50% glycerol, 45%; 25% feces, 50% glycerol, 25% tetrathionate broth, 63%; 25% feces, 50% glycerol, 25% buffered peptone water (BPW), 66%; 50% feces, 50% glycycerol/Tris buffer, 58%; 50 % feces, 50% BPW, 30%. When fresh (not autoclaved) feces were used, inoculated with a nalidixic acid resistant S. Typhimurium (WI-73), 4% of the inoculum was recovered from undiluted frozen feces while the addition of 50% BPW before freezing increased recovery to 27%.

In a 2x2x2 fully randomized block factorial study, fresh fecal samples were inoculated with 10^3 CFU UW-73 /g feces. These samples were processed undiluted or with the addition of glycerol and/or BPW before freezing. The addition of 20%-40% of each compound simultaneously resulted in increased recovery of UW-73 when compared with undiluted fecal samples (p<0.05). The addition of 40% BPW and 20% glycerol in combination resulted in the highest recovery (83%). It is concluded that the addition of 20-40% glycerol and 20-40% BPW before freezing may be effective cryopreservatives for *Salmonella* in porcine fecal samples, allowing for simplified and more economical laboratory enumeration.

Introduction

Freezing of bacteria can result in cell death due to increased osmotic pressure and the formation of ice crystals. A cryoprotective agent (e.g. glycerol or dimethyl sulfoxide) can depress the temperature at which this occurs (Gherna, R., 1994). Effective and economical cryopreservation of fecal samples would simplify application of conventional culture techniques, permitting sampling and laboratory work to be conducted on asynchronous schedules. Further, costs of large scale quality assurance evaluations may be reduced due to lower transportation costs for overnight delivery.

While freezing of ileocolic lymph nodes resulted in no detected change in sensitivity of qualitative microbial culture of *Salmonella* in a study using a double enrichment system (Bahnson et al., 2006), no effective systems for cryopreservation of fecal samples have been reported. Anecdotal evidence suggests that freezing reduces survival. For example, from pigs with known exposure to Salmonella, the organism was detected in 19 of 20 non-frozen samples, but in only 5 of 20 paired frozen fecal samples. The mean log CFU/g was 2.0 in non-frozen and 0.5 in frozen feces (unpublished observations).

Our objective was to test whether the addition of cryopreservatives protected salmonellae in frozen (-70°C) fecal samples. Initial trials indicated that the addition of 20% volume / weight glycerol improved survival. When autoclaved porcine fecal samples diluted with 50% glycerol were inoculated with approximately 10^3 CFU S. Derby / g fecal weight before freezing, the Log CFU / g was 4.49 and 3.87 in the unfrozen and frozen samples, respectively (unpublished observations).

Following up on these preliminary observations, we designed two studies to identify possible cryoprotective storage protocols. In study I, we evaluated combinations of glycerol, buffered

Session 6

peptone water (BPW), tetrathionate broth, and TRIS-HCI (MgSO4 buffer ("TRIS buffer"). In study II, we determined which concentrations of the two most effective cryoprotective agents from Study I would result in a higher % recovery in frozen samples.

Material and Methods

Study 1. Differing combinations of glycerol, buffered peptone water (BPW), tetrathionate broth (TT), and Tris buffer (ACTUAL CONCENTRATION INGREDIENTS) were added to either autoclaved or fresh porcine feces as follows: A, 10 g feces only; B, 5 g feces plus 5 ml glycerol; C, 2.5 g feces plus 2.5 ml TT and 5 ml glycerol; D, 5 g feces plus 2.5 ml BPW and 5 ml glycerol; E, 5 g feces plus 5 ml TRIS buffer; and F, 2.5 g feces plus 7.5 ml BPW. S. Derby WI-9 was mixed with autoclaved feces from growing pigs while S. Typhimurium WI-73, a naladixic acid resistant strain that was isolated from ileocolic lymph node tissue from a normal slaughtered pig, was added to fresh feces (Table 1). The inoculum for each sample was adjusted in BPW prior to addition to the feces so that each sample would contain approximately 10^3 CFU/g of the final fecal/cryopreservative mixture. The size of the inoculum was determined by triplicate plate counts on blood agar for autoclaved feces and on XLT-4 w/ 25 µg/mL naladixic acid. For mixing the feces with the various additions and the inoculum, the samples were placed in a paddle blender (Stomacher 80, Seward), for 2 minutes on the high setting. Immediately after mixing, 100 µL of each sample was plated in triplicate to determine the number of organisms present. The remainder of the sample was immediately frozen at -70C for at least 24 hours. The frozen samples were thawed at 37C in a water bath and then plated as for the unfrozen samples. The autoclaved feces samples were plated on Blood Agar, while the fresh feces samples were plated on XLT-4 agar with 25 µg naladixic acid/ml to select for S. Typhimurium WI-73. Results are reported as CFU observed / CFU expected.

Study II. Since in Study I the two additives with highest % recovery following freezing were glycerol and BPW (see below), we designed a randomized incomplete block study to test the hypothesis that certain combinations of these two compounds would result in higher % CFU recovery after freezing than others. Fresh feces from ~50 kg growing pigs were collected <6 h before inoculation. Four final concentrations (0%, 20%, 40%, and 60%) of each additive were evaluated.

The inoculum was prepared and enumerated for each test condition as described for Study I and was kept on ice or in a cold room at all times during before mixing with the feces and cryopreservative agents. The final concentration of organisms in each fecal mixture contained ~10^3 CFU / g feces, to approximate what might occur in fresh animal feces from *Salmonella* shedding commercial swine. The fecal mixtures were immediately frozen after 100 µL of the fecal mixture was plated on XLT-4 agar containing 25 µg/ml naladixic acid. Results are reported as the % of expected *Salmonella* CFU per g fecal sample. Statistical analysis was by SAS PROC MIXED, with levels of treatments treated as nominal variables. Pairwise comparisons used the Tukey-Kramer adjustment to guard against inflated experiment-wise error rate.

Results

Study I. For autoclaved feces, the highest number of CFU / mL mixed solution were detected before freezing in samples comprised of 2.5 g feces and 7.5 g BPW. After freezing the highest CFU / g was detected in samples comprised of 5 g feces, 2.5 mL glycerol and 2.5 mL BPW (Table 1).

Table 1. The % recovery of *Salmonella* Typhimurium from porcine feces (autoclaved or fresh) with, or without the addition of glycerol, tetrathionate broth (TTB) or buffered peptone water (BPW) after freezing. Treatment groups A-F were plated on blood agar and treatment groups (G-H) were plated on XLT-4 agar containing 25 µg naladixic acid / mL. Results are reported as the % of expected *Salmonella* CFU per g fecal sample.

Treatment Group	Cryopreservative Agent	Autoclaved Feces	Fresh Feces	Salmonella strain	% of expected CFU recovered
A	-	+	-	Derby WI-9	11%
B	Glycerol	+	-	Derby WI-9	45%
C	Glycerol, TTB	+	-	Derby WI-9	63%
D	Glycerol, BPW	+	-	Derby WI-9	66%
E	Glycerol, Tris buffer	+	-	Derby WI-9	58%
F	BPW	+	-	Derby WI-9	30%
G	-	-	+	Typhimurium WI-73	4%
H	BPW	-	+	Typhimurium WI-73	27%

Study II.

The average percentage recovery varied from 11% for samples frozen without BPW or glycerol to 83% for samples frozen with BPW (40% final concentration) and glycerol (20% final concentration. The addition of any of tested glycerol (p = 0.01) or BPW concentrations (p < 0.01) to the fecal mixture before freezing resulted in a higher recovery of Salmonella after freezing. When compared to other combinations of glycerol and BPW, 40% BPW plus 20% glycerol resulted in the highest recovery of Salmonella from frozen feces. This combination, when compared with all specific treatment combinations higher recover than samples frozen with feces only (p < 0.01), 20% BPW and 20% glycerol (p = 0.02), 40% BPW and 0% glycerol (p = 0.01), and 0% BPW and 20% glycerol (p = 0.07).

Discussion

Freezing of fresh or autoclaved feces spiked with Salmonella without the addition of a cryopreservative agent resulted in poor recovery of Salmonella. We failed to recover 89% of the inoculum in autoclaved feces and 96% of the inoculum in fresh feces (Table 1). These results are in agreement with a prior report in which approximately 85% of Salmonella were non-culturable from fresh bovine feces inoculated with S. Typhimurium after freezing at -70 or -20C (Daniels).

Study I results suggest that the addition of glycerol immediately prior to freezing may protect Salmonella from the deleterious effects of freezing and that this protection is greatest when TTB or BPW, both of which contain peptones, are also added. BPW has been commonly used to increase sensitivity of conventional culture for Salmonella after freezing. TTB is commonly used as a first step in Salmonella enrichment bacterial culture.

Study II confirmed that glycerol and BPW are both protective during freezing, used either alone or in combination. 20-40% final concentration of each compound added in combination resulted in the highest recovery. This observation suggests that the protective effects of glycerol and BPW are additive.

Conclusions

The addition of glycerol and BPW may result in an increased rate of recovery of Salmonella from frozen fecal samples. Thus, these or other cryopreservatives may be useful to improve the logistics and to reduce the costs of epidemiologic studies. Since porcine fecal samples are expected to contain low numbers of Salmonella and because available quantitative techniques are cumbersome and/or costly, it may be advantageous to screen fecal samples qualitatively first, freeze paired samples, then thaw and enumerate only those which test positive. This may reduce

Session 6

the cost of epidemiologic studies and enable *Salmonella* quantification as a practical outcome for quality assurance or food safety programs.

References

Bahnson P.B., Damman D.J., Isaacson R.E., Miller G.Y, Weigel, R.M., Troutt H.F. 2006. Prevalence and serovars of *Salmonella enterica* isolated from ileocecal lymph nodes of market pigs reared in selected Midwest US swine herds. J. Swine Health and Production, 14:182-188.

Daniels EK, Woollen NE, Fryda-Bradley SJ. 1994. *Salmonella* viability in frozen bovine feces. Bovine Practitioner, 27:166-167.

Gherna, R., 1994. Culture preservation. In: Gerhardt, P., Murray, R.G.E., Wood, Willis A., Krieg, N.R., eds. Methods for general and molecular bacteriology. Washington, D.C.: American Society for Microbiology.

The QseBC Quorum Sensing System is Involved in *Salmonella enterica* serovar Typhimurium Colonization of the Swine Gastrointestinal Tract

Bearson, B.L.*[1], Bearson, S.M.D.[2],

[1]National Soil Tilth Lab, ARS, USDA, NSRIC-2103, 2150 Pammel Drive, 50011, Ames, IA, USA
[2]National Animal Disease Center, ARS, USDA, 2300 Dayton Avenue, 50010, Ames, IA, USA
*corresponding author:bearson@nsric.ars.usda.gov

Abstract

The response of bacteria to hormone-like, chemical molecules is termed quorum sensing, a mechanism for cell-to-cell communication that includes sensing the host environment. In the gastrointestinal tract, at least two quorum sensing molecules are present that activate the bacterial QseBC quorum sensing system, autoinducer-3 (AI-3) and norepinephrine (NE). AI-3 is produced by bacteria, whereas NE is produced by the host, often during stress. We have demonstrated that the motility of *Salmonella enterica* serovar Typhimurium is enhanced in the presence of NE and 10% pre-conditioned medium (AI-3) from the wild-type strain. Additionally, DNA microarray and qRT-PCR analyses revealed transcriptional induction of motility genes in the presence of NE. The enhanced motility of *S.* Typhimurium to both NE and AI-3 requires the *qseC* gene, encoding the QseC sensor kinase. To determine whether the QseBC quorum sensing system is involved in colonization of the swine gastrointestinal tract, a competitive index (CI) experiment was performed. Swine were intranasally inoculated with a 1:1 ratio of a *qseC* mutant and the wild-type strain. Fecal samples were obtained for quantitative bacterial culturing on 1 through 7 days post-inoculation (d.p.i.). The mean CI (*qseC* mutant/wild-type ratio) for fecal samples (n=6) was 0.13, 0.09, 0.03, 0.11, 0.11, 0.06, and 0.22 at 1, 2, 3, 4, 5, 6, and 7 d.p.i., respectively (p≤0.01). At 7 d.p.i., necropsies (n=3) were performed and tissue samples obtained for quantitative bacterial cultures. The mean CI of the *qseC* mutant/wild-type strain for cecum, tonsil, ileal Peyer's Patches, and ileocecal lymph nodes at day 7 were 0.02, 0.4, 0.04, and 0.07, respectively (p≤0.05). This research demonstrates that the QseBC system of *S.* Typhimurium is important for colonization of the swine gastrointestinal tract and porcine tissues.

Introduction

The endocrine system in higher eukaryotes uses hormones as messengers for cellular communication within the body. Thus, distant cells can work in concert to respond to chemical signals and alter physiology. In an analogous manner, bacteria are able to communicate via cell-to-cell communication systems termed quorum sensing (QS) (Waters and Bassler, 2005). Quorum sensing utilizes small hormone-like molecules called autoinducers (AIs) to monitor the environment. As bacteria produce and release AIs, the signal molecules accumulate in the environment. Accumulation of the quorum sensing signal permits the bacterial cells to respond to the AI as a population instead of as individual cells. Typically, the response to an AI involves the modulation of gene expression.

Multiple quorum sensing systems have been demonstrated, with AIs produced by *E. coli* (both commensal and pathogenic), *Shigella* sp, *Salmonella* sp, *Klebsiella pneumoniae* and *Enterobacter cloacae*, as well as the microbial intestinal flora cultured from stools of healthy human volunteers (Walters and Sperandio, 2006). It has been proposed that intestinal bacteria may utilize AIs for interspecies communication and may aid pathogenic bacteria by signaling the appropriate time for expression of virulence determinants within the gastrointestinal tract (Clarke and Sperandio, 2005).

Similar to AIs being produced by the bacterial cell, neurotransmitters are produced by the mammalian host. Several neurotransmitters are released by the sympathetic nervous system including norepinephrine. The gastrointestinal tract is highly innervated, with the sympathetic nervous system controlling motility, secretion and vasoregulation (Furness, 2000). Therefore, the presence of norepinephrine in the gastrointestinal tract, in addition to AIs (produced by the microbial flora), may serve as quorum sensing signals to *E. coli* and *Salmonella*.

Session 6

In *E. coli*, the *qseBC* two-component system modulates the quorum sensing response to AI-3, epinephrine and norepinephrine (Sperandio et al, 2002). QseC is a histidine sensor kinase and QseB is a response regulator that increases motility in the presence of these QS signals. In this study, we investigated the role of the *qseBC* two-component system in *Salmonella enterica* serovar Typhimurium swine colonization using an in vivo competitive assay comparing a *qseC* mutant to the wild-type strain.

Material and methods

Bacterial strains and media. The *Salmonella enterica* serovar Typhimurium strain χ4232 and its *qseC::cat* (BBS10) derivative were used in this study. Strains were grown in Luria-Bertani (LB) broth or 1.5% agar medium. Where indicated, chloramphenicol was used at a concentration of 30 µg/ml. Cultures were grown and assays performed at 37°C.

Competitive index animal experiment. Six piglets from *Salmonella* spp.-free sows were weaned at 12 days of age, shipped to the National Animal Disease Center, Ames, IA and raised in an isolation facility. Pigs were confirmed to be negative for *Salmonella* spp by bacteriological culture. At 13 weeks of age (day zero), all pigs received an intranasal inoculation of 1 ml PBS containing two S. Typhimurium strains, χ4232 (1.2 X 10^9 CFU) and BBS10 (1.3 X 10^9 CFU). Pig fecal samples were obtained on days 1-7 for quantitative and qualitative *Salmonella* culture analysis. The *qseC* mutant strain was differentiated from the wild-type (WT) strain based upon chloramphenicol resistance. On days 7 and 14, pigs (n=3) were necropsied and tissue samples (cecum, ileal Peyer's Patch, ileocecal lymph nodes, tonsil) were placed on ice for quantitative and qualitative *Salmonella* culture. All procedures involving animals were lawful and approved by the USDA, ARS, NADC Animal Care and Use Committee.

Quantitative and qualitative *Salmonella* culture analysis. For quantitative bacteriology, one gram of pig feces was combined with 5 ml PBS, vortexed and 100 µl directly plated to brilliant green agar with sulfadiazine (BGS, Difco, Detroit, MI) containing nalidixic acid, ferric ammonium citrate (0.8 g/L) and sodium thiosulfate (6.8 g/L) with and without chloramphenicol. For tissue samples, one gram of each tissue was combined with 2 ml of PBS in a whirlpak bag, pounded with a mallet and homogenized in a Stomacher (Seward, Westbury, NY) for 1 minute. One hundred microliters of the resulting solution was aliquoted onto BGS with and without chloramphenicol. One hundred microliters of a ten-fold dilution of each fecal and tissue sample were also plated, and additional dilutions were performed when necessary. Following 24 hours of incubation at 37° C, black colonies were enumerated and a single colony from each plate was confirmed to be *Salmonella* by serogroup antiserum agglutination (Beckton, Dickinson and Co., Sparks, MD).

Qualitative bacteriology of *Salmonella* was performed as follows: 1 gram (fecal) or 100 µl (homogenized tissue) samples were inoculated in 10 ml of GN-Hajna (GN, Difco, Detroit, MI) broth and tetrathionate (TET, VWR, Rutherford, NJ) broth for 24 and 48 hours of growth at 37°C, respectively. Following incubation, 100 µl of each culture was transferred to 10 ml Rappaport-Vassiliadis medium (RV, Difco, Detroit, MI) and incubated at 37°C for 18 h. The cultures were streaked on BGS with and without chloramphenicol. Colonies suspicious for *Salmonella* were confirmed by serogroup antiserum agglutination.

Statistical Analysis. For calculation of the competitive index (CI), the output ratio (*qseC* CFU/WT CFU) was divided by the input ratio (1.0833) of the mutant to the wild-type strain. To incorporate samples that only had qualitative data (too few *Salmonella* for quantitative detection) into the calculations for competitive index and *p* value, the highest possible value was given for the level of detection. For example, the lowest possible value for quantitative detection was 50 colony forming units (CFU) per gram of feces and 20 CFU per gram of tissue. Therefore, samples negative in the quantitative analysis but positive in the qualitative testing were given the highest possible value for a quantitative negative/qualitative positive sample (50 CFU for fecal or 20 CFU for tissues) to determine CI and *p* values. The level of detection for the qualitative assay was 1 CFU/g; therefore, quantitative negative/qualitative negative samples were given the highest possible value of 1

CFU/g to determine CI and *p* values. For statistical analysis, the CI data (output/input ratio) for each pig sample was log normal transformed and the data analyzed by SAS Analyst (Cary, NC) using the One Sample t-test for a Mean.

Results

QseC is involved in *S*. Typhimurium colonization of swine. In *E. coli*, the QseBC quorum sensing system regulates motility and the expression of virulence genes. Additionally, QseBC is important for *E. coli* pathogenicity in a rabbit model (Clark et al, 2006). Our research has shown an up-regulation of motility gene expression in *Salmonella enterica* serovar Typhimurium in response to norepinephrine exposure and the *qseBC* genes are required for norepinephrine-enhanced motility in *S*. Typhimurium (data not shown). To determine if the *S*. Typhimurium *qseC* gene is important for swine colonization, an in vivo competition assay was performed. Fecal samples on days 1-7 post-inoculation revealed a decrease in shedding of the *qseC* mutant compared to the wild-type strain (**Table 1**). Furthermore, fewer colony forming untis of the *qseC* mutant than the wild-type strain were recovered from the tonsils, ileal Peyer's Patches, ileocecal lymph nodes and cecum at 7 days post-inoculation (**Table 2**); thus, a competitive disadvantage of the *qseC* mutant in vivo indicates an important role for the quorum sensing sensor kinase, QseC in swine colonization. Most of the samples at 14 days post-inoculation were only qualitatively positive. Since competitive index and *p* values could not be calculated for day 14, the data is not presented.

Table 1. Competetive Index of Fecal Shedding

	Day1	Day2	Day3	Day4*	Day5*	Day6*	Day7*
Mean CI	0.13	0.09	0.03	0.11	0.11	0.06	0.22
P value	0.0019	0.0017	0.0002	0.0051	0.0115	0.0015	0.0128

*qualitative data was used to estimate CFU/gram of feces for some samples
n=6

Table 2. Competetive Index at Day 7 in Tissues

	Cecum	ICLN*	PP*	Tonsil
Mean CI	0.02	0.07	0.04	0.40
P value	0.046	0.056	0.015	0.009

*qualitative data was used to estimate CFU/gram of tissue for some samples
n=3

Discussion

Mammalian cells communicate through hormones, and in a similar manner, bacteria produce hormone-like molecules for cell-to-cell communication, termed quorum sensing. Cross-talk between these cell communication molecules may occur when bacteria reside in a mammalian host (Sperandio et al, 2003), suggesting that host hormones such as norepinephrine may signal to the microorganism of their in vivo environment. Our competition experiment comparing the colonization potential of the *qseC* mutant to the wild-type strain in swine indicated that the competitive fitness of the *qseC* mutant was not as robust as the wild-type strain. Additional animal experiments need to be performed to determine whether a *qseC* mutant is attenuated for virulence in the swine model of infection. Our in vivo competition experiment suggests that sensing AI-3/epinephrine/norepinephrine in the swine gastrointestinal tract environment is important for optimal colonization by *Salmonella*.

Conclusions

Salmonella has a ubiquitous distribution in animals, including pigs. Although pigs colonized with *Salmonella* can exhibit clinical symptoms, they are usually asymptomatic carriers of the pathogen. *Salmonella*-carrier pigs are a serious food safety concern because they have the potential to shed the pathogen in their feces, contaminating penmates and the environment. Furthermore, during times of stress, pigs produce hormones such as norepinephrine, that

Session 6

Salmonella may sense and respond to, such as activating virulence mechanisms. A possible result of in vivo exposure of *Salmonella* to the stress hormone, norepinephrine (produced by the pig during transportation and marketing) is recrudescence from carrier pigs and shedding during lairage, resulting in pen contamination and exposing concurrent and subsequent pigs to the pathogen immediately prior to entering the processing plant. Thus, a scenario could be envisioned whereby *Salmonella* shed in the environment (expressing virulence genes due to norepinephrine exposure) are ingested by stressed pigs with decreased peristaltic activity of the gastrointestinal tract (due to stress-induced norepinephrine release), thereby retaining the "primed" pathogen in its preferred site of invasion. Identifying genes that play a role in this response will enhance our understanding of *Salmonella* colonization of the gastrointestinal tract and elucidate potential targets for development of intervention strategies.

References

CLARKE, M. B., SPERANDIO, V., 2005. Events at the host-microbial interface of the gastrointestinal tract III. Cell-to-cell signaling among microbial flora, host, and pathogens: there is a whole lot of talking going on. *American Journal of Physiology. Gastrointestinal and Liver Physiology*, 288, G1105- G1109.

CLARKE, M. B., et al., 2006. The QseC sensor kinase: a bacterial adrenergic receptor. *Proceedings of the National Academy of Sciences of the United States of America*, 103 (27), 10420-10425.

FURNESS, J.B., 2000. Types of neurons in the enteric nervous system. *Journal of the Autonomic Nervous System*, 81, 87-96.

SPERANDIO, V., et al.. 2003. Bacteria-host communication: the language of hormones. *Proceedings of the National Academy of Sciences of the United States of America*, 100 (15), 8951-8956.

SPERANDIO, V., TORRES, A.G., KAPER, J. B., 2002. Quorum sensing *Escherichia coli* regulators B and C (QseBC): a novel two-component regulatory system involved in the regulation of flagella and motility by quorum sensing in *E. coli. Molecular Microbiology*, 43 (3), 809-821.

WALTERS, M., SPERANDIO, V., 2006. Quorum sensing in *Escherichia coli* and *Salmonella*. *International Journal of Medical Microbiology*, 296, 125-131.

WATERS, C. M., BASSLER, B. L., 2005. Quorum sensing: cell-to-cell communication in bacteria. *Annual Reviews of Cell and Developmental Biology*, 21, 319-346.

Associations of the porcine immune response and genetic polymorphisms with the shedding of *Salmonella enterica* serovar Typhimurium

Bearson, S.[*][(1)], Uthe, J.[(1,2)], Wang, Y.[(2)], Qu, L.[(2)], Dekkers, J.[(2,3)], Nettleton, D.[(3,4)], Bearson, B.[(5)], Tuggle, C.[(2,3)]

[(1)]USDA, ARS, National Animal Disease Center, Ames, IA, 50010, USA
[(2)]Department of Animal Science, Iowa State University, Ames, IA, 50011, USA
[(3)]Center for Integrated Animal Genomics, Iowa State University, Ames, IA, 50011, USA
[(4)]Department of Statistics, Iowa State University, Ames, IA, 50011, USA
[(5)]USDA, ARS, National Soil Tilth Lab, Ames, IA 50011 USA

Shawn M.D. Bearson: sbearson@nadc.ars.usda.gov

Abstract

A major focus of our collaborative research is to investigate the porcine response to infection with *Salmonella* to 1) identify porcine genes differentially regulated during infection and 2) identify and associate genetic polymorphisms within these genes with infection status across swine populations. In the current study, 40 crossbred pigs were intranasally inoculated with *Salmonella enterica* serovar Typhimurium and monitored for *Salmonella* fecal shedding and blood immune parameters at 2, 7, 14 and 20 days post-inoculation (dpi). Using a multivariate permutation test, a positive correlation was observed between *Salmonella* shedding and interferon-gamma (IFNG) levels at 2 and 7 dpi ($p<0.05$), with a greater number of *Salmonella* shedding in the animals with higher IFNG levels. In addition, a positive correlation was observed between IFNG levels and the number of circulating neutrophils at 7 and 14 dpi, mature banded neutrophils at 2 dpi, monocytes at 7 dpi and white blood cells (WBCs) at 7, 14 and 20 dpi. We have further performed association studies of immune response parameters or shedding status of the *Salmonella*-infected pigs with single nucleotide polymorphisms (SNPs) in 9 genes: VCP, CCT7, LCP1, CD47, SCARB2, CD163, CCR1, TLR4 and TYROBP. Expression of these genes was identified by our group as differentially-regulated during *Salmonella* infection, and assays for these SNPs have been developed in our laboratories. Specifically, preliminary analysis suggests a positive association ($p<0.05$) of SNP genotype A/G at nucleotide 1026 (relative to start codon) of the CCT7 gene with circulating neutrophils and WBCs and with *Salmonella* shedding at 7 dpi compared to the G/G heterozygote genotype. CCT7 encodes a molecular chaperone involved in tubulin folding and protection. Thus, our analyses are linking the porcine immune response to *Salmonella* infection with specific genes and genetic polymorphisms, thereby providing potential markers for carrier pigs as well as targets for disease diagnosis, intervention and prevention.

Introduction

Currently, the most frequently applied methods for disease control in livestock involve the use of antibiotic drugs and/or vaccines. However, these approaches are not always effective (1); furthermore, antibiotic use is being regulated more strictly and may be banned from food products in the future. This creates a real need for alternative approaches to disease control to protect the food supply. One such approach is the identification and use of animals with enhanced disease resistance. If genes can be identified from animals which are naturally more resistant to microorganisms (such as *Salmonella),* direct improvement in food safety as well as animal disease can be achieved by selecting favorable animals to breed disease-resistant offspring.

A major problem in pre-harvest food safety is contamination on the farm or slaughter plant environment by animals shedding pathogenic bacteria such as *Salmonella enterica* (2,3). An additional challenge is the difficulty in identifying which animals are carriers and, therefore, will in turn be shedders. Since the current technology is not entirely efficient in detecting *Salmonella*-infected pigs, the goal of this study was to investigate specific molecular parameters for their contribution to *Salmonella* shedding. The transfer of this information may assist in developing diagnostic assays for carrier animals, as well as help develop *Salmonella*-resistant lines of pigs.

Materials and methods

Animal study. Forty conventionally raised, mixed sex piglets from sows identified as fecal-negative for *Salmonella* spp. were weaned at 10 days of age, shipped to the NADC, Ames, IA and raised in climate-controlled, fully enclosed isolation facilities. At seven weeks of age, the *Salmonella*-free pigs were intranasally challenged with 1×10^9 cfu of serovar Typhimurium χ4232 grown in Luria Bertani (LB) broth at 37°C. At 2, 7, 14, and 20 days post-inoculation (dpi), rectal temperatures and clinical signs of infection (lethargy, loss of appetite and diarrhea) were recorded and fecal and blood samples were taken for each animal. At 21 dpi, tissue samples from the ileocecal lymph nodes (ICLN) were aseptically collected for quantitative bacteriology. Blood samples were collected for the following procedures: DNA extraction, CBC analysis (ISU Veterinary Diagnostic Laboratory), and serum preparation for cytokine assays.

Bacteriology. For quantitative bacteriology, one gram of pig feces was combined with 5 ml PBS, vortexed and 100 µl directly plated to brilliant green agar with sulfadiazine (BGS, Difco, Detroit, MI) containing nalidixic acid. For tissue samples, one gram of ICLN was combined with 2 ml of PBS in a whirlpak bag, pounded with a mallet and homogenized in a Stomacher (Seward, Westbury, NY) for 1 minute. One hundred microliters of the resulting solution was aliquoted onto brilliant green agar plates with sulfadiazine (BGS) containing nalidixic acid. Following 24 hours of incubation at 37°C, colonies indicative of *Salmonella* were enumerated and a single colony from each plate was confirmed to be *Salmonella* by serogroup antiserum agglutination (Beckton, Dickinson and Co., Sparks, MD). The total number of cfu for each quantitative tissue or fecal sample was calculated per gram of sample by obtaining the number of *Salmonella* per plate and multiplying by the dilution factor. For qualitative bacteriology of *Salmonella*, the following was performed: 1 gram (fecal) or 100 µl (homogenized tissue) samples were inoculated in 10 ml of GN-Hajna (GN, Difco, Detroit, MI) broth and tetrathionate (TET, VWR, Rutherford, NJ) broth for 24 and 48 hours of growth at 37°C, respectively. Following incubation, 100 µl of each culture was transferred to 10 ml Rappaport-Vassiliadis medium (RV, Difco, Detroit, MI) and incubated at 37°C for 18 h. The cultures were streaked on brilliant green agar plates with sulfadiazine (BGS) containing nalidixic acid. Colonies suspicious for *Salmonella* were stabbed/streaked to triple sugar iron agar and lysine iron agar and further confirmed by serogroup antiserum agglutination.

ELISA assay for interferon-γ (IFNG). To determine concentration of circulating IFNG, serum of 40 experimental pigs at day 2 p.i. was analyzed by ELISA using the porcine IFNG (Pierce, Rockford, IL) ELISA kit according to the manufacturer's instructions.

SNP identification. Several sequence analysis tools were employed to investigate potential SNPs in selected genes, including analysis of available bioinformatics data in web databases such as TIGR pig gene index search tool (http://compbio.dfci.harvard.edu/tgi/cgi-bin/tgi/gimain.pl?gudb=pig) and NCBI SNP database (http://www.ncbi.nlm.nih.gov/projects/SNP/) as well as the software program Sequencher (Genecodes, Ann Arbor, MI), to compare published sequence data of the selected genes (gene sequences available at http://www.ncbi.nlm.nih.gov/entrez/query.fcgi?db=unigene). SNPs identified by computational means were further verified using our experimentally *Salmonella*-infected pig population. To confirm potential SNPs and to reveal polymorphic allele frequencies in the population, target sequence regions were amplified by PCR followed by sequencing of 4 DNA pools, created by sampling litters from sows with similar breed backgrounds. After the target SNP was confirmed by DNA sequencing, the entire experimental population was genotyped using restriction fragment length polymorphism (RFLP).

Correlation and association analyses. The correlation of serum levels of IFNG with *Salmonella* shedding as well as different blood cell counts was statistically analyzed using the multivariate permutation test for Goodman and Kruskal's Gamma correlation, with family-wise error rate (FWER) controlled at 0.05. Association analysis of each SNP to *Salmonella* shedding and blood cell counts was performed by one-way ANOVA (model: $y = \mu + genotype + \varepsilon$) followed by Student t tests, with FWER controlled at 0.05 by multivariate permutation tests

Results

Identifying non-shedder and persistent shedder pigs. Forty 7 week old pigs were intranasally inoculated with *Salmonella enterica* serovar Typhimurium and monitored for fecal shedding over a 3 week period. Four pigs were identified as non-shedders based on their initial *Salmonella* fecal positive status at 2 days post-inoculation (dpi) and lack of *Salmonella* shedding at 2 out of the 3 samplings at 7, 14, and 20 dpi, including 20 dpi. Six pigs were classified as persistent shedders based on their high numbers of cfu of *Salmonella* per gram of feces at all four sample time points.

Pig #	Classification	2 dpi (cfu/g feces)	7 dpi (cfu/g feces)	14 dpi (cfu/g feces)	20 dpi (cfu/g feces)	21 dpi (+ or -)
101	Non-shedder	100	112	-	-	-
105	Persistent shedder	120000	2526	373	194	+
106	Non-shedder	+	76	-	-	-
108	Persistent shedder	13800	3077	94	313	-
115	Persistent shedder	3500	11782	4330	413	+
118	Persistent shedder	13000	421	1778	175	+
134	Persistent shedder	30000	4928	21667	54054	+
140	Non-shedder	+	-	-	-	-
142	Persistent shedder	320000	151515	1393	238	+
143	Non-shedder	+	-	+	-	-

Blood analyses of *Salmonella* infected pigs. As shown by our research group and others (5), the level of interferon-γ (IFNG), a potent T helper 1 cytokine important in the host's immune response to infection, is elevated during infection with *Salmonella*. We have recently shown that the level of IFNG during serovar Typhimurium infections increases during the first 48 hours post-inoculation, then drops to the level of non-infected pigs by 7 dpi. Using an ELISA assay, the levels of IFNG in blood were determined for the 40 pigs at 2 dpi. To determine if a connection exists between the levels of IFNG at 2 dpi and shedding of *Salmonella* from the infected pigs, correlation analysis was performed. A significant positive correlation (FWER<0.05) was found for IFNG levels at 2 dpi with bacterial shedding at 2 and 7 dpi ($p<0.05$). In other words, the higher

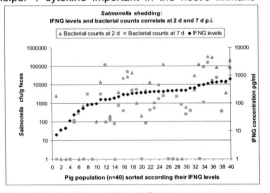

the IFNG level in pigs at 2 dpi, the greater the *Salmonella* shedding at 2 and 7 dpi.

Blood was also quantitatively analyzed for cells involved in immune response to infection. Correlation analyses identified positive correlations between IFNG levels at 2 dpi with: white blood cell counts at 7, 14 and 21 dpi ($p<0.05$); circulating neutrophils at 7 dpi and mature banded neutrophils at 2 dpi ($p<0.01$); monocytes at 7 dpi ($p<0.01$).

Identifying Single Nucleotide Polymorphisms in porcine genes differentially expressed during *Salmonella* infection. Over the last few years, our research group has employed various molecular techniques to identify many genes that are differentially regulated in the pig during infection with *Salmonella*. As potential candidates for affecting the porcine response to *Salmonella* (and, thus, the outcome of

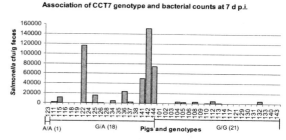

Association of CCT7 genotype and bacterial counts at 7 d p.i.

disease), several of these genes were chosen for sequence analysis to search for sequence variants. SNPs were identified in the following genes: CXCL10, SDCBP, ARPC2, HSPH1, CXCL2, CCT7, LCP1, VCP, CD47/IAP, SCARB2, CD163, MARCO, CCR1, IL8, TYROBP and NCF2. The identified SNPs were tested for their association to *Salmonella*-shedding levels, serum levels of IFNG and the various blood cell counts. Statistical analysis indicated a positive association of SNP genotype G/A of the CCT7 gene with *Salmonella* shedding ($p=0.0012$) as well as circulating neutrophils ($p=0.0102$) and WBCs ($p=0.0152$) at 7 dpi compared to the G/G genotype in our 40 pig experiment. As shown in the graph, pigs shedding *Salmonella* at higher levels were more likely to have genotype G/A than genotype G/G.

Discussion

Salmonella can establish a carrier state in pigs, thereby providing a reservoir for the pathogen. Once the *Salmonella*-carrier pig is placed under stressful conditions (i.e. transportation, mixing, etc.), the pathogen can re-emerge from the animal and be shed in the feces to contaminate/infect pen mates as well as the environment. Therefore, it is not only important to identify pigs that are carriers and may become shedders, but it is also important to prevent carrier status and eliminate *Salmonella* shedding. The goals of this research project were to address these issues by 1) investigating porcine genes that may play a role in *Salmonella* shedding and 2) characterizing genetic variations in porcine response genes that may associate with *Salmonella* shedding in swine. Our data suggests an important role for IFNG, a cytokine involved in stimulating Th1 immunity, during *Salmonella* infections, since higher levels of IFNG correlated with greater numbers of circulating immune cells and with *Salmonella* shedding. Furthermore, genetic variation in the gene encoding CCT7, a molecular chaperone involved in protein folding (4) and identified by our group as up-regulated in *Salmonella*-infected pigs (5), was associated with *Salmonella* shedding. Since the pigs used in this study were of mixed breed composition, this association could represent breed differences and must be validated in other populations. Investigating factors in the pig that control the ability of the animal to combat disease will assist in developing diagnostic tools for classifying potential carrier pigs as well as identify genetic markers to select for *Salmonella* resistant pigs.

Conclusions

From this study, our preliminary conclusions are as follows:
1. During acute infection with *Salmonella*, pigs with higher IFNG levels are more likely to shed greater numbers of *Salmonella*.
2. During an acute *Salmonella* infection, pigs with higher IFNG levels have greater circulating white blood cells, neutrophils and monocytes.
3. Within the studied mixed breed population, pigs with the SNP genotype G/A in the CCT7 gene are more likely to shed *Salmonella* than pigs with the G/G genotype.

Our current research goal is to test these associations in a larger pig population.

References

1. Beloeil P., et al., 2004. Risk factors for *Salmonella enterica* subsp. *enterica* shedding by market-age pigs in French farrow-to-finish herds. *Preventive Veterinary Medicine*, 63,103-20.

2. Ebner, P., et al., 2000. Effects of antibiotic regimens on the fecal shedding patterns of pigs infected with *Salmonella typhimurium*. *Journal of Food Protection*, 63,709-14.

3. Hurd, H., et al., 2001. The effect of lairage on *Salmonella* isolation from market swine. *Journal of Food Protection*, 64, 939-944.

4. Lopez-Fanarraga, M., et al., 2001. Review: postchaperonin tubulin folding cofactors and their role in microtubule dynamics. *Journal of Structural Biology*, 135, 219-229.

5. Uthe, J., et al., 2007. Porcine differential gene expression in response to *Salmonella enterica* serovars Choleraesuis and Typhimurium. *Molecular Immunology*, in press.

Effect of antimicrobial use on the resistance of *Escherichia coli* in faecal flora of pigs

Belloc, C.*, Dinh, N.L., Lezé, V., Beaudeau, F., Creignou-Péron, V. and Laval, A.

Veterinary School, F-44000, Nantes, France

*corresponding author: belloc@vet-nantes.fr

Abstract

The antimicrobial use in veterinary medicine is of concern because of possible transmission of resistant bacteria to humans. However the relation between use and occurrence of resistance is poorly documented in the field. Sixteen farrow-to-finish herds were selected and classified on the frequency of antimicrobial administrations (low (LU), medium (MU) and high (HU) users). Indicative *Escherichia coli* strains were isolated from faeces of sows (5 per herd) and young pigs (3 per sow) at several times during animals' life and tested for resistance to amoxicillin, gentamicin, trimethoprim-sulfamids and tetracyclin. The percentages of resistant strains were compared between herd groups.

The frequency of resistant strains was higher during the lactating and post-weaning periods for sows and young pigs respectively. The level of antimicrobial use was associated with the percentage of resistance although variations were observed depending on antimicrobials. Tetracyclin resistance was very frequent: from 63 to 93.2% in sows and from 65.8 to 99% in young pigs. Similar kinetic although lower frequencies were obtained with trimethoprim-sulfamids: from 37.4 to 74% in sows and from 32.7 to 84.6% in pigs. On the other hand amoxicillin resistance was lower and highly variable depending on the sampling time: from 15.5 to 59% in sows and from 7 to 70.3% in pigs. Lowest frequency values were observed for gentamicin with up to 19.3 and 25.3% in sows and pigs respectively.

Although we demonstrated that low antimicrobial use is associated with less frequent resistance in faecal *E coli*, both antimicrobial family and administration scheme have to be taken into account when considering the influence of treatments.

Introduction

The antimicrobial use in veterinary medicine is a major concern because of possible selection and transmission to humans of resistant bacteria. However the relation between use and the occurrence of resistance is poorly documented in the field. Such data could thus help to identify treatment schemes associated with less frequent resistant strains.

In swine production the antimicrobial use is rather standardized between herds since major part of the administrations occur during the lactation period for sows and the post-weaning period for piglets. Methods for the quantification of antimicrobial use have been developed in human medicine but are not available for treatments administered to food animals (Chauvin, 2001).

For this study we selected farrow-to-finish commercial herds in which antimicrobial use was representative of the French swine production. Occurrence of resistance was monitored by faecal sampling several times during sows' and pigs' life. Indicative *Escherichia coli* strains were isolated from faecal content and tested for antimicrobial susceptibility.

Materials and Methods

Sixteen herds located in west of France were selected and classified depending on the number of systematic collective antimicrobial treatments administered to sows and pigs. In each herd five sows and three piglets per sow were selected and piglets were ear tagged. Faecal samples were collected from sows before farrowing (D0) and then 7, 30 and 60 days after farrowing. Piglets were sampled once during the lactating period (D7), twice during the post weaning period (D30 and D60) and at the end of the fattening period (D150). After plating of faeces on selective medium, four *E. coli* strains were selected per faecal sample and tested for antimicrobial susceptibility using the standard disk diffusion method. Tested antimicrobials were the following: amoxicillin, gentamicin, trimethoprim-sulfamid and tetracyclin.

Herds were scored (s) depending on both the number of antimicrobials used (x_i) and the number of administrations of each antimicrobial (n_i) with $s=\Sigma n_i x_i$. Depending on the s value herds were classified as low users (LU) if $s\leq2$, medium users (MU) if was equal to 3 or 4 or high users (HU) if $s\geq4$. Statistical analysis was carried out to compare percentages of resistant strains in the groups (LU, MU and HU) using logistic regression (macro GLIMMIX, SAS Institute Inc, 1999) with $p<0.05$.

Results

		Sows				Pigs			
		D0	D7	D30	D60	D7	D30	D60	D150
Amoxicillin	PU	15.5	24.3	26.1	18.8	19.9	19.3	31.8	7
	MU	34.2	58.9	50.7	28.3	54.1	48.5	70.3	26.6
	HU	26	33.9	46.2	36.6	49.1	67.8	57.2	42.9
	p	0.01	<0.0001	0.0006	0.01	<0.0001	<0.0001	<0.0001	<0.0001
Tetracyclin	PU	79.3	82	72.2	88.4	65.8	80.1	84.9	80.5
	MU	73.7	93.2	74	63	76.1	88.7	99	91.5
	HU	87.8	79.8	83.2	87.5	86.2	92.7	95.1	90
	p	0.03	0.04	0.1	<0.0001	<0.0001	<0.0001	<0.0001	0.002
Trimethoprim-sulfamids	PU	45.7	49.6	37.4	39.3	32.7	38.3	40.5	28.8
	MU	55.3	65.8	74	39.1	58.4	58.8	84.6	46.8
	HU	60.2	60.5	60.1	67.9	62.9	74.7	79.6	66.4
	p	0.07	0.06	<0.0001	<0.0001	<0.0001	<0.0001	<0.0001	<0.0001
Gentamicin	PU	0	0.9	0	3.6	0	5.1	6.1	0.8
	MU	1.3	4.1	1.4	0	1.4	0.5	21.5	0
	HU	6.5	15.3	19.3	7.1	17.7	23.2	25.3	0.4
	p	0.006	<0.0001	<0.0001	0.11	<0.0001	<0.0001	<0.0001	0.6

Table 1 Percentage of antimicrobial resistant strains in sows and young pigs at different sampling times

The number of herds classified as LU, MU and HU were six, four and six respectively.

Antimicrobial susceptibility results were available for 1200 strains from sows and 3099 strains from young pigs and resistance levels at the different sampling times are presented in Table 1.

In sows the percentage of amoxicillin resistant strains varied from 15.5% (LU herds at D0) to 58.9% (MU, D7) and tended to increase when sows were in the farrowing unit and to decrease thereafter. In young pigs it ranged from 7% (LU, D150) to 70.3% (MU, D60) with maximal resistance during the post weaning period. The effect of level of antimicrobial use was always statistically significant.

Tetracyclin resistance levels were high (from 63% to 93.2% in sows and from 65.8% to 99% in young pigs) with a significant effect of the level of antimicrobial use except for sows at D30.

Trimethoprim-sulfamid resistance was also frequent with values ranging from 37.4% (PU, D30) to 74% (MU, D60) in sows and from 32.7% (LU, D7) to 84.6% (MU, D60) in pigs. Statistically significant differences were constantly observed for pigs and for sows at D30 and D60.

Gentamicin resistance was less frequently observed. Highest percentages were 19.3% at D30 and 25.3% at D60 for HU herds in sows and pigs respectively. The difference was statistically significant except for the following sampling times: sows at D60 and for pigs at D150.

For some antimicrobials the relationship between antimicrobial use and resistance was not linear between groups of herds. Indeed at some sampling times the percentages were higher in herds with lower antimicrobial use (for example amoxicillin resistance in sows at D0).

Discussion

Our results describe the kinetic evolution of antimicrobial resistance during sows' production cycle and pigs' life. In sows whatever the level of antimicrobial use the highest percentages of resistant strains were observed during the lactating period (D7 and D30) and decreased thereafter. In pigs the highest values were found during the post-weaning period (D30 and D60) and were lower at the end of the fattening period (D150). These differences between sampling times were more noticeable for antimicrobials with less frequent occurrence of resistant strains such as amoxicillin and gentamicin. These periods are those during which antimicrobial administrations occur most frequently in the field. However previous studies have shown that other factors such as farrowing or weaning stress can induce the occurrence of resistance (Moro et al, 2000).

Levels of resistance observed were different depending on the antimicrobial. Tetracyclin resistance was very common as demonstrated previously by others even in herds that did not use this antimicrobial class (Dunlop et al, 1998).

In our study the level of antimicrobial use estimated using a score value was frequently associated with the percentage of antimicrobial resistant *E coli* in the faecal content of pigs since in most cases the low user herds exhibited the lowest levels of resistance. However some discrepancies were noticed. For example amoxicillin resistance in young pigs at D7 and D60 was higher for the MU group than for the HU one. This is probably due to the fact that using our scoring method, beta-lactam using herds were included in both the MU and the HU groups. Consequently the resulting amoxicillin resistant strains were observed independently of the use of other antimicrobials.

Our scoring method did not take into account several parameters such as administration moment in animal's life, duration or route of administration. However it consisted in a rapid and easy approach of antimicrobial use. These observations emphasize the need for further studies on the association between antimicrobial use and resistance.

References

CHAUVIN, C., MADEC, F., GUILLEMOT, D. and SANDERS, P. (2001). The crucial question of standardization when measuring drug consumption. Veterinary Research, 32, 533-543

DUNLOP, R.H., Mc EWEN, S.A., MEEK, A.H., BLACK, W.D., FRIENDSHIP, R.M., and CLARKE, R.C. (1998). Prevalence of resistance to seven antimicrobials among fecal *Escherichia coli* in thirty-four farrow to finish farms in Ontario, Canada. Preventive Veterinary medicine, 34, 265-282

MORO, M.H., BERAN, G.W., GRIFFITH, R.W. and HOFFMAN, L.J. (2000). Effect of heat stress on the antimicrobial drug resistance of *Escherichia coli* in the intestinal flora of swine. Journal of Applied Microbiology, 88, 836-844

Detection and count of *Salmonella enterica* in pork meat products

Bonardi S. *[1] , Salmi F. [1], Salsi A. [1], Bacci C. [1], Brindani F. [1]

[1] Animal Health Department, Section of Food Inspection, Faculty of Veterinary Medicine, University of Parma, Via del Taglio 8, 43100 Parma, Italy.
*corresponding author: silvia.bonardi@unipr.it

Abstract

A direct plating technique for the enumeration *S. enterica* in 90 pig meat samples was evaluated in comparison with a three tube-MPN procedure. For the detection of *S. enterica* the ISO 6597:2002 method was employed. Pork samples were collected at retail level in northern Italy. A total of 15 (16.7%) *Salmonella* positive samples were detected. By the use of the MPN method, *S. enterica* was countable in 12 (80.0%) samples, while the direct count gave positive results in two (13.3%) samples only. The ISO 6597:2002 method identified 12 (80.%) contaminated samples out of 15.The enumeration levels of *S. enterica* ranged from 0.03 MPN/g to > 110 MPN/g by the MPN method, and from 10 CFU/g to 180 CFU/g by direct plating. Seven *Salmonella* serovars were detected: *S.* Typhimurium, *S.* Derby, *S.* Give, *S.* Rissen, *S.* Livingstone, *S.* Brandenburg and *S.* London, with *S.* Typhimurium and *S.* Derby as the predominant ones.

Introduction

Salmonella enterica is responsible for several foodborne outbreaks all over the world and its transmission to the consumers is mainly linked to raw or undercooked meat products and raw or unpasteurized egg products. The micro-organism is often present in the pork meat production chain, *i.e.* from the live animal to the final meat product.

The major goal of this study was the evaluation of the prevalence of *S. enterica* in pork meat at retail level, together with the count of the micro-organism in positive samples. Quantification of the contamination level is, on our opinion, very important for the evaluation of the real risk for the consumer.

Material and methods

From January to December 2006, 90 samples of pig meat products were collected at retail level from 36 different stores in Parma, Modena, Cremona and Bergamo provinces, northern Italy. The samples were represented by 48 sausages, 20 different fresh pig meat samples, 14 minced meat samples, 4 dry cured salami, 3 offal samples (tongue, heart and kidney) and one bacon fat sample. All samples were tested for *S. enterica* by using the ISO 6597:2002 method.

In order to quantify the presence of the micro-organism, both a three tube-MPN procedure and a direct count method were employed. For the MPN counting method, a 10 g-aliquot of the meat samples was diluted in 90 of Buffered Peptone Water (BPW) and the following dilutions were set up in tubes containing 9 and 9.9 of BPW, respectively. This procedure, *i.e.* a three-tube MPN representing 1.0, 0.1 and 0.01 g of sample, was applied to the first 25 samples; thereafter, a three-tube MPN representing 10, 1.0 and 0.1 g of sample was combined with the previous one, in order to count very low levels of *S. enterica*. The MPN dilution series were incubated at 37 °C $\pm$ 1 °C for 18 $\pm$ 2 h. After incubation, a 0.1-aliquot of each tube was seeded into 10 of Rappaport-Vassiliadis Soya broth, incubated at 41.5 °C $\pm$ 1 °C for 24 $\pm$ 3 h. The broth-cultures were then plated onto XLT4 agar dishes, incubated at 37 °C $\pm$ 1 °C for 24 h plus 24 h. Suspect colonies were subjected to biochemical and serological tests.

For *Salmonella* direct count, a 10-fold dilution of each sample was set up in BPW, followed by direct plating onto XLT4 agar, incubated at 37 °C $\pm$ 1 °C for 24 h plus 24 h. Suspect colonies were counted and at least five ones per sample were subjected to biochemical and serological confirmation tests, to evaluate the number of *Salmonella* CFU/g.

For *Salmonella* genus identification the API-20 E® (bioMérieux) biochemical system was employed. Serotyping of *Salmonella* strains was performed by the National Reference Laboratory for *Salmonella* (CRNS) of the Istituto Zooprofilattico Sperimentale delle Venezie, Italy.

Results

A total of 15 (16.7%) out of 90 pig meat samples were contaminated by *S. enterica*. In particular, we detected *S. enterica* in 5 out of 48 sausages (10.4%), in 3 out of 20 meat samples (15.0%) and in 3 out of 14 minced meat samples (21.4%). In addition, each offal sample and the bacon fat were contaminated by the micro-organism (Table 1). As shown in Table 2, seven *Salmonella* serovars were detected: *S.* Typhimurium, *S.* Derby, *S.* Give, *S.* Rissen, *S.* Livingstone, *S.* Brandenburg and *S.* London. In one sausage sample three different serovars were identified (*S.* Give, *S.* Brandenburg, *S.* London). The *S.* Typhimurium isolates were phage-typed and they all belonged to DT NT (nontypeable). As far as *S.* Typhimurium antimicrobial susceptibility is concerned, all strains were resistant to ampicillin, streptomycin, sulphonamide compounds and tetracycline (ASSuT). The enumeration levels of *S. enterica* ranged from 0.03 MPN/g to > 110 MPN/g by the MPN method, and from 10 CFU/g to 180 CFU/g by direct plating. By the use of the three-tube MPN procedure, *S. enterica* was countable in 12 (80.0%) out of 15 contaminated samples. On the other hand, the direct count gave positive results in two (13.3%) samples only. The detection of *Salmonella* by the ISO 6597:2002 method was positive in 12 (80.%) samples (Table 1).

Discussion

The contamination rate of pork samples by *S. enterica* was rather high, particularly in minced meat and offal samples. On the other hand, the enumeration level by *Salmonella,* although variable, was rather low. The direct plating and the MPN method gave different results, even in the same sample unit, and therefore we could hardly estimate the number of viable micro-organisms per g of meat. Further studies are therefore needed to compare the MPN and direct count methods.

A very important step in our study was the choice of the most reliable selective medium for MPN and direct count methods. The XLD agar and BGA, employed at the beginning of the study as the first one is recommended by ISO 6579:2002, were soon replaced by XLT4 agar only. Suspect colonies grown on the latter medium were, in fact, more easily recognized and picked up than *Salmonella* colonies grown on the former ones. As a matter of fact, even if *Salmonella* colonies grown on XLD agar were similar to the pink colonies with a black centre grown on XLT4 agar, and therefore easy to select, XLT4 medium gave better performances if compared to XLD alone. On the other hand, the pink colonies grown on BGA dishes were not easily recognizable as *Salmonella* suspect ones, because of the lack of the black centre, that was very useful for the selection of colonies in presence of background flora.

As the enumeration level of *S. enterica* was particularly low, in the direct plating it was impossible to dilute samples more than 1:10. On the other hand, 1:10 pig meat dilutions were heavily contaminated by background flora and therefore the high number of non-target colonies grown on the selective agar dishes made both count and picking up of suspect colonies very difficult. Therefore, the characteristics of the selective medium (sensibility, sensitivity, colonies features) were crucial for the good performance of the direct count.

As shown in Table 1, the simultaneous use of both the ISO 6579:2002 method for the detection of *Salmonella* and the MPN method as counting procedure gave the best results for the identification of contaminated products. As in some pig meat samples the *Salmonella* level exceeded 110 MPN/g, while in others the level was as low as 0.03 MPN/g, we suggest to set up a three-tube MPN representing at least 10, 1.0, 0.1, 0.01 and 0.001 g of sample.

S. Typhimurium is one of the most relevant *S. enterica* serovars for public health, as identified by the European Commission (Reg. 1003/2005/CE). Although *S.* Typhimurium was detected in 5 (33.3%) out of 15 positive samples, its levels were low, ranging from 0.4 MPN/g in bacon fat to 19 MPN/g in sausages. Higher values were detected for *S.* Livingstone in the tongue sample (> 110 MPN/g), for *S.* Derby and *S.* Brandenburg simultaneously present in a fresh sausage (> 110 MPN/g) and for *S.* Derby (180 CFU/g) in another sausage sample.

Conclusions

As reported by EFSA (2006) and the CRNS (Centro di Referenza Nazionale per le Salmonellosi; Italian Reference Centre for Salmonellosis), pig meat could be a source of zoonotic agents for humans, particularly *S. enterica*. The predominat *Salmonella* serovars isolated from pig meat in the EU in the last years, *i.e. S.* Typhimurium and *S.* Derby, were the most common serovars even in this study. As the *Salmonella* contamination level in the examined samples was generally low, any risk assessment procedure should not ignore the quantitative evaluation of *S. enterica* in pork products.

References

EFSA, 2006. *Trends and sources of zoonoses, zoonotic agents and antimicrobial resistance in the European Union in 2004.*
Enter-VET 2005. Annual report. Eds. Ricci A., Mancin M., Cibin V. Padua: Centro Referenza Nazionale Salmonellosi (CNRS), Istituto Zooprofilattico Sperimentale delle Venezie.
ISO 6579:2002. *Horizontal method for the detection of Salmonella spp.* Geneve: International Organization of Standardization.

Table 1 – Detection and enumeration of *S. enterica* in pig meat samples

Sample	MPN Determination	Direct Count	ISO 6579:2002
Minced meat	0.7 MPN/g *S.* Typhimurium	< 10 CFU/g	*S.* Typhimurium
Bacon fat	0.4 MPN/g *S.* Typhimurium	< 10 CFU/g	*S.* Typhimurium
Sausage	12 MPN/g *S.* Typhimurium	< 10 CFU/g	*S.* Typhimurium
Minced meat	0.3 MPN/g S. Derby	< 10 CFU/g	-
Sausage	19 MPN/g *S.* Typhimurium	< 10 CFU/g	*S.* Typhimurium
Sausage	< 0.03 MPN/g	< 10 CFU/g	*S.* Typhimurium
Sausage	> 110 MPN/g *S.* Give *S.* Brandenburg	< 10 CFU/g	*S.* London
Pig meat	0.03 MPN/g *S.* Give	< 10 CFU/g	*S.* Give
Minced meat	0.04 MPN/g *S.* Derby	10 CFU/g *S.* Derby	*S.* Derby
Pig meat	< 0.03 MPN/g	< 10 CFU/g	*S.* Derby
Pig meat	0.3 MPN/g *S.* Derby	< 10 CFU/g	-
Tongue	> 110 MPN/g *S.* Livingstone	< 10 CFU/g	*S.* Livingstone
Heart	< 0.03 MPN/g	< 10 CFU/g	*S.* Rissen
Kidney	0.2 MPN/g *S.* Rissen	< 10 CFU/g	*S.* Rissen
Sausage	0.9 MPN/g *S.* Derby	180 CFU/g *S.* Derby	-
Positive samples: *Total number (%)*	12 (80.0%)	2 (13.3%)	12 (80.0%)

Table 2 – Distribution of *S. enterica* serovars in pig meat samples

Serovar	Sausages	Pig meat	Minced meat	Dry salami	Offal samples	Other	Total	%
S. Typhimurium	3	0	1	0	0	1	5	29.41
S. Derby	1	2	2	0	0	0	5	29.41
S. Give	1	1	0	0	0	0	2	11.77
S. Rissen	0	0	0	0	2	0	2	11.77
S. Brandenburg	1	0	0	0	0	0	1	5.88
S. London	1	0	0	0	0	0	1	5.88
S. Livingstone	0	0	0	0	1	0	1	5.88
Total	7	3	3	0	3	1	17	100

E. Coli, K. Pneumoniae and Providencia Rettgeri ESBLs producing isolated from pigs in the Veneto region, Italy.

Chiaretto, G., *(1) Perin, R., (2), Bettini, F., (3)., Sturaro, A., (2) Corrò, M. (2), and A. Ricci(1)

(1)National Reference Laboratory for Salmonella,
(2)Laboratory of Diagnostic Microbiology,
(3)Laboratory of Virology -Research and Development, Istituto Zooprofilattico Sperimentale delle Venezie, Legnaro (PD) Italy.
*corresponding autor: gchiaretto@izsvenezie.it ; tel +39-0-0498084286

Abstract

Twelve *Enterobacteriaceae* (n=10 *E. coli*, n=1 *K. pneumoniae* and n=1 *P. rettgeri*) resistant to cefotaxime and/or ceftazidime were isolated from ten sick piglets in the same pig farm in October 2006. All the strains were multi-drug resistant and confirmed as ESBLs producers by synergy tests. PCR and sequencing were carried out to detect the *bla* genes. The *E. coli* isolates and *P.rettgeri* harboured the $bla_{CTX-M-1}$; the *K. pneumoniae* isolate were positive for SHV *bla* gene (99% of omology with bla_{SHV-28}). All the isolates but *P. rettgeri* carried a TEM-1 β-lactamase as well.
This study represents the first report of *Enterobacteriaceae* ESBLs-producing other than *E. coli* and *Salmonella* in veterinary microbiology.

Introduction

The spread of resistance to Extended-Spectrum Cephalosporins (ESC) is an issue of growing concern in human medicine (Paterson D. L., 2006). This class of β-lactams as well as fluoroquinolones are antimicrobials widely used in the therapy of complicated infections indeed. Although ESC are not drugs frequently used in veterinary practice, the number of reports recording *E. coli* and *Salmonella enterica* ESC-resistant isolates from animals has recently increased in Europe.

E. coli ESBLs-producing have been isolated from poultry in Spain and Italy (Brinäs et al. 2003,2005, Chiaretto et al. 2006), from cattle in UK (Liebana et al. 2006,) and from companion animals in Italy and Portugal (Carattoli et al. 2005, Costa et al. 2004, Chiaretto et al. 2006). On the other hand, only few recent studies reported the recovery of *E. coli* with ESBL phenotype from pigs (Meunier et al. 2006, Blanc et al. 2006).

The class A ESBLs belong mainly to TEM, SHV and CTX-M family. The CTX-M enzymes, described in late '80 for the first time, have become the most prevalent ESBLs worldwide in humans (Cantón and Coque, 2006). The recovery of *E. coli* and Salmonella carrying bla_{CTX-M} genes has been also repored from different animal sources (poultry, cattle, pig, pet) in Europe (Weill et al. 2004, Liebana et al. 2006, Meunier et al. 2006, Riaño I., et al., 2006 Carattoli et al. 2005).

The aim of this study was to characterize at a molecular level ESBLs-producing enterobacteria isolated from ten piglets with septicaemia at the same pig farm. This study is the first report of *Enterobacteriaceae* ESBLs-producing other than *E. coli* and *Salmonella* in veterinary microbiology.

Material and Methods

Bacterial Strains

Twelve ESBLs-producing strains (n=10 *E. coli*, n=1 *K. pneumoniae* and n=1 *P. rettgeri*) were isolated from different organs of ten sick pigs (ranging from 30 to 80 days old) after post-mortem examination, in October 2006. The isolates were identified biochemically by routine laboratory procedure and Api20E system (Biomerieux).

Susceptibility tests

The antimicrobial susceptibility was evaluated by disk diffusion with 16 different antimicrobial drugs (Becton Dickinson Microbiology Systems Cockeysville, MD, USA) on Mueller-Hinton (MH) agar, according to the recommendations of the CLSI (formely NCCLS). The following antimicrobials were

Session 6

tested: colistin (CL 10 µg), trimethoprim-sulfamethoxazole (SXT 23,75+ 1,25 µg), kanamycin (KAN 30 µg), gentamicin (GEN 10 µg), cefotaxime (CTX 30 µg), amoxicillin-clavulanic acid (AMC 30 µg), nalidixic acid (NAL 30 µg), tetracycline (TET 30 µg), ampicillin (AMP 10 µg), streptomycin (STR 10 µg), chloramphenicol (CHL 30 µg), spectinomycin (SPT 100 µg), enrofloxacin (ENO 5 µg), sulfisoxazole (G 25 mg), aminosidin (AN 60 µg), apramycin (APRA 15 µg). The strains were also tested against three extra β-lactams: ceftiofur (30 µg), cefoxitin (FOX 30 µg), imipenem (IMP 30 µg)). The ESBL phenotype was assayed according to CLSI tests using ceftazidime and cefotaxime (30 µg) and the same cephalosporins plus clavulanic acid (10 µg). The enhancement of the oxymino-β-lactams inhibition zone (≥ 5 mm) caused by clavulanate revealed the ESBL-producing strains. *E. coli* ATCC25922 and *K. pneumoniae* ATCC 700603 were used as quality control strains for the ESBL phenotype screening tests.

Genetic characterization of *bla* genes.
Total DNA was extracted with InstaGene matrix kit (Bio-Rad) in accordance with the manufacturer's recommendation. The detection of *bla*TEM, *bla*SHV, *bla*CTX-M genes was carried out by PCR assays.The primers used were either adapted from those previously published (Liebana et al. 2004, Weill et al. 2004) or designed by using computer analysis of available β-lactamase sequences (GenBank) (Table 2).

Table 2: Primers and PCR conditions used in PCR analysis

PCR target	Primer	Sequence (5'-3')	$T_a(°C)$	PCR products	Reference
*bla*TEM	TEM-F	TCGTGTCGCCCTTATTCCCTTTTT	60	425 pb	Liebana 2004
	TEM-R	GCGGTTAGCTCCTTCGGTCCTC			
	TEM-B-F	AGTCACAGAAAAGCATCTT	52	576 pb	This study*
	TEM-B-R	GAGTAAACTTGGTCTGACAG			
*bla*SHV	SHV-F	CGGCCCCGCAGGATTGACT	60	409/849 pb	Liebana 2004
	SHV-Fmod**	GATGTATTGTGGTTATGCGTT			
	SHV-R	TCCCGGCGATTTGCTGATTTC			
*bla*CTX-M	CTX-M-F	C(A/G)ATGTGCAG(C/T)ACCAGTAA	53	540 pb	Weill 2004
	CTX-M-R	CGC(A/G)ATATC(A/G)TTGGTGGTG			
*bla*CTXM Group1	CTX-M-F-1	ATGGTTAAAAAATCACTGC	53	886 pb	This study***
	CTX-M-R-1	CGTTTCCGCTATTACAA			

*primers TEM-B-F position: 315-333, TEM-B-R position: 862-881; EMBL accession number AY529705.
**primers SHV-Fmod position: 185-205; EMBL accession number AF124984.
***primer CTX-M gruppo1, CTX-M-F position: 63-81, CTX-M-R position 871-887; EMBL accession number X92506

Sequencing
The purified PCR fragments were sequenced on both strands with the "BigDye terminator v3.1 cycle sequencing" kit (Applied Biosystems) using the same set of primers as for the PCRs (Table 1). Sequence analysis was performed on an 3100-Avant Genetic Analyzer (Applied Biosystems) and analysed using the software SeqScape v2.1.1. The obtained nucleotide sequences and the derived amino acid sequences were compared with those previously described from the GeneBank database www.ncbi.nlm.nih.gov and www.lahey.org/studies/webt.html, respectively.

Results

Ten *E. coli*, one strain of *K. pneumoniae* and one strain of *P. rettgeri* were identified by biochemical tests. All the strains showed a multi-drug resistant phenotype (summarized in table 1) and were confirmed as ESBLs producers by synergy tests. All the *E. coli* strains and the *P. rettgeri* isolate carried a CTX-M enzyme classified as CTX-M-1 by DNA sequencing.
The *K. pneumoniae* isolate was positive to a *bla*SHV gene, the sequence analysis of the amplicon revealed an omology of 99 % with the *bla*SHV-28 gene. All the isolates but the strain of *P. rettgeri* possessed the β-lactamase TEM-1. The results of genetic characterization are shown in table 1.

Discussion

The CTX-M β –lactamases have become the most widely spread ESBLs worldwide (Cantón and Coque, 2006). In this study, we found multi-drug resistant strains (*E. coli* and *P. rettgeri*) positive for the CTX-M-1 β –lactamase. Among the CTX-M enzymes, CTX-M group1 are recognized mainly in Europe. In particular, the CTX-M-1 β–lactamase is the most prevalent variant reported in human *E. coli* and has been already reported in animals in Italy (Mugnaioli et al. 2006, Carattoli et al. 2005). Furthermore, we found that in the same animal a strain of *Klebsiella pneumoniae* SHV positive and a strain of *E. coli* CTX-M –1 producing coexisted. This study represents the first report of *Enterobacteriaceae* ESBLs-producing other than *E. coli* and *Salmonella* in veterinary microbiology

The strains were isolated from piglets coming from different areas in the same pig farm and we reported also the isolation of two different species (*E. coli* and *P. rettgeri*) carrying CTX-M-1 from the same animal. It is worth noting that the dissemination of CTX-M genes can follow different ways (Cantón and Coque, 2006). In the farm under study, this could be due to the presence of a specific clone and/or mobile genetic elements. Further molecular investigations and monitoring will be needed to ascertain the mechanism/s of CTX-M-1 positive *E. coli* spreading and check the efficacy of the control actions adopted.

Conclusion

The antibiotic resistance is a issue of growing concern in human and veterinary medicine. In particular, antimicrobials such as cephalosporins and fluoroquinolones represent major therapeutical options in complicated human infections. The recovery of ESBLs- producing *Enterobacteriaecae* animal-associated demands surveilaence actions focused on cephalosporins resistance to understand the interplay among animals and humans related to the diffusion of cephalosporin resistance genetic determinants. On the other hand, the prudent use of antimicrobials remains the first action to preserve their effectiveness.

Table 1: ESBLs- producing strains isolated from sick piglets (Dicember 2006)

Strain	Species	Resistance	β-lactamases
3593	*E. coli*	SXT-KAN-GM-CTX-AMC-TET-AMP-STR-CHL-SPT-G-AN-EFT	CTX-M-1, TEM-1
3595	*E. coli*	SXT-KAN-GM-CTX-AMC-TET-AMP-STR-G-AN-APRA-EFT	CTX-M-1, TEM-1
3616	*E. coli*	SXT-KAN-GM-CTX-AMC-TET-AMP-STR-G-AN-EFT	CTX-M-1, TEM-1
3620	*E. coli*	SXT-KAN-GM-CTX-AMC-TET-AMP-STR-CHL-SPT-G-AN-EFT	CTX-M-1, TEM-1
3622	*E. coli*	SXT-KAN-CTX-AMC-NAL-TET-AMP-STR-CHL-G-AN-EFT	CTX-M-1, TEM-1
3623	*E. coli*	SXT-KAN-CTX-AMC-CTX-NAL-TET-AMP-STR-CHL-G-AN-EFT	CTX-M-1, TEM-1
3623	*K. pneumoniae*	SXT-KAN-CTX-AMC-NAL-TET-AMP-CHL-ENO-G-EFT	bla_{SHV}, TEM-1
3696	*E. coli*	SXT-KAN-GM-CTX-AMC-NAL-TET-AMP-STR-G-AN-EFT	CTX-M-1, TEM-1
3857	*E. coli*	SXT-KAN-GM-CTX-AMC-NAL-TET-AMP-SPT-CHL-ENO-G-AN-EFT	CTX-M-1, TEM-1
3858	*E. coli*	SXT-KAN-GM-CTX-AMC-NAL-TET-AMP-SPT-CHL-ENO-G-AN-APRA	CTX-M-1, TEM-1
3859	*E. coli*	SXT-KAN-GM-CTX-AMC-TET-AMP-STR-C-SPT-G-AN-EFT	CTX-M-1, TEM-1
3859	*P. rettgeri*	CL-SXT-KAN-CTX-AMC-TET-AMP-STR-C-SPT-G-AN-APRA-EFT	CTX-M-1

CL: colistin, SXT: trimethoprim-sulfamethoxazole, KAN: kanamycin, GEN: gentamicin, CTX: cefotaxime, AMC: amoxicillin-clavulanic acid, NAL nalidixic acid, TET tetracycline, AMP ampicillin,

Session 6

STR streptomycin, CHL: chloramphenicol, SPT spectinomycin, ENO: enrofloxacin, G: sulfisoxazole, AN: aminosidin, APRA: apramycin, EFT: ceftiofur.

References

BLANC V., et al., 2006. ESBL- and plasmidic class C β-lactamase-producing E. coli strains isolated from poultry, pig and rabbit farms. *Veterinary Microbiology*, doi: 10.1016/j.vetmic.2006.08.002.

BRINÄS L., et al., 2005. Monitoring and characterization of extended-spectrum β -lactamases in Escherichia coli strains from healthy and sick animals in Spain in 2003. *Antimicrobial Agents and Chemotherapy* 49, 1262-1264.

BRINÄS, L., et al., 2003. Detection of CMY-2, CTX-M-14, and SHV-12 β-lactamses in Escherichia coli fecal-sample isolates from healthy chickens. *Antimicrobial Agents and Chemotherapy*, 47, 2056-2058.

CANTÓN R and T. M. COQUE, 2006. The CTX-M β-lactamase pandemic. *Current Opinion in Microbiology*, 9, 466-475.

CARATTOLI A., et al., 2005. Extended-spectrum β-lactamses in Escherichia. coli isolated from dogs and cats in Rome, Italy, from 2001 to 2003. *Antimicrobial Agents and Chemotherapy*. 49, 833-835

CHIARETTO G., et al., 2006. Monitoring and molecular characterization of ESBLs-producing Enterobacteriaceae of veterinary origin in northern Italy. 1. *Proceedings of 13S International Symposium Salmonella and Salmonellosis*, 237-239.

COSTA, D., et al., 2004. Detection of CTX-M-1 and TEM-52 β-lactamases in Escherichia coli strains from healthy pets in Portugal. *Journal of Antimicrobial Chemotherapy*, 53,418-431.

LIEBANA E., et al., 2004. Characterization of β-lactamases responsible for resistance to extended-spectrum cephalosporins in E. coli and Salmonella enterica strains from food-producing animals in United Kingdom. *Microbial Drug Resistance*. 10, 1-9.

LIEBANA E., et al., 2006. Longitudinal farm study of extended-spectrum β-Lactamases-mediated resistance. *Journal of. Clinical Microbiology*. 44,1630-1634.

MEURNIER D., et al., 2006. CTX-M-1-and CTX-M-15 type β-lactamases in clinical Escherichia coli isolates recovered from food-producing animals in France. *International Journal of Antimicrobial Agents* 28, 402-407.

MUGNAIOLI C., et al., 2006 CTX-M-Type Extended-Spectrum β-lactamases in Italy: molecular epidemiology of an Emerging countrywide problem. *Antimicrobial Agents and Chemotherapy* 50, 2700-2706.

NATIONAL COMMITTEE FOR CLINICAL LABORATORY STANDARDS. 2002. Performance standards for antimicrobial disk and diluition tests for bacteria isolated from animals; Approved Standard-second edition. M31-A2. National Committee for Clinical Laboratory Standards, Wayne, PA.

NATIONAL COMMITTEE FOR CLINICAL LABORATORY STANDARDS. 2003. Performance standards for antimicrobial disk susceptibility test: approved standards-8th edition.M2-A8. National Committee for Clinical Laboratory Standards, Wayne, PA.

PATERSON D. L., 2006. Resistance in gram-negative bacteria: Enterobacteriaceae. *American Journal of Infection Control*, 34 (5), 20-28.

RIAÑO I., et al., 2006. Detection and characterization of extended –spectrum β-lactamases in Salmonella enterica strains of healty food animals in Spain. *Journal of Antimicrobial. Chemotherapy*. 58: 844-847.

WEILL, F., et al, 2004. Emergence of Extended-Spectrum-β-lactamase (CTX-M-9)-producing multiresistant strains of Salmonella enterica serotype Virchow in poultry and human in France. *Journal of. Clinical Microbiology*. 42, 5767-5773.

Salmonella prevalence and antimicrobial resistance in swine from 5 US states from 2003 to 2005

Bailey, J.S[1]., Fedorka-Cray, P.J[1]., Wineland, N.E[2]., and Dargatz, D.A[2].

[1]USDA, ARS, Athens, GA, USA
[2]USDA, APHIS, Fort Collins, CO , USA
*corresponding author: stan.bailey@ars.usda.gov

Abstract

The Collaboration in Animal Health and Food Safety Epidemiology (CAHFSE), a USDA joint program of ARS, APHIS, and FSIS was established to track food borne pathogens and monitor animal health issues. Fecal samples (n=9020) were collected and cultured for *Salmonella* from pens of pigs near slaughter weight (generally $\geq$ 22 weeks old) from swine farms in five U.S. states. A prevalence of 8.0, 10.1, and 8.5% was observed in 2003, 2004, and 2005, respectively. The top 10 serotypes accounted for 94% of the total *Salmonella* isolates with *S.* Derby (45%), *S.* Typhimurium var. 5- (15%), and *S.* Heidelberg (9%) comprising the top three serotypes each year. *Salmonella* Give was found in 8% of samples in 2003, 3% of samples in 2004, but was not found in the top 10% of isolates in 2005. The percentage of *Salmonella* isolates that were susceptible to all of the 16 antimicrobials tested increased from 6% in 2003 to 15% in 2005. At the same time, the percentage of isolates resistant to 10 or more antimicrobials increased from 1% to 15%. The increase in multiple drug resistance was coincident with an increase in the percentage of *S.* Derby isolates. Overall, frequency of resistance to individual antimicrobials was relatively stable from 2003 to 2005 and observed differences were related to changes in serotypes over time, which highlights the importance of reporting resistance data by individual serotype. CAHFSE provides a mechanism to monitor changes in serotypes of *Salmonella* as well as antimicrobial resistance patterns over time.

Introduction

Salmonella have been linked to food animal production and pork products are considered to be potential sources of *Salmonella* (White, et al. 2001). Nontyphoidal *Salmonella* spp. are estimated to account for 1.4 million cases of gastroenteritis in humans annually in the United States (Mead et al. 1999). Most cases result in self-limiting diarrheal disease. However, prolonged duration of illness, septicemia or altered immune function in some individuals may warrant use of antimicrobial therapy (Conte, 1995). Therefore, it is important to maintain an effective array of antimicrobials for potential treatment of bacterial infections.

The emergence of antimicrobial resistance in zoonotic bacteria associated with food producing animals, and evidence of human infections from animal sources (Fey, et al., 2000; Cohen and Tauxe, 1986) has spurred public health officials and scientists to reassess antimicrobial use in food animal production (FDA, 1998; WHO, 1997). In food animal production, antimicrobials are used both therapeutically and non-therapeutically. It is believed that therapeutic treatment of individual animals plays a minor role in the development of resistance. However, prolonged exposure of animals to non-therapeutic levels of antimicrobials for the prevention of disease and performance enhancement is believed to have the potential to increase antimicrobial resistance.

The results of the National Animal Health Monitoring System's (NAHMS) Swine 2000 study indicated antimicrobials were given in feed to grower/finisher pigs on 88.5% of the swine operations (APHIS, 2002) accounting for 95.9% of the grower/finisher pigs in the United States. Thus, antimicrobial use and related issues are a major concern to the pork industry. The merit and consequences of both therapeutic and non-therapeutic use of antimicrobials is under increasing scrutiny, but little information is available comparing the effects of these usage levels on the development and persistence of antimicrobial resistance among food borne pathogenic bacteria.

Session 6

Previous monitoring programs have consisted of short-term studies of the presence of antimicrobial resistant populations, particularly in zoonotic pathogens associated with farm animals. To enhance and expand these initial monitoring efforts, a multi-agency "Public Health Action Plan to Combat Antimicrobial Resistance" was developed to address the potentially adverse effects of using antimicrobials in food animal production. The United States Department of Agriculture (USDA) responded by developing the Collaboration on Animal Health and Food Safety Epidemiology (CAHFSE), a partnership among USDA agencies; Animal and Plant Health Inspection Service (APHIS), Agricultural Research Service (ARS) and Food Safety and Inspection Service (FSIS). The primary objectives of CAHFSE are: 1) to enhance the overall understanding of pathogens that pose a food-safety risk by tracking these pathogens from the farm to the plant and 2) to monitor critical diseases in food-animal production. These objectives and critical issues related to the relationship between antimicrobial susceptibility and antimicrobial use will be addressed on a long term continuous basis under the CAHFSE program. Swine were the first commodity tested in the CAHFSE program.

Materials and Methods

On-Farm Sampling

CAHFSE sampling began in July, 2003 and by December 31, 2005, a total of 9020 fecal samples from 5 states (Iowa, Minnesota, Missouri, North Carolina and Texas) were tested for the presence of *Salmonella*. Selection criteria for soliciting farm participation included production types (indoor farrow-to-finish, outdoor farrow-to-finish, indoor finish only, and outdoor finish only) and size (number of pigs marketed per year; small $\leq$ 2,000, medium > 2,000 and $\leq$ 7,500, large > 7,500). Samples and data were collected quarterly. During each site visit, a questionnaire regarding animal inventory, animal health, management practices and antimicrobial use was completed.

Up to 40 pen floor fecal samples were collected from pigs at least 22 wks old for isolation and subsequent characterization of *Salmonella*. At least 5 samples per pen (center and at each corner) were taken for each of 8 pens. When there were less than 8 pens, then two or more sets of samples were taken from the same pen. Approximately 25 gm fecal samples were collected with a clean tongue depressor and placed in Whirl Pack bags. Liquid diarrhea fecal samples were placed in 50 ml centrifuge tubes, the screw caps were tightly secured and also placed in Whirl Pack bags. Samples were then shipped overnight on frozen cold packs to the Richard B. Russell Agriculture Research Center in Athens, Georgia.

Salmonella

Feces (1 g) was incubated in 10 mL of GN Hajna (Difco, Becton Dickenson, Sparks, MD) for 18-24 h at 37° C, and Tetrathionate broth (Difco) for 40-48 h at 37° C. After the initial enrichments, aliquots (100 µl) were transferred to 10 mL of Rappaport-Vassiliadis R10 broth (Difco) which were incubated for 18-24 h at 37° C. Ten microliter aliquots of Rappaport-Vassiliadis R10 broth were then streaked onto Xylose-Lysine-Tergitol-4 (Difco) and BG Sulfa (Difco) agar for isolation of *Salmonella*. Plates were incubated for 18-24 h at 37° C. Isolated colonies characteristic of *Salmonella* were inoculated into triple sugar iron and lysine iron agar slants for biochemical confirmation. Presumptive positive isolates were serogrouped using serogroup specific antisera (Difco) and were then sent to the National Veterinary Services Laboratory (Ames, IA) for serotyping.

Antimicrobial Susceptibility Testing

Salmonella, generic *E. coli* and *Enterococcus* antimicrobial susceptibility testing were conducted using the SensititreTM System (Trek Diagnostics, Inc., Westlake, Ohio) as per manufacturer's directions. Antimicrobials included those used in both human and veterinary medicine and were configured in a 96 well custom made panel. National Committee for Clinical Standards (NCCLS) (renamed to Clinical and Laboratory Standards Institute's (CLSI)) guidelines and resistance breakpoints were used throughout the testing procedure.

Results

Salmonella were recovered from 8.0, 10.1, and 8.5% of tested U.S. pigs in 2003, 2004, and 2005, respectively (Table 1).

Table 1: *Salmonella* prevalence 22 wk-old-pigs from five U.S. states

	2003	2004	2005
Samples tested	1.763	3,377	3,881
Number of positives	143	338	330
Prevalence	8.1%	10.0%	8.5%

The top 10 serotypes accounted for 94% of the total *Salmonella* isolates with *S.* Derby (45%), *S.* Typhimurium var. 5- (15%), and *S.* Heidelberg (9%) comprising the top three serotypes each year. *Salmonella* Give was found in 8% of samples in 2003, 3% of samples in 2004, but was not found in the top 10% of isolates in 2005 (Table 2).

Table 2: Predominate serotypes of *Salmonella* from U.S. pigs, 2003-2005

Rank	2003 n=146		2004 n=356		2005 n=346	
	Serotype	Percent	Serotype	Percent	Serotype	Percent
1	Derby	31.0%	Derby	45.21%	Derby	43.93%
2	Typh var 5-	27.6%	Typh var 5-	13.86%	Heidelberg	11.85%
3	Heidelberg	8.97%	Heidelberg	7.92%	Typh var 5-	11.56%
4	Give	7.59%	Typhimurium	6.60%	Typhimurium	7.51%
5	Mbandaka	6.90%	Untypable	4.29%	Mbandaka	6.65%
6	Typhimurium	4.83%	Give	3.96%	Agona	4.62%
7	Untypable	3.45%	Mbandaka	3.30%	Worthington	3.47%
8	Infantis	2.07%	Anatum	3.30%	Untypable	2.60%
9	Worthington	1.38%	Bovis-Morbificans	2.64%	4,5,12:i:-	2.02%
10	Bovis-Morbificans	1.38%	Worthington	2.31%	Newport	1.16%

The percentage of *Salmonella* isolates that were susceptible to all of the 16 antimicrobials tested increased from 6% in 2003 to 15% in 2005. At the same time, the percentage of isolates resistant to 10 or more antimicrobials increased from 1% to 15%. The increase in multiple drug resistance was coincident with an increase in the percentage of *S.* Derby isolates (Table 3).

Table 3: Multiple antimicrobial susceptibility of *Salmonella* from U.S. pigs, 2003-2005

No. of ABX	2003 n=146	2004 n=356	2005 n=346
Pan-Susceptible	5.5	5.3	15.0
1	29.7	33.3	10.7
> 2	64.8	61.4	74.3
> 5	21.4	28.7	30.6
>10	1.4	9.5	15.2

Discussion

Salmonella prevalence in swine fecal samples were similar to earlier reports (Bush et al., 1999). In addition *Salmonella* serotypes recovered in this study were typical of those reported in U.S. swine production. Resistance among *Salmonella* isolates was observed most frequently among antimicrobial agents used extensively in the past (streptomycin, sulfonamides, and tetracycline). Overall, frequency of resistance to individual antimicrobials was relatively stable from 2003 to 2005 and observed differences were related to changes in serotypes over time, which highlights the importance of reporting resistance data by individual serotype. Quinolones are not approved for use in swine in the U.S. and no isolates resistant to ciprofloxacin were observed. Since any use of antimicrobials can result in selection of resistant bacterial populations, antibiotics should only be used when warranted to treat disease or to enhance the healthy growth of animals.

CAHFSE provides a mechanism to monitor changes in serotypes of *Salmonella* as well as antimicrobial resistance patterns over time.

References

Animal and Plant Health Inspection Services (APHIS) Info Sheet. 2002. Preventive Practices in Swine: Administration of Iron and Antibiotics. APHIS webpage, March 2002. http://www.aphis.usda.gov/vs/ceah/cahm/

Bush, E.J., B. Wagner, and P.J. Fedorka-Cray. 1999. Risk Factors Associated with Shedding of *Salmonella* by U.S. Finishing Hogs. Proceedings of the 3rd International Symposium on the Epidemiology and Control of Salmonella in Pork, Washington D.C., August 5-7, 1999. p.106-108.

COHEN, M.L., and TAUXE, R.V. 1986. Drug-Resistant Salmonella in the United States: An Epidemiologic Perspective. Science 234: 964-969.

CONTE, J. E. 1995. Manual of antibiotics and infectious diseases. Williams & Wilkins, Baltimore.

FEY, P.D., et al., 2000. Pediatric Ceftriaxone-Resistant Salmonella infection acquired from infected cattle in the United States. New England J. Med. 342:1242-1249.

Food and Drug Administration (FDA) Center for Veterinary Medicine (1998): Antimicrobial use in veterinary medicine. FDA position paper.

KIN. J.Y., et al., 1999. Salmonella prevalence in market weight pigs before and after shipment to slaughter. Proceedings of the 3rd International Symposium on the Epidemiology and Control of Salmonella in Pork, Washington D.C., August 5-7, 1999. p.137-139.

MEAD, P.S., et al., 1999. Food-related illness and death in the United States. Emerg Infect Dis.5:607-625.

Weigel, R.M., et al., 1999. Reservoirs of *Salmonella* infection on swine farms in Illinois. Proceedings of the 3rd International Symposium on the Epidemiology and Control of Salmonella in Pork, Washington D.C., August 5-7, 1999. p.180-183.

White, D.G., et al., 2001. The Isolation of Antibiotic-Resistant Salmonella from Retail Ground Meats. N Engl J Med. 345:1147-1154.

World Health Organization (1997): The Medical Impact of the Use of Antimicrobials in Food Animals, Report of a WHO meeting, WHO/EMC/ZOO/97. 4, Berlin, Germany, 13-17 October, 1997.

Genetic comparison of *Campylobacter coli* resulting from pigs and poultry with isolates resulting from human campylobacteriosis..

Denis, M. [1]*, Chidaine, B. [1], Laisney, M-J. [1], Kempf, I. [2], Mégraud, F. [3], Rivoal, K. [1], Fravalo, P. [1]

(1)   AFSSA, Unité HQPAP, 22440 Ploufragan, France
(2)   AFSSA, Unité MB, 22440 Ploufragan, France
(3)   CNR-CH, CHU Pellegrin, 33076 Bordeaux Cédex, France

* m.denis@ ploufragan. afssa.fr

Abstract

133 isolates of *Campylobacter coli* isolated from Brittany in France and collected in 2003 were analysed by RFLP/PFGE. They came from pig (65), poultry (56) and human campylobacteriosis (12). No pulsotype common to the 3 origins could be detected but the analysis of the genetic similarity at 80% of the isolates made it possible to build 19 groups of similarity. In 3 cases, poultry isolates were found in groups containing human isolates. Nevertheless, the pig isolates were always in groups different from the poultry isolates and the human ones. These results tend to indicate that the two animal productions would have their own genotype and that the campylobacters from pigs are rarely responsible of human campylobacteriosis.

Introduction

Campylobacter sp. is one of the most frequent causes of human gastro-enteritis. The poultry meat is mainly accused; it would be responsible for at least 40% of the human campylobacteriosis (Vellinga and Van Loock, 2002). In France, *C.jejuni* species represents 76% of the human isolates against 17% for *C coli* (Gallay *et al*, 2005) and pigs are known to be frequently infected with *C coli* (Magras *et al*, 2004). It was thus interesting to genetically compare *C. coli* from human campylobacteriosis with *C. coli* isolates resulting from pig and poultry productions in order to estimate the importance of these animal productions in the human infections at *Campylobacter coli*.

Material et methods

Isolates

The isolates of *Campylobacter coli* analyzed in this work were collected in Brittany in France and during the year 2003. Twelve *C. coli* of human origin were provided by Pr F Mégraud of the CNR-CH of Bordeaux. Each isolate comes from an analysis carried out on a patient presenting gastro-enteritis. The 121 isolates of animal origin (56 poultry *C. coli* and 65 pig *C. coli*) come from samples collected in farm, slaughter-house, and supermarket. Only one isolate was retained by analyzed sample.

Methods

The typing of the isolates was carried out by RFLP/PFGE as described by Rivoal *et al*., (2005). Two enzymatic profiles were obtained by isolate : a *Kpn*1profile and a *Sma*1 profile. The combined profile resulting from the 2 enzymes was coded KS.
Electrophoretic patterns were compared by BioNumerics® (Applied Maths). Similarities between profiles, based on band positions, were derived from the Dice correlation coefficient with a maximum position tolerance of 1%. A dendrogram of the analysis of the combined *Kpn*1- and- *Sma*1-digested DNA was constructed to reflect the similarities between the strains in the matrix. Strains were clustered by the Unweighted Pair-Group Method using the Arithmetic Mean (UPGMA) (Struelens, 1996). Isolates with high similarity were considered as deriving from the same parent strain (Tenover *et al*., 1995). In this study, clusters were defined for a genetic similarity equal or superior to 80%.
The index of Simpson (Hunter, 1990) was calculated to estimate the diversity of the sample.

Results

Table 1 gives the number of genetic profiles per enzyme, and origin on the number of isolates, as well as the Index of Simpson.

Table 1 : number of genetic profiles
per enzyme, and origin

enzyme	Origin		
	Human	Poultry	Pig
Kpn 1	11 / 12	52 / 56	62 / 65
Sma 1	11 / 12	47 / 56	60 / 65
KS	**11 / 12**	**53 / 56**	**64 / 65**
Simpson index	0,984	0,998	0,999

Eleven, 53 and 64 combined KS profiles were obtained respectively for 12, 56, and 65, human, poultry and pig isolates.
For the 3 origins, the index of Simpson is very close to 1 what indicates that our sampling has a very great diversity.

Table 2 : number of isolates per cluster and origin

clusters	N° isolates per origin			N° isolates per cluster
	pig	poultry	Human	
C1	2			2
C2	2			2
C3	2			2
C4		2		2
C5		2		2
C6		2		2
C7		1	1	**2**
C8	12			12
C9			3	3
C10		3		3
C11		4	1	**5**
C12		4		4
C13		6	2	**8**
C14		2		2
C15		4		4
C16		2		2
C17		2		2
C18	2			2
C19	2			2
Total	22	34	7	63

No pulsotype common to the 3 origins could be detected but the analysis of the genetic similarity at 80% of the isolates made it possible to build 19 groups of similarity coded clusters C1 to C19 (table 2) which contained 47,6 % of the total isolates.

In 3 cases (in fat in the table), poultry isolates are in the same clusters containing human isolates. On the other hand, the pig isolates are always in clusters different from those containing poultry and / or human isolates.

The figure 1 represents the dendrogram obtained from the analysis of KS profiles by BioNumerics®.

Discussion

The genetic comparison by RFLP/PFGE of *Campylobacter coli* from pig and poultry productions with isolates resulting from the human campylobacteriosis showed genetically close isolates between the poultry production and the human cases. In spite of the importance of the sampling of the isolates from the pig production and its diversity, it was not possible in our study to highlight identical or very close isolates between this animal production and the human isolates. In addition, the *C coli* from pigs are always in clusters different from those containing poultry and / or human isolates.
This result consolidates other studies which show the implication of the poultry in the human campylobacteriosis (Steinhauserova *et al*, 2002; Nadeau *et al*, 2002; Kärenlampi *et al*, 2003; Michaud *et al*, 2005). Genetic separation between *C. coli* from poultry and *C. coli* from pig were described by Hopkins *et al*., (2004) and by Siemer *et al*., (2005). The latter, moreover, showed that *C. coli* resulting from the poultries are in the same genetic groups as the isolates resulting from human campylobacteriosis.

Session 6

This result is in agreement with the results of Guévremont *et al.*. (2004). For the same period and the same geographical area in Canada, Guévremont compared 660 isolates resulting from feces of pigs taken in slaughter-house with 24 isolates resulting from patients. No isolate genetically identical and commun to the two origins was found.

Conclusions

These results tend to indicate that the two animal productions would have their own genotypes and that the campylobacters resulting from the pig would not be implied in the human campylobacteriosis. The probability of human *Campylobacter* contamination by pig thus seems very weak.

References

GALLAY A., PROUZET-MAULÉON V., MÉGRAUD F. 2005. Les infections à Campylobacter en France : bilan de surveillance du réseau de laboratoire de villes et hospitaliers. *Rapport CNRCH, INVS*, Octobre 2005, 9 pages

GUÉVREMONT, E., HIGGINS, R., QUESSY, S. 2004. Characterization of *Camplylobacter* isolates recovered from clinically healthy pigs and from sporadic cases of camplylobacteriosis in humans. *Journal of Food Protection*, Vol. 67, N°2, p. 228-234

HOPKINS, KL, DESAI M, FROST JA, STANLEY J, LOGAN JMJ 2004. Fluorescent Amplified Fragment Length Polymorphism Genotyping of *Campylobacter jejuni* and *Campylobacter coli* strains and its relationship with host specificity, serotyping, and phage typing. *Journal of Clinical Microbiology*, vol 42, n°1, 229-235

HUNTER P. 1990. Reproductibility and indices of discriminatory power of microbial typing methods. *Journal of Clinical Microbiology*, 28 : 1903-5.

KÄRENLAMPI, R., RAUTELIN, H., HAKKINEN, M., HÄNNINEN, M.L. 2003. Temporal and geographical distribution and overlap of Penner heat-stable serotypes and pulsed-field gel electrophoresis genotypes of *Camplylobacter jejuni* isolates collected from humans and chickens in Finland during a seasonal peak. *Journal of Clinical Microbiology*, Vol. 41, N°.10, p. 4870-4872

MAGRAS C., GARREC N., LAROCHE M., ROSSERO A., MIRCOVICH C., DESMONTS M-H., FEDERIGHI M. 2004. Sources of *Campylobacter* sp. Contamination of piglets in farrowing units of farrow-to-finish farms : first results. *International Society for Animals Hygiene*, Saint-Malo, 2004

MICHAUD S., MÉNARD S., ARBEIT R.D. 2005. Role of real-time molecular typing in the surveillance of *Campylobacter* enteritidis and comparison of pulsed-field gel electrophoresis profiles from chicken and human isolates. *Journal of Clinical Microbiology*, 43, 1105-1111

NADEAU, E., MESSIER, S., QUESSY, S. 2002. Prevalence and comparison of genetic profiles of *Campylobacter* strains isolated from poultry and sporadic cases of campylobacteriosis in humans. *Journal of Food Protection*, Vol. 65, N°.1, p. 73-78

RIVOAL, K., RAGIMBEAU, C., SALVAT, G., COLIN, P. ERMEL, G. 2005. Genomic diversity of *Campylobacter coli* and *Campylobacter jejuni* isolates recovered from free range broiler farms. Comparison with isolates of various origins. *Applied and Environmental Microbiology*, 2005 Oct 71(10):6216-27.

SIEMER B.L., NIELSEN E.M., ON S.L.W. 2005. Identification and molecular epidemiology of *Campylobacter coli* isolates from humans gastroenteritis, food and animal sources by amplified fragment length polymorphism analysis and Penner serotyping. *Applied and Environnemental Microbiology.*, 2005 Apr;71(4):1953-8.

STEINHAUSEROVA I., CESKOVA J., NEBOLA M. 2002. PCR/Restriction fragment length polymorphism (RFLP) typing of human and poultry *Campylobacter jejuni* strains. *Letters in Applied Microbiology* 34, 354-358

STRUELENS, M.J., Members of the European Study Group on Epidemiological Markers (ESGEM), 1996. Consensus guidelines for appropriate use and evaluation of microbial epidemiologic typing systems. *Clinical Microbiology and Infection*, 2 : 2-11

VELLINGA A., VAN LOOCK F. 2002. The dioxin crisis as experiment to determine poultry-related *Campylobacter* enteritis. *Emergent Infectious Diseases* 8, 19-22

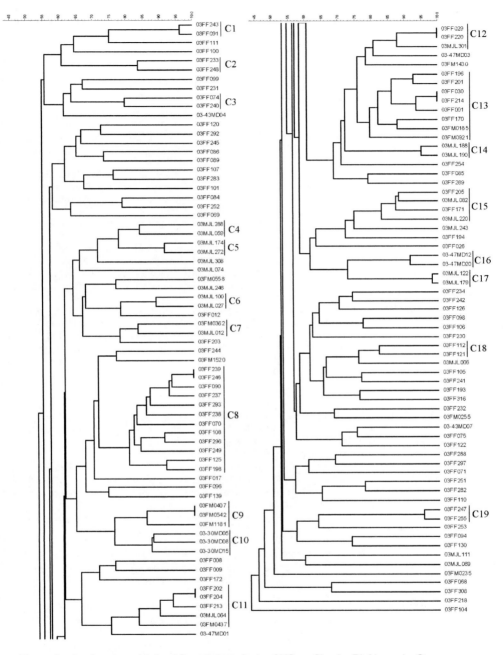

Figure 1 : dendrogram obtained from the analysis of KS profiles by BioNumerics®.
C1 to C19 : clusters defined for 80% of similarity

Acknowlegment

This project was financed by the Brittany Area and the "Syndicat Mixte du Zoopole" from Ploufragan.

Session 6

Colistin: alternative for the treatment of swine colibacillosis with the respect of human health protection

Jaunet H.*[1], Domps P.[1], Deflandre A.[1]

[1]Ceva Santé Animale, BP 126, 33501 Libourne, France
*corresponding author: herve.jaunet@ceva.com

Abstract

From suckling up to slaughter, pigs experience frequently enteritis outbreaks caused by various pathogens, most of them from bacterial origin. Preliminary epidemiological studies have shown that *Escherichia coli* are the most often isolated bacteria during diarrhoeas.

Quinolones and penicillins are the most frequently used treatments when colibacillosis is suspected. Many reports have shown these bacteria became frequently resistant when these antibiotics were massively used. Moreover, many cross resistances were demonstrated in these antibiotic families, leading to a major zootechnical and zoonotic concern.

However, some antibiotics, like colistin, are effective to treat swine enteritis while they are known to involve no or few resistance.

This article discusses some trial results that illustrate the observation of particular mechanisms of resistance of colistin that make it less susceptible to antibiotic resistance. In an experiment on the efficacy and safety of colistin for the treatment of colibacillosis in weaned piglets in an infected environment, no resistant strain of *E. coli* against colistin were isolated on rectal swabs after the treatment.

Colistin is not only clinically effective alternatives to quinolones and penicillins for the treatment of swine colibacillosis but also its use does not involve any antibiotic resistance profile. Colistin is therefore of great interest to overcome the situation of antibioresistance currently established in the intensive swine production after a massive use of the more traditional antibiotics, aminosides and macrolides, that can lead to a major risk for human health.

Introduction

From suckling up to slaughter, pigs experience frequently enteritis outbreaks caused by various pathogens, most of them from bacterial origin. Preliminary epidemiological studies have shown that *Escherichia coli* is the most often isolated bacteria during diarrhoeas.

If quinolones and penicillins are among the most frequently used treatments when colibacillosis is suspected, many reports have shown these bacteria became frequently resistant when these antibiotics were massively used. Moreover, many cross resistances were demonstrated in these antibiotic families, leading to a major zootechnical and zoonotic concern.

However, some antibiotics, like colistin are effective to treat swine enteritis while they are known to involve no or few resistance.

In an experiment on the efficacy and safety of colistin for the treatment of colibacillosis in weaned piglets in an infected environment, some bacteriological analysis are conducted at the end of the clinical study to check the emergence of resistant strains of *E. coli* against colistin.

Material and methods

In a farm with history of post-weaning diarrhoea caused by *E. coli*, piglets weaned between 21 and 28 days of age were randomly split into 2 groups.

When at least 10% of the piglets showed sign of colibacillosis, they were treated (Table 1) through drinking water either with a placebo, either with COLIVET® (Colistin, Ceva Santé Animale, France) for 5 days.

All sick animals (having shown clinical signs of diarrhoea at the beginning or during the experiment) were identified.

Among different criteria to assess efficacy of COLIVET®, some bacteriological analysis were performed on feces collected by rectal swab at the end of the trial (Day 6) on all animals identified as sick during the experiment :
- Isolation and identification of haemolytic *E.coli* strains,
- Antibiogram to evaluate *E. coli* resistance to colistin after treatment.

Table 1: Protocol

	Group A	Group B
Treatment	Placebo	COLIVET®
Daily dosage regimen	0.5 ml/10 kg BW in 2 administrations (Volume equivalent to group B)	100,000 IU colistin/ kg BW in 2 administrations
Duration	5 days	5 days
Monitored parameters on Day 6	1- Isolation and identification of haemolytic strains of E. coli 2- Test of sensitivity (antibiograms)	

Results

Beside the clinical cure rate that was significantly higher in group B (1), the search of haemolytic strains of *E. coli* showed they had completely disappeared in group B while 47.7% of the E. coli strains isolated on animals of group B were haemolytic (Graph 1).
100% of this haemolytic strains isolated in group A were the serotype K88.

In addition, 100% of the *E. coli* strains isolated in both group and tested on antibiograms were all susceptible to colistin.

Graph 1: Number of haemolytic E. coli strains (%) isolated at the end of the treatment (Day 6)

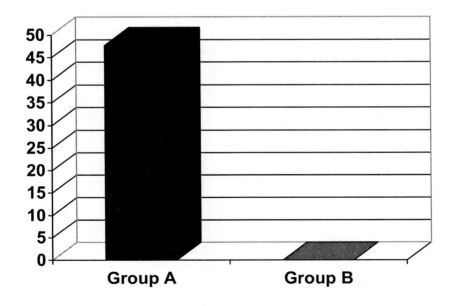

Discussion

This trial showed not only the efficacy of colistin (COLIVET®) at the applied dose for the treatment of post-weaning colibacillosis but also evaluated the risk of development of *E. coli* resistance to this anti-infective after treatment. Its use did not induce any antibiotic resistance profile.

This result confirms that the occurrence of resistance to colistin are very rare, as reported in various studies (2).

Colistin is therefore of great interest to overcome the situation of antibioresistance currently established in intensive swine production after a massive use of more traditional antibiotics (such as quinolones and penicillins) that can lead to a major risk for human health.

References

1. DEFLANDRE, A. et al., 2006. Efficacy evaluation of colistin for the treatment of colibacillosis in weaned piglets. 19th IPVS proceedings, Vol. 2:238

2. SOGAARD, H., 1982. The pharmacodynamics of polymyxin antibiotics with special reference to drug reference liability. J. Vet. Pharmacol. Therap., 5, 219-231

Influence of light exposure on horizontal transmission of *Salmonella typhimurium* in weaned pigs

Edrington, T.*, Callaway, T., Genovese, K., Anderson, R., and Nisbet, D.

USDA-ARS, Food and Feed Safety Research Unit, 2881 F&B Road, College Station, TX, 77845, USA
*Corresponding author: edrington@ffsru.tamu.edu

Abstract

The objective of the following experiment was to examine the effect of light exposure on horizontal transmission of *Salmonella typhimurium* in weaned pigs. Twenty crossbred pigs (average BW = 15 kg) were housed in isolation rooms (10 pigs/room) and randomly assigned to one of two lighting regimes: Low (8 h light, 16 h dark) or High (16 h light, 8 h dark). Pigs were adjusted to their respective lighting treatments for six days and on the seventh day, two randomly selected pigs/room orally inoculated with 5 ml of tryptic soy broth containing 18×10^8 cfu *Salmonella typhimurium*/ml. Rectal swabs were collected from each pig daily over the next eight days for direct plating and plating following 24-h enrichment. On day nine, following inoculation of the seeder pigs, all pigs were euthanized and necropsied. Luminal contents were collected from the ileum, colon, cecum and rectum (quantification and qualification of inoculated strain) and tissue samples collected from the above gut segments as well as the tonsils, ileo-cecal lymph nodes, spleen and liver (qualification only). The number of rectal swabs positive for the inoculation strain of *Salmonella* was higher ($P = 0.003$) in the High lighting treatment (25 versus 5.4% positive) compared to the Low treatment when examined across sampling days. No differences ($P > 0.10$) were observed in the percentage of fecal swabs positive for *Salmonella* following enrichment. Serial dilutions of luminal contents were not statistically different with very few samples containing quantifiable amounts of *Salmonella*. However, following enrichment, the percentage of positive luminal content samples was higher ($P < 0.05$) in the colon and rectum and tended to be higher ($P = 0.07$) in the cecum, in pigs exposed to 16 h of light. The percentage of tissue samples from the ileum and colon that were *Salmonella* positive was also higher ($P < 0.05$) in the High lighting treatment compared to those receiving 8 hours light. No other differences were observed in tissue or luminal contents. Body weights were similar among treatments prior to initiation of lighting treatments and weight gains were not different ($P > 0.10$) among treatments. Results of this research indicate that lighting exposure may play a role in the horizontal transmission of *Salmonella typhimurium* among weaned pigs.

Introduction

Previously research conducted by our laboratory demonstrated light exposure influenced fecal shedding of *E. coli* O157:H7 in feedlot cattle (Edrington et al., 2006) and that melatonin was likely involved in population dynamics of this pathogen (Edrington et al., 2005). The idea that hormones are involved in microbial systems is not a new one as others have demonstrated the involvement of the catecholamines in a bacterial quorum sensing system used by *E. coli* O157:H7 (Sperandio et al., 2003). Melatonin, produced by the pineal gland, plays a role in a number of physiological processes including the control of biological rhythms, immune response, cell proliferation and division (Kvetnoy et al., 2002). Based on our previous research examining the role of light exposure and hormones associated with light exposure on foodborne pathogens, we designed an experiment to examine the effects of lighting on horizontal transmission of *Salmonella typhimurium* in growing pigs. We hypothesize that reducing the amount of light exposure should increase melatonin secretion, thereby stimulating the immune system and reducing the susceptibility of pigs to *Salmonella* transmission and colonization.

Material and methods

Twenty crossbred pigs (barrows and gilts; avg. BW = 15 kg) were purchased locally and transported to our facilities at the Food and Feed Safety Research Unit in College Station, TX. Immediately upon arrival (day 1), piglets were weighed, ear-tagged, and randomly assigned to one of two rooms (10 pigs/room; sex equally distributed across treatments) providing either 8 h light, 16 h dark (Low Light) or 16 h light, 8 h dark (High Light) for the duration of the experimental period. Fecal samples were collected from all pigs on day 1 and plated on brilliant green agar containing novobiocin and naladixic acid (25 and 20 µg/mL, respectively; BGA_{NN}) to screen for the presence of antibiotic resistant wild-type *Salmonella* prior to experimental infection. Feed and water were provided for *ad libitum* consumption throughout the experimental period. On day 7, two randomly selected pigs per room were experimentally-infected with 18×10^{-8} cfu/ml *Salmonella typhimurium* via oral gavage and returned to their respective rooms. The challenge strain of *Salmonella* was made resistant to novobiocin and naladixic acid. Rectal swabs were collected daily for 9 days following inoculation of the seeder pigs and then all pigs were humanely euthanized and tissue and luminal contents collected from the ileum, cecum, colon and rectum. Tissue samples were also collected from the ileocecal lymph nodes, tonsils, spleen, and liver for qualification of *Salmonella*. Body weights were recorded at the beginning and end of the study. Fecal samples and luminal contents (1 g) were serially diluted, plated on BGA_{NN} agar and incubated overnight (24 h, 37° C). Tissue samples were enriched in tetrathionate broth (24 h, 37° C) followed by a second enrichment in Rapport-Vassilidis broth (100 µl in 5 ml, 42° C, 24 h) prior to plating on BGA_{NN} for qualitative determination of the challenge strain. Daily fecal shedding data were analyzed as repeated measures using the MIXED procedure of SAS (SAS Inst. Inc., Cary, NC). Chi-square analysis using the FREQ procedure of SAS, was used to determine influence of treatment on qualitative bacterial enumeration of tissue samples. *Salmonella* populations in luminal contents and BW were subjected to analysis of variance appropriate for a completely randomized design. Least square means were compared using Duncan's mean separation statement when significant ($P < 0.05$) differences detected.

Results

Prior to challenge with the experimental *Salmonella* strain, all rectal swab samples were negative for wild-type *Salmonella* capable of growth on BGA_{NN}. The number of rectal swabs positive for the challenge strain of *Salmonella* in pigs exposed to the seeders is presented by day in Figure 1. *Salmonella* shedding was detected in the rectal swabs of more pigs exposed to 16 h of light during the first six days of the experiment. When averaged across the experimental period, *Salmonella* shedding (as detected by direct plating of rectal swabs) was higher ($P < 0.01$) in pigs exposed to 16 versus 8 h light (Table 1).

Populations of *Salmonella* in the luminal contents of the ileum, cecum, colon and rectum were mostly undetectable or very low following serial dilution and therefore were not analyzed statistically. Table 1 presents the percentage of luminal content samples and tissue samples that were *Salmonella* positive following enrichment. A greater ($P < 0.05$) percentage of colon and rectal contents were *Salmonella* positive in pigs exposed to 16 h of light and a similar trend was observed for cecal ($P = 0.07$), but not ileal contents ($P > 0.10$). A greater ($P < 0.05$) proportion of tissue samples collected from the ileum and colon were *Salmonella* positive in pigs exposed to 16 h of light compared to those receiving 8 h of light exposure.

Body weights were similar among treatments at the beginning and end of the experimental period with pigs in both treatments gaining an average of 4 kg BW (Table 1). Feed intakes were not measured, however no obvious differences were noted with both treatments exhibiting normal, healthy appetites.

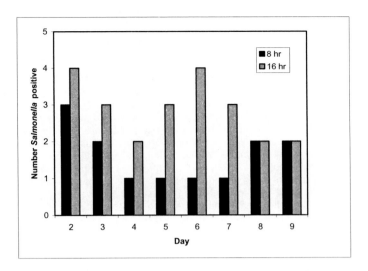

Figure 1. Daily number of rectal swabs positive (following direct plating) for *Salmonella* in feeder pigs exposed to experimentally-infected seeder pigs and maintained under 8 or 16 h light exposure.

Table 1. Percentages of rectal swabs (direct plating), luminal contents and tissue samples positive for *Salmonella,* and BW change in growing pigs, following exposure to seeder pigs experimentally-inoculated with *Salmonella typhimurium* and different levels of light exposure.

| | Light Exposure | | |
	Low (8 h)	High (16 h)	*P*-value
Daily rectal swabs	5.4	25.0	0.003
Luminal contents			
Ileum	42.9	60.0	0.56
Cecum	28.6	75.0	0.07
Colon	57.1	100	0.04
Rectum	28.6	100	0.005
Tissue enrichments			
Cecum	85.7	87.5	0.92
Ileum	57.1	100	0.04
Colon	57.1	100	0.04
Rectum	42.9	50	0.78
Lymph nodes	57.1	62.5	0.83
Spleen	28.6	12.5	0.44
Liver	14.3	12.5	0.92
BW (kg)			
Initial	14.1	15.6	0.26
Final	18.1	19.5	0.52
Change	4.0	3.9	0.93

Discussion

In the United States, virtually all swine production occurs indoors in environmentally controlled buildings, with light exposure closely regulated. In most species, pineal melatonin production increases at the beginning of darkness and peaks most often during the middle of the night (Bubenik 2002). Taken together, controlling light exposure as a means to regulate melatonin production may have practical application. By decreasing light exposure we hoped to increase melatonin concentrations and subsequently reduce *Salmonella* colonization. Results of the current research confirmed our hypothesis that varying light exposure may be a viable means to reduce horizontal transmission of *Salmonella* among growing pigs. Whether the differences observed in this study are a result of increased melatonin, stimulation of the immune system or other factors is unclear. Determination of serum melatonin concentrations is currently in progress. The GIT is a major producer of melatonin (Bubenik 2002) and GIT melatonin has been suggested as playing a protective role in GIT disorders such as irritable bowel syndrome and gastroesophageal reflux disease (Talley 1992), intestinal colic in newborns (Weissbluth and Weissbluth, 1992), and gastric mucosa ulceration by its antioxidant action, immune system stimulation and by fostering microcirculation and epithelial regeneration (Bubenik 2001). Possibly one or a combination of the above melatonin-induced responses might explain the differences observed in the current research.

Conclusions

While the effects observed in the current study are modest, they indicate further research is warranted. Increasing the numbers of animals used and thereby the sensitivity and ability to detect differences, may yield more insight into the effects of lighting exposure and melatonin concentration on pathogen populations. Manipulation of light exposure to growing pigs may provide the producer with an economically viable alternative for reducing *Salmonella* transmission and carriage. Obviously, although no differences were observed for BW gain among treatments in this research, changing lighting in a commercial setting could have substantial effects on performance and will need to be examined further.

References

BUBENIK, G.A., 2001. Localization, physiological significance and possible clinical implication of gastrointestinal melatonin. *Biological Signals and Receptors*, 10, 350-366.

BUBENIK, G.A., 2002. Gastrointestinal melatonin. Localization, function, and clinical relevance. *Digestive Diseases and Sciences*, 47, 2336-2348.

EDRINGTON, T.S., et al. *Effect of exogenous melatonin on fecal shedding of E. coli O157:H7 in naturally-infected beef cattle*. 15th International Congress of Comparative Endocrinology, Boston, MA. May 2005.

EDRINGTON, T.S., et al., 2006. Seasonal shedding of *Escherichia coli* O157:H7 in ruminants: A new hypothesis. *Foodborne Pathogens and Disease* 3, 413-421.

KVETNOY, I.M., et al., 2002. Gastrointestinal melatonin: Cellular identification and biological role. Neuroendocrinology Letters, 23,121-132.

SPERANDIO, V., et al., 2003. Bacteria-host communication: The language of hormones. Proceedings of the National Academy of Science, 100, 8951-8956.

TALLEY, N.J., 1992. Review article: 5-hydroxytryptamine agonists and antagonists in the modulation of gastrointestinal motility and sensation: clinical implications. Alimentary Pharmacology and Therapeutics, 6,273-289.

WEISSBLUTH, L., et al., 1992. Infant colic: the effect of serotonin and melatonin circadian rhythms on the intestinal smooth muscle. Medical Hypotheses 39, 164-167.

The Characterization of Salmonella isolated from Pig Meat in Northern Ireland by PFGE and Antibiotic Resistance Profiles

Egan D. [(1), (2)*], Spence S. [(3)], Dooley J. [(2)], Naughton P. [(1), (2)]

[(1)] Northern Ireland Centre for Food and Health, [(2)] University of Ulster, BT52 1TD, Coleraine, Northern Ireland
[(3)] Agri-Food and Bioscience Institute (AFBI), Newforge Lane, BT9 5PX, Belfast, Northern Ireland
* corresponding author: Egan-D@ulster.ac.uk

Abstract

The emergence of antibiotic resistance and especially multiple antibiotic resistance Salmonella has become a concern for the pig industry throughout the EU. Pig herds and pork are considered as principal reservoirs for the multi-resistant Salmonella type Typhimurium DT104, which has acquired resistance to ampicillin, chloramphenicol, streptomycin, sulphonamides and tetracycline. This resistance pattern is also known as ACSSuT. In this study Porcine Salmonella strains were isolated between December 2005 and December 2006. The strains originated from an abattoir study sampling the 'oyster' cut. The Antimicrobial Resistance Profiles of all Salmonella isolates in this study were determined by disk diffusion tests. Twelve antibiotics were utilized throughout the profiling procedure. Pulsed Field Gel Electrophoresis (PFGE), which is regarded as the "Gold Standard" for the typing and strain identification of Salmonella isolates, was used to determine DNA fingerprints of the Salmonella isolates using the restriction enzyme XbaI (Invitrogen). The fragments were then separated by PFGE in a Chef DR II system (Bio-Rad). This enabled comparison of Salmonella isolated in this study.

Introduction

There are over 2,300 serotypes of Salmonella worldwide (Foley et al., 2001, 2000). In 2005 there were 176 reported cases of human salmonellosis in Northern Ireland. This has been the lowest level reported in the past 12 years, but in 2004 there were three major outbreaks of Salmonella in the Northern Ireland involving S. tyhimurium DT104, S. virchow and S. newport (CDSC, 2006). These outbreaks are a reminder of how important it is to monitor and control Salmonella in our food animals. Over the past five years Salmonella typhimurium has consistently been the second most common cause of human salmonellosis. S. typhimurium type DT104 has also been the most commonly isolated Salmonella on the island of Ireland and in Great Britain (CDSC, 2006)(Randall et al., 2003) (Foley et al., 2000). There were 33 reported cases of Salmonella typhimurium in Northern Ireland alone, of which the most frequently reported phage type was Salmonella typhimurium DT104 (CDSC, 2006). It has been established that multi-drug resistant S. typhimurium DT104 has acquired antibiotic resistance to ampicillin, chloroamphenicol, streptomycin, sulphonamides and tetracycline's. This resistance profile has been abbreviated to ACSSuT resistance (Alban et al., 2001) (Threlfall, 2000). An abattoir study undertaken in the UK in 2003 to determine the carriage of food borne pathogens in food animals reported the prevalence of Salmonella carriage at slaughter was 23.4% for pigs (DEFRA, 2004). Studies in The Netherlands into the distribution of sero- and phage types of Salmonella strains found that the serovar Typhimurium was the predominant serovar in pigs between the years 1984 and 2001 (Duijkeren et al., 2002). This information suggests that pigs may be one of the main reservoirs of Salmonella and more importantly a reservoir of the multi-drug resistant S. typhimurium definitive phage type DT104. Wide spread antibiotic resistance has become a serious public health risk over the last decade and multi antibiotic resistance has been reported in many food borne pathogens including Salmonella. Antibiotic resistance profiles for strains of Salmonella spp. isolated from the pork samples in Northern Ireland were determined using an agar disk diffusion technique.

Session 6

The aim of this research is to:

1. Assess antibiotic resistance among *Salmonella* spp. isolated from pigmeat in Northern.
2. Generate PFGE macro-restriction fingerprints of the *Salmonella* spp. isolated from pig meat in Northern Ireland. PFGE is regarded as the "Gold Standard" for the typing and strain identification of *Salmonella* isolates (Brown *et al.*, 2006) (Tamada *et al.*, 2001).

Material and methods

All *Salmonella* isolates were examined by the "Modified Stoke's Technique" a disc diffusion method testing isolates for sensitivity to 12 antibiotics: Amikacin (AK 30µg), Ampicillin (AMP 10µg), Apramycin (APR 15µg), Cefotaxime (CTX 30µg), Ceftazidime (CAZ 30µg), Chloramphenicol C 10µg, Ciprofloxacin (CIP 1µg), Compound Sulphonamides (S3 300µg), Furazoldidose (FR 15µg), Streptomycin (S 25µg), Sulphamethoxazole/trimethoprim (SXT 25µg) and Tetracycline (TE 10µg). PFGE macrorestriction fingerprint images are created using the PulseNet protocols (CDC, 2006). This molecular technique is used to create an individual DNA fingerprints for all *Salmonella* isolates.

Results

Antibiotic resistance was demonstrated in 29 isolates. The antibiotics with least effect were Tetracycline (74%), Streptomycin (29%), Sulphamethoxazole/trimethoprim (26%), Compound Sulphonamides (26%) and Ampicillin (11%). Two of the *S. typhimurium* isolates displayed the ACSSuT phenotype associated with multidrug resistant *S. typhimurium* DT 104. These two *Salmonella* isolates also displayed resistance to Sulphamethoxazole/trimethoprim.

Discussion

In this study the antibiotic resistance profiles for strains of *Salmonella* spp. isolated from the pork samples in Northern Ireland were determined using the Modified Stokes technique. Comparison of the antibiotic resistance of the salmonellae tested in this project suggested that antibiotic resistance was observed in 76% of all serovars tested. A high resistance to tetracycline (74%) was observed, this result may be attributed to tetracycline being the most common therapeutic drug used by the pork industry (Burch, 2005). The second most common therapeutic antibiotic used in the pig industry a sulphamethoxazole and trimethoprim (Burch, 2005) which also exhibited a high antibiotic resistance profile, with over a quarter (26%) of all the *Salmonella* isolated from pork in Northern Ireland displaying resistance. Ampicillin and apramycin are also commonly used therapeutically throughout the pig industry (Burch, 2005) (DEFRA, 2007). In all 18 of the 19 *S. rissen* isolates were resistant to tetracycline. This result was supported by a Spanish study that concluded that a *S. rissen* isolated from pork harboured the tet(A) resistant gene (Ioana *et al.*, 2006). A high level of intermediate resistance was observed in 6 out of the 12 antibiotics analysed in this study. This may suggest an increase in the number of antibiotic resistant *Salmonella* spp. in years to come. PFGE has become a valuable tool for the epidemiological typing of all *Salmonella* including *S. typhimurium*. The majority of multi-resistant DT104 has the distinctive *Xba*I generated macrorestriction fingerprint that can be detected by PFGE (Threlfall, 2000) (Doran *et al.*, 2005). PFGE images were generated for all the *Salmonella* isolates in this project.

Conclusion

76% of *Salmonella* spp. isolated in this study had resistance to one or more of the antibiotics tested. These results highlight the need for continual monitoring and control of *Salmonella* in food animals.

References

ALBAN, L., OLSEN, A.M., NIELSEN, B,, SORENSEN, R., JENSEN, B. 2001. Qualitative and quantitative risk assessment for human salmonellosis due to multi-resistant *Salmonella typhimurium* DT104 from consumption of Danish dry-cured pork sausages, *Preventative Veterinary Medicine,* (52), 251-265

BROWN, D.J., MATHERS, H., COIA, J.E., 2006. Three years experience of "real time" pulsed field gel electrophoresis and plasmid profiling for molecular typing of *Salmonella enterica* subspecies *enterica* in a national reference laboratory, *International Symposium Salmonella and Salmonellosis.* 99-100

BURCH, D. 2005. Problems with antibiotic resistance in pigs in the UK
http://www.thepigsite.com/articles/1/health-and-welfare/1266/problems-of-antibiotic-resistance-in-pigs-in-the-uk

Centers of Disease Control and Prevention (CDC). 2006. What is the role of PulseNet?
www.cdc.gov/PulseNet/whatis.htm

Communicable Disease Surveillance Centre Northern Ireland (CDSC). 2006.
http://www.cdscni.org.uk/

Department of the Environment Food and Rural Affairs (DEFRA). 2007. *Defra antimicrobial resistance coordination group.*
http://www.vmd.gov.uk/General/DARC/antimibacterials.pdf

DORAN, G., MORRIS, D., O'HARE, C., DELAPPE, N., BRADSHAW, P., CORBETT-FEENEY G., CORMICAN, M. 2005. Cost-effective application of pulsed-field gel electrophoresis to typing of *Salmonella enterica* serovar typhimurium, *Applied Environmental Microbiology,* (71) 8236-8240

FOLEY, B., CORMICAN, M., FITZGERALD, M., MCKEOWN, P., 2000. *Salmonella* in Ireland, 2000. Report: National Disease Surveillance Centre.

FOLEY, B., CORMICAN, M., MCKEOWN. 2001. *Salmonella* in Ireland, 2001. Report: National Disease Surveillance Centre.

IOANA, R., MIGUEL, A.M., TIRUSHET, T., YOLANDA, S. 2006. Detection and characterization of extended-spectrum [beta]-lactamases in *Salmonella enterica* strains of healthy food animals in Spain. *The Journal of Antimicrobial Chemotherapy.* 58 (4) 844

TAMADA, Y., NAKAOKA, Y., NISHIMORI, K, DOI, A., KUMARI, T., UEMURA, N., TANAKA, K., MAKINO, S., SAMESHIMA, T., AKIBA, M., NAKAZAWA, M., UCHIDA, I. 2001. Molecular typing and epidemiological study of *Salmonella enterica* serotype typhimurium isolates from cattle by flourescent amplified-fragment length polymerphism fingerprinting and pulsed-field gel electrophoresis, *Journal of Clinical Microbiology* (3) 1057-1066

THRELFALL, E.J. 2000. Epidemic *Salmonella typhimurium* DT104 – a truly international multiresistant clone, *Journal of Antimicrobial Chemotherapy* (40) 7-10

VAN DUIJKEREN, E., WANNET, W.J.B., HOUWERS, D.J., VAN PELT, W., 2002. Serotype and phage type distribution of *Salmonella* strains isolated from humans, cattle, pigs, and chickens in The Netherlands, *Journal of Clinical Microbiology* (40) 3980-3985

Molecular epidemiology of *Salmonella* Typhimurium DT104 on Ontario swine farms

Farzan, A *[1], Friendship, R [1], Poppe, C [2], Martin, L.[2], Dewey, C [1], Gray, J [3], Funk, J.[4]

[1]Department of Population Medicine, University of Guelph, N1G 2W1 Guelph, ON Canada
[2]OIE Reference Laboratory for Salmonellosis, Public Health Agency of Canada, N1G 3W4 Guelph, ON, Canada
[3]Department of Microbiology, Des Moines University, 3200 Grand Ave., Ryan Hall 272, Des Moines, IA 50312-4198;
[4] National Food Safety and Toxicology Center, Michigan State University, 165 Food Safety and Toxicology Building, East Lansing, MI 48824-1302
*corresponding author: afarzan@uoguelph.ca

Abstract

This study was conducted to investigate the diversity in antimicrobial resistance (AMR), plasmid profiling, and pulsed field gel electrophoresis (PFGE) of 81 *S*. Typhimurium and S. Typhimurium var. Copenhagen DT 104 strains recovered from pig and environmental fecal samples on swine farms in Ontario. No resistance was observed to amoxicillin and clavulanic acid, apramycin, carbadox, cephalothin, ceftriaxone, ceftiofur, cefoxitin, ciprofloxacin, nalidixic acid, trimethoprim, and tobramycin. However, the isolates exhibited resistance against 4 to 10 antimicrobials with most frequent resistance to sulfonamides (Su), ampicillin (A), streptomycin (S), spectinomycin (Sp), chloramphenicol (C), tetracycline (T), and florfenicol (F). Thirteen distinct AMR patterns and 10 different plasmid profiles were determined. 88% of isolates shared the typical resistance pattern "ACSpSSuT". The isolates were classified into 7 and 18 different genotypes by PFGE-*Spe*I and PFGE-*Bln*I, respectively. However, 23 distinct genotypes were generated by means of PFGE-*Spe*I+*Bln*I. The isolates recovered from pig samples in 18 pens on 10 different farms were discriminated from the isolates recovered from environmental samples from these same pens by PFGE. The highest diversity (discriminatory power) was 0.92 (95% CI: 0.88, 0.93) for PFGE while plasmid profiling had the lowest discriminatory power to differentiate the isolates.

Introduction

Multi-drug resistant *Salmonella* Typhimurium DT104 was first reported from a human case in the UK (Threlfall et al., 1994), and since then it has been isolated from humans and other sources including food-producing animals around the world and has become a worldwide public health concern (Helms et al., 2005). *S*. Typhimurium DT104 first demonstrated a typical penta-resistance pattern to (A), (C), (S), (Su), and (T) but it has more recently displayed additional resistance to other antimicrobials. Multi-drug resistant *S*. Typhimurium DT104 has been also the first or second most common *Salmonella* serovar reported from human and food-producing animals in Canada (Michel et al., 2006; Khakhria et al., 1997; Public Health Agency of Canada, 2004), and it has been found to be associated with increased hospitalization, mortality and consequent economic cost (Martin et al., 2004; Travers and Barza, 2002). During the recent past, *S*. Typhimurium DT 104 has been the most frequent strain isolated in epidemiological studies on swine farms (Farzan et al., 2006; Rajic et al, 2005) and in pork slaughterhouses (Perron et al., 2006). However, since *S*. Typhimurium DT 104 isolates might not be distinguished based on phenotypic characteristics, the source of DT 104 infection in humans has remained unknown. For the control purposes it is very important to understand how the DT 104 isolates are introduced, transmitted, and maintained on farms, as well as to have knowledge of the source-specific attributable fraction for human salmonellosis. Therefore, there is a need for molecular techniques to discriminate *S*. Typhimurium DT 104 strains in order to perform further epidemiological investigation. The objective of this study was to investigate the AMR and molecular characteristics of *S*. Typhimurium DT 104 strains recovered from apparently healthy pig on swine farms in Ontario. Also the discriminatory power of AMR testing, plasmid profiling, and PFGE for distinguishing DT 104 strains was studied.

Material and methods

In total 81 isolates, including 74 *S.* Typhimurium Copenhagen, 5 *S.* Typhimurium, and one *S.* I:4,12:i:-) isolates recovered from pig fecal samples on 17 swine farms in Ontario were used in this study. The isolates were phage type DT 104 (42 isolates), DT 104a (23 isolates), and DT 104b (15 isolates). Antimicrobial susceptibility of *Salmonella* isolates was tested by the agar dilution method (Poppe et al., 2001). Plasmid finger printing was performed as explained elsewhere (Poppe et al., 2002). PFGE was performed as described previously by the Centers for Disease Control and Prevention (CDC) (2001). Agarose slices containing whole DNA were digested for 18 hr with, *Spe*I and *Bln*I. Results were analyzed with BioNumerics (Applied Maths, Austin, Texas) using the Dice similarity coefficient. Also the similarity coefficient used to create the dendograms using UPGMA with optimization of 1.5% and 2.5% position tolerance. The Simpson's index (Hunter and Gaston, 1988) was used in order to compare diversity among the *S.* Typhimurium DT 104 isolates and the discriminatory power of the methods.

Results

All isolates were susceptible to amoxicillin and clavulanic acid, apramycin, carbadox, cephalothin, ceftriaxone, ceftiofur, cefoxitin, ciprofloxacin, nalidixic acid, trimethoprim, and tobramycin. However, the isolates exhibited resistance against 4 to 10 antimicrobials with most frequent resistance to Su (100%), A (99%), S (99%), Sp (97%), C (96%), T (93%), and F (93%). Thirteen distinct AMR patterns (R-type 1 to 13) were determined (Table). The typical R-type "ACSpSSuT" was common among 88% of isolates. Except for resistance to (T) which was exhibited by 100% of isolates recovered from environmental samples compared to 88% of "pig samples" ($P < 0.05$), and resistance to gentamicin (G) and nitrofurantoin (Nit), which was exhibited only by the strains isolated from pig samples, there was no significant difference in antimicrobial resistance between DT 104 isolated from pig and environmental samples. The resistance to (K) and (N) was significantly correlated to phage type in that 91% of DT104a phage types displayed resistance to these two antimicrobials compared to 19% and 7% of DT104 and DT 104b phage types, respectively ($P < 0.0001$).

Overall, 10 different plasmid profiles (P-type: a to j) were determined (Table). The 62MDa was statistically associated to resistance against (A), (C), (Sp), (S), (Su), and (T) ($P < 0.0001$) and the 2.1 MDa plasmid seemed to be related with resistance against (K) and (N) ($P < 0.0001$). In fact, all isolates susceptible to (K) and (N) lacked the 2.1MDa plasmid while 93% of isolates resistant to these two antimicrobials had this plasmid. The isolates were classified into 7 and 18 different genotypes by PFGE-*Spe*I and PFGE-*Bln*I, respectively. However, 23 distinct genotypes were generated by means of PFGE-*Spe*I+*Bln*I with Dice similarity index between 35% and 100%. In total, the isolates recovered from pig samples in 18 pens on 10 different farms were discriminated from the isolates recovered from environmental samples from these same pens by PFGE. However, these isolates were identical based on phage type, antimicrobial resistance pattern, and plasmid profile. Only isolates recovered from pig and environmental samples from 2 pens on 2 different farms had identical PFGE patterns. The highest diversity (discriminatory power) was 0.92 (95% CI: 0.88, 0.93) for PFGE followed by 0.67 (95% CI: 0.52, 0.77) and 0.56 (95% CI: 0.37, 0.68) for AMR and plasmid profiling, respectively. Except diversity in antimicrobial resistance, there was no significant difference in diversity among the isolates recovered from pig samples compared to those isolated from environmental samples.

Discussion

We found 88% of isolates shared the typical R-type "ACSpSSuT", which has been frequently reported in association to DT 104 isolates from different sources in Canada (Poppe et al, 2002) and other countries (Ridley and Threlfall, 1998; Baggesen et al, 2000; Foley et al., 2006; Gebreyes and Altier, 2002). The variation in AMR between isolates from different sources might represent

Session 6

some level of true diversity among DT 104 isolates. However, this might be partly due to the between laboratory variation and if this systematic error could be minimized, the S. Typhimurium DT 104 isolates might not be differentiated based on the antimicrobial resistance patterns. The 62MDa which was detected in almost 90% of ACSpSSuT-resistant isolates, has been found to carry the Salmonella plasmid virulence genes (spv), not the antimicrobial resistance genes (Gulig et al., 1987). This indicates a significant correlation between AMR and virulence in S. Typhimurium DT 104 isolates. The plasmid profiling and AMR testing had a lower discriminatory power than PFGE which might be due to the instability of the plasmid and lower diversity in extra chromosomal DNA compared to the chromosomal DNA (Fernandez et al., 2003). We used the difference in at least one band to define a genotype. On the other hand, if one defined genotype as the difference in 5-7 bands, which was suggested by Tenover et al (1997), there would then be only one identical clone of DT104 spreading on 17 Ontario swine farms despite the fact that the isolates belonged to three distinct phage types, 15 plasmid patterns, and 15 antimicrobial resistance patterns. We could discriminate DT 104 isolates with similar phage type, AMR, and plasmid profile into different genotypes by PFGE and find a difference in PFGE-genotypes among the DT 104 isolates recovered from pig samples compared to those isolated from environmental samples. These findings might be used to track the source of DT104 on swine farms and find out different gates by which the multi-resistant DT104 is introduced and maintained on swine farms.

Table: AMR, plasmid patterns, and PFGE of 81 DT104 isolates on swine farms in Ontario

Resistance pattern	No. of isolates	Plasmid pattern (MDa)	No. of isolates	PFGE group	No. of isolates
ACFSpSSuT	43	62, 2.1	50	D	12
ACFKNSpSSuT	21	62	21	H	11
ACGKNSpSSu	3	62, 3.0	3	M	10
ACFKNSpSSu	3	4.8, 2.1	1	E	7
ACFNitSpSSuT	2	50, 40, 38	1	S	6
ACFSpSSuT	2	62, 2.8	1	G	4
ACFKNNitSpSSuT	1	62, 36, 2.1	1	K	4
ACFNitSpSSuT	1	62, 4.0, 2.1	1	T	4
AFKNNitSpSSuT	1	65	1	A	2
ACFSpSSu	1	65,1.4	1	C	2
SpSuSxtTm	1			F	2
ACFKNSSuT	1			I	2
ASSuT	1			L	2
				Q	2
				R	2
				B,J,N,O,P,U,V, W	8

Acknowledgements

We would like to thank the Public Health Agency of Canada, the Ontario Ministry of Agriculture, Food and Rural Affairs, Ontario Pork, the Canadian Research Institute for Food Safety (CRIFS) for the financial and technical support. We also thank the research technicians, and producers who participated in the project, Linda Cole, and Betty Wilkie in OIE Reference Laboratory for serotyping Salmonella isolates.

References

BAGGESEN, D.L., et al., 2000. Characterization of Salmonella enterica serovar Typhimurium DT104 isolated from Denmark and comparison with isolates from Europe and the United States. Journal of Clinical Microbiology, 38 (4), 1581-6.
CDC, 2001. Standardized molecular subtyping of foodborne bacterial pathogens by pulsed-field gel electrophoresis. CDC, Atlanta.

FARZAN, A., et al. 2006. Antimicrobial resistance (AMR) of *Salmonella* spp. on Ontario swine farms, 2004. Proc of the 19th IPVS Congress (Copenhagen, Denmark), Vol 1, pp. 196.

FERNANDEZ, J., et al., 2003. Analysis of molecular epidemiology of Chilean *Salmonella* enterica serotype enteritidis isolates by pulsed-field gel electrophoresis and bacteriophage typing. Journal of Clinical Microbiology, 41 (4), 1617-22.

FOLEY, S.L., et al., 2006. Comparison of subtyping methods for differentiating *Salmonella* enterica serovar Typhimurium isolates obtained from food animal sources. Journal of Clinical Microbiology, 44 (10), 3569-77.

GEBREYES, W.A., et al., 2002. Molecular characterization of multidrug-resistant *Salmonella* enterica subsp. enterica serovar Typhimurium isolates from swine. Journal of Clinical Microbiology, 40 (8), 2813-22.

GULIG, P.A., et al., 1987. Plasmid-associated virulence of *Salmonella* Typhimurium. Infection and Immunity, 55 (12), 2891-901.

HELMS, M., et al., 2005. International *Salmonella* Typhimurium DT104 infections, 1992-2001. Emerg Infect Dis 11, 859-67.

HUNTER, P.R., et al., 1988. Numerical index of the discriminatory ability of typing systems: an application of Simpson's index of diversity. Journal of Clinical Microbiology, 26 (11), 2465-6.

KHAKHRIA, R., et al., 1997. *Salmonella* isolated from humans, animals and other sources in Canada, 1983-92. Epidemiology and Infection, 119 (1), 15-23.

MARTIN, L.J., et al., 2004. Increased burden of illness associated with antimicrobial-resistant *Salmonella* enterica serotype Typhimurium infections. The Journal of Infectious Diseases 189 (3), 377-84.

MICHEI, P., et al., 2006. Regional, seasonal, and antimicrobial resistance distributions of *Salmonella* Typhimurium in Canada: a multi-provincial study. Canadian Journal of Public Health 97 (6), 470-4.

PERRON, G.G., et al., 2007. Genotypic diversity and antimicrobial resistance in asymptomatic *Salmonella* enterica serotype Typhimurium DT104. Infection, Genetics and Evolution, 7 (2), 223-8.

POPPE, C., et al., 2001. Trends in antimicrobial resistance of *Salmonella* isolated from animals, foods of animal origin, and the environment of animal production in Canada, 1994-1997. Microbial Drug Resistance 7 (2), 197-212.

POPPE, C., et al., 2002. Diversity in antimicrobial resistance and other characteristics among *Salmonella* Typhimurium DT104 isolates. Microbial Drug Resistance, 8 (2), 107-22.

PUBLIC HEALTH AGENCY OF CANADA, 2004. Annual Summary Reports 2000-2003. National Enteric Surveillance Program.

RAJIC, A. et al., 2005. Longitudinal study of *Salmonella* species in 90 Alberta swine finishing farms. Veterinary Microbiology 105 (1), 47-56.

RIDLEY, A., et al., 1998. Molecular epidemiology of antibiotic resistance genes in multiresistant epidemic *Salmonella* Typhimurium DT 104. Microbial Drug Resistance, 4 (2), 113-8.

TENOVER, F.C., et al., 1997. How to select and interpret molecular strain typing methods for epidemiological studies of bacterial infections: a review for healthcare epidemiologists. Molecular Typing Working Group of the Society for Healthcare Epidemiology of America. Infection Control and Hospital Epidemiology, 18 (6), 426-39.

THRELFALL, E.J., et al., 1994. Epidemic in cattle and humans of *Salmonella* Typhimurium DT 104 with chromosomally integrated multiple drug resistance. The Veterinary Record, 134 (22), 577.

TRAVERS, K., et al., 2002. Morbidity of infections caused by antimicrobial-resistant bacteria. Clinical Infectious Diseases, 34 (3), S131-4.

Comparison of multidrug resistant *Salmonella* between intensively- and extensively-reared antimicrobial- free (ABF) swine herds

Thakur, S. [1], Tadesse, D. [2], Morrow, M. [3], Gebreyes, W. *[2]

[1] Division of Animal and Food Microbiology, Office of Research, Center for Veterinary Medicine, U. S. Food and Drug Administration, 20708, Laurel, Maryland, USA
[2] Department of Veterinary Preventive Medicine, College of Veterinary Medicine, The Ohio State University, 1920 Coffey Road, 43210, Columbus, Ohio, USA
[3] College of Agriculture and Life Sciences, Department of Animal Sciences, North Carolina State University, 4700 Hillsborough Street, 27606, Raleigh, North Carolina, USA
*corresponding author: gebreyes.1@osu.edu

Abstract

This cross-sectional study was conducted to determine the prevalence and antimicrobial resistance of *Salmonella* species in swine reared in the intensive (indoor) and extensive (outdoor) ABF production systems at farm and slaughter in North Carolina, U.S.A. We sampled a total of 279 pigs at farm (Extensive 107; Intensive 172) and collected 274 carcass swabs (Extensive 124; Intensive 150) at slaughter. *Salmonella* species were tested for their susceptibility against 12 antimicrobial agents using the Kirby-Bauer disk diffusion method. Serogrouping was done using polyvalent and group specific antisera. A total of 400 salmonellae were isolated in this study with a significantly higher *Salmonella* prevalence from the intensive (30%) than the extensive farms (0.9%) ($P <$ 0.001). At slaughter, significantly higher *Salmonella* was isolated at the pre and post-evisceration stages from extensively (29 % pre-evisceration and 33.3 % post-evisceration) than the intensively (2 % pre-evisceration and 6 % post-evisceration) reared swine ($P < 0.001$). The isolates were clustered in six serogroups including B, C, E1, E4, G and R. Highest frequency of antimicrobial resistance was observed against tetracycline (78.5%) and streptomycin (31.5%). A total of 13 antimicrobial resistance patterns were observed including the pentaresistant strains with ampicillin, chloramphenicol, streptomycin, sulfamethoxazole, tetracycline resistance pattern observed only among isolates from the intensive farms (n=28) and all belonged to serogroup B. This study shows that multidrug resistant *Salmonella* are prevalent in ABF production systems despite the absence of antimicrobial selection pressure.

Introduction

Swine have been shown to be colonized with different serovars of *Salmonella* and responsible for outbreaks in humans (Valdezate et al., 2005; Bucholz et al., 2005). Resistance to important antimicrobials has been reported previously in *Salmonella* isolated from swine reared in conventional production systems where antimicrobials are routinely used for growth promotion and treatment (Gebreyes et al., 2004). However, there is scarcity of information on the status of *Salmonella* in pigs that are reared in ABF systems including the outdoor (extensive) and indoor (intensive) systems. The primary objectives of this study were to determine the prevalence and the antimicrobial susceptibility of *Salmonella* isolates from the two types of ABF production systems at farm and slaughter.

Materials and methods

In all the ABF swine production systems included in the current study, no antimicrobials were used post-weaning. Under the extensive ABF system, pigs have free access to the environment and are placed in barricaded fields till slaughter. Pigs in the intensive system are placed in confined barns with concrete slatted floors. We collected approximately 10 grams of fresh faecal samples per rectum with gloved hands from 30 pigs within 48 hours of slaughter. Ten individual carcass swabs were collected at each of three processing stages: pre-evisceration, post-evisceration and post-chill. The extensively reared pigs were slaughtered in a smaller slaughter plant (800 pigs processed/ day) with the carcasses cooled overnight at 1-4°C for 18 hours. Pigs reared under the intensive system were processed in a large scale plant (9,000 pigs/ day) and employed the modern blast chilling method (-30 °C) to cool the carcass surface within two hours. Both the plants processed pigs from the conventional production systems as well. However, to avoid cross-contamination, the plants were cleaned with disinfectant over the weekend and the ABF pigs were processed separate from pigs from conventional system. *Salmonella* isolation from the fecal samples and carcass swabs was done following the method described previously (Gebreyes et al., 2004, 2006). Multiple colonies (up to five) from each positive sample were tested on triple sugar iron (TSI) and urea agar media (Difco, Becton Dickinson) for biochemical testing. Serogrouping was done following the manufacturer recommendations (Statens Serum Institut, Copenhagen, Denmark). Antimicrobial susceptibility testing and MIC determination for 12 antimicrobials were done using the Kirby-Bauer disk diffusion method as described previously (Gebreyes et al., 2006; NCCLS, 2002). We used the χ^2 test (Minitab Inc. PA, USA) to compare the *Salmonella* prevalence, antimicrobial resistance profile and pattern between the two ABF systems. Strength of association between serogroup and resistance pattern as well as type of ABF system was determined using the odds ratio (OR) with a 95 % confidence interval. A value of $P < 0.05$ was considered statistically significant.

Results

The overall *Salmonella* prevalence at the farm and slaughter was 24% and 15% respectively with significantly higher prevalence at farm ($P < 0.001$). A single pig from the extensive ABF farm was positive for *Salmonella* compared to 51 (30%) pigs from the intensive farms. At slaughter, in contrast to the on-farm findings, significantly higher prevalence was found from the extensive production system at both the pre-evisceration (29 %) and post-evisceration (33.3 %) stages ($P < 0.001$). There was no significant difference in prevalence between the two systems at the post-chill level ($P = 0.19$).

Resistance was observed against eight of the 12 antimicrobials tested. Overall, the highest frequency of resistance was observed against tetracycline (78.5%) followed by streptomycin (31.5%) (Table1).

Table 1
Antimicrobial resistance frequency comparison among the *Salmonella* isolates from Extensive and Intensive reared ABF pigs at farm and slaughter.

Production Stage	ABF System	Isolates Tested	Number of isolates resistant to antimicrobials (%) [a]							
			AMP	CHL	STR	SXT	TET	AMX	CEF	KAN
Finishing Farm	Extensive	1	1 (100)	0	1 (100)	0	1 (100)	0	1 (100)	0
	Intensive	226	31 (13.8)	30 (13.2)	64 (28.3)	48 (21.2)	202 (89.3)	2 (0.8)	0	1 (0.4)
Slaughter										
Pre-evisceration	Extensive	43	0	0	24 (55.8)[1]	23 (53.4)[2]	17 (39.5)[3]	0	0	0
	Intensive	5	0	0	0	0	5 (100)	0	0	0
Post-evisceration	Extensive	73	3 (4)	0	24 (32)[1]	22 (29.3)[2]	57 (78)[3]	2 (2.6)	2 (2.6)	0
	Intensive	12	0	0	1 (10)	1 (10)	8 (66)	0	0	0
Post-chill	Extensive	25	4 (16)	0	9 (36)	5 (20)	19 (76)[4]	2 (8)	3 (12)	0
	Intensive	15	0	0	3 (20)	0	5 (33.3)[4]	0	0	0
Total Isolates		400	39 (9.7)	30 (7.5)	126 (31.5)	99 (24.7)	314 (78.5)	6 (1.5)	6 (1.5)	1 (0.2)

Antimicrobials with number of isolates showing resistance against; percentage resistance is shown in parenthesis. AMP, ampicillin; AMX, amoxicillin/clavulanic acid; CEF, cefalotin; CHL, chloramphenicol; KAN, kanamycin; STR, streptomycin; SXT, sulfamethoxazole; TET, tetracycline. For each antimicrobial, figures sharing common numerical superscripts were significantly different at $P < 0.05$ (chi-square test and Fisher's exact two-tailed). No resistance was observed against AMK, amikacin; CRO, ceftriaxone; CIP, ciprofloxacin and GEN, gentamicin at any stage.

On comparing the two ABF systems at slaughter, significantly more isolates were resistant to sulfamethoxazole and tetracycline at all the three stages (pre-evisceration, post-evisceration, post-chill) among the extensively reared pigs ($P < 0.001$). Thirteen different resistance patterns were observed including 10 patterns that were multidrug resistant (MDR; resistant to $\geq$ three antimicrobials). Streptomycin, sulfamethoxazole, tetracycline were the most common MDR pattern (10.5%) and significantly more frequent in isolates from the carcass of extensively reared swine at all the three stages of slaughter ($P < 0.001$). Isolates with the pentaresistant MDR pattern ampicillin, chloramphenicol, streptomycin, sulfamethoxazole, tetracycline were found from the intensive production system (n = 28). Frequency of MDR *Salmonella* isolation at slaughter was significantly higher among the extensively reared pigs ($P < 0.001$). A total of 71 isolates (17.7%) were pansusceptible.

Among the 400 isolates, a total of six serogroups (B, C, E1, E4, G and R) and 13 untypable were found. Serogroup B was the most predominant found in 174 (43.5%) isolates. All the 28 isolates with the pentaresistant MDR pattern ampicillin/chloramphenicol/streptomycin/sulfamethoxazole/tetracycline were clustered under serogroup B. We did not find any association between serogroup B and production system (OR of 1.03; 95 % CI 0.68-1.56). However, serogroup B was strongly associated with tetracycline resistant isolates (n=58) from the intensive farms with an OR of 21.38, 95 % CI (12.10-37.77).

Discussion

This study was conducted to determine the dynamics of *Salmonella* in swine population reared in ABF production system. Only a single pig from the extensive (outdoor) ABF system was positive for *Salmonella* compared to 51 from the intensive farms. Contrary to this finding, the risk of *Salmonella* infection in organic pigs reared outside has been shown to increase if the environment is contaminated (Jensen et al., 2006). Based on our finding, though prevalence on-farm was higher in intensive units, the risk of foodborne infection to humans was higher on products from extensive units as recovery of *Salmonella* from these herds was higher. This finding underscores the significance of periharvest and postharvest cross-contamination. The low level of *Salmonella* isolation from extensive swine farms may be attributed to the fact that these farms were relatively newly established and the environment including soil and water were not exposed to high level of *Salmonella* shedding.

The intensive farms were all-in all-out based system of production with the primary aim of reducing transmission of infectious agents such as *Salmonella* between different batches. However, *Salmonella* has been shown to persist on the farm floor of such systems even after it has been cleaned with disinfectants (Funk et al., 2001). A recent study conducted over a two year period to determine *Salmonella* prevalence in diverse environmental samples reported 57.3% of samples from swine production environment being positive for *Salmonella* (Rodriguez et al., 2006). Therefore, it is possible that the intensive ABF pigs get exposed to *Salmonella* once they are transferred to new farms as reflected in the significantly higher prevalence compared to the extensive farms. In addition, intensively reared pigs originated from a production pyramid system with those of conventional ones and are more closely confined which could help in the vertical and horizontal transmission of the pathogen.

High prevalence at extensive slaughter could be due to the slaughter plant effect. The slaughter houses were not dedicated to ABF farms only and did process swine from conventional herds. Therefore, the potential cross-contamination existed at these slaughterhouses (Beloeil et al., 2004). We isolated *Salmonella* from the post-chill carcasses from both the ABF systems. This indicates that *Salmonella* is able to survive freezing temperatures, be it overnight or blast chilling. Overall, the high frequency of antimicrobial resistance seen in *Salmonella* isolates without antimicrobial selection pressure indicates other sources of transmission. This was clearly illustrated in 13.2 % chloramphenicol resistant isolates from the intensive farms. Chloramphenicol has not been used in any swine production system for the last two decades. This shows that antimicrobial resistant *Salmonella* can exist in the environment even in the absence of selection pressure and have the potential to transmit to other swine over a long period of time. We observed specific resistance patterns that were observed only at slaughter (Table 2). It is possible that these isolates were either not isolated at the farm level, were shed at slaughter under increased stress or were transmitted at lairage. Few MDR patterns were observed only in isolates from the slaughter plant suggesting phenotypic diversity based on the stage of sample processing.

The predominant pentaresistant pattern ampicillin, chloramphenicol, streptomycin, sulfamethoxazole, tetracycline was seen only in isolates from the intensive farm. This pattern is commonly observed among *S.* Typhimurium DT 104 strains which are commonly associated with the presence of Class I integrons. Previous studies conducted in the same geographical region on conventional farms have shown this pattern to be associated with *S.* Typhimurium DT 104 phage types (Gebreyes et al., 2004, 2006). It is not possible to conclude whether these isolates are DT 104 since we did not serotype and phage type them. However, *S.* Typhimurium DT 104 belongs to serogroup B and all the 28 isolates with this pattern in this study were clustered under serogroup B. It is therefore possible that these isolates are *S.* Typhimurium DT 104.

Conclusions

This study shows that MDR *Salmonella* strains exist in the ABF production system both at farm and slaughter even in the absence of the antimicrobial selection pressure and has important implications from food safety perspective. We recommend conducting detailed epidemiological based studies to determine the role played by environment in dissemination of *Salmonella* in swine reared in ABF production systems.

References

BELOEIL, P., et al., 2004. Impact of *Salmonella* status of market-age pigs and the pre-slaughter process on *Salmonella* caecal contamination at slaughter. Veterinary Research, 35 (5), 513-530.

BUCHOLZ, U., et al., 2005. An outbreak of *Salmonella* Muenchen in Germany associated with raw pork meat. Journal of Food Protection, 68 (2), 273-276.

FUNK. J., et al., 2001. Risk factors associated with *Salmonella* enterica prevalence in three-site swine production systems in North Carolina, USA. Berliner und Münchener tierärztliche Wochenschrift. 114 (9-10), 335-358.

GEBREYES, W., et al., 2004. Trends in antimicrobial resistance, phage types and integrons among *Salmonella* serotypes from pigs, 1997–2000. Journal of Antimicrobial Chemotherapy, 53 (6), 997-1003.

GEBREYES, W., et al., 2006. Comparison of Prevalence, Antimicrobial Resistance and Occurrence of Multidrug-Resistant *Salmonella* in Antimicrobial-Free and Conventional Pig Production. Journal of Food Protection, 69, 743-748.

JENSEN, A., et al., 2006. Survival and transmission of *Salmonella* enterica Serovar Typhimurium in an outdoor organic pig farming environment. Applied Environmental Microbiology 72 (3), 1833-1842.

NATIONAL COMMITTEE FOR CLINICAL LABORATORY STANDARDS, 2002. Performance Standards for Antimicrobial Disk and Dilution Susceptibility Tests for Bacteria Isolated from Animals- Second Edition: Approved Standard M31-A2. NCCLS, Wayne, PA, USA, 2002.

RODRIGUEZ, A., et al., 2006. Prevalence of *Salmonella* in diverse environmental farm samples. Journal of Food Protection, 69 (11), 2576-2580.

VALDEZATE, S., et a., 2005. *Salmonella* Derby clonal spread from pork. Emerging Infectious Diseases, 11 (5), 694-698.

Session 6

Inhibition of *Salmonella* Typhimurium by medium chain fatty acids in an in vitro simulation of the porcine caecum

Goris, J.[1], Dierick, N.[2], Herman, L.[1], Heyndrickx, M.[1], Messens, W.*[1]

[1]Institute for Agricultural and Fisheries Research (ILVO), Technology and Food Unit, Brusselsesteenweg 370, 9090 Melle, Belgium
[2]Ghent University, Department of Animal Production, Laboratory for Animal Nutrition and Animal Product Quality (LANUPRO), Proefhoevestraat 10, 9090 Melle, Belgium
*corresponding author: winy.messens@ilvo.vlaanderen.be

Abstract

To lower the contamination of pork meat with *Salmonella*, feed additives such as medium chain fatty acids (MCFA's) can be applied at the primary production level. An *in vitro* continuous culture system, simulating the porcine caecum, was developed for investigating the effect of MCFAs on the pig intestinal microbial community. The system was monitored by plating on selective media, 16S rDNA PCR denaturing gradient gel electrophoresis (PCR-DGGE) and HPLC analysis of fermentation products. In a simulation of the porcine caecum without MCFA treatment, with *Salmonella* Typhimurium added after stabilization of the microbial community, the strain could establish itself at a stable population size of about 5 log cfu/ml. The effect of selected MCFAs was observed from all monitored parameters and depended on chain length and concentration applied. At a dose of 15 mM, caproate and caprinate did not show any pronounced effect, while a clear *Salmonella* inhibiting effect (3 log units reduction) was found for caprylate. Doubling the caprylate dose did not result in enhanced *Salmonella* inhibition.

Introduction

In Belgium, 49.4% of the human salmonellosis cases were identified as Salmonella Typhimurium (STM) in 2006. STM is the most common serovar isolated from pigs. In pig stables, complex Salmonella contamination cycles occur, in which Salmonella-free animals are contaminated through direct or indirect contact with faeces of infected animals. Therefore, if the gastrointestinal tract (GIT) of the pig can be made an unfavorable environment for Salmonella growth e.g. through the use of feed additives, this will result in decreased pathogen shedding, which at its turn will reduce carcass contamination. This will attribute to reduce the prevalence of human salmonellosis cases due to consumption of pork meat.

MCFAs show some promising beneficial effects for use as these feed additives have been postulated to modulate the porcine gut bacterial ecosystem, resulting in healthier gut mucosa and improved zootechnical parameters of piglets (Dierick et al., 2002a,2002b,2003). For caprylate, an inhibitory effect on Salmonella was obtained in standard bacteriological media (Skrivanova et al., 2004). Although MCFA preparations are commercially available and are used in practice, their effect on the gut bacterial ecosystem remains largely unknown.

In this study, the effect of selected MCFA's on the GIT microbial community was evaluated, with special emphasis on their inhibitory activity against STM. For this purpose, an in vitro model of the porcine caecum based on continuous culture was developed and validated.

Material and methods

The fiber- and mucin containing incubation medium for porcine caecum simulation was as described by Dierick et al. (2002a), with minor modifications. The medium was acidified to pH 2 and kept at 4°C and under constant agitation to prevent precipitation of the fiber. Caecal contents were used as inoculum; directly after slaughter, caecal contents from 12 pigs (originating from 7 different farms) were pooled, homogenized and divided in aliquots of 15 ml to which 15% glycerol was added and frozen at -80°C. Equipment for continuous culture consisted of a BioFlo110 unit (New Brunswick Scientific) with a 1.3 l fermentor vessel. Fresh medium was added via a peristaltic pump at a constant rate of about 1.8 ml/min and spent culture liquid was wasted at the same rate to maintain a constant working volume of 500 ml (i.e. 4.6 h retention time). Temperature was kept at 37°C and pH at 6.2. The culture was constantly agitated at 300 rpm. Anaerobic conditions were maintained by flushing the headspace of the vessel with 20 ml/min of 20% CO_2+80% N_2. After inoculation with pooled caecal contents (15 ml), the fermentor was operated in batch mode for 24 h. Continuous culture was then started by switching on the peristaltic pumps. Ten ml of an overnight grown STM strain in Müller-Hinton broth was added after the switch to continuous culture. The strain was originally isolated from pig colon (Botteldoorn et al., 2003) and belongs to phage type DT104. After several days, MCFAs (caproate, caprylate, caprinate) were added to the medium at a final concentration of 15 and 30 mM. Bacterial populations were monitored by plating on general and selective media: Reinforced Clostridial Medium, Tryptone Soy Agar, de Man, Rogosa & Sharpe medium, MTPY (Rada and Petr, 2000), Slanetz and Bartley medium, MacConkey agar and Xylose-Lysine-Desoxycholate agar (all from Oxoid) for enumeration of total anaerobes, total aerobes, lactic acid bacteria, bifidobacteria, streptococci, coliforms and Salmonella, respectively. Cultivation-independent community analysis was done by PCR-DGGE, as described by Boon et al. (2000). Organic acids formed during fermentation were quantified by HPLC analysis using an Aminex HPX-87H column (BioRad) as described previously (Van Coillie et al., in press). MCFAs were purchased from Sigma as sodium salts.

Results

In a simulation of the porcine caecum without MCFA addition (control experiment), with the STM strain added after stabilization of the microbial community, the strain could establish itself at a stable population size of about 5 log cfu/ml for at least 13 days. Before addition of the STM strain, no black colonies on XLD agar were observed.
The effect of different MCFAs was first evaluated at a final concentration of 15 mM in the in vitro caecum model, after an ecological equilibrium was obtained. In one experiment, the STM strain was added immediately after switching to continuous culture. After seven days of operation, the incubation medium stock was replaced by a stock containing 15 mM caproate and this treatment was maintained until the end of the experiment. No clear effects on the microbial counts or produced organic acids were observed. From day 6 on, Salmonella counts remain relatively steady at around 104-105 cfu/ml. When this experiment was performed with caprinate, results were similar. However, for reasons of solubility, a lower dose than 15 mM was evaluated. Gradual replacement of the regular medium in the fermentor vessel by caprylate-containing medium resulted in a rapid decrease of the Salmonella population from 6.8 to 2.2 log cfu/ml (Fig. 1).

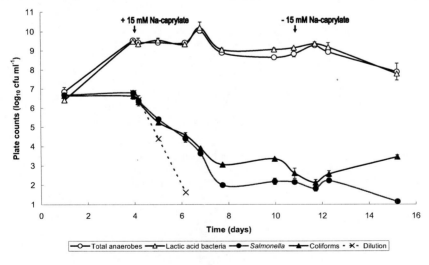

Fig. 1: Effect of 15 mM caprylate on the in vitro porcine caecum simulation. Bacterial populations as determined by plating. The start of continuous culture, addition and withdrawal of caprylate are indicated.

When after 13 days of operation, the feed was switched back to medium without caprylate, no concomitant increase of the Salmonella population was observed. Propionic and butyric acid production decreased after addition of caprylate, while lactic acid production increased. The effect on formic acid production was less clear. Acetic acid concentrations seemed to gradually increase in the course of the caecum simulations. When caprylate treatment was stopped, propionic, butyric and lactic acid production returned to their initial levels. Cultivation-independent microbial community analysis via PCR-DGGE for this experiment is shown in Fig. 2. At day 1 (directly after the start of continuous culture) equilibrium is obviously not reached yet, as shown by a pattern quite distinct from all other. From day 3 on, DGGE profiles are all quite similar, indicating a relatively stable ecosystem. During caprylate treatment, one band seems to be more prominent in the DGGE pattern. A treatment with 30 mM caprylate resulted in very similar findings as obtained with 15 mM caprylate.

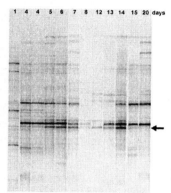

Fig. 2: PCR-DGGE patterns of the microbial populations in the experiment described in Fig. 1. The arrow indicates the position of a band that seems to be correlated with the presence of caprylate in the incubation medium.

Discussion

The use of an in vitro model facilitates the study of the GIT microbial community and circumvents animal to animal variation encountered in slaughter trials. Existing continuous culture GIT models are often operated on particle free medium with a chemical composition that is quite distinct from actual chymus. In our model, we tried to mimic the physiological conditions in the porcine caecum as closely as possible through the use of a cellulose (non-digestible fiber) and mucin (glycoproteins isolated from the porcine stomach)-containing incubation medium. The caecum was specifically selected, because a pronounced proliferation of several bacterial groups occurs in this compartment of the GIT. The rationale is that, if Salmonella outgrowth can be suppressed here, this would result in reduced excretion via the faeces.

The original pooled caecal contents inoculum evolved in the in vitro model within 2-3 days after the onset of continuous culture into a relatively stable microbial ecosystem with stable fermentation characteristics, as observed from plating results, PCR-DGGE analysis and organic acid production. When operated under normal conditions (i.e. after stabilization and without MCFA added), average population densities of total anaerobic bacteria, lactic acid bacteria, coliforms and streptococci were 8.7, 8.6, 5.8 and 7.6 log cfu/ml, respectively. Organic acid concentrations were 0.7, 11, 94, 14 and 26 mM for lactic, formic, acetic, propionic and butyric acid, respectively. Bacterial counts as well as organic acid concentrations in our model corresponded well with literature data available for the porcine caecum (Mikkelsen et al., 2004). Since Salmonella was not detected prior to the deliberate inoculation with the STM strain, the in vitro simulation can be used to specifically monitor the behavior of the inoculated strain via enumeration on XLD agar plates.

The effect of MCFA on Salmonella and other microbial populations was investigated in the in vitro caecum model. At a dose of 15 mM, caproate and caprinate did not show any pronounced effect, while a clear Salmonella inhibiting effect was found for caprylate. Earlier, Skrivanova et al. (2004) found caprylic acid to be the only Salmonella-inhibiting compound among the 15 fatty acids tested in liquid cultures. Doubling the caprylate dose did not result in enhanced Salmonella inhibition in our experiments. The observed effect does not seem to be Salmonella-specific, since the coliform counts showed a similar inhibition in response to caprylate.

Conclusion

Our study indicates that caprylate addition to the medium at a dose of 15 mM, corresponding to about 1% in a feed, has potential for reducing Salmonella excretion in pig faeces.

Acknowledgements
The authors wish to thank the Institute for the Promotion of Innovation by Science and Technology in Flanders for financial support and Jessy Claeys for excellent technical assistance.

References
BOON, N., GORIS, J., DE VOS, P., VERSTRAETE, W., and TOP, E.M., 2000. Bioaugmentation of activated sludge by an indigenous 3-chloroaniline-degrading Comamonas testosteroni strain, I2gfp. Applied and Environmental Microbiology, 66, 2906-2913.

BOTTELDOORN, N., HEYNDRICKX, M., RIJPENS, N., GRIJSPEERDT, K., and HERMAN, L., 2003. Salmonella on pig carcasses: positive pigs and cross contamination in the slaughterhouse. Journal of Applied Microbiology, 95, 891-903.

DIERICK, N.A., DECUYPERE, J.A., and DEGEYTER, I., 2003. The combined use of whole Cuphea seeds containing medium chain fatty acids and an exogenous lipase in piglet nutrition. Archives of Animal Nutrition, 57:49-63.

DIERICK, N.A., DECUYPERE, J.A., MOLLY, K., VAN BEEK, E., and VANDERBEKE, E., 2002a. The combined use of triacylglycerols (TAGs) containing medium chain fatty acids (MCFAs) and exogenous lipolytic enzymes as an alternative for nutritional antibiotics in piglet nutrition. I. In vitro screening of the release of MCFAs from selected fat sources by selected exogenous lipolytic enzymes under simulated pig gastric conditions and their effects on the gut flora of piglets. Livestock Production Science, 75, 129-142.

DIERICK, N.A., DECUYPERE, J.A., MOLLY, K., VAN BEEK, E., and VANDERBEKE, E., 2002b. The combined use of triacylglycerols (TAGs) containing medium chain fatty acids (MCFAs) and exogenous lipolytic enzymes as an alternative for nutritional antibiotics in piglet nutrition. II. In vivo release of MCFAs in gastric cannulated and slaughtered piglets by endogenous and exogenous lipases; effects on the luminal gut flora and growth performance. Livestock Production Science, 76, 1-16.

MIKKELSEN, L.L., NAUGHTON, P.J., HEDEMANN, M.S., and JENSEN, B.B., 2004. Effects of physical properties of feed on microbial ecology and survival of Salmonella enterica serovar Typhimurium in the pig gastrointestinal tract. Applied and Environmental Microbiology, 70, 3485-1492.

RADA, V., and PETR, J., 2000. A new selective medium for the isolation of glucose non-fermenting bifidobacteria from hen caeca. Journal of Microbiological Methods, 43, 127-132.

SKRIVANOVA, E., SAVKA, O.G. e MAROUNEK, M., 2004. In vitro effect of C2-C18 fatty acids on Salmonellas. Folia Microbiologica (Praha), 49, 199-202.

Van Coillie, E., Goris, J., Cleenwerck, I., Grijspeerdt, K., Botteldoorn, N., Van Immerseel, F., De Buck, J., Vancanneyt, M., Swings, J., Herman, L., and Heyndrickx, M. Identification of lactobacilli isolated from the cloaca and vagina of laying hens and characterization for potential use as probiotics to control Salmonella Enteritidis. Journal of Applied Microbiology, in press.

Session 6

2005 French "*Salmonella*" Network data on antimicrobial resistance in the swine channels

Granier, S. A.*,   Danan, C., Moury, F.,Fremy, S., Oudart, C., Piquet, C.,Pires-Gomes, C., Brisabois, A.

Bacterial Characterization and Epidemiology Unit, AFSSA-Lerqap, 23 avenue du General de Gaulle, 94706 Maisons-Alfort Cedex, France.
* *corresponding author : s.granier@afssa.fr*

Abstract

The "*Salmonella*" Network is gathering, on a voluntary participation scheme, from approximately 150 public and private laboratories disseminated throughout France, *Salmonella* strains and/or epidemiological information. Those non-human *Salmonella* strains are isolated either from animal health and production or food, feed and the Environment sectors.

Thus, in 2005, a total of 527 isolations from the swine channels were reported. The top 5 prevalent serotypes were : Typhimurium, Derby, Manhattan, Infantis and Kedougou. Two-hundred and ninety five strains were received at the laboratory and, after double clearance, 185 strains were tested for their antimicrobial resistance against 16 antibiotics by the disk diffusion method. Twenty-one strains were associated to the animal health and production sector and 164 to the food sector.

No noticeable differences in antimicrobial resistance phenotype has been detected between the two sectors. No wild type (fully susceptible) strain has been detected. The rate of beta-lactamase detection (ampicillin resistant strains) was under 25% and no resistance to third generation cephalosporin has been detected. Fluoroquinolone resistance was approximately of 2%. The ASCTSu phenotype (resistance to ampicillin, streptomycin, chloramphenicol, tetracycline and sulphonamides) has been detected in 14% of the *Salmonella* spp strains; 24 out of those 26 strains were identified as *S.* Typhimurium.

All those figures are stable if compared to 2004 data. Those data should now be combined with the one of other food animal channels and human origin in a perspective of risk assessment studies for public health management.

Introduction

The "*Salmonella*" network is now 10 years old. Over those past years, it has been collecting either strains or epidemiological data of *Salmonella* isolates from non-human sources throughout France. "Non-human" wording gathers 4 sectors : animal health and production, food, feed and the Environment. This collection is based on a voluntary participation scheme.

For the year 2005, the Network has gathered a total amount of 13673 data. After double clearance 3041 strains have been tested for their antimicrobial resistance phenotypes.

Concerning the swine channels for the year 2005, a total of 527 isolations were reported. The top 5 prevalent serotypes were : Typhimurium, Derby, Manhattan, Infantis and Kedougou. Two-hundred and ninety five strains were received at the laboratory and, after double clearance, 185 strains were tested for their antimicrobial resistance phenotype.

Twenty-one strains were associated to the animal health and production sector and 164 to the food sector.

Material and Methods

Strain selection : double clearance has been performed on the collection as follows : all salmonella strains of the same serotype, isolated from the same product type, in the same department, by the same laboratory and provided in the same parcel were considered as doubles. In this case, only one strain was taken into account.

Antimicrobial susceptibility tests have been performed by the disc diffusion method as recommended by the Antibiogram Comity of the French Society for Microbiology (http://www.sfm.asso.fr/). 16 antimicrobials have been tested : Ampicillin, Amoxicillin + clavulanic acid, cephalothin, cefotaxime, ceftazidime, chloramphenicol, tetracycline, streptomycin, kanamycin, gentamicin, sulfamides, cotrimoxazole, nalidixic acid, ofloxacin, enrofloxacin, colistin. Automatic reading have been performed by OSIRIS system (BioRad).

Results

No noticeable differences in antimicrobial resistance phenotype has been detected between the animal health and production sector and the food sector. No wild type (fully susceptible) strain has been detected.

The rate of beta-lactamase detection (ampicillin resistant strains) was under 25% and no resistance to third generation cephalosporin has been detected. Fluoroquinolone resistance was approximately of 2%.

The ASCTSu phenotype (resistance to ampicillin, streptomycin, chloramphenicol, tetracycline and sulphonamides, characteristic of *S.* Typhimurium DT104) has been detected in 14% of the *Salmonella* spp strains; 24 out of those 26 strains were identified as *S.* Typhimurium.

Conclusion and Discussion

All those figures are stable if compared to 2004 data.

Those data should now be combined with the one of other food animal channels and human origin in a perspective of risk assessment studies for public health management.

Antimicrobial susceptibility of S. aureus strains isolated from a ham plant in France.

Granier, S. A.*, De Buyser, M.-L., Dorwling-Carter, M., Kerouanton, A., Brisabois, A.

Bacterial Characterization and Epidemiology Unit, AFSSA-Lerqap, 23 avenue du General de Gaulle, 94706 Maisons-Alfort Cedex, France.
* corresponding author : s.granier@afssa.fr

Abstract

As MRSA (methicillin resistant *Staphylococcus aureus*) were recently isolated from pigs in the Netherlands (1), we were incited to evaluate the resistance gene circulation inside *S. aureus* strains isolated from swine food products.

A study, build in 2002, established the biodiversity of *S. aureus* isolates originated from a single raw ham industrial unit located in western France. Biotypes and pulsotypes from 106 isolates from raw material ham, end product and plant environment were determined. Isolates split up into 7 biotypes and about forty pulsotypes, which delineated a total of 23 sub-groups with 80% of homology and indicated the presence of numerous *S. aureus* strains in the plant.

Antimicrobial resistance phenotype was determined by the disk diffusion method for 40 strains representing 39 distinct pulsotypes.

Forty three percent of those strains presented no resistance at all to the 16 antimicrobials tested. Seventeen percent were resistant to at least two antibiotics. On the other hand, 12 strains were suspected to display a reduced susceptibility to glycopeptides and eight strains to be MRSA. The cross check of those suspected phenotypes is currently being performed as recommended by the Antibiogram Comity of the French Society for Microbiology.

Anyway, resistance rates observed in this study seem to be considerably lower than the one observed for human clinical *S. aureus* strains.

Introduction

As MRSA (methicillin resistant *Staphylococcus aureus*) were recently isolated from pigs in the Netherlands (1), we were incited to evaluate the resistance gene circulation inside *S. aureus* strains isolated from swine food products.

A study, build in 2002, established the biodiversity of *S. aureus* isolates originated from a single raw ham industrial unit located in western France. The strain collection constituted during this study was also studied for its antimicrobial resistance profiles.

Material and Methods

Bacterial identification and **Biotyping** has been performed as previously described (2).

Pulsed field electrophoresis has been performed as previously described (3).

Antimicrobial susceptibility tests have been performed by the disc diffusion method as recommended by the Antibiogram Comity of the French Society for Microbiology (http://www.sfm.asso.fr/). 16 antimicrobials have been tested : Penicillline G, Cefoxitin, Fosfomycin, Teicoplanine, Erythromycin, Lincomycin, Tetracyclin, Fusidic acid, Pristinamycin, Neomycin, Gentamicin, streptomycin, ciprofloxacin, Sulfamides, Cotrimoxazole, Rifampicin.

MRSA confirmation was performed, as recommended by the Antibiogram Comity of the French Society for Microbiology, by PCR detection of *mecA* gene as previously described Predari et al. (4)

GISA confirmation have been performed as recommended by the Antibiogram Comity of the French Society for Microbiology (http://www.sfm.asso.fr/), using MH agar plates containing 5µg/mL of Teicoplanine.

Results
Strain typing :
Biotypes and pulsotypes from 106 isolates from raw material ham, end product and plant environment were determined. Isolates split up into 7 biotypes and about forty pulsotypes, which delineated a total of 23 sub-groups with 80% of homology and indicated the presence of numerous *S. aureus* strains in the plant.

Antimicrobial resistance determination :
Forty three percent of those strains presented no resistance at all to the 16 antimicrobials tested. Seventeen percent were resistant to at least two antibiotics.

On the other hand, 12 strains were suspected to display a reduced susceptibility to glycopeptides and eight strains to be MRSA. After further investigations **no MRSA** have been detected. As a matter of fact, mec A gene has not been detected in any of the strains displaying a reduce diameter to cefoxitin. Gisa investigation is still in progress.

Conclusion and Discussion

Resistance rates observed in this study seems to be considerably lower than the one observed usually for human isolates.
In respect to the recent public health concern in the Netherlands, it is absolutely clear that a study in a unique plant is not enough to assess the low level of resistance observed.
The *S. aureus* strains associated to the swine channels should be now further investigated from the farm to the fork.

References

(1) Huijsdens et al., 2006, *12th ISSSI*, Maastricht, NL.
(2) Kerouanton, A., J. A. Hennekinne, et al. (2007). Characterization of *Staphylococcus aureus* strains associated with food poisoning outbreaks in France. *Int J Food Microbiol.,* Epub ahead of print.
(3) Hennekinne, J. A., A. Kerouanton, et al. (2003). Discrimination of Staphylococcus aureus biotypes by pulsed-field gel electrophoresis of DNA macro-restriction fragments. *J Appl Microbiol*, **94**(2): 321-9.
(4) Predari, S. C., M. Ligozzi, et al. (1991). Genotypic identification of methicillin-resistant coagulase-negative staphylococci by polymerase chain reaction. *Antimicrob Agents Chemother* **35**(12): 2568-73.

Session 6

SPI-2 of *Salmonella* Typhimurium is not necessary for long term colonization of pigs

Haesebrouck F.*[1], Boyen. F.[1], Volf J.[1], Botteldoorn N.[2], Adriaensen C. [3], Hernalsteens J.-P.[3], Ducatelle R.[1], Van Immerseel F.[1], Heyndrickx M.[2], Pasmans F. [1]

[1] Department of Pathology, Bacteriology and Avian Diseases, Faculty of Veterinary Medicine, Ghent University, Merelbeke, Belgium.
[2] Center for Agricultural Research Ghent, Department for Animal Product Quality and Transformation Technology, Brusselsesteenweg 370, 9090 Melle, Belgium
[3] Viral Genetics Laboratory, Faculty of Sciences, Vrije Universiteit Brussel, Pleinlaan 2, 1050 Brussels, Belgium.
*corresponding author: freddy.haesebrouck@UGent.be

Abstract

Unravelling the role of *Salmonella* virulence factors in the porcine host could greatly contribute to the development of control measures such as vaccination. The virulence genes located on the *Salmonella* Pathogenicity Island 2 (SPI-2) are indispensable for the induction of systemic disease and persistence in BALB/c mice. The role of this pathogenicity island in the pathogenesis of *Salmonella* Typhimurium infections in pigs is not documented. Therefore, in the present study, the interactions of a porcine field strain of *Salmonella* Typhimurium and a non-polar isogenic SPI-2 (*ΔssrA*) deletion mutant were compared in both *in vitro* and *in vivo* models. The *ssrA* mutant strain displayed decreased SPI-2 expression levels *in vitro* and was attenuated in a mouse model after oral inoculation. No difference was seen in the expression of SPI-1 related virulence genes. Through flowcytometric analysis, the *ssrA* mutant strain was found to be moderately attenuated in intracellular replication in porcine macrophages *in vitro*. In an infection experiment, 2 groups of 10 piglets were orally inoculated with the wild type or the *ssrA* mutant strain. The infection of the animals inoculated with the *ssrA* mutant strain followed a similar course as the animals infected with the wild type strain. At days 5 and 28 post inoculation, the animals of both groups were infected to the same extent in the gut and gut-associated lymphoid tissue, as well as in the internal organs. These results suggest that SPI-2 of *Salmonella* Typhimurium may not contribute to the colonization of pigs to the same extent as it contributes to the colonization of BALB/c mice.

Introduction

Salmonella Typhimurium is the most frequently isolated serotype from pigs and pork (Botteldoorn et al, 2003). Carrier pigs can shed *Salmonella* for at least 28 weeks (Wood et al., 1989) and pose an important threat to animal and human health. The mechanism of this carrier state is not yet known. The virulence genes located on the *Salmonella* Pathogenicity Island 1 (SPI-1) are of great importance in the invasion of intestinal cells in various animal species (Zhou and Galan, 2001). The virulence genes located on the *Salmonella* Pathogenicity Island 2 (SPI-2) are indispensable for the induction of systemic disease and persistence in mice after both oral and intraperitoneal inoculation (Shea et al., 1999). The role of this pathogenicity island in the pathogenesis of *Salmonella* Typhimurium infections in pigs is not documented. It was the aim of the present study to determine the importance of SPI-2 in the colonization and persistence in pigs.

Material and Methods

Salmonella Typhimurium strain MB2486, isolated from a pig in Belgium, was used as the wild type strain (WT) to construct the *hilA* and *ssrA* deletion mutants, according to the one step inactivation method with lambda red for use in *Salmonella* Typhimurium (Boyen et al., 2006). The intracellular expression of the *ssrA* gene and of the SPI-2 effector gene *sifB* was quantified by real-time reverse transcription PCR, using SYBR Green, as described before (Botteldoorn et al., 2006). The SPI-1 expression level (*hilA*, coding for the major regulating protein of SPI-1; *sipA*, coding for a

SPI-1 effector protein) was measured in a late logarithmic culture in Luria-Bertani broth, also by real-time reverse transcription PCR, using SYBR Green. *In vitro* invasion and cytotoxicity assays were conducted on porcine pulmonary alveolar macrophages (PAM), as described before (Boyen et al., 2006). BALB/c mice (6 weeks old, 2 groups of 8 animals) and conventional *Salmonella* negative piglets (5 weeks old, 2 groups of 10 animals) were inoculated orally with approximately 10^8 and 10^7 colony forming units respectively of the wild type strain or the *ssrA* deletion mutant. As a control group, 4 animals were sham-inoculated with PBS. Four mice of each *Salmonella* inoculated group were humanely euthanized at day 1 and day 4 post inoculation. Five piglets of each *Salmonella* inoculated group were humanely euthanized at day 5 and day 28 post inoculation. Control animals were euthanized together with the last group of *Salmonella* inoculated animals. Internal organs of mice and piglets as well as faecal samples collected daily from the piglets were examined for the presence of *Salmonella* by means of plating ten-fold dilutions on Brilliant Green Agar. To assess the intramacrophagal replication deficit of the *ssrA* mutant strain, PAM were inoculated with the wild type strain or the *ssrA* mutant strain carrying the green fluorescent protein (GFP) expressing plasmid pFPV25.1. After 30 min incubation at 37°C under 5% CO_2, the flasks were washed and fresh medium supplemented with 100 µg/ml gentamicin was added. After an additional 60 min incubation, cells were released using trypsin and maintained on ice, protected from light until use (T=0h). To assess intracellular growth, fresh medium supplemented with 15 µg/ml gentamicin was added and at 6 hours after inoculation, cells were released and handled as described (T=6h). Flow cytometry measurements were made using a FACScanto™ cytometer. Macrophages were discriminated from bacteria and debris based on forward (FSC) and side (SSC) light scatter. GFP fluorescence was recorded using the FL1 channel (emission wave length: 515-545 nm).

Results

The complete coding sequence of the *ssrA* gene was deleted, which was confirmed with PCR and sequencing of the surrounding area. The *ssrA* mutant strain displayed no intracellular *ssrA* expression and a decreased *sifB* expression level *in vitro*. The expression levels of 2 SPI-1 encoded proteins were not altered (Table 1).

Table 1: Relative expression levels of SPI-1 and SPI-2 related genes in the wild type, the ssrA mutant and the hilA mutant strain

Relative expression	Wild type	*ssrA* mutant	*hilA* mutant
Intracellular SPI-2 expression	ssrA: 1.0 sifB: 10.4	ssrA: 0.0 sifB: 2.6	Not Determined
SPI-1 expression in a logarithmic culture	hilA : 1.00 sipA : 0.10	hilA : 1.06 sipA : 0.07	hilA : 0.00 sipA : 0.01

In the murine *in vivo* model, the caeca of both groups of mice were colonized to the same extent 1 day post inoculation. Four days after inoculation, however, the internal organs of the mice inoculated with the *ssrA* mutant strain were colonized with a 100-fold reduction compared to the wild type strain (Table 2). The infection of the piglets inoculated with the *ssrA* mutant strain followed a similar course compared to the piglets infected with the wild type strain. The daily faecal excretion levels of both strains were not significantly different (p>0.05; non-parametric Kruskal-Wallis test; Table 3). At days 5 and 28 post inoculation, the animals of both groups were infected to the same extent in the gut and gut-associated lymphoid tissue, as well as in the internal organs (Table 3). All sham inoculated animals, mice as well as piglets, remained negative for *Salmonella* throughout the experiment.

Table 2: The colonization of different organs of BALB/c mice with the Salmonella Typhimurium wild type or ssrA mutant strain (log(10) cfu/gram tissue +/- sd)

Organ	Wild type	ssrA mutant
Caecum day 1	5.88 (+/- 1.13)	6.39 (+/- 1.20)
Caecum day 4	4.91 (+/- 1.43)	3.96 (+/- 0.39)
Liver day 4	3.02 (+/- 1.27)	1.03 (+/- 1.20)
Spleen day 4	3.79 (0.98)	1.37 (+/- 1.64)

Table 3: The colonization of different organs of piglets with the Salmonella Typhimurium wild type and ssrA mutant strain (* frequency = number of pigs positive/number of pigs inoculated)

	Tissue	Wild type strain		ssrA mutant strain	
		Frequency*	Log_{10} cfu g^{-1} ± sd	Frequency*	Log_{10} cfu g^{-1} ± sd
Day 5 pi	Tonsil	3/5	1.33 ± 1.57	4/5	3.14 ± 1.77
	Liver	4/5	0.8 ± 0.45	2/5	0.4 ± 0.55
	Spleen	2/5	0.58 ± 0.86	1/5	0.2 ± 0.45
	Ileocecal ln.	5/5	3.69 ± 0.62	5/5	4.04 ± 0.79
	Ileum	5/5	4.92 ± 0.52	5/5	5.17 ± 1.39
Day 28 pi	Tonsil	2/5	0.76 ± 1.23	4/5	1.88 ± 1.74
	Liver	0/5	0 ± 0	1/5	0.2 ± 0.45
	Spleen	0/5	0 ± 0	2/5	0.4 ± 0.55
	Ileocecal ln.	4/5	1.32 ± 1.34	4/5	0.98 ± 0.68
	Ileum	5/5	1.72 ± 1.61	5/5	1.18 ± 0.41

Six hours after inoculation, the mean and median green fluorescence of PAM inoculated with the GFP expressing ssrA mutant strain was significantly lower compared to PAM inoculated with the GFP expressing wild type strain (Table 4).

Table 4: Mean and median fluorescent values of infected porcine macrophages at 0 h and 6 h after inoculation. The average values of 3 independent experiments ± sem are shown. Both the mean and median fluorescent values of the PAM infected with the ssrA mutant strain at 6 h pi were statistically significant lower (*; $p < 0.05$) than the values of the PAM infected with the wild type strain.

	Mean fluorescence ± sd			Median fluorescent value ± sd	
	0h	6h		0h	6h
WT	1165 ± 110	3236 ± 488		831 ± 26	1862 ± 189
ΔssrA	1073 ± 124	1594 ± 298*		801 ± 57	1042 ± 166*

Discussion

In NRAMP$^{-/-}$ laboratory mice, SPI-2 has an important and highly documented impact on the pathogenesis of *Salmonella* Typhimurium infections, particularly on the systemic phase of the infection (Hensel et al., 1998; Shea et al., 1999), but also on the enteric phase (Coburn et al., 2005). Data describing the importance of SPI-2 in the systemic phase of infection obtained in food producing animals are less extensive. For host-restricted or host adapted serotypes (ex. Pullorum, Dublin, Choleraesuis) SPI-2 is a prerequisite for virulence and colonization in their respective hosts (Dunyak et al., 1997; Bispham et al., 2001; Jones et al., 2001; Wigley et al., 2002). However, for broad range serotypes, such as Enteritidis and Typhimurium, the role of SPI-2 in the pathogenesis of *Salmonella* infections in food producing animals is less described and less straightforward (Tsolis et al., 1999; Zhao et al., 2002; Morgan et al., 2004). In accordance, our results suggest that SPI-2 of *Salmonella* Typhimurium may not contribute to persistence in pigs to the same extend as it does in laboratory mice.

Conclusions

In conclusion, we have shown that a *ssrA* deletion mutant of a porcine field strain of *Salmonella* Typhimurium, that is attenuated *in vitro* and in an *in vivo* mouse model, is still capable of colonizing pigs and establishing a long term persistent infection. This work contributes to the recent insights in the serotype- and host-dependent pathogenesis of *Salmonella* infections in food producing animals.

This work was supported by the Institute for the Promotion of Innovation by Science and Technology in Flanders and by the Research Foundation-Flanders.

References

BISPHAM et al., 2000. *Salmonella* pathogenicity island 2 influences both systemic salmonellosis and *Salmonella*-induced enteritis in calves, Infection and Immunity, 69, 367-377.
BOTTELDOORN et al., 2003. *Salmonella* on pig carcasses: positive pigs and cross contamination in the slaughterhouse. Journal of Applied Microbiology, 95, 891-903.
BOTTELDOORN et al., 2006. Real-time reverse transcription PCR for the quantification of the *mntH* expression of *Salmonella enterica* as a function of growth phase and phagosome-like conditions. Journal of Microbiological Methods, 66, 125-135.
BOYEN et al., 2006. Role of SPI-1 in the interactions of *Salmonella* Typhimurium with porcine macrophages. Veterinary Microbiology, 113, 35-44.
COBURN et al.,2005. *Salmonella* Typhimurium pathogenicity island 2 is necessary for complete virulence in a mouse model of infectious enterocolitis. Infection and Immunity, 73, 3219-3227.
DUNYAK et al.,1997. Identification of *Salmonella* Pathogenicity Island 2 (SPI2) genes in Salmonella choleraesuis using signature-tagged mutagenesis. Abstr 97th ASM congress, 76.
HENSEL et al., 1998. Genes encoding putative effector proteins of the type III secretion system of *Salmonella* pathogenicity island 2 are required for bacterial virulence and proliferation in macrophages. Molecular Microbiology, 30, 163-174.
JONES et al., 2001. Salmonella enterica serovar Gallinarum requires the Salmonella pathogenicity island 2 type III secretion system but not the Salmonella pathogenicity island 1 type III secretion system for virulence in chickens. Infection and Immunity, 69, 5471-5476.
MORGAN et al., 2004. Identification of host-specific colonization factors of Salmonella enterica serovar Typhimurium, Molecular Microbiology, 54, 994-1010.
SHEA et al., 1999. Influence of the *Salmonella* typhimurium pathogenicity island 2 type III secretion system on bacterial growth in the mouse. Infection and Immunity, 67, 213-219.
TSOLIS et al., 1999. Contribution of *Salmonella* typhimurium virulence factors to diarrheal disease in calves. Infection and Immunity, 67, 4879-4885.
WIGLEY et al., 2002. Salmonella Pullorum requires the *Salmonella* pathogenicity island 2 type III secretion system for virulence and carriage in the chicken. Avian Pathology, 31, 501-506.

Session 6

WOOD et al., 1989. Distribution of persistent *Salmonella* typhimurium infection in internal organs of swine. The American Journal of Veterinary Research, 50, 1015-1021.

ZHAO et al., 2002. Identification of genes affecting *Salmonella* enterica serovar enteritidis infection of chicken macrophages. Infection and Immunity, 70, 5319-5321.

ZHOU & GALAN, 2001. *Salmonella* entry into host cells: the work in concert of type III secreted effector proteins. Microbes and Infection, 3, 1293-1298.

A model to visualize attachment and survival of Yersinia enterocolitica in superficial and deep structures of pig carcasses before and after decontamination

Krag, R.[1,2][*], Olsen, J.E. [2] and Aabo, S.[1]

[1]National Food Institute, Technical University of Denmark, Moerkhoej Bygade 19, DK-2860 Soeborg, Denmark.
[2]Department of Veterinary Pathobiology, Faculty of Life Sciences, University of Copenhagen, Groennegårdsvej 15, st, DK-1807 Frederiksberg C, Denmark.
*Corresponding author: rkxyz@food.dtu.dk

Abstract

At the slaughterhouses carcasses are often contaminated with pathogenic bacteria. End point carcass decontamination is found to be effective to reduce the number of bacteria on the carcasses and may improve food safety. Attachment of bacteria to the carcass surface is the first step in contamination of the final food product, and understanding of the adherence and survival of bacteria in relation decontamination is essential for the development of effective decontamination methods.

Yesinia enterocolitica is used as a model organism for studying attachment of pathogenic bacteria to superficial and deep structures of pig carcasses. A plasmid, constitutively expressing green fluorescent protein (GFP), has been transformed into wildtype Yersinia enterocolitica serotype O:3. Pig skin, inoculated with GFP-Yersinia enterocolitica, were cryosectioned horizontally and vertically and visualization of bacteria attachment to the skin surfaces was done by Confocal Scanning Laser Microscopy. By this technique it was possible to determine the three dimensional location of the bacteria on skin and meat structures (e.g. crevices, hair follicles and sweat glands). In order to visualize the effect of decontamination, a method, which is able to discriminate between live and dead bacteria, is essential. By staining the decontaminated pig skin, inoculated with GFP-Yersinia enterocolitica, with CTC (5-cyano-2,3-ditolyl tetrazolium chloride) BacLight[TM] RedoxSensor[TM] CTC Viability Kit (Molecular Probes), a red fluorescent formazan (CTF) will be formed intracellular in active respiring (live) bacteria, while dead bacteria will continue to be green fluorescent.

Introduction

During slaughter and subsequence handling at the slaughterhouses the carcasses are potentially contaminated with pathogenic bacteria from faeces and oral cavity of the pig. Yersinia enterocolitica is a foodborne pathogen isolated from pig, and in Denmark serotype O:3 is the predominant isolate (Anonymous, 2000). In this study Yersinia enterocolitica serotype O:3 were used as a model organism for pathogenic bacteria on pig carcasses.

Most decontamination methods focus on washing and sanitizing of the carcass. It is found to be effective to reduce the number of bacteria, but do not provide a total elimination of the foodborne pathogens. The bacterial reduction may depend on the structures bacteria attached to and to which depth bacteria are able to penetrate. A common approach to determinate bacteria attachment is by culturing (Benito et al., 1997;Bouttier et al., 1997;Conner and Bilgili, 1994). However, culturing methods are not able to determinate which surface sites the bacteria attach to or to quantify the proportion of the bacterial populations left at the surfaces after detachment. An alternative method, Confocal Scanning Laser Microscopy (CSLM), has been used to study bacterial attachment and is promising for studying in situ localization of bacteria in various kinds of food e.g. beef and pork, chicken skin, apples and carrots (Auty et al., 2005;Burnett and Beuchat, 2002;Chantarapanont et al., 2003;Delaquis et al., 1992). CSLM provide the opportunity to visualize the location of the bacteria, at multiple depths without or little mechanical sectioning of the sample. Furthermore CSLM make it possible, simultaneously, to visualize both the bacteria and the tissue

Session 6

structures, which makes it possible to study the localization of the bacteria as a part of the bacteria- tissue interactions (Auty et al., 2005). Another potential advantage of microscopy is the ability to differentiate between live and dead cells by certain staining techniques. Some drawbacks are, however, that the laser illumination can be destructive to viable tissue and fluorophore photobleaching. Furthermore the autofluorescence of the skin will result in some background (varez-Roman et al., 2004).

Attachment of bacteria to meat and skin surfaces of both poultry and beef has been investigated by CSLM, while only a few studies deal with attachment of *Yersinia enterocolitica* to pork meat and skin. Chantarapanont et al. (2003) used CSLM and *gfp*-marked *campylobacter* for studying location of bacteria on chicken skin. The study showed that after rinsing; bacteria were primarily located in crevices and inside the feather follicles (in a water phase), and in the water film on the surface. In addition more bacteria where located in the feather follicles compared to the channels at same depth. Bacteria were found more numerous in the upper 10µm compared to 30µm-50µm depth. Water absorption by chicken skin has been shown to cause capillary-size channels to open in the surface layer, leading to entrapment of bacteria in cleft, crevice and feather follicles by capillary forces. Even after very thorough decontamination, bacteria were shown to retain in water film in feather follicles (Kim et al., 1996;Thomas and McMeekin, 1982;Thomas and McMeekin, 1984). Kim et al. (1996) found, that the location of *Salmonella* was similar to the location of *Campylobacter* in the study of Chantarapanont et al. (2003), but showed bacteria in a depth of 140µ. Similar studies have not been done on pig skin.

Material and methods

Bacteria strain, plasmid and inoculum preparation
A wildtype *Yersinia enterocolitica* serotype 0:3 isolated from a pig carcass was used. A plasmid, constitutively expressing green fluorescent protein (GFP) pFPV25.1Gm, was constructed by inserting a gentamycin resistance cassette from pUCGM in HindIII site at pFVP25.1 (Valdivia and Falkow, 1997). The plasmid was transformed into wildtype *Yersinia enterocolitica* serotype O:3 in order to get a GFP-*Yersinia enterocolitica*. GFP-*Yersinia enterocolitica* was maintained on brain heart infusion (BHI) agar (Oxoid) with a supplement of 30µg of gentamycin per ml. Inoculum was prepared by growing cells in BHI Broth (Oxoid) at 37°C for 18 hours. Bacteria were wash one time and resuspended in PBS with 0.1% glucoses.
CTC staining
CTC (5-cyano-2,3-ditolyl tetrazolium chloride) BacLight[TM] RedoxSensor[TM] CTC Viability Kit (Molecular Probes) was used at a final concentration of 5mM. CTC produces a red fluorescent formazan (CTF) intracellular in active respirating bacteria (Chantarapanont et at., 2003)
Pig skin
Fresh porcine skin from the jaw was obtained from a slaughterhouse (Danish Crown, Ringsted, Denmark). Skin was cut in pieces at 1.5X2.5 cm and heated for 10 minutes at 37°C. Afterwards skin was placed in sterile Petri dishes. Four artificial crevices were made by needle pricks. The skin was inoculated with $1X10^7$ CFU/cm² and left at room temperature for 30 min to allow attachment. Afterwards, skin was rinsed with 30 ml 0.9% Sodium Chloride using a 60 ml syringe and 50 µl of a 5mM CTC was applied for 30 min at room temperature in the dark, either directly to the GFP-*Yersinia enterocolitica*-inoculated skin or after decontamination with 80°C hot water for 5 or 15 seconds. Vertically and horizontally 40 µm skin sections were made by using a cryostat at -25°C (Leica CM1900). The cryostat blade was swabbed with ethanol to sterile the blade after each section and sections was mounted on microscopy slides (Superfrost+, Menzel Gläser, Germany)
Visualization of GFP-Yersinia on pig skin
A TCS SP1 three channel confocal scanning laser microscope (Leica Microsystems Heidelberg GmbH, Germany) equipped with an argon laser (458 nm, 476 nm, 488 nm and 514 nm wavelength) and two HeNe lasers (543 nm and 633 nm wavelength) was used for microscopic observation. The observations were done on both cryosectioned and non-sectioned skin before and after rinsing and decontamination the skin. The microscope was equipped with a X5 objective (numerical aperture = 0.12, Leica), a X10 objective (numerical aperture = 0.40, Leica) and a X63 oil immersion objective (numerical aperture = 1.32, Leica). A laser excitation at 458 and 488 nm was used and the emitted light (495 to 530 nm) was assigned a green colour for the GFP image;

and a 610 - 670 nm emission was assigned a red color for the CTC-formazan image. The Leica Confocal Software TCS SP/NT version 2.5.1347 was used to process images.

Results

GFP-*Yersinia enterocolitica,* applied to the skin surface in a liquid suspension, were moving on the surface and drawn into hair follicles and cleft by capillary like forces (Figure 1). Skin-cryosections showed bacteria located on the surfaces with a tendency of bacteria to cluster in rough areas and clefts. Bacteria were located in high numbers in hair follicles (Figure 2), artificial crevices and other deep structures of the skin and meat surface. After removing reversible attached bacteria by rinsing, fewer bacteria was identified on superficial layers. Most bacteria was then found in deeper tissue structures, and as illustrated on Figure 3 and 4 more bacteria was found in the needle pricks compared to hair follicles. It appeared that decontamination; by 80°C water rinsing, of the GFP-*Yersinia enterocolitica* inoculated surface, reduced the number of bacteria in relation to surface structure, but it did not eliminate all bacteria. After decontamination bacteria was found especially in relation to deeper structure at the skin surfaces. To discriminate between live and dead bacteria after decontamination, skin surfaces were stained with CTC. Preliminary results indicate that the main population of bacteria present after decontamination are dead bacteria both superficially and in the depth of the skin.

   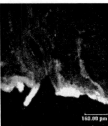

Figure 1: CSLM. Hairfollicle with GFP-*Yersinia enterocolitica* moving on the surface. X10

Figure 2: CSLM. Vertically cryosectioned pig skin. Hair follicle with GFP-*Yersinia enterocolitica.* Before rinsing the skin. X63

Figure 3: CSLM. Vertically cryosectioned pig skin. Artificial crevice with GFP-*Yersinia enterocolitica.* After rinsing the skin. X5

Figure 4: CSLM. Vertically cryosectioned pig skin. Hair follicle. After rinsing the skin. X10

Discussion

CSLM is a useful tool for studying bacteria location on surfaces and deeper structure of pig skin. Bacteria applied to the skin surface in a liquid suspension are entrapped in cleft, needle pricks and hair follicles by capillary like forces like earlier studies had described for bacteria on chicken skin (Chantarapanont et al., 2003). Studying of cryosectioned pig skin with irreversible attached bacteria showed bacteria mostly located in deeper structures on the surface which support the theory that capillary forces drawn bacteria to the depth and can made it difficult to effective decontamination by rinsing the surface. More bacteria were found in needle prick compared to hair follicles. This is in contrast to studies made on chicken skin where feather follicles were the primary reservoir for bacteria in the depth. The explanation could be that pig hair follicles are thinner than feather follicles. The present method do not determine which tissues bacteria attach to, however, by combining the present technique with tissue specific staining visualization of tissue specific attachment may be possible.

Conclusion

CSLM of cryosectioned pig skin inoculated with GFP-*Yersinia enterocolitica* is a potential useful method to determine the attachment site and the depth of location of bacteria on pork meat. Bacteria were found both superficially located, in clefts, in needle pricks and in hair follicles. Capillary-like forces seems to be responsible for the location of bacteria in these places. After decontamination bacteria were fewer in number and were preferentially located in deeper tissue structures. Staining decontaminated surfaces with CTC is a potential method for discrimination of live and dead bacteria; however, the applicability of the method has still to be investigated. Future studies may include investigation for specific attachment sites and/or bacterial factors essential for the attachment.

References

ANONYMOUS. Annual report on Zoonoses in Denmark 1999. 2000. Ref Type: Report

AUTY M., DUFFY G., O'BEIRNE D., MCGOVERN A., GLEESON E., JORDAN K., 2005. In situ localization of Escherichia coli O157 : H7 in food by confocal scanning laser microscopy. Journal of Food Protection 68(3), 482-486.

BENITO Y., PIN C., LUISA M., GARCIA M.L., SELGAS M.D., CASAS C., 1997. Cell surface hydrophobicity and attachment of pathogenic and spoilage bacteria to meat surfaces. Meat science 45(4), 419-425.

BOUTTIER S., LINXE C., NTSAMA C., MORGANT G., BELLON-FONTAINE M.N., FOURNIAT J., 1997. Attachment of Salmonella choleraesuis choleraesuis to beef muscle and adipose tissues. Journal of Food Protection 60(1), 16-22.

BURNETT S.L., BEUCHAT L.R., 2002. Comparison of methods for fluorescent detection of viable, dead, and total Escherichia coli O157:H7 cells in suspensions and on apples using confocal scanning laser microscopy following treatment with sanitizers. International Journal of Food Microbiology 74(1-2), 37-45.

CHANTARAPANONT W., BERRANG M., FRANK J.F., 2003. Direct microscopic observation and viability determination of Campylobacter jejuni on chicken skin. Journal of Food Protection 66(12), 2222-2230.

CONNER D.E., BILGILI S.F., 1994. Skin Attachment Model for Improved Laboratory Evaluation of Potential Carcass Disinfectants for Their Efficacy Against Salmonella Attached to Broiler Skin. Journal of Food Protection 57(8), 684-688.

DELAQUIS P.J., GARIEPY C., MONTPETIT D., 1992. Confocal scanning laser microscopy of porcine muscle colonized by meat spoilage bacteria. Food Microbiology 9, 147-153.

KIM K.Y., FRANK J.F., CRAVEN S.E., 1996. Three-dimensional visualization of Salmonella attachment to poultry skin using confocal scanning laser microscopy. Letters in Applied Microbiology 22(4), 280-282.

THOMAS C.J., MCMEEKIN T.A., 1984. Effect of water uptake by poultry tissues on contamination by bacteria during immersion in bacterial suspensions. Journal of Food Protection 47(5), 398-402.

THOMAS C.J., MCMEEKIN T.A., 1982. Effect of water immersion on the microtopography of the skin of chicken carcasses. Journal of the Science of Food and Agriculture 33, 549-554.

VALDIVIA R.H., FALKOW S., 1997. Fluorescence-based isolation of bacterial genes expressed within host cells. Science 277(5334), 2007-2011.

VAREZ-ROMAN R., NAIK A., KALIA Y.N., FESSI H., GUY R.H., 2004. Visualization of skin penetration using confocal laser scanning microscopy. European Journal of Pharmaceutics and Biopharmaceutics 58(2), 301-316.

The influence of fatty acids on the expression of virulence genes of *Salmonella* Typhimurium and the colonization of pigs

Lardon, I*., Boyen, F., Ducatelle, R., Van Immerseel, F., Haesebrouck, F., Pasmans, F.

Department of Pathology, Bacteriology and Poultry Diseases, Faculty of Veterinary Medicine, Ghent University, B-9820 Merelbeke, Belgium
*corresponding author: Isabelle.Lardon@UGent.be

Abstract

Salmonella Typhimurium infections in pigs are a major source of human foodborne salmonellosis. To reduce the number of infected pigs, acidified feed or drinking water can be administrated. A study was carried out to evaluate the use of short-chain fatty acids (SCFA) and medium-chain fatty acids (MCFA) for the control of *Salmonella* Typhimurium infections in pigs. Short-chain fatty acids formate, acetate, propionate and butyrate (pH 6, osm 600, conc 10mM) and medium-chain fatty acids caproic, caprylic and capric acid (pH6, osm 600, conc 2mM) were used.
First, the effect of these acids on the invasion rate of *Salmonella* Typhimurium in porcine intestinal epithelial cells and on the expression of the virulence genes *fimA* and *hilA* was assessed *in vitro*.
The expression of *hilA* was decreased by butyrate, propionate, caproic and caprylic acid. Caproic and caprylic acid also decreased the expression of *fimA*. Contact of bacteria with butyrate, caprylic and caproic acid decreased invasion in porcine intestinal epithelial cells *in vitro*.
Since butyrate and caprylic acid resulted in the strongest attenuation of *Salmonella in vitro*, these acids were further tested in an *in vivo* trial. In order to reach the large intestine, the tested acids were coated. Coated butyrate showed a strong reduction of *Salmonella* excretion (approximately 100 times lower on average compared to the control group). Coated caprylic acid also showed a reduction of shedding (10 times lower on average compared to the control group). Neither butyrate nor caprylic acid decreased the colonization of the tonsils by *Salmonella* Typhimurium. In conclusion, coated butyrate lowers the shedding of *Salmonella* Typhimurium by pigs. Coated butyrate and, to a lesser extent coated caprylic acid, decreased the colonization of the intestinal tract but did not affect the colonization of tonsils.

Introduction

Salmonella Typhimurium is known as one of the most important zoonotic organisms and causes many cases of human salmonellosis each year worldwide. An important source of salmonellosis in humans is the consumption of *Salmonella* contaminated pork.
The use of SCFA and/or MCFA could contribute to control the colonization of pigs by *Salmonella* Typhimurium by influencing the expression of virulence genes, such as *fimA* (2) and *hilA* (1). Both genes are essential for an efficient colonization in pigs by *Salmonella* Typhimurium (1, 2).
In this study, the influence of SCFA and MCFA on the expression of the virulence genes *fimA* and *hilA* and the invasion rate of *Salmonella* Typhimurium in porcine intestinal epithelial cells was determined *in vitro*. Those acids which attenuated the *Salmonella* Typhimurium strain to the highest degree were selected for an *in vivo* trial. In this trial, the effect of the selected acids on the colonization of pigs by *Salmonella* Typhimurium was determined.

Material and methods

1) Influence of SCFA and MCFA on the expression of the *Salmonella* Typhimurium virulence genes *hilA* and *fimA*
Salmonella Typhimurium strain MB 2486, isolated from a pig stool sample was used in all *in vitro* experiments. Strains of MB 2486 carrying plasmids containing a *fimA-luxCDABE* or a *hilA-luxCDABE* transcriptional fusion were used to determine the gene expression. These transcriptional fusions result in light production when *fimA* or *hilA* is transcribed. Therefore, light production can be a marker for gene expression (4).

Session 6

Light production was measured in an Ascent luminometer. The expression of *fimA* and *hilA* was compared between *Salmonella* Typhimurium grown in LB-broth with or without acid supplementation. Osmolarity and pH were corrected after the addition of the acids.

Short-chain fatty acids formate, acetate, propionate and butyrate (pH 6, osm 600, conc 10mM) and medium-chain fatty acids caproic, caprylic and capric acid (pH6, osm 600, conc 2mM) were used.

2) Influence of SCFA and MCFA on invasion of *Salmonella* Typhimurium in porcine intestinal epithelial cells

The effect of SCFA and MCFA on the invasion capacity of *Salmonella* Typhimurium in a porcine intestinal epithelial cell line (IPI-2I) was determined in a standard gentamicin protection assay.

3) Effect of SCFA and MCFA on the colonization of pigs by *Salmonella* Typhimurium

This study was conducted on 24 weaned piglets, from a serologically negative breeding herd, that were negative for *Salmonella* at faecal sampling. The piglets were randomly divided into 3 groups: a control group, a group that received feed supplemented with coated butyrate (10 mM) and a group that received feed supplemented with coated caprylic acid (2mM). Acids were coated to avoid absorption in the proximal intestine. Twelve days after the piglets were given the different feeds, the animals were orally inoculated with 5×10^7 CFU of an invasive nalidixic acid resistant derivative of *Salmonella* Typhimurium strain MB 2486. Fecal samples were collected daily and animals were monitored for clinical disease signs. At 4 days post infection (p.i.), all piglets were euthanized and samples were taken from various organs for bacteriological analysis.

Results

1) Influence of SCFA and MCFA on the expression of the *Salmonella* Typhimurium virulence genes *hilA* and *fimA*

Salmonella Typhimurium grown in LB-broth containing butyrate, propionate, caproic or caprylic acid showed a significantly (p<0.01) lower expression of the gene *hilA* compared to *Salmonella* Typhimurium grown in plain LB-broth. The expression of *fimA* was significantly (p<0.01) lower when bacteria were grown in LB-broth containing caproic or caprylic acid compared to *Salmonella* Typhimurium grown in LB-broth without acid supplementation. These results are summarized in figures 1 and 2.

Figure 1: Expression of *hilA* of *Salmonella* Typhimurium grown in acidified LB-broth relative to *Salmonella* Typhimurium grown in plain LB-broth

Figure 2: Expression of *fimA* of *Salmonella* Typhimurium grown in acidified broth relative to *Salmonella* Typhimurium grown in plain LB-broth

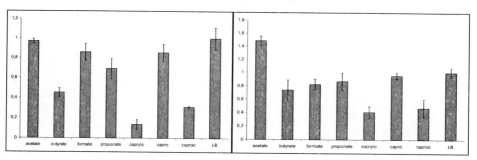

2) Influence of SCFA and MCFA on invasion of *Salmonella* Typhimurium in porcine intestinal epithelial cells.

Contact of *Salmonella* Typhimurium with butyrate, caprylic acid or caproic acid resulted in a significant (p<0.01) decrease of invasion capacity in the porcine intestinal epithelial cells *in vitro*. These results are presented in figure 3.

Figure 3: Invasion rates in the IPI-2I cell line of *Salmonella* Typhimurium grown in acidified LB-broth relative to *Salmonella* Typhimurium grown in LB-broth

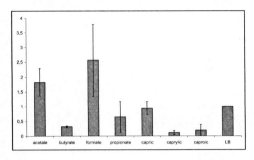

3) Effect of SCFA and MCFA on the colonization of pigs by *Salmonella* Typhimurium

In the *in vivo* trial, coated butyrate showed a strong decrease of *Salmonella* excretion at days 2 and 3 p.i. (approximately 100 times lower on average compared to the control group). Moreover, the colonization of the internal organs was also decreased when coated butyrate was supplemented (p<0.1). Coated caprylic acid showed a reduction of *Salmonella* shedding (10 times lower compared to the control group), mainly at day 2 p.i. Neither butyrate nor caprylic acid influenced the colonization of the tonsils. The results are summarized in figures 4, 5 and 6.

Figure 4: Fecal shedding of *Salmonella* Typhimurium at 3 days post infection

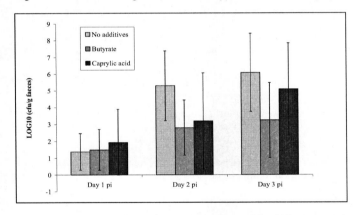

Figure 5: *Salmonella* Typhimurium colonization in tonsils, liver and spleen

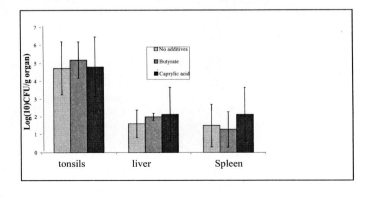

Figure 6: *Salmonella* Typhimurium colonization of the intestinal organs

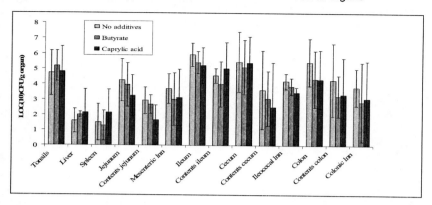

Discussion

The pronounced lower *hilA* expression of *Salmonella* Typhimurium grown in LB-broth supplemented with butyrate, caproic or caprylic acid and the lower *fimA* expression of *Salmonella* Typhimurium grown in LB-broth supplemented with caproic or caprylic acid were reflected in the gentamicin protection assay, in which bacteria grown in LB-broth supplemented with the same acids showed a reduced invasion capacity.

Supplementation of feed with coated butyrate or coated caprylic acid was also efficient in reducing fecal shedding of *Salmonella* Typhimurium. Application of fatty acids is thus one of the possible measures to decrease the number of infected pigs. However, a combined approach with other different control measures (hygiene, vaccination...) is necessary to control the *Salmonella* problem in pigs.

Conclusions

In this study, coated butyrate and to a lesser extent coated caprylic acid have proven to be useful tools for decreasing fecal shedding and colonization of the intestinal organs by *Salmonella* Typhimurium in pigs. Colonization of the tonsils was, however, not influenced.

This work was supported by the Institute for the Promotion of Innovation by Science and Technology in Flanders and by the Research Foundation-Flanders.

References

1. BOYEN, F. et al., 2006. Salmonella SPI-1 genes promote intestinal but not tonsillar colonization in pigs. Microbes and Infection 8, 2899-2907
2. LICHTENSTEIGER, C.A., Vimr, E.R., 2003. Type 1 fimbrae of Salmonella enterica serovar Typhimurium bind to enterocytes and contribute to colonization of swine in vivo. Microbial Pathogenesis 34, 149-154
3. VAN IMMERSEEL, F. et al., 2004. Medium-chain fatty acids decrease colonization and invasion through hilA suppression shortly after infection of chickens with Salmonella enterica serovar Enteriditis. Application of Environmental Microbiology 70, 3582-3587
4. VAN IMMERSEEL, F. et al., 2006. The use of organic acids to combat Salmonella in poultry: a mechanistic explanation of the efficacy. Avian Pathology 35(3), 182-188

Impact of use of Tylosin and Virginiamycin on antimicrobial agents resistance profiles of *Enterococcus* spp. and *E. coli* isolates from swine in field conditions.

Desranleau U., [1], Quessy, S.[1], Topp, E. [2], Laplante, B. [3], Letellier, A*[1],

[1]Faculté de Médecine Vétérinaire de l'Université de Montréal, 3200 Sicotte, J2S 7C6, St-Hyacinthe, Canada.
[2] Agriculture and Agri-Food Canada, 1391 Sandford Str. London ON, N5V 4T3, Canada.
[3] F. Ménard Inc., 251 route 235, Ange-Gardien, Québec, J0E 1E0, Canada.
*corresponding author : ann.letellier@umontreal.ca

Abstract

Enterococcus spp. and *E. coli* are recognized as indicator microorganisms for the human and animal intestinal flora, and are also known to be potential reservoirs of antimicrobial resistance genes. Among the various use of antimicrobial agents that can promote antibioresistance, on farm use of growth promoters raises public health concerns. The aim of this study was to evaluate the impact of the use of selected growth promoters on antimicrobial resistance profiles of *Enterococcus* spp. and *E. coli* isolates from swine in field conditions. *Enterococcus* and *E. coli* isolates obtained from pooled fecal samples of pigs receiving Tylosin (44 ppm, n = 100) and Virginiamycin (22 ppm, n = 100) were compared to isolates obtained from a control group (n = 100) fed without growth promoters, in field conditions. Comparison was done between isolates obtained in the first week of treatment and isolates obtained in the 15th week. All isolates were tested for susceptibility to 20 antimicrobial agents using the disc diffusion method according to NCCLS guidelines. For *Enterococcus* isolates, an increase in resistance was observed for Chloramphenicol (C) and Gentamycin (CN) in the Tylosin fed group and for Ampicillin (AMP) for both Virginiamycin fed and control groups. For *E coli.* isolates, no increase of resistance was observed in the control group but an increase of resistance for Chloramphenicol (C) and Cephalotin (KF) was noted for both Virginiamycin and Tylosin fed groups. Other significant increases of resistance were also noted for Erythromycin (E) and Sulfamethoxazol (RL) in Virginiamycin group and for Neomycin (N) and Kanamycin (K) in Tylosin group. A treatment effect (CTL, Virginiamycin or Tylosin feeding) was also noted for each increase of observed resistance. The results indicated that for E. coli isolates, Tylosin had higher effect on K and N resistance than Virginiamycin while Virginiamycin had higher effect on E resistance than Tylosin. It suggest that both *Enterococcus* and *E. coli* antimicrobial profiles varry with the age of pigs and that antimicrobial resistance profiles can be modified through growth promoter administration.

Introduction

Among major factors that can influence the spread of antibiotic-resistant bacteria are the therapeutic use of antibiotics in human medicine and their use in livestock for therapy, prophylaxis and growth promotion. The use of veterinary antibiotics has many benefits for the livestock industries ensuring animal health and welfare, but their use at sub-therapeutic and growth promoter levels also exerts selective pressure on emergence of resistant bacteria (Hart et al 2004). Resistance to more than one antibiotic is common in enteric bacteria but the role of GP in the acquisition of resistance determinants in field conditions is not clear since it is quite rare that GP are used alone without any therapeutic level use. In this study, we wanted to evaluate the impact of the use of selected GP, commonly used in Canada, on antibiotic resistance profiles of *E. coli* and *Enterococcus* at farm level.

Material and Methods

For this study, 2 separate trials were performed; each trial was done with 300 cross-bred (F4) pigs of 7 weeks of age, all originating from the same lineage and nursery. Pigs were assigned to one of

Session 6

the three groups, Control, Tylosin or Virginiamycin, to obtain 3 homogenous groups of 100 pigs. Each group was then distributed in 10 different pens. During 15 weeks, each group was fed with the same specific diet: group 1 was fed without growth promoter; group 2 was fed with Virginiamycin at 22 ppm and group 3 was fed with Tylosin at 44 ppm. Theses concentrations are related to the commercial use of these growth promoters in swine in Québec. Any pig that had to be treated with therapeutic dosage of antibiotics during the trial was removed from its pen and from the trial. Biosecurity measures were put in place to avoid contamination between sections in the barn and each person visiting the barn was advised to change footwear when moving from one test group to another. Fecal samples were collected from each pen (1 g of fecal material from 5 sites were pooled for each pen) in each group and kept on ice for a maximum period of 24 hours before analysis. E. coli and Enterococcus strains were then isolated as described in the standard Health Canada procedure from each pool. Briefly, E. coli were isolated using Nutrient Broth (ratio 1:10) as enrichment broth followed by a McConkey Agar plating. Typical colonies were selected and biochemical tests (TSI, Citrate, Indole, API 20E) were done to confirm the identification of E. coli. For Enterococcus, fecal material samples in Peptone Buffered water (ratio 1:10) were mixed with Enteroccocosel broth for the enrichment and incubated for 24 h at 37 °C, followed by a striking on Enteroccocosel Agar plate. Typical colonies were put on CBA and biochemical tests (tetrazolium and sugar utilization) were used to confirm the identification of Enterococcus. For each trial and for both microorganisms, 30 isolates from every test group (15 from the first week and 15 from the15th week) were then screened for antimicrobial resistance toward 20 antibiotics using the disc diffusion test according to NCCLS guidelines. Antibiotics used in the disc diffusion test were: AMP: ampicillin (10 µg), AMC: Amoxicillin (30 µg), APR: Apramycin (15 µg), B: Bacitracin (10U), C: Chloramphenicol (30 µg), CIP: Ciprofloxacin (30 µg), CN: Gentamicin (10 µg), E: Erythromycin (15 µg), ENR: Enrofloxacin (5 µg), FOX: Cefoxitin (30 µg), K: Kanamycin (30 µg), KF: Cephalotin (30 µg), N: Neomycin (30 µg), NA: Nalidixic acid (30 µg), RL: Sulfamethoxazol (25 µg), S: Streptomycin (25 µg), SXT: Trimethoprim-sulfas (25 µg), TE: Tetracyclin (30 µg), VA: Vancomycin (30 µg), XNL: Ceftiofur (30 µg). The proportion of resistant isolates were analysed for each antibiotic tested and an increase of resistance was noted when the proportion of resistant isolates was higher at the 15th week in comparison to the first week of the trial.

Results

In both trials, some modification of the antimicrobial resistance profiles for E. coli and Enterococcus were observed. In the group fed without growth promoter (Control group), no increase of resistance was noted for all antibiotics tested for E. coli but an increase of resistance for Enterococcus spp. was noted for AMP and KF. A decrease of resistance for APR-CN-K and AMP had also been observed respectively for Enterococcus and E. coli in the control group. For GP fed groups, increase of resistance was noted in E. coli for C-E-K-KF-N and RL and AMP-C-CN-KF and RL for Enterococcus, as described in details in Table 1. Overall, these results suggest that use of Tylosin and Virginiamycin was associated with an increased of the resistance in E. coli only.

Table 1. : Effect of Growth Promoters administration on proportion of antibiotics resistance in E. coli and Enterococcus groups, after 15 weeks (T= Tylosin, C= Control, V= Virginiamycin)

	ATB*	Group 1-C (p value)	Group 2-V (p value)	Group 3-T (p value)	Effect of GP (p value)
E. coli	AMP	Decrease (0,03)	-	-	T>C (0,02)
	C	-	Increase (0,02)	Increase (0,01)	-
	E	-	Increase (0,002)	Decrease (0,003)	C>T, V>T (0,001)
	K	-	Decrease (0,051)	Increase (0,0008)	T>C, T>V (<0,0001)
	KF	-	Increase (0,052)	Increase (0,02)	T>C, V>C (0,01)

	ATB				
	N	-	-	Increase (0,01)	T>C, T>V (0,0001)
	RL	-	Increase (0,049)	-	-
	Te	-	Decrease (0,01)	-	-
Enterococcus spp.	AMC	-	-	-	C>T, C>V (0,01)
	AMP	Increase (0,005)	Increase (0,02)	Decrease (0,046)	C>T, C>V (0,002)
	APR	Decrease (0,0007)	Decrease (0,04)		C<V, C<T (0,003)
	B		Decrease (0,0001)		T>V, C>V (<0,0001)
	C			Increase (0,03)	T<V (0,01)
	CIP		Decrease (0,001)	Decrease (0,03)	C>T, C>V (0,0001)
	CN	Decrease (0,007)	-	Increase (0,049)	C<T, C<V (0,002)
	ENR	-	-	Decrease (0,02)	-
	K	Decrease (0,03)	-	-	-
	KF	Increase (0,0003)	Increase (0,01)	-	-
	RL	-	-	Increase (0,02)	-
	SXT	-	Decrease (0,006)	Decrease (0,04)	C>T (0,04)
	XNL	-	-	-	C>T (0,02)

*ATB: antibiotics used, description in the material and method section.

Discussion

Results obtained in this study indicated that resistance profiles of *E. coli* and *Enterococcus* can be influenced by use of Tylosin and Virginiamycin as growth promoters at farm level. In *Enterococcus*, it was quite difficult to assess the impact of the use of these GP given the fact that we observed an increase in resistance to some antimicrobial agents while we observed a decrease for others. Furthermore, for the groups that received Virginiamycin, isolates showed surprisingly a decreased in resistance for 4 of the tested antimicrobials while an increase was noted in only 2. Further research to characterize genetic determinants coding for resistance will be necessary to elucidate these discrepancies. It is possible, for instance, that resistance determinants cotransferred with other antibiotic resistance genes on a plasmid or other mobile genetic elements had influenced the results (Rice et al., 1998)

For E. coli, however, it was quite clear that the use of both GP resulted in an increased resistance to many antimicrobial agents suggesting that the negative impact of the use of GP is more important for this bacterial species. However, one should be prudent in the interpretation of such field study since many external factors can influence microflora. Indeed, the age, health status of pigs, biosecurity measures, barn design and time of sampling are important factors susceptible to influence the bacterial microflora and resistance profiles. In addition, even if every efforts were made to appropriately disinfect the premises, it is possible that some flora from the past production lots may have transmitted some genetic determinants to the strains carried by entering animals.

Session 6

Conclusion

Results obtained in this study suggest that use of GP altered significantly the resistance profiles of the strains. While the use of both GP was found to be detrimental for the E. coli resistance profiles, overall a reduction of resistance was observed in *Enteroccocus*. It will be therefore important to continue the study of other bacterial species and/or to determine the number of copy of the resistance genes in the entire bacterial population by quantitative PCR to better assess the real impact of these GP in the development of resistance to antimicrobials agents.

References

ERIC A. Auerbach et al. 2007. Tetracycline resistance genes in activated sludge wastewater treatment plants. Water Res. 40:1143-1151.

HART, WS, et al. 2004. Antimicrobial resistance in Campylobacter spp., E. coli and Enterococci associated with pigs in Australia. J Vet Med B Infect Dis Vet Public Health. 51: 216-221

RICE, LB., 1998. Transfer of Tn5385, a composite, multiresistance chromosomal element from Enterococcus feacalis. J Bacteriol. 180:714-721.

A comparative study on the effect of subtherapeutic tylosin administration on select feral or domestic porcine gut microflora grown in continuous-flow culture

N. Ramlachan, R.C. Anderson*, Kate Andrews and D.J. Nisbet

USDA-ARS, Southern Plains Agricultural Research Center, Food & Feed Safety Research Unit, College Station, TX, 77843, USA, Ph: 979-260-9429
*corresponding author: anderson@ffsru.tamu.edu

Abstract

Continuous flow cultures of feral (culture FC) and domesticated (culture RPCF) pig gut microflora were established in steady state. Cultures, in duplicate, were continuously infused subtherapeutic (25 µg/ml) levels of tylosin and sampled at intervals to assess effects on total culturable anaerobes, *Bacteroides* spp. and *Enterococcus* spp. via plating on serial 10-fold dilutions to anaerobic Brucella blood agar, Bacteroides bile esculin agar, and M Enterococcus agar supplemented without or with 100 µg tylosin/ml, the later to assess bacterial sensitivity to tylosin. Concentrations of total culturable anaerobes within culture FC decreased ($P < 0.05$), albeit slightly, following 7 days tylosin administration. Concentrations of *Bacteroides* and *Enterococcus* decreased ($P < 0.05$) to near or below detectable levels (1.0 $\log_{10}$ CFU/ml) in culture FC following 7 days tylosin administration, and tylosin-insensitive colonies were recovered at low numbers (≤ 2 $\log_{10}$ CFU/ml) and did not persist. In contrast, concentrations of total culturable anaerobes, *Bacteroides* and *Enterococcus* in culture RPCF, while initially decreased upon initiation of tylosin administration, began to increase ($P < 0.05$) by as early as 4 days thereafter, with tylosin-insensitive colonies recovered as one of predominant populations. The results of this study illustrate that under the conditions of this test, subtherapeutic administration of tylosin promoted the enrichment of tylosin-insensitive bacterial populations (capable of growing on media supplemented with 100 µg tylosin/ml) within RPCF cultures (originating from a traditionally reared domesticated pig) but not from FC cultures (originating from a feral pig).

Introduction
Macrolide antibiotics are commonly used in human and veterinary medicine, primarily to treat infections caused by Gram-positive bacteria and also as a feed additive to improve production efficiency in swine (Gaynor and Mankin, 2003). Resistance can occur via acquisition of *erm* methyltransferases, which catalytically inactivate the macrolide's targeted binding site, via acquisition of multidrug efflux pumps or even, albeit infrequently, via point mutations in the microbe's genome (Chopra and Roberts, 2001; Gaynor and Mankin, 2003; Karlsson et al., 2004; Poole, 2005). Recovery of bacteria harbouring *erm* genes from domestic swine and swine production habitats is not uncommon (Chee-Sanford et al., 2001; Wang et al., 2005) but less is known regarding the quantitative acquisition and selection of resistance in bacteria, particularly within swine not reared traditionally (Stanton and Humphrey, 2004). Continuous flow culture of intestinal microorganisms has been used to study competitive interactions between commensal and pathogenic microflora (Harvey *et al.*, 2002; Hume *et al.*, 2001; Nisbet *et al.*, 2000) as well as to investigate potential factors affecting spontaneous acquisition of antibiotic resistance (Kim *et al.*, 2005). In this study, a continuous flow chemostat model established with mixed populations of porcine gut bacteria was used to assess the effects of subtherapeutic tylosin administration on select populations of resident bacteria.

Materials and Methods
Two separate mixed populations of porcine gut bacteria were established in continuous flow culture as previously described (Harvey et al., 2002; Hume et al., 2001). The RPCF culture had been previously established with cecal contents obtained from a traditionally reared pig and its initial characterization has been reported previously (Harvey et al., 2002). The other culture, defined as FC, was established under similar conditions except with cecal contents from an

Session 6

adolescent feral boar killed near Caldwell, Texas, USA, approximately 2 to 4 h prior to necropsy. Both parent cultures of RPCF and FC were established and maintained in BioFlo chemostats (New Brunswick Scientific Company, Edison, NJ) with a culture volume of 550 ml. The culture medium was Viande Levure broth which was prepared and maintained anaerobically under a stream of O_2-free CO_2 and infused at 0.40 ml/min which corresponds to a 24 h vessel turnover. Cultures were incubated at 39°C and agitated at 100 rpm. Once established in steady state, initial characterization of culture FC was accomplished using traditional bacteriological culture methodologies and antibiotic susceptibility testing was performed as described in the National Committee for Clinical Laboratory Standards (now known as the Clinical and Laboratory Standards Institute [CLSI]) (NCCLS, 2004). Both parent cultures were used to provide inoculum to establish separate RPCF and FC cultures, in duplicate, which after at least 14 vessel turnovers, were continually infused with culture medium containing 25 µg tylosin/ml. Fluid samples collected immediately before and during tylosin infusion were quantitatively cultured, via plating of 10-fold serial dilutions, to the following media, each prepared with or without 100 µg tylosin/ml: anaerobic Brucella blood agar and Bacteroides bile esculin agar (Anaerobe Systems, Morgan Hill, CA), for detection of total anaerobes and *Bacteroides* spp., respectively, and M Enterococcus agar (Becton Dickinson and Company, Sparks, MD) for detection of *Enterococcus* spp. Inoculated media were incubated 48-72 h at 37 °C and colonies propagated with and without tylosin selection were enumerated. Specific identification of bacteria from select colonies was achieved using rapid ID 32 STREP, rapid 20E, 20NE, 20A, and rapid ID 32 A identification strips (bioMérieux, Hazelwood, MO). Indole spot tests (Anaerobe Systems, Morgan Hill, CA), E-test™ (AB Biodisk, Piscataway, NJ) and gas chromatography were also used in this analysis. Samples containing no detectable colonies of bacteria were given a value of 1.0 $\log_{10}$ CFU/ml. $\log_{10}$ transformations of bacterial concentrations obtained from duplicate cultures were analyzed for main effects of day, culture type (i.e., RPCF or FC culture) and the possible interaction using a repeated measures analysis of variance (Statistix®8 Analytical Software, Tallahassee, FL, USA). Multiple comparison of means was accomplished using a Tukeys procedure.

Results and Discussion

Characterization of microflora in culture FC. Culture FC achieved steady state after 14 days continuous flow culture and the bacteriological composition was found to include *Streptococcus bovis, Proteus mirabilis, Staphylococcus epidermidis, Alcaligenes denitrificans*, and members of *Bacteroides, Lactobacillus, Enterococcus*, and *Clostridium. Campylobacter* and *Salmonella* were never detected in the feral culture and *E. coli* that was initially isolated from the cecal contents was never recovered once the culture had achieved steady state. *Enterococcus hirae, Streptococcus bovis, Proteus mirabilis, Staphylococcus epidermidis, Alcaligenes denitrificans* were susceptible to tylosin and erythromycin; *Bacteroides uniformis* and *Bacteroides stercoris* were resistant to gentamicin, ciprofloxacin, ceftriaxone and ampicillin. *Clostridium hathewayi* showed resistance to tylosin at MIC >512 µg/ml and was the predominant anaerobe recovered on anaerobic Brucella blood agar.

Effect of tylosin on select bacterial populations. Recovery of anaerobes from non-selective Brucella blood agar was not affected ($P > 0.05$) by culture; however, main effects of day and day by culture interaction were observed ($P < 0.01$) on recovery of anaerobes from nonselective Brucella blood agar due to a decrease in anaerobes in the FC and an increase in RPCF cultures (Figure 1A). Main effects of culture, day and a day by culture interaction were observed ($P < 0.01$) on recovery of anaerobes from tylosin-selective Brucella blood agar due to a temporary increase in tylosin-insensitive anaerobes, which were prominent even before tylosin administration, from the FC culture and a gradual enrichment of tylosin-insensitive anaerobes from the RPCF culture (Figure 1A). The prominent tylosin-insensitive anaerobe was *Clostridium hathewayi*. Main effects of culture, day and a day by culture interaction were observed ($P < 0.05$) on recovery of *Bacteroides* from Bacteroides bile esculin agar supplemented with or without tylosin (Figure 1B) due to higher *Bacteroides* concentrations in the RPCF cultures prior to administration of tylosin and to an enrichment of tylosin-insensitive *Bacteroides* spp. beginning by day 3 of tylosin administration (Figure 1B). In the case of total anaerobes and *Bacteroides*, tylosin-insensitive populations were prominent in RPCF cultures even before initiation of tylosin administration. Conversely, tylosin-insensitive *Enterococcus* spp., were not apparent prior to tylosin administration; however, upon initiation of treatment recovery was highly variable between the two RPCF cultures regardless of culturing on M Enterococcus agar supplemented with or without tylosin. This indicates that the two RPCF cultures contained markedly different enterococcal populations. For instance, even though mean concentrations of tylosin-insensitive *Enterococcus* recovered from the RPCF cultures began to increase markedly beginning 4 days after initiation of tylosin administration (Figure 1C) this increase occurred in only one of the cultures. As a consequence, main effects of culture, day or day by culture interactions on quantitative recoveries on M Enterococcus agar supplemented with or without tylosin were not observed ($P > 0.05$) (Figure 1C).

In conclusion, results from this study revealed that subtherapeutic administration of tylosin promoted the enrichment of tylosin-insensitive bacterial populations (capable of growing on media supplemented with 100 µg tylosin/ml) within RPCF cultures (originating from a traditionally reared domesticated pig) but not from FC cultures (originating from a feral pig).

Acknowledgements

The authors thank M. Reiley Street, Clayton Myers, Jim Snodgrass and Matthew Quatrini for technical support. This work was funded in part by the National Pork Board.

References

CHEE-SANFORD, J.C., AMINOV, R.I., KRAPAC, I.J., GARRIGUES-JEANJEAN, N., MACKIE, R.I., 2001. Occurrence and diversity of tetracycline resistance genes in lagoons and groundwater underlying two swine production facilities. *Applied and Environmental Microbiology,* 67,1494-1502.
CHOPRA, I., ROBERTS, M., 2001. Tetracycline resistance: mode of action, applications, molecular biology, and epidemiology of resistance. *Microbiology and Molecular Biology Reviews,* 65,232-260.
GAYNOR, M., MANKIN, A.S., 2003. Macrolide antibiotics: binding site, mechanism of action, resistance. *Current Topics in Medicinal Chemistry,* 3,949-961.
HARVEY, R.B., DROLESKEY, R.E., HUME, M.E., ANDERSON, R.C., GENOVESE, K.J., ANDREWS, K., NISBET, D.J., 2002. *In vitro* inhibition of *Salmonella enterica* serovars Choleraesuis and Typhimurium, *Escherichia coli* F-18, and *Escherichia coli* O157:H7 by a porcine continuous-flow competitive exclusion culture. *Current Microbiology,* 45:226-229.
HUME, M.E., NISBET, D.J., BUCKLEY, S.A., ZIPRIN, R.L., ANDERSON, R.C., STANKER, L.H., 2001. Inhibition of in vitro *Salmonella* Typhimurium colonization in porcine cecal bacteria continuous-flow competitive exclusion cultures. *Journal of Food Protection,* 64,17-22.
KARLSSON, M., FELLSTRÖM, C., JOHANSSON, K.-E., FRANKLIN, A., 2004. Antimicrobial resistance in *Brachyspiira pilosicoli* with special reference to point mutations in the 23S rRNA gene associated with macrolide and lincosamide resistance. *Microbial Drug Resistance,* 10,204-208.
KIM, W.K., KARABASIL, N., BULAJIC, S., DUNKLEY, K.D., CALLAWAY, T.R., POOLE, T.L., RICKE, S.C., ANDERSON, R.C., NISBET, D.J., 2005. Comparison of spontaneous antibiotic frequency of *Salmonella* Typhimurium growth in glucose amended continuous culture at slow and fast dilution rates. *Journal of Environmental Science and Health Part B,* 40,475-484.
NCCLS, 2004. Methods for Antimicrobial Susceptibility Testing of Anaerobic Bacteria; Approved Standard, 6th Ed., NCCLS document M11-A6, Wayne, PA: National Committee for Clinical Laboratory Standards.
NISBET, D.J., ANDERSON, R.C., CORRIER, D.E., HARVEY, R.B., STANKER, L.H., 2000. Modeling the survivability of *Salmonella typhimurium* in the chicken cecae using an anaerobic continuous-culture of chicken cecal bacteria. *Microbial Ecology in Health and Disease,* 12,42-47.
POOLE, K., 2005. Efflux-mediated antimicrobial resistance. *Journal of Antimicrobial Chemotherapy,* 56,20-51.
STANTON, T.B., HUMPHREY, S.B., 2004. Tetracycline resistant bacteria in organically raised and feral swine. *Abstract of the 104th American Society for Microbiology General Meeting,* Z-029.
WANG, Y., WANG, G., SHOEMAKER, N.B., WHITEHEAD, T.R., SALYERS, A.A., 2005. Distribution of the *ermG* gene among bacterial isolates from porcine intestinal contents. *Applied and Environmental Microbiology,* 71,4930-4934.

Session 6

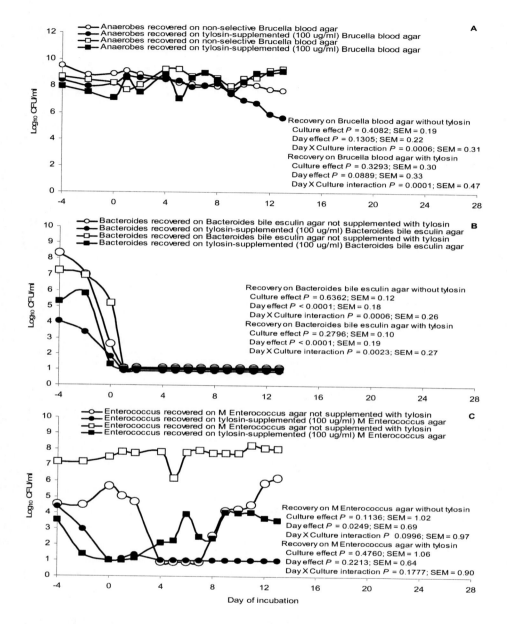

Figure 1. Effects of subtherapeutic (25 µg/ml) tylosin administration on populations of anaerobes, *Bacteroides* spp., and *Enterococcus* spp. from continuous flow cultures of mixed populations of porcine gut bacteria obtained from feral (culture FC, circles) or domestic (culture RPCF, squares) swine. Bacteria were quantitatively recovered on anaerobic Brucella blood agar, Bacteroides bile esculin agar and M Enterococcus agar each supplemented without (open symbols) or with (closed symbols) 100 µg tylosin/ml.

The influence of pig carcass processing of the efficacy of sponge swab sampling

Richards, P. and Dodd, C. E. R.*

University of Nottingham, Sutton Bonington, UK.
*Corresponding author: christine.dodd@nottingham.ac.uk

Abstract

The efficacy of different methods of sampling have been widely compared in the literature. Whilst it is recognised that swabbing and sponging leave a residual bacterial population, the levels that are left are difficult to evaluate and may be influenced by other factors such as changes to the skin due to processing. In this Food Standards Agency funded study we have used bacterial bioluminescence as a visual marker of the presence of bacteria to evaluate the efficacy of different sampling methods on the removal of bacteria. Pig skin was spiked with a strain of *E. coli* or *Salmonella* Typhimurium made bioluminescent by the introduction of the *luxCDABE* genes from *Photorhabdus luminescens* on a plasmid construct. Samples were visualized under a light sensitive camera before and after sponging or swabbing and the levels of the bacteria removed evaluated. Methods compared were agitated sponging, using cellulose acetate sponges, against traditional sponging and a double-swabbing technique, using cotton tipped bud swabs. Results indicate that damage to skin can lead to 'hot spots' of contamination, where residual bacteria are not easily removed by further physical abrasion.

Introduction

Microbiological sampling and testing of carcasses has been introduced in many countries to verify that HACCP schemes effectively control plant processing. Whilst many studies have compared the efficiency of different sampling methods (excision, sponging, wet-dry) (Hutchison et al., 2005; Pepperell et al., 2005), few studies have been undertaken on the efficiency of alternative sponge-sampling methods. The UK Food Standards Agency (FSA) requires that *Salmonella* sampling of carcasses can only be undertaken using sponges. These are seen as easier to use, particularly on a moving line, less affected by operator variability and as cost effective because only one set of sampling consumables is required for all of the statutory tests. For testing using sponges the recommended approach is to agitate the sponge by moving it by a few centimetres using a side-to-side movement (Anon, 2006). Here we evaluate the efficacy of agitated sponging against a technique in which multiple sponge passes are made through a delineated area and against wet-dry swabbing with cotton-tipped swabs.

To allow the removal of bacteria to be monitored easily, we have spiked pork rind with *Escherichia coli* or *Salmonella* Typhimurium engineered to carry the *lux* genes making the bacteria bioluminescent. The presence of such bacteria on a surface can then be viewed using a light sensitive camera.

Materials and methods

Sampling

Sponge sampling was carried out using cellulose acetate sponges; swabbing was carried out using cotton tipped bud swabs. Agitated sponge sampling was performed on a section of pork rind over a 10 x 10 cm area in a single pass. The sponge was agitated from side-to-side across the whole area in the fashion recommended by the FSA. Traditional sponge sampling was performed by rubbing the sponge firmly across the rind surface with 10 strokes in each of the horizontal and vertical directions, with no side-to-side agitation. Wet-dry swab sampling was undertaken by rubbing a swab moistened in maximum recovery diluent firmly across the rind surface with 10 strokes in each of the horizontal, vertical and both diagonal directions. Swabs were rolled between the thumb and index finger as they were rubbed across the rind surface. Immediately, after rubbing with the moistened swab, the procedure was repeated within the sample template with a dry swab.

Efficacy of carcass surface sampling methods

Samples of pork rind were inoculated with an *Escherichia coli* or *Salmonella* Typhimurium strain which constitutively express *luxABCDE* genes from *Photorhabdus luminescens* on a plasmid construct. Bacteria were inoculated to a final concentration of approximately 1×10^5 cfu ml^{-1}. Following inoculation the pork rind was incubated at 37°C for 1 hour so that the bacteria could adhere to the pork rind surface. Before and after sampling, photographs were taken of the skin and sponge/swab using a Night Owl CCD camera (EG & G Berthold, Bad Wildbad, Ger.). Two minute integration times were used.

Results

Agitated Sponge Sampling

A

B

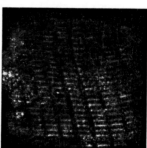

Figure 1. Bioluminescence image of a 100cm^2 section pork rind inoculated with 1×10^5 cfu cm^{-2} bioluminescent *E. coli* (A) prior to sampling (B) following agitated sponging.

From Figure 1 comparison of the sample before and after agitated sponge sampling demonstrates a significant reduction in light output. This demostrates the method removes a large proportion of the bacteria present on the rind surface. Examination of the sponges confirmed that bacteria had been removed and were present on the sponge surface (data not shown). The residual light on the rind surface appears to be associated with micro-topological features created by an undetermined aspect of the slaughter process. After two further rounds of sponging (data not shown), the reduction in bacterial bioluminescence, relative to the intensity of light emission visualized after one round of agitated sponging, was minimal. This suggests the remaining bacteria are firmly adhered to the surface.

Traditional sponge sampling

A

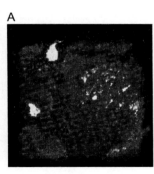

B

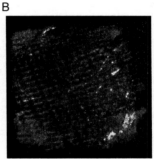

Figure 2. Bioluminescence image of a 100cm^2 section pork rind inoculated with 1 x 10^5 cfu cm^{-2} bioluminescent *E. coli* (A) prior to sampling (B) following traditional sponging.

Post-sampling, the level of bioluminescence emitted from bacteria on the rind surface (Figure 2B) is not noticeably different to that remaining following agitated sponging (Figure 1B). However, the traditional sponging technique is more time consuming and involves more actions than agitated sponging making it a less easy to use method when sampling from carcasses in slaughterhouses during processing.

Wet-dry swab sampling

A

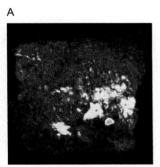

B

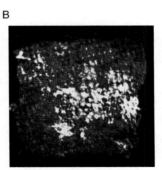

Figure 3. Bioluminescence image of a 100cm^2 section pork rind inoculated with 1 x 10^5 cfu cm^{-2} bioluminescent *E. coli* (A) prior to sampling (B) following swabbing.

Following swab sampling there was very little change in the levels of bioluminescence produced, indicating that a substantial proportion of the inoculant remained on the rind surface. Bacterial removal by the swabs was confirmed by further testing.

Discussion

Although an essentially qualitative approach, the use of bioluminescent bacteria does give a simple evaluation of the effectiveness of different sampling methods. Both sponge sampling methods tested were more effective at removing bacteria than swab sampling, probably because of the larger surface area sponges have in contact with the skin. The agitated sponge method is also quicker, needs less skill to carry out and gives less variation between operators. Repeated sampling of an area never completely removed the bacteria, particularly where these were associated with micro-topological features. This suggests that some contamination may be firmly attached which may be protected from physical methods of removal such as washing.

Session 6

Reference

Anon. 2006. Red carcass sampling. Food Standards Agency. London, UK. http://www.ukmeat.org/RedSampling.htm

Hutchison, M.L., Avery, S.M., Walters, L.D., Reid, C.A., Wilson, D., Howell, M., Johnston, A.M. and Buncic, S. 2005. A comparison of wet-dry swabbing and excision sampling methods for microbiological testing of bovine, porcine, and ovine carcasses at red meat slaughterhouses. *Journal of Food Protection* 68(10). 2155-62

Pepperell, R., Reid, C.A., Solano, S.N., Hutchison, M.L., Walters, L.D., Johnston, A.M. and Buncic, S. 2005. Experimental comparison of excision and swabbing microbiological sampling methods for carcasses. *Journal of Food Protection* 68(10).2163-8.

Use of ELISA HerdChek® Swine Salmonella for Evaluation and Monitoring Salmonella in Swine Herds

A. Rossi*, A.Ballagi and C. Goetz

* IDEXX Switzerland AG, Stationsstrasse 12, CH-3097 Liebefeld-Bern
email: alessandro-rossi@idexx.com; fax:+41 31 970 62 79

Abstract

The epidemiology of salmonellosis in swine must be viewed as not only the problem of the disease of pigs, but also as the problem of infected pork carcasses and food products. Clinical disease outbreaks occur most often in intensively reared weaned pigs. High animal density and stress of transportation increase the shedding by carriers and also the susceptibility of exposed pigs. Both clinically diseased and healthy pigs can shed high numbers of bacteria in their feces, the major source of the disease spreading. Healthy carriers that spread the Salmonella are the major source of carcass infection in slaughterhouses. Therefore, the control of Salmonella in pigs should be the first line of attack. The final goal of control programs should be the production of Salmonella-free pigs slaughtered in Salmonella-free slaughterhouses.

In general, the herd prevalence is high and varies between 30–60%. Five to ten percent of the slaughter pigs are positive for Salmonella. The Salmonella infection in these herds is not equally distributed and affects only groups of animals (cluster). The so-called intra-herd prevalence is actually fairly low.

Control programs based on serological monitoring and isolation of Salmonella aim not only for the reduction of infection prevalence, but also could serve as valuable tools to change slaughterhouse routines in order to decrease food contamination. The goal of control programs is actually not eradication, but preventing Salmonella spp. from entering the food chain. Simple measures such as selecting herds with low prevalence of low seropositive animals to slaughter first and leaving the highly infected ones for last could make a significant difference.

Recent field experience from Germany and Austria during last year 2005 confirmed that the HerdCheck Swine Salmonella kit is a valuable tool for monitoring the progress of salmonella control program especially in countries where a low prevalence is already reached.

Introduction

Salmonellosis is one of the major causes of food-borne infections in humans in industrialized countries, and is often associated with pork production. Several countries have introduced monitoring and control programs. Easy, robust and technically simple diagnostic methods can make those efforts more efficient. The IDEXX HerdChek Swine Salmonella Test Kit has proven to be a practicable and efficient test for monitoring Salmonella during field investigation and reducing risks of carcass contamination during slaughter and processing.

The IDEXX HerdChek Swine Salmonella Antibody Test Kit is an indirect ELISA that was developed and evaluated in collaboration with the Dutch Animal Health Service. The test is based on a mixture of serogroups B, C1 and D Salmonella lipopolysaccharide antigens to ensure the detection of a broad range of species and strains of the bacteria. The kit is able to detect different Salmonella serotypes corresponding to the requirement of the most important Salmonella mentioned by the new EU regulation (Table 1).

Serum, plasma and meat juice samples can be tested.
• All reagents are ready-to-use.
• Results can be obtained in 90 minutes, or samples can be incubated overnight for convenience.
• The cutoff value can be adapted to the purpose of the testing and local guidelines or regulations.

Session 6

Table 1

(Salmonella serotype detected by the HerdChek Swine Salmonella ELISA kit)

Serotype	Group	Designation	Serum Origin	Country	Result
S. Typhimurium	B	National Reference	STM 1, 2, 3	Germany	+
		Deventer Reference	SW-TYP	The Netherlands	+
		ELISA Calibration Sera	1, 2, 3	Denmark	+
		Ring Test Sample	24 - 30	The Netherlands	+
S. Derby	B	Weybridge Reference	194, 195	United Kingdom	+
S. Brandenburg	B	Ring Test Sample	11 - 13	The Netherlands	+
S. Cholerasuis	C1	National Reference	SCS 1, 2, 3	Germany	+
S. Livingstone	C1	Deventer Reference	SW-LIV	The Netherlands	+
		Ring Test Sample	19 - 20	The Netherlands	+
S. Infantis	C1	ELISA Calibration Sera	4	Denmark	+
		Weybridge Reference	199, 253, 254	United Kingdom	
S. Panama	D	Weybridge Reference	259, 260	United Kingdom	+
		Ring Test Sample	10	The Netherlands	
S. Enteritidis	D	Field Sample		Denmark	+

Material and Methods

The test was evaluated in several negative populations from different geographical areas in Europe and in the US. These herds in the study were under strict management and the serum and meat juice samples were collected carefully in order protect against undesirable effects due to a poor quality. Reference sera provided by different European Reference Laboratories were used to measure serotype detectability (groups B, C and D).

Additional evaluation was conducted with samples from different abattoirs in Germany (during a regular control program between 2003 and 2005) and from Austria (1) between the summer and winter of 2005. The goal was to evaluate the kit capacity to match the expected results of low Salmonella prevalence (Figure 2,3).

Results

The HerdChek Swine Salmonella kit specificity demonstrated excellent performance with a narrow distribution profile and mean OD% values close to zero (Figure 1).

Recent field experience from Germany (Figure 2) and Austria during last year 2005 (Figure 3) confirmed that the HerdCheck Swine Salmonella kit is a valuable tool for monitoring the progress of salmonella control program especially in countries where a low prevalence is already reached.

Figure 1

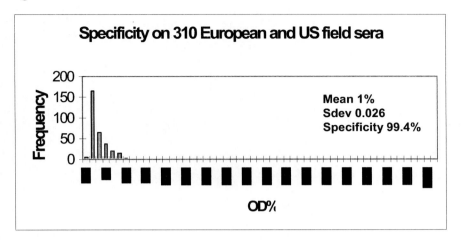

Figure 2

(Germany, temporal evaluations 2003-2005. The kit was introduced as routine screening tool during May 2004)

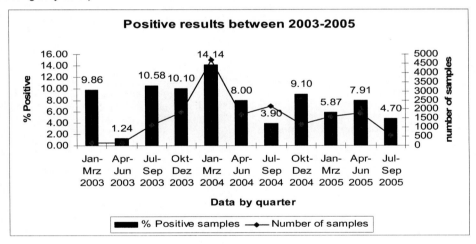

Figure 3

(Austria, the kit correspond to the meat juice expected prevalence (total of 2318 samples)

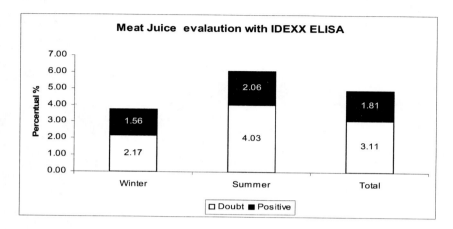

Discussion

The performance of the IDEXX HerdCheck Swine Salmonella ELISA kit supports that the kit is a good diagnostic tool for national swine salmonella control programs as defined by the EU regulations. The kit has serum, plasma and meat juice claim and its flexible protocol is adapted to the local purpose of the testing.

Conclusion

These field experiences confirmed that serological screening determines the animal's previous exposure to salmonella, although it has no relevance to the carrier status or the probability of shedding. The program n place in Germany and Austria using also IDEXX HerdCheck Swine Salmonella ELISA kit clearly shows the serological screening is easy to run on large scales, it is used for estimating and reducing the herd prevalence.

Reference

1. E.Wilhem et al. 2005. *Fleischwirtschaft,* 5, 97-99.

Antibiotic resistance patterns of faecal indicator organisms and occurrence of *Salmonella* spp. in wild boar (*Sus scrofa scrofa*) in Italy.

M. Rossi[1], M. Delogu[1], F. Ostanello[1], A.Caprioli[2], R. G. Zanoni[1]*

[1]Dept. Veterinary Public Health and Animal Pathology, University of Bologna, Italy; [2]Laboratorio di Medicina Veterinaria, Istituto Superiore di Sanità, Rome, Italy.

* Dept. Veterinary Public Health and Animal Pathology, Via Tolara di Sopra, 50, 40064, Ozzano Emilia, Bologna, Italy; e-mail: zanoni@vet.unibo.it, fax: 0039.051.2097039.

Abstract

In order to monitor antibiotic resistance in faecal indicator organisms and evaluate the occurrence of *Salmonella* spp., faeces from 110 wild boars (*Sus scrofa scrofa*), killed during a demographic control program in two different regional parks in Bologna province, were collected from September 2002 to June 2003. A single isolate of *Escherichia coli, Enterococcus faecalis* and *Enterococcus faecium* from each sample was tested for antibiotic susceptibility using the agar diffusion method recommended by CLSI (formerly, NCCLS). A total of 110 *E. coli*, 48 *E. faecium* and 5 *E. faecalis* strains were isolated and submitted to antibiotic susceptibility tests. Antibiotic resistance patterns were similar in wild boar populations from both parks. Multiple antibiotic-resistance to ciprofloxacin, rifampin and erythromycin was found with high frequency in *Enterococcus* spp. strains. *E. coli* isolates showed a low antibiotic resistance level. Two *Salmonella arizonae* and one *Salmonella* spp. strains, isolated from wild boars of one park, didn't show any resistance concerning the antibiotics tested.

Introduction

Antibiotics have become commonplace in our environment in consequence of their wide use in animal husbandry, medical therapy. Although data concerning antibiotic resistance in wild animals are scarce, some surveys have demonstrated the presence of multi-resistant indicator organisms in their faeces (Middleton and Ambrose, 2005; Poeta et al., 2005). The aim of this study was monitoring antibiotic-resistance in faecal indicator organisms isolated from wild boar (*Sus scrofa scrofa*) population living in two natural Regional Parks of Bologna province. Furthermore, occurrence and antibiotic resistance of *Salmonella* spp. were evaluated .

Materials and Methods

From September 2002 to June 2003, faeces from 55 wild boars (*Sus scrofa scrofa*) from Gessi Bolognesi Regional Park (48.15 Km^2) and 55 from Monte Sole Regional Park (69.34 Km^2) located in the Emilia-Romagna Region were collected. No contact between the different populations of the two parks had been recorded. The possibility of interactions and hybridisation between wild boars and domestic pigs was demonstrated in both parks, by capturing hybrid phenotype animals. Faecal samples were collected directly from the rectum, placed in BBL-Cary-Blair Transport Medium (Becton and Dickinson and Co., BD), stored at 4°C, transported to the laboratory and processed within 24 h after collection. In order to isolate *E. coli*, faeces were streaked directly onto BBL-MacConkey Agar (BD) and incubated at 37°C for 18-24 h. Strains identification was carried out by API 20E (BioMérieux). For the isolation of *E. faecalis* and *E. faecium*, 1 g of faeces was suspended in 4 ml of saline solution and serially 10-fold diluted until 10^{-4}; 0,1 ml of each dilution was then inoculated on Difco-Bile Esculin Azide Agar (BD) and incubated at 37°C for 72 h. Isolates were identified at genus level on the basis of colony morphology, Gram staining, catalase production, esculin hydrolysis, growth in 6,5% NaCl, bile tolerance and L-pyrrolydonyl-β-naphtylamide hydrolysis (Manero e Blanch 1999; Devriese et al, 1993). Identification of *E. faecium* and *E. faecalis* isolates was performed by PCR as described by Dutka-Malen *et al.* (1995a;1995b). In order to isolate *Salmonella* spp. 5 g of each sample were inoculated in Difco-Muller-Kauffmann Tetrathionate Broth (BD) and Selenite Broth (Oxoid) and incubated at 42°C and 37°C for 24 h respectively. Enrichment broth's culture were then seeded onto two different media: Brilliant Green Agar (Oxoid) and XLT4 Agar (BD). *Salmonella* suspect colonies were identified by commercial system API 20E (BioMérieux). A single isolate of *E. coli*, *E. faecalis*, *E. faecium* and *Salmonella* spp. from each sample was tested for antimicrobial susceptibility using the agar diffusion method recommended by CLSI (NCCLS, 2002).The following 16 antimicrobial agents were included in the study for *E. coli* and *Salmonella* spp. using BBL Sensi-Disc (BD): amikacin, amoxicillin-clavulanic acid, ampicillin, cefazolin, cefotaxime, chloramphenicol, colistin, enrofloxacin, gentamicin, kanamycin, nalidixic acid, spectinomycin, streptomycin, sulfisoxazole, tetracycline and trimethoprim-sulfamethoxazole The antibiotic susceptibility of *Enterococcus* spp. was assessed using the following molecules: ampicillin, chloramphenicol, ciprofloxacin, erythromycin, penicillin, rifampin, tetracycline and teicoplanin. CLSI interpretative standards (NCCLS, 2004) for *Enterobacteriacae* and *Enterococcus* were used and the intermediate category was considered, in this study, as resistant. Multiple resistance was defined when resistance to three or more unrelated antimicrobial agents was found. Vancomycin and the high level aminoglycoside resistances of *E. faecalis* and *E. faecium* were evaluated by the screening test described by CLSI (NCCLS, 2004).

Results

From the 110 wild boars tested a total of 110 *E. coli*, 48 *E. faecium* and 5 *E. faecalis* strains were isolated. Differences in isolation rate from the animals living in the two Regional parks were observed for *Enterococcus* spp: *E. faecium* was isolated from 33 subjects from Gessi Bololgnesi Park and 15 animals from Monte Sole Park while *E. faecalis* was isolated only from 5 wild boars in Monte Sole Park. Resistance rates of *E. coli*, *E. faecium* and *E. faecails* strains from wild boars living in the two regional parks are showed in table I. Multiple antibiotic resistance was observed in 83% of *E. faecium* and in all *E. faecalis* isolated. No multiple resistance was found in *E. coli*. No significant difference in antibiotic resistance rates between isolates from both parks was detected. No vancomycin and high level aminoglycoside resistance were observed in enterococci. Two *Salmonella enterica arizonae* and 1 *Salmonella* spp. strains were isolated from wild boar from Monte Sole Park ; any antibiotic resistance was detected in these strains.

Table I: Antibiotic resistance rates (%) of the faecal isolates from wild boars from two regional parks obtained by agar diffusion method. Absolute numbers are presented under brackets.

	AN	S	K	GM	ENO	NA	CL	SPT	SXT	G	CZ	CTX	AMC	AM	C	Te	CIP	E	P	RA	TEC
Gessi Bolognesi Regional Park																					
E. coli (n=55)	0	24 (13)	4 (2)	2 (1)	0	0	0	2 (1)	0	2 (1)	0	0	0	0	0	4 (2)	.	.	.	.	.
E. faecium (n=33)	.	.	.	.	.	.	.	.	.	.	.	.	.	0	0	15 (5)	97 (32)	94 (31)	9 (3)	76 (25)	0
Monte Sole Regional Park																					
E. coli (n=55)	0	40 (22)	0	0	0	2 (1)	0	0	2 (1)	2 (1)	0	0	0	2 (1)	0	7 (4)	.	.	.	.	.
E. faecium (n=15)	.	.	.	.	.	.	.	.	.	.	.	.	.	0	0	13 (2)	100 (15)	87 (13)	13 (2)	100 (15)	0
E. faecalis (n=5)	.	.	.	.	.	.	.	.	.	.	.	.	.	0	20 (1)	0	100 (5)	80 (4)	0	80 (4)	0

AN: amikacin; S: streptomycin; K: kanamycin; GM: gentamicin; ENO: enrofloxacin; NA: nalidixic acid; CL: colistin; SPT: spectinomycin; SXT: trimethoprim-sulfamethoxazole; G: sulfisoxazole; CZ: cefazolin; CTX: cefotaxime; AMC: amoxicillin-clavulanic acid; AM: ampicillin; C: chloramphenicol; Te: tetracycline; CIP: ciprofloxacin; E: erythromycin; P: penicillin; RA: rifampin and TEC: teicoplanin.

Conclusion

In this study, *E. coli* and *Salmonella* strains showed a low antibiotic resistance level. Relative low levels of antibiotic resistance were also detected in enterococcal isolates when compared with those detected in enterococci of farm animals and human (Poeta et al., 2005). In particular no vancomycin or high level aminoglycoside resistances were observed in this study. Multiple antibiotic-resistance to ciprofloxacin, rifampin and erythromycin was found with high frequency in *Enterococcus* spp. strains, however further research should be carried out in order to investigate the molecular mechanisms of these resistances as well as to evaluate if the high rates are eventually due to strain clonality.

References

Devriese et al., 1993. Phenotypic identification of the genus Enterococcus and differentiation of phylogenetically distinct enterococcal species and species groups. *Journal of Applied Bacteriology*, 75(5):399-408

Dutka-Malen et al., 1995a. Detection of glycopeptide resistance genotypes and identification to the species level of clinically relevant enterococci by PCR. *Journal of Clinical Microbiology,* 33(5):1434.

Dutka-Malen et al., 1995b. Detection of glycopeptide resistance genotypes and identification to the species level of clinically relevant enterococci by PCR. *Journal of Clinical Microbiology* 33(1):24-7. Erratum in: J Clin Microbiol 1995 May;33(5):1434.

Manero A and Blanch AR, 1999. Identification of Enterococcus spp. with a biochemical key. *Applied and Environmental Microbiology*, 65(10):4425-30.

Middleton JH and Ambrose A., 2005. Enumeration and antibiotic resistance patterns of fecal indicator organisms isolated from migratory Canada geese (Branta canadensis). *Journal of Wildlife Diseases*, 41(2):334-41.

National Committee for Clinical Laboratory Standards (NCCLS), 2002. Performance standards for antimicrobial disk and dilution susceptibility tests for bacteria isolated from animals, Second edition: Approved Standard M31-A2, NCCLS, Wayne, PA pp. 80.

National Committee for Clinical Laboratory Standards (NCCLS), 2004. Performance Standards for Antimicrobial Susceptibility Testing. Fourteenth Informational Supplement: Approved Standard M100-S14, NCCLS, Wayne, PA pp. 156.

Poeta P et al., 2005. Characterization of antibiotic resistance genes and virulence factors in faecal enterococci of wild animals in Portugal. *Journal of Veterinary Medicine Series B,* 2005 Nov;52(9):396-402.

Pulse-field-gel-electrophoresis development for *Salmonella* species using PaeR7 I enzyme

Thompson, C.*, McKean, J., O'Connor, A.

Veterinary Diagnostic and Production Animal Medicine, Iowa State University, Ames, USA

Curt Thompson: *curtt@iastate.edu*

Abstract

Pulse field gel electrophoresis (PFGE) currently has been preformed on 22 *Salmonella spp.* isolates using a new method that distinguishes between different species of *Salmonella* and gives reproducible results using Pae R7 1 enzyme. This PFGE data, when using the Pae R7 1 enzyme, was compared to the Xba 1 restriction enzyme that is used by CDC (Center for Disease Control) for *Salmonella spp.* isolate comparisons. PFGE results were analyzed using cluster analysis and results were comparable between Pae R7 1 and Xba 1 enzymes for distinguishing differences.

Introduction

Salmonellae is a major cause of food-borne illness in the United Sates (1). Pulse-field gel electrophoresis (PFGE) is one of several approaches available for determining relationship between isolates (2). For our purpose, PFGE represents an opportunity to evaluate the relationship between *Salmonella* isolates associated with sample collected at the farm and at the packing plant. The pattern associated with PFGE is enzyme and isolate unique and should be useful in discriminating isolates. Several enzymes are available and the goal of this project was to evaluate the discrimination ability of Pae R7 1 compared to the Xba 1 restriction enzyme. The null hypothesis was that a cluster of isolates identified by Xba 1 would be identified as a cluster using Pae R7 1.

Materials and methods

Salmonella isolates were obtained from rectal swabs, lymph tissue, skin, gut and head meat swabs from swine slaughter at a commercial plant. Isolates identified as *Salmonella* were then grown overnight on blood agar plates then resuspended in cell suspension buffer (100 mM Tris-HCL, 100 mM EDTA, pH8.0) to obtain an absorbance reading of 1.2 to 1.4. 300 ul of suspension was added to 15 ul of proteinase K (20 mg/ml) and 300 ul of 1.2% SeaKem agarose (FMC Bioproducts), mixed, and then allowed to solidify in a 100-µl plug mold (Bio-Rad Laboratories). Plugs were incubated for 2 hours at 55°C in 5 ml of Cell lysis buffer (50 mM Tris-HCl [pH 8.0], 50 mM EDTA [pH 8.0], 1.0% SDS, and 25 ul proteinase K [20 mg/ml]), washed twice for 15 min with ddH$_2$0 followed by four 15 minute washes with TE buffer (10 mM Tris-HCl [pH 8.0], 0.1 mM EDTA). A 2 mm slice of each plug was incubated in 200 µl of restriction buffer (Buffer 4, BSA and PaeR7 I) at 37°C for 2 to 4 h. The DNA fragments were separated on 1.0 % agarose (FMC Bioproducts). Electrophoresis was performed on CHEF Mapper XA system (Bio-Rad) for 32 h at 14°C at 6V/cm in 0.5xTBE buffer with varying pulse times (begin - 0.47s, end - 10.0s). MidRange1 PFG marker (NEB) was used as DNA size marker. The DNA restriction patterns were compared using BioNumerics software (Applied Math).

For Xba 1 enzyme the procedure was provided by Centers for Disease Control.

Results

22 isolates were available for comparison. The number of bands produced by the Pae R7 1 was greater than the Xba 1 enzyme. On average, 20 - 25 bands are identified with Pae R7 1 and 10 -12 with Xba 1. Results for seven similar isolates using Pae R7 1 enzyme showed 90% correlation by

BioNumerics software analysis whereas Xba 1 enzyme showed 88% correlation between these same isolates. Another group of 4 isolates showed 96% similarity when using the Pae R7 1 enzyme and 82% similarity between these isolates when using the Xba 1 enzyme. A third group of 3 isolates showed a 76% correlation between isolates for Pae R7 1 and a 73% correlation between isolates when using Xba 1. When individually comparing isolates to each other for each enzyme and taking into account that similar isolates had been ran on different gels then both enzymes were able to group the 22 isolates into the same 11 groupings. However, the relationships between isolates, of different banding patterns, are not always the same when comparing the 22 patterns generated by Pae R7 1 and Xba 1.

Discussion

In studies directed at looking for clusters of organisms the use of Pae R7 1 may be comparable to Xba 1. However, epidemiological studies examining association between isolates using Xba 1 or Pae R7 1 would likely reach different conclusions due to differences between cluster associations identified by the enzymes. A draw back of the Pae R7 1 enzyme is the increased processing time required. Pae R7 1 analysis of 11 isolates required 32 hours and used shorter pulse times (0.47 seconds to 10 seconds) compared to just 18 - 20 hours and longer pulse times (.47 seconds to 63 seconds) for Xba 1.

Conclusion

Initial use of the Pae R7 1 enzyme gives comparable results to Xba 1 enzyme. This procedure has been comparable at distinguishing *Salmonella* isolates for the purpose of strain relatedness. When comparing banding patterns of individual isolates to each other both enzymes identify the same 11 groups. When using the BioNumerics Software similar correlations between similar isolates are seen between the two enzymes. Initial results may show more variation between runs due to laboratory conditions and experience of technicians. However, continued comparisons of these two procedures are still taking place and final analysis of results is still to be determined.

References

1. Mead, P. S., L. Slutsker, V. Dietz, L. F. McCaig, J. S. Bresee, C. Shapiro, P. M. Griffin, and R. V. Tauxe. 1999. Food-Related Illness and Death in the United States. Emerging Infectious Diseases 5:607-625.

2. Tenover, F. C., R. D. Arbeit, R. V. Goering, P. A. Mickelsen, B. E. Murray, D. H. Persing, and B. Swaminathan. 1995. Interpreting Chromosomal DNA Restriction Patterns Produced by Pulsed-Field Gel Electrophoresis: Criteria for Bacterial Strain Typing. Journal of Clinical Microbiology 33(9):2233-2239.

Application of a 23S rRNA Fluorescent *In Situ* Hybridization method for rapid detection of *Salmonella* sp. in slaughtered pigs

Vieira-Pinto, M. M.[1*]; Oliveira, M.[2]; Martins, C.[1] and Bernardo, F.[2]

[1*]Lab. Inspecção Sanitária & T.P.A., Departamento das Ciências Veterinárias, CECAV, Universidade de Trás-os-Montes e Alto Douro Apartado 1013. 5001-911 Vila Real, Portugal.
[2] CIISA/Laboratório de Inspecção Sanitária, Faculdade de Medicina Veterinária, Lisboa, Portugal.
[*] corresponding author: mmvpinto@utad.pt

Abstract

Pork products contamination during the slaughter process represents an important vehicle of *Salmonella* sp. dissemination to humans. It's urgent to develop rapid, sensitive and accurate methods that allow the detection of a large number of *Salmonella*-positive samples, in order to control these risks efficiently and in a practical time. This study evaluates the suitability of Fluorescent *In Situ* Hybridization (FISH) method as a rapid screening tool for *Salmonella* sp. detection in pork carcasses, as well in some risk tissues (ileum, ileocolic and mandibular lymph nodes and tonsils), which could be involved in *Salmonella* contamination during slaughter process. For that, FISH was comparatively analysed with the labour intensive reference microbiological culture method (ISO 6579:2002) whose results were previously published by the same authors. From the 69 (13.7 %) positive samples identified by the culture method, 58 were also identified by FISH, 7 hours after the pre-enrichment step. Additionally, FISH has detected *Salmonella* sp. in more 135 samples (26.7%), being this difference highly significant (p-value<0.001). These results indicate FISH as a promising tool for rapid *Salmonella* sp. detection in pork samples, which could be considered an important ally concerning to the actual European Regulation in matter of *Salmonella* sp. control in slaughtered pigs. Nevertheless, this study must be considered as a base line work that must be improved with additional studies in order to evaluate the origin of the higher number of positive results.

Introduction

Programs to reduce *Salmonella* sp. transmission to meat in the slaughterhouse should be implemented in order to promote food safety. To guarantee the efficacy of those programs is fundamental the use of sensitive methods that provide results more rapidly without a prohibitive cost. Only in this way it is possible the implementation of corrective measures in due time avoiding additional costs associated to storage of materials and products prior to use and distribution. According to Fang et al., (2003), FISH is a potential method that could be successfully implemented in food microbiology due to its favorable characteristic, such as: less prone to inhibitory substances, rapid availability of quantitative results, identification of genetic markers (greater sensitivity and specificity), the possibility of simultaneous identification of different species in the same sample and the relatively low cost per experiment.

In 1997, studies developed by Nordentoft et al. (1997) revealed that FISH using Sal3, a fluorescence-labelled oligonucleotide probe, combined with a simple hybridization protocol, could be used to rapidly and accurately detect *S. enterica* serovars. Subsequently, other studies, related to the application of FISH with Sal3, indicated its potential as a sensitive and specific rapid method for *Salmonella* detection in food samples (Oliveira and Bernardo; 2002, Fang et al., 2003; Vieira-Pinto et al., 2005a). The objective of this study was to evaluate the efficacy of a 23S rRNA Fluorescent *In Situ* Hybridization (FISH) method, using Sal3, as a rapid screening tool for *Salmonella* sp. detection in pork carcasses and in some risk tissues (e.g. ileum, ileocolic and mandibular lymph nodes and tonsils) that can be involved in *Salmonella* sp. contamination during slaughter. The use of FISH as rapid method for *Salmonella* sp. detection at the slaughter level could constitute an important ally concerned to the actual European Regulation (Regulation (EC) N°. 2160/2003 and Regulation (EC) N°.2073/2005) in matter of *Salmonella* sp. control in slaughter pigs, as well as an important tool to be use within Hazard Analysis Critical Control Point (HACCP) programmes.

Material and methods

From June 2003 to September 2004, a randomly selected group of 101 pigs was sampled in an abattoir in the North of Portugal during the slaughter procedure. In each pig, samples of the ileum (25g), ileocolic lymph nodes (25g), mandibular lymph nodes (10g) and tonsils (10g) were collected. In the corresponding half carcass, an internal surface swab was performed, with a cotton sterilised gauze (hydrated in 25 ml of Buffered Peptone Water with 0.1% Tween) (Vieira-Pinto et al., 2005a).

At the laboratory, four hours after sample collection, samples were suspended in Buffered Peptone Water (BPW, Merk®, 1.07228) (1:10) and homogenised during 90 seconds in the Stomacher. The isolation of *Salmonella* was performed according to ISO 6579:2002 Norm, as already described by Vieira-Pinto et al. (2005a).

For the rapid *Salmonella* detection, a specific 23S rRNA oligonucleotide probe was used, Sal3 (5'-AATCACTTCACCTACGTG-3'; *E. coli* 1713→1730; Nordentoft *et al.*, 1997; Vieira-Pinto *et al.*, 2005b). The probe was synthesized and labeled with fluorescein in the 5'-end (MWG-Biotech, Ebersberg, Germany). The cells from 1 ml of the suspensions of each dilution in BPW were recovered by centrifugation (14000 rpm, 10 min; HERMLE Z233M-2, HERMLE AG, Gosheim, Germany) and fixed with a 4% paraformaldehyde (w/v) solution in PBS for four hours.

Ten µl of the fixed suspensions were placed on the wells of teflon slides (Heinz Herenz, Hamburg, Germany) and air dried, after which were dehydrated with ethanol at 50%, 80% and 96%, during 3 minutes at each concentration. After drying, 10 µl of hybridization buffer (0,9 M NaCl, 20 mM Tris-HCl, pH 7,2, 0,01% SDS) containing 5 ng/µl of the Sal3 probe were added. The slides were incubated in a humid chamber at 45 °C during 3 hours. After incubation, the slides were washed in a buffer solution (0,9 M NaCl, 20 mM Tris-HCl, pH 7,2, 0,1% SDS) at 45 °C during 15 min. The slides were mounted in Vectashield® Mounting Medium (Vector Laboratories, H1000) and immediately visualized by fluorescent microscopy at x1000 (objective HCX PLAN APD) in a Leica DMR microscope (Leica Microsistemas Lda., Portugal).

Positive deviations (false-positive results), negative deviations (false-negative results), sensitivity and specificity of FISH comparatively to ISO 6579:2002 method, were determined according to ISO/FDIS 16140:2000(E) Norm which specify the protocol validation of alternative microbiological methods for food and animal feeding stuffs.

A McNemar test (using Chi-square approach with Yates correction) for matched samples (D'Hainaut, 1992) was applied in order to determine the significance level of the difference between the results achieved using FISH and ISO method, with respect to the ratio of positive to negative results. Differences were considered significant at $P<0.05$.

Results

The results concerned to the detection of *Salmonella* sp. in the 505 pork samples determined by both methods and the statistical analysis are summarized in Table 1.

Table 1 - Results and statistical analysis concerned to the detection of *Salmonella* sp. determined by the reference microbiological method and FISH.

Tissue	Carcass	II. Ln.	Ileum	Mand. Ln	Tonsils	Total
	n=101	n=101	n=101	n=101	n=101	n=505
Method						
Microbiological	13 (12.9%)	19 (18.8%)	14 (13.9%)	13 (12.9%)	10 (9.9%)	69 (13.7%)
FISH	41 (40.6%)	47 (46.5%)	39 (38.6%)	40 (39.6%)	26 (25.7%)	193 (38.2%)
McNemar test	22.781***	21.441***	19.862***	21.806***	11.250***	103.623***
Posit. deviation	30 (29.7%)	31 (30.7%)	27 (26.7%)	29 (28.7%)	18(17.8%)	135 (26.7%)
Neg. deviation	2 (2.0%)	3 (3.0%)	2 (2.0%)	2 (2.0%)	2 (2.0%)	11 (2.2%)

II. – Ileocolic; Ln. – Lymph nodes; Mand. – Mandibular; Posit. – Positive; Neg. – Negative; *** - p-value <

0.001 (Highly significant difference)

According to the results presented in Table 1, the difference among the results from the two methods were highly significant (p-value<0.001).
Sensitivity and specificity of FISH comparatively to ISO 6579:2002 method determined according to ISO/FDIS 16140:2000(E) Norm, using the results presented in Table 1, was 84% and 69%, respectively.

Discussion

FISH allowed *Salmonella* sp. detection in approximately 7 hours (necessary time for fixation, hybridization and observation of the samples), with a consumable cost of 0.45 to 3.0 euros per sample, which is in accordance with previous results reported by Oliveira and Bernardo (2002) and Blasco et al. (2003).
Concerned to the differences in results obtained by FISH, comparatively to those achieved by the culture method, it was observed that, from the 69 samples where *Salmonella* sp. was isolated by the culture method, FISH detected 58 failing in detection of 11, corresponding these ones to the false-negatives or negative deviations. The number of negative results are inversely related with the sensitivity value of FISH, that in our study was 84%. Fang et al. (2003) also found false-negative results using the FISH method for detection of *Salmonella* in food. False negatives or weak signals can be obtained when small numbers of the target molecules are present, since the reduced number of bacteria in the sample can limit the FISH applicability because only a small part of the specimen is viewed within a reasonable time, or when the accessibility of the target molecules is insufficient (Stender et al. 2001; Fang et al. 2003).In our case we believe that the lower number of *Salmonella* sp. presented in the original sample as well as the presence of debris in the suspension observed trough FISH, were the main responsible for the occurrence of false-negative results.
Additionally to the 58 positive samples detected simultaneously by FISH and by the culture method, the Hybridization method has detected more 135 positive samples (26.7%) where no *Salmonella* was isolated by the cultural method, corresponding these cases to the false-positive samples or positive deviation. Several authors previously reported higher number of positive results by hybridization comparatively to the standard culture method (Bottari et al., 1995 and Eckner et al.; 1994). Particularly to the application of FISH to food samples, Fang et al. (2003) previously reported that in 56 positive samples screened by FISH (using Sal3), *Salmonella* was not recovered in 28 samples of them by the conventional cultural method.
The large number of positive deviations achieved in this study, leaded to a low value of FISH specificity (69%). In view of these reduced value, two important questions must be prompt: Could these results be related to the FISH detection of other bacteria rather than *Salmonella* sp. or could these bacteria be dead? or this result reflects a ISO method limitation concerned to *Salmonella* sp. isolation in these kind of samples due to the presence of injured cells (viable but not cultivable) or a high competitive flora?

With regard to the large number of false-positive results verified, it is necessary to understand its origin and, most of all, to investigate if the noncultivable cells detected by FISH are viable. The presence of viable bacterial cells in food is of extreme importance to the food industry and to the consumers. To correspond to these expectations the authors suggests an optimization of the FISH method, in order to allow a reliable detection of viable cells, based on the work of Buchrieser and Kaspar (1993). These authors showed that the previous sample incubation with inhibitory antibiotics of the DNA gyrase, generated a significative cellular elongation in the physiologic active cells and increased the fluorescent intensity of the hybridized viable cells through the increase of the intracellular rRNA.

Conclusions

The FISH results, previously described, corroborated and increased the culture results, allowing the quick (7 hours) observation of individual cells by epifluorescent microscopy.
From the 505 samples analyzed, FISH allowed the detection of a superior number of positive samples (193 samples) comparatively to ISO method. The larger number of positive results detected by FISH that should be confirmed by the cultural method should not be an imposing limitation, since the negative results are most often encountered in food analysis. In addition, the use of FISH as a screening method would avoid an unnecessary waist of time and material in the

analyses of these negative samples, as well as expedite the results in a proper time to allow adequate consumers protection from the microbiological risk.

The results from this study suggests that FISH could be considered an important rapid screening tool for *Salmonella* sp. detection in pork samples, constituting an important ally concerned to the actual European Regulation (Regulation (EC) Nº. 2160/2003 and Regulation (EC) Nº.2073/2005) in matter of *Salmonella* sp. control in slaughter pigs, as well as an important tool to be use within Hazard Analysis Critical Control Point (HACCP) programs. Nevertheless, additional studies should be performed in order to evaluate the origin of the high number of the positive results and to eliminate the false-negative results.

References

BLASCO, L., FERRER,S. e PARD, I. 2003. Development of specific fluorescent oligonucleotide probes for *in situ* identification of wine lactic acid bacteria. FEMS Microbiol. Letters, 225, 115-123

BOTTARI, D. A., EMMET, C. D., NICHOLS, C. E., DURBIN, G. W., e REYNOLDS, G. N. 1995. Comparative study of a colorimetric DNA hybridization method and conventional culture procedure for the detection of *Listeria* spp. in foods. J. Food Prot, 58(10), 1083-1090.

BUCHRIESER, C. e C. W. KASPAR. 1993. An improved direct viable count for the enumeration of bacteria in milk. Int. J. Food Prot, 20, 227-236

D'HAINAUT, L. (Editor) 1992: Conceitos e métodos da estatística. Fundação Calouste Gulbenkian. Lisboa. Portugal

ECKNER, K. F. e FLOWERS, R. S. 1994. Enhanced recovery and isolation of *Salmonella* and *Listeria* using a novel culture-transfer-inoculation device. J. Food Prot, 57(8), 725-731.

FANG, Q., BROCKMANN, S., BOTZENHART, K. e WIEDENMANN, A. 2003. Improved detection of *Salmonella* spp. in foods by fluorescent *in situ* hybridization with 23S rRNA probes: a comparison with conventional culture methods. J. Food Prot., 66, 723-731

NORDENTOFT, S., CHRISTENSEN, H. e WEGENER, H. C. 1997. Evaluation of a fluorescence-labelled oligonucleotide probe targeting 23S rRNA for *in situ* detection of *Salmonella* serovars in paraffin-embedded tissue sections and their rapid identification in bacterial smears. J. Clin. Microbiol. 35, 2642-2648

OLIVEIRA, M. e BERNARDO, F. 2002. "Fluorescent *In Situ* Hybridization" aplicado à detecção rápida de *Salmonella* de origem alimentar e ambiental. Revista Portuguesa de Ciências Veterinárias. 97, 81-85

VIEIRA-PINTO, M. M., TEMUDO, P. e C. MARTINS, 2005a. Occurrence of Salmonella in the ileum, ileocolic lymph nodes, tonsils, mandibular lymph nodes and carcasses of pigs slaughtered for consumption. J. Vet. Med. B. 52, 476-481.

VIEIRA-PINTO M. M., OLIVEIRA, M., BERNARDO, F. e MARTINS, C. 2005b. Evaluation of fluorescent in situ hybridization (FISH) as a rapid screening method for detection of *Salmonella* in tonsils of slaughtered pigs for consumption: a comparison with conventional culture method. J. Food Safety. 25 (2), 109-11.

Session 6

Antimicrobial resistance in fecal generic *Escherichia coli* in 90 Alberta swine finishing farms: prevalence and risk factors for resistance

Varga, C.,[1] Rajić, A..,[*1,2] McFall, M.,[3] Avery, B.,[4] Reid-Smith, R.,[1,2] Deckert, A.,[1,2] Checkley, S.[3] and McEwen, S.[1]

[1]Department of Population Medicine, University of Guelph, Ontario N1G 2W1
[2]Laboratory for Foodborne Zoonoses, Public Health Agency of Canada, Guelph, Ontario N1G 3W4
[3]Food Safety Division, Alberta Agriculture, Food and Rural Development, Edmonton, Alberta T7H 4P2

The objective of this retrospective study was to determine the prevalence of antimicrobial resistance (AMR) in generic *Escherichia coli* isolates obtained from 90 Alberta finisher swine farms, and to evaluate the potential associations between on-farm antimicrobial use (AMU) practices and observed AMR. The farms were visited three times, approximately one month apart (n=269 farm visits). In total, 5 pen fecal samples were collected per each visit and mixed into one pool per visit. Conventional culture and susceptibility testing were employed. Reported AMU practices through feed, water and injection in different phases of pig production, were collected using a questionnaire. Of the 1322 isolates, 166 (12.56%) were susceptible to all 15 antimicrobials. No resistance to amikacin, ceftiofur, ceftriaxone, ciprofloxacin, or naladixic acid was observed. This is an encouraging finding from a public health perspective. Lower frequencies of resistance were observed to gentamicin (1.1%), amoxicillin/clavulanic acid (0.7 %), and cefoxitin (0.7 %). Higher frequencies of resistance were observed for tetracycline (78.9%), sulfisoxazole (49.9%), streptomycin (49.6 %), ampicillin (30.6%), chloramphenicol (17.62%), kanamycin (10%), and trimethoprim/sulfamethoxazole (6.4 %). Most of the aforementioned antimicrobials are members of drug classes frequently used in veterinary medicine. Therefore, both judicious antimicrobial selection and use is needed when treating animals to preserve their efficacy. The most common multidrug-resistant patterns (resistance to ≥ 2 antimicrobials) were streptomycin-tetracycline (9.38%), streptomycin-sulfisoxazole-tetracycline (6.20%), and ampicillin-streptomycin-sulfisoxazole-tetracycline (6.15%). More clustering (less variation) in AMR was observed at the farm visit than the farm level indicating that sampling more farms with longer periods of time between farm visits might be required for better understanding of shifts in AMR over time. Risk factor analysis on the potential associations between certain on-farm AMU practices and observed AMR has been initiated and the results will be presented at the Symposium.

*Laboratory for Foodborne Zoonoses
Public Health Agency of Canada
160 Research Lane, Unit 103
Guelph, Ontario N1G 5B2
Phone: 1-519-826-2980
Fax: 1-519-826-2255
E-mail: andrijana_rajic@phac-aspc.gc.ca

Molecular epidemiology of Salmonella Typhimurium and Salmonella 4,5,12:i:- isolated from pig farms in Spain.

Vidal, A.,[1*] Rubio, P.,[2] Carvajal, A.[2] & Liebana, E.[1]

[1]Department of Food and Environmental Safety, Veterinary Laboratories Agency Weybridge, Addlestone, Surrey, UK
[2]Department of Animal Health, University of Leon, Campus de Vegazana s/n, 24071, Leon, Spain
*corresponding author:a.vidal@vla.defra.gsi.gov.uk

Abstract

The genetic diversity of 194 salmonella isolates belonging to different phagetypes of S. Typhimurium and S. 4,5,12:i- isolated from both healthy slaughter (157) and diarrhoea-affected (37) pigs was assessed using molecular typing (plasmid profiling and PFGE). The aim of this study was to elucidate the sources of infection, and to follow the spread of specific clones within the infected farms. In spite of the genetic diversity observed amongst the isolates, some clones were more prevalent and widely distributed in the pig population, being detected in several slaughter batches from the same and different farms. This finding suggests the existence of multiple and recurrent infection sources, as well as mechanisms favouring survival, persistence and spreading of certain clones within and between pig farms.

Introduction

Salmonella is an important human pathogen worldwide. The primary route of human infection is via contaminated foods of animal origin. Pigs are important reservoirs for different serotypes of salmonella and the importance of pork as a source of human salmonellosis has been increasingly recognised in the last two decades (Wegener & Baggesen, 1996).

Serovar Typhimurium is the second most frequent type of Salmonella isolated from human, food and animal samples in Spain (Usera et al., 2001). In 1997, the Spanish National Reference Laboratory for Salmonella first reported on the emergence of a new Salmonella serovar with the antigenic formula 4,5,12:i:-, which became the fourth most frequently isolated Salmonella serotype in Spain. This serotype has often been found in pigs and pork products in this country (Usera et al., 2001).

Molecular techniques have been developed and used to investigate the epidemiology and ecology of Salmonella in animal populations. Limited information is available about the genetic diversity of Salmonella within the pig population in Spain. This study was undertaken to determine the distribution and persistence of different Salmonella clones within and between pigs farms.

Material and methods

A total of 194 Salmonella isolates belonging to different 'phagetypes of Salmonella Typhimurium and Salmonella 4,5,12:i:- were characterized. Most of the isolates (157) were obtained from slaughter pigs from 23 batches and 11 farms located in the North-West region of Spain that belonged to the same pig production company. Additionally, 37 isolates recovered from diarrhoea-affected pigs belonging to 20 epidemiologically unrelated farms were included in the study..

Salmonella cultures were serotyped following a microagglutination method (Poppoff & Le Minor, 2001) and 'phage typed (Anderson et al., 1977) at the National Reference Laboratory for Salmonella and Shigella in Spain.

Pulsed Field Gel Electrophoresis (PFGE) was performed according to the "One-Day (24-28 h) Standardized Laboratory Protocol for Molecular Subtyping of Non-Typhoidal Salmonella by PFGE"

(Pulse-Net, CDC, Atlanta, USA) (CDC, 2002). Chromosomal DNA was digested with *Xba*I and *Bln*I. Macrorestriction patterns were compared by using Bionumerics software. A difference of at least one restriction fragment in the patterns was considered the criterion for distinguishing between different clones or strains.

Plasmid DNA was obtained by the alkaline lysis method according to Kado & Liu (1981). Samples were analysed by electrophoresis in 1X TBE buffer at 150 V on 0.8 % agarose gels with recirculation at 20ºC. Plasmids were compared by the use of BioNumerics software.

Results

PFGE. Electrophoresis of DNAs from the 194 isolates digested with either *Xba*I or *Bln*I generated thirty-six different macrorestriction profiles. The PFGE types obtained with each of the restriction enzymes did not coincide, and a combination of both profiles (*Xba*I/*Bln*I) allowed for a better discrimination. In total, 53 XbaI/BlnI combined types were identified of which 35 were found only in a single isolate from specific farms. In contrast, 6 genomic types accounted for more than 65% of the isolates and were found on different farms and in several batches within the same farm.

Plasmid profile. Thirty-six different plasmid profiles with 0 to 6 plasmids were identified. Thirteen plasmid profiles, containing the serotype-specific plasmid (approximately 90.6 Kb), were frequently found in isolates belonging to S. Typhimurium. The remaining plasmid profiles showed a larger plasmid of about 120 or 140 Kb and predominated in isolates of S. 4,5,12:i:-.

Combination of fingerprinting profiles. The use of various typing methods identified different groups of clones. Therefore, their results were combined to obtain a detailed overall fingerprint type. With the combination of the results described above we were able to identify a total of 79 combined types (CT). The 157 isolates from slaughter pigs were differentiated into 56 CTs, most of them (45 of 56) were represented by one single isolate, while 4 CTs accounted for 60% of the isolates. The vast majority of the CTs were found only in individual batches with the exception of 5 CTs (CT53, CT70, CT55, CT6 and CT23) that were found in several batches from different farms and 4 CTs (TC55, TC23, TC47 and TC14) which were recovered from different batches within the same farm. The 37 isolates belonging to diarrhoea-affected pigs were divided into 25 CT. Only CT18, that was found in 7 S. 4,5,12:i:- isolates, was recovered from more than one farm.

Discussion

Both molecular techniques (PFGE and plasmid profile), individually, discriminated among isolates belonging to different 'phagetypes of S. Typhimurium and S. 4,5,12:i:-. However, when used simultaneously a higher discriminatory power was achieved. S. 4,5,12:i:- strains, both from healthy and diarrhoea-affected pigs, formed a genetically homogeneous cluster closely related to contemporary S. Typhimurium isolates.

The heterogeneity of *Salmonella* isolates between and within pig slaughter batches has been reported previously (Wonderling *et al.*, 2003). In spite of the genetic diversity observed among the isolates from slaughter pigs, some clones were more prevalent and widely distributed among the population being detected in several batches of the same and different farms.

The high percentage of types isolated less frequently during the study period could have resulted from minor alterations in the genetic material of the predominating strains, which may or may not be maintained in the population. It has also been suggested that rarely isolated types could result from rare exposures or introductions of types, which fail to persist. In addition, some strains may be recovered at a different frequency due to differential performance of sampling and isolation techniques. The much higher isolation frequencies of relatively few types are consistent with the description of predominating strains on pig farms and slaughterhouses (Wonderling *et al.*, 2003). Types that were more frequently isolated and shared between several batches of the same or different farms may represent frequent common exposures or may be more apt to survive, be maintained and propagate in the population.

Only one of the combined types isolated from diarrhoea-affected pigs was found in more than one epidemiologically-unrelated farm which suggests a possible pathogenic role of these strains in pigs.

Molecular characterization of *Salmonella* isolates, complemented by conventional epidemiological information is a valuable tool for investigation of the sources of infection and transmission mechanisms of *Salmonella* within pig populations. The information provided is essential for the implementation of efficient control measures within pig production.

References

Anderson, E.S., Ward, L. R., De Saxe, M. J. & De Sa, J., 1977. Bacteriphage-typing designation of *Salmonella Typhimurium*. J. Hyg., 78, 297-300.

CDC (2002) Standardized Molecular Subtyping of Foodborne Bacterial Pathogens by Pulsed-Field Gel Electrophoresis. Centres for Disease Control and Prevention, Atlanta, Georgia.

Kadou, C. I. & Liu, S. T. 1981. Rapid procedure for detection and isolation of large and small plasmids. J. Bacteriol., 145, 1365-1373.

Poppoff, M. Y. & Le Minor, L. 2001. Antigenic formulas of the *Salmonella* Serovars, 8th revision, WHO Collaborating Centre for Reference and Research on *Salmonella*, Institute Pasteur, Paris.

Usera, M. A., Aladueña, A. Diez, R. M., De la Fuente, M., Gutierrez, F, Cerdan, R. & Echeita, A. 2001. Analisis de las cepas de *Salmonella* spp. aisladas de muestras clinicas de origin no humano en España en el ano 2000. Bol. Epidemiol. Semanal., 9, 221-224.

Wegener H. C., Baggesen D. L., 1996. Investigation of an outbreak of human salmonellosis caused by *Salmonella enterica* ssp. *enterica* serovar Infantis by use of pulse-field gel electrophoresis. *Int. J. Food Microbiol.* 32, 125-131.

Wonderling, L., Pearce, R., Wallace, F. M., Call, J. E., Feder, I., Tamplin, M. & Luchansky, J. 2003. Use of pulsed-field gel electrophoresis to characterize the heterogeneity and clonality of Salmonella isolates obtained from the carcasses and feces of swine at slaughter. Appl. Environm. Microbiol., 69(7), 4177-4182.

Antimicrobial resistance in non-pathogenic *E. coli* isolated from slaughter pigs

Wasyl, D.*, Hoszowski, A.

National Veterinary Research Institute, Pulawy, Poland

*corresponding author: wasyl@piwet.pulawy.pl

Abstract

An increasing antimicrobial resistance in bacteria of animal origin is recognised as a public health threat. Resistant pathogens directly affect infected host and can lead to therapeutic failures whereas commensal flora may serve as a reservoir and vector of resistance genes in a population. The incidence of resistant non-pathogenic bacteria may also indirectly indicate the intense of antimicrobial use in animal husbandry. A five-year resistance monitoring project covering an indicator E. coli was run at the National Veterinary Research Institute since autumn 2003. The study was designed to collect yearly up to 1000 samples from healthy bovine animals, pigs, broilers, turkeys and geese at slaughter. Standard isolation and identification procedures were applied for E. coli detection in bovine and swine rectal swabs and poultry caecum contents referred to the laboratory. Agar diffusion method according to CLSI recommendations was used for antimicrobial resistance testing of 1692 strains, including 676 swine isolates. Resistance ranged from 0.9% of tested strains (Cefuroxime) to 33.7% (Streptomycin). Certain year-to-year variations in the occurrence of antimicrobial resistance were noted. Resistance to at least 1 antimicrobial was found in 49.5% of strains isolated from pigs, compared to 16.6% of bovine and 89.1% of broiler isolates. Multiresistance was recorded in 6.4% of swine isolates in comparison with 2.7% and 39.7% found, respectively, in cattle and broilers. Eighty-two resistance profiles covering up to 9 out of 11 tested antimicrobials were observed in pigs isolates. The resistance in non-pathogenic E. coli depended on source of isolation. Swine isolates were more often resistant than bovine strains, but less frequently resistant than those obtained from poultry. It might be due to different intensity and prudence of antimicrobial use in animal husbandry.

Introduction

An increasing antimicrobial resistance in bacteria of animal origin is recognised as a public health threat. Resistant pathogens directly affect infected host and can lead to therapeutic failures. Commensal flora may serve as a reservoir and vector of resistance genes in a population. The incidence of resistant non-pathogenic bacteria may also indirectly indicate the intense of antimicrobial use in animal husbandry [3,6]. Those are the major rationale for monitoring and control of antimicrobial resistance. On the other hand knowledge on resistance and resistance patterns may be used as an effective empirical treatment during acute outbreaks of disease when an antimicrobial admission in needed as early as possible [2,5].

The problem is well known in bacterial pathogens although the occurrence of resistance varies between countries and regions [3,4]. A few and mostly point prevalence studies on the resistance among indicator bacteria originating from healthy animals are known and they support only limited information over a phenomenon within a longer time period.

The need for data on antimicrobial resistance was recognised in Poland in early 2000s. As a response a five-year resistance monitoring project was lunched at the National Veterinary Research Institute in autumn 2003. It covers E. coli, Salmonella, Staphylococcus, and Streptococcus. Nowadays the project provides an information on antimicrobial resistance in bacteria of animal origin crucial to the national program for antibiotics protection initiated in 2005 by the National Institute of Public Health and Ministry of Health.

The paper presents the resistance to a range of antimicrobials of non-pathogenic E. coli isolated from pigs, discusses the scope of the resistance, and compares the phenomenon in pigs and other animal species.

Material and methods

The study was designed to collect yearly up to 1000 samples from healthy animals sampled at slaughter in selected slaughterhouses located in 21 counties. Pigs were sampled by county veterinary officers at 8 slaughterhouses, whereas cattle, broilers, turkeys and geese at, respectively, 10, 5, 5, and 4 locations.

Standard isolation and identification procedures were applied for E. coli detection in samples referred to the laboratory. Rectal swabs (cattle and pigs) or a loopfull of caecum contents (poultry) were suspend in saline and streaked directly onto MacConkey agar. The plates were incubated in 37°C for 18±2h and a single lactose-fermenting colony was selected for biochemical confirmation. The number of isolates tested during the subsequent years were given in Table 1.

Agar diffusion method according to CLSI recommendation was used for ART. Mueller-Hinton agar and antimicrobial discs were manufactured by Oxoid. The antimicrobials and breakpoints used are listed in Table 2. Growth inhibition zone diameters were automatically read with OSIRIS (BioRad Laboratories) and the results were transferred to WHONet software for analysis.

Table 1. Number of isolates tested, by year and source of isolation

Year	pigs	cattle	broilers	turkey	Geese	total
2004	278	184	93	46	47	648
2005	306	181	59	24	36	606
2006	92	193	21	116	16	438
total	676	558	173	186	99	1692

Results

The E. coli isolation rate in the collected samples was high. Few samples yelled no lactose-positive culture growth on MacConkey plates and the only reduction in number of samples was due to motile Proteus spp cross-contamination.

The average resistance in pig isolates ranged from 0.9% to 33.7% in, respectively, cefuroxime and streptomycin (Table 2). In general, the percentage of resistant strains increased within 3-years period in the case of cefuroxime, chloramphenicol, gentamicin and TMP/Sulfamethoxazole, but only in the laser compound the change was significant ($P \leq 0.01$). The resistance to quinolones and sulfonamides ($P \leq 0.05$) peaked in 2005. In the same year the decrease in resistance for streptomycin and tetracycline ($P \leq 0.001$) was noted. A non-significant decline in the percentage of resistant strains within the study period was observed in the case of ampicillin and trimethoprim.

No matter the antimicrobial used, swine isolates were usually more resistant than bovine and less frequently resistant than poultry isolates.

Pig isolates showed 82 out of 191 noted resistance profiles and they were the most variable compared to other sources (data not shown). The percentage of fully susceptible isolates diminished from year to year and on average 49.5% showed any resistance (Table 3). The resistance profiles comprised up to 9 antimicrobials of all classes tested. The resistance to 5 and more antimicrobials, although higher than in cattle, was several times lower than in poultry isolates.

Table 2. Percentage of antimicrobial resistant E. coli, by source and year of isolation

Antimicrobial [code & concentration (µg)]	break point	pigs 2004	2005	2006	average 2004-2006	cattle	broilers	turkey	geese
Ampicillin AMP (10)	14-16	10.4	9.2	8.7	9.6	9.3	61.3	41.4	33.3
Cefuroxime sodium CXM (30)	15-17	0.7	1.0	1.1	0.9	0.4	4.1	1.1	0.0
Chloramphenicol CHL (30)	13-17	1.8	4.2	4.3	3.3	0.5	11.3	10.8	5.0
Nalidixic acid NAL (30)	14-18	4.0	6.9	6.6	5.6	1.6	72.1	34.9	30.7
Enrofloxacin ENR (5)	17-22	0.4	2.6	2.2	1.6	0.4	33.5	11.8	3.1
Gentamicin GEN (10)	13-14	0.4	2.0	2.2	1.3	0.4	5.4	2.2	0.0
Streptomycin STR (10)	12-14	36.0	30.6	37.0	33.7	5.6	54.3	18.1	24.7
TMP/Sulfamethoxazole SXT (1.25/23.75)	11-15	6.9	11.8	18.7	10.7	4.3	26.6	13.3	20.8
Sulfonamides SSS (300U)	13-16	15.8	21.6	9.8	17.6	4.3	37.8	21.3	28.0
Trimethoprim TMP (5)	11-15	7.6	6.9	6.5	7.1	3.2	16.8	11.9	21.2
Tetracycline TCY (30)	15-18	34.6	20.1	44.0	29.2	8.7	53.8	44.6	22.2

Table 3. Percentage of susceptible, resistant and multiresistant E. coli strains, by source and year of isolation

Strains characteristics	pigs			cattle		broilers	turkey	geese
	2004	2005	2006	average 2004-2006				
susceptible	52.5	51.1	42.4	50.5	83.4	10.9	32.8	47.5
resistant to 1 antimicrobial	14.4	23.1	21.7	19.4	9.5	16.7	23.1	14.9
resistant to 2 antimicrobials	15.8	10.1	13.0	12.9	1.4	9.2	9.1	5.9
resistant to 3 antimicrobials	9.4	4.9	13.0	7.8	1.3	12.6	9.1	7.9
resistant to 4 antimicrobials	2.2	3.3	5.4	3.1	1.8	10.9	7.5	5.9
resistant to 5 and more antimicrobials	5.8	7.5	4.3	6.4	2.7	39.7	18.3	17.8

Discussion

Antimicrobial resistance surveillance programs run in some countries usually use diverse sampling frame, strain selection criteria, testing methodology. Therefore obtained results may not be comparable [2,3,7,8]. Being aware of the limitations we carefully discuss the general trends rather than the percentage of resistant strains observed in our study in comparison with those available from other EU countries.

Resistance to ampicillin, streptomycin, sulphonamides and tetracycline were the most common in E. coli both in Poland and other countries no matter the animal species considered [1,4,6]. Presented data show cephalosporins were the most active antimicrobial. Similar observations were found in Denmark [3] although the Dutch studies showed an increase of cefotaxime resistance in poultry isolates [6]. Some authors report the resistance levels of indicator E. coli tend to increase [3,6,7].

Certain year-to-year variations in the occurrence of antimicrobial resistance were noted during the study but the trends were mostly inconclusive. The resistance in pig isolates increased during the study period in the case of 8 antimicrobials tested although only TMP/Sulphametoxazole showed a significant change. An increasing trend in resistance was also observed in the stains originating from, respectively, cattle, turkey and geese (data not shown). No increase in resistance was observed in broiler isolates. Similar variations were described by others [3,6,8].

Host animal species and animal production system highly influenced the level of resistance. Poultry isolates showed higher resistance than those from swine. Similar tendency was observed in the Netherlands [6] whereas swine isolates were the most resistant in Sweden [8]. Cattle strains were usually the less resistant although compared to other antimicrobials the observed frequency of ampicillin resistance should be emphasized [1]. Penicillins usage in mastitis treatment might be the explanation. Quinolone resistance in broilers and other poultry species was higher than in to swine isolates [1,6]. Relatively infrequent gentamycin resistance served as an example of the lower selection pressure of the compound which is rarely used in animals [2,3]. Cattle are usually extensively reared whereas pigs and chicken are mostly housed under intensive conditions resulting in a higher proportion of resistance [1,6].

Antimicrobial resistance reflected regional differences in animal husbandry and antimicrobial usage [4]. For example, DANMAP [3] reported higher resistance in indicator E. coli isolated from imported broiler meat compared to the domestic ones. Prudent policy for antimicrobial use in Sweden results in a lower resistance. Therefore as much as 78% of indicator E. coli isolated from pigs were sensitive to all antimicrobials tested [8]. Similar conclusions can be drawn from Norwegian experiences [7]. A high antimicrobial consumption in Spain and the Netherlands is reflected by the higher incidence of resistance [2,6]. In our study nalidixic acid and enrofloxacin resistant E. coli indicate quinolone overuse in broilers whereas a short production period gives a limited opportunity for reduction of resistance once selection took place [6].

Conclusions

A harmonised antimicrobial monitoring and control programmes are needed throughout all Member States. Monitoring of antimicrobials consumption, restrictions and prudent antimicrobial use in food animals will reduce public health impact of drug resistant bacteria. It also concerns antimicrobial therapy in humans and the need for collaboration among veterinary, food hygiene and public health authorities.

References

1.   ITAVARM 2003. Italian Veterinary Antimicrobial Resistance Monitoring. First Report., 2004, Instituto Zooprofilattico Sperimentale delle Regioni Lazio e Toscana, Centro Nazionale di Referenza per l'Antibioticoresistenza, Italy.
2.   Bywater R, Deluyker H, Deroover E, de Jong A, Marion H, McConville M, Rowan T, Shryock T, Shuster D, Thomas V, Valle M, Walters J., 2004, A European survey of antimicrobial susceptibility among zoonotic and commensal bacteria isolated from food-producing animals. *J Antimicrob Chemother,* 54, 744-54.
3.   DANMAP 2004 - Use of antimicrobial agents and occurrence of antimicrobial resistance in bacteria from food animals, foods and humans in Denmark. 2005.
4.   The Community Summary Report on Trends and Sources of Zoonoses, Zoonotic Agents, Antimicrobial Resistance and Foodborne Outbreaks in the European Union in 2005. *The EFSA Journal* 2006, 94.
5.   Hendriksen R S, Mevius D J, Schroeter A, Teale Ch, Meunier D, Butaye P, Battisti A, Utinane A, Amado A, Moreno M, Greko Ch, Stärk K, Berghold Ch, Myllyniemi A L, Wasyl D, Sunde M, Aarestrup F M., 2007, Occurrence of antimicrobial resistance among bovine bacterial pathogens and indicator bacteria in different European countries from year 2002-2004; the ARBAO-II study. *International Journal of Antimicrobial Agents* (submitted).
6.   Mevius D J, Pellicaan C, van Pelt W., 2005, MARAN-2004 Monitoring of Antimicrobial Resistance and Antibiotic Usage in Animals in The Nederlandes in 2004. available from: www.vwa.nl and www.cidc-lelystad.nl.
7.   NORM/NORM-VET 2004, 2005, Usage of Antimicrobial Agents and Occurrence of Antimicrobial Resistance in Norway. Tromso /Oslo, Norway.
8.   SVARM 2005, Swedish Veterinary Antimicrobial Resistance Monitoring, 2006, The National Veterinary Institute (SVA), Uppsala, Sweden.

Session 6

Antimicrobial resistance in *Salmonella* isolates recovered from swine: A NARMS report

Fedorka-Cray, P.J.[1], Dargatz, D.A.[2], Anandaraman, N.[3], Wineland, N.E.[2], Frye, J.[1], and Bailey, J.S.[1]

[1]USDA, ARS, Athens, GA, USA
[2]USDA, APHIS, Fort Collins, CO, USA
[3]USDA, FSIS, Washington, DC, USA
*corresponding author: paula.cray@ars.usda.gov

Abstract

In 1996 the Food and Drug Administration Center for Veterinary Medicine established the National Antimicrobial Resistance Monitoring System – Enteric Bacteria (NARMS) as a post-approval monitoring program. From 1997 through 2005, 10,565 *Salmonella* isolates originated from swine slaughter/processing (n=3,848), diagnostic (n=4,579) and on-farm (n=2138) sources as part of the animal arm of NARMS. Relative to 2005, the top five *Salmonella* serotypes from slaughter/processing (in decreasing frequency) were *S.* Derby, *S.* Typhimurium var. 5-, *S.* Infantis, *S.* Anatum, and *S.* Johannesburg while diagnostic serotypes were *S.* Typhimurium var. 5-, *S.* Choleraesuis var. kunzendorf, *S.* Derby, *S.* Typhimurium, and *S.* Heidelberg. Increased antimicrobial resistance was most often observed for diagnostic versus slaughter/processing isolates although there were exceptions for some drug and serotype combinations. For all years, greater than 55% of the slaughter/processing isolates were either pan-susceptible or resistant to only one antimicrobial, which was most often tetracycline. Since 1997, approximately 41% of the isolates exhibited multi-drug resistance, defined as resistance to ≥ 2 antimicrobials. Of the 723 *S.* Typhimurium DT104 isolates from swine only 24% (n=176) originated from slaughter/processing. These data reaffirm that overall patterns of resistance are highly dependent on the *Salmonella* serotype distribution and is variable when measured at different points along the farm to fork continuum.

Introduction

Salmonella species, which are ubiquitous in nature, have been recovered from meat and meat products (including swine), poultry, and eggs, as well as from fruits, vegetables and non-food sources. Food-borne illness attributed to *Salmonella* infections is one of the leading causes of gastroenteritis in the United States and elsewhere. The acquisition of multiple antimicrobial resistant *Salmonella* in animals and humans can impact treatment regimens for infections requiring antimicrobials. Treatment failures can result in increased morbidity, requiring revision of recommended therapies and an increase in healthcare costs.

The National Antimicrobial Resistance Monitoring System (NARMS) was established in 1996 by the Food and Drug Administration (FDA), the United States Department of Agriculture (USDA), and the Centers for Disease Control and Prevention (CDC) to monitor changes in antimicrobial susceptibilities of zoonotic pathogens from humans and animal diagnostic specimens, from healthy farm animals, and from raw product collected from federally inspected slaughter and processing plants. Non-typhoid Salmonella were selected as the sentinel organism and have been continuously tested for antimicrobial susceptibility to a panel of antimicrobials of human and veterinary importance since 1997. This poster focuses on antimicrobial resistance observed in *Salmonella spp.* isolated from swine as part of the NARMS program from1997 through 2005.

Materials and Methods

Isolates
Slaughter samples were collected and cultured by USDA-FSIS and diagnostic samples were collected and cultured by state veterinary laboratories throughout the United States or obtained from the USDA-APHIS National Veterinary Services Laboratories (NVSL), Ames, IA.

Testing
Antimicrobial susceptibility testing was conducted using the Sensititre™ semi-automated system (Trek Diagnositic Systems, Inc., Cleveland, Ohio) as per manufacturer's directions. Antimicrobials were configured in a 96 well custom made panel for susceptibility testing using the broth microdilution method. Clinical and Laboratory Standards Institute's (CLSI) guidelines were followed throughout the testing procedure. The following quality control strains were used: *E. coli* ATCC 25922, *P. aeruginosa* ATCC 27853, and *E. faecalis* 29212 (*S*.aureus ATCC 29213 replaced *P*.aeruginosa in 2004).

Results

From 1997 through 2005, 10,565 *Salmonella* isolates originated from swine slaughter/processing (n=3,848), diagnostic (n=4,579) and on-farm (n=2138) sources as part of the animal arm of NARMS. Rankings of top isolated serotypes differed depending on animal status although five serotypes were common to both diagnostic and slaughter (Anatum, Derby, Heidelberg, Infantis, and Typhimurium var. 5-) (Table 1).

Table 1. Top isolated *Salmonella* serotypes from swine in 2005 – diagnostic and slaughter

Diagnostic (n=495)	Percent	Slaughter (n=301)	Percent
Typhimurium var. 5-	23.0%	Derby	28.2%
Choleraesuis var. kunzendorf	14.5%	Typhimurium var. 5-	12.0%
Derby	12.3%	Infantis	9.0%
Typhimurium	9.5%	Anatum	5.3%
Heidelberg	7.1%	Johannesburg	5.0%
Agona	3.6%	Reading	3.7%
Infantis	3.0%	Saintpaul	3.7%
Anatum	2.8%	London	3.7%
Untypable	2.6%	Adelaide	3.3%
6,7:Nonmotile	1.8%	Heidelberg	2.7%

Overall, increased antimicrobial resistance was most often observed for diagnostic versus slaughter isolates with the highest levels of resistance seen to streptomycin, sulfonomides, and/or tetracycline. The largest disparity in antimicrobial resistance between animal status was seen with ampicillin where almost four times more diagnostic isolates were resistant than slaughter isolates (Figure 1).

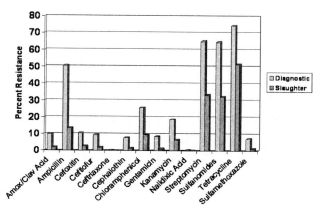

Figure 1. Percent resistance of *Salmonella spp.* isolated from swine by status
(1997 – 2005)

For all years, greater than 55% of the slaughter/processing isolates were either pan-susceptible or resistant to only one antimicrobial, which was most often tetracycline (Table 2). From 1997 through 2005, an average of 10% of the isolates was resistant to greater than five antimicrobials with no significant variations observed throughout the years.

Table 2. Multiple drug resistance from *Salmonella spp.* isolated from swine - slaughter

	1997	1998	1999	2000	2001	2002	2003	2004	2005
Total n Tested	111	793	876	451	418	379	211	308	301
Total (%) Pan Susceptible	44.1	49.2	48.9	43.2	43.3	40.1	53.6	37.3	44.5
Total (%) R = 1*	11.7	16.0	15.6	12.2	16.5	16.6	12.3	21.1	15.0
Total (%) R ≥ 5*	16.2	11.9	9.1	12.0	8.4	9.2	10.0	13.0	11.6
Total (%) R ≥ 10*	0.0	0.0	0.3	0.9	1.4	1.9	1.0	0.3	0.7

* Refers to the number of antimicrobials isolates are resistant to

Two-thirds (64%, n=460) of confirmed *Salmonella* DT104 isolates from swine (n=723) from 1997 through 2005 came from diagnostic animals while 24% (n=176) were from slaughter isolates (Figure 2).

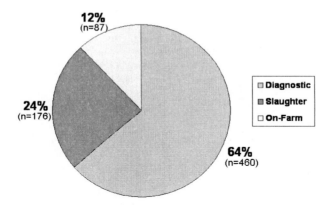

Figure 2. Distribution of *Salmonella* DT104 from 1997 – 2005 by source

Discussion

- *Salmonella* Derby and S. Choleraesuis var. kunzendorf are among the top 5 serotypes of isolates tested from swine but are not found in the top 20 serotypes identified from humans by the NARMS program (CDC, 2003).
- Animal status influences serotype distribution
- The percentage of *Salmonella* isolates from swine slaughter samples that were susceptible to all tested antimicrobials did not significantly change throughout the years
- Antimicrobial resistance is dependent upon serotypes (data not shown)
- The predominant source of *Salmonella* DT104 is diagnostic animals which are not entering the food chain
- Because of the number of human *Salmonella* cases attributed to food sources, further monitoring and analysis of resistance trends should continue but sample factors affecting resistance such as geographical or seasonal distribution, processing methods or husbandry practices should always be considered.

References

CDC. National Antimicrobial Resistance Monitoring System for Enteric Bacteria (NARMS): 2003 Human Isolates Final Report. Atlanta, Georgia: U.S. Department of Health and Human Services, CDC, 2006.

USDA. National Antimicrobial Monitoring System for Enteric Bacteria (NARMS): 1997-2003 Annual Reports. United States Department of Agriculture, ARS, BEAR. Available at the following web page: http://www.ars.usda.gov/Main/docs.htm?docid=6750

Summarizing the evidence of the performance of diagnostic tests for *Salmonella* spp. in swine: A systematic review approach.

[1]Wilkins, W.*, [2,5]Rajić, A., [1]Parker, S., [2,5]Waddell, L., [2,4]Sanchez, J., [2,3]Sargeant, J., [1]Waldner, C.

[1]Western College of Veterinary Medicine, Saskatoon, Saskatchewan, Canada; [2]Public Health Agency of Canada, Guelph, Ontario, Canada; [3]McMaster University, Hamilton, Ontario, Canada; [4]Atlantic Veterinary College, Charlottetown, Prince Edward Island, Canada; [5] Ontario Veterinary College, Guelph, Ontario, Canada
*corresponding author: Wendy.Wilkins@usask.ca

Abstract

A systematic review was undertaken in order to identify, critically appraise and synthesize the existing literature on the diagnostic performance (e.g. Se and Sp of the test) and agreement (e.g. kappa and correlation coefficients) of conventional bacterial culture, enzyme-linked immunosorbent assays and polymerase chain reaction assays used to detect and monitor *Salmonella* spp. in swine. 2110 citations were identified and 160 were relevant to the research objectives. Quality assessment is complete for 150 of these references; 73 were excluded due to estimates of test performance not being clearly reported and insufficient raw data available for post-hoc analysis. Although the review is still in progress, early experiences indicate problems with lack of standardization in the design, conduct and reporting of studies of diagnostic test evaluation in this area. This review will provide valuable information by identifying gaps in existing research and providing direction for future work on the standardization of tests examined in this review.

Introduction

Recent initiation or consideration of *Salmonella* control programs in swine in many European pig-producing countries has created an impetus for other pork producing countries to investigate the epidemiology of *Salmonella* infection in their pig populations and to evaluate the feasibility of potential control options. Although the Danish surveillance program for *Salmonella* in swine has been in place for almost a decade (Mousing et al. 1997), it has been only recently that the international research community has started to address some basic research questions related to the validity and accuracy of existing sampling strategies and testing protocols, particularly at the farm level.

A systematic review is an overview of primary studies which contains an explicit statement of objectives, materials, and methods and has been conducted according to explicit and reproducible methodology (Greenhalgh 1997). This methodology has been increasingly used in human medicine to synthesize the results of studies of diagnostic test accuracy; however, quality systematic reviews in general in the areas of animal health and agri-food public health are limited (Sargeant et al. 2006). The application of systematic reviews in these areas is complicated by the use of challenge studies and observational studies, as well as the lack of randomized controlled trials (Sargeant et al. 2006). While these factors present an additional challenge to researchers, the obstacle is not insurmountable. Through the process of addressing the review question the researchers may also set precedence for review protocol.

In human health and medicine, diagnoses are made to predict prognosis and to guide treatment decisions. In animal health and agri-food public health, diagnostic tests are more often used to evaluate herd prevalence and to classify herds for monitoring and control programs. The main objectives of this systematic review were to identify, critically appraise and synthesize the existing literature on the diagnostic performance (e.g. Se and Sp of the test) and agreement (e.g. kappa and correlation coefficients) of conventional bacterial culture, enzyme-linked immunosorbent assays and polymerase chain reaction assays used to detect and monitor *Salmonella* spp. in swine.

Material and methods

The initial objective of the literature search was to identify all publications reporting the evaluation of one or more tests used to detect *Salmonella* infection in domestic swine. In addition, we sought to identify all studies where two or more of these tests had been used simultaneously on the same subject/sample to detect *Salmonella*, recognizing that these studies potentially contain data that could permit the evaluation/comparison of the tests being used even though test evaluation was not one of the objectives of the research being reported. Thus a broad search was performed, designed to have a high sensitivity for any abstract reporting the use of a diagnostic test for *Salmonella* in swine. The databases searched, search terms and results for each database were recorded. The search was restricted to 1980 and onward, as it was thought that tests after this date would be most representative of tests in current use.

Two reviewers independently reviewed all references at each step of the review process. First, the titles and abstracts of all articles were screened to identify potentially relevant articles. Articles reporting the evaluation of one or more tests (ELISA/serology, bacterial culture or PCR) were retained for further evaluation, as were articles reporting the use of two or more of these tests to detect the presence of *Salmonella* in swine. These abstracts were then subject to a 2nd level relevance screening, where non-English references and non-primary research articles were excluded.

Next, quality assessment was done using the full texts of articles passing through relevance screening. Questions pertaining to study quality were restricted to those items which the review team deemed to be critical inclusion criteria, in order to expedite the review process. Other non-critical questions pertaining to study quality were included in the subsequent data extraction process. Finally, data was extracted from references surviving the quality assessment phase. The data extracted included general study information (including non-critical study quality questions), details of test protocols and reported measures of test performance or agreement, and/or raw test data, if available.

The review process was carried out using an electronic systematic review (eSR) program developed by TrialStat© (www.trialstat.com). All review forms were developed *a priori* and pre-tested prior to use. Disagreements were resolved by discussion between reviewers until consensus was reached.

Results

A total of 2110 citations were identified, uploaded to the eSR database and screened for relevance. 160 of these references were deemed relevant to the research objectives. Quality assessment is nearly complete, with screening of 10 references still in progress.

Of the 150 references for which quality assessment is complete, 73 have been excluded due to estimates of test performance not being clearly reported and insufficient raw data available for post-hoc analysis. Preliminary exploration of the data indicates that approximately 50% of research reporting the evaluation of one or more tests used to detect *Salmonella* infection in domestic swine did not report actual estimates of test performance or agreement, nor did they provide raw data in a manner which permits post-hoc analysis. Similarly, approximately 50% of the studies which were included because two or more of these tests had been used simultaneously on the same subject/sample contained no useable data with which to perform post-hoc analysis.

The remaining 77 references are in the process of data extraction. While there are insufficient data to explore at this time, early experiences point to potential difficulties with future data synthesis attempts. Some of the potential problems include: insufficient/no detail on test protocol(s); inconsistent use of reference tests; pooling of results from different populations or from different tests; and failure to specify the population from which samples were obtained.

Discussion

Systematic reviews evaluating diagnostic tests important in veterinary and agri-food public health are virtually non-existent in the published literature, despite the fact that review methodology in the human health fields is well developed. To illustrate, a simple search of the PubMed database, using the search string "systematic review AND diagnostic test", will return 52 results (as of

February, 2007); in contrast, using the same search string and combining it with veterinary or animal related terms will return no results. This failure to utilize systematic reviews in non-traditional areas is regrettable, as the use of systematic reviews to synthesize the current body of knowledge on targeted food safety issues – in this case diagnostic test performance - can provide increased credibility to findings in the field (Sargeant et al. 2005).

The principles that apply to evaluating diagnostic tests in human health also apply in animal and agri-food public health; therefore, it is possible to adapt existing tools for systematic reviews of diagnostic tests and modify these tools for application in these areas. One such tool is the QUADAS tool (Whiting et al. 2003), which provides criteria for assessing the quality of studies of diagnostic test evaluation. As mentioned previously, the use of challenge studies and observational studies, and the lack of randomized controlled trials present a challenge to reviewers in veterinary and food safety fields(Sargeant et al. 2006), and subsequent modifications to tools such as the QUADAS tool must take this into consideration.

A major variation to the diagnostic test review protocol that was made in this review was the decision to include all studies where two or more of these tests had been used simultaneously on the same subject/sample to detect *Salmonella*, even though test evaluation was not an objective of these studies. For those studies that report the results of each test in a manner that allows extraction of this information into a two-by-two contingency table, estimates of test performance (percent agreement, kappa, sensitivity, specificity) can be calculated. This methodology may be particularly useful in cases where there is a scarcity of published studies regarding the performance of a diagnostic test.

Another variation to the more traditional systematic review protocol that we made was to include studies of all levels of evidence. In the human health field, studies included in systematic reviews are typically of the highest level of evidence – randomized control trials which are published in peer-reviewed journals (ref). In our review, studies of any design were included if they contained information relevant to the review question. Studies from "grey-literature" sources (non-published research, e.g. conference proceedings) were also included, in contrast to more traditional systematic reviews. The impact of study design and literature type will be examined once data extraction is complete.

Early experiences with data extraction have hinted at potential problems with future data synthesis attempts. Insufficient detail of test protocol, a wide range of potential reference tests, pooling of results from different populations or from different tests, and failure to specify the population from which samples were obtained are examples of some of the problems encountered so far. Many of these types of problems are due to a lack of standardization in the design, conduct and reporting of studies of diagnostic test evaluation. This lack of standardization has been a problematic in the human health fields as well, and efforts have been made to encourage the research community to use a more structured approach (Meyer 2003). The anticipated outcome of the current systematic review is to perform a meta-analysis to calculate summary estimates of the diagnostic performance and agreement of these diagnostic tests; however if insufficient data are available, qualitative systematic review will still provide valuable information by identifying gaps in existing research and providing direction for future work on the standardization of tests examined in this review.

Conclusions

Systematic reviews are under-utilized in animal health and agri-food public health, and systematic reviews of diagnostic tests are virtually non-existent in these areas. The use of these tools in non-traditional areas is encouraged, as the use of systematic reviews to synthesize the current body of knowledge can provide increased credibility to findings in these fields, in addition to identifying gaps in existing research and providing direction for future work.

Acknowledgments

We would like to thank Janet Harris and Lindsay Downey for their contributions to this project. This project was funded by the Public Health Agency of Canada.

References

Greenhalgh T. Papers that summarise other papers (systematic reviews and meta-analyses). BMJ 1997; 315 (7109):672-5.

Meyer GJ. Guidelines for Reporting Information in Studies of Diagnostic Test Accuracy: The STARD Initiative. Journal of Personality Assessment 2003; 81 (3):191–3.

Mousing J, Jensen PT, Halgaard C et al. Nation-wide Salmonella enterica surveillance and control in Danish slaughter swine herds. Preventive Veterinary Medicine 1997; 29 (4):247-61.

Sargeant J, Amezcua R, Rajic A et al. Conducting Systematic Reviews in Agri-Food Public Health. http://www.fsrrn.net/UserFiles/File/conductingsysreviewsenglish[1].pdf 2005.

Sargeant JM, Rajic A, Read S et al. The process of systematic review and its application in agri-food public-health. Preventive Veterinary Medicine 2006; 75 (3-4):141-51.

Whiting P, Rutjes AW, Reitsma JB et al. The development of QUADAS: a tool for the quality assessment of studies of diagnostic accuracy included in systematic reviews. BMC Med Res Methodol. 2003; 3:25.

Session 6

Assessment of the diagnostic accuracy of bacteriological culture and the *invA*-gen-based PCR for the detection of *Salmonella* organisms from caecal content from slaughtered pigs through Bayesian approaches

Mainar-Jaime, RC.*[1], Atashparvar, N.[2], Chirino-Trejo, M.[3]

[1]Unidad Sanidad Animal, Centro de Investigación y Tecnología Agroalimentaria –CITA-, Gobierno de Aragón. Apdo. Correos 727. 50080 Zaragoza, Spain.
[2]Departament of Microbiology, School of Veterinary Medicine, Lorestan University Khorram-Abad, Iran P.O.BOX:465.
[3]Department of Veterinary Microbiology, WCVM, University of Saskatchewan, 52 Campus Drive, Saskatoon, Saskatchewan S7N 5B4 Canada
*Corresponding author: rcmainar@aragon.es

Abstract

The goal of this study was to determine the accuracy of a culture technique and the *invA*-gen-based PCR, for the detection of *Salmonella* spp from caecal samples from slaughtered pigs. For this purpose a Bayesian approach was used. Two hundred and three pigs were used. Animals were grouped into 2 populations: 96 from small farms and 107 from large farms. Sensitivity was 56% (95% Credible Interval: 40-76) for culture and 91% (95%CI: 81-97) for PCR. The specificity of the PCR was 88% (95%CI: 80-95). According to these estimates, the percentage of pigs with *Salmonella* organisms in their faeces at slaughter in this population was at least 25.5%. It is concluded that bacteriology on caecal samples alone is a poor diagnostic method to carry out studies on the prevalence of salmonellosis in pigs, and that the sensitivity of this technique would be probably lower if the procedure is simplified or is carried out on non-stressed pig populations. PCR was considered a reliable screening method for the diagnosis of pig salmonellosis but prone to some misclassifications that should be considered if this technique is used.

Introduction

The accuracy of bacteriology for the isolation of *Salmonella* organisms from faeces from subclinically-infected pigs is a current matter of research. A large number of pre-enrichment, enrichment, and selective media have been described, and different combinations of them have been used for isolation of *Salmonella*, apparently showing large variations in terms of sensitivity (Hoorfar and Mortensen, 2000; Rostagno et al, 2005). Moreover, asymptomatic pig salmonellosis is characterized by intermittent shedding, thus culture may yield false negative results simply because the organism is absent from the sample collected. Thus, bacteriology is considered to have low sensitivity (Se). In contrast, its specificity (Sp) is 100%. Polimerase chain reaction (PCR) based on the *invA*-gen of *Salmonella* spp. is considered a rapid and reliable diagnostic test for the detection of *Salmonella* organisms (Rahn et al, 1992; Malorny et al, 2003). It appears to show high Se, although its Sp is sometimes questionable (Arnold et al, 2004). However, if the assessment of its accuracy is based on direct comparison to bacteriology it will yield biased estimates of Se and Sp. An alternative to estimate the accuracy of 2 tests in absence of a gold standard is the use of latent-class approaches. They allow for the estimation of Se and Sp of the tests by cross-classifying their results after applying them to individuals from 2 populations with different prevalences, and assuming constant Se and Sp of the tests across populations (Enøe et al, 2000). We estimate the accuracy of culture and PCR for the detection of *Salmonella* organisms on caecal samples from slaughtered pigs using a latent-class (Bayesian) approach.

Material and methods

A total of 203 slaughtered pigs from 19 producers were sampled between September 2005 and March 2006 from 3 abattoirs in Saskatchewan, Canada. Ten pigs were randomly chosen from one of the producers delivering animals the day of sampling. Pigs were grouped into 2 populations: 96

from small farms (<2,000 hogs/year) (P_A), and 107 from large farms (>2,000 hogs/year) (P_B). Caecal content was collected and 10 grams submitted to qualitative *Salmonella* isolation following a culture method based on pre-enrichment with buffered peptone water (BPW), 3 selective enrichment media (tetrathionate –TT-, selenite, and Rappaport-Vassiliadis –RV- broths) and 4 selective, solid media (Xylose-Lysine-Tergitol-4, *Salmonella/Shigella*, Hekton-Enteric, and MacConkey). Isolates were further submitted to the National Laboratory for Bacteriology and Enteric Pathogens in Ottawa, for serotyping. Aliquots from the RV and TT broths were subjected to DNA extraction through a phenol-chloroform method, and a PCR targeting the *invA* gene of *Salmonella* spp was used following the method described by Malorny et al (2003) with slight modifications. A summary of the procedures is outlined in Figure 1.

Figure 1: Flow diagram of the methods used to isolate *Salmonella* in samples from caecal content from slaughtered pigs.

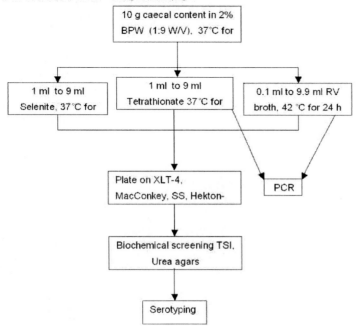

Priors for the Bayesian analysis were based on published literature. For Se of the culture (Se_{cul}) we used a mode of 75% with a 5th percentile as low as 40% (beta distribution defined by α= 5.29 and β=2.43); Sp of the culture (Sp_{cul}) was considered to be 100%; a reasonable prior for sensitivity of PCR (Se_{PCR}) was 85% with a 5th percentile as low as 65% (α=15.13 and β=3.49); same beta distribution was used for Sp of the PCR (Sp_{PCR}); a mode of 35% was used for P_A and P_B, with a minimum prevalence of 6.25% for P_A and 21.5% for P_B, thus the corresponding beta distributions were α=1.21, β=1.39 for P_A and α=9.31, β=16.44 for P_B. The conditional independence model for two tests, two populations was used (Branscum et al, 2005). To check for consistency of results and assess the influence of priors on the estimates the model was further repeated using non-informative priors (α=1, β=1). Posterior inferences were based on 100,000 iterations. Convergence was assessed by visual checking of the Kernel density and trace plots for each parameter, and by running multiple chains from dispersed starting values and further estimate the Gelman and Rubin statistic (Gelman and Rubin, 1992).

Results

Salmonella spp was isolated from 6.25% of the samples of P_A, and 21.4% of P_B. The cross-classification of results of the 2 tests for both populations is shown in Table 1. All culture-positive samples were PCR-positive except one. Out of 67 PCR-positive samples, only 28 (41.8%) were culture positive. Table 2 shows the posterior medians obtained with the different models used. When prior information was used for all parameters (model 1) posterior medians were 56% (95%CI=40, 76), 91% (95%=81, 97), 88% (95%=80, 95), 11% (95%CI=4, 20), and 40% (95%=28, 51), for Se_{cul}, Se_{PCR}, Sp_{PCR}, P_A, P_B, respectively. Results were similar when non-informative priors were used for the Se_{cul} (model 2), with the estimate of Se_{cul} in this model decreasing to 52% (Table 2). When non-informative priors were also included for Se_{PCR} and Sp_{PCR} (model 3), the Se_{cul} dropped to 50% but Se_{PCR} and Sp_{PCR} estimates went up (95% and 92%, respectively). If all the priors, except those for Sp_{cul} were non informative (model 4), the Se_{cul} decreased even more (48%). When all priors used were non-informative, including those for Sp_{cul}, the results obtained were similar to those from model 4, with median Sp_{cul} being 99% (95%CI=96, 100) (results not shown).

Table 1. Cross-classification of the results of the bacteriological culture and *invA*-gen-based PCR for the detection of *Salmonella* organisms in caecal samples from two populations of slaughtered pigs.

		P_A		P_B		TOTAL
		PCR		PCR		
		+	-	+	-	
Culture	+	6	0	22	1	29
	-	11	79	28	56	174
TOTAL		17	79	50	57	203

Table 2. Results from different Bayesian models[a] of sensitivity of the bacteriological culture (Se_{cul}), and sensitivity (Se_{PCR}) and specificity (Sp_{PCR}) of the *invA* gen-based PCR for the detection of *Salmonella* spp in caecal samples, and prevalences for two populations of slaughtered pigs (P_A and P_B).

	Se_{cul}	Sp_{cul}	Se_{PCR}	Sp_{PCR}	Prevalence P_A	Prevalence P_B
Model 1[b]	56 (40, 76)	100	91 (81, 97)	88 (80, 95)	11 (4, 20)	40 (28, 51)
Model 2[c]	52 (36, 73)	100	91 (81, 97)	89 (81, 96)	11 (5, 21)	41 (29, 52)
Model 3[d]	50 (35, 71)	100	95 (83, 99)	92 (82, 99)	13 (5, 23)	42 (30, 53)
Model 4[e]	48 (34, 70)	100	94 (82, 99)	93 (82, 99)	13 (5, 23)	45 (31, 57)

95%CI: 95% credibility intervals;
[a]Models 1 to 4 were based on the assumption of conditional independence between Se_{cul} and Se_{PCR}. Sp_{cul} was considered 100%.
[b]Model 1 uses the following informative priors: Se_{cul}: beta(5.29, 2.43); Se_{PCR}: beta(15.13, 3.49); Sp_{PCR}: beta(15.13, 3.49); prevalence P_A: beta(1.21,1.39); prevalence P_B: beta (9.31, 16.44);
[c]Model 2 uses non-informative (1, 1) priors for Se_{cul};
[d]Model 3 uses non-informative (1, 1) priors for Se_{cul}, Se_{PCR} and Sp_{PCR};
[e]Model 4 uses non-informative (1, 1) priors for Se_{cul}, Se_{PCR}, Sp_{PCR}, and prevalences.

Discussion

This study would confirm the low Se_{cul} (56%) Since we used an important amount of caecal content (10g) which was cultured on 3 different broth media for selective enrichment (after a pre-enrichment with BPW), and further plated on 4 selective, solid media, we think that the ability of this culture technique to recover *Salmonella* organisms should have been enhanced considerably. Should other simpler culture techniques were used then a likely lower Se_{cul} would be expected. Se_{cul} is also affected by the number of organisms shed by animals, which is positively influenced by stressors such as handling, commingling of pigs, transportation, food deprivation or lairage (Williams and Newell, 1970; Craven and Hurst, 1982). The Se of this culture method may have been even lower if performed on faecal samples from pigs at the farm. According to our estimate of Se_{cul} the expected percentage of pigs shedding *Salmonella* in their faeces at slaughter in this population was at least 25.5%. By contrast, PCR has been considered a technique of high Se for the diagnosis of *Salmonella* infection in faecal samples after enrichment in proper media (Malorny et al, 2003; Myint et al, 2006), but of questioned Sp (Arnold et al, 2004). PCR positive results from samples from which *Salmonella* cannot be isolated can be due to nonviable *Salmonella* organisms (i.e. due to the presence of inhibitors of *Salmonella* growth in the faeces, previous treatment of the animal with antimicrobials, or because the animal has consumed nonviable organisms from the environment), or as a result of cross-reactivity with *Salmonella*-like bacterium (Ward et al, 2005). Although the results from this study showed that Se_{PCR} was clearly superior to that of the culture (91%), the Sp_{PCR} would be however much inferior, misclassifying around 12% of the negative samples. The *invA*-gen-based PCR is a rapid diagnostic method that, despite the lower Sp shown, detected 96.5% (28 out of 29) of the culture positive samples. It seems reasonable to think that it could be used as screening tool in *Salmonella* surveillance schemes. Bacteriology (on caecal samples) alone should be considered a very poor diagnostic method to carry out studies on the prevalence of salmonellosis in pigs, but useful as a confirmatory test and for further identification and characterization of the *Salmonella* isolates.

Acknowledgements

The authors thank Sask Pork and the government of Saskatchewan (Saskatchewan Agriculture and Food Disease Surveillance) for the partial funding of this project.

References

ARNOLD, T., SCHOLZ, HC., MARG, H., et al, 2004. Impact of invA-PCR and culture detection methods on occurrence and survival of *Salmonella* in the flesh, internal organs and lymphoid tissues of experimentally infected pigs. *Journal of Veterinary Medicine B*, 51, 459-63.

BRANSCUM, A.J., GARDNER, I.A., JOHNSON, W.O. 2005., Estimation of diagnostic-test sensitivity and specificity through Bayesian modeling. *Preventive Veterinary Medicine*, 68, 145-63.

CRAVEN, J.A., HURST, D.B., 1982. The effect of time in lairage on the frequency of Salmonella infection in slaughtered pigs. *Journal of Hygiene*, 88, 107-11.

ENØE, C., GEORGIADIS, M.P., JOHNSON, W.O., 2000. Estimation of sensitivity and specificity of diagnostic tests and disease prevalence when the true disease state is unknown. *Preventive Veterinary Medicine*, 45, 61-81.

GELMAN, A., RUBIN, D.B., 1992. Inference from iterative simulation using multiple sequences. *Statistical Science*, 7, 457-511.

HOORFAR, J., MORTENSEN, A.V., 2000. Improved culture methods for isolation of *Salmonella* organisms from swine feces. *American Journal of Veterinary Research*, 61, 1426-9.

MALORNY, B., HOORFAR, J., BUNGE, C., et al, 2003. Multicenter validation of the analytical accuracy of *Salmonella* PCR: towards an international standard. *Applied Environmental Microbiology*, 69, 290-6.

MYINT, M.S., JOHNSON, Y.J., TABLANTE, N.L., et al, 2006. The effect of pre-enrichment protocol on the sensitivity and specificity of PCR for detection of naturally contaminated *Salmonella* in raw poultry compared to conventional culture. *Food Microbiology*, 23, 599-604.

RAHN, K., DE GRANDIS, S.A., CLARKE, R.C., et al, 1992. Amplification of an *invA* gene sequence of *Salmonella typhimurium* by polymerase chain reaction as a specific method of detection of Salmonella. *Molecular Cell Probes*, 6, 271-9.

ROSTAGNO, M.H., GAILEY, J.K., HURD, H.S., et al, 2005. Culture methods differ on the isolation of *Salmonella enterica* serotypes from naturally contaminated swine fecal samples. *Journal of Veterinary Diagnostic Investigation*, 17, 80-3.

Session 6

WARD, M.P., ALINOVI, C.A., COUETIL, L.L., et al, 2005. Evaluation of a PCR to detect *Salmonella* in fecal samples of horses admitted to a veterinary teaching hospital. *Journal of Veterinary Diagnostic Investigation*, 17, 118-23.

WILLIAMS, L.P., NEWELL K.W., 1970. *Salmonella* excretion in joy-riding pigs. *American Journal of Public Health*, 60, 926-9.